Media Selling

FIFTH
EDITION

Media Selling

Digital,
Television,
Audio,
Print and Cross-Platform

CHARLES WARNER
WILLIAM A. LEDERER
BRIAN MOROZ

WILEY Blackwell

Registered Office
John Wiley & Sons, Inc., 111 River Street, Hoboken, NJ 07030, USA

Editorial Office
111 River Street, Hoboken, NJ 07030, USA

For details of our global editorial offices, customer services, and more information about Wiley products visit us at www.wiley.com.

Wiley also publishes its books in a variety of electronic formats and by print-on-demand. Some content that appears in standard print versions of this book may not be available in other formats.

Library of Congress Cataloging-in-Publication Data

Names: Warner, Charles, 1932– author. | Lederer, William, author. | Moroz, Brian, author.
Title: Media selling : digital, television, audio, print and cross-platform / Charles Warner, William Lederer, Brian Moroz.
Description: 5th Edition. | Hoboken : Wiley, 2020. | Revised edition of Media selling, 2009. | Includes bibliographical references and index.
Identifiers: LCCN 2020013130 (print) | LCCN 2020013131 (ebook) | ISBN 9781119477396 (paperback) | ISBN 9781119477464 (adobe pdf) | ISBN 9781119477419 (epub)
Subjects: LCSH: Selling–Broadcast advertising. | Advertising, Newspaper. | Internet advertising. | Advertising, Magazine. | Advertising, Outdoor.
Classification: LCC HF5439.B67 W37 2020 (print) | LCC HF5439.B67 (ebook) | DDC 659.13068/8–dc23
LC record available at https://lccn.loc.gov/2020013130
LC ebook record available at https://lccn.loc.gov/2020013131

Cover Design: Wiley
Cover Image: Grey Bokeh Background © cyb3rking/iStock.com, Set of flat design concept icons © VLADGRIN/Getty Images

Set in 11/13pt Dante by SPi Global, Pondicherry, India

V10019598_070320

This book is dedicated to my wife, Julia, whose loving care and support sustained me and to the memory of my mother and father who would be proud of me for being productive in my dotage.

Charles Warner

Contents

About the Authors

Charles Warner teaches in the Media Management Program in the School of Media Studies at The New School in New York. He is also the Goldenson Chair Emeritus at the University of Missouri School of Journalism.

Until he retired in 2002, Charlie was Vice President of AOL's Interactive Marketing division. Before joining AOL, he was the Goldenson Endowed Professor at the Missouri Journalism School for 10 years where he taught media management, media economics and finance, and media sales, and where he created and ran the annual Management Seminar for News Executives.

Charlie has also served as a management and sales consultant and trainer for CBS, ABC, ESPN, MTV, TCI, Fox, AH Belo, Hearst Magazines, Microsoft's MSN, Cox Cable, The Hyperfactory, and many other major media and online companies. He has also been VP, General Manager, of WNBC-AM (now WFAN) in New York, WMAQ-AM (now WSCR) and WKQX-FM in Chicago, WWSW-AM and WPEZ-FM in Pittsburgh, and CBS Radio Spot Sales.

William A. Lederer co-founded and serves as Chairman and CEO of iSOCRATES, the Global leader in Programmatic Resource Planning and Execution™ that serves publishers, marketers, agencies, and their suppliers. iSOCRATES has two lines of business: Strategic and Operations Consulting and Managed Services (Managed Service Platforms and Business Process Outsourcing). The company is owned by its employees, is headquartered in Saint Petersburg, Florida, and has its global delivery center in Mysuru, Karnataka, India.

Previously, Bill founded and served as Chairman and CEO of MediaCrossing Inc., a pioneering programmatic media trading company. Prior to MediaCrossing, he was CEO, Kantar Video, a global online and mobile video data, measurement and analytics innovation unit of Kantar, a global media and market research holding company of WPP Group. He also served as a board member of WPP Digital and of Kantar Digital. Bill had been Global Chief Development Officer and COO of North America at Kantar Media Audiences (formerly, TNS Media Research), and earlier VP, Corporate Development at Kantar Media (formerly, TNS Media NA). He was the Founder of Art. com, the leading e-commerce retailer, which he sold to Getty Images where he led as CEO of its Consumer Division.

Bill is an Adjunct Professor in the graduate Media Management Program in the School of Media Studies, The New School in New York. He is author or co-author of four Wiley texts on media selling or finance, including this 5th edition of *Media Selling*.

Brian Moroz is a senior creative strategist at Google. He has held several positions there during his decade-plus tenure both in the sales and agency groups and in the sales training group where he led North American new hire training in New York for all new employees.

Brian has particular expertise in strategic planning for complex online marketing campaigns and is expert in online video, search, and display as well as emerging technology in the digital media space. His current focus is on understanding how Google users interact with and take value from online marketing.

Previous to his work at Google, Brian worked in a postgraduate MBA startup and in finance. He has worked in the US and in Europe with consulting roles in Asia and was an Adjunct Professor in the graduate Media Management Program at The New School in New York.

Acknowledgments

Special thanks go to Haze Humbert, former Wiley Executive Editor, who urged me to write a fifth edition of *Media Selling* and to current Executive Editor, Todd Green, who has been so patient and supportive through several missed deadlines. Kudos to Wiley project manager Ajith Kumar and to the meticulous copy-editor Katherine Carr for making me seem like a much better writer than I really am.

Buckets of kudos and thanks go to my two co-authors, Bill Lederer and Brian Moroz; a fifth edition of *Media Selling* would not have been possible without their insights and expertise. And thanks to Scott Pompe of the *Austin American-Statesman* for his multiple insights into best practices in local cross-platform selling, to John Zimmer of Zimmer Marketing Group for his team's insights in local cross-platform selling, to Leo MacCourtney of Katz Television, to Tim Warner (no relation) of WRTH-TV in Indianapolis, and to Zorik Gordon, co-founder of Reach Local for being so candid in my interviews with them. Also, thanks to Will Warner for designing some of the coolest graphics in the book.

The book was also guided by the thoughtful reviews of several of my academic colleagues, and I would like to thank them for their efforts and encouragement.

Charles Warner
New York, August 2019

Preface

Updating the fourth edition of *Media Selling*, published in 2009, has been challenging because of the exponential changes in the media, especially in digital advertising, which in 2016 toppled television as the numberone advertising medium, and in the time since the fourth edition, Google and Facebook have dominated the digital advertising media environment. In 2017 and 2018 the two Internet giants amassed approximately 90 percent of the increase in digital advertising investment over the previous year, leaving hundreds of thousands of advertising-supported websites and apps struggling to survive by dividing the crumbs of the remaining 10 percent of the digital advertising yearly increase. It is difficult to keep up with accelerating changes in the media and in advertising because these changes are driven mostly by advances in artificial intelligence (AI), but this edition includes many of the changes up until August of 2019. With that in mind, we (the authors) have tried to avoid predicting the future beyond 2019. We have included a list of the most relevant references at the end of each chapter. We have also provided a list of resources that includes the URLs of websites and industry newsletters, blogs, apps, and websites where readers can keep up to date on current information.

Focus of the Book

Media Selling focuses on several basic concepts:

- Selling media has changed irreversibly since the advent of Google's self-serve Ad Words (called Google Ads from July 24, 2018) and the rise of programmatic buying and selling of media ad inventory. In 2019, over 80 percent of all digital inventory (desktop and mobile) was bought by computer-to-computer online programmatic trading. There are now two basic types of media selling: (1) in person, or via Skype or FaceTime, face-to-face educating, on which this book focuses and (2) programmatic trading, which is covered in a separate chapter. People selling legacy media (television, radio, newspapers, magazines, and out-of-home) today must understand both their own medium and the complexity of programmatic, including a basic knowledge of programmatic's underlying ecosystem and technology because virtually all of the legacy media, both nationally and locally, are sold on a cross-platform basis that includes a digital component.

- Personal selling without tricks or manipulation – with authenticity – is essential in order to build and maintain relationships based on trust.
- The imperative of honesty, integrity, and ethics in selling in this era of government, corporate, and media misdeeds and erosion of confidence in the media, and in this new era of social media in which it is virtually impossible to erase the digital footprint of misdeeds or impulsive comments.
- Attitudes control successful sales performance, and attitudes are controllable by using sound goals and objectives to motivate salespeople and help them achieve their dreams.
- Developing emotional and social intelligence – self-awareness, self-management, social awareness, and relationship management – is necessary for success in educating customers and helping them.
- Solution and insight educating and selling means selling solutions to marketing and advertising problems.
- Because some of the in-person business in the media is still conducted by means of negotiating, today's successful media salespeople must be competent negotiators.
- Understanding the basic concepts of marketing and advertising is crucial to developing appropriate solutions and insights.

Unique Features

The fifth edition of *Media Selling* has several unique features:

- A fully integrated and organized selling approach – AESKOPP – that enables salespeople and sales managers to organize and evaluate sales efforts.
- A strategic personal selling approach that emphasizes giving customers insight and solving customers' problems by developing trusting, long-term relationships using the wisdom of emotional intelligence.
- Definitions of the five or six steps of personal selling (depending on the type of selling) that focus on discovering and understanding customers' and buyers' personalities, needs, and wants; solving advertising and marketing problems; and, most important of all, getting results for customers.
- A thorough chapter on negotiating and closing.
- Tips on time management.
- A chapter that covers the history and practices of programmatic trading.
- A website (www.mediaselling.us) with a Downloads section that contains many useful documents such as ad-sales ratios, RFPs, and blank planners.

Most books on personal selling emphasize discovery and qualifying customer needs and viability, crafting proposals that meet those needs, and techniques for closing a deal, often by creating a false sense of urgency. In the current era of Big Data, micro-targeting, and buying individuals instead of broad audiences via programmatic, old-fashioned sales techniques do not tend to work. Today's media salespeople must concentrate on educating clients and helping them get results. Rather than being just sellers and closers, media salespeople must be educators and helpers.

Style of the Book

The three authors have attempted to write this book in a relatively informal and personal style. We have used the term salesperson throughout this book instead of account executive, seller, account manager, or business development person in order to be consistent, because they are all virtually equivalent in meaning.

1

The Marketing/Media Ecology

Charles Warner

Anyone taking a moment to ponder the $2 trillion marketing and advertising sector of the economy "can't avoid the inescapable truth that capitalism could not exist without marketing," Ken Auletta writes in *Frenemies: The Epic Disruption of the Ad Business (and Everything Else)*.[1] The marketing process is vital to the vigor of the American economy, and the media are integral elements in that marketing process and, thus, to the economy's health and stability. Consumer demand is what drives the economy, and it is marketing that fuels demand. Advertising is a major component of marketing, and it is through the media that consumers and businesses receive advertising messages about products and services. Also, "in the United States each dollar spent in advertising alone spawned nineteen dollars in sales and supported sixty-seven jobs across many industries…"[2]

Furthermore, advertising keeps a brand healthy and growing in a highly competitive marketplace. In a March 4, 2019 issue of *Ad Age* an article titled "The end of austerity" detailed how "The stunning tumble of Kraft Heinz has caused pain for investors … after Kraft Heinz took a $15.4 billion write-down of its assets."[3] The article goes on to report how Kraft Heinz owner, Brazilian investment firm 3G, went into a cost-cutting mode and used a zero-based budgeting process to cut advertising investments drastically. After the Kraft Heinz huge write-down on assets, a JP Morgan analyst said, "Investors for years have asked if 3G's extreme belt-tightening model ultimately would result in brand equity

Media Selling: Digital, Television, Audio, Print and Cross-Platform, Fifth Edition.
Charles Warner, William A. Lederer, and Brian Moroz.
© 2020 John Wiley & Sons, Inc. Published 2020 by John Wiley & Sons, Inc.

erosion."[4] So not only is advertising a major element in the fuel that drives consumer demand, lack of sufficient advertising investment can stunt a brand's growth.

If any one of the three elements (marketing, advertising, and the media) is not healthy, the other two cannot thrive. This chapter will examine the ecosystem-like interdependent relationships among marketing, advertising, and the media and how the Internet disrupted that ecosystem.

What Is Marketing?

In his influential book, *The Practice of Management*, Peter Drucker, "the Father of Modern Management," presented and answered a series of simple, straightforward questions. He asked, "What is a business?" The most common answer, "An organization to make a profit," is not only false, but it is also irrelevant to Drucker. "There is only one valid definition of business purpose: to create a customer," Drucker wrote.

Drucker pointed out that businesses create markets for products and services: "There may have been no want at all until business action created it – by advertising, by salesmanship, or by inventing something new. In every case it is a business action that creates a customer." Furthermore, he said, "What a business thinks it produces is not of first importance – especially not to the future of the business and to its success." "What the customer thinks he is buying, what he considers 'value,' is decisive – it determines what a business is, what it produces and whether it will prosper." Finally, Drucker said, "Because it is its purpose to create a customer, any business enterprise has two – and only these two – basic functions: marketing and innovation."[5]

Notice that Drucker did not mention production, suppliers, or distribution, but only customers. That is what marketing is – a customer-focused business approach.

A production-focused business first produces goods and then tries to sell them. In the book *Marketing 3.0: From Products to Customers to Human Spirit*, Philip Kotler and his two co-authors refer to a product-focused approach as Marketing 1.0.[6] A customer-focused business approach produces goods or services that it knows will sell based on market research and data that reveal customers' aspirations, wants, needs, tastes, and preferences. In *Marketing 4.0: Moving from Traditional to Digital*, Kotler, who is often referred to as "the father of modern marketing," and his co-authors refer to a customer-focused approach as Marketing 2.0.[7] In Chapter 15: Marketing and Chapter 16: Advertising, you will learn more about how marketing has further changed from Marketing 1.0 (product focused), to Marketing 2.0 (customer focused), to Marketing 3.0 (human centricity), and to Marketing 4.0 (customer collaboration), but for now, we will concentrate on customer-focused Marketing 2.0.

Another leading theorist, former Harvard Business School Professor Theodore Levitt, wrote an article in 1960 titled "Marketing myopia" that is perhaps the most influential single article on marketing ever published. Levitt claims that the railroads went out of business "not because the need [for passenger and freight transportation] was filled by others ... but because it was not filled by the railroads themselves. They let others take customers away from them because they assumed themselves to be in the railroad business rather than in the transportation business."[8] In other words, the railroads failed because they did not know how to create and keep customers; they were not marketing-oriented.

Where would makers of buggy whips be today if they had decided they were in the vehicle acceleration business or in the transportation accessory business instead of being in the buggy whip business?

As a result of the customer-focused, marketing approach espoused by Drucker, Levitt and other leading management and marketing theorists, in the 1960s, 1970s, and 1980s many companies asked themselves the question, "What business are we in?" and subsequently changed their direction to focus more on marketing and customers rather than on products. After the Internet became widely adopted by consumers in the late 1990s, entrepreneurs such as Larry Page and Sergey Brin (Google), Mark Zuckerberg (Facebook), and Jeff Bezos (Amazon) asked "What business do our customers want us to be in?". Existing businesses that survived after the Internet disruption had a heightened sensitivity to customers and changed the old-fashioned outlook of, "Let's produce this product because we've discovered how to make it." The Internet opened the door to a new digital age in human history, and from a business perspective, successful businesses and entrepreneurs in the digital age put the preferences, wants, and needs of customers and consumers first as these customer-first businesses shot past traditional companies in market value.

In today's digital-age economy consumers rule because the availability of information on the web has switched the information asymmetry that existed in favor of marketers prior to the Internet to be in favor of consumers in the post-Internet, digital era. Before the Internet and search, someone who wanted to buy a car had to depend on car dealers and their salespeople to provide information about a car's features, benefits, condition, and price. The information asymmetry favored the salesperson.

Today, consumers can search for the information about the make, model, features, benefits, condition, and price of a car on the Internet and can be armed with thorough information before walking into a dealership, often with more information than a dealer salesperson has. Therefore the information asymmetry has switched to the consumer in the digital era. Any company that does not recognize that customers now rule and put them on a pedestal, wow them, and delight them with an excellent experience will disappear from the business landscape.[9]

The Internet and Ad Words: Disrupting Marketing and Advertising

The Internet completely disrupted marketing. It switched the focus of marketing from mass marketing in the mass media to marketing to one individual at a time in customized, personalized, and fragmented media. In addition, the Internet allowed marketers to appeal to a narrow market of just one person out at the end of the long tail; to sell less of more, as Chris Anderson writes in *The Long Tail*.[10]

Not only did the Internet allow marketing to be more precise and more highly targeted, it also allowed consumers to discover a new product or service, to get more information about the product in the moment, without going to a retail store or dealership, and, probably most important, it allowed consumers to purchase a product online without going to a retail checkout counter. Thus, elements in the old value chain were upended; distribution costs and transaction costs were reduced to virtually zero – an enormous disruption.

Charles Warner

THE VALUE CHAIN

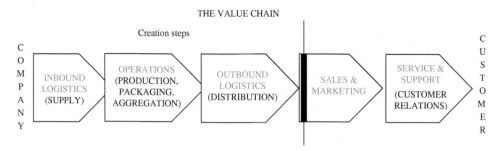

Figure 1.1   The value chain

Let's look at the steps in the value chain that companies had to go through in order to be successful:

The top step in each box (in gray, no parentheses) is the original one identified by Michael Porter in his 1998 book *Competitive Advantage*.[11] Porter's value chain obviously refers to a manufacturing or retail company, not a media or Internet company. The steps in the value chain that are in parentheses are more familiar and helpful in understanding the value chain process as it exists today, especially in companies such as Google, Facebook, and Amazon.

Before the advent of the Internet, large companies that were vertically integrated could control the three creation steps in the value chain (supply, production, and distribution) and could gain monopoly-like market power, charge higher prices, and, therefore, achieve huge profit margins. For example, newspapers that controlled the scarce supply of news (skilled reporters who wrote news stories), owned expensive printing presses and delivery trucks and, thus, controlled production and distribution; therefore, they often gained monopoly-pricing control over advertising. Newspapers, because they had an elastic supply of advertising inventory (they could add pages if demand for advertising went up), charged a fixed, non-negotiable price and gave volume discounts to large advertisers. In other words, newspaper pricing strategy rewarded advertisers for buying more advertising lineage and buying it more frequently, and the newspapers could just add pages as demand went up. This pricing strategy was extremely profitable for newspapers, and also favored large advertisers, such as department stores that could buy advertising more cheaply than small retailers because of volume discounts. Thus, it was an advantage to be a large advertiser; the small corner dry cleaner couldn't afford to advertise in a major newspaper and had to find other ways to market its business, such as advertising in Yellow Pages.

Another example of pre-Internet advertising pricing strategies was how television networks determined pricing. Television programming had an inelastic supply of advertising inventory because programs were formatted for a fixed amount of advertising. Thus, a half-hour news program was formatted for eight minutes of commercial time. Because of the inelastic supply of advertising slots and because there was high demand for a limited supply of television ad inventory, prices were not fixed and were determined by demand. The market determined prices, and thus each television commercial schedule was negotiated anew at the time an advertising campaign was placed. It was a pricing model based on scarcity and demand.

The prices for all media advertising were based on some version of a cost-per-thousand (CPM) model in which advertisers paid on the basis of having the opportunity to capture readers', viewers', or listeners' attention. Advertisers purchased the *opportunity* for exposure, not based on whether anyone read, watched, or listened to an ad. Mass media advertising was, in a sense, a gamble that someone would see and respond to an ad immediately or sometime in the future.

John Wanamaker, a Philadelphia department store owner, famously said in the early 1900s, "I know that half my advertising is wasted. The problem is I don't know which half." So Wanamaker and other advertisers doubled down on advertising hoping that at least half of it would work.

Therefore, newspaper readers and television viewers were inundated with advertising whether or not the ads were relevant to their individual aspirations, needs, or desires. Television advertising was especially intrusive, but most viewers put up with it because of an implicit contract between television stations and networks and their viewers who got free entertainment and news in return for their attention.[12]

The introduction of the digital video recorder (DVR) in 1999 by TiVo allowed viewers to record programs and fast-forward through commercials in the programs they recorded. This fast-forwarding highlighted the fact that people were not happy about intrusive, irrelevant advertising and wanted to skip it.

Google

About the same time that TiVo introduced the DVR, Larry Page and Sergey Brin, who were PhD candidates at Stanford University in the Computer Science department, started a company in their dorm room. The two had come up with a way to organize keyword search results on the Internet based on how many other web pages had links to the website the keyword appeared on. They called their system PageRank after Larry Page.[13]

Both Page and Brin knew they had to find a way to monetize their search results, but they both disliked traditional, intrusive advertising. After Google got funding from two major Silicon Valley venture capital funds, the new company's first business plan was not written by either Page or Brin, who were both focused on the product and the user experience. The business plan articulated three streams of revenue: (1) Google would license its search technology to other websites, (2) it would sell a hardware product that would let companies search their own content very rapidly, and (3) it would sell advertising.[14] Google's first effort to sell ads was in July 1999.[15] Page and Brin felt that information in advertising should be as valuable to users as the search results Google provided.

From 1999 to 2002 Google sold advertising in the traditional way to major advertisers and their agencies through salespeople who sold on the basis of a CPM pricing model. However, in October 2000, Google "launched a product catering to smaller operations that had not previously contemplated an online buy."[16] Google named the self-service system AdWords.[i]

Initially, the automated system allowed advertisers to buy on a CPM basis and pay more for ads positioned at the top of the search results area on the right side of the page.[17]

---

[i] Google changed the name of AdWords to Google Ads effective July 24, 2018.

Although the system was fairly popular, it was easy to game, and Page and Brin felt it was not scalable. Therefore, Google adopted an online auction system similar to one used by a competitor in the online search space, GoTo. The major difference between Google's system and GoTo's system was that the GoTo auction was a traditional auction model in which the highest bidder won. The GoTo auction model is referred to as a first-price auction. However, Google developed a modified Vickrey second-price auction system. In a second-price auction, the highest bidder on a keyword won the bid, but paid only what the second-place bidder bid plus a penny.[ii] This model, counterintuitively, causes people to make higher bids than in a first-price auction, thus raising the final price because bidders know they will pay less than the price they actually bid.[18]

The second-price auction was a stroke of genius because it eliminated buyer's remorse, which often happened after a buyer won a traditional auction.[19] Google made another decision that finalized the earth-shattering effect AdWords had on marketing. Instead of charging on a CPM model, it adopted GoTo's model of charging an advertiser only when someone clicked on an ad. It was a cost-per-click (CPC) model.[20]

The third innovation, and one that was purely Google's was its quality score. A quality score is determined by a complex algorithm that determines how relevant a website is to users. If someone clicks on a keyword search result ad, and goes to a site that is not relevant, that site gets a lower quality score. For example, if someone searches for "jobs," does Google put up a result about Apple founder Steve Jobs or does it put up results about employment opportunities? The beauty of the ad quality score is that "it makes the advertiser do the work to be relevant," according to the 2002 Google head of advertising, Sheryl Sandberg, who in March, 2008, was named the COO of Facebook.[21]

On January 24, 2002, Google tested the new AdWords auction system and soon not only small businesses with a credit card were buying search results on a self-help, second-price online auction and CPC model, but also major advertisers such as P&G and Coca-Cola were participating. The immediate, runaway success of AdWords not only led to Google's first profitable year at the end of 2002, but it changed the entire marketing/media ecosystem and the way media would be bought and sold from that time on.

By mid-2018 Google was the most valuable media company and the third most valuable company in the United States. It had more than twice the market capitalization of older production-oriented companies such as General Motors and General Electric *combined*.[iii] In 2018 Google was by far the largest media company in the world, garnering an estimated $136.5 billion in revenue in 2018, 86 percent of which was from advertising. Google 2018 ad revenue was almost two-and-a-half times more than the second largest media company in terms of advertising revenue, Facebook, which had an estimated $56 billion in advertising revenue. In 2018 the largest traditional media company in terms of advertising revenue was Comcast's NBCUniversal division, which had roughly $33 billion in advertising revenue.

[ii] In March, 2019, Google announced it was abandoning the second-price auction system and was adopting a first-price auction system that is standard practice in programmatic, RTB bidding for available inventory.

[iii] Market capitalization, or market cap, is determined by multiplying a company's stock market price times the number of outstanding shares of stock.

For the purposes of this book, we are defining media companies as those that are supported primarily by advertising and are ranking them according to the amount of advertising revenue they generate. Bloomberg *BusinessWeek,* other financially oriented publications, and many Wall Street analysts consider Google and Facebook to be technology companies, and both Google and Facebook's top management also consider their companies primarily tech companies. However, for the purposes of this book, Google and Facebook, often referred to in the advertising and marketing business as "the duopoly," are considered media companies because Google and Facebook's incredible success as advertising platforms clearly demonstrates that the Internet became the major factor in virtually all businesses' advertising and marketing efforts, and the duopoly dominates in digital advertising. Also, Google and Facebook might claim that they are technology companies or platforms and often deny they are media companies, but both are conduits for content that flows between advertisers and consumers – a medium as it were – and both are supported primarily by advertising, as most media companies are.

In 2007, the growth trajectory of the digital era veered in a new direction because of two innovations: (1) the iPhone and (2) programmatic buying and selling of digital ad inventory. The iPhone fueled Apple's rise to becoming the most valuable company in the world in 2012 and almost every year since then. In mid-2018 Apple exceeded a market valuation of $1 trillion, the first company in the world to reach that market-cap valuation. Technology business analyst Ben Thompson, author of the *Stratechery* newsletter, calls the iPhone "the most successful product *ever.*"[22] Also, the iPhone drove the phenomenal growth of smartphones and the Internet from being desktop, PC dominated to being mobile dominated, as approximately six billion global mobile phone users "have replaced the desktop and television as the dominant [advertising] platform."[23]

Also, 2007 was the year that the first real-time bidding (RTB) by Right Media occurred that "allowed advertisers to know in advance exactly whom they are presenting to and on exactly which site it will appear and at what time."[24] The ability to address specific individuals rather than broad audiences created the rapid growth of programmatic trading that has irrevocably changed media buying and selling practices (See Chapter 17: Programmatic Marketing and Advertising for more detailed information about RTB, programmatic, and automation). Furthermore, in 2007 Facebook shifted its focus from appealing just to college students to letting everyone join its popular social media platform, which gave its growth an atomic blast upwards to eventually become the second largest advertising platform.

Aggregation theory

In 2015 Ben Thompson in his "Stratechery" newsletter articulated aggregation theory, a concept that explained the phenomenal success of digital-era companies such as Google, Facebook, Amazon, Netflix, Snapchat, Uber, and Airbnb. Thompson wrote:

> First, the Internet has made distribution (of digital goods) free, neutralizing the advantage that pre-Internet distributors leveraged to integrate with suppliers. Secondly, the Internet has made transaction costs zero, making it viable for a distributor to integrate forward with end users/consumers at scale.

This has fundamentally changed the plane of competition: no longer do distributors compete based upon exclusive supplier relationships, with consumers/users an afterthought. Instead, suppliers can be aggregated at scale leaving consumers/users as a first order priority. By extension, this means that the most important factor determining success is the user experience: the best distributors/aggregators/market-makers win by providing the best experience, which earns them the most consumers/users, which attracts the most suppliers, which enhances the user experience in a virtuous cycle. The result is the shift in value predicted by the Conservation of Attractive Profits.[25]

Previous incumbents, such as newspapers, book publishers, networks, taxi companies, and hoteliers, all of whom integrated backwards, lose value in favor of aggregators who aggregate modularized suppliers – which they don't pay for – to consumers/users with whom they have an exclusive relationship at scale.[26]

Customers Versus Consumers

You have been reading about "customers" and "consumers," and the two terms seem to have been used almost interchangeably. It is time to clear up any confusion and accurately define the terms: a customer buys a product; a consumer uses a product. Consumers on the Internet are often referred to as users. Sometimes a customer and a consumer are the same person, for example, when a man buys an electric shaver for himself and uses it. Sometimes they are different people, for example, when a teenager says she wants an iPhone and her mother buys it for her. Proctor and Gamble (P&G) year after year is the world's largest advertiser; P&G's customers are retailers such as Walmart and their consumers are people who buy Crest. By advertising to consumers and creating demand for Crest, P&G pulls the product through the distribution system. Some manufacturers do not advertise their products but sell them to wholesalers who then sell the product to retailers and, thus, push products through the distribution system. In the media business, the customer is the advertiser and the consumer is the user, viewer, reader, or listener.

In today's marketing ecosystem, many companies, such as Facebook, are referring to customers as partners, and this trend toward partnership selling will be discussed more thoroughly in Chapter 2.

You will also find a more detailed discussion of marketing in Chapter 15 and of advertising in Chapter 16 because media salespeople must have a deeper understanding of marketing and advertising than is provided here in this introductory section in order to be effective problem-solvers and solutions sellers for the media.

What Is Advertising?

"In a non-state-run economy advertising is the bridge between seller and buyer."[27] This quote by media writer Ken Auletta in *Frenemies* defines advertising perfectly and concisely. Theodore Levitt also explains branding advertising well. Levitt changed the direction of marketing with his 1960 article "Marketing myopia," and he changed the perception of branding advertising 10 years later with his article "The morality (?) of advertising." Levitt wrote that, "In curbing the excesses of advertising, both business and government must distinguish between embellishment and mendacity." He presents a philosophical treatment of the human values of advertising as compared with the values of other "imaginative" disciplines.[28]

Levitt defended advertising against critics who would constrain advertising's creativity, who want less fluff and more fact in advertising. Many critics of advertising come from: (1) high-income brackets in business and government whose affluence was generated in industries that either create advertising (advertising agencies) or distribute it (the media), (2) industries that have grown through the use of effective advertising, or (3) by using advertising to promote themselves (politicians). Thus, advertising's critics must look carefully at their own glass houses when throwing stones at advertising.

Furthermore, advertising's critics, Levitt claims, often view the consumer as a helpless, irrational, gullible couch potato, which is far from the truth, especially in a digital age when consumers often have more product information than sellers do. As David Ogilvy, the advertising genius and practitioner par excellence, wrote to his advertising agency copywriters in his book, *Confessions of an Advertising Man*, "the consumer is not an idiot, she's your wife."[29] Obviously, when Ogilvy made the comment in 1963, most copywriters were men, which is no longer the case.

Levitt, too, believed that "most people spend their money carefully" and are not fooled by advertising's distortions, exaggerations, and deceptions. He writes that rather than deny that distortion and exaggeration exist in traditional branding advertising, these properties are among advertising's socially desirable purposes. Levitt goes on to say "illegitimacy in advertising consists only of falsification with larcenous intent." Levitt's thesis is that branding advertising is like poetry, the purpose of which is "to influence an audience; to affect its perception and sensibilities; perhaps even to change its mind." Branding advertising, like art, makes things prettier. "Who wants reality?" Levitt asks. When most people get up in the morning and look at reality in the mirror, they do not like what they see and try to change it by shaving, using hair gel, or applying makeup. These things give people hope that they will be better accepted, more attractive and, thus, happier. They aspire to a better version of themselves. The goal of the poet, the artist, and the composer are similar to the goal of most ads – creating images and feelings. Much advertising, especially on television and in video, is about feelings and emotions. It is about trying to make people feel good about a product. Levitt writes that, "Advertisements are the symbols of man's aspirations."[30] So, Madison Avenue (as the advertising industry is often referred to), like Hollywood, is selling dreams, and dreams and hope are essential to people's well-being.

In the digital era Google extended the definition of advertising to include search, or keyword, advertising, and Google's search advertising is primarily direct-response advertising, which is different from branding advertising, which sells the dreams mentioned in the paragraphs above. Direct-response advertising tries to close a sale or a transaction in real time. Branding advertising, on the other hand, invests in building brand equity and attempts to establish a brand's value proposition in consumers' minds. The return on direct-response advertising investment will often occur immediately with a click and a sale, the return on branding advertising investment will take longer, sometimes years, to pay off.

However, both types of advertising can develop demand for goods and services, and, as mentioned above, consumer demand drives the economy. Furthermore, the Internet reduces the cost of distributing digital goods and reduces the transaction costs to buy goods. Therefore, advertising can be a major contributor to reducing manufacturing costs, search costs, distribution costs, transaction costs, and, thus, ultimately, retail prices for goods. Many products such as personal computers and eyeglasses steadily come down in price as the market for them grows larger and as manufacturing, distribution, and transaction savings are passed on to consumers in the form of lower prices. Consumers get information about reduced prices and increases in features and value through both direct-response and branding advertising.

Advertising is a vital part of the nation's economy, and as the nation's population increases and products proliferate, marketers and their ad agencies will invest more and more in media advertising, especially in the digital media, to influence consumers and to introduce new products and services to highly fragmented media audiences. Therefore, media salespeople must understand the complexities and technologies that create and distribute advertising in order to effectively sell it. You will find out more about how advertising works in Chapter 16, and in that chapter and other chapters that follow, we will try to help you navigate through the maze of those complexities and technologies.

The Media

Advertising is one of the integral elements of the marketing process. We might look at advertising as the mass selling of a product. Where is advertising seen or heard? In the media. For the purposes of this book, as mentioned earlier in this chapter, the authors will define the media as businesses that are wholly or in part supported by advertising, e.g. Google, Facebook, ABC, CBS, FOX, NBC, ESPN, CNN, iHeart Media (radio), *The New York Times*, *Cosmopolitan*, the *New Yorker*, and BuzzFeed.

When people talk about the media, they are typically referring to the distributors of news and entertainment content – digital media such as Google and Facebook, plus television, newspapers, radio, magazines, and podcasts. The vast majority of media businesses are dependent in full or in part on advertising, and advertising, as an integral part of a larger marketing system, is co-dependent on the media. Without the media to reach large numbers of consumers with advertising, marketers would have to go door-to-door to try to sell their goods one-on-one through personal selling and, similarly, consumers would have to wander from store to store or website to website wondering which sold the product they needed – both very expensive and time-consuming undertakings. Advertising agencies would not exist if there were no media to distribute the ads they create.

The reason marketers and advertisers are dependent on the media is because the media are pervasive and popular with consumers (users, viewers, readers, listeners), and the media are consumers' link to the global village. People love their media and depend on their media – their favorite search engine, such as Google; their favorite social media platforms, such as Facebook or Instagram; their favorite television program, such as "Empire;" their favorite magazine, such as *People*; their favorite country music radio station; or their favorite newspaper, like the *Wall Street Journal*. Because of this affection and dependency, the media are actually the most powerful businesses in the country –more powerful than the celebrities, industries, or politicians they cover, expose, and glorify.

It is because of this enormous power coupled with a perception that the media emphasize negative news, poor-quality user-generated video, fake news, or sex and violence that many people probably have such a low opinion of the media. Americans seem to blame most of the ills of society on "the media," by which they typically mean the news media. It is for this reason that we have devoted a separate chapter in this book to ethics. Chapter 3 emphasizes the importance for media salespeople to deal with customers ethically, because the reputation of the media is at stake, and that reputation needs to be improved.

One of the roles of the media is to expose consumers to advertising, not to guarantee sales or results to advertisers. The media are just that – a medium, a connection between advertisers and consumers.

In most of the world's countries, the media are supported and/or controlled by government; however, most of the media in the United States are kept free from government control and interference because the majority of their revenue consists of advertising. The media from which the American public gets the vast majority of its information and entertainment are free or relatively inexpensive because they are supported by advertising. If Google were not supported by advertising, people would have to pay a few cents for each search. If Facebook were not free, people would have to pay for posting a selfie in a bar with friends.

Finally, in spite of a love-hate relationship between the public and the media, or perhaps because of it, most large media companies are profitable. Many of the great fortunes in the in the world have been built in the media, especially the digital media, for example Google, Facebook, Amazon, and Snapchat. Even if new products do not survive in the marketplace, the media still receive the advertising dollars invested to introduce a product, just as the media get the advertising revenue from political candidates who eventually lose. The profit margins in successful media companies are, as rule, higher than in many other industries. For example, Facebook's quarterly profit margins are often higher than 50 percent because it does not pay for content (its supply, which users create), does not pay for operations (producing the content), and does not pay for distribution (it's on the Internet). Also, top-rated radio and television stations in major markets often have profit margins of 40 percent or greater.

The reason for these profit margins is because in an advertising-supported medium such as Google, Facebook, radio, television, digital newspapers, and digital magazines, the cost of adding an additional ad has no or extremely low incremental costs involved. For example, in television, the time for commercials is baked into most programming, so if a commercial is not scheduled in a commercial pod, a promotion or public service announcement will run. A television station does not expand the programming time if it does not have commercials to run. Thus, at a television station, it costs nothing to add a commercial – there are no incremental, or marginal costs involved. On the other hand, if an automotive manufacturer sells a car, it has to build one with all of the incremental, marginal costs involved such as labor, materials, transportation, and so forth. Once a radio or television station or a website has sold enough advertising to cover its cost of operations and debt payment, if any, all additional advertising sold is virtually 100 percent profit. In digital newspapers and digital magazines, which often have an additional subscription revenue stream, once the cost of operating is recovered, the incremental cost of adding an ad is very low in comparison to the cost of the ad to an advertiser.

What this profitable economic model means for salespeople is that advertising revenue can be quite profitable and, therefore, there is more money to distribute to salespeople in the form of compensation than in less profitable industries. Media salespeople are among the highest paid of any industry.

Although media buying and selling functions are being automated by artificial intelligence (AI) and programmatic trading (see Chapter 17), research about jobs in the future indicates that jobs with more emphasis on clerical and service work (selling is service work) and jobs with more emphasis on communications and critical thinking (sales, again) are jobs that are less likely to be eliminated by automation and (AI). Furthermore, strategic media planning and selling-as-educating jobs will take on new importance in the future and, thus, are much less likely to be automated or computerized.[31] Chapter 2 will cover the concept of media selling as educating, which replaces the traditional practice of selling the inexact "magic" of the media in the pre-Internet era.

Hypocrites Not Allowed

If you agree that advertising is a vital part of the American economy and that advertising supports free Google searches, free Facebook posts, and free broadcast television and local radio programming, then you must believe in the value and efficacy of advertising. If so, then you cannot be hypocritical and use ad-blocking software. If you are selling advertising in any medium, including a digital medium, you must not only support, embrace, watch, listen to, and read all advertising you are exposed to but also understand enough about advertising to be able to evaluate, appreciate, and intelligently critique all the advertising you see or hear. Ad blocking is not allowed if you are a media salesperson.

Test Yourself

1. What is purpose of a business?
2. In marketing, what is the primary focus?
3. What was AdWords?
4. Why is Facebook so profitable?
5. What is the difference between a customer and a consumer?
6. Why are many media companies potentially so profitable?

Project

Make a list of all of the local media in your market: radio stations, television stations, cable systems, newspapers (daily, weekly, shoppers, suburban, ethnic, etc.), local magazines or journals (e.g. local business journals), outdoor companies, bus or subway posters, and local websites that sell advertising. Interview one or two sales managers or advertising directors of some of the media that have revenue in addition to advertising (newspapers subscriptions or a website's e-commerce, for example) and get a rough estimate of what percentage of revenue comes from advertising and what percentage comes from other revenue sources such as subscriptions. Then write some notes about what surprised you in this exercise.

References

Anderson, Chris. 2006. *The Long Tail: Why the Future of Business Is Selling Less of More*, New York: Hachette.

Auletta, Ken. 2018. *Frenemies: The Disruption of the Ad Business (and Everything Else)*, New York: Penguin Books.

Drucker, Peter. 1954. *The Practice of Management*, New York: Harper & Row.

Kotler, Philip, Kartajaya, Hermawan, and Setiawan, Iwan. 2010. *Marketing 3:0: From Products to Customers to Human Spirit*. Hoboken, NJ: Wiley.

Kotler, Philip, Kartajaya, Hermawan, and Setiawan, Iwan. 2017. *Marketing 4:0: Moving From Traditional to Digital*. Hoboken, NJ: Wiley.

Levitt, Theodore. 1960. "Marketing myopia." *Harvard Business Review*, July–August.

Levitt, Theodore. 1970. "The morality (?) of advertising." *Harvard Business Review*, July–August.

Levy, Steven. 2011. *In the Plex: How Google Thinks, Works, and Shapes Our Lives*. New York: Simon & Schuster.

Ogilvy, David. 1989. *Confessions of an Advertising Man*, 2nd ed. New York: Atheneum.

Porter, Michael. 1998. *Competitive Advantage: Creating and Sustaining Superior Performance*. New York: Free Press.

Smith, Mike. 2015. *Targeted: How Technology Is Revolutionizing Advertising and the Way Companies Reach Consumers*. New York: AMACOM.

Stewart, Thomas A. and O'Connell, Patricia. 2016. *Woo, Wow, and Win: Service Design, Strategy and the Art of Consumer Delight*. New York: Harper Collins.

Wu, Tim. 2016. *The Attention Merchants: The Epic Scramble to Get Inside Our Heads*. New York: Alfred A. Kopf.

Resources

Ad Age (www.adage.com)
MediaPost (media news) (www.mediapost.com)
Interactive Advertising Bureau (www.iab.com)
Ben Thompson's "Stratechery" newsletter (www.stratechery.com)

Notes

1   Auletta, Ken. 2018. *Frenemies: The Epic Disruption of the Ad Business (and Everything Else)*. New York: Penguin Books.

2   Ibid.

3   Schultz, E.J. and Wohl, J. 2019. "The end of austerity." *Ad Age*, March 4.

4   Ibid.

5   Drucker, Peter. 1954. *The Practice of Management*. New York: Harper & Row.

6   Kotler, Philip, Kartajaya, Hermawan, and Setiawan, Iwan. 2010. *Marketing 3:0: From*

Products to Customers to Human Spirit. Hoboken, NJ: Wiley.

7 Kotler, Philip, Kartajaya, Hermawan, and Setiawan, Iwan. 2017. *Marketing 4:0: Moving From Traditional to Digital.* Hoboken, NJ: Wiley.

8 Levitt, Theodore. 1960. "Marketing myopia." *Harvard Business Review,* July–August.

9 Stewart, Thomas A. and O'Connell, Patricia. 2016. *Woo, Wow And Win: Service Design, Strategy And The Art Of Customer Delight.* New York: Harper Collins.

10 Anderson, Chris. 2006. *The Long Tail: Why the Future of Business Is Selling Less of More.* New York: Hachette.

11 Porter, Michael. 1998. *Competitive Advantage: Creating and Sustaining Superior Performance.* New York: Free Press.

12 Wu, Tim. 2016. *The Attention Merchants: The Epic Scramble to Get Inside Our Heads.* New York: Alfred A. Kopf.

13 Levy, Steven. 2011. *In the Plex: How Google Thinks, Works, and Shapes Our Lives.* New York: Simon & Schuster.

14 Ibid.

15 Ibid.

16 Ibid.

17 Ibid.

18 Ibid.

19 Ibid.

20 Ibid.

21 Ibid.

22 Thompson, Ben. 2017. Episode 124, "Exponent." Retrieved from http://exponent.fm/esispode-124-thewatch-the-iphone-the-beatles.

23 Auletta, Ken. *Frenemies: The Epic Disruption of the Ad Business (and Everything Else).* New York: Penguin Books.

24 Smith, Mike. 2015. *Targeted: How Technology Is Revolutionizing Advertising and the Way Companies Reach Consumers.* New York: AMACOM.

25 Thompson, Ben. 2015. Retrieved from https://stratechery.com/2015/netflix-and-the-conservation-of-attractive-profits.

26 Thompson, Ben. 2015. Retrieved from https://stratechery.com/2015/aggregation-theory/.

27 Auletta, Ken. *Frenemies: The Epic Disruption of the Ad Business (and Everything Else).* New York: Penguin Books.

28 Levitt, Theodore. 1970. "The morality(?) of advertising." *Harvard Business Review,* July–August.

29 Ogilvy, David. 1989. *Confessions of an Advertising Man,* 2nd ed. New York: Atheneum.

30 Levitt, Theodore. 1970. "The morality (?) of advertising." *Harvard Business Review,* July–August.

31 Miller, Claire Cain and Bui, Quoctrung. 2017. "Switching Careers Is Hard: It Doesn't Have To Be." *New York Times.* Retrieved from http://www.nytimes.com/2017/07/27/upshot/switching-careers-is-hard-it-doesn't-have-to-be.html.

2

Selling in the Digital Era

Charles Warner

Chapter 1 covered the Internet's and Google's disruption of the marketing/advertising/media ecosystem. The Internet also disrupted the way media salespeople sell advertising. In his book *Googled: The End of the World As We Know It*, Ken Auletta writes about a July, 2003, meeting in Google's Mountain View, CA offices with Viacom's CEO Mel Karmazin and Google's Larry Page, Sergey Brin, and Eric Schmidt, then CEO of Google.

"Karmazin was among the first major executives from the old media to visit its headquarters. As CEO of Viacom, he represented the world's then fourth largest media company – the owner of the CBS network, of TV and radio stations, Paramount Studios, MTV and sister cable networks, Simon & Schuster publishers, Blockbuster video, and an outdoor advertising concern, among other holdings," Auletta wrote.[1]

During the meeting, the Google executives told Karmazin how the self-serve online second-price auction system worked – no advertising salespeople, no negotiating, and no relationships.[i] But what appalled Karmazin the most was the cost-per-click (CPC) pricing model that ensured that "advertisers were only charged when the user clicked on an ad."[2] It was Google's ambition, the founders and Schmidt liked to say, to provide an answer to Wanamaker's complaint that half his advertising was wasted. Therefore, Google offered

---

[i] In March, 2019, Google announced it was abandoning the second-price auction system and was adopting a first-price auction system that is standard practice in programmatic, real-time bidding (RTB) bidding for available inventory.

Media Selling: Digital, Television, Audio, Print and Cross-Platform, Fifth Edition.
Charles Warner, William A. Lederer, and Brian Moroz.
© 2020 John Wiley & Sons, Inc. Published 2020 by John Wiley & Sons, Inc.

their advertisers a free online tool called Google Analytics, which allowed them to track on a daily basis how many clicks and how many sales their search advertising produced, which meant they could easily calculate a return-on-investment (ROI) for their advertising.[3]

Karmazin's CBS salespeople sold advertising based on the theory that advertisers "paid their money and took their chances."[4] Advertisers did not know if their ads were going to work, and salespeople sold on the basis of emotions, relationships, and scarcity, not return-on-investment (ROI) metrics. However, the Google executives thought they could design a better system, one that was measurable and fair to all advertisers, not just to big advertisers. Karmazin could not believe what he heard from the Google executives, and he said, half in jest, to paraphrase his actual words, that they were messing (not his actual word) with the magic![5]

Indeed, Google's AdWords[ii] was not magic, it just reaffirmed how the Internet had disrupted advertising, marketing, the media, and the fundamentals of all media businesses, as indicated in Chapter 1 in the discussion of the value chain and aggregation theory.

What Changed?

A 2018 article in the *Harvard Business Review* titled "Ads that don't overstep" articulated how the Internet changed marketing and, thus, changed how media is sold:

> The Internet has dramatically expanded the modern marketer's tool kit, in large part because of one simple but transformative development: digital data. With users regularly sharing personal data online and Web cookies tracking every click, marketers have been able to gain unprecedented insight into consumers and serve up solutions tailored to their individual needs. The results have been impressive. Research has shown that digital targeting meaningfully improves the response to advertisements and that ad performance declines when marketers' access to consumer data is reduced.[6]

Mel Karmazin's magic has been replaced by data, which some experts have called *the new oil*, and which has made buying and selling media infinitely more complicated than it was before the Internet allowed marketers to micro-target consumers based on their Internet browsing and searching behavior and their intention to buy a product.

Complex digital-era selling requires new assumptions and approaches to media buying and selling, which we will examine in this chapter.

Digital-Era Media Are Still "The Media"

Even though the Internet spawned new ways to create, publish, and distribute news and entertainment content and new ways to buy advertising programmatically, the newly created media platforms such as Google and Facebook are still perceived to be "the

---

[ii] Google changed the name of AdWords to Google Ads effective July 24, 2018.

media" by the public. The media, including digital media, are ubiquitous and powerful, and they transmit advertising, political, cultural, social, and moral messages (either intended or unintended) to a mass audience. Over the years "the media" has been under attack from both the right and left of the political spectrum. In the 1960s, as you learned in Chapter 1, Theodore Levitt defended advertising from critics who thought it was creating a materialistic society. In the 1970s, conservative hawks accused "the media," particularly television, of vilifying the military and for the loss of the war in Vietnam. In the 1990s, liberals and Democrats accused "the media" of prosecuting President Bill Clinton. In the 2016 presidential election "the media" were accused of distributing fake news, especially by Donald Trump.

However, "the media" is not a single, monolithic entity. Media is a plural noun that includes a multitude of outlets – television, digital platforms, radio, newspapers, magazines, out-of-home advertising (billboards and posters), and digital and printed newsletters – that communicate in a multiplicity of voices, political orientations, and opinions.

Because of the complex and fuzzy combination of show business and public service, the media have always been and will continue to be loved and hated, praised and vilified, regulated and deregulated, and given credit or blamed for everything from keeping our nation free to poisoning the minds of our children. Salespeople in the media must learn to deal with all types of extreme reactions and to accept the fact that they, as representatives of their medium, will have to face these, often highly emotional, reactions on a daily basis.

The good news is that, as a salesperson for a medium, you will often have easy access to clients. The bad news is that your medium will be blamed for everything from a client's sore back to the election of an unpopular president, and you will have to listen to the reasons for your medium's and all of the media's failures. Many people tend to lump all the media together as a monolithic target for their anger, so it does not matter if you are selling for a website, a television network, a radio station, or a newspaper, you will probably get comments about how awful the media are. You will have to learn to listen non-defensively, not to take insults personally, and to respond unemotionally and good-naturedly to criticism.

New Assumptions for the Digital Era

The media industry is changing at an accelerated rate in terms of both technological advances and the audience's tastes and needs. As America continues its transition from a production-oriented, analog economy to an information-oriented, digital economy, consumers become more informed and more selective.

Assumption 1: The media are fragmented

In the past, the traditional media enjoyed virtually guaranteed profits, but today the media are becoming increasingly fragmented because of the disruption caused by the Internet. There is a plethora of media, especially digital media, chasing smaller and smaller market segments. As the audiences of traditional media such as newspapers, magazines, and television decline, the audience of digital media is exploding. Google, Facebook, Amazon, and other digital and mobile advertising-supported businesses are growing and, thus, gobbling up more and more of the available advertising dollars. Therefore, profits are declining in most of the traditional media as well as in marginal digital media. However, as the competition for advertising dollars increases, the need for effective salespeople increases.

Even though sales jobs at radio and television stations have declined in many markets, and sales jobs in newspapers and magazines have been reduced dramatically, sales positions in digital and mobile companies have exploded, so that the total number of media sales positions in America has increased overall. Also, media fragmentation has resulted in it being more difficult for the salespeople of smaller media companies and publishers to get traction with marketers and advertising agencies. Therefore, more and more small and medium-sized publishers are turning to selling their advertising inventory programmatically and, thus, are reducing their sales forces. On the other hand, sales jobs in data analytics companies, consultancies, exchanges, and platforms such as Google and Facebook have increased. There have never been so many opportunities for competent salespeople in the media; and yet today, selling is more difficult, complex, and competitive than ever before. To succeed, you must be better trained, better prepared, and better educated than was the case in the past.

Assumption 2: Automation changes the sales process

Over 80 percent of all digital ad inventory is sold on an automated basis, or programmatically. Programmatic refers to the real-time bidding (RTB) for an available online ad impression by a demand-side (advertiser) algorithm, the acceptance of a bid by a supply-side (media) algorithm, and the serving of a digital ad. This bid-ask–purchase–ad-serving process takes place while an ad impression is loading on a laptop or smartphone screen in 200 milliseconds, or in the blink of an eye. Chapter 17 explains in detail how programmatic buying and selling of ad inventory works.

It is estimated that by 2020 the vast majority of all media advertising will be automated – bought and sold programmatically – which means that the negotiating and transaction phase of the media buying and selling process will be done by algorithms in an artificial intelligence (AI) application, not by humans. Therefore, the nature of media selling will change as automation does many of the routine tasks involved in the prospecting, qualifying, researching, proposing, negotiating, and transacting phases of selling as well as the planning and executing of media buys done by marketers and ad agencies. Media selling will become more about educating marketers and media planners about the advantages and benefits of a medium or platform during the planning stage of advertising campaigns. It will be about coming up with innovative ideas regarding targeting, optimization, creative executions, promotions, endorsements, and events that appeal to a medium's specific audience and about connecting emotionally with everyone a salesperson calls on.

Assumption 3: The explosion of complexity makes media selling difficult

There are two main drivers of complexity in selling digital advertising: (1) the marketing ecosystem is more complex and (2) digital ad targeting adds even more layers of complication.

First, the marketing and advertising ecosystem has become infinitely more complex, as visualized in the Display LUMAscape graphic available at https://www.lumapartners.com/luma-institute/lumascapes/display-ad-tech-lumascape/.

The graphic shows the number of service companies that come between marketers such as P&G, AT&T, Amazon, and Ford and publishers such as *The New York Times*, The HuffPost, and NPR. These businesses include:

- Advertising agencies
- Retargeting companies
- Ad Servers
- Verification/Privacy companies
- Agency trading desks
- Creative optimization companies
- Demand-side platforms (DSPs)
- Media planning and attribution companies
- Measurement and analytics companies
- Exchanges
- Data-management platforms (DMPs) and data aggregators
- Data suppliers
- Ad networks (horizontal, vertical, and custom targeted)
- Performance and optimization companies
- Data-sharing and social tools
- Supply-side platforms (SSPs)
- Publisher tools companies
- Media management systems and operations companies

All of these businesses need salespeople who understand both the digital marketing ecosystem and the personal needs, problems, and challenges of media buyers, prospects, customers, and partners.

Second, the switch from broadcast, print, and US Postal Service distribution to Internet distribution has dramatically increased the amount of data available to marketers and, thus, has dramatically increased the ability of marketers to target individual consumers rather than advertise on traditional media like television or radio to broad demographics such as women 18–49. Cookies on web browsers, location data on smartphones, and the Internet Of Things (IOT) – chips in packages, in boxes of food, or in clothing – give marketers mountains of data to use to target specific individual consumers, for example a 34-year-old single woman who has recently looked online for outdoor camping equipment, who lives in the state of Washington, who uses one or more dating apps such as Tinder or Match.com, and who is planning a camping trip on a weekend in the next three weeks. Behavioral, life-style, location, purchase intent, exact age, marital status, and much more data are available about anyone in the US or in the world who uses the Internet on a desktop, laptop, mobile phone, gaming station, or smart TV (smart TVs are connected to the Internet).

The explosion of specific data on individuals has replaced sizzle, magic, wild promises, and broad demographics as the currency in the media. Today virtually all media selling includes a digital component, so media salespeople must understand how digital advertising works and how it is created, purchased by auction, placed, targeted, served, tested, measured, and verified.

Assumption 4: Much of digital advertising is unpopular

In a January 31, 2018 article in *The New York Times* titled "Tackling the Internet's central villain: The advertising business," technology reporter Farhad Manjoo writes, "There's a lot of dark stuff. In one corner, you have the Russian campaign to influence the 2016 presidential election with digital propaganda. In another, a rash of repugnant videos on YouTube…"[7] Manjoo further writes, "Then there's tech 'addiction,' the rising worry that adults and kids are getting hooked on smartphones and social networks despite our best efforts to resist the constant desire for a fix." Manjoo lays the blame for these problems on the advertising business. He suggests:

> Ads are the lifeblood of the Internet, the source of funding for just about everything you read, watch and hear online. The digital ad business is in many ways a miracle machine – it corrals and transforms latent attention into real money that pays for truly useful inventions, from search to instant translation to video hosting to global mapping.
>
> But the online ad machine is also a vast, opaque and dizzyingly complex contraption with underappreciated capacity for misuse…

Furthermore in 2018, a Kantar Millward Brown survey revealed that people believe digital ads are becoming more invasive. The study showed that 71 percent of respondents to the survey said that ads were more invasive than they were three years earlier. A similar number of respondents said they were seeing more ads overall, and even a larger percentage responded that they thought that ads were appearing in more places they visited.[8] So, consumers as well as media critics and reporters are attacking digital advertising, especially too much and too intrusive advertising.

Because of criticisms like that of Manjoo and of consumers, media salespeople, especially those selling digital media advertising, must make sure they are selling responsible, truthful, not overly intrusive advertising that appears in brand-safe content and that they are closely adhering to the Five Cs of Ethical Responsibility, as defined in the Chapter 3 of this book.

With these new assumptions in mind, let's look at several approaches to successful media selling.

Approaches

An old approach that still works

The question most asked by beginning salespeople is, "Where do I start?" The answer is to start with the AESKOPP approach.

AESKOPP is a mnemonic that will help you remember the following elements of successful selling:

- Attitude
- Emotional intelligence
- Skills
- Knowledge
- Opportunities
- Preparation
- Persistence

We will look at each element of the AESKOPP approach closely in Chapter 4.

New selling approaches for the digital era

Matthew Dixon and Brent Adamson's 2011 book, *The Challenger Sale: Taking Control of the Customer Conversation*, was "the most important advance in selling for many years," according to Neil Rackham the author *Spin Selling*, one of the most influential books ever written about selling, and the go-to book for sales training until *The Challenger Sale* was published.[9]

Dixon and Adamson were Executive Directors of the Corporate Executive Board's (CEB) Sales Executive Council (SEC), and in 2009 launched

> What was to become one of the most important studies of sales rep productivity in decades. Tasked by our members – heads of sales for the world's largest, best-known companies – we set out to identify what exactly set this very special group of top-performing sales reps apart. And having now studied that question intensively for the better part of four years, spanning dozens of companies and thousands of sales reps, we have discovered four core insights that have fundamentally rewritten the sales playbook and let B2B sales executives all over the world think differently about how they sell.[10]

Prior to the debilitating recession that hit America in 2008 as a result of the subprime mortgage meltdown, solution selling had been the preferred approach used by enterprise, or business-to-business (B2B), selling, which includes media selling. The fourth edition of *Media Selling*, published in 2009, espoused a solutions-based approach. However, the research of Dixon and Adamson showed that several trends had reduced the effectiveness of solution selling:

1 The customer burden of solutions
2 The rise of the consensus-based sale
3 Increased risk aversion
4 Greater demand for customization

These trends identified by authors of *The Challenger Sale* also broadly apply to selling media.

The customer burden of solutions   Solution selling requires a deep understanding of a customer's business, customer problems and challenges, customer strategy, and a customer's competitors, all of which require asking customers a lot of questions. This process of discovery and investigation consumes a great deal of a customer's time, which business customers are less and less willing to give. Furthermore, in the age of Internet disruption, many customers are unaware of some of their more pressing problems and especially of the opportunities available in digital media.

Also, advertising agencies purchase the majority of national media advertising by using a highly formalized request-for-proposal (RFP) process, although because of programmatic buying, the use of RFPs is declining. You can see examples of RFPs at http://mediaselling.us/downloads.html. Agencies email RFPs to media salespeople and expect proposed schedules emailed back that meet the criteria specified in the RFPs. Face-to-face selling is kept to a minimum because of the vast number of media outlets, and only salespeople from large media brands such as Google, Facebook, ABC, CBS, FOX, NBC, ESPN, BuzzFeed, Huff Post, or Snapchat, for example, can get personal selling time with major agency buyers and planners, who are neither interested in nor have time for solutions-based selling approaches; they only want to know the price, the medium's ability to deliver impressions to a specific target audience, the social-media support a schedule will be given, the appropriateness of the content, and the responsive service they will get. Effectively selling media to agencies requires conversations with agency planners and buyers before an RFP is crafted in order to affect the scope of the RFP so that it favors in some way the medium being sold. On the other hand, if a buy is being made programmatically and no RFP is going to be issued, effective selling to agencies requires educating the agency planners and buyers on the benefits of your medium so they will consider putting it in a media plan and buying it.

Local businesses that place ads in media, such as on radio and television stations or in local newspapers and magazines, are typically interested in solutions to their marketing problems and, thus, are willing to take the time to share information about their businesses with salespeople. Local advertisers will usually answer discovery questions and will be grateful for help in crafting solutions to their marketing problems and in navigating a complex and fragmented media environment.

John Zimmer and his brother, Don, own the Zimmer Radio and Marketing Group in the Columbia-Jefferson City, MO market. The group consists of nine radio stations, three magazines, creative services, website design and development, logo design, digital promotion, social media, print design, and jingle production – a complete integrated marketing communications offering. The Zimmer Group has 20 salespeople who are trained to assess the marketing and advertising needs of local businesses and propose integrated, cross-platform solutions, including being an advertising agency that plans and buys digital media, primarily Google and Facebook, in addition to placing radio, television, and magazine schedules.

The salespeople for the *American-Statesman* newspaper in Austin, TX, also sell on a cross-platform basis. Over 20 percent of the *American-Statesman's* total revenue comes from the digital edition of the paper and from two other websites, Austin 360, a things-to-do website and Ahora Si!, a Spanish-language version of the newspaper. The *American-Statesman* also offers an advertising agency service to its clients, similar to what the Zimmer Radio and Marketing Group offers.

These two media companies are bucking a trend of local radio and newspaper advertising revenue decline by offering cross-platform, full-service solutions to local advertisers. The Zimmer Radio and Marketing Group and the *Austin American-Statesman* are partnering with local businesses and helping both themselves and their partners grow.

The rise of the consensus-based sale   As the media have fragmented and buying so many media alternatives has become more complex, the need for consensus to get big media deals done has increased. A major shift in media placement strategy, for example moving significant ad dollars out of broadcast television or radio and placing it in digital media, is a decision that a chief marketing officer (CMO) is often not willing to make alone or without input from multiple sources, including the company's CEO. Dixon and Adamson's research for *The Challenger Sale* indicated that widespread support for a supplier across a decision-maker's team is the number-one thing senior executives look for in making a purchase decision.[11]

This need for consensus requires that for major media investments salespeople must call on and persuade multiple levels of client and agency personnel, which, of course, means an investment of a great deal of time and effort. This need for consensus also means that salespeople should be adept at and comfortable with establishing and maintaining relationships at multiple client and agency levels if the situation calls for it.

Increased risk aversion   According to Dixon and Adamson, "As deals have become more complex and more expensive, most customers are much more concerned about whether they'll *ever* see a return on their investment."[12] This general increase in risk aversion applies to the media, especially to buying programmatically, which is quite confusing to many marketers. Thus, in a risk-averse environment, media sellers need to establish a high level of trust in order to mitigate their clients' fear of uncertainty and of making a mistake. For example, on a national basis, even though a large advertiser, such as AT&T or its advertising agency, could buy Google keywords such as "mobile phone service" on the Google Ads (formerly AdWords) self-serve auction platform, Google has a sales team that handles the AT&T buying of keywords.

On a local basis, many media outlets such as the Zimmer Radio and Marketing Group and the *Austin American-Statesman* are partnering with clients and delivering full-service ad agency buying, designing, creative, and optimization functions in order to reduce their client's apprehension in placing cross-platform advertising.

Greater demand for customization   A one-size-fits-all solution is no longer a viable approach to selling in general, and particularly in the media. When selling media, every advertiser wants to feel special and that they are not only different from other businesses but especially different from their competitors. An offer for each customer must be customized according to the client's unique business goals and strategies and framed according to the unique personality of the decision-making individual.

Customization means that every sales call, every proposal, and every presentation has to be crafted differently and, of course, it takes time to do in-depth research to understand a client's industry, goals, strategies, creative approach, and personal needs. Also, one critical part of the customization process is analyzing a multitude of data available on a client to find insights that might help a client get better results through its advertising efforts.

New approach 1: Serving the customer

Chapter 9 in Daniel Pink's 2012 book titled *To Sell Is Human: The Surprising Truth About Moving Others* is titled "Serve." Pink writes: "[Servant selling]…begins with the idea that those who move others aren't manipulators but servants. They serve first and sell later."[13]

Facebook does not have a sales division; it has a partnership group. The difference is that a pre-Internet-era media sales department handled transactions, but the Facebook partnership group works with advertisers and marketers to educate them on the best way to use Facebook's ability to micro-target consumers on a wide range of behavioral, psychographic, gender, and preference dimensions.

A serving-the-customer, partnership approach means that both the buyer and the seller are interested in enhancing the growth and profitability of each. They are on the same side and have the same mission, goals, and strategies for growth and, most importantly, are not adversaries who are trying to maximize just their own profits.

The concept of selling as serving, or helping, customers is vital in the digital era. Media salespeople must take the approach that they are helping marketers be successful. Media salespeople help advertising agency buyers get what they want for their clients and help advertisers get results as advertisers define results.

The importance of the perspective of selling as helping others is reinforced dramatically in Johann Hari's 2018 book, *Lost Connections*, in which the author recaps several scientific studies that show that often people are happier when they do something for someone else than when they do something for themselves. This unexpected conclusion comes from studies by evolutionary biologists that suggest *homo sapiens* became the dominant species on earth primarily because we learned to cooperate, to help others, to be primarily concerned about the welfare of the tribe, or the community, rather than to be selfish and primarily concerned about our own, individual welfare. We learned to share, to cooperate, in order to survive.[14]

Thus, many people (not all) are happiest and feel more fulfilled when they are helping and serving others. They get more *intrinsic* value from connecting with people and helping them. Also, when you sell local media advertising, you are helping to fuel the economy and enabling your community to remain prosperous by helping local businesses be successful.[15]

Some definitions   Following are some definitions that will clarify the concepts of selling as serving and clients as partners:

Buyers are divided into three types: prospects, customers, and partners.

> *Prospects* are people who have not bought a product for a variety of reasons, ranging from never having heard of it to disliking it; prospects require *missionary selling*. In the media, prospects might be those people who: (1) have never before advertised because they have an established business that they feel does not need advertising; (2) have never advertised before because they are starting a new business; (3) advertise but not in your medium; or (4) advertise in your medium but do not use your platform, website, mobile app, network, station, newspaper, cable system, or magazine.

> *Customers* are people who have either decided to buy a product or who have already bought a product and are going to buy it again. Customers require outrageous service that will delight them and make them "raving fans."[16]

> *Partners* are customers who have collaborated with a media company to conduct business based on mutual trust and, in a sense, to help each other to be more successful by cooperating in discovering innovative solutions that connect a partner to a medium's audience in a way that delivers partner-defined results and jointly builds the business of both companies.

Investments are advertising dollars placed in the media. In the past advertising money has been "spent" in the media; however, many marketers and their advertising and media agencies have realized that advertising is an investment in future sales of a product. Major media agencies promote the concept of advertising as an investment. For example, WPP's media agency Group M refers to itself as "the world's largest investment group."[17] Media salespeople should always refer to advertising as an investment. Thus, rather than asking a prospect, "How much money do you spend in advertising?" ask, "How much money do you invest in advertising?" It is important for media salespeople to educate marketers about the fact that their advertising is an investment.

Products are either tangible or intangible. Tangible products are goods that can be seen and touched, such as automobiles, personal computers, or cosmetics. Intangible products are services that cannot be seen, touched, or tested in advance, such as insurance, financial services, or advertising. Tangible products can be experienced and they are usually easy to demonstrate – product features and benefits are apparent before a purchase. However, even tangible products have some degree of intangibility, as pointed out by Theodore Levitt, "You can't taste in advance or even see sardines in a can or soap in a box. This is common for frequently purchased moderate- to low-priced consumer goods. To make buyers more comfortable and confident about tangibles that can't be pre-tested, companies go beyond the literal promises of specifications, advertisements, and labels to provide reassurance."[18]

Packaging is one common tool used to make the intangible elements of products more tangible in a consumer's mind – for example, putting pickles in a glass jar so purchasers can see them. Advertising is another tool used to communicate advance assurances that a product is what it says it is.

It is harder to keep customers satisfied with intangible products than with tangible ones. The biggest problem with intangible services – such as advertising, insurance, or banking services – is that customers are usually not aware of the full range of services they are getting until they no longer get them. Therefore, they rarely appreciate the positives, and the negatives tend to be blown out of proportion. This situation means that intangibles require more service and greater efforts on the part of salespeople. From now on all products and services will be referred to as *products*, whether they are tangible or intangible.

New approach 2: Focus on customer success

In 2003 Mel Karmazin's CBS television and radio salespeople's approach had not changed since I was Eastern Sales Manager and then VP and General Manager of CBS Radio Spot Sales from 1967 to 1971. The approach was internally focused, and its sole purpose was to maximize revenue for CBS and the stations Radio Spot Sales represented. This maximizing revenue approach meant that salespeople sold the "magic," which was typically audience estimate numbers (ratings) and promises of ad positioning that they often could not keep. For example, a media buyer would place an order with a local television station salesperson for a schedule of 12 spots a week that were to run for a month in morning, early, and late news programs. However, one-third of the scheduled 48 spots would be preempted (not run) for various phantom reasons such as "technical difficulties." Station sales managers would preempt a part of virtually all schedules to take subsequent orders placed at higher rates. Therefore, an inordinate amount of salespeople's time was spent negotiating makegoods with media buyers, who were made furious over this preemption-and-makegood process. This system was highly inefficient, ethically questionable, and totally self-serving, not customer serving or customer focused. Such a system was based on the leverage that local television and high-rated radio stations and television networks took advantage of because they had scarce ad inventory that was in high demand.

However, the birth and unprecedented growth of Internet advertising reduced the leverage of television and radio stations by expanding to virtual infinity the amount of available advertising inventory. This expansion changed the marketing ecosystem from one of scarcity before the Internet to one of abundance, and when Google introduced the self-serve online auction model with AdWords,[iii] advertisers had direct access to advertising inventory on which the auction market, not media sales management, set ad prices that were affordable and guaranteed to run as ordered.

Google, then Facebook and other Internet advertising platforms, led the way to a different approach. Instead of an old-fashioned media sales department's focus being *internal* – to maximize revenue – a contemporary media sales department's focus has to be *external* – on a customer's success.

[iii] Google changed the name of AdWords to Google Ads effective July 24, 2018.

New approach 3: Selling as educating

Adopting serving-the-customer and focus-on-customer-success approaches led to a third new approach to selling in the digital era, that of selling as educating.

Media Selling, 4th Edition recommended a systematic approach to selling that broke down the sales process into six steps: (1) prospecting, (2) identifying problems, (3) generating solutions, (4) presenting, (5) negotiating and closing, and (6) servicing. These steps have changed because of the disruptions caused by the Internet. You have learned from reading about *The Challenger Sale* research above that the identifying problems and generating solutions steps are no longer viable in the digital-era selling process because they put too much burden on prospects who do not have time for answering questions about their problems to which salespeople can offer ready-made solutions. Prospects want customized solutions, but only after they understand more about the complexities and possibilities of advertising in the digital age.

Virtually all media selling today includes some element of cross-platform selling, for example selling both the print and digital editions of *The New York Times*. Therefore, the old presenting step of selling has been replaced by an educating step because the presenting step was based on an assumption that prospects were familiar with the medium being presented and were able to evaluate one-size-fits-all solutions.

An educating step makes no such assumption and focuses on teaching prospects about the complexities and opportunities of digital or cross-platform advertising. Also, prospects and buyers want to be kept up to date on the rapidly changing media ecosystem and technology. In a 2018 column in *Radio Inc*, Beasley Broadcasting's VP/Sales, Bob McCurdy writes:

> I recall several years back when Kim Vasey, a Senior Partner Director of Radio at GroupM addressed our sales staff and reinforced this message, stressing the need to continue to "educate and re-educate" clients and ad agencies, citing turnover and the difficulty of staying on top of all the new developments in media. This challenge is even more acute in 2018.[19]

Therefore, educating and re-educating prospects, customers, planners, and buyers not only meets the needs of those selling media but also meets the needs of those buying media.

New approach 4: Algorithms and AI are the competition

Because the majority of mobile, online, and soon television, radio, and large, national newspaper ad inventory will be bought programmatically by artificial intelligence (AI) and algorithms, a media salesperson's biggest competition is not other media salespeople, it is the algorithms in AI applications. There are three choices today for buying advertising: (1) buy programmatically indirectly via a network of third-party providers, (2) buy programmatically direct from publishers or buy by means of an online, automated, self-serve auction (e.g. Google, Facebook), or (3) buy through a salesperson. If advertising buys are made programmatically or on an online auction, algorithms do the bidding, do the negotiating, complete the transactions, serve the ads, and optimize the creative – untouched by human hands...or hearts.

Media salespeople must ask themselves, "What can I, as a human, offer that artificial intelligence cannot?" Algorithms and AI are "designed to work in a rigid environment."[20] Human beings prefer to connect emotionally with other human beings; AI cannot do that. "Humans are able to make analogies or recognize similarities in different contexts," which gives them much better judgment and allows them to be flexible.[21] AI is not yet warm or cuddly or flexible and does not know how to connect emotionally to a prospect or buyer; therefore, salespeople have an obvious advantage – they can laugh with buyers when the buyers are happy, they can cry with prospects when the prospects are unhappy, they can hug a customer when the customer needs a hug. AI can only deal with data. AI cannot give hugs...yet, although AI applications such as IPsoft's Amelia are getting closer to connecting emotionally every day with applications such as sentiment analysis and tone analysis (see IBM's Watson Tone Analyzer at https://www.ibm.com/watson/developercloud/tone-analyzer/api/v3/curl.html).

In later chapters you will learn how to understand people and their personal needs, and how to connect with them emotionally.

Mission, Objectives, Strategies, and Tactics

The transition to an Internet-dominated, digital economy created a shifting emphasis for media salespeople from that of selling and getting an order toward one of building relationships, solving problems, and educating customers based on insights coming from analyzing data. Meanwhile, there was less time available for preparation, planning, and purchasing as advertising campaigns ran for shorter and shorter periods of time, and buyers often wait until the last minute to place schedules or buy programmatically.

The new approaches explained above also require an understanding of a hierarchical set of concepts: a sales organization's *mission, objectives, strategies,* and *tactics.* As in any military or business organization, in a sales organization the salespeople must understand these four concepts and follow their precepts in order to have consistent and meaningful selling-as-serving, focus-on-customer-success, selling-as-educating, and connecting-emotionally approaches.

Another important reason for emphasizing a sales organization's mission that includes such values as selling-as-serving, focus-on-customer-success, and selling-as-educating is because having a job that is serving-oriented and meaningful is what a large majority of young people entering the job market today are looking for. A 2018 *Harvard Business Review* article titled "9 out of 10 people are willing to earn less money to do more-meaningful work" details the many advantages to companies of providing meaningful, purpose-driven work to employees.[22]

However, before a sales organization (division or department) can articulate sales-specific mission, objectives, strategies, and tactics, it must answer the purpose question about the company or organization it is a part of. The purpose question is, "What is our reason for existence?"

Peter Drucker's view of a company's only purpose being "to create a customer" was written in 1954, and was helpful for businesses in that era, but people and their needs have changed over the 65 years since Drucker made that often-quoted statement. Drucker's intent almost certainly was to shift businesses, particularly manufacturing businesses, from an internal, production-focused approach to an external, customer-focused, marketing-oriented approach, which many of them subsequently did. In the 1970s, 1980s, and 1990s, most major businesses took a customer-focused, marketing approach to their businesses.

But in the early 2000s the Enron and Worldcom scandals put a spotlight on corporate greed and deception as a new generation of employees entered the workforce. This new generation wanted more from their employers than just a paycheck. Many of them wanted meaning in their work at the same time as the Internet was changing the world. Internet companies, in order to attract talented young people, began to adapt purpose or mission statements that gave meaning to the work the young people did.

Google adopted a motto of "don't be evil" and articulated a purpose or mission to express the reason for its existence: "To organize the world's information and make it universally accessible and useful." Google has since dropped the slogan "don't be evil," but still is driven by its meaningful and inspiring mission, which is one of the many reasons in 2017 Google topped the list of *Fortune* magazine's list of the best companies to work for in America for the eighth time in 11 years.

Facebook is also considered by many young people to be one of most desirable companies to work for in America. In LinkedIn's 2018 list of top companies at which people wanted to work, Facebook ranked number three, behind Amazon and Alphabet (Google's parent company). One of the reasons for Facebook's popularity is its mission statement: "Making the world more open and connected." However, in 2018, Facebook CEO Mark Zuckerberg announced a change in the mission statement. It is now: "Bring the world closer together," which is still inspiring and positive and more in tune with Facebook's effort to reduce fake news and divisive posts, some of which were attributed to Russia during the 2016 US presidential election.

Google and Facebook's mission statements have been widely covered in the general and trade press. Why? Because the concept of a business doing well by doing good, in other words, having a commitment, or cause, of serving their communities and doing something good for humanity has been shown to be good business because it attracts and keeps good, purpose-driven employees. Having a meaningful cause also appeals to consumers and suppliers.

For example, Facebook surveys its workforce twice a year, asking employees what they value most. After examining hundreds of thousands of answers over several years, the company identified three primary motivators: career, community, and cause. In a *Harvard Business Review* online article written by Facebook HR executives and Adam Grant, cause was defined as follows: "Cause is about purpose: feeling that you make a meaningful impact, identifying with the organization's mission, and believing that it does some good in the world. It's a source of pride."[23] These findings from Facebook reinforce the notion that having a meaningful purpose, or cause, is a significant motivator for employees.

Even many traditional manufacturing companies have adopted socially conscious mission, or purpose, statements. For example, the mission statement of P&G, one of the world's largest advertisers, is: "We will provide branded products and services of superior quality and value that improve the lives of the world's consumers."

One of the reasons for the corporate emphasis on meaningful mission, or purpose, statements is the realization that, in general, most people want a sense of meaning in their work, as Facebook discovered. In Daniel Pink's 2011 book, *Drive: The Surprising Truth About What Motivates Us*, the author writes that there are three things that motivate humans: *autonomy, mastery,* and *purpose*. People want autonomy because they do not like to be told what to do all the time. They seek mastery because there is an inherent drive to be good at something. They seek purpose to give meaning to their work.

Therefore, a sales organization must be in synch with its corporate mission, its corporate purpose. So, if you work for Google in sales, the purpose, or mission, of the company is, "To organize the world's information and make it universally accessible and useful," but Google's sales organization has its own mission to support its corporate mission.

Mission

The mission of a media sales organization is simple and direct, it is *to get customers and keep them*.

The mission of an old-fashioned media sales department was to maximize revenue, which is an internally focused mission that met a media company's economic need but did not give nourishing meaning to the work that salespeople do. Pink's three motivational drives do not include making money, making budget, or maximizing revenue because increasing revenue or making a revenue budget tends to make the owners of the media richer than it makes salespeople. Thus, working harder to make someone else richer does not seem to be terribly meaningful to the vast majority of media salespeople. In order to be motivational, a mission or purpose has to be meaningful. It has to give meaning to the work people do – to make them feel good about what they are doing – and for media salespeople, turning customers into partners and helping them get results and be successful makes them feel good about what they are doing.

Objectives

The four objectives of a media sales organization in order to fulfill its mission to get customers and keep them are:

1   To get results for customers
2   To develop new business
3   To retain and increase current business
4   To delight customers

To get results for customers   Results must be defined by customers – increased sales, reduced distribution costs, increased profit margins, increased share of market, high ROI, increased product awareness, or improved corporate image, for example. Salespeople must help customers get results for two reasons: (1) if customers do not get results, they will not renew their advertising schedules, and, thus, salespeople must take a long-term view and create renewable business, and they must get results for customers as the customers define results; and (2) helping people makes a salesperson's job more meaningful, and, therefore, makes both the customer and the salesperson happier.

Also, communicating the primary objective of getting results not only helps turn customers into partners, but also communicates that you care more about them than about yourself, your commissions, or maximizing revenue for your company. But getting results for customers and partners also leads to you and your company making more money because virtually all advertising budgets are based on a percentage of total sales. For example, in 2017 beverage industry companies averaged investing 4.1 percent of their total sales in advertising, and department stores invested 4.0 percent of their total sales in advertising.[24] These percentages of sales invested in advertising by industry tend to remain relatively stable over time, which means that if a customer or partner gets results and sales go up, say 10 percent, its advertising budget is almost certain to go up 10 percent. Therefore, the customer's investment in your medium will probably go up 10 percent or more.

To develop new business   That is, to turn prospects into customers and then partners. A sales organization must continually develop new business from agencies and clients not only to replace accounts that are lost each year due to normal account attrition but also to ensure growth. Another important reason for constantly developing new business is to create demand, because it is demand that largely determines the price of media advertising.

To retain and increase current business   Managing customers obsessively in order to delight them and getting them to renewal is vital. Just as important is to continually pre-sell and provide clients and agencies with solid evidence, reasons, and, especially, ideas, for them to increase their investment in your medium. Your best prospects are your current partners, and continually showing them the benefits of your medium and getting an increased investment from them is crucial for growth.

On every account contact, always present customers with ideas that will lead to an increased investment and will reinforce the value of their current investment. Remember that advertising is an intangible product that requires more reinforcement, servicing, and reassurance than a tangible product would. Partners require constant attention if you are going to retain and increase current business.

To delight customers   If you are going to put customers first, get results for them, and get all-important renewals, then you are going to have to woo, wow, and delight them, as described in Tom Stewart and Patricia O'Connell's *Woo, Wow, and Win: Service Design, Strategy and the Art of Customer Delight*.[25] When Steve Jobs was CEO of Apple, he made delighting customers his mantra and, in his book *The Leader's Guide to Radical Management*, Steve Denning states the first principle of radical management: "The goal of work is to delight clients."[26] More and more sales organizations of major companies are evaluating and compensating their salespeople based on levels of customer satisfaction, service, success, and, in effect, delight. That means that salespeople must not only make a sale, but also delight customers and partners by means of excellent service after the sale. Chapter 14: Customer Success covers the techniques of delighting customers and partners.

In some smaller organizations with a limited sales staff, all four of the above objectives might be assigned to a single salesperson. However, in larger media organizations such as Facebook, CBS, or iHeart Media some of the above objectives might be divided into separate and discrete functions. For example, getting results for partners might be the overall objective of all sales job functions, but developing new business might be the objective given to a business development or partnership staff, retaining and increasing current business might be the objective of an agency sales staff, and delighting partners might be the objective of an account management or customer success staff.

Strategies

Strategies are long-term, overall operating concepts and principles that guide actions toward stated objectives. In order to achieve the above sales objectives, salespeople should follow these sales strategies:

1 Create value
2 Research and develop insights into prospects' and customers' problems, challenges, pain points, and competitive positioning
3 Become an expert about how your medium works and solves marketing and advertising problems
4 Become the preferred supplier
5 Innovate

Create value   A salesperson's most important sales strategy is to create value for their product, to create a perception of a *differential competitive advantage* of their product in prospects', buyers', and customers' minds. Creating value means telling a compelling story and educating your prospects, buyers, and customers about your product and medium. Here's an example of creating value with a sales story:

1 A new kids' toothpaste is blue and tastes like bubble gum.
2 A revolutionary new product that is a glistening, bright, cool, deep blue color that shimmers with flecks of silver, making it interesting, exciting, and fun for children to

push out of a dispenser that is easy for small hands to manipulate. Its foaming action in the mouth is new and different; it is thicker and foamier, as if something important is really working in kids' mouths to fight cavities and to make their breath smell great so their mommies will know they really did brush their teeth. When the kids first taste their very own type of new toothpaste that is not for adults, they experience a taste sensation unlike any other. It is not toothpaste; it is bubble gum! Kids cannot wait to brush their teeth several times a day. They are likely to say after lunch, "Well, I think I'd better go brush my teeth."

Which of the above two sales stories about a new kids' toothpaste creates more value for the product? Which sales story is better? Which story is more likely to make the sale? The second description tells a story and creates value for the product, which is positioned according to its benefits to the kids.

You must become a brand evangelist for your product.[27] You will find a much more thorough discussion of the many ways to create value in Chapter 7: Influence and Creating Value.

Research and develop insights into prospects' and customers' problems, challenges, pain points, and competitive positioning   Potential advertisers do not care about a website or app's underlying code, a broadcast station's power or antenna height, a cable system's type of commercial insert equipment, or a magazine or newspaper's press size or color-separation ability – these are all features. What prospects care about is how advertising is going to help them solve marketing or advertising problems and challenges. Solutions to these problems are benefits. Therefore, salespeople must learn to position their offerings in such a way that they always answer prospects' question, "What's in it for me (WIIFM)," as is covered in depth in Chapter 10: Researching Insights and Solutions and Chapter 11: Educating.

Become an expert about how your medium works and solves marketing and advertising problems   Effective selling is a lot more than just building and managing relationships; it requires being an expert about how your medium or product works and solves marketing and advertising problems. Effective selling requires being an expert in teaching prospects how to use your medium, tailoring your proposals to the needs of your prospects, and taking control of the sales conversation in order to give insights into how your solutions work.

Become the preferred supplier   Salespeople must create so much value for their medium or product that they become the preferred supplier with both a partner and that partner's advertising agency if they have one. It is highly probable that clients will eventually change advertising agencies, so salespeople should create value and establish relationships at the client level. In order to become the preferred supplier, or preferred partner, salespeople must provide more and better information and service than any other salesperson from any other medium so the customer will think of them first when they need information or want to invest in advertising.

Innovate   In the *Harvard Business Review* article titled "The best salespeople do what the best brands do," author Denise Lee Yohn writes that "the best brands ignore trends. Great salespeople don't imitate, they innovate...[they] offer their customers unique perspectives and often seek to push their thinking. They present a differentiated sales experience by challenging customers' status quo and teaching them something new and valuable."[28] Every product and medium must also continually innovate: new packages, new ad formats, new promotions and contests, new content, new special sections, new functionality, new ways to access information, and new events. New products and opportunities such as those mentioned give salespeople a reason to make another call on a customer or agency, they create excitement, and they provide new ways to solve marketing and advertising problems.

Key tactics

A salesperson has three key tactics to use on a day-to-day basis to help them carry out their broader strategies:

1   To create a differential competitive advantage
2   To build relationships
3   To solve problems

To create a differential competitive advantage   Salespeople who cannot find ways to create differential competitive advantages for their product and for themselves are merely order-takers or clerks who wait on customers and process transactions, and they will not build a long-term career in the highly competitive environment of media selling.

To build relationships   A relationship must be built on mutual trust and respect, and salespeople must take the long view when managing a relationship. The relationship between a salesperson and a customer does not end when a sale is made; it is just beginning of the relationship from the customer's point of view. The relationship should intensify over time and help to determine a customer's buying choices.

To solve problems   Salespeople must be creative in solving advertising problems that get results for customers. The objectives of a salesperson begin with getting results for customers, and a salesperson's key functions end with solving problems for them. You cannot get results unless you learn first to discover and then solve problems.

Related functions   A salesperson has three functions that support the key tactics:

1   To monitor the marketplace
2   To recommend tactics
3   To cooperate

To monitor the marketplace.   Salespeople must provide information to their management and other salespeople about competitors in all media – their pricing, strategies, content or format changes, management and ownership changes, advertising and promotion strategies, and sales strategies and tactics. Competitive intelligence is vital to your management in determining your company's competitive strategy.

To recommend tactics.   A salesperson should recommend new selling tactics, new questions to ask, new packages, promotions, and changes in selling approaches to their management as a result of what they learn on the street about what competitors and other media are doing.

To cooperate.   It's important for all salespeople in your department to learn from each other's experiences – successes and failures; to help the sales department meet its strategic selling objectives; to cooperate in completing reports, expense accounts, and insertion orders (IO) accurately and on time; to help with promotions, parties, and events; and to cover for other salespeople who are absent. Departments in which the mode of operating is cooperative are more productive than those in which the operating mode is competitive, according to Alfie Kohn in his 1986 book, *No Contest: The Case Against Competition.*

These are the key tactics and related functions for salespeople. Their responsibility is to demonstrate an intelligent effort (DIE) in carrying out these tactics and functions. In other words, not only must digital-era salespeople do what they are supposed to do to carry out these tactics and functions, but they must also let their management know that they are doing so diligently, that they are implementing the company's strategy which management has designed to reach the company's objectives.

An outline of the above approaches, mission, objectives, strategies, key tactics, and related functions can be downloaded onto your smartphone so you can refer to it often and so it can act as a reminder at www.mediaselling.us/downloads.html.

Exhibit 2.1 details how the competencies of salespeople in the digital era have changed from those previously required. Hiring managers are now looking for people who can analyze data, think strategically, and learn the business.

Digital-era media salespeople also need to apply the competencies listed in Exhibit 2.1 to two different types of selling.

Types of Selling

Now that you have a foundation consisting of the assumptions about and approaches to digital-era media selling, you need to know how to apply them to different types of selling.

There are two basic types of selling: *missionary selling* and *service selling*. Successful salespeople must apply a selling-as-educating approach to whichever type of selling they are engaged in. Often salespeople are described as *hunters* or *farmers* depending on the type of selling they do.

Exhibit 2.1   Salespeople require different competencies than they did two decades ago

Percent appearance in job profiles				Percent appearance in job profiles			
Top competencies in the past	Pre-2000	2000–2009	2010–2014	Top competencies today	Pre-2000	2000–2009	2010–2014
Develops sales leads	30%	12%	8%	Prioritizes tasks through logical analysis	10%	15%	17%
Commits time and effort to ensure success	20%	12%	6%	Embraces strategic vision/implements corporate direction	0	8%	13%
Qualifies prospects with standard probes	45%	9%	7%	Ability to learn the business	0	2%	10%
Willingness to deal with multiple tasks	20%	7%	3%	Controlled work approach	5%	3%	8%

Source: Cespedes, Frank V. and Weinfuter, Daniel. 2015. "The best ways to hire salespeople." *Harvard Business Review*. Used with permission.

Hunters are salespeople who have the personality, motivation, experience, and preference to do missionary selling which involves developing new business – finding new partners to a medium (television, online, for example) and to a media outlet (a station or a website, for example) – and typically involves calling on customers, including local retailers, and not calling on advertising agencies. Missionary selling is also commonly referred to as *direct selling*.

Farmers are salespeople who have the personality, motivation, experience, and preference to do service selling, which includes calling on, servicing, and getting increased business from current customers. Service selling typically involves calling on advertising agencies.

Both types of selling require the ability to build trusting relationships with different types of customers and partners.

Two types of customers

In their *Harvard Business Review* article "Make sure your customers keep coming back," F. Stewart DeBruicker and Gregory Summe identify two types of customers: inexperienced generalists and experienced specialists.[29] In media selling, examples of inexperienced generalists are smaller customers, often retailers and others called on direct (those who do not have an advertising agency), who are new to advertising in a medium. Examples of experienced specialists are advertising agency media buyers. DeBruicker and Summe point out that selling and creating value strategies to these two types of customers must be different.

Inexperienced generalists typically do many jobs in their businesses. For example, a small, owner-run retailer might keep the books, set up displays, and do personal selling as well as place advertising. If this retailer, who we will call John, is unfamiliar with radio, for instance, he wants to know how to buy it, how to schedule it, how to write copy, and how to best position his store to appeal to his target customers. John is more interested in expert marketing and advertising advice and in results (selling more goods) than in price; therefore, a salesperson must provide expert advice in those areas in which John needs help.

Experienced specialists typically specialize in one activity. For example, an agency media buyer does only one thing – place media buys – and is an expert in that activity. If this buyer, who we will call Jane, is making a television buy in a market, she is primarily interested in price and service – fast, responsive service. Jane is not interested in marketing or advertising advice or in advice about writing effective copy; she is interested in a different type of results – ratings, circulation, cost-per-points, cost-per-thousands, cost-per-clicks, reach, and frequency, all of which you will learn about in Chapter 18: Measuring Advertising.

As inexperienced direct accounts gain experience, their needs shift from asking for marketing and advertising advice to asking for responsive service and competitive prices. However, one thing direct accounts, especially retailers, will always focus on is results, which will always be more important to them than ratings, circulation, or research data. In the following sections of this chapter, you will learn more about strategies for calling on direct accounts and on agencies.

Missionary selling

Missionary selling most often involves calling on the principle owner, the CEO, or director of marketing or advertising of an account. Calling directly on an account and not on the account's advertising agency, if the account has one, is referred to as *direct selling*. Often, direct selling, particularly in local media, entails calling on retail businesses. The information that follows is for calling on retail businesses, but it also applies to most direct selling.

The retail business   Retailers are the middlemen between manufacturers and consumers, and advertising plays an important role because retailers sell their goods in a highly competitive environment. Few businesses that start up survive; two out of every three new retail businesses will fail within one year. Changes in the nation's demographics, lifestyles, and buying habits have caused many of the more traditional retailers to rethink their strategies, especially because of Amazon's dominance in online shopping. Single-brand loyalty has declined, and mass-marketing techniques have been developed to accommodate the proliferation of new products. Consumer groups that used to share homogeneous tastes have now splintered into many groups, all demanding different products to meet their different and changing needs.

Amazon's incredible growth, customer focus, ease of use, and fast home delivery policies have decimated large and small retail businesses, as have the proliferation of direct-to-consumer marketed products such as Harry's shaving products, Quip toothbrushes, and Blue Apron's meal kit service.

Retailers have had to change their ways of doing business to satisfy and attract consumers who are generally better educated, more cynical of product claims, and more demanding of quality. To entice these consumers, advertising and promotion have become more important than ever before, and most retailers now use digital advertising, especially search advertising on Google, to reach consumers who are looking for a product online because they are in the market to buy the product. When someone is in the market to buy a product, they are referred to as *intenders*. If retailers want to reach intenders, they will almost certainly buy self-serve search advertising in a Google Ads auction.

If retailers want to buy demographically – for consumers who are in the precise targeted demographic – they will almost certainly buy ads on Facebook. Therefore, salespeople who sell for other media such as local radio, local television, or newspapers must be prepared to help their customers buy Google and Facebook ads and be able to show how their medium complements ads on these two giant online platforms.

Selling to retailers   Retail is a broad category for which there is no standard definition; stores (hard goods, soft goods, food), services (insurance companies, banks, dry cleaning), entertainment (theaters, clubs, bars), and restaurants all normally come under the general classification of retail. In this book, all types of retail establishments and sellers of services are referred to as *stores*. For example, those businesses that are results-oriented should be designated as retail clients, or retail accounts, and have missionary salespeople calling on them. A retailer may have an advertising agency that buys according to the dictates of a store owner who cares only about results and who directs the agency to buy in a particular pattern that has proven to be successful in the past. These types of agency and direct accounts should be called on by a retail specialist. A retail specialist is a salesperson who thoroughly understands the retail business and who might have had experience working in retail.

A retail salesperson must be patient and not always seek a fast sale or a quick close. It may take much longer to sell to a retailer who is trying to fit advertising into a complex marketing and merchandising mix than to an advertising agency that is merely trying to make an efficient media buy.

Service selling

Service selling entails calling on existing customers and partners, and most often involves calling on advertising agencies.

The advertising agency business   Advertising agencies came into existence in the 1880s when they sprang up as sales representatives for newspapers and magazines. As sales representatives for the media, they kept a 15 percent commission on the amount of money advertisers spent with them in the media they represented. Thus, an advertiser might spend $1,000 for ads in a magazine and the agencies would keep $150 and give $850 to the magazine. As time went on, the agencies got close to their advertisers and began to create advertising for them and to advise where to place it. The agencies maintained the practice of keeping 15 percent of the amount the advertisers spent in the media through the late 1980s, when the agency business began to change as more and more independent agencies were purchased by large agency holding companies such as WPP, Omnicom, Publicis, IPG, Havas, and Dentsu. As competition for large accounts intensified, the holding company agencies began to compete for business on price, or lower commissions and fees. The fierce competition among the holding company agencies accelerated a trend of decreasing commissions. This trend was acerbated by large advertisers that often turned over the negotiating of agency commissions and fees to their purchasing departments, which brought on the use of negotiated fees based on scope of work (SOW).

Agencies also make money by adding a 15 percent commission to the material, services, and production they purchase for a client, a practice that is referred to as *grossing up* a charge. For example, if an agency purchases $850 worth of photography for a client, it would gross it up 17.65 percent (or multiply $850 by 1.1765) and charge the client $1,000. (You may recall from basic high school algebra that you cannot take a 15 percent discount off the price of some product and then multiply the discounted price by 1.15 to get the original number; the two values will not be equal. For example, 15 percent less than 100 is 85, but 1.15 times 85 equals only 97.7.)

Fee arrangements   Advertising agencies are service businesses and their expenses are mostly for people: copywriters, designers, art directors, media buyers, media planners, account management people, and so forth. The fees ad agencies charge are typically based on the following: (1) a monthly retainer fee against which media commissions are credited, (2) an agreed-upon charge per hour for work performed, or (3) a complex formula related to the amount of work the agency performs for a client as a percentage of the agency's total overhead. One reason that the fee arrangement is preferred by many advertisers is that they do not want their agency's income to depend on how much money they invest in the media. Advertisers want to make sure the agencies place their ad dollars as efficiently as possible and that the agencies buy the most effective, not necessarily the most expensive, media.

Agency structure.   Advertising agencies vary in size from large conglomerates with more than 50,000 employees in offices throughout the world and with media billings in the tens of billions of dollars to local, one-person agencies in smaller towns with media billings in the thousands of dollars.

Basic functions.   The work in the typical agency is broken into three basic functions: creative, media, and account management. These functions are supported in larger agencies by plans groups and by research, production, traffic, and accounting departments:

The creative function is handled by art directors, copywriters, and creative directors who create advertising. Typically, the account executive will present a client's advertising problem to the creative group, normally an art director and a copywriter, who will mull it over and then recommend an overall campaign or a single ad or commercial approach. Ideas are often the result of brainstorming among art directors, copywriters, account people, and media people in the agency. The account executive then will present the idea to the client. If the client accepts the approach, the creative people will proceed to create the advertising and arrange for its production.

The media function is carried out by media planners, media buyers, and media directors who evaluate media and place advertising. Planners recommend what media and how much of each should be used. Media buyers evaluate and select which digital platforms, networks, stations, magazines, newspapers, or websites to buy; and they are the people on whom media salespeople typically call on. However, in recent years planners have become more important in the evaluation process and salespeople have been calling on planners more often in order to get ahead of the process.

Media departments and media agencies are organized in various ways depending on the agency. Some are organized by product, and buyers buy all markets around the country and the digital platforms for a certain product or brand. Other agencies organize on a regional basis and have buyers specialize in buying one or more markets for all of the agency's products. Furthermore, large media agencies usually have buyers who specialize in a particular medium: network television buyers, spot television buyers, radio buyers, print buyers, and digital buyers, for example.

The account management function is carried out by account executives, account supervisors, and management supervisors who are the primary contact people between agency and client. The account management team usually solicits clients and services them once they are signed up.

Digital agencies.   A digital agency is one that specializes in creating and placing advertising in the online media. Large, multinational, conglomerated agencies, such as WPP, typically have divisions that specialize in online advertising. Buying digital advertising, including search advertising, is quite complex and requires special, often highly technical, expertise. With the growth of programmatic buying, there are also media agencies that specialize in buying programmatically, and these are called *trading desks*. The largest agency holding company, WPP, has a trading desk, Xaxis, that buys programmatically for over 3,000 clients.[30]

Television bias   In most large- and medium-sized agencies, there is a bias in favor of television in general and network television in particular. A typical large national advertising agency might place up to 40 percent of its total US media dollars in broadcast network television. The reason advertising agencies try to sell the benefits of letting their agency handle the advertising for large users of network television (both broadcast and cable) is because if clients can afford the networks, they will generate large fees, especially production fees for commercials. The media department likes to buy network television because it can spend and administer huge amounts of money with fewer people than it would take to place a similar amount of money in, say, lower-priced radio advertising.

Moreover, creative people do not get higher-paying jobs by producing beautiful newspaper ads or static banner ads; they move up the ladder to become high-paid creative directors by developing a reel of award-winning television commercials.

However, the network television bias is eroding as television network audiences shrink and as millennials cut the cord of cable television and watch streaming entertainment and sports content on their smartphones and smart TVs connected to the Internet. Furthermore, with digital advertising's ability to precisely target individual consumers, the appeal of broad-reach, non-micro-targeted television advertising has diminished for many marketers.

Selling to agencies   Advertising and media agencies are typically efficiency oriented and require a service-oriented (farmer) salesperson who understands and is experienced operating in a numbers- and data-analytics-oriented selling environment. Most advertising agency buyers do not care much about results; they are experienced specialists who are mostly interested in the type of audience a medium has, price, and responsive service.

Agencies depend on the media for their existence. Their incomes are based to some degree on how much advertising they buy; conversely, the media depend on agency buying decisions for much of their revenue. As a result, agencies and media continually perform a ritualized, arm's-length waltz: Agencies try to buy at the lowest prices possible, and the media try to sell at the highest prices possible. This is a good example of an ambivalent, co-dependent, love-hate relationship.

A further complication is that agencies tend to be defensive about their accounts because of the tenuousness of agency–client relationships. Although clients and agencies have contracts that normally spell out the financial details of relationships, rarely is a long-term commitment involved. Agencies will serve their clients because of an advertiser's trust, faith, and, too often, whim.

Advertisers might drop an agency for a number of reasons: advertiser personnel changes (a new person at the client wants to make a change); new personnel at the agency (the client does not like an agency's new creative director); agency plunder (agencies target other agencies' clients); or moving the digital media buying in house. Salespeople who call on agencies must learn to deal with the complex needs and behaviors of agency people, particularly of media buyers.

Media buyers are in the bottom echelon of an agency's media department. They are typically overworked, unappreciated, and underpaid. They are the agency's infantry troops slogging through mountains of media research and media proposals. There is little wonder that buyers tend to be defensive, given the pressure under which they work. They are particularly touchy about salespeople calling on their clients.

Calling on clients.   Some media salespeople, especially those from magazines and television networks, frequently make sales calls on both the advertising agency and the agency's clients with the blessing, or at least the grudging cooperation, of an agency. Generally, the larger the agency, the more secure it is with its relationship with clients. The higher the position of a person in the agency hierarchy, the less that person usually objects to media salespeople calling on the agency's clients because they hope the salesperson can convince the client to increase the client's advertising budget. However, buyers, who are far down on the organizational ladder, normally do not like salespeople calling on their clients, especially if it is to complain about a buy or to make waves of any sort.

If you feel it is necessary to stir things up to get your message across to a client, and a buyer has told you not to call on the client, then sell your way up through the agency's media department (through the associate media director to the media director to the vice president in charge of media). All along the way, tell your medium's story; tell the agency why you want to see its client and exactly what you are going to tell the client. Someone higher up will finally give you permission to see the client because he or she will realize that, in the final analysis, the agency cannot keep you away if the client agrees to see you, plus, you might get the client to invest more in advertising.

The secret of getting agencies' permission to call on their clients is to keep the agencies involved all along the way and to go over your proposals with them so they will be assured you are not going to make them look bad.

Numbers and data are a security blanket.   As mentioned previously, agency selling is numbers- and-data-oriented selling, as opposed to direct selling, which is usually results oriented. Since an agency's performance is difficult to measure, anything that has a number associated with it is eagerly grasped as a measurement device. In broadcasting and cable, ratings are used as a tool to evaluate an agency's media-buying performance. Online, impressions are currently the quantitative criteria, and in print magazines and newspapers, circulation is generally the quantitative criterion.

If a buyer can bring in a campaign on budget for the desired audience or impressions level, the agency and the buyer have a way of quantifying their performance to their clients. The agency and their clients feel secure with the numbers because they are tangible evidence of the fact that the agency performed its service and exercised good buying judgment. Therefore, do not expect agencies and their clients to give up their security blankets. You have to play the game using their rules, and their rules place emphasis on numbers and data, not on results.

Still, if agencies and their clients take refuge in the security of numbers and make their media buys based on ratings, impressions, and circulation, you might well ask how a salesperson makes a difference. It is because numbers are so absolute and finite that salespeople can make a difference. In fact, in a numbers-oriented selling situation, salespeople are the only difference, because a 10 rating is a 10 rating is a 10 rating and 1,000 impressions are 1,000 impressions are 1,000 impressions. Buyers continually need reassurance that what they are buying will turn out to be what they hoped for. In their hearts, they know that numbers do not walk through doors and buy products, but that people do. Buyers know that ultimately they will be judged by their clients on the overall effectiveness of their advertising campaigns. If buyers buy very efficiently in media that have the wrong demographics or to which no one pays attention, then their campaigns will not be successful. So, agency buyers depend on media salespeople to help them by keeping them thoroughly informed about the various media: demographics, attentiveness and engagement levels, programming and content changes, demographic changes, and anything that will help them evaluate the media better and make better buys. In other words, agencies want excellent, helpful, and responsive service.

Communication skills.   The International Radio and Television Society (IRTS) conducted a survey among important agency media buyers in New York City several years ago. The buyers were asked to name and rank the characteristics they thought were most important for a salesperson to have. The following list resulted from the study:

1   Communication skills – clarity and conciseness, not oral skills or flamboyance, were ranked as most important
2   Empathy – insight and sensitivity
3   Knowledge of product, industry, and market
4   Problem-solving ability – using imagination in presentations and packaging

5 Respect
6 Service.
7 Personal responsibility for results
8 Not knocking the competition

Summary

Personal selling for a media company is a fascinating and worthy craft that involves dealing with people, who are complex and basically trustworthy. Even though the media are often under attack, selling for a media outlet often gives salespeople access to high-level executives who appreciate the media's ability to grab their customers' attention.

Virtually all media selling involves digital advertising in some manner, and digital advertising is highly complex and requires new approaches for the digital era. The serving-the-customer, focus-on-customer-success, and selling-as-educating approaches require teaching prospects about your product and the complexities of digital advertising, tailoring your offers to customers' individual needs, and taking control of the conversation. Exhibit 2.2 summarizes the new assumptions, new approaches, and trends that have been brought on by the Internet, the increase of digital advertising, and the growth of automation and artificial intelligence (AI) that will be covered in more detail in later chapters.

Because media selling today requires focusing on a customer's success, a salesperson's number one objective is *to get results for customers*. Other objectives are *to develop new business, to retain and increase current business*, and *to delight customers*. The numberone sales strategy to accomplish these objectives is *to create value for your product*. Other strategies are *to research and develop insights into prospects' and customers' problems, challenges, pain points, and competitive positioning*. Key tactics are *to create a differential competitive advantage, to build relationships*, and *to solve problems*, and functions related to the key tactics are *to monitor the marketplace, to recommend tactics*, and *to cooperate*.

Exhibit 2.2 Assumptions, approaches, and trends

New assumptions	New approaches	Trends
• The Internet caused a fragmen tation of the media.	• A teaching, tailoring, and taking-control approach	• The customer burden of solutions
• The Internet increased the opportunity to target customers.	• A serving, partnership approach	• The rise of the consensus sale
• Programmatic disintermediated buying and selling.	• A selling-as-educating approach	• Increased risk aversion
• The Internet caused an explosion of complexity in the advertising ecosystem.	• Algorithms-as-the-competition approach	• Greater demand for customization
• Internet advertising is under attack.		• AI is changing all steps of selling

Much of the remainder of this book will be spent helping you develop the attitudes, emotional intelligence, skills, knowledge, opportunities, preparation, and persistence necessary to become a salesperson who can help both direct buyers and agency buyers make effective and efficient media investments.

Test Yourself

1. What are the three old and four new assumptions that this book makes about media selling?
2. What are the elements in the AESKOPP approach to selling?
3. What are the four approaches for the digital era?
4. What is the difference between tangible and intangible products?
5. What is the mission of a sales organization?
6. What are the four objectives of a sales organization?
7. What are the five strategies, three key tactics, and three related functions of a media salesperson?
8. What is the difference between missionary and service selling?
9. What are the two types of customers, and what are the differences between them?
10. What are the main differences between what direct clients and agency buyers want?

Project

Make an appointment with the person responsible for purchasing advertising at a large advertiser in your market (not at an advertising agency). This person might be the sales manager of a large automobile dealer or the head of marketing at a large hospital. Interview this person and ask him or her what they expect of media salespeople, what attributes they would like to see, and what kind of service they expect. Make a list of these answers and compare them to the answers that professional media buyers gave in the IRTS survey in this chapter. Are there any differences? What are they? What did you learn from this exercise?

References

Auletta, Ken. 2009. *Googled: The End of the World As We Know It*. New York: Penguin Press.

Blanchard, Ken and Bowles, Sheldon. 1993. *Raving Fans*. New York: William Morrow.

Dixon, Matthew and Adamson, Brent. 2011. *The Challenger Sale: Taking Control of the Customer Conversation*. New York: Portfolio/Penguin.

Hari, Johann. 2018. *Lost Connections: Uncovering the Real Causes of Depression—and the Unexpected Solutions*. New York: Bloomsbury.

Kohn, Alfie. 1986. *No Contest: The Case Against Competition*. Boston, MA: Houghton Mifflin.

Pink, Daniel. 2011. *Drive: The Surprising Truth About What Motivates Us*. New York: Riverhead Books.

Pink, Daniel. 2012. *To Sell Is Human: The Surprising Truth About Moving Others*. New York: Riverhead Books.

Stewart, Tom and O'Connell, Patricia. 2016. *Woo, Wow, and Win: Service Design, Strategy,* and the Art Of Customer Delight. New York: Harper Collins.

Weinberg, Mike. 2013. *New Sales Simplified: The Essential Handbook for Prospecting and New Business Development*. New York: AMACOM.

Resources

Examples of RFPs (http://www.mediaselling.us/downloads.html)

Notes

1   Auletta, Ken 2009. *Googled: The End of the World As We Know It*. New York: Penguin Press.

2   Ibid.

3   Ibid.

4   Ibid.

5   Ibid.

6   John, Leslie K., Kim, Tammi, and Barasz, Kate. 2018. "Ads that don't overstep." *Harvard Business Review*, January–February.

7   Manjoo, Farhad. 2018., "Tackling the Internet's central villain: The advertising business," *The New York Times*, January 31.Retrieved from https://www.nytimes.com/2018/01/31/technology/internet-advertising-business.html.

8   Benes, Ross. 2018. "People Believe Ads Are Becoming More Intrusive." Retrieved from https://www.emarketer.com/content/people-believe-ads-are-becoming-more-intrusive.

9   Rackham, Neil. 1988. *Spin Selling*. New York: McGraw-Hill.

10 Dixon, Matthew and Adamson, Brent. 2011. *The Challenger Sale: Taking Control of the Customer Conversation*. New York: Portfolio/Penguin.

11 Ibid.

12 Ibid.

13 Pink, Daniel. 2012. *To Sell Is Human: The Surprising Truth About Moving Others*. New York: Riverhead Books.

14 Hari, Johann. 2018. *Lost Connections: Uncovering the Real Causes of Depression – and the Unexpected Solutions*. New York: Bloomsbury.

15 McCurdy, Bob. 2018. "What's your purpose?" Retrieved from https://radioink.com/2018/02/18/whats-your-purpose.

16 Blanchard, Ken and Bowles, Sheldon. 1993. *Raving Fans*. New York: William Morrow.

17 www.groupm.com.

18 Levitt, Theodore. 1983. *The Marketing Imagination*. New York: Free Press.

19 McCurdy, Bob. "An educated client is a more valuable Client." Retrieved from https://radioink.com/2018/07/15/blog-an-educated-client-is-a-more-valuable-client.

20 Agrawal, Ajay, Gans, Joshua, and Goldfarb, Avi. 2018. *Prediction Machines: The Simple Economics of Artificial Intelligence*. Boston, MA: Harvard Business School Press.

21 Ibid.

22 Achor, Shawn, Reece, Andrew, Kellerman, Gabriella Rosen, and Robichaux, Alexi. 2018. "9 out of 10 people are willing to earn less money to do more-meaningful work." Retrieved from https://hbr.org/2018/11/9-out-of-10-people-are-willing-to-earn-less-money-to-do-more-meaningful-work.

23   Goler, Lori, Gale, Janelle, Harrington, Brynn, and Grant, Adam. 2018. "The three things employees want: Career, community, cause." Retrieved from https://hbr.org/2018/02/people-want-3-things-from-work-but-most-companies-are-built-around-only-one.

24   "2017 Ad-to-sales ratios." Retrieved from http://mediaselling.us/2017Ad-Sales-Ratio.pdf.

25   Stewart, Tom and O'Connell, Patricia. 2016. *Woo, Wow, and Win: Service Design, Strategy, and the Art Of Customer Delight.* New York: Harper Collins.

26   Denning, Steve. 2010. *The Leader's Guide to Radical Management: Reinventing the Workplace for the 21st Century.* New York: Jossey-Bass.

27   Yohn, Denise Lee. 2016. "The best salespeople do what the best brands do." *Harvard Business Review.* Retrieved from https://hbr.org/2016/08/the-best-salespeople-do-what-the-best-brands-do.

28   Ibid.

29   DeBruicker, F. Stewart and Summe, Gregory L. 1985. "Make sure your customers keep coming back." *Harvard Business Review*, January–February.

30   www.xaxis.com.

3

Sales Ethics and Transparency

Charles Warner

The Sales Executive Council (SEC) is a private membership-based research consortium serving approximately 300 of the world's largest sales organizations, including IBM, Coca-Cola, GE, McGraw-Hill, Microsoft, and the Walt Disney Company. The SEC is a division of the Corporate Executive Board and its mission is to assist executives in enhancing the effectiveness of their sales strategy and operations, from sales productivity and strategic account management to sales training and compensation. The SEC's primary tool is conducting research on sales problems its members face and producing case studies of best practices that companies use to solve these problems.

One of the SEC's reports dealt with sales force retention and motivation. In one survey that was a part of this report, it asked 2,500 senior sales executives in major industries worldwide to rank the attributes, from most important to least important, that they felt were necessary to be successful as a salesperson and as a sales manager.[1]

The most important attribute, by far (63 percent inclusion versus 50 percent inclusion for the second ranked attribute) was *honesty/integrity*.[2]

In 2016, Dr. Sunnie Giles, an organizational scientist and President of the Quantum Leadership Group surveyed 195 leaders in 15 countries in over 30 global organizations. Survey participants were asked to choose the 15 top leadership competencies from a list of 74. The number one competency, rated by 67 percent of the leaders, was "high ethical and moral standards."[3]

Media Selling: Digital, Television, Audio, Print and Cross-Platform, Fifth Edition.
Charles Warner, William A. Lederer, and Brian Moroz.
© 2020 John Wiley & Sons, Inc. Published 2020 by John Wiley & Sons, Inc.

No matter whether you are a salesperson or in a sales leadership position, the most important attribute or competency is ethical behavior – honesty and integrity.

How does one know how to be ethical, honest, and act with integrity? What are the rules for honesty? In business the rules usually come from codes of standards or codes of ethics.

Sales Ethics in the Advertising-Supported Media

A ballad made famous in the late 1930s by Jack Teagarden, titled "A Hundred Years Today," has been used by countless young men to woo their dates and to convince them not to wait to give out their kisses (and more), because who would ever know what they had done in a hundred years. It was a pitch for a one-night stand, not a long-term relationship. It was probably an effective short-term tactic because two people were not going to live another hundred years and were more than likely able to keep their actions secret if they wanted to.

However, clever short-term tactics are unwise for corporations for three reasons: (1) corporations, by charter, are immortal – they last forever – and, therefore, they want to do business a hundred years from today, (2) corporations have multiple relationships with customers and suppliers thus making it highly unlikely that they can keep details of these relationships secret for very long, and (3) in the age of transparency[4] created by the Internet, "…Information is like a toddler: It goes everywhere, gets into everything, and you can't always control it."[5] These reasons are especially important for large public corporations that file detailed reports with the Securities and Exchange Commission. Some of these reports contain information on contracts with key strategic partners and are available to the public from https://www.sec.gov/edgar/searchedgar/webusers.htm – an example of transparency.

These three factors are magnified several times with media companies because their revenue depends on maintaining the long-term trust of their advertisers, subscribers, and audiences. Major advertisers provide the lion's share of revenue for most media businesses. Furthermore, major advertisers such as Proctor & Gamble (P&G), General Motors (GM), and AT&T not only have long memories, but they will also be around in a hundred years. As Warren Buffett, known as the country's most astute investor, has said, "Trust is like the air we breathe. When it's present, nobody really notices. But when it's absent, everybody notices."[6] It is not smart business to undo a trusting relationship and bite the hand that will feed your company in future years. If media salespeople lie, cheat, gouge, or overpromise and underdeliver in order to make their short-term numbers, they jeopardize revenue far into the future. Simply put, advertisers do not buy from someone they do not trust – they are not looking for one-night stands; they prefer long-term partnerships.

There is also a good chance that if you deceive any of these large customers, they will tell others, especially your competitors and the press. The press loves stories about corporate bullies, liars, and cheaters, and as Dov Seidman writes in his book *How*, "Corporate scandals, celebrity breakups, political corruption: Each day's news – delivered instantly via television, radio, website, cell phone … exposes the transgressions of the icons of the day…once we've gotten a taste of scandal we can't seem to get enough."[7] The public has become scandal addicted.

It seems that many corporations, politicians, and people today either do not know about or care about rules, norms, standards, or ethics. Perhaps they go along with unethical behavior because of group pressure or peer pressure or perhaps they rationalize to themselves "everyone does it," "it's standard practice in this business (or political campaign)," or "no one will know; I won't get caught." Maybe they think, "My manager said to do what it takes to make the quarter," or "If I don't take their money, someone else will." Such callous rationalization of lying, cheating, and stealing is typical sociopathic or malignant narcissistic behavior.

Within the last several years, I know of a salesperson for a major media company who forged a client's signature on a contract. The salesperson was certain the customer would eventually sign the contract, and the salesperson wanted to start the campaign early in order to meet his quarterly quota and, thus, make more money. When the advertiser got the first invoice, the surprised reply was, "What's this, we never bought anything or signed anything?" Why did the salesperson forge a signature? Was there pressure from management to close business early or did greediness motivate the salesperson? What was the root cause of this unethical behavior? Of course, being a sociopath or a narcissist clearly can lead to unethical behavior, but people not suffering from these personality disorders sometimes behave unethically. Why?

Reasons people do not follow the rules

There are many reasons for unethical behavior, but among the most common are these. (1) People have a strong tendency to bow to authority and follow orders from higher-ups, giving them the excuse that "I was just following orders." (2) People have a strong tendency to bow to the social pressure and conformity of their peer group, perhaps a left-over tendency from their teenage years, leading to the excuse of "everyone does it." (3) Unethical behavior is often due to an absence of clearly defined and communicated rules of behavior, standards, norms, or codes of ethics in a peer group, organization, company, or an industry, particularly for salespeople, allowing people to say "nobody told me." (4) They are unaware that, "Every keystroke on your computer is there, forever and ever"[8] in the age of transparency and the likelihood of getting caught is exceedingly high. (5) Corporate cultures that encourage employees to wink at their company's code of standards or mission statement can justify their actions by saying, "no one will know; I won't get caught." (6) They believe their celebrity, fame, and power is so great that on impulse they can do anything they want.

While people who bow to authority may have to give up their individual free will and autonomy for the sake of the organization they work for, they do not have to turn their conscience and their self-esteem over to that company or to anyone else. "Just following orders," as we learned in the Nuremberg trials, is not a valid, acceptable excuse for doing the wrong thing. On the other hand, people who cave in to peer pressure in order to conform negate their own free will and autonomy and hand over their conscience and individuality to the crowd. "Everybody does it" is not an acceptable excuse for breaking the rules or for unethical behavior. An absence of clearly defined standards and codes of ethics can lead to unethical behavior because people can use the cop-out "nobody told me." This excuse is hollow because ethical behavior is implied and assumed in all of our daily social interactions. For example, we do not go around killing people because nobody said "Don't kill anyone today." Most people know what we are supposed to do and not to do, and know what the norms of decent behavior are.

Groups, organizations, and companies must create and communicate ethical standards to guard against these abuses and, even more importantly, to follow up with practices and behavior at the highest levels of the organization that adhere to stated corporate standards. Unfortunately "Do as I say, not as I do," can be as effective on employees as it was on me as a teenager when my father told me not to smoke cigarettes as he puffed away on one of his 40 Camels a day. For example, Enron had a clearly defined code of conduct that it communicated to everyone in the company and posted on its website. Enron's top executives obviously viewed this code as public relations, not as a set of rules they should follow, thinking arrogantly and cynically, "No one will know."

Employees of an unethical company whose executives do not follow the rules should strongly consider leaving the company and looking for another job. Leaving an unethical, corrupt company is probably in your long-term self-interest because when the company's ethical problems come to light, your pension fund or 401(k) plan will be worthless if it is invested in the stock of a company that declares bankruptcy. Also, your reputation will be tainted in the job market. Therefore, select the companies you work for very carefully and choose ones that will enhance your reputation not detract from it.

What Are Ethics?

Ethics are clearly defined and published standards and norms of right and wrong that are expressed as guidelines for behavior. There are three general types of ethical standards. First, most organizations, companies, and professions have written codes of ethics or standards of conduct. Next are accepted beliefs and modes of conduct among various social and ethnic groups. Finally, individuals have their own standards of right and wrong that they use to make daily judgments, which are based on a combination of deep-seated personal values and beliefs inculcated from the first moment parents say "bad boy" or "bad girl."

Why Are Ethics and Rules Important?

With heightened press coverage of corporate, Wall Street, government, and political scandals, the public has become increasingly concerned about the ethical behavior of the representatives of our important institutions. Therefore, if ever there was a time when ethical behavior for business and for salespeople was important, it is now. And it is vital to the health and credibility of American business to do the right thing rather than to do things right. Companies should perceive ethical behavior and doing the right thing as enlightened self-interest because they preserve a company's long-term reputation, which is its greatest asset.

Doing the right thing and being trustworthy is not only the top priority for companies, but also for leadership. If salespeople want to get promoted and eventually be in a leadership position, they must be trustworthy. Adam Bryant, who wrote the weekly Corner Office column for *The New York Times,* interviewed 525 CEOs over the years for the column. In October of 2017, Bryant wrote a final column titled "How to be a C.E.O., from a decade's worth of them." In the column he wrote, "if you were to force me to rank the most important qualities of effective leadership, I would put trustworthiness at the top."[9] He goes on to write:

> We all have a gut sense of our bosses, based on our observations and experiences: Do we trust them to do the right thing? Will they be straight with us and not shave corners of truth? Do they own their mistakes; give credit where credit is due; care about their employees as people as opposed to assets?[10]

If you substitute "customers" for "employees" in the last sentence, you have excellent guidelines for ethical behavior for media salespeople and their bosses.

Five Ethical Responsibilities for Media Salespeople

1. Responsibility to consumers

As defined in Chapter 1, consumers use a product and the consumers of the media are the audiences – users, readers, viewers, listeners, or subscribers.

In 2018 the information industry credibility hit an all-time low, according to the Center for Media Research.[11] Criticism of fake news came from all sides of the political spectrum, especially from the right. So to avoid being labeled fake news and to attract audiences desirable to advertisers, the media must put the needs of the majority of its consumers first. If a media outlet does not put the interests of its consumers or audience first, the audience will eventually gravitate to sources of information and entertainment that do. If a media outlet does not tell the truth, withholds important information from consumers, sells shoddy products, or erodes consumers' values and sense of self-esteem, these consumers will eventually turn to information, entertainment, and opinion sources that provide what they want, what they agree with, and that they find truthful, useful, interesting, and convenient.

Audiences want something in which they can believe. Therefore, the media should not transmit false or misleading news or advertising. General rules for media salespeople should include not accepting advertising for products that are unsafe. People do not like to be deceived, especially by the media. Thus, when a medium lies to its audience and loses its credibility, it eventually loses its audience, and can no longer be advertiser supported. Putting the consumers first is at the heart of the marketing concept, and is the essence of ethical behavior in the media.

In 2017 Facebook hired 8,500 people to manually review content that had been rejected for publication by Facebook's algorithms. Facebook also changed its algorithms in its News Feed to show users fewer news items and more personal items. Facebook made these changes because Facebook users, critics in the media, and critics in the government were concerned about fake news, and Facebook wanted to regain the trust of users, critics, and politicians. Facebook's attempts to address the problem of fake news without government passing restrictive regulations was an example of an important medium where people get a large portion of their news self-regulating, of putting the needs of consumers first, before its own need for profits.

2.   Responsibility to their conscience

All salespeople are responsible to themselves for doing what they believe is good or bad, right or wrong, and is based on their own conscience or moral standards. John Wooden, the legendary UCLA basketball coach, said that there is no pillow as soft as a clear conscience. Purposely acting unethically will erode a salesperson's self-esteem. By acting ethically, salespeople increase their self-esteem, self-image, and self-confidence and do the same for their company. By acting ethically, salespeople develop a long-term perspective, which benefits their mental health and their company as well as the customers and consumers.

Unfortunately, some salespeople and sales organizations are more motivated by greed, in making money or "getting the stock price up," than in building a highly respected personal or company reputation. Such greed inevitably produces cheating, which is a cancer that erodes a person's or a company's reputation and eventually will kill the company. Those who conduct business unethically know they are doing so, but they continue doing the wrong thing because they believe they will not get caught. However, they are playing an ethical lottery in which the odds of being discovered are high, as we saw with Enron and Harvey Weinstein. Practicing ethical behavior every business day is the only sure way of maintaining a reputation, and self-esteem grows as the result.

3.   Responsibility to customers

Customers (advertisers) do not buy from or partner with media companies and salespeople they do not trust. Thus, media salespeople should concentrate on building trust and managing relationships for the long term, not merely selling for a one-shot deal. Salespeople must underpromise and overdeliver.

Customer-oriented rules for media salespeople – the Don'ts

- Don't lie to advertisers.
- Don't sell anything that customers do not truly need.

- Don't allow clients to feel like they lost in a negotiation ("Leave something on the table.")[12]
- Don't be unfair to advertisers.
- Don't sell something customers cannot afford.
- Don't use bait-and-switch tactics (selling something that they know is not available just to get the money in the door).
- Don't recommend or accept advertising that is in bad taste or that will harm a client's image.
- Don't accept false or misleading advertising.
- Don't give kickbacks (a euphemism for bribes) to customers. Kickbacks often come in the form of unauthorized rebates or other cash payments given by salespeople from their own pockets. Kickbacks are illegal, and there are serious consequences to violating the law, including fines and imprisonment.

Rules for media salespeople – the Dos

- Do represent your clients. Media salespeople's responsibility is to publish the best possible advertising for their clients and to try to get the clients the best, fairest deal they are entitled to according to a medium's official pricing and positioning policies. Salespeople should be their client's advocates inside their organizations.
- Do keep privileged information confidential. Salespeople must keep privileged information to themselves, including details about advertisers' strategy, budgets, creative plans, special sales, and media plans until the campaign has broken and the information is readily available from outside sources. When a client or advertising agency requests competitive information, salespeople should not give it out before the campaign starts. If salespeople have done their selling job properly, they have sold themselves as solutions providers, which implies a privileged relationship, such as that between a doctor and patient. Customers have a right to assume that salespeople are experts whose recommendations are given with their customers' best interests in mind.
- Underpromise. It is salespeople's responsibility not to promise what advertising by itself cannot deliver. The media can deliver exposure to an audience. But the media cannot be certain of generating sales results, so it should not promise results to advertisers. Rather, salespeople should promise only what they can deliver. The rule to remember is "underpromise and overdeliver."

4. Responsibility to the community

The word community has many meanings, but in this context, it is limited to four: (1) the global community, (2) the general business community, (3) an industry community, and (4) a local community.

- *The global community.* Each corporation and individual ultimately has a responsibility to the world community. We owe it to society to act in a way that provides the greatest good for the greatest number of people, that enhances the environment, that improves the human experience and condition, and that, in the words of the Hippocratic oath, does no harm. To answer questions about our social responsibility, we should always ask ourselves the question, "Suppose everybody did this?"[13]

- *The business community.* As members of the free-market business community salespeople must behave responsibly so that investors, regulators, and the general public have faith in our capitalistic system. All companies have, or should have, published rules, codes, or standards that prohibit unethical behavior such as selling stock based on inside knowledge, shredding documents or deleting computer files to avoid prosecution, cooking the books to inflate revenue, and avoiding sexual harassment. In business, as well as in society, salespeople must ask: "Suppose everybody did this? Would the regulators, investors, and the public maintain their faith in the free-market system and in business?"

- *An industry community.* The media have a special responsibility to the public because in many cases the media deliver the news to Americans. The public also forms many of their social values, beliefs, attitudes, and opinions from the digital, social, electronic, and print media. This enormous power makes it more imperative that the media wield that power responsibly. As a country, we altered our aggregate opinions about racial prejudice, about the war in Iraq, and about women's rights while we watched images of these issues mesmerize, indoctrinate, and change us. The advertising messages between these images guaranteed the freedom of the press that bigots, the government, and non-egalitarian people might not want us to have. If any one of these groups had controlled the media, we might not have been exposed to these issues and the truth would not have worked its torturous way into our collective consciousness. Therefore, media companies and their salespeople have the responsibility of keeping the media and the press free by fueling it with the advertising revenue it needs to remain so. Without a free, advertising- or subscriber-supported media, there cannot be a free exchange of ideas. This exchange of ideas leads to an informed electorate, the foundation of our democracy. As a salesperson, you might say, "The high-minded notion of protecting democracy is fine if you're selling "60 Minutes" or CNN or the Washington Post, but I'm selling commercials on a Rock 'N Roll radio station." But no one program, no one news story, or no one medium is necessarily more important than another, rather it is the free-market, advertising-supported system that is important. By selling within that free-market system, media salespeople are sustaining a market for advertising that supports all information and entertainment content. Salespeople must be ethical and play by the rules not only because public attention is focused on corporate ethics, but also because attention is intensely focused on the media. The believability of the media in general and journalism specifically has been eroding in recent years, and advertising has never been at the top of the list in the public's esteem. Thus, the media must attempt to turn around the image, esteem, and credibility of its product (information, entertainment, and opinion) and its supporting buttress, advertising, if the media hope to thrive.[14]

- *A local community.* All companies, organizations, and people have a responsibility as citizens to act responsibly and ethically towards their neighbors in the community where they live and work. The simple rule is, "Don't foul your own nest. Don't cheat your neighbor." The local media must first serve their communities, for without local support, local media cannot thrive or even exist. Remember that broadcast media are given licenses based on their promise to serve their communities, so their obligation is not only a moral, social one, but also a regulatory one.

5.   Responsibility to a company

Media salespeople represent their companies to their customers and because they are selling an intangible product, they become the personification of, the surrogate for, their product. Salespeople are often the only contact a customer will have with anyone from a company. Therefore, they have to face the kill-the-messenger attitude many people have about the media. Because of this unique situation, a company's credibility depends on its salespeople's credibility, which to a large degree depends on their personal conduct and integrity. Salespeople must be law abiding, respectful of civil liberties and actions or statements that are potentially offensive to others, as well as be moderated in their personal habits. It is the responsibility of salespeople to build and maintain customer relationships based on dependability, reliability, believability, integrity, and ethical behavior.

Salespeople must give their job their full attention, not steal company's assets, not waste its resources (which includes efficient and reasonable use of entertainment and transportation money), not file false expense reports, and not offer special deals to get business away from others within their own organization.

Salespeople have a responsibility to their company to generate revenue by getting results for clients, to sell special promotions and packages, and to keep customers and get renewals. There are times when the responsibility to a company to generate revenue can come into conflict with a salesperson's duty to his or her customers, to his or her conscience, and to the various communities. When such conflicts occur, salespeople should remember the hierarchy of responsibilities and that their company is at the bottom of that hierarchy, because it is in the company's best long-term interest to be last. Good companies know that what goes around, comes around; that good karma returns home; that ethical behavior is good business; that employees are happier working for ethical companies; and that consumers keep coming back to products and companies they believe are ethical, do the right thing, and are sustainable.

Great media companies understand that, if they take care of their audience that usage, readership, and ratings will go up, which means advertising revenue will go up. Also, if advertisers trust salespeople and their companies, most advertisers will pay higher prices for better service from these trusted partners. If salespeople do the wrong thing, it results in lost customers, expensive employee turnover, high lawyers' fees, large court costs, and, perhaps, even time in jail.

Unfortunately, many companies set up rewards for salespeople that unwittingly reinforce doing the wrong thing. These include compensation systems that reward getting an order regardless of what's best for the customer, contests that reward selling special promotions or events regardless of advertisers' needs, and bonuses for making sales budgets regardless of what is reasonable.[15] Beware of chief finance officers (CFOs) and top management that recommend accounting practices that "preserve a company's assets"; they often have the wrong assets in mind. A company's and a salesperson's most precious asset is an excellent reputation, which is preserved by always doing the right thing all of the time.

The Five Cs of ethical responsibility

The Five Cs of ethical responsibility are:

1   Consumers
2   Conscience
3   Customers
4   Community
5   Company

An Ethics Check[16]

Is it legal? When salespeople conduct an ethics check, the first question to ask is: "Is what I am considering doing legal?" The term "legal" should be interpreted broadly to include any civil or criminal laws, any state or Federal regulations, any industry codes of ethics, or any company policy. If salespeople do not know or have any doubts about the legality of what they are doing, they should ask their boss and the company's legal department.

Is it fair? Is it rational, as opposed to emotional, and balanced, so that there are no big winners and big losers? Is it fair to all: to both sides, to the consumer, to the salesperson, to the advertiser, to the various communities, and to the company? If the company had an open-book policy, would all of its customers think everyone got a fair shake? Are all customers getting fair rates, placements, rotations, and makegoods? To test for fairness, ask yourself the question, "Suppose everybody did this?"

What does my conscience say? Salespeople should ask themselves, "How would I feel if what I am doing appeared in the *Wall Street Journal* or *The New York Times*? How would it make me feel about myself? According to my personal moral standards, is what I am doing OK?"

A company's and a salesperson's most valuable assets are their reputations and their relationships with their customers. Reputations and relationships are built by consistently doing ethics checks on the way you do business, by taking a long-term view, and by not doing anything that would put you or your company in jeopardy, even a hundred years from today.

Transparency

Transparency is closely related to ethics because both concepts depend on being honest and having integrity. Transparency is being completely open about how you do business, in other words, being openly honest.

The concept of transparency in the media made headlines in the summer of 2016 with the release of the Association of National Advertisers' (ANA) Media Transparency Initiative: K2 Report.[17]

> From October 20, 2015, through May 31, 2016, K2 Intelligence, on behalf of the ANA, conducted an independent study of media transparency issues in the U.S. advertising industry. K2 was selected to lead the fact-finding portion of the study after a request for proposal process initiated by the ANA on June 17, 2015.
>
> Over the course of the study, K2 conducted 143 interviews with 150 individual sources, representing a cross-section of the U.S. media buying ecosystem. K2 kept the identities of all participating sources – and all the individuals and corporate entities named in their accounts – confidential from the ANA throughout the study.
>
> Results of the study were delivered by K2 in a comprehensive report. Among the key findings:
>
> - Numerous non-transparent business practices, including cash rebates to media agencies, were found to be pervasive in the U.S. media ad buying ecosystem.
> - There were systemic elements to some of the non-transparent behavior. Specifically, senior executives across the agency ecosystem were aware of, and mandated, some non-transparent business practices.
> - There was evidence of non-transparent practices across a wide range of media, including digital, print, out-of-home, and television.[18]

The ANA had commissioned the study because of a number of back-and-forth allegations in 2015 between major advertisers and large agency holding companies that the agencies' ad buying, especially with growing use of programmatic trading, had not been transparent, which had inflated the profit margins of the agencies at the expense of major advertisers who should have received credit for discounts and rebates that instead went to the agencies.

When the report was released, the Association of American Advertising Agencies (4A's) posted this response:

> The ANA today released a K2 report on media buying practices. Although the 4A's has worked collaboratively with the ANA via a joint task force, this report is anonymous, one-sided and paints the entire industry with the same negative brush. This statement further elaborates the 4A's position on this issue.
>
> A healthy and constructive debate about media buying can only happen with a bipartisan, engaged, industry-wide approach – and that is precisely the opposite of what the ANA has pursued. The immense shortcomings of the K2 report released today – anonymous, inconclusive, and one-sided – undercut the integrity of its findings.
>
> We call upon the ANA in the strongest terms to make available to specific agencies on a confidential basis all of the materials related to them. Without an opportunity for agencies

to assess and address the veracity of information provided to K2, sweeping allegations will continue to drive attention-grabbing headlines; this does nothing to foster a productive conversation or to move our industry forward.

Faced with a report that views media buying from the perspective of only one of the three parties to such transactions, agencies are hard-pressed to defend themselves, which could cause substantial economic damage to all media agencies.

The advertising ecosystem is increasingly complex, and *we are firmly committed to ensuring appropriate governance practices are in place.* In an effort to address today's challenges and modernize industry practices, the 4A's worked productively for six months with ANA last year. Our joint task force developed principles of conduct to establish clear standards for transparency in media buying. When the involvement of third parties in tackling this challenge was suggested by ANA, the 4A's was supportive, even offering to be a partner in the RFP process. The entire industry is harmed and at risk of further damage as a result of the path the ANA has chosen.

With or without ANA's collaboration, the 4A's is committed to taking a leadership role in achieving fairness and transparency in the marketplace for all parties to media buys. Despite the fact that our paths have diverged, the 4A's is determined to build upon the significant groundwork laid by the joint task force, including a number of agreed-upon principles, which we released in January of this year and which can be found here (link to https: //www.aaaa.org/4as-issues-transparency-guiding-principles-of-conduct/).[19]

I will let the reader make a judgment as to which side's argument is the most credible. However, to those knowledgeable about the issue, there is little doubt that at many major advertising agencies there had been a lack of transparency that had inflated the agency profits without their clients knowing about what was going on.

As a result of this dispute over transparency in media buying, in which the media was often complicit in order to kowtow to large agencies, many advertisers put in place highly specific contracts with their agencies that required transparency.

This conflict clearly demonstrates what happens when trust between two businesses or industries vanishes – handshakes are replaced by restrictive and complex contracts. The only people who benefit from such contracts are the lawyers who draw up the contractual agreements. It would have been much better for the marketing ecosystem (marketers, advertisers, agencies, and the media) if everyone had conducted an ethics check whenever they did business.

If there had been an ethics check, everyone's reputation would not have been tarnished and everyone would have made more money in the long run, as clearly pointed out in Fred Kiel's research detailed in his 2015 book, *Return on Character*. The research by KRW International found that CEOs whose employees gave them high marks for character (honesty, integrity, responsibility, forgiveness, and compassion) had an average return on assets (ROA) over the two-year period studied of 9.35 percent, which was almost five times as much as that of those companies with CEOs who had low character ratings; their ROA averaged only 1.93 percent.

The result of the research can be summarized as showing that character and doing the right thing is more profitable in the long run. Good ethics are good business.

Test Yourself

1. What are the five rationalizations some people use for their unethical behavior?
2. What are the four reasons why people are inclined to behave unethically?
3. What are the Five Cs of ethical responsibility for media salespeople?
4. What are the Don'ts for media salespeople?
5. What are the Dos for media salespeople?
6. What are the three rules of the Ethics Checklist?
7. Explain transparency.

Projects

Project #1: Go to the Web and search the websites of several major media companies and see if you can find any statements about ethical behavior, standards of conduct, corporate citizenship, or corporate responsibility. Then, go to the websites of major advertisers such as ATT, P&G, Ford, Google, Apple, or Amazon, and see if they have any statements about ethical behavior, standards of conduct, corporate citizenship, or corporate responsibility. What did you discover?

Project #2: Go to the Downloads section of the *Media Selling* website (www.mediaselling. us) and download "A Salesperson's Dilemma." Read the case carefully and then complete the assignment at the bottom of the case.

References

Blanchard, Kenneth and Peale, Norman V. 1988. *The Power of Ethical Management*. New York: William Morrow.

Davis, Keith, Frederick, William C., and Blostrom, Robert L. 1980. *Business and Society: Concepts and Policy Issue*. New York: McGraw-Hill.

Gardner, Howard, Csikszentmihalyi, Mihaly, and Damron, William. 2001. *Good Work: When Excellence and Ethics Meet*. New York: Basic Books.

Kiel, Fred. 2015. *Return on Character*. Boston, MA: Harvard Business Review Press.

Seidman, Dov. 2007. *How: Why How We Do Anything Means Everything...in Business (and in Life)*. Hoboken, NJ: Wiley.

Resources

Dov Seidman's LRN corporate website (www.lrn.com/index.php)
Securities and Exchange Commission Public Company filing (www.sec.gov/edgar.shtml)
Association of National Advertisers
   (www.ana.net/content/show/id/industry-initiative-media-transparency-report)
Association of American Advertising Agencies (www.aaaa.org/4as-statement-media-transparency-recent-k2-report)

Notes

1 "Voice of the sales leader." 2001. *Leading the Charge*. Sales Executive Council.

2 Ibid.

3 Giles, Sunnie. 2016. "The Most important leadership competencies, according to leaders around the world." Retrieved from https://hbr.org/2016/03/the-most-important-leadership-competencies-according-to-leaders-around-the-world.

4 Seidman, Dov. 2007. *How: Why How We Do Anything Means Everything…in Business (and in Life)*. Hoboken, NJ: Wiley.

5 Ibid.

6 Ibid.

7 Ibid.

8 Stone, Brad. 2007. "Tell-all PCs and phones transforming divorce." Retrieved from http://www.nytimes.com/2007/09/15/business/15divorce.html.

9 Bryant, Adam. 2017. "How to be a C.E.O., from a decade's worth of them." Retrieved from https://www.nytimes.com/2017/10/27/business/how-to-be-a-ceo.html.

10 Ibid.

11 Loechner, Jack. 2017. "Information industry outlook, 2018." Retrieved from https://www.mediapost.com/publications/article/309126/information-industry-outlook-2018.html.

12 Bennak, Frank. 2019. *Leave Something on the Table: And Other Surprising Lessons for Success in Business and Life*. New York: Simon & Schuster.

13 Davis, Keith, Frederick, William C., and Blostrom, Robert L. 1980. *Business and Society: Concepts and Policy Issue*. New York: McGraw-Hill.

14 Gardner, Howard, Csikszentmihalyi, Mihaly, and Damron, William. 2001. *Good Work: When Excellence and Ethics Meet*. New York: Basic Books.

15 Jensen, Michael. 2001. "Corporate budgeting is broken – Let's fix it." *Harvard Business Review*.

16 Blanchard, Kenneth and Peale, Norman V. 1988. *The Power of Ethical Management*. New York: William Morrow.

17 "Media transparency initiative: K2 report." Retrieved from https://www.ana.net/content/show/id/industry-initiative-media-transparency-report.

18 Ibid.

19 "4A's statement on media transparency and the recent K2 report." Retrieved from https://www.aaaa.org/4as-statement-media-transparency-recent-k2-report.

4

The AESKOPP Approach, Attitude, and Goal Setting

Charles Warner

The AESKOPP approach was mentioned in Chapter 2 as one of the approaches to selling in the digital era. The AESKOPP approach is a generalization, a simplification of some underlying, universal sales principles and provides a framework for coaching, planning, executing, and evaluating sales performance. It posits that successful selling requires Attitude (A), Emotional Intelligence (E), Skills (S), Knowledge (K), Opportunities (O), Preparation (P), and Persistence (P):

$$A \times E \times S \times K \times O \times P \times P = Success$$

Notice that each element in the above formula is multiplied by the others. Just as in a mathematical formula, if any one of the elements is not present, then the result is zero success, because any element multiplied by zero is zero. Thus, all of the elements must be present for a successful result – getting customers and keeping them.

The AESKOPP Approach

Definitions

The following are definitions of each of the seven AESKOPP elements.

Media Selling: Digital, Television, Audio, Print and Cross-Platform, Fifth Edition.
Charles Warner, William A. Lederer, and Brian Moroz.
© 2020 John Wiley & Sons, Inc. Published 2020 by John Wiley & Sons, Inc.

Attitude   Attitude is having the desire and motivation to be a salesperson and having the proper mind-set to do it. If you have the skills, the knowledge, and the opportunities to sell but have no desire or motivation to do so, you will not be successful. Later in this chapter are more details on attitudes and how to control and improve them.

Emotional intelligence   Emotional intelligence is the ability to understand yourself and others so you can develop empathy and rapport with people and manage relationships successfully. Chapter 5 presents more details on how to increase your emotional intelligence.

Skills   Skills are the ability, improved through preparation and deliberate practice, to use your knowledge of sales techniques, methods, and tools. For salespeople, it is understanding the techniques of prospecting and qualifying, researching insights and solutions, educating, proposing, negotiating and, closing, and customer success (account management). Chapters 9 through 14 will have in-depth details about these skills and how to improve them.

Knowledge   Knowledge means knowing the product you are selling in depth – knowing more about it than your customers do so you can educate them. For salespeople, it means having information not only about their own product and its underlying technology, but also about measurement and data analysis, about marketing and advertising, about a customer's business, and about competitive media. Chapters 15 through 24 will cover these knowledge areas.

Opportunities   Opportunities are the circumstances in which you can use your tools – attitude, skills, and knowledge. Even if you have the tools and know how to use them, you cannot accomplish anything unless you have opportunities to put them to use. Salespeople may have a positive attitude, the skills to solve problems, and a storehouse full of product, marketplace, and competitive knowledge, but if they do not make sales calls and find the right prospective customers, they will lack the opportunities to put their skills and knowledge to work.

Preparation   A large part of preparation is getting organized to solve customer problems. Even if you have the attitude, emotional intelligence, skills, knowledge, and opportunities to sell, you will not solve problems or make many sales if you are not thoroughly prepared for every call and every presentation. There are two types of preparation: short term and long term. Short-term preparation is intense, thorough preparation for every sales call, every presentation, every negotiation, and every service call. A general rule of thumb is that you should spend a minimum of two hours of preparation for every 20-minute call or presentation, or six hours for every one-hour call or presentation. The type of preparation required for a call or presentation involved in a typical media selling situation is covered in Chapter 9: Prospecting and Qualifying. The aphorism that "the best prepared negotiator always wins" has been attributed to former Supreme Court Justice Arthur Goldberg, and this comment holds true for negotiators, lawyers, and, certainly, salespeople. Another example of almost obsessive preparation applies to 18-minute TED Talks, which often seem informal and off the cuff, but TED founder Chris Anderson writes in a *Harvard Business Review* article that, "We start helping speakers prepare their talks six months (or more) in advance so they'll have plenty of time to practice."[1]

Therefore, depending on the situation, the amount of time to spend preparing for a one-hour sales call or for an important formal presentation can range from six hours to six days.

On the other hand, long-term preparation requires *deliberate practice*. Malcolm Gladwell's book *Outliers* was number 17 on Amazon's list of the best-selling books of 2008.[2] Chapter Two of *Outliers* was titled "The 10,000-hour rule," and in it Gladwell wrote about the research that was done in Berlin's elite Academy of Music in the early 1990s by three psychologists. The researchers divided the school's violinists into three groups. In the first group were the stars – those with potential to become world-class soloists. In the second group were those students who were judged to be merely "good," according to the teachers at the school. The third group consisted of students who were deemed unlikely to ever play professionally.[3]

All of the students in all three groups started playing at roughly the same age, around five years old. In their first several years they all practiced about the same amount, about two or three hours a week. But when the students were around the age of eight, their practice habits changed. The students who would wind up in the best group began to practice more than everyone else. They practiced six hours a week by age nine, eight hours a week by age 12, 16 hours a week by age 14, "and up and up."[4] By the age of 20 they were practicing – "that is, purposefully and single-mindedly playing their instruments with the intent to get better – well over thirty hours a week. In fact, by the age of twenty, the elite performers had each totaled ten thousand hours of practice."[5] The merely good students had totaled 8,000 hours, and the third group of those judged to be unlikely to play professionally had practiced just over 4,000 hours.

All of the students were talented enough to get into the elite Berlin school. Thus, the only noticeable difference in the students was not inherent talent but the amount of time they had practiced. This research and other credible research came to the conclusion that in order to be a true expert a person has to have 10 years or 10,000 hours of practice, of preparation.

Also in 2008, another book, *Talent Is Overrated: What Really Separates World-Class Performers from Everybody Else*, by Geoff Colvin referred to the same research conducted at the Berlin Academy of Music. But Colvin wrote in more detail about the ten-years-or-thousand-hours rule and not only emphasized the importance of practice in developing expert performance, but also the necessity of that practice being well structured and highly repetitive – deliberate. Colvin quoted from the seminal research article on deliberate practice, "The role of deliberate practice in the acquisition of expert performance" by K. Anders Ericsson, Ralf Th. Krampe, and Clemens Tesch-Romer:

> The theoretical framework presented in this article explains expert performance as the end result of individuals' prolonged efforts to improve performance while negotiating motivational and external constraints. In most domains of expertise, individuals begin in their childhood a regimen of effortful activities (deliberate practice) designed to optimize

improvement. Individual differences, even among elite performers, are closely related to assessed amounts of deliberate practice. Many characteristics once believed to reflect innate talent are actually the result of intense practice extended for a minimum of 10 years. Analysis of expert performance provides unique evidence on the potential and limits of extreme environmental adaptation and learning.[6]

Deliberate practice is characterized by the following elements: (1) Activity designed specifically to improve performance, "often with a teacher's help;"[7] (2) an activity that can be repeated an infinite amount of time; (3) an activity on which feedback is continuously available; (4) an activity that is highly demanding mentally *and* physically; and (5) an activity that is not much fun.[8]

Deliberate practice is specifically designed to improve performance, not on an element of performance that a person is necessarily good at or likes, but one that is necessary to achieve expertise. And that particular performance element might not be fun, which is all the better, because the person doing it has to think about executing, has to concentrate, and, therefore, the practice does not become thoughtlessly automatic.

Colvin writes: "Identifying the learning zone, which is not simple, and then forcing oneself to stay continually in it as it changes, which is even harder – these are the first and most important characteristics of deliberate practice."[9]

So, if you want to become an expert performer in media selling, you need to develop the discipline to prepare thoroughly, both short-term preparation and long-term preparation through deliberate practice.

Persistence   Persistence means never giving up, sticking to it. Salespeople will get 10 times more "nos" than "yeses," so persistence and grit are vital and salespeople need to continue working on prospects past any initial uninformed "no" they might encounter. Reid Hoffman, the founder of LinkedIn, a Facebook board member, and head of the venture capital fund, Greylock Partners, has a podcast titled "Masters of Scale with Reid Hoffman." In one of his podcasts, Hoffman interviews Eric Schmidt, Chairman of Google, and he asks Schmidt what Google looks for when it hires people. Schmidt's answer is, "Persistence is the single best predictor of future success, so we look for persistence."[10] Google bases its hiring decisions on the analysis of massive amounts of data, so if Google has found that persistence is the single best predictor of future success, we should probably learn from Google and emphasize persistence in the AESKOPP approach to selling.

Key Elements and Core Competencies of the AESKOPP Approach

Each of the seven elements of the AESKOPP approach is made up of a group of core competencies – building blocks – that, linked together, lead to successful performance on that element. The core competencies are subject to change, depending on the media selling job involved. Some sales positions, such as in a large-circulation, up-scale national magazine – *Vanity Fair,* for example – require a high level of knowledge, especially about national advertising, the product, and magazine research, plus very strong relationships with major advertising agencies and advertisers. Other sales positions, such as in a local television station, might require an understanding of retail businesses – an automotive dealership, for example – and skills in negotiating with advertising agencies and customers.

Exhibit 4.1 shows the AESKOPP elements and the core competencies which form each element's building blocks.

Exhibit 4.1   Salesperson core competencies

Attitude
- Honest
- Positive/Optimistic
- Committed
- Confident
- Courageous
- Competitive
- Coachable (Open/Non-defensive)
- Curious
- Self-motivated
- Assertive
- Flexible
- Cooperative
- Nurturing

Emotional Intelligence
- Self-awareness
- Self-management
- Social awareness
- Relationship management
  - Internal
  - External

Skills
- Communicating
  - Internal
  - External
- Listening
- Understanding people
- Presenting
  - Individual
  - Groups
- Creating Value
  - Missionary selling
  - Service selling
- Persuasion
- Negotiating/Closing
- Account management
- Team leadership

Knowledge
- Financial/economic/business/category
- Marketing/Advertising/Research
- Market
- Product (your medium)
- Competitors
- Competitive media
- Programmatic
- Pricing
- Sales process
- Contract terms and conditions

Opportunity
- Prospecting/Getting appointments
- Identifying problems (Discovery)

Preparation
- Researching insights
- Solving advertising and marketing problems
- Organization
- Planning
- Time management
- Creating proposals and presentations

Persistence
- Getting feedback on areas of needed improvement
  - Internal feedback from bosses such as sales managers
  - External feedback from clients and buyers
- Expertly structured deliberate practice schedule
- Incredibly hard work
- Grit to keep going after being rejected or losing a sale

Each of the seven AESKOPP elements will be defined and explained much more thoroughly in subsequent chapters.

To use the AESKOPP approach effectively, you need to evaluate yourself based on your degree of expertise on each of the core competencies as listed in Exhibit 4.1. These AESKOPP elements and their corresponding core competencies will change with the type of media selling job, but the AESKOPP elements and core competencies in Exhibit 4.1 are a good place to start in order to define and evaluate a media salesperson's job.

Then, salespeople should study their modified list, evaluate themselves, and then develop a plan to improve those competencies in which they lack experience or have a deficit.

The term salesperson is used because it is inclusive of a wide variety of titles salespeople in the media are assigned by their organizations: sales representative, account executive, account manager, sales consultant, radio marketing consultant, business development director, director of new business, and many more. The preferred title is account executive or account manager, which implies managing customers' accounts, schedules, and campaigns according to what is best for a customer. Also, titles that include "consultant" should be avoided because customers need results more than advice. In this modern age of insight and solutions selling, "results generator" might be a suitable title. but this euphemism is akin to calling a janitor a maintenance engineer, so account executive or account manager are more appropriate titles. However, in this book, to avoid confusion, salesperson will be used in order to encompass all titles.

The most effective way to use this list of core competencies is to download it from the book's website (www.mediaselling.us) and use it as a coaching instrument.

The AESKOPP approach to selling provides salespeople with an excellent way to keep track of their strengths and opportunities for improvement. A positive way to say weakness or shortcoming is to frame it as an opportunity for improvement. The core competencies list is also a valuable tool for managers because, by using a modified core competencies checklist, sales managers will have an excellent coaching tool and snapshot of a salesperson's strengths and weaknesses and of who has high potential to become a manager.

Attitude and Goal Setting

We have been using the word attitude in this book in a positive context. You might hear sports commentators say that a particular athlete has an "attitude," which translated into everyday, non-sports speak means that the athlete has an aggressive, nasty, or arrogant attitude. However, the word attitude is not a singular noun as in sports-speak, but is an aggregate concept that encompasses all types of mind-sets, both positive and negative.

In this chapter we will answer the following questions about attitude:

1   What is attitude?
2   Why are attitudes important in selling?
3   Can I control and change my attitudes?
4   How can I motivate myself to maintain a positive attitude?

What is attitude?

An attitude is a point of view, either negative or positive, about an idea, situation, or person. We develop favorable attitudes about those ideas, situations, or people that are associated with positive rewards and benefits and unfavorable attitudes toward those that are associated with penalties or dislikes. An attitude is also an outlook on life or a mind-set about something.

An attitude has three components: what you *think*, what you *do*, and what you *feel*. To change your attitudes you can change the way you think, act, or feel. But changing the way you think and act is easier than changing how you feel, because attitudes have a strong emotional component despite being supported by varying degrees of fact. Thus, by correcting misconceptions or adding facts, you can change your attitude and those of others. For example, you can learn to like someone about whom you had a negative first impression by thinking about a positive attribute or characteristic and acting friendly at the next encounter, despite lingering negative feelings. Also, acting and thinking positively helps you begin to change the feelings part of your attitude.

Why are attitudes important in selling?

Attitudes are important in selling because performance in a job depends on a person's attitudes and attributes (see the definition of attributes further on in this section). Performance in selling is like performance in sports; it is a synchronization of mind, body, and action. Many of the characteristics of successful athletes and successful salespeople are similar – as is the jargon of selling and sports – both use the terms, "superstars," "heavy hitters," and "rookies."

Performance in any endeavor starts with a dream of successful accomplishment. Scientist/philosopher Buckminster Fuller said that people can accomplish anything they can imagine; but first they must have the courage and confidence to believe in their imaginations and to dream. Walt Disney put it another way: "If you can dream it, you can do it."[11] We translate our dreams into objectives and goals, and these objectives and goals are born in our minds as the result of the interaction of our mental attitudes.

You might think that performance comes about as the result of attitudes; but to the contrary, we tend to form attitudes because of how well we do things, because of our actions. Research has indicated that performance, which is a series of successful behaviors, often precedes attitudes. In other words, if we do something well, we tend to have a favorable attitude toward it. For example, if you are successful at a job, you are likely to have a favorable attitude about the company for which you work. In contrast, having a positive attitude about your company does not necessarily mean you will perform any better, because what determines job performance is mostly your internal drive or motivation to perform well, not external factors such as a pleasant work environment or company picnics.

Attitudes represent the mind portion of job performance and, more importantly, performance in selling. Attitudes can be useful in helping salespeople perform better because they can be changed, controlled, and directed from counterproductive attitudes to productive, objective-oriented ones to help improve performance. Thus, your actions can lead to a feeling of success, which, in turn, leads to a positive attitude.

I include *attributes* in this section about attitudes. Attributes are somewhat like attitudes in that attributes also have a significant impact on job performance. Attributes are inherent talents, characteristics, or qualities of a person. You are born with attributes, but you develop attitudes as you experience life. You can change attitudes, but you can only improve or enhance your attributes, you cannot change them. For the purpose of this book, we are combining the concepts of attitudes and attributes into one broad concept – attitude – to avoid confusion and so that the AESKOPP mnemonic is no longer than seven letters.

Attitude control and enhancement in sports is an obvious example of the importance of mental attitude. Experts estimate that sports performance is determined by about 75 percent inherent ability and about 25 percent attitude, with ability consisting of such inherent elements as size, speed, coordination, quickness, and endurance. Attitude is the head (or mind) portion of sports performance. Sales performance is also determined by ability and attitude, but, unlike sports, is split equally between the two.

While skills and knowledge are vital in selling, the following attitudes from the core competencies listed in Exhibit 4.1 are even more important. Successful media selling requires you to be the following:

Honest   Honest is technically not an attitude, it is an attribute – it means behaving with integrity and in an ethical, straightforward, morally upright, and truthful way. You trust honest people and feel that their word is their bond. Because so much media business is conducted by verbal agreements and not by signed contracts or insertion orders (IOs) (contracts sometimes do not get signed for weeks or months after an advertising campaign has started), being honest in media selling is of primary importance, which is why it is listed first.

Positive/optimistic   You cannot sell successfully if you do not have a positive outlook on life and, thus, have an optimistic attitude. An example of a positive attitude is Albert Einstein's comment that, "In the middle of difficulty lies opportunity"[12] – the glass-is-half-full attitude (instead of half-empty). On the other hand, negative people are downers, to themselves and others. Optimism is also directly related to self-esteem and confidence. People with high self-esteem and confidence believe they can affect the future and make things come out right. As Helen Keller said, "Optimism is the faith that leads to achievement. Nothing can be done without hope and confidence."[13]

Committed   Committed means you have absolutely no doubts and will give everything in support of an undertaking or a cause without turning back. As Myer Berlow, former President of AOL Interactive Marketing, says: "When you're eating ham and eggs for breakfast, the chicken was involved, but the pig was committed."[14] Generals have been known to burn bridges behind their troops to make retreat impossible and, thus, forced their soldiers to be totally committed and to fight for their lives.

Another dimension of commitment is passion for the cause and the task. Louis Gerstner, ex-CEO of IBM in his book, *Who Says Elephants Can't Dance*, which describes his incredible turnaround of IBM, wrote that "personal leadership is about passion."[15] He means a passion for or commitment to winning. Being committed also means that people accept responsibility and hold themselves accountable for their successes and failures.

Confident Feeling confident is vital in selling. Without confidence, or belief, in yourself, your product, and your offer, you cannot generate the enthusiasm required to reflect a positive image of your product to buyers. All training, all knowledge acquisition, all practice, all planning should be aimed at one thing – making you feel more confident about what you are selling.

Courageous Being courageous is a vital attribute for salespeople. Courageous does not mean you have no fear, it means you have the ability to overcome fear. You need courage to stand up to managers and others who might pressure you to do the wrong thing or to be dishonest. You need courage to set out every day to make 10 calls when you know you will probably face 10 rejections. You need courage to tell your boss the bad news that you did not get an order on a piece of business you had been working on for months. You need courage to be honest and tell the truth to your customers and to your management.

Competitive Being competitive means having a strong desire to win. However, the drive and passion for winning must be channeled into two areas: being self-competitive and being externally competitive. When you are self-competitive, you compete with yourself, pushing yourself to improve. In *Who Says Elephants Can't Dance?*, Louis Gerstner refers to this self-competitiveness as "restless self-renewal," or the motivation to constantly improve.[16] Self-competition is a prerequisite for improvement, which the Japanese call *kaizen*, meaning constant improvement in small increments, leading to huge improvements in the long run, as Toyota practiced religiously on the way to becoming the world's largest car maker.

Being externally competitive means having a strong desire to beat the competition, those direct competitors in your medium and competitive media. If you are a television station salesperson, you want to beat the salespeople from other television stations to get higher shares of business and get higher rates, while pulling advertising dollars away from websites and Internet platforms, newspapers, radio, and outdoor. Being externally competitive means winning by playing the game fairly and by the rules and not becoming overly competitive either within or out of your own company, which can lead to dishonest and unethical behavior, as described in Chapter 3. This attitude is probably better described as being ethically competitive, externally competitive, and self-competitive, and is exemplified by being a member of a 400-meter relay race in the Olympic Games. You cooperate with other team members on passing the baton, as you perfect your own running technique and set increasingly lower lap-time goals, while your overall goal is for the team to win the race.

Coachable (open/non-defensive)   Coachable means that you are open to feedback and coaching in the form of an evaluation or criticism with becoming defensive. Being open and not defensive is directly related to your self-esteem and self-confidence. People with low self-esteem and self-confidence take almost anything said to them in a negative way, as a criticism or slap in the face. Being coachable and not defensive will help you improve and grow and will make you more valued by your management.

Curious   Salespeople must be insatiably curious about all elements of their product, their company and its technology stack, their industry, advertising, and marketing. Curious people are not only open to coaching and training but they thirst for it. In the podcast "Masters of Scale With Reid Hoffman" mentioned earlier, Eric Schmidt's complete answer to the question of what Google look for in hiring people was "persistence and curiosity."[17]

Self-motivated   Being self-motivated means that you do not depend on others to spark your drive to achieve but that you have the discipline and courage to set your own goals and to improve yourself. Being self-motivated means you have a strong desire to work, to do a good job, to achieve, and to improve. Daniel Pink in his book *Drive: The Surprising Truth About What Motivates Us* writes that there are three things that motivate people: *autonomy, mastery,* and *purpose*.[18] People have an inherent motivation to get good at something, which, as Pink points out, is why after working hard on a job during the week, some people will spend the weekend practicing on their guitar because they are driven to improve. This craving for improvement is what drives self-motivation.

Assertive   Assertive does not mean aggressive. It means being firm in expressing your ideas, thoughts, and feelings. One need not be pushy; quiet determination and resolve can result in being heard, included, and recognized.

Flexible   Flexible means being willing to change your plans, your attitudes, your opinions, and your feelings about people and situations. It allows you to be less rigid, open to new ideas and ways of doing things. Flexibility is an attribute that you were either born with or not, but it can learned with practice.

Cooperative   Being cooperative means being a good team member, willing to help others and work towards company goals. The best analogy for cooperation I have ever read is, "We are all angels with only one wing, and the only way we can fly is by embracing each other."

Nurturing   Being nurturing means caring for others, wanting to help and mentor. Having a nurturing attitude is vitally important for media salespeople so that they will not forget about their customers after a sale and will care about getting results. This attitude helps salespeople overcome a tendency to hit-and-run after making a sale. Paperwork and production need to be completed properly, the schedule placed properly, and the customer contacted frequently and serviced after an ad or schedule runs.

Can I control and change my attitudes?

Attitudes can be changed and controlled, but you must have the will power and discipline to practice relentlessly and deliberately. Making any changes within ourselves takes self-discipline and practice. Techniques used by sports psychologists can help you control, manage, and change your attitude.

Positive framing　　This technique is based on the concept that verbal or written communication creates images, or pictures, in our heads that we cannot erase with mere language. If you tell people "do not think of an elephant" and then ask them what kind of an animal popped into their mind, they will invariably tell you they had an image of an elephant. They simply cannot think of a no elephant, zero elephant, or nothing elephant, as instructed.[19] Because we think visually, in pictures, you want to put positive pictures in your and your customers' minds.

Imagine if after losing a basketball game a coach uses a negative frame and says to his team, "Do not miss free throws! We lost the game because we missed too many free throws! You're a bunch of bums!" The team will get a picture implanted in their heads of missing free throws and will continue to miss free throws. On the other hand, it would form a positive image if the coach were to say after losing a game, using a positive frame, "Make your free throws. Free throws win ball games."

Always use positive frames in your inner dialogues with yourself and in external dialogues with others. When you use a positive frame, you put a positive spin on things and you create optimism in yourself. An example of a positive frame would be an offer by a gas station of a "cash discount" instead of informing consumers of a "credit card surcharge." Positive framing is a very valuable sales tool as we will see later in Chapters 11 and 13.

Visualization and mental rehearsal　　To use visualization, mobilize all of your senses and imagine a future sales call, down to how prospects will look and act while hearing your presentation. Visualize your prospects' reaction to your presentation – a big smile and a nod of the head. Next, mentally rehearse your presentation, including how you will create value for your product, and silently rehearse your proposals. Visualize the ideal outcome of your presentation and your reaction when your proposal is accepted. Will you jump up and click your heels? If so, practice this in your mind. Rehearse your presentation word for word, out loud over and over, visualizing prospects' reactions and your responses to their questions. Constant practice of visualization is a key to success and is an excellent confidence booster. While visualization has been referred to as instant replay, Spencer Johnson and Larry Wilson, in their best-selling book, *The One Minute Sales Person*, call this technique "the one minute rehearsal."[20]

Another dramatic example of the power of visualization was seen in a video series about athletes in the 2018 Winter Olympics who visualize their dream performance. Biathlon competitor Lowell Bailey looks "at the snow and imagines himself as a bow with an arrow drawn, ready to accelerate."[21] Before a cross-country race, Sadie Bjornsen, when she hears the countdown timer, "imagines herself as bird flying up the hills."[22] Brenna Huckaby "goes to her happy place," her home, and hears her mother's voice saying, "Come on, baby!"[23]

Do the right thing　　Behave ethically at all times. Integrity and honesty are not only good business practices that will help you manage relationships and build trust effectively over the long run, but also they are good for your soul. Conducting business with integrity improves your self-esteem, self-confidence, and health because you know that you are doing the right thing.

Using these three techniques requires mental discipline. Just as the dream of an Olympic gold medal helps athletes push their bodies to their physical limits time and again, they must channel their minds toward positive attitudes. Sales success requires the same persistence and mental discipline.

How can I motivate myself to maintain a positive attitude?

People's motivational drive comes more from internal forces than from external ones. While people who fail in sales often blame external elements, such as a company or its management, the vast majority of these people lack sufficient internal motivation to succeed. People who are successful in sales and in most other endeavors crave success and are, thus, high achievers.

High achievers

People who have strong internal motivation and drive for mastery are high achievers. Research has identified some common characteristics of high achievers:

1　They set goals and objectives.
2　They enjoy solving problems.
3　They take calculated risks.
4　They like immediate feedback on their performance.
5　They take personal responsibility for achieving their goals and objectives.

Looking at these characteristics, we can see that insight and solution selling is an ideal occupation for high achievers, who are more likely to satisfy their needs in sales jobs because of the nature of the tasks required in sales, especially in media sales. Selling requires a continual goal-setting process. High achievers like selling and are motivated by it because it gives them the opportunity to use their self-motivation to work to its peak while satisfying their needs to solve problems, help their customers, take risks, and receive immediate performance feedback.

Goal-Setting Theory and Objective-Setting Practice

Peter Drucker popularized the importance of setting goals and objectives in his classic book, *The Practice of Management*, published in 1954. While there is still some question about who first used the term *management by objectives* (MBO), it is generally conceded that the initial push came from Drucker, who attributes it to Alfred P. Sloan, the managerial and organizational genius who is credited with building up General Motors.

In the 1960s, Edwin A. Locke published a series of articles that detailed his research on goal setting and on how these motivate people. He not only explained why goals work but also proposed some basic rules for setting them. While Drucker, Locke, and most other goal-setting theorists put their work in a managerial context, these theories also apply to individual goal setting where competence and confidence grow as you get better at your own objectives and goals.

Goal-setting theory

Goals and objectives have a significant effect on performance if they have the following attributes: clarity, difficulty, and feedback. A goal has a time horizon of more than one year and an objective has a time horizon of less than a year. Therefore, one would set several short-term objectives to reach a long-term goal.

Goal clarity   Clarity is the single most important element in setting goals. Goals and objectives must be specific so they can be measured. A general objective of increasing the number of prospecting calls next month is vague, nonspecific, and virtually useless. A more specific objective would be to average two prospecting appointments per day for the next month.

Goal difficulty   Increasing the difficulty of goals and objectives generally amplifies the challenge, which, in turn, raises the effort to meet the challenge. This concept of goal difficulty creates confusion and is where defining the difference between goals and objectives becomes important. Because goals have a long-term time horizon, it is useful to set goals, and, thus, expectations, high. In the best-selling book, *Built to Last*, Collins and Porras's research shows that one of the things that highly successful companies have in common is that they set BHAGs – Big, Hairy, Audacious Goals. The authors write: "A BHAG should be so clear and compelling that it requires little or no explanation. Remember, a BHAG is a goal – such as climbing a mountain or going to the moon – not a 'statement.' If it does not get people juices going it is just not a BHAG."[24] One of the 18 built-to-last companies was Merck. Its BHAG was "to become the preeminent drug maker worldwide, via massive R&D and new products that cure disease."[25]

On the other hand, short-term objectives set by salespeople and their management should be set to make people feel like winners, a deep-seated need. Unfortunately, management often set BHAGs, or "stretch," short-term objectives, believing that they motivate people. Figure 4.1 shows the relationship between motivation and objective difficulty. Setting a very low objective has no motivating effect. On the other hand, setting an objective too high demotivates people because they give up the moment they realize that the objective is unachievable. Working hard to achieve an impossible objective creates cognitive dissonance, so people quit making an effort in order to bring thinking and action into internal harmony.

As you can see from Figure 4.1, the best objectives are moderately difficult, yet provide a challenge because they are perceived as attainable and are, thus, motivating. Contrary to

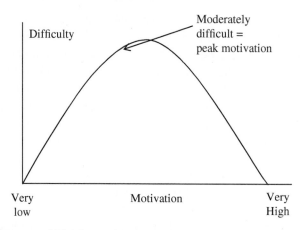

Figure 4.1   Objective difficulty and motivation

what many managers believe, the trick in setting objectives is to set them on the low side of the moderately difficult peak to ensure that they can be reached with a strong effort and, thus, allow people to feel successful. Unfortunately, too often managers set objectives on the high side of the moderately difficult peak and, thus, unintentionally reduce people's motivation. It is better, in fact, to be a little on the low side than to be a little on the high side because you want to make sure that the salespeople feel like winners.

Interestingly, people with low self-esteem often set unrealistically high goals because they expect failure. Already viewing themselves as losers, they are more comfortable reinforcing this view in advance. Claiming that "the objective was too high," allows them to quit before trying rather than attempting something difficult that they think they are bound to fail at.

The ideal is to set a series of moderately difficult, challenging objectives that get progressively more difficult and challenging as each objective is achieved (a critical element in deliberate practice). This series of realistic step-by-step, increasingly more difficult objectives will eventually lead you to your BHAG.

In 2018 in his annual letter to stockholders, Amazon CEO Jeff Bezos related a story that reinforced the importance of setting realistic goals. The title of his anecdote was "Perfect handstands," and read: "A close friend recently decided to learn to do a perfect free-standing handstand… In the very first lesson, the coach gave her some wonderful advice. … 'The reality is that it takes about six months of daily practice. If you think you should be able to do it in two weeks, you're just going to end up quitting.' Unrealistic beliefs…kill high standards."[26]

Setting objectives and goals that achieve high standards is an art. Achieving high standards takes work, analysis, thought, and incredible persistence when faced with an unpredictable future.

Goal feedback   You need to get feedback – a reading on how you are doing. You receive feedback from yourself by successfully solving problems and closing sales, by analyzing what you did right, or by failing and analyzing what you did wrong. For example, analyzing statistics about your ratio of total calls to successful calls will give you feedback on how you are doing. Furthermore, you should get feedback on your objectives and goals from your manager on a regular basis. You have the right to know how you are doing and what your manager thinks you can do to improve.

Objective-setting practice

Sound individual objectives must be:

1 Measurable
2 Attainable
3 Demanding
4 Consistent with company goals
5 Under the control of the individual
6 Deadlined

Here is a mnemonic for setting objectives – MADCUD. I will provide you with more details about using and prioritizing the MADCUD objectives on a daily and weekly basis in Chapter 25: Time Management. But for now, here are the elements' definitions:

Measurable   The measurable criterion relates to the concept of clarity. Objectives and goals must be specific enough to be measurable, for example, "to increase sales by 15 percent" or "to increase your number of face-to-face presentations from a current average of 10 per week to an average of 15 per week." Notice that objectives always begin with "to," which implies an action you are going to take.

Setting specific, measurable, revenue objectives is not necessarily a good idea, although it is common practice. Rather than setting the final objective as a revenue objective, it is more productive to set a series of specific, measurable, smaller objectives that will help you reach a desired monthly revenue level. In the chapter "A bias for action" in *In Search of Excellence*, Thomas J. Peters and Robert H. Waterman, Jr. quote the president of one successful company who says he has his managers focus on a few important activity-based objectives. If they have this task-oriented focus, he says that "the financials will take care of themselves."[27]

Attainable   Set moderately difficult but attainable objectives. If objectives are reasonable, challenging, and attainable, they are motivating. If people perceive objectives to be unattainable, they will not work hard to achieve them. It is important to give time and thought to setting realistic, attainable objectives so that when you accomplish them you will feel successful.

Demanding   Demanding, like attainable, is related to difficulty. As seen in Figure 4.1, an objective has to be not only attainable but also sufficiently demanding to be challenging. High achievers are particularly motivated by demanding goals that challenge them. For high achievers the big payoff is the conquest and feeling like a winner, more so than any money that might be involved.

Consistent with company goals   Individual objectives should be consistent with company objectives and goals. For example, broadcast salespeople sometimes work at cross-purposes to their sales departments by concentrating on selling rates that are too low or by "cherry picking" inventory, which means only selecting the highly rated advertising slots or special low-price offers to sell. Such practices would be inconsistent with an overall company goal of maximizing revenue, for example.

Under control of the individual   Another seemingly self-evident criterion for sound objectives states that they must be under the control of the individual. Instead of setting a revenue objective, set objectives for the number of calls you will make or for the number of presentations you will give. These are activity objectives. Too often, the concept of setting activity objectives is overlooked, especially by beginning salespeople. For example, objectives that would not be under the control of salespeople would be "to increase revenue next month by 25 percent." But what if that next month's ratings on your television station went down 30 percent or last month was the bottom month in a yearlong advertising slowdown. You cannot control ratings or the general economy; you can only control how hard you work and your own activities.

Deadlined   Your goals and objectives must be deadlined; they must have a due date. Without clear deadlines, goals and objectives become amorphous. Here is an example of some objectives a radio salesperson might write: "Next month I will increase my average rates from last month by 10 percent; I will increase the number of prospecting calls I make in the average week from 10 to 15; and I will make 25 percent more face-to-face presentations." These goals are measurable, attainable, demanding, consistent with company goals, under the control of the person, and deadlined. Notice the phrase "a radio station salesperson might write." Objectives that are not written down are worthless because they are merely intentions. A further way to increase your commitment to your objectives is to give your manager a copy of your written objectives.

Remember to keep your objectives flexible. If they are carved in stone and unchangeable, your objectives can lose their motivating effect particularly if they turn out to be unreasonable because of economic conditions, because of a shift in competitive positioning, or because of a change in your organization's priorities or strategy.

Take Full Responsibility for Your "Cycle of Success"

High achievers set demanding objectives and goals, enjoy solving problems, take calculated risks, want immediate feedback on their performance, and take personal responsibility for their own "cycle of success" (see Figure 4.2).

The cycle of success is an ongoing cycle of ever-more demanding objectives and goals that lead to ever-increasing success. But just as the AESKOPP formula for success was multiplicative in the sense that if any of the seven AESKOPP elements were not present, success could not be achieved, so it is with the cycle of success in that all of the elements are inextricably linked.

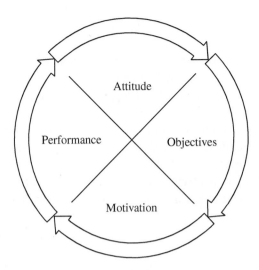

Figure 4.2 The Cycle of Success

The cycle is *your* cycle. You own it and must take full responsibility for keeping it moving. What drives it, the motor for this cycle, is your dream. Remember the words of Walt Disney earlier in this chapter: If you can dream it, you can do it.

Your dream, your mission

You cannot win an Olympic gold medal if you do not or cannot dream of winning one. Dennis Waitley in his inspirational book, *Empires of the Mind*, writes about the dreams of accomplished and successful people. Waitley suggests that writing a personal mission based on your dream can help you realize it. Write it down, keep it in your wallet, backpack, or purse, and let it drive your cycle of success.

Test Yourself

1. What do the various letters in AESKOPP mean?
2. Do all of the seven AESKOPP elements have to be present for successful selling?
3. What are some of the core competencies of Skills?
4. What are the two types of Preparation?
5. How can a salesperson use the core competencies rating system to improve performance?
6. Name two ways a sales manager can use the core competencies rating system.
7. What is an attitude?
8. Which comes first, attitude or performance? Why?
9. What is the difference between a goal and an objective?
10. What are the six criteria for sound objectives?
11. What are the four elements in the cycle of success?

Project

First, rate yourself on all of the core competencies, make a list of the five you need to work on most, and then assign yourself some monthly learning goals. For example, "to improve my market knowledge by reading Chamber of Commerce material and Census data next month."

Second, choose a task, such as writing a term paper or a sales presentation, or an activity, such as dating, and write a MADCUD objectives statement that will help you complete the task or activity successfully.

Last, write a BHAG for yourself – several years in the future – and then write a personal mission statement that will help you focus on and achieve your BHAG, your dream.

References

Drucker, Peter F. 1954. *The Practice of Management.* New York: Harper & Row.

Collins, James C. and Porras, Jerry. 1994. *Built to Last: Successful Habits of Visionary Companies.* New York: Harper Business.

Colvin, Geoff. 2008. *Talent Is Overrated: What Really Separates World-Class Performers for Everybody Else.* New York: Portfolio.

Garfield, Charles A. with Bennett, Hal Zina. 1984. *Peak Performance: Mental Training Techniques of the World's Greatest Athletes.* New York: Warner Books.

Gerstner, Louis V. Jr. 2002. *Who Says Elephants Can't Dance? Inside IBM's Historic Turnaround.* New York: Harper Business.

Gladwell, Malcolm. 2008. *Outliers: The Story of Success.* New York: Little, Brown and Company.

Johnson, Spencer and Wilson, Larry. 1984. *The One Minute Sales Person.* New York: William Morrow.

Locke, Edwin A. 1966. "The ubiquity of the technique of goal setting." *Behavioral Science,* Vol. II.

Locke, Edwin A. and. Bryan, J.F. 1967. "Goal setting as a means of increasing motivation." *Journal of Applied Psychology,* Vol. 51.

Locke, Edwin A. 1968. "Toward a theory of task motivation and incentives." *Organizational Behavior and Human Performance,* Vol. 3.

Locke, Edwin A., Cartledge, Norman, and Kerr, Claramae S. 1970. "Studies in the relationship between satisfaction, goal setting and performance." *Organizational Behavior and Human Performance,* Vol. 5.

Peters, Thomas J. and Waterman, Robert H. Jr. 1982. *In Search of Excellence: Lessons from America's Best Run Companies.* New York: Harper & Row.

Pink, Daniel. 2009. *Drive: The Surprising Truth About What Motivates Us.* New York: Riverhead Books.

Waitley, Dennis. 1995. *Empires of the Mind.* New York: William Morrow.

Resources

Daniel Goleman's website and blog (www.danielgoleman.info)
Lessons for Living website (www.lessons4living.com)
Core competencies (www.mediaselling.us/downloads.html)

Notes

1   Anderson, Chris. 2013. "How to give a killer presentation." *Harvard Business Review,* June.

2   Retrieved from https://www.amazon.com/gp/bestsellers/2008/books.

3   Gladwell, Malcolm. 2008. *Outliers: The Story of Success.* New York: Little, Brown and Company.

4   Ibid.

5   Ibid.

6   Retrieved from http://projects.ict.usc.edu/itw/gel/EricssonDeliberatePracticePR93.PDF.

7   Colvin, Geoff. 2008. *Talent Is Overrated: What Really Separates World-Class Performers From Everybody Else.* New York: Portfolio.

8   Ibid.

9   Ibid.

10   "Masters of scale with Reid Hoffman." Retrieved from https://www.stitcher.com/podcast/stitcher/masters-of-scale/e/53503384.

11   Retrieved from https:///.brainyquote.com/lists/authors/top_10_walt_disney_quotes.

12   Ben-Shahar, Tal. 2007. *Happier: Learn the Secrets to Daily Joy and lasting Fulfillment.* New York: McGraw-Hill.

13   Keller, Helen. 1903. *The Story of My Life.* Bantam Classics, reissue ed. 1991.

14   Personal conversation, October 2002.

15   Gerstner, Louis V. Jr. 2002. *Who Says Elephants Can't Dance? Inside IBM's Historic Turnaround.* New York: Harper Business.

16   Ibid.

17   "Masters of scale with Reid Hoffman." Retrieved from https://www.stitcher.com/podcast/stitcher/masters-of-scale/e/53503384.

18   Pink, Daniel. 2009. *Drive: The Surprising Truth About What Motivates Us.* New York: Riverhead Books.

19   Lakoff, George. 2014. *Don't Think of an Elephant: Know Your Values and Frame the Debate.* White River Junction, VT: Chelsea Green Publishing.

20   Johnson, Spencer and Wilson, Larry. 2002. *The One Minute Sales Person.* New York: William Morrow.

21   Retrieved from https://www.nytimes.com/video/sports/olympics/100000005699888/olympics-lowell-bailey.html.

22   Retrieved from https://www.nytimes.com/video/sports/olympics/100000005699977/olympics-sadie-bjornsen.html.

23   Retrieved from https://www.nytimes.com/video/sports/olympics/100000005700038/olympics-brenna-huckaby.html.

24   Collins, James C. and Porras, Jerry. 1994. *Built to Last: Successful Habits of Visionary Companies.* Harper Business.

25   Ibid.

26   "How Jeff Bezos leads." Retrieved from https://www.axios.com/jeff-bezos-amazon-leadership-seven-essentials-3c627861-b3ed-4335-baae-b8a768b24cc2.html.

27   Peters, Thomas J. and Waterman, Robert H. Jr. 1982. *In Search of Excellence: Lessons from America's Best-Run Companies.* New York: Harper & Row.

Emotional Intelligence

Charles Warner

In 1957, I got my first sales job at WSPA-TV, the CBS affiliate in Spartanburg, SC. My first sale was to Mr. Parrott of Parrott's Florist. The owner of WSPA-TV, Walter Brown, knew Mr. Parrot and bought flowers from him weekly for his home and for the station. Mr. Brown sent me to see Mr. Parrott because a CBS program, "See It Now" with Edward R. Morrow was sponsored on the network by Florist Telegraph Delivery (FTD). Because of the two men's relationship I got an order for a 20-second commercial that ran before the network program. When he gave me the order, Mr. Parrott said he'd "try it once," but when I returned to see Mr. Parrott the next day after his commercial ran and asked him if he would like to renew for another 13 weeks, he said, "No. I didn't get any results. No one called."

When I retuned downhearted to the station, my general sales manager asked, "How did it go? Did you close him?"

"No. He said he didn't get any results," I replied sheepishly.

"That's a common objection," replied my sales manager. "You should have asked him a bunch of questions that led him to the answer you wanted him to give you and then sold him sizzle!"

"Sizzle?"

"Yeah, you know, 'sell the sizzle, not the steak!'" My sales manager always spoke in exclamation points. It was his way of showing that he was enthusiastic.

"Enthusiasm, enthusiasm! Enthusiasm is what gets orders! Always sell the sizzle!" He might as well have said, "Sell him magic!" for all I knew. And with that, he reached back to his small bookshelf, took out a book, and handed it to me. "Read this!", said my sales

Media Selling: Digital, Television, Audio, Print and Cross-Platform, Fifth Edition.
Charles Warner, William A. Lederer, and Brian Moroz.

manager, "it's by Elmer Wheeler and it's called *Sizzlemanship*! It's the greatest book ever written about selling! Memorize it!"

Old-Fashioned Models of Selling

In 1957, books on selling, such as *Sizzlemanship!,* Frank Bettger's *How I Raised Myself from Failure to Success in Selling,* and Og Mandino's ode of humility, *The Greatest Salesman in the World,* preached a model of selling that was developed in the 1920s, 1930s, and 1940s. These books on selling urged the use of techniques and tricks that were relatively success-ful for products that could be sold in one encounter, that were often low-cost, and for which people could be badgered into buying, often just to get rid of the salesperson.

These outmoded selling models used simple mnemonics to guide salespeople, such as AIDA, which stood for Attention, Interest, Desire, and Action and ABC, which stood for Always Be Closing and which was made notorious by Alex Baldwin in the David-Mamet-scripted play and movie "Glengarry Glen Ross." The old-time sales practitioners urged outrageous, often silly, techniques for getting a prospect's attention and closing sales. They advocated manipulative techniques such as "sizzlemanship" to get interest and create desire (usually by overselling and overpromising). And they advocated a num-ber of techniques, such as ABC, that pressured prospects to act immediately and which allowed a salesperson to slam down a one-time sale. While there is nothing necessarily wrong with the AIDA and ABC mnemonics, these old-fashioned, hard-sell techniques, which include the "tell-and-sell" model, are largely responsible for the bad reputations that salespeople are often saddled with today.

Old Models Don't Work In the Digital Era

Carl Zaiss and Thomas Gordon point out in their excellent book, *Sales Effectiveness Training,* that old selling models do not work in a highly competitive, digital-oriented, and data-flooded business environment.

Rather than being seen as the manipulators and hard closers of the past, media sales-people need to be perceived as trusted and respected partners who provide insights and get results for their customers. Modern media salespeople must concentrate on long-term, trusting personal relationships with buyers and clients. Remember, the biggest competition for media salespeople is algorithms, so developing emotional intelligence is vital to differentiate you from the AI used in algorithms.

The Zeiss and Gordon non-manipulative advice might have been suitable for selling in the 1990s, but after the disrupting influence of the Internet and after 2003 when Google introduced its online auction AdWords[i] that featured a cost-per-click (CPC) pric-ing model, just being non-manipulative is not enough. Media salespeople have to be able

---

[i] Google changed the name of AdWords to Google Ads effective July 24, 2018.

to analyze data in order to come up with insights and solutions and to educate prospects about the benefits of their product.

The Current Model: Selling as Educating

The vast majority of buyers and customers of the media are hypersensitive to the tricks, manipulations, and the selling of "magic" in the past. With the highly complex digital advertising ecosystem, programmatic trading, and the explosion of available data, buyers need relationships with media salespeople based on a basic understanding of the underlying ad-delivery technology, familiarity with available data, and mutual trust. Establishing mutual trust is the first step for a successful digital-era, selling-as-educating model which, in turn, requires salespeople to have emotional intelligence in order to develop trusting relationships.

The Importance of Emotional Intelligence

The term *emotional intelligence* was popularized by Daniel Goleman, a Harvard-educated PhD in psychology, in his best seller, *Emotional Intelligence: Why It Can Matter More Than IQ*, which expanded on the work of the world-renowned educational psychologists, Howard Gardner, Robert Sternberg and others.

Gardner, Sternberg, and others questioned accepted definitions of intelligence and began to look beyond a number or intelligence quotient (IQ). After exploring the topic thoroughly, they realized that what IQ tests measured was only a person's ability to take an IQ test and was not the enormously complex construct that had been referred to in the past as "intelligence."

While Howard Gardner broadly defined intelligence as "the ability to solve problems or to create products that are valued within one or more cultural settings," in his influential book, *Frames of Mind, The Theory of Multiple Intelligences*, he identified seven facets of intelligence. These are linguistic, logical-mathematical, musical, bodily-kinesthetic, spatial, interpersonal, and intrapersonal. In his book, *Intelligence Reframed: Multiple Intelligences for the 21st Century*, he added three more facets of intelligence: naturalist, spiritual, and existential.

Daniel Goleman concentrated his research on the importance of the personal intelligences, which he labeled *emotional intelligence*. Beginning in *Emotional Intelligence*, published in 1995, and in three subsequent books, *Working With Emotional Intelligence*, *Primal Leadership: Realizing the Power of Emotional Intelligence*, and *Social Intelligence* Goleman has continued to refine and simplify his construct of emotional intelligence (referred to as EQ, emotional quotient) and social intelligence. In *Working With Emotional Intelligence*, Goleman defined emotional intelligence as the "capacity for recognizing our own feelings and those of others, for motivating ourselves, and for managing emotions well in ourselves and in our relationships."[1] His book, *Primal Leadership*, lays out an expanded definition that includes four dimensions of EQ, as defined in Exhibit 5.1 below:

Exhibit 5.1   Emotional intelligence domains and associated competencies

Personal competence: These capabilities determine how we manage ourselves.

Self-awareness

- Emotional self-awareness: Reading one's own emotions and recognizing their impact; using "gut sense" to guide decisions.
- Accurate self-assessment: Knowing one's strengths and limits.
- Self-confidence: A sound sense of one's self-worth and capabilities.

Self-management

- Emotional self-control: Keeping disruptive emotions and impulses under control.
- Transparency: Displaying honesty and integrity; trustworthiness.
- Adaptability: Flexibility in adapting to changing situations or overcoming obstacles.
- Achievement: The drive to improve performance to meet inner standards of excellence.
- Initiative: Readiness to act and seize opportunity.
- Optimism: Seeing the upside in events.

Social competence: These capabilities determine how we manage relationships.

Social awareness

- Empathy: Sensing others' emotions, understanding their perspective, and taking an active interest in their concerns.
- Organizational awareness: Reading the currents, decision networks, and politics at the organizational level.
- Service: Recognizing and meeting...client or customer needs.

Relationship management

- Inspirational leadership: Guiding and motivating with a compelling vision (for media salespeople this would translate into creating value with an inspiring vision for your medium and your media outlet).
- Influence: Wielding a range of tactics of persuasion.
- Developing others: Bolstering others' ability through feedback and guidance.
- Change catalyst: Initiating, managing, and leading a new direction.
- Conflict management: Resolving disagreements.
- Teamwork and collaboration: Cooperation and team building.

Source: Goleman, Daniel, Boyatzis, Richard, and McKee, Annie. 2002. *Primal Leadership: Realizing the Power of Emotional Intelligence*. Boston, MA: Harvard Business School Press. Used with permission.

How important is emotional intelligence in selling?

Goleman makes the case that, contrary to previously held theories, IQ might not be an accurate predictor of life success. "At best IQ contributes about 20 percent to the factors that determine life success, which leaves 80 percent to other forces. As one observer notes, 'The vast majority of one's ultimate niche in society is determined by non-IQ factors, ranging from social class to luck.'"[2] A study of Harvard graduates in the fields of law, medicine, teaching, and business found that scores on entrance exams, a surrogate for IQ, had zero or negative correlation with eventual career success.

A study initiated in 1968 by the Stanford Graduate School of Business reinforced the importance of emotional intelligence for success in business. It conducted in-depth interviews with the members of its graduating class, which examined the students' academic records and grades, their extracurricular and social activities, and their reputation among their fellow students. The school kept track of the graduates' careers and levels of success with re-interviews in 1978 and in 1988. When the school published the findings of its 20-year study in 1988, it concluded that the only two things that the most successful graduates (top five percent in title, position, money, for example) had in common was that all of the most successful graduates were in the bottom half of their class in grades and all of them were popular. In other words, relationship skills were more important for success than grades.

A major element of and success is optimism. A study of salesmen at Met Life by Martin Seligman revealed that,

> Being able to take a rejection with grace is essential in sales of all kinds, especially with a product like insurance, where the ratio of nos to yeses can be so discouragingly high. For this reason, about three quarters of insurance salesmen quit in their first three years. Seligman found that new salesmen who were by nature optimists sold 37 percent more insurance in their first two years on the job than did pessimists. And during the first year the pessimists quit at twice the rate of the optimists."[3]

Media salespeople sell an intangible product similar to what insurance salespeople sell, but media salespeople do not have quite the same rejection rate, which makes media selling more desirable and satisfying. However, the above research reinforces the importance of optimism in selling. Optimism is defined in terms of how people explain to themselves their own successes and failures. People who are optimistic believe failures are the result of something that can be changed so that they can be successful the next time around. Pessimists take personal blame for failures, attributing them to some inherent characteristic they are helpless to change.[4] Pessimists also often blame their parents or their bosses or even the weather for their failures. Their attitude is that they expect failure; therefore, they create failures and a disastrous future. On the other hand, optimists expect success, and therefore create a successful future. Seligman's research reinforces the importance of attitude in selling.

Do I have emotional intelligence?

Socrates said that all knowledge begins with, "Know thyself." Self-knowledge is the keystone of EQ. It is the awareness of one's feelings as they occur. Self-awareness is a nonreactive, nonjudgmental attention to one's inner states and feelings. To find out if you have emotional intelligence you have to ask yourself the following thee questions, as outlined by Daniel Goleman and Michele Nevarez in a 2018 *Harvard Business Review* article titled "Boost your emotional intelligence with these 3 questions."[5]

1 What are the differences between how you see yourself and how others see you?
2 What matters to you?
3 What changes will you make to achieve these goals?

What are the difference between how you see yourself and how others see you? Obviously, to answer this question you need feedback, and the first step in getting feedback is to get a sense of how your self-perception, or how you see yourself, differs from your reputation, or how others see you. This type of feedback is important because we can be blind to other people's reaction to us. For example, most people think they are good listeners, but very often that is not the case. Research shows that 90 percent of people who drive cars think they are above average drivers, which, of course, is mathematically impossible. Without some sort of external reality check, it is difficult for people to identify the ways in which they can improve.

Getting feedback from others can provide proof of the necessity of changing specific behaviors on one or all of the four dimensions of EQ: self-awareness, self-management, social awareness, and relationship management.

In order to gain the best idea of where the differences lie between your self-perception and your reputation, you should use some sort of 360-degree feedback assessment that takes into account the four dimensions of EQ such as the Emotional Intelligence Appraisal – Multi-Rater & 360° Editions available for purchase at https://www.talentsmart.com/products/emotional-intelligence-appraisal-mr.php.

You can also work with a professional coach, which is expensive, or work with a colleague or learning partner whose opinion you trust and who would be willing to talk over how you are doing on a regular basis.[6]

What matters to you? When you get your feedback from a test, a coach, or a trusted colleague, let that information tell you what you want to improve on. But you also have to consider what *your* goals are, or what you want to get better at now and in the future. Your own EQ is completely tied up in your own sense of self, so that being intrinsically motivated to make the effort to change matters more than simply learning a skill such communicating or closing. You have to have a long-term goal, such as attaining a leadership position of a sales manager or a CEO, or being a better team member, or getting better at managing yourself. When you have a specific goal it helps you have the discipline to focus on one of the four areas of EQ and make discernable, incremental changes. For example, let's say you get feedback that your are not a great listener, but you think you are. Instead of seeing this feedback as an attack, step back and consider your goal of becoming sales manager. Ask yourself if being a better listener would improve your chances of being a sales manager. Seeing feedback in this light can help you position it as an opportunity to take a step toward achieving your goal.

What changes will you make to achieve these goals? Once you have determined what EQ skills you want to focus on, you must then identify what specific actions you will take. If you are going to work on being a better listener, you might decide that whenever you are talking with someone that you will take the time to pause, listen thoroughly to what they have to say without interrupting, and check with them that you understand what they are saying before you craft a reply.

Hopefully your answers to the above questions placed you more than half-way toward the side of possessing EQ, which means that you know you have an opportunity for improvement. "Opportunity for improvement" is a positive frame for the concept of deficiency and your first lesson in the use of framing.

People are sometimes tempted to use personality tests to determine their EQ, but many of these tests, such as the Myers-Briggs Type Indicator (MBTI), do not have much value in predicting success, uncovering motivation, and understanding yourself and others. Instead, they attempt to pigeonhole people into types such as "feeling" or "thinking" or expressive." Most psychological tests are not designed to assess emotional intelligence, so if you are interested in improving your EQ, use tests specifically designed for that, such as the Emotional Intelligence Appraisal – Me Edition, available for purchase at https://www.talentsmart.com/products/emotional-intelligence-appraisal.php.

How can I apply emotional intelligence to selling media?

Now that you have learned about what emotional intelligence is and how EQ can help you improve your relationships, the next step is to relate EQ to selling. Using the three Golden Rules of Selling is the optimum way to apply EQ to selling.

Rule #1: Do unto others as they would have others do unto them   Unlike the Bible's Golden Rule, this does not make the assumption that others like the same things that you like. Modern psychology and EQ indicate that it is better to recognize people's diversity and differences and to value their needs, wants, desires, and preferences. Empathy requires that you find out how others feel, what they like, what they want and then base your response to them according to how *they*, not you, want to be treated.

Rule #2: People like and trust people exactly like themselves   This rule reinforces the notion that people are most comfortable with other people who are similar, a fact we observe everyday as people gather in groups and cliques.

Rule #3: People don't care how much you know until they know how much you care   This rule reminds us that feeling and communicating a sense of caring for another person comes first in any relationship. In other words, you put another's concerns before your own.

These rules should be applied in the following steps:

Step 1: Just before sales conversations or meetings, ask yourself how you feel at that moment and then pause, exhale, and proceed. It is important to exhale because when we are nervous or tense, we tend to hold our breath, which tightens us up and makes fluid movement difficult. Exhaling is a sports training technique in which athletes release tension and improve performance. Taking time to recognize your feelings, to relax, and to exhale will allow you to manage your emotions consciously, and to control and use your emotions and your tensions to help you.

Step 2: Sense the mood and the emotional climate of the person or group you are meeting with. Beginning salespeople are usually nervous and anxious when they meet with customers, particularly the first time, and are unaware that customers are probably as nervous, anxious, and uncomfortable as they are. Effective leaders, politicians, and entertainers develop a knack for sensing the mood of a crowd or audience and playing to it. Salespeople must develop similar radar.

Step 3: Set the mood, the emotional tone and climate, for the meeting. Emotion is contagious, so by taking charge and energetically exuding a sense of confidence and enthusiasm (yes, "enthusiasm!" like my first sales manager often repeated) you infect the others with your contagious enthusiasm and positive vibes. Enthusiasm does not have to be the loud, excited, highly demonstrated type we often associate with back-slapping, broad-grinning used-car salesmen, but honest enthusiasm can come through in a restrained, calm, confident way that is in harmony with the emotional state of the other person or people in a meeting.

As Goleman points out *in Emotional Intelligence*:

> We transmit and catch moods from each other in what amounts to a subterranean economy of the psyche in which encounters are toxic, some nourishing. This emotional exchange is typically at a subtle, almost imperceptible level; the way a salesperson says 'thank you' can leave us feeling ignored, resented, or genuinely welcomed and appreciated. We catch feelings from one another as though they were some kind of social virus."[7]

Make sure the viruses you transmit are positive, caring ones.

Step 4: Let the person or people you are meeting with know that you care. The best way to accomplish this step in a first meeting with a person is to begin by being very open about yourself. The goal is to reach out with personal details about yourself to enable the other person to get to know you. At that point you can ask the question, "How about you?" to learn more about the other person. People will normally reciprocate with openness and talk about themselves, their families, their hobbies, and interests. As they are talking, you must search for common interests and associations, such as being married, having children, or loving sports. This is an application of Rule #2, "people like and trust people exactly like themselves," and your job is to talk about and emphasize those things in each of your personal lives that are similar. By showing a genuine sense of caring about their personal interests, they will know that you care. After the meeting, write down all the personal details for future reference. Always keep in mind the greatest advantage you have over algorithms is your ability to connect emotionally with people.

Also, be prepared to encounter different responses from men and women, for as Goleman writes, men generally "take pride in a lone, tough-minded independence and autonomy" and women generally "see themselves as part of a web of connectedness."[8] These gender differences are pointed out to encourage you to be aware of your own tendencies and to know what you might expect in an initial encounter with someone to be more like them and to build rapport. You can and probably should change these gender generalizations and initial stereotypes once you have had the opportunity to get to know someone better.

Also, when meeting with a group of people for the first time, it pays large dividends to research their personal backgrounds and interests prior to your meeting.

Step 5: Listen with "emotional synchrony," as Goleman calls it. "The degree of emotional rapport people feel in an encounter is mirrored by how tightly concentrated their physical movements are as they talk… One person nods just as the other makes a point, both shift chairs at the same moment, or one leans forward as the other leans back."[9]

This type of synchrony is a major way to transmit a "social virus" or emotional state or mood. It is also makes you more similar to the other person in the conversation, gets you closer, and makes them feel that you care.

Having learned about the importance of emotional intelligence in building relationships in this chapter, in the next chapter you will learn how to put your EQ knowledge to work in communicating with, listening carefully to, and understanding what makes people tick.

Test Yourself

1. Why don't old-fashioned sales techniques work in today's media selling environment?
2. What is emotional intelligence?
3. Why is EQ more important for success in business and other fields than IQ?
4. What are the four major elements of EQ?
5. Why is optimism important in selling?
6. What are the three EQ rules of selling?
7. What are the five steps in applying the EQ rules?

Project

Select a week in your life (next week might be good) in which you commit yourself to taking notes on encounters you have with people during the week whose job it is to serve you and be pleasant: waiters in restaurants or retail salespeople, for example. Take notes in two columns. In the first column, note the type of or lack of emotional intelligence you observe in each of the service people you encounter. Did the person try to connect with you, did the person cause you to leave the encounter feeling put off, angry, dissatisfied, happy, or pleased? In the second column, makes notes on your feelings and your ability to control your emotions in reaction to those encounters. You might copy into your notebook the EQ elements in Exhibit 5.1 and use it as a guide. At the end of the week, look over your notes and see if you picked out those people who displayed EQ and how they were different from those who did not display EQ and if you were able to recognize your emotions.

Resources

EQ at Work website (www.eqatwork.com.au)
The Consortium on Emotional Intelligence in Organizations at Rutgers University (www.eiconsortium.org)

References

Alessandra, Tony PhD, Wexler, Phil, and Barerra, Rick. 1992. *Non-Manipulative Selling*, 2nd ed. New York: Fireside Books.

Gardner, Howard. 1983. *Frames of Mind: The Theory of Multiple Intelligences*. New York: Basic Books.

Gardner, Howard. 1993. *Multiple Intelligence: The Theory in Practice*. New York: Basic Books.

Gardner, Howard. 1999. *Intelligence Reframed: Multiple Intelligences for the 21st Century*. New York: Basic Books.

Goleman, Daniel. 1995. *Emotional Intelligence: Why It Can Matter More Than IQ*. New York: Bantam Books.

Goleman, Daniel. 1998. *Working with Emotional Intelligence*. New York: Bantam Books.

Goleman, Daniel. 2006. *Social Intelligence: The New Science of Human Relationships*. New York: Bantam Books.

Goleman, Daniel, Boyatzis, Richard, and McKee, Annie. 2002. *Primal Leadership: Realizing the Power of Emotional Intelligence*. Boston, MA: Harvard Business School Press.

Sternberg, Robert J. 1988. *The Triarchic Mind: A New Theory of Human Intelligence*. Viking Penguin.

Zaiss, Carl D. and Gordon, Thomas PhD. 1993. *Sales Effectiveness Training*. New York: Dutton.

Notes

1 Goleman, Daniel. 1998. *Working With Emotional Intelligence*. New York: Bantam Books.

2 Ibid.

3 Ibid.

4 Ibid.

5 Goleman, Daniel and Nevarez, Michelle. 2018. "Boost your emotional intelligence with these 3 questions." Retrieved from https://hbr.org/2018/08/boost-your-emotional-intelligence-with-these-3-questions

6 Ibid.

7 Ibid.

8 Ibid.

9 Ibid.

6

Effective Communication, Effective Listening, and Understanding People

Charles Warner

The following is a review of several things we have covered so far.

The three Golden Rules of Selling from Chapter 5 are:

1   Do unto others as they would have others do unto them.
2   People like and trust people exactly like themselves.
3   People don't care what you know until they know you care.

Next, are the determinants of success in the AESKOPP system in Chapter 4:

1   Establish and maintain trusting relationships with prospects, customers, and partners.
2   Provide insights and solve advertising and marketing problems for them.
3   Get results for them (as they define results).

If you remember the International Radio and Television Society (IRTS) survey of media buyers noted at the end of Chapter 2, the number one characteristic that the buyers wanted in a salesperson was "communication skills." If the most important skill in selling is communicating with people, then understanding and mastering communication skills is the logical next step in becoming a successful salesperson. Understanding your customers' businesses and your product and its capabilities are secondary because if you cannot

Media Selling: Digital, Television, Audio, Print and Cross-Platform, Fifth Edition.
Charles Warner, William A. Lederer, and Brian Moroz.
© 2020 John Wiley & Sons, Inc. Published 2020 by John Wiley & Sons, Inc.

Exhibit 6.1   The communication process

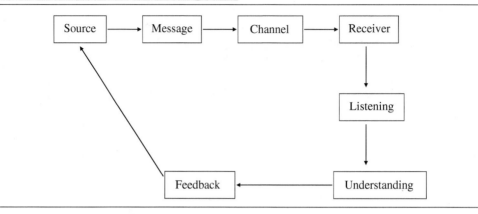

effectively communicate with people in order to gain their trust, you will never get to the point of being able to discover what their problems are, let alone solve those problems.

Communication

To begin to understand the communication process, see Exhibit 6.1.

Source

Communication begins with a *source*, the initiating origin of information in the communication process. The credibility of the source of information is its most important characteristic. Source credibility is multidimensional and a weakness in one dimension, or characteristic, can be offset by strength in another. Communication research has shown there are seven characteristics that enhance source credibility:

1 *Trustworthiness.*
2 *Competence.*
3 *Objectivity.* Having the ability to see and understand both sides of an issue, position, or argument. Source credibility can be enhanced by the use of a two-sided argument, a technique effective with people who are initially opposed to your point of view. The two-sided argument features an on-the-one-hand this and on-the-other-hand that approach, always giving the argument counter to your own point of view first. This technique signals that you are objective and candid and have considered the alternative point of view. Recent research indicates that if a sales or advertising message uses a two-sided presentation by beginning with several candid points about a product's weaknesses, subsequent points about the product's strengths are much more likely to be believed. Initial candor is a powerful tool for enhancing objectivity. Salespeople should remember this technique.

4 *Dynamism.* The more dynamic, energetic, and enthusiastic sources are, the more credible they are. It follows that if people are enthusiastic others are likely to say to themselves, "Well, if she believes in it so much, it must be a good product."

5 *Expertise.* Expertise comes from experience and in-depth knowledge of a product, process, medium, industry, or any area of knowledge.

6 *Physical attractiveness.* Of course, beauty is always in the eye of the beholder, but communications research has clearly shown that people generally perceive a source of information to be more credible if the source is physically attractive, according the beholder's standards of beauty. This fact probably explains why we rarely see ugly people delivering the news on television and why network television anchors and reporters are often chosen as much for their good looks and pleasant personalities as for their journalistic expertise. Salespeople can enhance their physical attractiveness by good grooming. How many customers have scruffy beards, green hair, dreadlocks, visible tattoos, or body piercing and how many don't? Think about it and go with the numbers.

7 *Similarity.* Recall Golden Rule of Selling #2 that "people like and trust people exactly like themselves"? People are simply more comfortable with people like themselves in age, gender, race, cultural background, and tastes and interests.

How do you use the seven characteristics of source credibility to enhance your ability to build a trusting relationship? As mentioned earlier, these characteristics are multidimensional and they work together in an intricate and complicated way. Some characteristics might be more important to some customers than others are. You must listen to and observe your prospect, customer, or person with whom you want a relationship, understand what characteristics and behaviors they seem to be comfortable with, and then emphasize your strengths in those areas.

For example, if you are a young female salesperson, there might not be similarity between you and an older male customer from a different cultural background. In this situation, you would emphasize your *competence* in how you present your case; your *expertise* in what you are selling; your *dynamism and enthusiasm* for your product and how it can solve the customer's problems. Finally, you would demonstrate your *objectivity* by using a two-sided argument and presenting some drawbacks of your medium or product first before presenting its many strengths. These positive attributes can go a very long way toward overcoming your lack of similarity.

Message

The second element in the communication process is the *message*. After establishing your source credibility, you want to work on the strength of your message. Because it is critical that customers comprehend the information you are verbally communicating, what you communicate should be kept relatively simple and easy to understand. *Repetition* is a key factor in the strength of information and its comprehension, and during a conversation or presentation, you must find ways to repeat your important points. For example, regularly summarizing the three major points you are trying to make in a discussion or in a written or oral presentation is an excellent way to repeat your points and make them more memorable. The notion of repeating *three* points is an important one. Just as repetition is effective in advertising, it is also effective in discussions and presentations.

Ordering effects can have an impact on your message's comprehension and make it more memorable. There are two ordering effects: *primacy* and *recency*. People tend to remember best those elements they see or hear first (primacy) in a conversation, television newscast, or sales presentation and what they see or hear last (recency). Recency effects are especially important when people have to consider carefully and weigh all information in a sequence. Thus, arrange your material with your most important points first and repeat them at the end of a presentation in a concise summary.

Channel

Channel effects are the third element in the communication process. The most effective channel of communication for simple messages is face-to-face, the second most effective is sight-plus-sound (such as film, television, or video), the third is sound only (for instance, radio, podcast, or telephone), and the last is sight only (newspapers, magazines, and all printed materials). However, exactly the reverse is true when dealing with complex messages and material. Thus, complex presentations that contain a large number of facts, statistics, and complicated logical arguments have a much better chance of being comprehended and remembered when they are in writing. The lesson here is that simple messages and presentations that tend to appeal to the emotions are best remembered when presented in person or on video. Complex sales presentations are best remembered when they are in writing, a PowerPoint presentation or comb-bound booklet or both, supplemented by a face-to-face discussion that engages people emotionally and that reinforces the major points of your written argument. Always keep in mind the KISS rule – keep it short and simple – and eliminate extraneous points and material from your communications whenever possible.

Receiver

There are two characteristics of a receiver in the communication process that are important – intelligence and self-confidence. People who are not very intelligent and suffer from low self-confidence tend to be slower in comprehending the benefits and advantages of your product, but, on the other hand, they have a greater tendency to accept and to yield to your attempts to persuade them. Also, people with low intelligence and, especially, low self-confidence tend to believe the last person they talk to. Therefore, if you are calling on such a buyer or client, be sure to be the last salesperson to talk to them. If you have intelligent and self-confident customers, they are likely to understand the material you present, but will require from you a good deal of source credibility, objectivity, expertise, strong evidence, and message strength to get them to accept your proposal. Remember that, while intelligent people might comprehend your points better and faster, they will also come up with a greater number of counterarguments and objections. When calling on a buyer or client that is highly intelligent and self-confident, you might want to be the first salesperson to talk to them because of primacy, which means they are apt to remember your presentation better than those that follow. Thus, know your buyers' and customers' relative level of intelligence and self-confidence so you can position the timing of your discussions most effectively.

Listening

Listening is the keystone of the communication process and is the foundation on which the vast majority of relationships are based. Listening is the basis for Golden Rule #3, "people don't care how much you know until they know how much you care," which requires that you not only listen but also observe. You are listening to gain understanding of what is being communicated verbally, but we know that nonverbal communication and body language contain a great deal of the meaning of any message. Therefore, this is why observing is included in listening – you listen for verbal clues and messages and you observe nonverbal messages communicated through body language.

You are also listening and observing to discern what a person's personality traits are. Understanding a person's personality traits is vital because it will determine how you interact with, communicate with, and, most importantly, how you can influence that person. Chapter 7 will cover techniques for influencing others and creating value for your product.

Inevitably, the most effective and successful salespeople are those who have mastered the skills of good listening and observing. Unfortunately, as much as I and other sales trainers and authors write and teach about the primacy of listening in the sales process, and as many times as I have done sales training seminars over the years, I still see too many salespeople nod their heads when they hear about the importance of effective listening and then go right on talking too much, trying to sell as prospects desperately try to get a word in edgewise. Perhaps this unfortunate situation comes about because people who like to talk a lot are attracted to selling and are unable or unwilling to change their behavior.

In over 60 years of being a salesperson, managing salespeople, training salespeople, and teaching sales and sales management, the most successful salespeople I have known have been world-class listeners and live by the adage: "Nature has given us one tongue, but two ears so that we hear from others twice as much as we speak." In Exhibit 6.2 you will see what world-class listeners do and what they do not do.

Exhibit 6.2   The Dos and Don'ts of world-class listeners

What world-class listeners do:

They adopt the proper attitude. They are optimistic; they tell themselves that they are going to like the person they're calling on and that they are going to have a positive outcome. They are positive, confident, friendly, open, and intensely curious.

They shut up and listen.

They are conscious of their body language. World-class listeners are conscious of their posture and how they sit when they listen to someone. They try to make sure their body language indicates they are fascinated and eager to learn more – often leaning forward and nodding.

They respect the other person's point of view. World-class listeners are able to put themselves in another person's shoes. They see both sides of an argument and respect others' views; they don't denigrate or belittle others' views.

They listen and look for emotional cues. World-class listeners observe how someone says something and looks for clues that reveal underlying feelings. People often say things that try to cover up how they are really feeling. World-class listeners listen and observe carefully and with empathy and understanding for how the person is feeling. World-class listeners look for nonverbal clues as to how other people feel and what they really mean to say. World-class listeners listen for *how* people say something, not so much *what* they say.

They listen for and look for buying cues. World-class listeners watch very carefully for any little sign or movement that indicates another person has made a decision to agree with them or to buy – a slight leaning forward, a tiny nod of the head, a sudden tension that signals an intent to buy and a desire to begin negotiating.

They match speech, listening patterns, and movements to the speaker. World-class listeners let the other person set the pace. They talk and listen at the other person's pace, not theirs. They do the adapting and speeding up or slowing down; they don't make other people adjust to them. This type of listening is referred to academically as synchronic listening or listening in synchrony, and it merely means being "in synch" with someone else. By being in synch, world-class listeners show respect for the other person, for their style, and even or for cultural differences.

They are patient. World-class listeners know that if they listen patiently and courteously to everything others have to say, without interrupting, that others will usually reciprocate and give them a courteous hearing.

They pause often. World-class listeners pause after someone says something to make sure the other person is finished. Like any good interviewer, they know that a pause often prompts others to talk more – often revealing more than they intend to.

They listen actively. See Exhibit 6.3 for details

They summarize well. Periodically through a discussion, they pause and summarize the points of agreement. Brief summaries not only make points memorable through repetition, but they also focus the discussion and get it back on track if it has wandered.

What world-class listeners don't do:

They don't listen judgmentally. See Exhibit 6.3 for details

They don't interrupt and step on sentences. The biggest giveaway of poor listeners is that they constantly step on other people's sentences – they interrupt or finish a statement for others. They cannot wait to be heard. These people spend their time during a conversation thinking of what they want to say next and are more concerned with their need to express themselves than with listening. Poor listeners don't let the other person finish what they are saying, especially if the other person talks slowly. World-class listeners don't make these errors.

Exhibit 6.2	The Dos and Don'ts of world-class listeners (cont'd)

They don't think of a rebuttal. Allied to stepping on sentences is thinking of what the next comment or a rebuttal is going to be while someone is talking. We often have a tendency to do this while we are listening to a speech or lecture to which we cannot respond; we engage ourselves mentally in the game of forming a reply to a particular point. This is a nonproductive game to play. World-class listeners pay full attention to the speaker and concentrate on listening carefully to every word without thinking of their comeback or rebuttal.

They don't respond too soon. World-class listeners let others finish a discussion and make as many points, as many objections as they feel inclined to do. They let people get all the negatives out on the table before responding. By responding too soon, they know they look defensive and may even be interrupting.

They don't react emotionally. We learned about the importance of self-management in Chapter 5: Emotional Intelligence. World-class listeners understand that an excellent place to practice self-control is while they are listening. In Chapter 11 we will go into more detail about negotiating and how sometimes manipulative negotiators will purposely try to get people angry so emotions will kick in and they will make a bad – emotional – decision. World-class listeners know the best way to counteract an attempt to make them angry or to get a rise out of them is to stay calm and never react emotionally – that is the way they turn the tables on others who try to manipulate them.

They don't become distracted. Too often people do not concentrate on looking at the person who is talking; they allow their attention to be diverted to other things. They doodle, look out the window, glance at some attractive person in the next office, or conduct other discourteous and disconcerting behavior. Some people keep their cell phones on, and, worse, constantly check them, which gives the speaker the silent message that they are not interested in the speaker. World-class leaders put their smartphones away and focus intently on speakers, look them in the eye.

They don't respond to negatives. World-class listeners know better than to respond too quickly to negative statements because they understand it makes them look defensive and that they might give some credence to the negatives. They ignore negatives and reinforce positive statements or compliments.

They don't ask leading questions. They don't try to use manipulative questioning and selling techniques or try to trick people into saying things they don't intend to say.

They don't take notes. In 60 years of selling and watching Hall of Fame media salespeople sell, I've rarely seen any of them take notes. They preferred to focus intently on the other person and do their best to build empathy and rapport, which note-taking makes difficult. Taking notes is a distraction from rapport building. Of course, the Hall of Famers were all very bright and had memories good enough to remember what was said in a conversation. These great salespeople typically made detailed notes on important calls after a call was over. Times when note-taking is a good idea is during complicated negotiations over programmatic details, targeting, and contract conditions, for example. By the time negotiating starts, though, you should have built sufficient rapport and know your customer well enough to be able to take notes. The rule on taking notes is: Don't take notes unless you have to in order to remember complicated factual details and, even then, keep the notes as brief as possible.

Nonverbal communication

Another type of communication is nonverbal communication. Research has shown that as much as 65 percent of communications between people can be nonverbal. In other words, *how* people say something is often more important than *what* they say. Part of the process of listening entails being sensitive to and observing all the nonverbal, often unconscious, hints people give you about how they feel about you and your medium or product. In the lingo of professional poker players, they call these hints tells. People's posture and body language, their facial expressions, their eye contact and movement, their tone of voice and pitch, and their pace of talking usually tell more about how they feel than the content of their verbal messages do. Salespeople must not only develop skills in picking up nonverbal messages and observing body language closely but also in using nonverbal communication to give messages.

When selling, look for the attributes and postures described below that might indicate how the other person is receiving your message. As you get to know your prospects and customers better, you will learn to understand their body language as well as you understand their words.

Use gestures, space, enthusiasm, openness, proximity, eye contact, and your body language to help you emphasize your sales points and to show customers that you care about them and are interested in them, but make sure your gestures are in sync with the person with whom you are talking. Of course, you can overdo the use of gestures. You can become too excited and animated with a shy, quiet prospect, for instance. One particular gesture to avoid is finger pointing. This gesture implies "I'm telling you what to do" or "Shame on you" or other authoritarian messages that impede open communication.

A *Harvard Business Review* Tip of the Day posted a paragraph on body language that was adopted from the book *How to Increase Your Influence at Work* by Rebecca Knight:

> If you want people at work to trust and respect you, regardless of your title or authority, pay attention to your body language. How you stand, sit, and speak all affect whether people are open to being influenced by you. For example, standing up straight with your shoulders back helps you come across as confident and commanding, while slouching and looking down at your feet have the opposite effect. When meeting with someone you don't know well, keep your arms uncrossed, your hands by your sides, and your torso open and pointed at the other person. This sends the message that you are open and trustworthy. And try pitching your voice a little lower than you normally would, to connote power. This can counteract the effect of nervousness, which tends to push the tone of your voice higher.[1]

Feedback

To be an effective listener, you have to close the feedback loop in the communication process. You must listen actively and give responsive feedback. You must give both verbal and nonverbal feedback, including gestures and expressions and communicate the appropriate enthusiasm as you actively encourage people to open up. The most important single thing you can do in giving responsive feedback is to smile. A smile says, "I like you; I care about you; I'm interested in what you're saying; I'm glad I'm here with you; I approve of you." Nodding your head in agreement is another effective feedback mechanism. Use it often.

In his 2018 book, *The Culture Code: The Secrets of Highly Successful Groups*, author Daniel Coyle gives excellent listening and feedback advice:

> **Listen Like a Trampoline:** Good listening is about more than nodding attentively; it's about adding insight and creating moments of mutual discovery, Jack Zenger and Joseph

Folkman, who run a leadership consultancy, analyzed 3,492 participants in a manager development program and found that the most effective listeners do four things:

1 They interact in ways that make the other person feel safe and supported.
2 They take a helping and cooperative stance.
3 They occasionally ask questions that gently and constructively challenge old assumptions.
4 They make occasional suggestions to open up alternative paths.

As Zenger and Folkman put it, the most effective listeners behave like trampolines. They aren't passive sponges. They are active responders.[2]

Techniques for Effective Listening

All knowledge, all learning about a customer begin with a question such as, "How's business?", or "How can I help you?", "What are your marketing goals?", or "How about those Patriots?" Therefore, all effective listening techniques begin with a question. These techniques work in a business or a personal conversation, but it is a good idea to practice them often at the beginning in personal situations, with family and friends, and become comfortable and adept at these listening techniques before attempting them with customers. Here are guidelines and exercises that will help you become a world-class effective, non-judgmental listener.

Exhibit 6.3 Techniques for active, non-judgmental listening

1 *Ask a question.*
2 *Listen to the answer carefully, actively.* For example, wave your hand toward yourself, which gives the message, "tell me more." Notice what gestures the people you are listening to use. Are they very expressive and do they motion with their hands a lot? Use their gestures. Are they calm and analytical? Do they lean back and ponder things with their fingers intertwined and their chins resting on their folded hands. Get in synch with them.
3 *Respond non-judgmentally.* Non-judgmental listening is non-defensive listening. Don't argue or defend your point view, but nod, smile, and encourage them to continue talking.
   • *Develop a non-threatening, non-confrontational approach.* You want people to feel secure in opening up, revealing personal information, so be have open body language to encourage people to unwind.
   • *Offer personal information first.* People will reciprocate by giving you personal information.
   • *Find something you have in common.* Similar interests such as kids, sports, or pets, for example.
   • *Similar interests create common bonds.* Common bonds create openness, honesty, and trust.
   • *Vary your responses.* Otherwise your responses become a monotonous and recognizable as

Exhibit 6.4   Barriers to active, non-judgmental listening

1   *Never ask "why?"* "Why?" questions are challenging to someone. When you ask "Why?" you sound like you doubt what they are saying or are testing them. "Why?" questions send bad emotional vibes.

2   *Never ask leading questions.* Leading questions like "Have you stopped beating your wife?" or "Are you still paying those outrageously high newspaper rates?" are challenging and produce frustration and anger.

3   *Never minimize a problem.* This response seems natural, as though you are trying to help someone feel better, that things are not as bad as they seem. However, you are being judgmental and making an assumption than you know more than the person complaining does. Furthermore, you are there to help solve their marketing problems, so the bigger the problems are, the more you can help, so don't minimize problems. Finally, some people love to complain, so do them a favor and let them –"feel their pain."

4   *Never cheer up or reassure.* These responses make you seem happier or more knowledgeable than the person who is speaking. It may be counterintuitive, but telling someone to cheer up maybe unrealistic. It's better to share their misery; develop empathy and demonstrate your supportive feelings.

5   *Never criticize or moralize.* These responses are highly judgmental and frustrate and anger other people.

6   *Never argue or defend.* Argumentative and defensive responses are completely counterproductive and move a conversation backward, not forward. The moment you become defensive, you lose control of the agenda of a conversation and lose rapport and credibility – you are seen as not being objective (and you aren't).

7   *Never be aggressive.* Aggressive responses make you appear competitive instead of cooperative and look as though you are trying to get what you want instead of what the other person wants.

8   *Never respond with "you" statements.* "You" responses are those that begin with "you," such as "you shouldn't be paying those high rates on other stations." "You" statements appear to be accusatory or seem to be telling other people what they "should" do. Never, never use the word "should" in a response, it is completely judgmental.

Source: Many of the "Never" responses are based on suggestions in. Zaiss, Carl D and Gordon, Thomas. 1993. *Sales Effectiveness Training*. New York: Dutton.

Use all of the techniques for effective listening to achieve the goal of developing mutual trust with your clients. Always return to the question, "Am I behaving and listening in a manner that my customer believes I am a trusted helper and am not merely trying to sell something."

Exhibit 6.5 provides you with an effective listening exercise that you should practice regularly using deliberate practice techniques.

Use the techniques of deliberate practice to master effective listening as outlined in Exhibit 6.5. Remember, deliberate practice consists of: (1) activity designed specifically to improve performance, (2) lots of repetition, (3) feedback continuously available, (4) highly demanding mentally, and (5) not much fun. These guidelines for deliberate practice seem like they were aimed specifically to help you practice effective listening over and over and over and over again until you become comfortable with variations on the feel-felt-found technique and are an expert listener. You can download all of the exhibits in this chapter, which appear in one file titled "Effective Listening" from www.mediaselling.us/

Exhibit 6.5   Effective listening exercise

1   *Listen carefully, actively to objections, questions, or statements.*
2   *Repeat or rephrase the objection, question, or statement.*
   A.   "Let me make sure I understand your position…you feel our rates are too high?" Put the burden of understanding on yourself. By repeating or rephrasing an objection, you let your customers know that you are listening and that you heard what they were saying – they like that.
3   *Get their agreement that you understand.*
   A.   "Is that correct?" This is a powerful step in the process because by getting agreement that you understand objection, question, or statement and that you are on their side. You are encouraging them to say "yes," a habit you want them to get into. If they say, "no" then you must follow up and clarify their objection or question, and keep doing so until you get it right and they agree that you understand.
4   *Respond with a form of an "I understand" statement (vary your responses).*
   A.   "I understand how you feel, other advertisers have felt the same way, but they have found that our rates are based on market demand and the size of our audience. We have the largest audience in town and the largest number of advertisers of any station in the area, and those advertisers are paying our rates and getting great results." The feel-felt-found responses are incredibly powerful because with the "feel" response you are acknowledging your customers feeling and respecting them. The "felt" response reinforces and legitimizes their objections so they don't feel silly, out of line, or alone. The "found" response gives you the opportunity to mention the benefits and advantages of what you are offering in the context of the success enjoyed by other advertisers – comforting knowledge for a prospective advertiser.

downloads. By downloading these exhibits, you can have them all in one packet to make them easier to study and review. There are media salespeople who put these exercises on their smartphones so they can review them before making sales calls.

The Power of Questions

Good listening requires good questions. Lots of them. In a *Harvard Business Review* article titled "The surprising power of questions," authors Alison Wood Brooks and Leslie K. John report on ground-breaking research into the effectiveness of questions in building, maintaining, and improving relationships, especially in selling situations:

> There are few business settings in which asking questions is more important than sales… [Research] shows a strong connection between the number of questions a salesperson asks and his or her sales conversion rate (in terms of both securing the next meeting and eventually closing the deal). This is true even after controlling for the gender of the salesperson and the call type (demo, proposal, negotiation, and so on). However, there is a point of diminishing returns. Conversion rates start to drop off after about 14 questions, with 11 to 14 being the optimal range.

> The data also shows that top-performing salespeople tend to scatter questions throughout the sales call, which makes it feel more like a conversation than an interrogation. Lower performers, in contrast, frontload questions in the first half of the sales call, as if they're making their way through a to-do list.
>
> Just as important, top salespeople listen more and speak less than their counterparts overall. Taken together, the data …affirms what great salespeople intuitively understand: When sellers ask questions rather than just make their pitch, they close more deals.

Asking good questions spurs learning and the exchange of ideas, and it builds rapport and trust. By asking questions, you naturally improve your emotional intelligence, which in turn makes you a better questioner – a virtuous cycle.

Dale Carnegie in his classic 1936 book, *How to Win Friends and Influence People*, recommends that you "Ask questions the other person will enjoy answering." Research conducted over 80 years after the book was written reveals that most people still do not follow Carnegie's wise advice and do not ask enough questions. Most people typically do not ask enough questions because they often tend to be egocentric and eager to impress others that they are the smartest person in the room and because they do not comprehend how important good questioning is, how it unlocks learning and improves interpersonal bonding.

People have conversations for two main reasons, according to the authors of "The surprising power of questions:" (1) information exchange and (2) impression management (liking). Current research suggests that asking questions achieves both.

Therefore, it is a good idea when trying to connect to someone else to ask lots of questions, and the type of questions, your tone of voice, the sequence of the questions, and the questions' framing are also important, as is whether the conversation is cooperative or competitive. In a cooperative conversation or negotiation, the major objective is to build a relationship. In a competitive conversation or negotiation the major objective is to serve your own interests first, so you want to be careful about revealing too much information.

Conversations fall along a continuum from purely competitive to purely cooperative. For example, discussions about the allocation of scarce resources tend to be competitive; those between friends and colleagues are generally cooperative; and others, such as managers' check-ins with employees, are mixed – supportive but also providing feedback and communicating expectations. Exhibit 6.6 shows some of the challenges that commonly arise when asking and answering questions and also gives tactics for handling them in different types of conversations.

Favor follow-up questions: In Exhibit 6.6 under "Competitive Conversation/When you're asking," one of the instructions under "Tactics" is "Ask detailed follow-up questions." In all conversations follow-up questions are particularly effective because they solicit more information and show that you are attentively listening, which is always a good signal to the person talking that you care.

Open-ended or closed-end questions: In the "Tactics" section of a "Cooperative Conversation/ When you're asking," the first item is "Ask open-ended questions." Open-ended questions are effective in learning something new. Closed-end questions (those requiring

Exhibit 6.6   Conversational goals matter

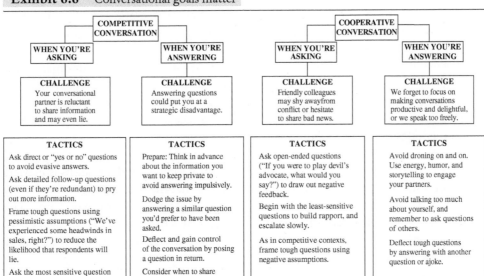

Source: Brooks, Alison Wood and John, Leslie K. 2018. "The surprising power of questions." *Harvard Business Review*. Used with permission.

either a "yes" or a "no") tend to restrict the information you get and, to the other person, can feel like you are grilling them. On the other hand, closed-end questions in competitive conversations avoid evasive answers. Furthermore, in such a conversation, people are less apt to lie if questioners make pessimistic assumptions. For example, rather than asking an optimistic question such as "The delivery will be on time, right?" ask a pessimistic question such as "The delivery will probably not be on time, right?"

Get the sequence right: You must also think about the sequence of the questions you ask. In Exhibit 6.6 notice that in a "Competitive Conversation" you ask the most sensitive, the toughest questions first and then have the questions get progressively easier. People are more willing to reveal sensitive information when questions are asked in a decreasing order of intrusiveness.

Get the tone right: Use the right tone of voice when you ask questions. People tend to be much more forthcoming when you ask in a casual, almost off-hand tone that when you ask in a stiff, formal, officious tone.

Pay attention to group dynamics: Conversational dynamics can change considerably depending on whether you are talking to a group or one-on-one to a single person. Members of a group tend to follow others in the group, so if one person speaks up, others will follow as a herd of horses follows a lead horse. Also, in a group it only takes a few closed-off for questions to lose their power, but as soon as one person answers, others will follow. Therefore, when addressing a group of people, especially a large group (over 25), it is important to get some to answer your first question. Use a forcing mechanism such as pointing at someone and asking them directly while nodding and smiling. And, most important, reward the person who answers with a compliment such as "That was a really good, smart answer!" Another way to get people in a group to reveal information (it works one-on-one as well) is to reveal something embarrassing or very personal about yourself because it shows you are transparent and vulnerable.

Keeping something private: Of course there will be times when you and your organization would be better off by keeping your cards close to your chest and not revealing sensitive information. You want to deal with difficult questions without lying, so artfully dodge them like politicians do. Deflect or redirect a probing question by asking another question or by telling a joke.

An excellent summary of the power of listening and asking good questions is in Mark Goultson's superb book, *Just Listen.* Goulston wrote that the best questions to ask were those that let the other person tell you: "This is what I think," "This is who I am," "This is what I want to achieve," or "This is how you can play a part in making my life better." In other words, all good listening starts when a conversation is all about the other person and not about you.

Understanding People

If you are an effective, world-class listener and question asker, that is great, but what are you listening for and questioning about? You are trying to understand why people behave as they do, and, even more important, you want to predict how they will respond to the information, insights, and proposals you offer. If you have good emotional intelligence and can predict how your proposals will appeal to prospects and customers, you can frame your proposals in such a way that they are much more likely to be accepted.

The personality-type or personality-trait approach

One way we can try to understand people is to use a personality-type or personality-trait approach. A personality trait refers to differences among individuals who have a "typical tendency to behave, think, or feel in some conceptually related ways."[3] There are several well-known personality-type descriptive models, probably the most recognized being the Myers-Briggs Type Indicator (MBTI) which divides people into four classifications and then into two preferences within each classification. The classifications are:

1   How people direct their energy: Extroversion (E) or Introversion (I)
2   How people prefer to process information: Sensing (S) or Intuition (N)
3   How people prefer to make decisions: Thinking (T) or Feeling (F)
4   How people prefer to organize their life: Judgment (J) or Perception (P)[4]

Myers-Briggs personality types are then defined by a combination of these four preferences, such as an ISTP (perhaps a journalist) or an ENTJ (perhaps a business executive).

Although the Myers-Briggs Type Indicator (MBTI) is used by many organizations for hiring, structuring teams, improving communications within and among teams and departments, and, in some cases, to identify leadership potential, many psychologists believe that the MBTI has some severe limitations. The biggest problem with the MBTI is that it does not predict performance; it does not predict how well people will perform on a job, how hard they will work, or how fast they will learn. Also, "the MBTI exhibits significant psychometric deficiencies, notably including poor validity (i.e. not measuring what it purports to measure) and poor reliability (giving different results for the same person on different occasions)."[5]

The MBTI was not developed by academically trained psychologists; a mother and daughter interested in the teaching of psychologist Carl Jung developed the Myers-Briggs Type Indicator in the late 1920s before the era of modern psychology. In the 1980s a group of prominent psychologists developed the Big Five personality types, which they referred to as personality traits, after exhaustive research into adjectives people used to describe behavior such as outgoing, bold, talkative, energetic, reliable, practical, hardworking, or careful. The Big Five personality traits have some correlation to the four scales used in the MBTI, but became a more commonly accepted framework for describing personality types or traits.[6] Eminent psychologist Lewis Goldberg named the traits the Big Five: Extraversion (E), Agreeableness (A), Neuroticism (N), Conscientiousness (C), and Openness (O).

These personality traits were developed by using a lexical approach, which means using a dictionary as a source of personality characteristics and developing a list of descriptive adjectives, and then using a statistical technique called *factor analysis* to see which adjectives correlated with each other. The Big Five personality traits were the result of using a lexical approach and computer-powered factor analysis. However, the Big Five traits came from an analysis of only English language adjectives and were derived from factor-analyzing adjectives in an era (the 1980s) that had limited computing power.

In the 2000s, several leading psychologists, using high-powered computing, factor analyzed descriptive adjectives in several languages, including Croatian, Dutch, Filipino, German, French, Greek, Hungarian, Italian, Korean, Polish, and Turkish. The psychologists consistently found a six-factor solution with a new personality trait they named *honesty-humility*. This new trait also showed up when factor analyzing English adjectives with high-powered computers.

Therefore, many psychologists today subscribe to the HEXACO (Honesty-Humility, Emotionality, eXtraversion, Agreeableness, Conscientiousness, Open to Experience) personality trait descriptions as in Exhibit 6.7.

Steps in assessing personality traits

With practice, concentrated listening, and careful observation salespeople can learn to infer what their prospects' and customers' personality traits are and can recognize the dominant personality traits that seem to drive people's behavior; and if you have

Exhibit 6.7 Personality traits

Honesty-Humility	Emotionality	eXtraversion	Agreeableness	Conscientiousness	Open to Experience
Sincere	Fearful	Social self-esteem	Forgiving	Organized	Aesthetic appreciation
Fair	Anxious	Social boldness	Gentle	Diligent	Inquisitive
Faithful	Dependent	Sociable	Flexible	Prudent	Creative
Avoids greed	Nervous	Lively	Patient	Perfectionist	Imaginative
Modest	Sentimental	Extroverted	Tolerant	Thorough	Unconventional
- versus -	- versus -	- versus -	- versus -	- versus -	- versus -
Sly	Brave	Shy	Ill-tempered	Sloppy	Shallow
Deceitful	Tough	Passive	Quarrelsome	Negligent	Unimaginative
Greedy	Independent	Withdrawn	Stubborn	Reckless	Conventional
Pretentious	Self-assured	Introverted	Choleric	Lazy	Close-minded
Hypocritical	Insensitive	Reserved	Headstrong	Irresponsible	Simple
Boastful	Stable	Inhibited	Temperamental	Absent-minded	

Source: Personality traits based on those shown in Ashton, Michael. 2018. *Individual Differences and Personality*, 3rd ed. Academic Press; and Lee, and Ashton, Michael C. 2012. *The H Personality Factor: Why Some People Are Manipulative, Self-Entitled, Materialistic, and Exploitative – And Why It Matters to Everyone*. Waterloo, ON: Wilfred Laurier University Press.

identified a customer's dominant personality traits correctly, you have gained a powerful tool to position yourself and your product to have a competitive advantage.

Following are the steps to take in assessing the personality of a person you are dealing with. However, it is vitally important that your assessment be as objective and emotion-free as possible, which is difficult. We all love our celebrities and politicians, our favorite singers or movie actors, our favorite sports stars and family members, but we have to put our fandom, our hero worship, and even our loyalties aside when trying to objectively assess those to whom we want to persuade or influence. We have to step out of fan shoes and into perhaps an unfamiliar pair of emotion-free, loyalty-free, and bias-free shoes. These shoes may not fit everyone, but it is vital to try to be as prejudice-free as possible. Remember, you are trying to serve your customers, educate your customers, and get results for your customers. In other words, you are trying to do what is best for your customers, which means you are going to have to appeal to their emotional side as well as their rational side. And their emotional side, which you will learn more about in Chapter 11, is guided by their personality traits to a large degree. Therefore, in order to help your customers, you must understand them.

Here the steps for assessing a person's personality traits:

Step #1: Familiarize yourself thoroughly with the six personality traits in Exhibit 6.7.
Step #2: Listen to and observe a person carefully with the six personality traits in mind.
Step #3: Fill out the personality trait scale in Exhibit 6.8.
Step #4: Select the three traits with the highest scores and consider those the dominant traits of the HEXACO model.

Exhibit 6.8   Personality trait scale

Put a check next to the appropriate number in each scale to indicate where a person falls on the personality scale for each trait and its opposite.

Honesty-Humility
Sincere, Fair _10_9_8_7_6_5_4_3_2_1 1_2_3_4_5_6_7_8_9_10_ Hypocritical, Deceitful

Emotionality
Fearful, Anxious _10_9_ 8_7_6_5_4_3_2_1 1_2_3_4_5_6_7_8_9_10_ Self-assured, Stable

Extraversion
Social Self-Esteem, Sociable _10_9_8_7_6_5_4_3_2_1 1_2_3_4_5_6_7_8_9_10_ Shy, Introverted

Agreeableness
Forgiving, Gentle __10_9_8_7_6_5_4_3_2_1 1_2_3_4_5_6_7_8_9_10_ Headstrong, Temperamental

Conscientiousness
Organized, Diligent _10_9_8_7_6_5_4_3_2_1 1_2_3_4_5_6_7_8_9_10_ Lazy, Irresponsible

Open to experience
Creative, Imaginative _10_9_8_7_6_5_4_3_2_1 1_2_3_4_5_6_7_8_9_10_ Conventional, Shallow

---

Putting it all together

After you have taken the four steps above in defining a person's three dominant (highest scoring) personality traits, you are ready to take the final step in the personality assessment process. One of the traits should be Honesty-Humility because this trait indicates whether or not you can trust somebody, which is absolutely critical when trying to consummate a deal. In the book *The H Personality Factor: Why Some People Are Manipulative, Self-Entitled, Materialistic, and Exploitative – And Why It Matters to Everyone*, the authors write that it vital to know if someone is honest and trustworthy or is greedy and manipulative because trust depends on this personality factor and is the basis for how you respond to people and whether you should be trusting or skeptical.[7]

Step #5: Now that you have made a reasonably good guess of the three dominant personality traits, choose two adjectives from the end of each scale of the traits you have selected. For example, after listening to and observing the behavior of a prospect, you guess that the person is at the opposite end of the Honesty-Humility scale and the adjectives that describe the prospect are greedy and boastful. On the eXtraversion scale, you guess that the two adjectives that fit are social-boldness and extroverted. On the Agreeableness scale you suspect the two best adjectives are quarrelsome and headstrong – see Person B in Exhibit 6.9. Now you have a pretty good verbal personality profile of your prospect and can position your offers so that they will appeal to that prospect.

Exhibit 6.9   Personality profiles

Person A

Dominant personality traits	Descriptive adjectives
Honesty-Humility	Fair
	Faithful
Conscientiousness	Organized
	Thorough
Agreeableness	Tolerant
	Patient

Person B

Dominant personality traits	Descriptive adjectives
Honesty-Humility	Greedy
	Boastful
eXtraversion	Social boldness
	Extroverted
Agreeableness	Quarrelsome
	Headstrong

Exhibit 6.9	Personality profiles (cont'd)

Person C

Dominant personality traits	Descriptive adjectives
Honesty-Humility	Sincere
	Modest
Emotionality	Nervous
	Fearful
Conscientiousness	Prudent
	Diligent

Person D

Dominant personality traits	Descriptive adjectives
Honesty-Humility	Deceitful
	Hypocritical
Open to Experience	Creative
	Unconventional
Agreeableness	Temperamental
	Stubborn

Personality profile comparisons Exhibit 6.9 compares the personality profiles of four fictitious people. I have not necessarily used any famous people as my models, but have tried to choose four different types of people that you might encounter in selling situations.

In order to practice completing a Personality Profile, you can download a blank one at www.mediaselling.us/downloads.html. In Chapter 7 you will learn more about a Benefit Matrix that will help you frame your insights, solutions, presentations, and proposals according to their personality profile.

Positioning your product to align with personality traits Remember the second key tactic of a salesperson from Chapter 2 is to build relationships. The first step in building any relationship is getting another person to trust you. The best way to build trust, to a large degree, is to listen to them carefully, to ask questions, to understand their personality traits, and then to frame and position your offers to align with their personality profile, as you will learn in the Chapter 7.

Test Yourself

1. What are the three Golden Rules of Selling?
2. What are the three determinates of success in the AESKOPP system?
3. What are the seven elements of communication?
4. What are seven characteristics that enhance source credibility?
5. Name two ordering effects and what do they mean?

6. What are the most effective channels of communication for a message that is not highly complex?
7. What are two receiver characteristics to keep in mind when calling on a buyer or customer?
8. What are the four steps in the effective listening exercise?
9. What are some of the benefits of asking questions?
10. What are the six HEXACO personality traits?

Project

Go to the Downloads section of the *Media Selling* website at www.mediaselling.us and download "A Salesperson's Dilemma," a Blank Personality Profile, and a Blank Personality Trait Scale. Read "A Salesperson's Dilemma" carefully and then fill out a personality trait scale based on the personality traits detailed in Exhibit 6.9 for both Sy Abell and Harry Godowski. Then create a personality profile of both Sy Abell and Harry Godowski.

References

Ashton, Michael. 2018. *Individual Differences and Personality*, 3rd ed. Academic Press.

Barondes, Samuel. 2011. *Making Sense of People: Decoding the Mysteries of Personality*. Upper Saddle River, NJ: FT Press.

Brooks, Alison Woods and John, Leslie K. 2018. "The surprising power of questions." *Harvard Business Review*.

Goulston, Mark. 2010. *Just Listen: Discover the Secret to Getting Through to Absolutely Anyone*. New York: AMACOM.

Lee, Kibeom and Ashton, Michael C. 2012. *The H Personality Factor: Why Some People Are Manipulative, Self-Entitled, Materialistic, and Exploitative – And Why It Matters to Everyone*. Waterloo, ON: Wilfrid Laurier University Press.

Notes

1 "Does your body language convey confidence?" Retrieved from https://hbr.org/tip/2018/04/does-your-body-language-convey-confidence.

2 Coyle, Daniel. 2018. *The Culture Code: The Secrets of Highly Successful Groups*. New York: Bantam Books.

3 Ashton, Michael. 2018. *Individual Differences and Personality*, 3rd ed. Academic Press.

4 Retrieved from https://en.wikipedia.org/wiki/Myers%E2%80%93Briggs_Tye_Indicator.

5 Barondes, Samuel. 2011. *Making Sense of People: Decoding the Mysteries of Personality*. Upper Saddle River, NJ: FT Press.

6 Ibid.

7 Lee, Kibeom and Ashton, Michael C. 2012. *The H Personality Factor: Why Some People are Manipulative, Self-Entitled, Materialistic, and Entitled – And Why It Matters To Everyone*. Waterloo, ON: Wilfred Laurier University Press.

7

Influence and Creating Value

Charles Warner

When I made the first sales call of my career on Parrott's Florist, as described in Chapter 5, the first question Mr. Parrott asked after he figured out I was trying to sell him a television commercial, was, "How much is it?" The how-much-does-it-cost question is typically the first one people ask when they are considering a purchase. If they are inexperienced buyers, they often ask the price question defensively because they do not want to go over an arbitrary price limit they have set. If they are experienced buyers, they often ask the price question because they want to react negatively to any response in an attempt to scare the seller and keep the price as low as possible. Experienced buyers also try to convince sellers that they are selling a commodity.

A commodity is a product that is interchangeable with other products, widely available, and differentiated only by price. Because commodities are interchangeable with other products and are undifferentiated, that means there are many substitutes and it is difficult to charge a higher price than other similar products charge. Because commodities are widely available and a surplus of supply exists, it is hard to maintain price levels. Because commodities are products that are differentiated only by price, commodities are sold to the highest bidder at a price only marginally higher than the next highest bid. Examples of commodities are wheat, corn, and soybeans, which are typically sold in commodity markets such as the Chicago Board of Trade.

Advertising agency media buyers and price-conscious advertisers naturally want to convince media salespeople that they are selling undifferentiated commodities and they, invariably, start negotiations over price as quickly as possible and with a low offer.

The hallmarks of weak or inexperienced media salespeople are that they do not know how to position their products effectively, that they readily accede to buyer demands,

Media Selling: Digital, Television, Audio, Print and Cross-Platform, Fifth Edition.
Charles Warner, William A. Lederer, and Brian Moroz.
© 2020 John Wiley & Sons, Inc. Published 2020 by John Wiley & Sons, Inc.

and that they sell based only on price. The sales pitch of weak salespeople is "I have the lowest price," a position that does not add value.

World-class media salespeople do not sell their product as a commodity; they create value with insights and solutions gathered by means of thorough data analysis.

In this chapter, you will learn more about some persuasive techniques that can influence people, you will discover why creating value is important, and you will learn how to create value for your medium, for your company, and for yourself.

The Psychology of Influence

In 1984, Robert Cialdini wrote an extremely important book, *Influence: The Psychology of Persuasion*. In 2001, he published the fourth edition of the book, retitled *Influence: Science and Practice*. Perhaps he dropped the word persuasion from the title because the term has a negative, manipulative connotation.

The concept of persuasion somehow indicates that people are persuaded to do something they would rather not do or that is against their better judgment. *Media Selling* deals with persuasion gingerly in order to emphasize ethical persuasion and to be consistent with the book's educational, helping approach to selling. Therefore, I will advocate that any attempt at persuasion should be viewed as influence, suggesting that people are being swayed to do something consciously and willingly, which is more suitable to the approach advocated in this book.

Cialdini studied compliance practitioners and professionals such as salespeople, fundraisers, and advertisers. He studied compliance using participant observation and gained experience in organizations that practiced persuasion techniques, such as organizations selling encyclopedias, vacuum cleaners, portrait photography, and dance lessons – some of the worst examples of manipulative persuasion techniques. Over a three-year period, Cialdini observed thousands of different tactics that compliance practitioners employed to produce a yes, and he found the majority fell into six basic categories. "Each of these categories is governed by a fundamental psychological principle that directs human behavior, and in so doing, gives the tactics their power."[1]

I have modified Cialdini's list of six principles by combining two, *liking* and *authority*, and have added one, which I call *automatic responses*, which was not on Cialdini's original list. I believe this modified list makes it easier to understand, to remember, and to use.

Exhibit 7.1 shows a modified list of the six principles of influence.

Let's now look at each of the six principles of influence separately. While you are reading the descriptions, think of ways that you might use them honestly and ethically to influence people.

Automatic responses

Being trained in psychology, Dr. Cialdini begins his research by looking at animals, fish, and insects. He writes about the many animals that have instincts that cause them to act in certain fixed action patterns that involve intricate sequences of behavior, such as in

Exhibit 7.1	Principles of influence

1   Automatic responses
2   Reciprocation
3   Commitment and consistency
4   Social proof
5   Scarcity
6   Liking and authority

Source: Cialdini, Robert B. 2001. *Influence: Science and Practice*. Boston, MA: Allyn and Bacon.

mating rituals. Cialdini refers to these instinctual behaviors in animals as pre-programmed tapes and believes that humans, too, have pre-programmed tapes that can trigger unconscious, automatic responses of compliance, sometimes at the wrong times.[2] An example that Cialdini uses to support his thesis is research conducted by social psychologist Ellen Langer and her colleagues, which reinforces the "well-known principle of human behavior that says when we ask people to do us a favor we will be more successful if we provide a reason."[3]

Langer demonstrated this need for a reason by asking a small favor of people waiting in line to use a copy machine: "Excuse me, I have five pages. May I use the Xerox machine because I'm in a rush?" Langer reports that this request plus a reason was successful 94 percent of the time, compared to the 60 percent success rate of the request "Excuse me, I have five pages. May I use the Xerox machine?" In another experiment Langer used another "because" phrase that added no new or even any logical information to a request: "Excuse me, I have five pages. May I use the Xerox machine because I have to make some copies?" The result was 93 percent compliance. There is no logical explanation for the high compliance rate; therefore, a "because" explanation must trigger an instinctual response that, as human beings, we have been preconditioned to make.

We see another automatic response in the use of the *contrast principle*, which is often used in automotive sales, real estate sales, and retail clothing sales. An example would be new car salesperson who tries to sell us a $32,000 car and then adds on, one at a time, options that seem to be a minor expense when contrasted to the $32,000 price of the car. But the options add up, and soon the car costs $40,000. Another example would be a real estate salesperson who shows prospective buyers three houses that are dumps and then shows them a reasonably clean house that looks spotless in comparison. In the retail clothing business salespeople are taught to use the contrast principle by showing expensive items first so that subsequent, lower priced items seem like a bargain in comparison. If customers say they are interested in several items, say a suit and some socks, salespeople are taught always to sell the most expensive item first, in this case the suit, then to show them expensive cashmere socks. Why? Because cashmere socks, when compared to regular socks, would seem expensive; but compared to what a suit costs, the socks are not perceived to be overpriced. Many prospective buyers are not perceptive enough to see the effects of the contrast principle working.

Another example Cialdini uses is one from one of his students who relates that while waiting to board a flight at O'Hare airport, the student heard a gate attendant announce that the flight was overbooked. In an attempt at humor, which some airlines such as Southwest Airlines encourage, the gate attendant announced that anyone willing to take a later flight would be compensated with a voucher worth $10,000. Because people waiting at the gate knew it was a joke, they all laughed, but when the attendant then offered a $100 voucher, no one took it. Why? Because compared to $10,000, $100 seemed measly. No one took a $200 or $300 voucher either and the attendant had to raise the ante to $500 to get any takers. Had the attendant started with a ridiculous $5 joke offer, there probably would have been many takers for a real offer of $100 because, compared to $5, $100 would have seemed generous – a good deal.

Used appropriately, the contrast principle is a legitimate method of positioning your offers when selling media. For example, compare the price of your offer to much more expensive prices of competitive media such as the $5.2 million cost of a 2018 30-second Super Bowl commercial. Or, make your first offer or proposal unreasonably high so that the second one seems reasonable, regardless of its actual value. Or, make your first offer very low and refer to it as cheap, which will imply not only a low price, but low quality, and then show that subsequent offers, each more expensive, are better, of higher quality, which might include more precise demographic or behavioral targeting.

Reciprocation

Noted archeologist Richard Leakey ascribes the essence of what makes us human to the principle of reciprocation. The rule of reciprocity is that *we must provide to others the kind of actions they have provided us*. We learn reciprocity as the major motivation for cooperation, which is essential to the functioning of society. It creates a web of indebtedness that allows for the division of labor, the exchange of diverse forms of goods and services, and the interdependence that binds people together into workable units, groups, and cultures.[4] The concept of indebtedness, or future obligation, allows people to exchange goods without fear of loss and to build sophisticated systems of aid, gift giving, defense, and trade.

We are taught from early childhood that if someone gives us something, we have an inviolable future obligation to return the gift or favor, no matter how small, whether or not we asked for the favor. The rule of reciprocity is overpowering. "The rule possesses awesome strength, often producing a yes response to a request that, except for an existing feeling of indebtedness, would surely be refused," writes Cialdini.[5] People who do not reciprocate are held in the lowest possible esteem and are seen as welshers or moochers.

According to Cialdini, probably the most notorious abuse of the rule of reciprocity occurs with the Hare Krishnas when they solicit donations by first giving a target person a gift of a book, a flower, or a magazine. Even if targeted, passersby are initially repulsed by the look of the Krishnas, when they have flowers given to them or pinned to their lapels, and say, "No, thank you," they are told that the gift cannot be taken back, that, "It is our gift to you." That is when the overpowering rule of reciprocity kicks in and the vast majority of people feel obligated to make a reciprocal gift because refusing it would be against our nature. It is an automatic, uncontrollable response. There are two overwhelming obligations involved: to accept a gift and to reciprocate. So, of course, people take the flower and then feel obligated to make a contribution.

We can see the reciprocity rule used in a myriad of circumstances. Waiters who leave a gift of a candy mint know that it will increase tips, grocery stores that offer free samples of food know that sales will increase significantly, and marketers that give away free samples of their products know future use of a product will increase.

The reciprocity rule works both ways. Not only is there an obligation to reciprocate when someone gives you a gift or does you a favor, but also there is an obligation for the gift-giver to provide an opportunity for the gift-receiver to repay the debt or return the favor. A socially satisfactory closure only occurs when a gift has been given and the receiver's reciprocation is accepted. "Thank you" must be followed by "You're welcome."

This rule applies to concessions also, and it is called the rule of reciprocal concessions. Imagine that I am heading our college class fundraising drive and I call you up, introduce myself, and then say, "How are you doing today?"

You respond by saying, "Just fine, thanks, Charlie."

"We have a huge big fundraising goal this year. Can you pledge $500 because I want our great class to win the competition for raising the most money?"

You decline by saying, "Gee, that's a lot. I just can't afford it now?"

"So $500 is a little steep?"

"Yes."

"I certainly understand; a lot of our classmates are in a similar position. Could you give $10, then we stand a good chance of winning the competition for the highest percentage of participation, and could you volunteer for three hours a week to help me solicit our classmates on the phone?"

How can you not give $10 and three hours of your time, during which you will raise more than $500 using the same technique I used on you: I asked for something, you felt a little guilty but declined. I then came back with a lower ask, a concession to my original ask, to which you felt obligated to reciprocate with a concession – a small gift of money and time.

In Chapter 13 we will show you how to use reciprocation tactics to your advantage in the closing step of selling, which often requires negotiating to help you counteract people's tendencies of material self-interest (getting the most for the least amount) and receive a fair price and reasonable terms for what you are selling.

Commitment and consistency

Cialdini reports on a study of people placing bets on horses at a racetrack. They were much more confident of their horses' chances of winning after placing a bet than before. The same thing happens with voters; they believe much more strongly that their candidate will win after they vote than before they vote. The need for our beliefs to be consistent with our actions lies deep within us and directs our actions with quiet power. As Cialdini writes: "Once we make a choice or take a stand, we will encounter personal and interpersonal pressures to behave consistently with that commitment."[6]

But in order for people to be consistent, they must take a stand – have something to be consistent about. Commitment comes first. There are several techniques to get

people's commitment. Telemarketers and fundraisers understand the power of commitment when they call and ask, as I did in the conversation above, "How are you doing
today?" or "How are you feeling?" If you say, "Fine," or something similar, you are
responding to the apparent concern about you that has been expressed and you will find
it difficult to be subsequently grouchy or stingy. Other ways to intensify commitment is
to *get people to say yes to small things first*, to give a small amount of money or to volunteer
or both. This works even better if you can *get people to write something down*, put a check
mark in a box, or sign their name to a petition. The third way to strengthen commitment
is to *get people to tell someone else*. All of these techniques are powerful ways to increase
commitment.

One of the best illustrations of the principles of commitment and consistency comes
from research by psychologists Jonathan Freedman and Scott Fraser. They reported on
the results of an experiment in which a researcher, posing as a volunteer, went door-to-
door in a residential California neighborhood. They first asked people if they were in
favor of driver safety, and, if so, to sign a petition. Everyone signed. Who could be
against safe driving? Then the researcher asked if the homeowners would put a small
sign on their lawns that read BE A SAFE DRIVER. It was such a trifling request that
nearly everyone agreed to it. Two weeks later the "volunteer" returned and said that
speeding on local streets had not diminished and asked if people would put up a very
large, poorly lettered sign that read DRIVE CAREFULLY. The sign almost completely
obstructed the view of their house from the street. Seventy-six percent of the people
who had put up the small sign agreed to put up the ugly, massive sign. Even the researchers were amazed at how well the consistency principle worked. Once people committed
to being involved in a safe driving campaign, they went all out.[7] This technique of getting people to agree to a small request and then to larger and larger ones is called the
foot-in-the-door technique.

In a follow-up experiment, the researchers went to another neighborhood and asked
homeowners if they supported safe driving. If the answer was yes, they showed pictures of the houses with the huge, ugly DRIVE CAREFULLY signs on the lawns, and
asked homeowners if they would be willing to put the signs up. Interestingly, only 17
percent said yes, which not only demonstrates the power of the foot-in-the door technique, but also shows the importance of getting an original commitment to, in this
example, safe driving.[8]

The researchers then went to another neighborhood and tried a different procedure.
First, they asked homeowners to sign a petition that favored "keeping California beautiful." Naturally, nearly everyone signed it because everyone believes in maintaining the
quality of the environment. Two weeks later, the people who signed the "keep
California beautiful" petition were asked to put the big DRIVE CAREFULLY sign on
their lawn. The response of the homeowners astounded the researchers; over fifty percent of those asked said yes. Freedman and Fraser finally realized after examining the
data that when people signed the beautification petition, they changed their view of
themselves to public-spirited citizens who acted on their civic principles and who supported good causes.[9]

If Freedman and Fraser had first gone to homeowners and asked them if they supported safe driving, and, if they said yes, then asked them to put a huge DRIVE

CAREFULLY sign, the results would have been different. The majority of the home-owners would have refused them. And, if the researchers had returned in two weeks and asked homeowners to put up a smaller four-feet-by-three-feet sign, they might have received over 75 percent compliance using this *door-in-the-face technique*.

Finally, the technique of making a public commitment is an important one to amplify commitment. For example, if you want to stop smoking, tell everyone you know that you have stopped. Cialdini writes that Chicago restaurant owner Gordon Sinclair low-ered his no-show rate for reservations from 30 percent to 10 percent by simply changing "Please call us if you change your plans," to "Will you please call us if you change your plans" and then paused to wait for a response. When people responded with a yes, they were publicly expressing their commitment.[10] The pause was the key to this technique because the pause gave people a little time to consider the request. Public commitments work especially well with people with high levels of pride, self-esteem, or public self-consciousness because their egos are involved.

For media salespeople these lessons are important ones to keep in mind when you make present proposals and offers.

Social proof

According to Cialdini, the principle of social proof states that *people determine what is correct by finding out what other people think is correct*. The principle applies especially to the manner in which we decide what constitutes correct behavior. "We view behavior as correct in a given situation to the degree that we see others performing it."[11] Whether it is when to laugh in a movie, how to eat chicken at a dinner party, or whether to help someone lying on a sidewalk, the actions of others is what guides our behavior.

Examples of compliance practitioners using social proof are all around us: street per-formers who salt their empty fiddle case with a five-dollar bill and public radio and pub-lic television stations during pledge weeks that constantly give us the names of people who contribute. This technique tells us that, "everyone is doing it, so it must be the right thing to do." Nightclub owners will keep a long line waiting outside even when there are plenty of seats inside to increase the perception that it is a hot place. Advertisers inform people that their product is "the fastest growing" or "number one" because they do not have to convince us directly that that their product is good; they need only to convince the public that others think it is good.

Social proof has particularly strong influence under two conditions: *when we view oth-ers to be similar to ourselves* and *when people feel unfamiliar or insecure in a specific situation*. In other words, in the first instance monkey see, monkey do, but not when a monkey sees an elephant do it. And in the second instance of monkey see, monkey do, the mon-key copies if the monkey is not sure what to do. Therefore, in media selling give evi-dence of what other people who are similar to a customer or buyer has done, and always give evidence or social proof to people who seem to be insecure or lack confidence. Using advertiser success case studies is one of most effective sales tools because it involves using the principle of social proof.

Scarcity

For media salespeople who are selling broadcast television and radio inventory that is not bought programmatically, the scarcity principle is probably the principle they will use most often. Cialdini states the scarcity principle as: *opportunities seem more valuable to us when they are less available.* We are familiar with this principle because we see it operating in everyday life in collecting baseball cards, in scalping tickets outside a big game, in choosing wine, in the dating game. Everyone knows that when you tell people they cannot have something, that something becomes even more desirable.[12]

However, there are several interesting corollaries to the basic scarcity principle. The first one is that people are more motivated by the thought of losing something than the thought of gaining something of equal value. The threat of a potential loss looms especially large under conditions of risk and uncertainty. So, when people are faced with a great deal of risk or uncertainty about the future, they worry about loss and do not think of a possible gain.

For this reason, Cialdini suggests the limited-number tactic is particularly effective. When people are informed that there are only a limited number of tickets or shares of stock left to purchase and they are then urged to make a decision quickly, they usually make an immediate decision and say yes. This tactic is so powerful that unethical salespeople often use it even when it is not true. Keeping with the spirit of this book, we urge media salespeople to use the limited number tactic only when it is true, but when it is true, use it, because it works.[13] You are doing a service to your buyers and partners to inform them that a desirable opportunity such as the Super Bowl, special website content, or the last episode of a hit television program has only a few slots left. If you have done your job of creating value, they will be motivated by fear of losing it.

In addition to time, *information* and *data*, particularly if they are scarce, can be valuable. Businesses know that data is their most valuable resource, and data is more valuable if it is scarce, that is, if very few have it. And having exclusive information is even more precious, more powerful, and, therefore, provides greater opportunities for misuse and corruption, as seen in the continuing insider trading scandals on Wall Street.

What kind of information can media salespeople use ethically with customers and buyers in order to influence decisions? Certainly not inside information about a competitor's advertising before it runs, as we pointed out in earlier in Chapter 3. You also cannot lie to customers and tell them that competitors are interested in something the customers are considering if it is not true. Also, do not promise customers and buyers exclusive information for their eyes only. On the other hand, it is your responsibility to tell customers if others, particularly their competitors, are considering buying what you are offering. The rule is simple, always play it straight and be honest. You must be fair to everyone and make any relevant information available to everyone.

What you can share with your customers and partners is non-exclusive and non-proprietary information that they might not be aware of, information about advertising trends, information in email newsletters and trade journals about new products, or information about new creative approaches that customers would find valuable. It takes time to dig for this kind of information, but it is worth the effort. Give it to customers and partners, and they will appreciate it and you will take a big step toward becoming the preferred supplier.

The final corollary to the scarcity principle is that limited resources become even more valuable when other people are competing for them, which is why online auctions such as Google's Ads are so effective. Frantic bargain-basement shoppers grab up merchandise when they see others competing for the same merchandise, and the ardor of an indifferent lover surges with the appearance of a rival, for example. So, when competition really does exist for a scarce resource that you are selling, make sure everyone knows about the competition.

Liking and authority

The liking principle is straightforward and comes as no surprise: *we prefer to say yes to people we know and like*, which is similar to the second Golden Rule of Selling, people like and trust people exactly like themselves. Dale Carnegie's book, *How to Win Friends and Influence People*, was first published in 1937 and became the best-selling self-help book of all time. Even though the book is simplistic, Carnegie's essential point was that the best way to influence people is to get them to like you. This is an effective approach if you are a likable, credible, caring person, but it does not work if you are insincere or not authentic.

Cialdini refers to the principle of authority as *directed deference*. The great power of the authority principle is that for a society to function, we must obey the rules of that society and, therefore, obey its designated authority figures and symbols. Thus, we are trained from childhood on to obey the commands and requests of legitimate authority figures: our parents, policemen, fireman, government officials, judges, and tax collectors.

There are many symbols that communicate authority: titles, clothes, and trappings.[14] Titles are important because they communicate status, prestige, success, power, and authority. When I was a Vice President in AOL's Interactive Marketing Division, I remember the constant battles our top management had with AOL's inflexible HR department attempting to get the regional sales managers and business development (BD) salespeople titles of Vice President. The sales managers and BD salespeople used the valid argument that they called on CEOs and Senior VPs of Marketing and Advertising and that these high-level people wanted to deal only with correspondingly high-level executives, not merely salespeople. Although HR held firm for several years, the regional managers and business development salespeople had a simple solution; they called themselves Vice Presidents on their calling cards. It worked and it became easier to get appointments with top executives. Unfortunately, what this title-consciousness leads to is title inflation and eventually everyone is a Senior Vice President calling on Senior Vice Presidents. But title inflation is rooted in the basic principle that people do tend to defer to and be impressed with authority.

Clothes are another symbol of authority, status, and power. Clothes, like titles, can trigger compliance. A policeman's uniform, a doctors' coat, and a pilot's uniform are all symbols of authority. Trappings of authority such as Rolex watches, huge offices and desks, and luxury cars all add to the cache of authority and power in some circles, particularly in urban centers such as New York. In Silicon Valley, black turtlenecks, hoodies, jeans, and sneakers might be the symbols of power. But salespeople must be sensitive to these subtle displays of power and keep in mind the second basic rule of selling that people like and trust people exactly like themselves, including people who dress like they do.

There are two reasons to learn about the principles of influence – offensive and defensive. Offensively, it is a good idea for you to use the principles of influence when it is appropriate in order to influence people legitimately. But be mindful of the *law of instrument*, which was defined by Abraham Kaplan in *The Conduct of Inquiry*, as "give a small boy a hammer, and he will find that everything he encounters needs pounding."[15] In other words, now that you know a little about the theory of influence and the power of automatic responses, reciprocity, commitment and consistency, social proof, scarcity, and liking and authority, do not use them as a hammer in every sales situation. However, do use them when appropriate to position your products and proposals effectively to create value for them.

I strongly recommend that you read Robert Cialdini's book, *Influence: Science and Practice*, study it carefully, and become an expert at using and recognizing the tactics of influence. Also, by recognizing these principles you can defend yourself against others who use them. Customers and buyers in their attempt to get more for less will often use one or all of these principles to get you to give them more, lower your prices, give them better position, say yes to a deal that is good for them, or to defer to their power and authority. The best defense against the use of these principles of influence is to recognize them for exactly what they are, to stop before you respond automatically, to name the tactic ("that's reciprocation" or "the buyer is using social proof to try to influence me"), and then to exhale and respond appropriately and rationally.

Creating Value

Understanding the techniques of influence can be used defensively to alert you to being influenced and can be used offensively to influence others. Understanding the techniques of influence also prepares you for being able to create value for your product or medium more effectively.

As you go forward learning about value creation, keep in mind the first Rule of Creating Value:

Creating Value Rule #1: Create value before mentioning price and before negotiating As I mentioned at the beginning of this chapter, the first question most experienced buyers ask is, "How much does it cost?" They ask the cost question in order to get you in the mindset that you are selling a commodity, a product that is only differentiated by price. Do not fall for this ploy. Create value before you discuss price, because *the more value you create, the higher price a buyer will pay*. After you create value, you can discuss price and then begin to negotiate over price, terms, and conditions.

Why creating value is vital

Also, remember from Chapter 2 the strategy that a salesperson's most important job is to create value for their product, to create a positive, *differentiated* perception and image of their product in prospects' and customers' minds. In the following section you will learn some techniques to help you create value.

Creating Value Rule #2: Selling media as if what you are selling is a commodity does *not* create value   Do *not* sell media advertising as though it were a commodity – an undifferentiated product that is bought only on the basis of price. If price is the only consideration, advertising can be bought and sold programmatically and by means of online auctions. Programmatic trading and online auctions disintermediate salespeople who sell media as if it were a commodity. Media salespeople's job selling in the digital, programmatic era is to create value for their product by differentiating it with insights and solutions, which when implemented will get results for their customers and will create a positive return on investment (ROI).

Creating Value Rule #3: Creating value enhances your credibility and builds trust   In the process of creating value, you display your expertise, which builds your source credibility. You demonstrate that you understand customers' needs (personality), businesses, their marketing goals and problems, your product, your market, media trends, buyers' and customers' business needs, and buyers' and customers' personal needs based on their personality traits. All of these elements build trust.

Creating Value Rule #4: Creating value helps you control your customers' expectations   When people contemplate investing in advertising, they do so with the expectation that their business will increase. And because their hopes are high, their expectations usually rise to meet their hopes. In other words, there is a natural tendency for people to expect too much from their advertising. Part of creating value is creating *realistic* value in the minds of customers, which typically means lowering their expectations. The lower their expectations, the more pleased they will be with their results, as they define them.

What is value?

The formula for perceived value is:

$$\text{Perceived value}\,(PV) = \frac{\text{Quality}\,(Q) + \text{Results}\,(R) + \text{Service}\,(S)}{\text{Price}(P)}$$

In order to increase the *perceived value* to a customer, you must increase the value of the numerator in the above equation (quality, results, and service) and not lower the denominator (price). In fact, if salespeople are expert in creating value and in increasing the perception in a buyer's mind of the value of quality, results, and service, then the price customers are willing to pay will increase.

Quality. Quality is a subjective concept. Like the concept of beauty, quality is in the eye of the beholder. Perceptions of quality are defined by several attributes of a medium. For example, a magazine might be perceived to be of high quality because of glossy paper stock, beautiful four-color photographs, a pleasing layout and design, and eye-catching, tasteful photos and graphics. A newspaper might be perceived to be high quality because of the up-scale demographics of its audience and because of the many Pulitzer Prizes it has won. A radio station might be perceived to be a high-quality station because it plays classical music. A television network might be perceived to be high in quality because its season kick-off parties and presentations are eye-popping, expensive, and include multiple television stars and celebrities. A website might be perceived to be a high-quality site because of its design and its non-cluttered look. The concept of a platform such as YouTube or Facebook having brand-safe content is another badge of quality. The more attributes that a medium and its salespeople can promote to create a perception of quality, being brand-safe, and having desirable demographics, the higher the site's perceived quality is and the higher prices the site can charge for each impression whether it is purchased programmatically or direct from a salesperson.

Results. Results in a media context means, primarily: Does advertising in that medium get an acceptable ROI and get results as defined by the customer? Customer-defined results vary a great deal by media and by customer. In some cases, results can mean beautiful reproduction and display of four-color ads. At other times, results can mean direct response, or sales. With some clients, results can mean recall of specific product claims in an ad or commercial. With others, results can be measured by increased stock price. And with other clients, results mean an increase in market share.

With advertising agencies, results might mean fast response times to RFPs (requests for proposals), presenting proposals that meet their buying criteria, or excellent service and follow up.

By understanding a customer's definition of results, salespeople can demonstrate how their medium in general and their specific media outlet can improve results.

Service, account management, and customer success. These form a product attribute that is becoming more and more important to customers. In fact, with many products, especially those that are either highly undifferentiated or are intangible, customers consider service to be the most important differentiator. Also, as an industry matures, customers migrate from being inexperienced generalists to being experienced specialists. Inexperienced generalists are interested in learning more about a product, understanding how to use it, and figuring out how to buy it, and because of the FUD factor – fear, uncertainty, and doubt – will often be predisposed to pay a premium price in order to gain experience. On the other hand, experienced specialists, such as agency media buyers, generally know a product or medium well. They know how to use it and how to buy it, and price and responsive service are most important to them. To experienced specialists, who have multiple substitutes for virtually all media, the single most important differentiator, after price, is service.[16]

By emphasizing the importance of quality, results, and customer success, salespeople can get customers and buyers to focus on attributes other than price.

Value is a perception   Every person or potential buyer places a different weight on the relative importance of the quality/results/service mix and, thus, has a different definition of the value of that mix. Therefore, value is a perception that is unique to each individual. Thus, the price people will pay for a product is a result of their unique solution to the perceived value formula. For example, a commercial on a local television station news program may be worth $1,000 to one advertiser based on how many adults between the ages of 18 and 49 a newscast reaches. On the other hand, the same newscast might be worth $2,000 to another advertiser who wants to have the company's name associated with a station's newscast or sports segment within that newscast, who desires to reach mature, male business decision-makers, and who likes an association with sports. Therefore, paying a premium for sponsoring a sports segment that features a brief opening billboard such as "Sports brought to you by Warner Ford," makes economic sense to that advertiser – a good perceived value.

Value signals   Value signals reinforce the perception of value. Here is a list of some value signals:

1 *Company image and reputation.* Does a company's management have a track record of success and a philosophy that stresses dedication to excellence and high business standards? Google and Amazon have excellent reputations, Comcast a bad one, for example.
2 *Media outlet reputation. The New Yorker* magazine has an excellent reputation; the *National Inquirer*'s is not so good.
3 *Ethical practices.* Does the media outlet have a reputation for treating its customers fairly? Is its word its bond? Do advertisers trust it?
4 *Awards and prizes.* How many awards for excellence or Pulitzer Prizes has a media outlet amassed? Awards and prizes are the one of the best proofs of quality and brand safety.
5 *Content.* Editorial or programming content. *The New York Times, The Washington Post*, and National Public Radio (NPR) are perceived to have high-quality reporting and content.
6 *Insights.* New information about their business that customers were unaware of can be valuable insights that can help them increase the effectiveness of their advertising.
7 *Sales promotion material.* Slick, well-designed, tasteful, informative sales brochures, media kits, and one-page sell sheets speak volumes about an organization.
8 *Continuity.* The number of years a company has been in business, the number of years a television news anchorperson has been on the air, the number of years a website or app has been in existence, or the tenure of a magazine editor all impart a perception of value.

9 *Advertisers*. The presence of well-known, prestigious advertisers gives a medium credibility and value – they reinforce the idea that "you are known by the company you keep," an example of social proof.

10 *Audience or user quality and quantity*. Examples include high-income readers of *Vanity Fair* magazine or the huge audience of Facebook or a Super Bowl telecast.

11 *Price*. The higher the price of a product, the higher the perceived value (expensive equals good). Patek Philippe watches are perceived to have more value than Casio watches, for example.

12 *Management*. The better the reputation of top management and the more visible managers are in the business community, the more favorably a company is viewed. Think of Jeff Bezos and Amazon.

13 *Production values*. Well-produced YouTube videos, slick magazine ads, and well-produced radio, podcast, and television commercials add value.

14 *Sales presentations*. Well-written, problem-solving, and graphically arresting proposals and presentations not only help make a product tangible, they also add value. See Chapter 12 for guidelines for generating winning proposals.

15 *Salespeople*. One survey asked media buyers what first came to mind when the call letters of a radio or television station were mentioned. Seventy-five percent of all buyers gave the name of the salesperson who called on them. Thus, salespeople are the surrogate for the product and can tangibilize intangible media advertising and, thus, create value.

16 *Creative approaches*. Ideas for arresting creative executions can add value for direct clients without advertising agencies. Agencies usually do not appreciate suggestions for creative approaches in copy and art because they see creative execution as their prerogative.

Positioning value

Positioning is creating a unique perception of your product to have a differential competitive advantage in the mind of your customers. As marketing guru Philip Kotler says, "Having a competitive advantage is like having a gun in a knife fight."[17]

When you position your company and your product to have a competitive advantage, a competitor's image is as important as your own image, if not more so, because you are positioning your product against the image of your competitor's medium and product. If you position properly, you can accomplish two things: you position your product to have an advantage and you position your competitors' products to have a disadvantage.

A classic example of this double positioning was AOL's slogan in the late 1990s, "So easy to use, no wonder we're number one." This slogan, or tag line, not only positioned AOL as easy to use but also positioned its competitors as hard to use.

You must clearly establish a differential competitive advantage in the minds of potential customers for your medium, your company, your product, and yourself. To do so, you should begin the positioning process by asking yourself the following questions:

1 What position, if any, does my product already occupy in the mind of my customer? Of course, the best way to find out is to ask.

2   What position do I want to occupy? It must be unique and concise. It must have an easily definable and differential competitive advantage that clearly makes a difference; if it takes too long to explain, customers will not stick around or stay awake long enough to find out how good it is. The slogan "So easy to use, no wonder we're number one" is a good example of a unique and concise slogan that defines a competitive advantage that was important to consumers who were new to the Internet.

Create value in both types of selling

No matter what type of selling you are engaged in – missionary/development selling or service/agency selling – you must always find ways to create value. In missionary selling creating value comes by generating actionable insights and solutions to marketing problems and creating arresting, informative presentations and proposals. In service selling creating value comes by generating actionable insights, by creating arresting, informative presentations that address the criteria set forth in an RFP or creative brief, and by giving outrageously excellent service, as detailed in Chapter 14.

Five steps for creating value

Because the vast majority of media advertising inventory is bought and sold programmatically via automation, you must position your product to create the perception of value before your inventory is bought programmatically, and the best way to increase the value of what you are selling is to follow the five steps for creating value. As part of the creating value process, it is a good idea to have a customizable general presentation (GP). Many media organizations have a GP, which is an introduction to their product that reinforces the product's history, reputation, and combination of advantages and benefits. To see an example of a local GP, go to http://www.mediaselling.us/downloads. html and look at the presentation for the *DeSoto Times*, a small community newspaper.

The five steps of the creating value process parallel a salesperson's primary sales strategies.

1   Reinforce your expertise as an insight provider and problem solver.
2   Reinforce the value of advertising.
3   Reinforce the value of your medium.
4   Reinforce the value of your product (your website, platform, or app, your network, or your television station, for example).
5   Frame the advantages and benefits of your product according to the personality traits of the buyer.

Reinforce your expertise as an insight provider and problem solver   You want your prospects to consider you as a marketing and advertising expert who can provide new insights into their business challenges and recommend solutions to their advertising and marketing problems. Chapter 10 goes into detail about how to conduct research and come up with insights and solutions. In order to demonstrate your expertise, you should show your broad-based knowledge of national and international economic and business trends, economic and business trends in your market, economic and business trends in the media and in your medium, and economic and business trends in your customers' businesses.

Also, demonstrate your knowledge of marketing and advertising – the goals, strategies, and tactics of not only your customers and their competitors, but also of *your* competitors.

Finally, provide your customers with the latest research available. Do not just present reams of data, but put research information in a concise, summarized, easy-to-read format. Customers will appreciate and reward you for your consideration and respect for their time.

Your goal in providing new information is to become your customers' preferred supplier – the salesperson and organization your customers would most like to do business with, and, more important, the salesperson they will always call first when they want information.

Reinforce the value of advertising   In most cases, especially with advertising agencies, you do not have to reinforce the value of advertising because, obviously, the agencies are doing just that with their clients. However, at times you will find a marketer that is spending a majority of its marketing dollars in promotion rather than in advertising. Remember, frame advertising is an investment, but frame promotion is a less desirable expense – a subtle example of how framing can position advertising more positively than promotion.

The difference between advertising and promotion is more than just a matter of framing; there are substantial differences. Advertising tells consumers *why* to buy a product and has long-lasting effects in creating brand value. Promotion tells consumers *when* to buy a product and has only short-term effects, which do not build brand value. Promotions are often based on a "buy-now" appeal of lower prices, or contests such as *Star Wars* cups at McDonalds.

In 1978, 60 percent of all marketing dollars were invested in advertising, 40 percent spent in promotion. In 2017, it was estimated by some experts that about 50 percent of all marketing dollars were spent in promotion, 50 percent invested in advertising. The migration of marketing dollars from advertising to promotion hurt the growth rate of advertising over those years. Salespeople should continually reinforce advertising's positive long-term effects and the value of advertising to build brand image. Exhibit 7.2 shows seven problems with promotions that you can discuss with your customers that might help stem the tide of advertising dollars being switched to promotion.

Furthermore, the majority of promotions involve some inducement for consumers to act immediately and purchase a product. Inducements invariably involve a price reduction in some form such as rebates, coupons, or free merchandise, for example.

Examples of promotions that have hurt the profit margins of entire industries are the costly rebates American automotive manufacturers at times offer.

These losses due to rebates – essentially a price cut – back up and reinforce the claim that "the cost to a manufacturer of a 1-percent reduction in price is always far greater than the cost of a 1-percent boost in advertising expenditure."[18] Do your customers want to increase sales? Recommend that they raise their advertising investment and do not reduce their prices.

Exhibit 7.2 The seven problems with promotions

1 *Short-term effects.* There is overwhelming evidence that "the consumer sales effect is limited to the time period of the promotion itself." Contrary to some marketers' belief, there is no residual effect of a promotion. Consumers do not turn into long-term customers. "When the bribe stops, the extra sales also stop."

2 *Promotions mortgage future sales.* By encouraging consumers to take action immediately, a promotion brings forward sales from a future period and, therefore, future sales are lower than forecast because of problem #1 above.

3 *Promotions encourage stockpiling.* Savvy consumers stock up on low-priced promotion items, which cannibalizes future full-price sales, which lower margins.

4 *Promotions train consumers not to pay full price.* Price-conscious consumers are aware of continual promotions and wait for them – they become trained never to pay full price – which lowers profit margins.

5 *Promotions devalue a brand's image.* Continual promotions create a low-price, even "cheap," image and often appear to be desperate measures of a sinking brand in trouble. If consumers believe price cuts come from an oversupply, they will often wait for an even lower price.

6 *Promotions are addictive.* Marketers become dependent on more and more quick fixes in a vicious circle of more and more promotions at lower and lower prices at shorter and shorter intervals. Unilever describes this circle as "promotion, commotion, and demotion."[i]

7 *Continual use of promotions leads to retaliation.* Promotions "fuel the flames of competitive retaliation far more than other marketing activities."[ii] Competitors join the price war to defend their position. The long-term result of price wars can lead to the elimination of both retailers' and an entire industry's profit margins.[iii]

[i] Jones. John Phillip. 1990. "The double jeopardy of sales promotions." *Harvard Business Review*, September–October.
[ii] Ibid.
[iii] Srinivasan, Shuba, Pauwels, Koen, Hansses, Dominique, and Dekimpe, Marnik. 2002. "Who benefits from price promotions?" *Harvard Business Review*, September–October.

Of course, all of these reasons why cutting prices is not a good idea for customers doubly reinforce why media salespeople should not cut their rates if they are selling direct (not programmatically).

Reinforce the value of your medium   In many cases, you may not think you have to sell the value of your medium to a current advertiser who is a heavy user. However, keep in mind that competing media salespeople are calling on your advertisers and doing their best to switch your customers' advertising to their medium. It is a good idea to reinforce the value of your medium, and you can do this in three ways with current advertisers:

- At yearly renewal times, or at mid year, make a stewardship presentation that shows the advertising an advertiser ran during the previous year and what results they got, and remind them of the excellent service they received from you.
- Ask advertisers for testimonial letters or, better, to participate in a case study. Go to www.mediaselling.us/downloads.html to read a paper titled "How to Write an

Advertising Success Case Study." Helping you write a case study reinforces an advertiser's excellent judgment in buying your medium.

- Invite advertisers to your industry's trade association presentations. Associations such as the Interactive Advertising Bureau (IAB), the Television Bureau of Advertising (TVB), and the Radio Advertising Bureau (RAB) regularly make presentations touting their medium in cities around the country. It is the job of these associations to sell the value of their media and they do it well.

You should also make presentations to advertising agencies, especially to media planners, on the value of your medium if you sell for a medium other than television. As you read in Chapter 2, agencies have a bias in favor of television. If you are not selling television, selling the value of your medium to agencies is important in the long term, even though it may not produce an immediate order.

Another reason for reinforcing the value of your medium to both agencies and clients is to attempt to get them to invest more dollars in your medium – increase the size of the advertising dollar pie in your medium. You should sell the value of your medium first and worry about your share of the pie later. In many markets, there are radio or television station associations that cooperate in an attempt to get new advertisers into their particular medium and away from another, such as newspapers.

Reinforce the value of your product   One of the best examples of a company that positions itself superbly is Patek Philippe, the Swiss watchmaker. Go to the company's website at www.patek.com and notice how the company promotes its history, its collection, its customers, and its complicated watches, but price is never mentioned. After seeing how Patek Philippe positions itself and creates value for its watches, ask yourself if you would like to own one and if you would rather sell these watches than sell Casio watches.

Just as the Patek Philippe website reeks of quality, you want your customers to get the same sense of quality when you talk about your product. One way to create the perception of quality is to repeat the word, to use it in every possible context, such as "We have a quality news website and quality contributors," or "We have a quality production department that produces the highest quality commercials."

Remember, you are trying to position the quality, results, and service of your product to have a competitive advantage. After quality, comes results; stress that your medium gets results, and the best way reinforce this concept is with case studies. These cases studies are not only good for positioning the value of your medium with an advertiser who is involved in developing the case study with you, but they are also powerful sales tools. You will find case studies are an effective proof of performance that your medium gets results for advertisers. Case studies are also powerful stories that connect with people emotionally.

Too often, inexperienced media salespeople sell on the basis of the features of their product and do not place enough emphasis on advantages and benefits. Here are the definitions of these elements:

Features.   Features are descriptive. Features are facts and information about your product and its various parts. The features of a platform such as Facebook is that its users spend a great deal of time with it and that its ads are not overpowering. The features of a radio station, for example, are its tower, its transmitter, its programming format, its personalities, its coverage, its audience, and its ratings. Features describe what you have to sell, but they do not indicate or imply if the features are good or bad or why a customer should care about them. Customers do not buy based on product features, they want to know "What's in it for me?" (WIIFM).

Advantages. Advantages are comparative. They describe why the features of your product are better. Customers are interested in a feature's advantages and consider these advantages when they make a purchase (or in the case of advertising, an investment) if they feel the features are relevant. Use the contrast principle when you present advantages.

Exhibit 7.3 shows an example of dramatizing ratings advantages for a television station schedule.

Exhibit 7.3   Ratings of a TV newscast

Poor WAAA-TV display of ratings

	Adults 25–54 Nielsen Rating WAAA-TV
Early news	3.0

Fair WAAA-TV display of ratings (shows a comparative advantage)

	Adults 25–54 Nielsen Rating WAAA-TV	Adults 25–54 Nielsen Rating WBBB-TV
Early news	3.0	2.0

Good WAAA-TV display of ratings (quantifies a comparative advantage)

	Adults 25–54 Nielsen Ratings WAAA-TV	Adults 25–54 Nielsen Ratings WBBB-TV	WAAA-TV Difference
Early news	3.0	2.0	+ 1.0

Best WAAA-TV display of ratings (dramatizes a comparative advantage)

	Adults 25–54 Nielsen Ratings WAAA-TV	Adults 25–54 Nielsen Ratings WBBB-TV	WAAA-TV Advantage
Early news	3.0	2.0	+ 50%

WBBB-TV counterproposal display of ratings (minimizes a comparative disadvantage)

	Adults 25–54 Nielsen Ratings WAAA-TV	Adults 25–54 Nielsen Ratings WBBB-TV	WBBB-TV Disadvantage
Early news	3.0	2.0	– 33%

Notice the WBBB-TV proposal. WBBB-TV saw a copy of WAAA-TV's proposal that claimed WAAA-TV had a 50 percent lead over WBBB-TV, which is accurate.

However, WBBB-TV showed in its counterproposal that things weren't all that bad – that it only trailed WAAA-TV by 33 percent, which is also accurate. The lesson here is to learn how to use numbers to compare, maximize, and dramatize your advantages and to minimize your disadvantages.

Benefits. Benefits are reasons why the features and advantages of your product solve customers' problems. Benefits are what you should concentrate on selling because that is what customers buy – benefits. Peter Drucker explained succinctly that people do not buy quarter-inch drill bits, they buy quarter-inch holes. Every time you state a feature or advantage of your product or proposal, customers ask themselves the WIIFM question, "What's in it for me?" Benefits answer the WIIFM question. Don't let a customer ask the WIIFM question out loud, you must answer the question by attaching a problem-solving benefit to every feature you mention.

You should always frame your benefits so that they directly address marketing and advertising problems (it is better to refer to them as challenges when you make presentations to customers) and how your proposed solutions help customers get what they want – achieve their marketing and advertising goals and get results as they define results. There is also a subtle subtext involved that you should master. You must also frame your benefits and solutions in such a way that they appeal to customers based on your assessment of their dominant personality traits and corresponding descriptive adjectives. This type of subtle framing according to personality traits is where it gets a little more difficult. You can hardly say to a customer, "My proposal to run commercials in the Super Bowl on my television network will not only help you achieve your marketing goals of reaching the largest possible male audience and locking out your competitors from this valuable position, but it will also appeal to you because you are greedy and boastful." Or, "My proposal to invest in advertising on my newspaper's website will not only help you achieve your goal of making your advertising investments as efficient as possible, but it will also appeal to you because you are nervous and fearful about losing money."

No, you have to be careful and practice framing your benefits to match a prospect's or a buyer's personality traits as you assess them. Creating a personality profile, as discussed in Chapter 6 and seen in Exhibit 6.9, is the first step in framing benefits according to personality traits. The next step is to develop a Benefits Matrix, as seen in Exhibit 7.4. You can download a blank Benefits Matrix from www.mediaselling.us/downloads.html in order to practice completing a Benefit Matrix for important calls, such as in the Education step in missionary selling or after getting to know planners and buyers in service selling.

You will notice in the Benefits Matrix that the statements that frame the benefits reinforce the benefit in terms of both the customer's business challenges and personality traits. For example, in the first row the Communications VP of a health maintenance organization (HMO) is estimated to be fair, faithful, organized, thorough, tolerant, and patient; therefore, the health app's benefits are framed using

Exhibit 7.4 Benefits matrix

Customer	Customer business challenge	Customer descriptive adjectives	Your feature	Your benefit	Frame your benefit
Communications VP, HMO	HMOs perceived as hindering choice.	Fair Faithful Organized Thorough Tolerant Patient	Health app	Associated with positive concept such as health and wellness. Trusted content, credible advertisers. Reach wellness fans.	"It's a fair price." "Reach our faithful audience." "If you're patient, you'll get good long-term results."
CEO of beer brand	Increasing market share	Greedy Boastful Social boldness Extroverted Quarrelsome Headstrong	Live sports on TV	High reach in target audience, M 25–54.* Live; low DVR viewing. Fan loyalty to advertisers.	"You can tell everyone you're in the Super Bowl." "You'll get free seats in our private box." "You'll be in the box with other CEOs."
Agency buyer for a financial services client	Increase share of mind	Sincere Modest Nervous Fearful Prudent Diligent	News on radio	Ideal environment to improve brand image and credibility Reach decision makers. Reach up-scale income people.	"We're a safe buy." "Your company's executives listen to our news and will like that you bought it." "Buying into news is prudent choice."
Art gallery owner	Driving traffic to gallery	Deceitful Hypocritical Creative Unconventional Temperamental Stubborn	Local news website	Destination for people looking for different things to do. Reaches high-income collectors. Can test different creative approaches.	"Imagine all the ways you can take advantage of our unconventional ad sizes." "You can innovate with native ads." "Go crazy with creative."

*M = Men

some of the adjectives that describe the VP's personality: "It's a fair price," and "Reach our faithful audience."

In the second row, to the CEO of a beer brand, the benefits of advertising in the Super Bowl are rational and measurable, but the way you frame the obvious benefits is to appeal to the CEO's ego by reminding him how he can boast about being in the Super Bowl and be in a high-status private box with other important CEOs.

The home-run secret

The most important skill in media selling is being able to subtly frame the benefits of your product according to personality traits without being too obvious, as shown in the Benefits Matrix. You should create a Benefits Matrix for your key customers and buyers, and you should practice saying the right words to hit their hot buttons. If you can master the art of framing benefits in this manner, it is the biggest home run in media selling and, in fact, in all personal selling.

Two Don'ts in creating value

Don't promise results   The first principle of creating value is: *Advertising is not an expense* (or "spend"), *it is an investment*. The second principle is: *Underpromise and overdeliver*. One of the main things you accomplish when you create value is that you embed and, thus, control your customers' expectations. Do not be guilty of setting unrealistically high expectations in your customers' minds; it is the fastest way to lose credibility, create a furious client, and guarantee no renewal. You will have happy customers if you lower their expectations and then, as their advertising runs, if they have better results than they expected, you will get an enthusiastic renewal. Conversely, you will have an unhappy customer if you raise their expectations by hinting at or promising unreasonable results. If they have worse results than they expected, you will get an angry cancellation and possibly even a lawsuit.

Unfortunately, you cannot promise or even predict results with confidence or accuracy because there are many other marketing variables that affect customers' sales that you have no control over, as seen in Exhibit 7.5.

Don't knock the competition   The second "don't" of creating value is: *Don't knock the competition*. Its corollary is: Don't even mention the competition. Perhaps the best reason for not knocking the competition is because buyers do not like it. Unfortunately, in some highly competitive industries such as radio and magazines, weak and unprofessional salespeople habitually sell negatively. Exhibit 7.6 shows the reasons why not to knock or mention the competition and gives you some ways to deal with competitors when asked about them.

Exhibit 7.5 Marketing variables that affect sales

Variable	Description
Competitors' offers	Competitors might offer contests, sweepstakes, rebates, free delivery, cash back on purchases made elsewhere for less.
Competitors' advertising activity	No matter how much an advertiser invests, if a competitor invests substantially more, especially in the same medium, it's difficult to gain market share.
Competitors' creative	Competitors' effective and attention-grabbing creative approaches can blunt your customer's attempts to gain market share. Bud Light beat Miller Light over the years not only with heavier advertising weight but also with consistently brilliant, funny commercials that young men loved.
Customer's backend	Advertisers may have great creative and sufficient advertising weight, but if their backend cannot process orders efficiently or deliver on time, they lose customers and sales.
Competitors' backend	If competitors' have highly efficient backend systems, they might steal customers with faster delivery cycles, better after-purchase service.
Competitive pricing	No matter how much an advertiser invests, if competitors' prices are lower for similar quality, it is very difficult to increase sales.
Competitors' innovations	New, improved product lines and models from competitors can slow your customer's sales.
Purchasing cycle	No amount of advertising can change a product's historic purchasing cycle. No advertiser can sell bikini bathing suits in the middle of zero-degree cold spells in January.
Interest level, novelty	Some products are ho-hum products – they have low consumer interest. Household products such as toilet paper do not elicit a lot of interest from consumers. New, novel products like the Amazon Echo create interest. An advertiser with a ho-hum product can see sales fall when competitors introduce exciting new products.

If a buyer asks you a direct question about a competitor, rather than being negative, Exhibit 7.7 shows you how to respond.

Creating value ideas

To wind up this chapter, in Exhibit 7.8 you will find a list of creating value ideas. These are just a few of hundreds of ideas that can help you add value for your product, reinforce the perception of quality, results, and service for your company and for your product, and help you become a world-class media salesperson.

Exhibit 7.6   Reasons for not knocking (or even mentioning) the competition

Reason	Description
Buyers hate it.	How would you like it if every conversation you had during a business day were negative, nasty, and mean spirited? You would probably become depressed. Buyers feel the same way.
You tear down the image of your medium.	After buyers hear how bad several competitors are, they begin to have a negative impression of the whole medium. Knocking the competition is destructive to your medium.
You waste time.	Customers' and buyers' time is limited; you usually have just few minutes to get their attention and make a presentation. If you spend time knocking the competition, you waste valuable time. Remember the old adage, "You can't sell what your competitors don't have." You can only sell the benefits of what you have to offer, so get on with it.
You lose credibility.	When you knock the competition, you are perceived as not being objective. Buyers say to themselves, "Of course you're badmouthing the competition; you're trying to sell me something. Why should I believe you?" Therefore, when you knock competitors, you lose credibility.
You lower your image.	Selling negatively puts your down in the gutter with other negatively selling salespeople. Stay above it; refuse to throw dirt. Buyers will appreciate your positive approach and like you better for it. If your competition goes low, you go high.
You can touch hidden sore spots.	You may not know if a customer or buyer has invested in advertising with a competitor (in your medium or another medium), so if you knock a competitor a buyer has invested in, you are insulting the buyer's judgment. When this happens, buyers become defensive and entrenched, and they vigorously defend their past decisions. Also, a buyer may like a salesperson (may even be dating the salesperson) and when you knock that salesperson's medium, you are knocking the salesperson and the buyer will become very defensive and defend their friend's product (and dislike yours). Remember, the media are an intangible product and, thus, salespeople become the surrogate for their products – they are the products in the minds of buyers.
You build competitors' importance and image.	Did you ever see an ad in a magazine for Rolex that had a headline "We're better than a Timex?" Never mention the competition below you in rank position; all you do is elevate them to your level. If you mention competitors below you in rank position, buyers' reactions are "Why is this salesperson talking about that competitor? What is the salesperson afraid of?"

Exhibit 7.7 How to respond when asked about the competition

Response	Description
Compliment competition	Use a two-sided argument. The first side is to compliment the competitors (remember, you do not know if the buyer knows or likes the competition). By complementing, you boost the image of your own product or medium and come across as a positive, nice person. For example, if a buyer asks, "I understand BuzzFeed has lowered its prices. Is this true?" you might respond with, "I've heard that, too. It's a shame – pressure from Wall Street, I guess. BuzzFeed has broken some big stories and has a good reputation."
Talk about your strengths	Do what politicians do, do not answer the question directly, answer the question with information about the benefits of your product. For example, if a buyer says, "WAAA-TV's late news had a 20 percent drop in women 18–49 in the latest rating book," you might respond with "My station, WBBB-TV's late news had only a two percent drop in that demo even though it was a summer rating book and overall viewing in the demo was down 18 percent."
Expose generic weaknesses	The second side of a two-sided argument is an exposure of your competitor's generic weakness – weaknesses that are not specific to that individual competitor, but to a type or genre of products or media. For example, you might add to your response to #1 above to the question about BuzzFeed lowering its rates, the second side of the argument: "All news sites like BuzzFeed, the HuffPo, and even *The New York Times* have seen a drop in traffic as a result of Facebook tweaking its News Feed algorithms, and some sites are adjusting their rates accordingly."

Exhibit 7.8 Creating value ideas

1 Email customers and buyers useful, relevant trade articles and news (don't overdo it).
2 In your organization assign category, or vertical, sales specialists that are experts in their categories.
3 Conduct webinars on strategy for advertisers. For example, "How Retailers Can Use Television," or "How to Use Cable Television to Reach Upscale Viewers," or "How to Get Results Using Programmatic."
4 Have a website that offers advice and services to customers. See the Zimmer Radio and Marketing Group's website at zimmercommunications.com.
5 Offer business breakfasts once a quarter for local business leaders featuring well-known, expert speakers.
6 Offer dashboards, analytics, and trends information to customers if you sell a digital medium or platform.
7 Develop a system for the sales staff for presenting a predetermined number of speculative ads or speculative commercials per week.
8 Create SWAT teams of salespeople by category and have the team develop category presentations for the use of the whole sales staff.

Exhibit 7.8   Creating value ideas (cont'd)

9   Have exhibition booths at relevant industry trade shows such as truckers' conventions, retail trade conventions, or SXSW (South By Southwest conference).

10   Conduct creative execution seminars for advertisers and advertising agencies.

11   Offer joint promotions with a charity group, an advertiser, and your company.

12   Sponsor city association luncheons honoring advertisers and advertising agencies and present creative awards.

13   Create fun carnival days to promote your medium at local trade association or civic organization meetings.

14   In broadcasting, offer remote broadcasts to advertisers; call them marketing opportunities.

15   Distribute email newsletters about your company that contain news, gossip, and insights.

16   Develop a "Little Things Mean a Lot" list: top management follow-up calls; thank-you notes and birthday cards in invoices; Rolodex-shaped calling cards for salespeople with business, home, and cell phone numbers and email addresses on the cards; framed success letters (on your walls and on your customers' walls); and shopping bags for stores imprinted with your logo and theirs.

17   Develop a total customer responsiveness (TCR) mentality throughout your company, especially by those who answer the telephone. Distribute to the entire staff the "Close to the Customer on the Phone" paper found on www.mediaselling.us/downloads.html.

18   Provide an easy-to-buy, buy-your-way website (see http://espncms.com/advertise-on-espn.html).

19   Provide advertisers with several advertising success stories in their category.

20   Provide advertisers with marketing research by category.

21   Conduct media auctions for a charity to establish the value of your advertising rates: Donate impressions or time and then the charity auctions it off to advertisers, who use the time; the money goes to the charity and it establishes the value of your inventory.

22   Conduct shopping mall research among a store's customers asking them why they shop at competitors' stores.

23   Provide a list by category of your advertisers over the last year.

24   Conduct brainstorming sessions. Invite clients to your offices and let the sales staff create ideas for that client, not ideas why a client should purchase you, but ideas for promotions, positioning, slogans, or creative executions, for example.

25   Spend time in a customer's business. For example, bag groceries, wait on tables, or clean up a showroom.

Test Yourself

1.   What are the six principles of influence outlined in this chapter?
2.   Discuss what the meaning is of the two terms *foot-in-the-door* and *door-in-the-face*.
3.   What is the definition of a commodity?

4. What are the four Creating Value rules?
5. Give an example of an advertiser's positioning strategy as seen in an ad or a commercial?
6. What are the five steps of creating value?
7. What are the seven problems with promotions?
8. What are the differences between features, advantages, and benefits?
9. What are the two "don'ts" in creating value?
10. What are seven reasons for not knocking the competition?

Projects

Project #1: Select a week in your life in which you commit yourself to taking notes on encounters you have with compliance practitioners during the week, waiters in restaurants, telemarketers, retail salespeople, or fundraisers, for example. Take notes in two columns. In the first column, note which one of the six principles of influence, if any, the compliance practitioner used. In the second column, note whether the attempt to influence you was effective or, if the person did not use a principle of influence, which one might have been appropriate. At the end of the week, look over your notes and see: (1) if you identified different principles of influence and (2) if those principles of influence were effective in influencing you and, if not, which principles might have been used.

Project #2: Go to the Downloads section of the *Media Selling* website (http://www.mediaselling.us/downloads.html) and download "A Salesperson's Dilemma" and "Janet Creates Value" case studies. Read "A Salesperson's Dilemma" carefully and then read "Janet Creates Value" and complete the assignment at the bottom of "Janet Creates Value."

References

Cialdini, Robert. 1984. *Influence: The Psychology of Persuasion*. New York: William Morrow.

Cialdini, Robert. 2001. *Influence: Science and Practice*. Boston, MA: Allyn and Bacon.

Conger, Jay. 1998. "The necessary art of persuasion." *Harvard Business Review*, May–June.

Jones, John Phillip. 1990. "The double jeopardy of sales promotions." *Harvard Business Review*, September–October.

Jones, John Phillip. 1995. *When Ads Work: New Proof That Advertising Triggers Sales*. New York: Lexington Books.

Larson, Charles U. 1986. *Persuasion: Reception and Responsibility*. Belmont, CA: Wadsworth.

Ries, Al and Trout, Jack. 1981. *Positioning: The Battle for Your Mind*. New York: McGraw-Hill.

Resources

Advertise on ESPN (https://espncms.com/advertise-on-espn.html)
Zimmer Communications (https://zimmercommunications.com)

Notes

1   Cialdini, Robert. 2001. *Influence: Science and Practice*. Boston, MA: Allyn and Bacon.
2   Ibid.
3   Ibid.
4   Ibid.
5   Ibid.
6   Ibid.
7   Ibid.
8   Ibid.
9   Ibid.
10 Ibid.
11 Ibid.
12 Ibid.
13 Ibid.
14 Ibid.
15 Kaplan, Abraham. 1964. *The Conduct of Inquiry*. Scranton, PA: Chandler Publishing.
16 DeBruicker, F. Stewart and Summe, Gregory L. 1985. "Make sure your customers keep coming back." *Harvard Business Review*, January–February.
17 Kotler, Philip. 1999. *Kotler on Marketing*. New York: Free Press.
18 Jones, John Phillip. 1995. *When Ads Work: New Proof That Advertising Triggers Sales*. New York: Lexington Books.

8

The New Buying and Selling Process

Charles Warner

The old sales process model as described in the fourth edition of *Media Selling* was the same for both missionary and service selling. The old sales process had worked for decades until the Internet, Big Data, programmatic buying and selling, self-serve buying models, and artificial intelligence applications completely disrupted the old tried-and-true sales process model. Exhibit 8.1 shows the difference between the old, pre-Internet steps of selling and the new, post-Internet, digital-era steps of selling.

Remember from Chapter 2 that *missionary selling* is focused on developing new business, and missionary salespeople typically call direct on prospects who are not current advertisers. *Service selling* is focused on selling to current customers who are regular advertisers or to advertising agencies. There is also a hybrid selling model in which salespeople are required to do both missionary and service selling, to develop new business as well manage the accounts of regular advertisers and their agencies.

Missionary and service selling generally require salespeople with different personality traits, motivations, and skills. Missionary, new-business salespeople are hunters who tend to be motivated by competing and winning, and they enjoy the excitement and challenge of the hunt. Service, agency salespeople are farmers who tend to be motivated by relationships and collaborating, who are comfortable with data and numbers, and who enjoy helping their accounts be successful.

Because hunting and farming characteristically require different personality traits, motivations, and skills, a hybrid- or single-sales-role selling model often does not work as well as one which has a sales staff where hunters concentrate on developing

Media Selling: Digital, Television, Audio, Print and Cross-Platform, Fifth Edition.
Charles Warner, William A. Lederer, and Brian Moroz.

Exhibit 8.1   Sales process models

Old sales process steps of selling	New **missionary** sales process steps of selling	New **service** sales process steps of selling
1. Prospecting	1. Prospecting and qualifying	1. Finding decision-makers
2. Identifying problems	2. Researching insights and solutions	2. Educating
3. Generating solutions	3. Educating	3. Researching insights and solutions
4. Presenting	4. Proposing	4. Proposing
5. Negotiating and closing	5. Negotiating and closing	5. Negotiating and closing
6. Servicing	6. Customer success	6 Customer success

new business and farmers sell to current customers and to agencies. A single-sales-role selling model is often seen in smaller, local sales teams such as in medium- and small-market radio and television stations.

In a *Harvard Business Review* article titled "What subscription business models mean for sales teams," authors Andris Zoltners, P.K. Sinha, and Sally Lorimer lay out the pros and cons of a single-sales-role, or a hybrid structure, and a two-role sales structure.[1]

Sales Force Structure

The pros and cons of a single-sales-role sales force structure

There are several advantages to having the same salesperson who develops a new account also be the one who manages the ongoing relationship with that account and assures the account is successful:

- *It encourages customer focus and accountability.* There is no question of who is responsible for each account.
- *Customers like it.* They are not disappointed when they can no longer work with the person who sold to them initially.
- *Typically, salespeople like it.* Salespeople are motivated by owning the relationships with the accounts they develop.
- *Single-role selling is efficient.* There are few, if any, miscommunications and errors when handing off customer responsibility from one salesperson to an account management or customer success person.

On the other hand, the often challenging and important work of new business development gets shortchanged in a single-role sales model. Salespeople in this single role too often gravitate to the easy work of friendly "just-checking-in" calls or putting out fires for demanding accounts.

In some cases, training, incentives, and performance management can redirect sales-people's effort to new business development, but if such approaches do not work or are only partially effective, it is likely time to split the sales force into two roles.

The pros and cons of two roles

Having two sales roles, one for new business development and another for account management, or customer success, has several advantages.

- *Single-role salespeople are more effective.* Management can match salespeople's personality with the missionary selling role. Salespeople who are persistent, like to win, and prefer autonomy can take missionary selling roles. Those who are more patient, collaborative, and focused on maintaining relationships can do service selling, or in a larger sales organization can take a customer success role. Also, with two sales roles, management can train and develop salespeople on a more focused set of skills and competencies, allowing them to bring deeper expertise to customers.
- *Management has more control of selling strategy and effort.* If management wants more sales time devoted to new business development, it can put more people in missionary, new-business-development roles. With a single sales role, management can influence sales effort allocation with training, incentives, and performance management, but it takes constant diligence.
- *You can drive efficiency by using inside sales.* Often, the work required to support and retain customers can be performed remotely by utilizing an inside sales team that uses email, video, and text chat to work with customers. By assigning account management responsibility to less-expensive inside salespeople, or even to an automated virtual assistant, a company can obtain substantial cost-savings with little or no effectiveness loss if the inside-salespeople (or virtual assistants) are properly trained and monitored.

However, along with the benefits, a two-sales-role model creates some stresses and challenges that must be managed properly. Continuing effort is required to ensure efficient, effective, and seamless transfers of account responsibility from a missionary salesperson to an inside salesperson, to an account manager, or a customer success person or both. Account transfer requirements include:

- *Defining how and when the handoff should occur.* By specifying the transition steps required and which sales role is responsible for each step, management can see that nothing falls through the cracks in an account transition. If the handoff takes time, you may want the missionary salesperson to share incentives with an account manager for customer success person for a brief period. Developing handoff checklists is a must.
- *Ensuring customers see value in the transition.* Customers who have become comfortable with the salesperson who sold to them initially need to know the transition is aligned with their best interests. One strategy is to get the account manager or

customer success person involved during the implementation phase of the customer solution. That way, customer personnel get to know the customer success manager (and vice versa) and gain confidence they will be in good hands. Well-trained, talented, and motivated customer success people will be able to succeed in the transition.

Management must decide which model best fits its particular selling situation, but it is important to give a lot of thought to which sales-force structure aligns with an organization's overall sales strategy.

Missionary Selling

The buying process for missionary selling

Not only do these two types of selling require different type of salespeople, but also the buying and selling *process* is different in the two types of selling. The buying process for missionary, direct business consists of six steps, several of which were identified by Neil Rackham in his 1989 book *Major Account Selling*:

1   Recognition of needs[2]
2   Narrowing of alternatives
3   Evaluation of alternatives[3]
4   Resolution of concerns[4]
5   Purchase
6   Execution, optimization, and verification

Recognition of needs   Selling media is business-to-business (B2B) selling, which means one media business selling advertising to another business. Virtually every business advertises in order to get customers, so the basic need to advertise their product or service is endemic to virtually every business that wants to grow. Therefore, in most cases a media salesperson does not have to persuade a business to advertise, and, thus, the vast majority of missionary media selling is focused on persuading a business either to advertise in a particular medium or to invest more in that medium than in another medium.

Missionary selling is most prevalent at radio and television stations, at cable systems, at newspapers, at magazines, and at Internet-based businesses in small and medium-sized markets, because in large markets and in national media such as magazines, television and radio networks, and global platforms such as Google, Facebook, and Amazon, advertisers that can afford these media typically have advertising agencies that create and place their advertising.

Narrowing of alternatives   Once an organization recognizes the need to advertise, the next question is where, in which medium. Or a business might spend its marketing money in promotion, in which case a salesperson's role is to create value for advertising as opposed to promotion (see Figure 7.2 The seven problems with promotions).

The narrowing-of-alternatives step of buying has become much more complicated in the digital era. In the 1970s, 1980s, and 1990s for advertisers in small and medium-sized markets there were only a handful of choices: newspapers, television, radio, outdoor (posters and billboards), or direct mail. The digital era brought a multiple of new choices, for example local websites and global platforms such as Google, YouTube, Facebook, Instagram, and Amazon. Narrowing the alternatives for large advertisers is the task of advertising agencies, but at the local, small- and mid-sized-market level, it is the job of media salespeople to help businesses with the narrowing process like the salespeople at Zimmer Radio and Marketing Group or the *Austin American-Statesman* do, as described in Chapter 2. Many business people at the small- and mid-sized-market level tend to be inexperienced generalists and are not experts in marketing and advertising, so they need to be educated on the various media and the benefits, advantages, and technical requirements of those media.

Evaluation of alternatives   Once alternatives have been narrowed to a few media in which to advertise, those media need to be evaluated to determine which medium or combination of media makes the most sense based on an advertiser's objectives and strategy. For example, is direct-response or branding advertising the best approach? If direct-response advertising is called for, Google search terms are more than likely the first choice. If branding is called for, video ads on TV, You Tube, or Facebook or audio ads on radio or in podcasts might be the best choice.

Resolution of concerns   Once a medium or combination of media are selected as providing the best potential return on investment (ROI) or branding opportunity, the next step is to begin the purchasing process by negotiating or determining price, terms, and conditions of a potential advertising investment. This negotiating can be in person with a media salesperson or conducted programmatically online.

Purchase   When the concerns are answered and price, terms, and conditions agreed on, a purchase is made by emailing an insertion order (IO) or a signed contract to a salesperson at a selected medium or bought via a programmatic transaction.

Execution, optimization, and verification   Too often salespeople believe that when a customer makes a purchase, the buying and selling process is over. However, customers typically believe that when they make a media buy, the relationship is just beginning. Executing the advertising schedule is of vital importance. Are the TV or radio spots scheduled properly, does the medium have the creative? If the ad schedule is digital, the hard work is just beginning because, for the schedule to be as effective as it can be, it needs optimization – A/B testing of creative to see which wording, color combinations, and offers work best. One of the advantages of digital advertising is that different creative executions can be tested and optimized on a real-time basis, especially for direct-response copy, banners, or videos. With the vast majority of advertising being purchased programmatically, verifying that the purchased level of impressions were served properly and were viewable is necessary. Were the ads served, were they viewable, and were guaranteed impression levels met?

The selling process for missionary selling

The selling process for missionary selling consists of six steps that coordinate with the buying process that direct, non-agency prospects go through:

1 Prospecting and qualifying
2 Researching insights and solutions
3 Educating
4 Proposing
5 Negotiating and closing
6 Customer success

Prospecting and qualifying   Prospecting is finding potential customers; it is creating opportunities. Qualifying is finding the *right* potential customers, those who have the money to advertise, who pay their bills, for whom the timing is right (such as graduation season for jewelers who sell class rings), and who are logical fit with what you are selling. For example, if you are selling for a talk radio station that features Rush Limbaugh and other conservative pundits, you would look for businesses and organizations that wanted to appeal to older adults (55+), especially older men who live in a rural area, and that wanted to appeal to right-wing-leaning people who do not consider themselves elite. A Ford truck dealer would qualify as a good target account as would a local elder-care facility. Or, if you are selling for a radio station that features hip-hop and rap music – an *urban* format – you would look for businesses and organizations that wanted to appeal to fashion-oriented 12–24-year-old African American city-dwellers. A local shoe store that sells Air Jordan or LeBron James sneakers would be a good target account. Chapter 9 will go into more depth about the prospecting and qualifying step and determining target accounts.

Researching insights and solutions   Once you have qualified accounts that are a good fit for the medium you are selling and for whom the timing is right, the next step is to conduct research to learn about your target accounts' business model, seasonality, size, advertising problems, competitive challenges, and marketing and creative strategy. And then the next step is to analyze available data for some insights that might help the account be more successful and address some of its marketing and advertising problems. Also, included in insights is information about the person you will be calling on. Information such as where they have worked, where they went to school, and other information that can be gathered on LinkedIn or on other social media platforms. Chapter 10 will go into more depth about some techniques for researching insights and solutions.

Educating   In previous editions of *Media Selling*, this step of selling was referred to as *presenting*; however, as indicated in Chapter 2, approaches to selling in the digital era have changed dramatically. A selling-as-educating approach is now required for a number of reasons, including self-serve auction buying models and programmatic buying and selling of media advertising. Buying digital and mobile advertising direct from a salesperson or buying programmatically is extremely complex, and buyers need to be thoroughly educated on the advantages and benefits of the proposed solution. It is in the educating step of selling that you create value for your medium and for your eventual solutions. Remember, Rule 1 of Creating Value is that you create value before you mention price and before you negotiate. Chapter 11 will cover in detail techniques for educating both individuals and groups.

Proposing   Proposing is presenting a specific, tailored, customized solution or Big Idea and when you finally mention price, terms, and conditions. Chapter 12 will cover in-depth strategies for creating and presenting proposals.

Negotiating and closing   Negotiating and closing is the step of selling in which you get the order or a firm commitment to buy. If you are selling direct (not programmatically) to an account, this is the step in which you get acceptance of the price, terms, and conditions you have negotiated and get a signed contract or an insertion order (IO). If you are selling a schedule that the account will buy programmatically, you get a firm commitment to buy via an email. Chapter 13 will cover in-depth strategies for negotiating and for closing a deal.

Customer success   In the pre-Internet era this function was typically referred to as *account management* or *customer relationship management* (CRM), and in *Media Selling* editions 1–4, this final step of selling was referred to as *servicing*. However, with the rise of digital to pass television to become the number one advertising medium, managing an account became much more complicated than merely managing relationships. With digital advertising, the purchase is the somewhat less complicated part of the process; the harder part is execution of a schedule, optimization of the placement (especially, optimizing the creative approach), and finally, verification that the impressions were delivered, viewable, and in a brand-safe environment – all of these efforts are directed toward a single goal of customer success. Chapter 14 will go into depth about the details of the customer success function.

Service Selling

The buying process for service selling

The buying process for service selling is somewhat similar to the buying process for missionary selling, although one step shorter:

1 Recognition of needs
2 Evaluation of alternatives, Phase I
3 Evaluation of alternatives, Phase II
4 Purchase
5 Execution, optimization, and verification

Recognition of needs   We will make the assumption that in service selling you are selling to an advertising agency, typically to a media agency or the media department of an agency or client. In recent years, primarily because of programmatic buying, a trend has developed for large marketers to use programmatic buying in house rather than using an agency. Also, large consulting firms, primarily Accenture and Deloitte, have become more active in not only consulting on advertising and media strategy but also in creating and placing advertising, thus taking business from advertising agencies. However, for the sake of simplification, we will refer to agency selling, which will include selling to the media departments of large marketers and to consulting companies – to any entity that performs the advertising functions of planning, creating, and placing ads.

In the recognition-of-needs step, agencies have accounts that already have a budget for advertising, so in this first buying step agencies develop an overall media strategy that consists of determining, based on an allocated budget, which media to use and when to use them.

Evaluation of alternatives, Phase I   The first phase of evaluating alternatives consists of an agency developing a media plan that allocates dollars to the various media it has decided to use and sending out requests for proposals (RFPs) to the media selected.

Evaluation of alternatives, Phase II   The second phase of this buying step consists of comparing and evaluating the proposals that have been submitted in response to the RFPs that have been sent out. More and more often, this step is being eliminated by agencies because they do not use RFPs, they go directly to buying programmatically or on a self-serve basis from Google or Facebook or having one of these two platforms manage the auction-based buying for them.

Purchase   Once the media plan has been determined, the plan is executed either through a salesperson or programmatically.

Execution, optimization, and verification   The hard work of executing an advertising schedule, optimizing a digital buy, and verifying that the schedule ran as ordered will be covered in more depth in Chapter 19: Selling Digital and Cross-Platform Advertising.

The selling process for service selling

Even though the agency buying process is one step shorter than the missionary buying process, the selling process consists of the same number of, although slightly different, steps.

1   Finding decision-makers
2   Educating
3   Researching insights and solutions
4   Proposing

5   Negotiating and closing
6   Customer success

Finding decision-makers   In selling to advertising agencies, you do not have to prospect to find businesses that have advertising budgets, because the agencies have done the prospecting for you. If a business or non-profit organization has a budget for advertising, and if the budget approaches or is over seven figures or more, that organization more than likely hires an agency to create and place its advertising. Therefore, agencies are in business because they control advertising budgets, but finding what department in an agency and what person in a media department make media strategy and planning decisions and then identifying what person makes media buying decisions is the first step in the service selling process. There is a high turnover of personnel in agency media departments, especially in the planning and buying functions, and also agency organizational structures and job titles vary widely. Therefore salespeople calling on agencies, particularly large multinational agencies and agency holding companies, must keep in constant touch with their assigned agencies, familiarize themselves with the often Byzantine structure of an agency, and develop relationships with planners and buyers in these continually changing jobs. By far the best way to find advertising decision-makers in agencies and at clients is to subscribe to the database, The List, which provides updated agency and client information to subscribers.

Educating   The second step in service selling to agencies is educating. Salespeople must call on and create value for their medium with agency media strategists and planners, and in some cases creative directors, in order to get their medium and product on the list to be sent an RFP and evaluated. Chapter 11 will cover in-depth techniques for educating and presenting to individuals and to groups at agencies.

Researching insights and solutions   In addition to educating agency strategy, planning, and creative people on their medium (e.g. search, TV, radio, social media, magazines), media salespeople need to conduct research on insights and solutions for specific agency accounts that will convince those responsible for writing an RFP or creative brief to include a specific media outlet or platform (e.g. Google, ESPN, iHeart Radio, Facebook, or *Cosmopolitan*). Solutions can include a Big Idea such as a creative approach, event sponsorship, or a contest. Chapter 10, written by Brian Moroz of Google will give you some excellent tips on and resources for researching insights and solutions.

Proposing   The proposing step of service selling is essentially the same as in missionary selling: "presenting a specific, tailored, customized solution or Big Idea and when you finally mention price, terms, and conditions." Chapter 12 will cover strategies for creating and presenting proposals.

Negotiating and closing   This is also essentially the same as in missionary selling: "the step of selling in which you get the order or a firm commitment to buy. If you are selling direct (not programmatically) to an account, this is the step in which you get acceptance of the price, terms, and conditions you have negotiated and get a signed contract or an

IO. If you are selling a schedule that the account will buy programmatically, you get a firm commitment to buy via an email." Chapter 13 will cover strategies for negotiating and closing a deal. And even though negotiating is a skill that you may not use, because the vast majority of digital advertising is bought programmatically or by an auction model in which artificial intelligence (AI) does the negotiating, it is a skill that you should learn so you can negotiate effectively if and when a negotiating situation arises.

Customer success   Often previously referred to as *account management*, the customer success function in service selling is much the same as in missionary selling, and this step will be covered in depth in Chapter 14.

Figures 8.1 and 8.2 give a graphic representation of the missionary and service selling process that will help you conceptualize and visualize the two processes. Exhibitions 8.2 and 8.3 are rubrics for managing the steps in each type of selling. Note that the Step Management Guides do not include the customer success step of selling because that final step will be covered in depth in Chapter 14. Also, in many organizations, especially larger media companies, the customer success function is handed off to a separate department or virtual assistant.

The Step Management Guides are modeled after the Stage Management Guide, which you can find at http://firstround.com/review/this-sales-plan-moves-the-needle-on-every-success-metric. There are many advantages in developing a Step Management Guide, which you should do after reading Chapters 9–13 of this book. Some of those advantages are: (1) salespeople understand both the buying and the selling process, which are different and which must be aligned in order for salespeople to "help your

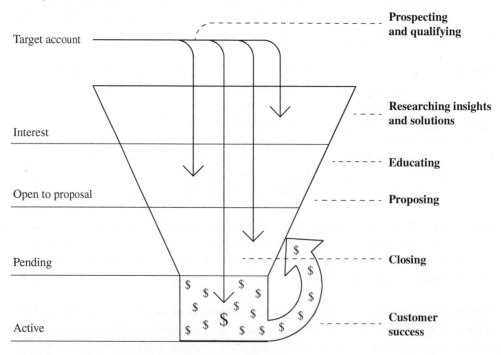

Figure 8.1   The sales funnel – missionary selling

Exhibit 8.2 Missionary selling Step Management Guide

STEP	Prospecting & qualifying	Researching insights & solutions	Educating	Proposing	Negotiating & closing
Objective	To establish your credibility and expertise and to move prospects from attention to interest.	To find insights or a Big Idea that will help solve marketing and advertising problems.	To teach your product's benefits and advantages and move prospects to active consideration.	To present a tailored proposal that includes price, terms, and conditions.	To get prospects to take action or give a firm commitment to purchase.
Key questions	"Are you satisfied with your current ads?" "Would you like to get better results?" "What keeps you up at night?" "What criteria do you use to make a decision on what media to invest in?"	(Conduct research so you understand prospect's industry, business, competitors, and advertising strategy and objectives.)	"Do you agree with the value in what I've presented so far?" "Do we have agreement on your decision criteria?" "Who else needs to see this solution?"	"Do you agree that the prices, terms, and conditions are fair and reasonable?"	"When would you like to start?" "If you have no other questions, shall we go ahead?"
Key gives	Give some new information and a success story in prospect's category.		(Create value for your benefits, solutions, Big Ideas.) More success stories.	(Negotiate on prices, terms, and conditions if appropriate. See Chapter 13.)	Give implementation details.
Key gets	Get appointment to present insights, solutions, or a Big Idea.		Get commitment to decision criteria. Get commitment to present a specific proposal to others involved in making a decision and to move forward.	Get agreement to move forward.	Contract signed, IO sent, firm commitment to purchase.
Next steps	Schedule appointment.	(Prepare customized presentation.)	Schedule appointment to make proposal.	Schedule closing appointment.	Send thank-you note.

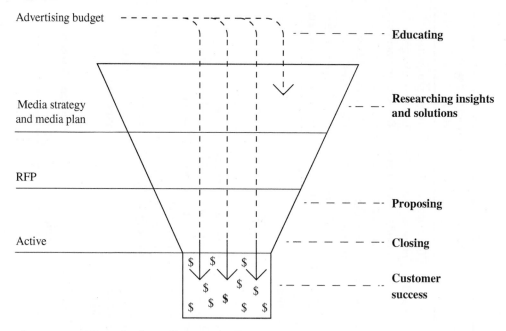

Figure 8.2   The sales funnel–service selling

customers through their buying journey, not push them through your process"[5]; (2) a Step Management Guide establishes a common language for internal sales communication and helps salespeople transition from being information providers and handling transactions "to a new role of being value-added consultants"[6]; and (3) pipeline management and forecasting become standardized and easier.[i]

The Step Management Guides in Exhibits 8.2 and 8.3 are general in nature and are meant to be illustrative more as a structural guide rather than to show explicit questions to ask. Questions must be customized for each separate media-selling situation. Sales organizations should develop their own unique Step Management Guide by getting input from experienced salespeople and from sales management. You can download these step management guides from www.mediaselling.us/downloads.html.

Decision Criteria

Notice the question about decision criteria in the prospecting and qualifying step in the Missionary Step Guide. It is important in this step to discover what criteria a prospect will use in evaluating media and making a decision to invest in advertising.

For example, if you are selling ads on a website or in an app, the criteria a prospect uses might be (1) cost-per-click (CPC) and (2) ROI based on sales. If you are selling for a local television station, the criteria might be (1) price based on a cost-per-thousand

---

[i]A pipeline is a system for managing the various stages of pending business and for forecasting revenue.

Exhibit 8.3 Service selling Step Management Guide

STEP	Finding decision-makers	Educating	Researching insights and solutions	Proposing	Negotiating and closing
Objective	To find the strategy, planning, and buying decision-makers at all agency and client levels.	To establish your credibility and expertise, to teach your product's benefits and advantages, and to move the agency to active consideration.	To find insights or a Big Idea that will help solve marketing and advertising problems.	To present a tailored proposal that includes price, terms, and conditions.	To get prospects to take action or give a firm commitment to purchase.
Key questions	"Who makes the media strategy, planning, and buying decisions for agency and client?" "What criteria do you use to purchase media?"	"Do you agree with the value of what I've presented? Who else needs to see this solution?"	(Conduct research so you understand account's industry, business, and competitors. See Discovery Questions at mediaselling.us)	"Does this meet your criteria on the RFP or in the brief?"	"When would you like to start?" "If you have no other questions, shall we go ahead?"
Key gives	New information.	Give success stories in account's category and show how to buy your medium.		(Negotiate on prices, terms, and conditions if appropriate. See Chapter 13.)	Give implementation details.
Key gets	Decision criteria for making media investments.	Get inclusion in a RFP or a creative brief.		Get agreement to move forward.	Contract signed, IO sent, firm commitment to purchase.
Next steps	Get on RFPs and RFIs.*	Appointment to present solution.	(Prepare customized presentation.)	Schedule closing appointment.	Send thank-you note.

*An RFI is a request for information; it is similar to an RFP (request for proposal).

(CPM) on a demographic, say, women 25–54 and (2) preferred content, such as news programming. If a prospect's decision criteria in your opinion will produce the desired results for the account, you do not need to attempt to change the decision criteria. However, if the criteria for evaluating a media investment are not ideal, you might need to educate the prospect on other decision criteria to consider that might produce better results.

Thus, if a prospect's decision criteria for a television buy are CPM, women 25–54, and you are selling for a CBS affiliate, you might try to educate the prospect on the importance of reaching a broader demographic of 25–64, to include 55–64 year olds, who tend to have more disposable income than younger people.

But, whatever a prospect's decision criteria are, you must know them or change them appropriately so that your eventual proposal helps them achieve their advertising objectives.

In service selling to an agency, you will typically know what the agency's decision criteria are. However, in the initial education steps, it is a good idea to get confirmation of a buyer's decision criteria and to understand how they evaluate a media buy.

In Chapter 16: Advertising, you will get a more detailed perspective on a number of decision criteria that can be used to make advertising more effective and efficient and, thus, get results for customers.

Test Yourself

1. What are the six steps of the buying process for missionary selling?
2. What are the six steps of missionary selling?
3. What are the five steps of the buying process for service selling?
4. What are the six steps of selling of service selling?
5. Why is prospecting and qualifying not necessary for service selling?
6. What are three advantages of developing a Step Management Guide?
7. What are decision criteria, and when should you try to change them?

Project

Develop a Step Management Guide for new business development (missionary selling) for a radio station in your market.

References

Antonio, Victor and Glenn-Anderson, James. 2018. *Sales Ex-Machina: How Artificial Intelligence Is Changing the World of Selling.* Alpharetta, GA: Sellinger Group.

Rackham, Neil. 1989. *Major Account Selling Strategies.* New York: McGraw Hill.

Resources

The List (www.thelistinc.com)
First Round Review (www.firstround.com/review/this-sales-plan-moves-the-needle-on-every-success-metric)

Notes

1 Zoltners, Andris A., Sinha, P.K., and Lorimer, Sally E. 2018. "What subscription business models mean for sales teams." *Harvard Business Review*. Retrieved from https://hbr.org/2018/06/what-subscription-business-models-mean-for-sales-teams.

2 Rackham, Neil. (1989). *Major Account Selling Strategies*. McGraw-Hill.

3 Ibid.

4 Ibid.

5 "This sales plan moves the needle on every success metric." Retrieved from http://firstround.com/review/this-sales-plan-moves-the-needle-on-every-success-metric.

6 Ibid.

9

Prospecting and Qualifying

Charles Warner

In Chapter 2 you learned that the overall objectives of a media sales organization are: (1) to get results for customers, (2) to develop new business, (3) to retain and increase current business, and (4) to delight customers. You learned in Chapter 8, in a Step Management Guide, that the objective of the prospecting and qualifying step is "to establish your credibility and expertise and to move prospects from attention to interest."

You also learned in Chapter 2 that there are two types of selling – missionary and service – and in Chapter 8 you learned that not only do the two types of selling generally require different types of salespeople but also that the sales process is different for each. Missionary, development selling has an extra step: prospecting and qualifying. This chapter covers that extra, first step, and you will learn techniques to improve your skills in prospecting and developing new business.

Outbound prospecting

Prospecting is developing leads – finding prospects who need to advertise and then reaching out to them. Mike Weinberg in his helpful book on developing new business, *New Sales Simplified*, writes at the beginning of the book:

> People and companies have needs. Those of us with sales responsibilities represent businesses with potential solutions to those needs…in sales, our incredibly important and

Media Selling: Digital, Television, Audio, Print and Cross-Platform, Fifth Edition.
Charles Warner, William A. Lederer, and Brian Moroz.
© 2020 John Wiley & Sons, Inc. Published 2020 by John Wiley & Sons, Inc.

incredibly straightforward job is to connect with these customers and prospective customers to determine if our solutions will meet their needs. The more and better we do that
simple job, the more successful we will be, and more we will sell.[1]

In media sales you are hired to do missionary selling, service selling, or a hybrid model
that includes both types of selling. If you are hired to do both, you must get guidance
from your sales manager as to what management's expectations are. For example, if you
are hired as one of six salespeople in a small-market (market number 150 or lower) television station, you might be given a list of 50 accounts, 5–7 of which are active. An
active account means that the account is currently running a schedule or has placed a
schedule in the last year and can be reasonably expected to run another schedule in the
next 12 months. In such a situation your sales manager might expect you to spend 20
percent of your time servicing your 5–7 active accounts and 80 percent of your time
developing new business from the remaining 43–45 accounts.

It is vital that you get expectations and priorities from management because you must
be able to plan your time according to management's priorities and then keep track of
your time. There is an almost unavoidable tendency to spend way too much time doing
the easy part of your job, service selling and nursing active accounts, and not spending
enough time on the hard part of the job, developing new business. You must discipline
yourself to stick to your plan and not only develop a strategy for prospecting but also do
the necessary hard work of digging for information.

Another thing to clarify with management is a common language, common definitions of terms. What is a "lead," a "prospect," or an "opportunity?" Generally, a *lead* is a
potential account that has not been contacted or even minimally qualified. A *prospect* is
an account that has been qualified in that (1) it can afford to advertise and (2) is a good
fit with what you are selling. You should scope out prospects using these two criteria
before you contact them. An *opportunity* is a prospect that can afford to advertise, is a
good fit, and that has not only shown interest but is also an account to which you have
given a proposal that is being seriously considered.

Where to find prospects

There are several ways to organize your search for prospects:

1   By current advertisers in other media
2   By season
3   By category
4   By geographic region
5   By advertisers in your medium
6   By inactive accounts
7   By current advertisers
8   By referrals
9   By civic, social, or professional organizations

By current advertisers in other media   The obvious first place to start looking for prospective customers is in other media. It is generally easier, and thus a more efficient use of your time, to sell to prospects who already have an advertising budget than to have to start from scratch with someone and sell them first on advertising, then on your medium, and then on your particular media outlet.

To prospect in other media, you should know something about their prices so you can estimate advertising budgets. Most markets have Kantar Media advertising, monitoring, and evaluation reports which many media companies and most large advertising agencies subscribe to. Each month Kantar publishes details of all radio and television advertising schedules that ran the previous month. If your market does not have monitoring services available, you can ask advertisers or their agencies for rate cards of other media outlets in your market and you and your fellow salespeople can monitor other media on a systematic basis.

For national media such as broadcast and cable network television, magazines, and websites and platforms with national and global appeal, if your company subscribes to the *Ad Age* Data Center reports, you can go www.adage.com/datacenter and get information on Leading National Advertisers (LNA) to get total investment levels by media and by the top 100 national advertisers. The leading national advertisers, through their advertising agencies are the most logical target accounts. You can use Bloomberg BusinessWeek Finance where you can find revenue, profit, and stock price information for public companies. Also, in the Downloads section of www.mediaselling.us you will find a "Media Business and Finance: Reading Financial Reports" article that will give you a basic familiarity with financial terminology and instructions on how to read a balance sheet so you can talk relatively knowledgeably to Chief Executive Officers (CEOs), Chief Finance Officers (CFOs), and Chief Marketing Officers (CMOs) if you find yourself doing so regularly. There are also artificial intelligence (AI) applications, such as Salesforce's Einstein, that can be programmed and used to do much of the grunt work in prospecting.

The most widely used database for prospecting in media sales is The List, which has up-to-date data on marketers, advertisers, and advertising agencies. The List also lists the agency of record of large marketers such as P&G and General Motors (GM), and features automated email notifications of personnel changes at these companies and agencies. Redbooks (generally referred to as the *Red Book*) is another frequently updated ad agency database that is easily searchable. Both The List and Red Book require a paid subscription. Links to all of the information resources mentioned in this chapter appear at the end of the chapter in Resources.

Next, in order to find advertisers that are a good fit for your medium, you should try to pick out the creative approaches different advertisers use, the image they are trying to project about their businesses, and the target audiences for their advertising. Kantar Media has a subscription-based creative monitoring service that will show creative executions for all major national accounts. You can also go to moat.com to see online creative executions for many brands. By evaluating creative approaches, you can assess which advertising is most appropriate for your medium and your medium's target audience. Moat also has a good database on marketers.

Websites for national associations are another good source of information. For example, if you sell for a mid-market TV station and are fortunate to have an auto dealer or two on your prospect list, there are several places you can go on the Internet to get a wealth of information. For example, the website for the National Automobile Dealers Association, has up-to-date news on auto industry trends. There are other industry associations, such as the American Beverage Association, that have informative websites. If you do not know whether or not a business or an industry association has a website, do a Google search on it.

If you work for a television station that is a member of the Television Bureau of Advertising (TVB), its website has many industry profiles and good information about categories of business such as consumer package goods (CPG) advertisers, as does the website of the Radio Advertising Bureau (RAB).

Once you have done your research on a potential target account's business and its creative approach, and have found the name of the person in charge of advertising, go to LinkedIn and get information about that person. LinkedIn is a very useful prospecting tool, because most people have a LinkedIn profile and keep their profiles updated. You should have a profile on LinkedIn so you can find mutual acquaintances who might introduce you or give you a referral to a prospect.

If you sell local broadcast, cable, or digital advertising, read newspaper ads carefully, for they are still fertile ground even though newspaper advertising in general has declined substantially in recent years. Look for a newspaper advertiser's selling points, image, creative approach, and target audience when you examine newspaper ads. If advertisers are continuously getting positions with low reader impact, such as bottom-left, back-of-the-section, or gutter positions (next to the fold), they might be ripe prospects.

If you sell for a local newspaper, radio station, or website, monitor your market's television stations for commercials for local businesses. Television is vulnerable because it is expensive and generally does not have the precise individual targeting capabilities that digital advertising has, and many local businesses, especially car dealers, tend to overinvest in television.

By season Prospecting by seasonal sales patterns is an effective way to organize your prospecting efforts. Most advertisers have seasonal sales patterns; therefore, advertisers should be contacted anywhere from three to six months before their peak selling seasons begin. A salesperson should find out when advertisers set their annual advertising budgets and make promotion plans and contact them at that time. November is obviously too late to start selling advertising for the Christmas season.

By category Another way to organize your prospecting is by category (categories are often referred to as *verticals*). Select a business category, a vertical, such as men's clothing, for example, and begin contacting as many of these businesses as you can. Combine this category-prospecting method with a seasonal one and choose a category that has a seasonal sales peak coming up. You will find that this category method is an excellent way to become an expert in a particular business category and helps you get referrals in that category. As you get prospects to tell you about their advantages over their competitors, you will also learn how to approach those competitors. You can also search on

Google for "ad-sales ratios" and get the latest advertising-to-sales ratios for over 200 business categories. The www.mediaselling.us website has the 2019 ad-sales ratio list in the Downloads section. Having information about the ad-sales ratio for a category, such as department stores (4 percent), helps you assist a department store in setting its overall media advertising budget and investment level in your medium.

Many successful media salespeople have carved out profitable careers by specializing in one or two categories, such as telecommunications, hospitals, supermarkets, automotive industries, banks, and so on.

By geographic region   It often makes sense to organize prospecting efforts geographically. Prospecting geographically is particularly effective in markets that are spread out physically, such as Los Angeles or Jacksonville, Florida. Isolate an area of town that looks promising and start making phone calls to set up appointments. When you do get your appointments, you will save time and gas money by going to one specific area. You can also use the Google Maps app to help you prospect in a new geographical area, because Google Maps typically lists businesses on its maps. For a national medium such as ESPN or Facebook, organizing accounts and prospecting by geographic region such as east, central, and west is sensible, and then within those regions prospecting can be organized using a combination of methods, such as by season and by category.

By advertisers in your medium   You can prospect in your own medium. However, this type of prospecting tends to encourage parasitic behavior and leads to hordes of media salespeople trying to carve up the same advertising pie, which, in turn, often leads to price cutting and overall lower rates. It is better to try to increase the size of the advertising pie by developing advertisers not in your medium whenever possible.

By inactive accounts   Prospect internally by looking at inactive account lists. Go back several years through the files of completed contracts and look for advertisers who were once active but are not currently running. You might be amazed when you ask someone why they are no longer advertising with you and the reply is, "No one asked for my business again." This inactive account would be another easy sale for the disciplined, well-organized prospector. Customer relationship management (CRM) software platforms such as Salesforce, Matrix, and Efficio (Matrix and Efficio are designed specifically for media selling) make it relatively easy to keep track of and reengage inactive accounts.

By current advertisers   Do not overlook the obvious: do not forget your current advertisers. While serving these customers, think of ways to get them to increase their investment with you. Sell promotional packages, special events, longer schedules, or more ads, but do not fail to look at current advertisers as potential prospects for new revenue. Platforms such as Salesforce, Matrix, and Efficio or any virtual assistant software have become a necessity for maintaining effective communications with current advertisers and, thus, being able to upsell them.

By referrals   You should never pass up the opportunity to ask a prospect, a customer, a partner, a friend, or an acquaintance to refer you to someone who might be a potential advertiser. The best referrals are from happy customers and partners, so get in the habit of politely asking for referrals, because you have nothing to lose and sales to gain.

By civic, social, or professional organizations   Arrange your prospecting efforts organizationally, by civil, social, or professional clubs or associations, or by sports, church, business, or fraternal organizations. Insurance salespeople often prospect this way, and so can media salespeople. In larger markets, it's usually a good idea to join Advertising Clubs and other advertising and marketing trade organizations because you get to know and establish relationships with employees and managers from local advertising agencies and marketers.

Prospecting and qualifying steps

Remember, *prospecting* is finding accounts that need to advertise; *qualifying* is finding the *right* accounts that have a good fit with your medium and discovering who the advertising decision-maker is. Whether you spend 20 percent, 50 percent, 80 percent, or 100 percent of your time prospecting, follow the steps below to develop new business:

1   Prioritize accounts according to potential investment, fit, and creditworthiness.
2   Discover who the target account's advertising decision-maker is.
3   Select specific target accounts with most potential.
4   Create a calendar based on seasonality.
5   Develop a tailored sales narrative.
6   Contact target accounts.

Prioritize accounts according to potential investment, fit, and creditworthiness
Determine which accounts have a logical fit with your medium's audience based on (1) the account's business and financial model, (2) an account's target consumer, and (3) its creative approach. Rank them A, B, and C, with A being the best, most logical fit. Next, assess which accounts have the largest potential to invest in advertising, which are typically the businesses with (1) the most revenue and (2) the highest ad-sales ratio. Rank them A, B, and C, with A being the ones with the highest potential. Finally, assess which accounts have good credit ratings and pay their bills on time. In most cases your accounting or business department will check an account's credit for you. Rank them A, B, and C, with A being the most creditworthy. Up-to-date CRM and AI platforms such as Salesforce's Einstein can do this ranking job for you in seconds.

Qualifying Questions. When doing research on an account's target consumer, business and financial model, creative approach, revenue, and ad-sales ratio, it is helpful to have a sense of the type of questions you should ask to determine if an account might be a good fit.

The 22 Qualifying Questions listed in Exhibit 9.1 were labeled *Discovery Questions* in *Media Selling, 4th Edition.* In the fourth edition, media salespeople were instructed to make several calls on an account, to ask the Discovery Questions in order to gather comprehensive information, and then to create solutions to address an account's marketing and advertising problems.

I first developed the Discovery Questions in 1999 when I was VP Sales Strategy and Development in AOL's Interactive Marketing division that sold over $1 billion of advertising. I crafted the questions to be used by the business development group, which sold large advertising deals that sometimes were valued at over $100 million. When selling deals for that much money, it is more than worth the effort to collect in-depth information in order to craft multilayered solutions that address a customer's complex challenges and that are aligned with that customer's goals and strategies.

However, as you learned in Chapter 2, research by the authors of *The Challenger Sale* discovered that in the digital era prospects and customers will generally not take the time to answer detailed questions about their business. *The Challenger Sale* authors, Dixon and Adamson, referred to this reluctance on the part of prospects as "the customer burden of solutions."[2] Also, for smaller, local accounts there is no need to have as much information as would be gathered by asking the 22 Discovery Questions.

On the other hand, when you are prospecting and qualifying an account, you should have as much information as you will find useful in determining if an account might be a good fit with what you are selling, which is why I have listed 22 Qualifying Questions in Exhibit 9.1; you should be able to answer as many of them as possible with a reasonable amount of research. Subsequently, you can gather additional relevant information on your first in-person meeting with a prospect.

Also, in the age of Big Data many sales organizations have a sales operations or sales analytics team that will conduct research on accounts in order to be more efficient and precise in determining appropriate target accounts, because as pointed out in *The Power of Sales Analytics* by Zoltners, Sinha, and Lorimer, good sales analytics can avoid "the overinvestment that many sales forces make in the bottom 30 percent of customers, [which] can cut profits by 50 percent over time."[3]

Furthermore, as noted earlier, AI applications can now do much of the prospecting and qualifying drudgery work. AI applications such as Salesforce's Einstein can do in seconds the type of prospecting and qualifying research as seen in Exhibit 9.1 that a decade ago might have taken days or weeks to complete.

Discover who the target account's advertising decision-maker is   In small businesses, the owner or proprietor typically makes decisions about how much and where to invest in advertising. In a mid-sized business, the decision-maker might be a sales manager, as in auto dealerships, or a marketing manager. In larger organizations, the decision-maker might be the Advertising Director, VP of Marketing, or an organization's advertising agency. Discovering who the advertising decision-maker is requires some digging in LinkedIn, The List, Red Book, or another database, or might take several calls to larger organizations, but it is a vital step in the process in order to avoid wasting time with people who cannot make a decision about advertising.

Select specific target accounts   Target accounts are the ones with most As, as designed by you or an AI application. In a list of 50 accounts you should have, roughly, 10 target accounts. Rank the list of target accounts by investment potential first, then by seasonality.

Exhibit 9.1   Qualifying questions

1 Before making a call, you should research the following information about a prospect.
   A   Size
       • Revenue (sales)?
       • Profit?
       • Number of employees?
2 In your research, you should also develop a profile of the company and find answers to the following questions.
   A   How long has the company been in business?
   B   Business structure? (For example, public company, privately held, corporation, partnership, sole proprietor, franchisor, franchisee
   C   Number of locations/outlets?
   D   Distribution channel? (For example, retail, direct marketing, wholesalers, online, catalogues.)
   E   Type of product/service? (For example, impulse purchase, planned purchase, high priced, low priced, middle range, mass consumer, luxury.)
   F   Peak selling season(s)?
       • Percent of yearly business at peak seasons
   G   Business cycle? (For example, purchase once a day, once a week, once a year, once in a lifetime.)
   H   Five largest customers?
   I   How has the business changed in the past year?
3 Before making a call, you should research the following information about a prospect.
   A   Total marketing budget?
       • Direct selling?
       • Advertising?
       • Promotion? (% trade, % consumer; advertising/promotion ratio)
       • Cause marketing, corporate relations, PR budget?
   B   Total advertising/direct marketing budget in dollars?
       • Advertising rank in industry? (Who is #1, #2, and #3?)
       • National, national spot, local budgets?
       • Digital budgets (search, social media, mobile)?
   C   Advertising as a percent of revenue (sales) – ad/sales ratio.
       • Ad/sales ratio rank in industry (Who is #1, #2, #3?)
       • Advertising rank in industry? ("What competitors spend more and in what media?")
4 Find answers to the following questions:
   A   Who in the organization will make the final decision?
       • A single decision-maker (e.g., CEO, Senior VP, Marketing)
       • The key influencers (e.g., CFO, Senior VP Advertising)
       • Influencers (e.g., ad committee, consultants)
   B   What is the organization's decision-making process like (e.g., fast, slow, consensus, CEO only, consultants)
5 What are the company's marketing goals? Examples:

Introduce new product/service	Create demand
Introduce line extension	Change customer attitudes
Develop/increase traffic	Feature specialty products
Maintain market dominance	Develop seasonal buying
Recapture old customers	Build destination
Expand target market	Build private label

Exhibit 9.1   Qualifying questions (cont'd)

Establish or re-establish image	Increase profit margins
Build brand awareness	Increase response level
Reinforce leadership position	Promote special sales
Promote special events	Increase market share
Increase usage	Move up one market rank
Expand size of pie (market)	Dominate a market

6   What challenges does the company have in achieving its marketing goals?

7   What are the company's primary marketing strategies? (For example, differentiation, focus/niche marketing, low-cost producer, easiest to use)

8   What are the company's secondary marketing strategies? (For example, defense, offense, flanker brand, fighting brand, guerrilla marketing, ambush marketing)

9   What is the company's current market position? (For example, dominant leader, number one, close second, follower, last)

10   Who the company's primary target customer?
   A   What percentage of its business is done by heavy users/big customers? (For example, 85% of product bought by 15% of customers.)
   B   Who are secondary target customers?
   C   Who are the most profitable customers?

11   Why do your customers buy from your company – what is the major appeal?

12   What messages or creative approaches have been most successful for the company in the past?
   A   Who (organization) does the company's creative?
   B   Who (organization) does the company's media planning?

13   What advertising media are the company currently using?
   A   How is budget allocated among the media?
      • Does this allocation reflect current media usage by consumers?
   B   How effective are the media currently being used?
   C   How are the results/response to the company's advertising tracked?"
   D   What advertising challenges are the company having and what are the priorities for addressing those challenges?
   E   Are there any perceptions about the company's brand that they would like to change?

14   What does the company want its advertising/direct marketing to do for it?
   A   What are its advertising goals? (For example, sales/transactions, branding, awareness, information, persuasion, or reminding/reinforcing)

15   Who are the company's three/five biggest competitors?

16   Why do its customers buy from each of the major competitors?
   A   What strategies does the company have to capture share from its competitors?
   B   How does the company differentiate itself from competitors? (For example, price, quality, convenience, location, selection, ease of use, free delivery)

17   What does the company do better than its competitors?
   A   What do the competitors do better than the company does?

18   What does the decision-maker think of your medium of advertising?
   A   Who owns the search terms most valuable to the company's business and industry?
      • Has the company been monitoring its competitors' advertising activity, campaigns, and creative?
   B   Are there any specific goals the company has in mind for its advertising? (For example, Low CPMS, low CPCs, promotions, brand safety)
   C   What advertising/marketing element has produced the best return on investment (ROI)?

Exhibit 9.1   Qualifying questions (cont'd)

---

19   What time of year does the company (A) plan and (B) buy advertising?

20   Does the company use promotions – if so what kind? (For example, sales, rebates, contests, sweepstakes, coupons, free samples)

   A   Is the decision to purchase a medium based on doing a promotion or added value (free)?

   B   Does the company create its own promotions or does it depend on the media or an outside agency or promotion company?

21   What are the company's criteria for judging the best media proposal?

   A   What are its metrics for a successful campaign (For example, sales, ROI, increase awareness)?

22   What do they think of my company?

   A   What is the likelihood that they'd buy from us?

For example, a local car dealer might be number one on your list based on potential investment and a jewelry store number four, but because you are organizing the list in January, you might move the jewelry store up to number one because you want to contact the jewelry store owner about a special Valentine's Day promotion idea before you contact the car dealer for which January and February sales are relatively slow. By the way, do not fall into the trap of thinking that because January and February have traditionally been low sales months for car dealers, a dealer should invest in those months to drive up sales. It will not necessarily work because it is extremely difficult to buck seasonal buying patterns.

Once you have selected your target accounts, it is a good practice to go to Google Alerts and create an alert about each of your target accounts. When you create a Google Alert, you will be sent emails detailing news about these accounts.

Create a calendar based on seasonality   Do some target accounts only advertise at certain times of the year such as a jewelry store that advertises prior to Christmas, Mother's Day, and graduation time? Arrange your target accounts on your calendar based on an account's seasonality, but be sure to give yourself enough lead time to contact each target account, typically three-to-four months before an account's peak season. Work with your marketing or content people to come up with seasonal packages and offerings that tie ad inventory to seasonal content. For example, your news website's editorial people are planning a special Academy Awards feature the day before the Oscar winners are announced on television, so you could put together a special Oscars promotion package that would run banners that surround the Oscars story for a local department store that features cosmetic advertising. AI applications also create the type of calendars mentioned above, if given instructions to do so.

Develop a tailored sales narrative   Now that you have target accounts and a calendar that indicates the best times to contact them, you need to develop the wording for an initial approach that is tailored, or customized, for each target account and that will highlight (1) who you are, (2) what you are selling, (3) how you have helped get results for similar businesses, and (4) why you want a meeting. The wording of your initial approach is not a complete sales story, but is a structured introductory narrative that should be designed to, first, get prospects' attention and, next, arouse their interest.

Later in this chapter, you'll learn how to structure scripts for your hunt for new business and turn prospects into opportunities.

Contact target accounts   There are four ways to make an initial contact (cold call) with prospect decision-makers: (1) in person, (2) on the phone, (3) via email, and (4) via social media.

On one hand, in-person contacts are very effective in terms of getting information about a prospect's marketing objectives, advertising problems (pain points), and competitive challenges in order for you to determine if there is a good fit with your medium and if you can help them. A cold call is defined as "calling on someone who doesn't know you and who isn't expecting your call."[4] The success ratio of getting to talk to a decision-maker and gathering useful information on in-person cold calls has been estimated at over 90 percent. On the other hand, in-person cold calls are not necessarily efficient because of the amount of time it takes to travel and to complete a call. In the same amount of time you can make 20–30 phone calls or send out hundreds or thousands of emails, especially if you use AI applications. In most media selling situations, with the exception being a small market where there is little travel involved in calling on accounts, phone and email prospecting are much more efficient than in-person calls.

Getting through to the decision-maker

Bob McCurdy, Corporate VP of Sales for the Beasley Media Group gave the following advice on how to get through to a decision-maker on his sales blog on "Radio Ink" on November 18, 2018:

> Getting through to the decision-maker is simply everything. The challenge is that these individuals are sometimes difficult to identify and once identified, are difficult to pin down.

> Miller Heiman's book, *Strategic Selling*, refers to key decision-makers as Economic Buyers (EB), the people who have veto power over a proposal and can release the money. Getting an audience with them is one of the most challenging aspects of any salesperson's job.
>
> The sale often begins and ends with the EBs, and it usually takes some creativity to get through to these individuals. A few suggestions:

> 1 Dig deeply and utilize all existing current contacts. Find out everything you can about the individual you want to meet. Build a dossier. We've all heard about six degrees of separation. Locally, it's more like two. Your entree to your EB could even be your next door neighbor, be sitting in your building or in your rolodex.
> 2 Scrub all of the social sites. Google everything written about them, articles, interviews, all of which provide insight as to the best way to initiate contact. Identify hobbies, family, college, charities, awards, etc. Chances are you will find something to "soften" your outreach.
> 3 Create an appointment prep profile. They can be most helpful in determining which type of approach might work best.
> 4 Compile all of this data/info in one place for easy review.

5   Some stalking is OK. Go where the EB goes, for what appears to them to be a random encounter. Be prepared to throw out some fact or insight so that you're remembered. It should sound off the cuff, but should be far from it.

6   Experiment with different approaches. Bob Dylan sang, "When you got nothing, you got nothing to lose." You are not yet on the EB's radar, so you have nothing to lose.

7   Work the family angle; spouse, kids, grandkids. Tickets, meet-and-greets, etc. that enable the EB to look good to their family go a long way.

In my previous professional life, one of my responsibilities was to get in front of marketing and advertising leaders and tell the radio story. I quickly discovered that this kind of meeting was far more important to me than to them, and that getting in front of these execs required some creativity and homework. What follows are a few ways we were able to make these meetings happen.

- The second year of Advertising Week in New York City, we dispatched limos to several high-level, difficult-to-reach agency execs to transport them to and from their various panels around town. They were not alone in the car.

- The CMO of a large automotive corporation was being non-responsive. A deep dive on this individual's work history uncovered that he had worked previously at a Southeast agency. We had the owner of that agency write an email to the CMO confirming we were not chipmunks. Meetings occurred.

- We wanted to discuss radio creative with a guy who had just been voted Worldwide Creative Director, not of the year, but the decade. He seemed like a cool dude. He had just finished a presentation at an industry event and was walking to the exit, which we had staked out. As he was passing by we said, "Great hair, man." He stopped. We talked. And subsequently did a number of radio creative seminars at his agency.

- We learned that a senior automotive marketing executive was flying to New York, arriving late in the evening, and was unable to meet with us. A limo was waiting that night and we had 45 minutes of uninterrupted discussion on the way to Manhattan.

- A hard-to-pin-down agency CEO appeared on the front page of ADWEEK as the industry's Executive of the Year. We wrangled his home address out of his assistant, promising to send a congratulatory gift. We then had a plaque created from ADWEEK's front page engraved with, "Congratulations Dad. You Are The Greatest, But Bob McCurdy Is Not Bad Either," for his kids to give to him. Getting an audience was no longer a problem.

- A senior soft drink marketing executive had moved to town with several teenaged daughters. We had one of our radio stations pull together a grab bag of cool station merchandise along with some concert tickets to assist her kids with their transition to a new city. A relationship was born.

- We got through to Howard Schultz, Starbuck's CEO, through an old coaching friend and the CEO of a major retailer in the Southeast via someone we had met at an ANA event who we had to track down in the UK.

Although these examples occurred a decade ago, if we are creative enough today, we can probably find a way to get through to most EBs. View it as a game. If we can land somebody on the moon, the chances are we can figure out a way to meet the people who control the purse strings and in many ways, our income. Though once we get in front of them, we must be sure to be worth their time or else it is over. Go to it![5]

Developing Prospecting Scripts

There is some controversy about whether it is a good idea for salespeople to use scripts for telling their sales narrative. In *New Sales Simplified*, Mike Weinberg answers the question about scripts with no and yes. The no answer is driven by the fact that when he hears the word "script," he thinks of theater and memorization, and he mentally hears someone reading to him. These are not reactions you want from prospects; therefore, in order to be authentic most salespeople shouldn't read directly from a script, according to Weinberg.[6]

On the other hand, Weinberg is a proponent of call outlines and scripted talking points. "Our calls should be logically structured, and we absolutely should have several key talking points scripted verbatim."[7] The author also points out that consistency matters. By using scripts you can judge what's working and what's not working, which you cannot do if you "change the flow or make up new questions with every call."[8]

Another reason for developing scripts to communicate your sales narrative is that the scripts provide a consistent voice for how a company wants to be perceived. Scripts, in a sense, help an organization control its public-facing tone and image.[9]

See Exhibit 9.2 for an example of a script for an initial in-person call on a target account decision-maker. Exhibit 9.3 is a sample script for a phone call. It is important to view the scripts for in-person calls and phone calls as outlines and talking points that can be customized for each encounter. Also, salespeople must create their own scripts so that they reflect that salesperson's individual personality and voice. Once the scripts are developed, they should not be memorized or read word-for-word, because it's vital to sound natural and authentic, and not come over as stiff and as if reading from a script. The best way to sound natural and conversational is to practice reading over the scripts dozens of times before the first call, or even better, have regular role-playing sessions with other salespeople to sharpen your skills in communicating naturally.

In-person cold calls

For the script in Example 9.2, several assumptions have been made: (1) that the salesperson has never met the prospect, Mike, (2) that Mike is not currently an advertiser and is a male lawyer who recently opened an office, (3) that the salesperson is from the Zimmer Radio and Marketing group in the Columbia-Jefferson City, MO market, (4) the salesperson is Jane Doe, a young female salesperson, and (5) that Mike knows Tami Benus, an advertiser who referred Jane to Mike. See https://zimmercommunications.com/ for details about the Zimmer Radio and Marketing Group.

Objectives of in-person cold calls   The objectives are (1) To establish rapport, (2) to pique curiosity and interest, (3) to establish your credibility and expertise, (4) to establish trust, and (5) to get a discovery/proposal meeting, preferably in person, but if not in person, in an online video conference call.

Exhibit 9.2 Sample script for initial in-person cold call

Introduction

"Good afternoon, Mike, I'm Jane Doe, and I'm with Zimmer Radio and Marketing Group. You might know our radio stations KTGR – Missouri basketball and football, The Eagle – Cardinal Baseball, and Y107, which is the most popular station in town. How are you doing today?

Referral

"Tami Benus suggested I call you because she thought you'd like to hear about how we helped her start her CPA practice."

Prospect/industry knowledge and challenge

"I read that you just opened your practice and that you're going to be specializing in personal injury and liability cases. I think it's certainly a good time to open an office because the number of fatal accidents in Missouri is up eight percent so far this year."

Case study

"When Tami Benus opened her CPA practice, she said the Zimmer Radio and Marketing Group was great with helping find the correct radio station for her target clients. She told me, 'They allowed me to reach my goals faster than I ever dreamed.'"

Directed questions

"Have you thought about the best way to get your name out to the public? Do you have a website yet? And is advertising in sports something you like and think might work for you?"

New information

"Are you a Mizzou sports fan?" (Pause)
"Then you know coach Cuonzo Martin just recruited a point guard who was ranked number seven among high school prospects."

Close

"I'd like to go back to the office and do some more research and generate a few ideas that might work for you. Can we set up an appointment now for me to come back with our Web designer and digital expert so we can explore specifically how we can help you have a successful launch?"

A closer look at the script sections

Introduction On the initial in-person call the first objective is to establish rapport. Therefore, use the decision-maker's first name because it is less formal, more conversational. Jane knew the prospect's name was Mike because she looked him up on LinkedIn, and she knew he's opening a new practice because she read it in a local business journal. However, if the prospect is older (over 55), use "mister" or "miz," or if the prospect has a title such as Dr., use that title. Be informal, but respectful on the first call. Typically, a person with a title will mention how they prefer to be addressed.

In the first meeting, it is usually best not to take notes. Taking notes while a prospect is talking is similar to tape recording the conversation; it makes many people nervous and usually unwilling to open up. Taking notes also requires concentrating on writing them and not concentrating on the prospect. However, immediately after the appointment, make detailed notes while the details are still fresh in your mind.

You never get a second chance to make a first impression. You have about 15 to 30 seconds to create a favorable first impression. Prospects will continue to judge you based on this first impression and reinforce their judgment the remainder of the time they know you. Your initial goal from the moment you lay eyes on your prospects is to get them to like you, which requires using the emotional intelligence, communication, listening, understanding people, and the influence skills you learned in Chapters 5, 6, and 7.

When you shake hands, do exactly what the other person does. If prospects have soft, limp handshakes, you reciprocate. People who have wimpy handshakes are not prone to enjoy aggressive handshakes that involve a tight grip, firm squeezing, and vigorous pumping. In contrast, if people grab your hand, squeeze, and pump heartily, follow their energetic lead. Remember, people like and trust people exactly like themselves. As you talk to prospects, synchronize with their speech patterns and pace.

In the next sentence after the greeting, introduce yourself and your product. If you represent a media outlet such as a well-known platform or website, a TV or radio station or group, a newspaper, or a popular podcast, that in itself will tend to pique interest. You are probably safe in making some stereotype assumptions in your intro about prospects' media consumption patterns. For example, you can make an initial assumption that men like sports, that older men like politics, that young women like popular music. So, in the script in Exhibit 9.2 the assumption is that the prospect, Mike, likes sports and is familiar with the radio stations mentioned, which will more than likely pique his interest in hearing what you have to say. In the first meeting pay particular attention to whether your stereotype assumptions were correct or not, and be prepared to adjust your thinking if they are not.

It is a good idea to end the in-person introduction section with the question "How are you doing today?" because it tends to trigger positive responses in later interactions. If a person responds positively that they are "fine," it is more difficult for them to respond negatively to future questions or statements because, unconsciously, they attempt to be cognitively consistent.

In the excellent book *Predictable Revenue*, the authors recommend that instead of repeating the phrase, "How are you doing today?", which they think is used too often and is hackneyed, the phrase, "Did I catch you at a bad time?" is the best one to use. Test both phrases and see which one you are most comfortable with and what works the best. You'll learn more about A/B testing later in this chapter.

Referral   Always try to use a referral for your initial contact with a prospect if you can get one. Referrals are excellent door openers because they are a socially acceptable way to make a personal connection. Referrals also help you meet the second objective of an in-person call, to pique curiosity and interest in who you are and in what you have to say. Obviously if you have not received permission to use a referral, do not make one up.

Prospect/industry knowledge and challenge   Remember from Chapter 6 how important source credibility is in the communication process? Showing a prospect that you have knowledge of their business or industry is a good way to fulfill the third objective, to establish your credibility and expertise. By demonstrating that you have done some research indicates that you have some level of expertise and it increases the prospect's curiosity about what you might have to offer. Mention the prospect's challenge, which in the above situation is to launch his legal practice.

Case study   A case study is a success story about how a business got results by advertising in your medium. See examples of case studies, or "performance stories," for different advertisers at the ESPN Customer Marketing website, https://espncms.com. Including a case study in a prospect's category or about a businessperson that the prospect knows is a vital element of the script because it serves as proof of performance, or at least a validation of your medium's ability to get results, which is what any prospect eventually wants. Also, note that the case study has a customer focus; it's about an obvious benefit of your product for a customer – results – not about the product's features, or advantages, or price.

Directed questions   A directed question is a way for you to begin to fulfill the fourth objective, to build trust by getting basic information that helps you identify some problems, challenges, and pain points the prospect has and sets the stage for you to do some research for insights and solutions that are customized for the prospect. A directed question also prompts prospects to give you more information.

New information   In a 2018 Radio Ink column, Bob McCurdy writes: "I was speaking last week with a client whom I had not previously met, and right after the introduction pleasantries, her first question was, "OK, so tell me something I don't know."[10] When you give a prospect some new information about your product, as in Exhibit 9.2 about Missouri basketball, you reinforce your expertise and continue to build trust. In effect, you are saying, "Hey, I know my business and am going to be a source of information for you now and in the future." Also, the new information might spark a conversation about what you mentioned. Does the prospect find the new information interesting and useful? Does the prospect react positively or negatively? You introduce new information in an attempt to find something that the prospect likes or dislikes so you can find areas of agreement.

A good way to prepare for a call and get new information you can pass on is to use Google Alert to gather news stories and tidbits about an account you plan to call on.

In your conversations with prospects, you may touch on a subject that you will disagree on. Do not be hypocritical and agree with something you really do not believe. Keep probing until you find something you can agree on and then say, "I agree 100 percent." Try to compliment your prospect on something specific, which usually gets prospects talking. If prospects brings up any negatives about salespeople in general, your medium, or your company, honor them and compliment them for bringing up the point. People will tend to trust you if you show confidence in yourself and in your product and are not afraid to deal with negative comments. The two-sided argument is particularly effective at this time. For example, if in a conversation a prospect makes a negative comment about radio, you might say, "Yes, that's a good point, Mike. Radio does have some limitations. You can't demonstrate or show products on radio or you can't show how you look. On the other hand, radio is far more cost efficient than television, radio is driven by a human voice, which means it can be warm, friendly, and intimate; and an effective creative approach can work wonders like it did for Tami Benus when she opened her CPA practice."

Close   In the close section, you are attempting to meet the fifth objective, to get a discovery/proposal in-person meeting. The second meeting is not necessarily to sell something, but, rather, to see if you can help the prospect and to present some alternatives based on research you are going to do. This helping approach puts you on the side of the prospect and tends to continue to build trust.

The Trust Equation is:

$$Trust = \frac{Credibility + Reliability + Authenticity}{Perception\ of\ Self - Interest}$$

The Trust Equation was developed by Anne Raimondi, former Director of Product at eBay, VP of Marketing at Survey Monkey, and Chief Operating Officer (COO) of Earnin.[11] Salespeople should always have the Trust Equation in the back of their minds when they are dealing with prospects, customers, and partners and realize that the more they are seen as being self-interested, the lower the level of trust is. This formula reinforces the importance of customer focus – putting the customer first, helping the customer get results – not putting yourself or your interests first.

It is conceivable that when you attempt to schedule a second discovery/proposal meeting that the prospect might be eager to get going right away. If this is the case, move forward by asking the prospect some basic discovery questions, such as (1) How much is their advertising budget and how much they think they ought to invest at this time? (2) What, specifically is their target audience? (3) Do they want traffic to their store or to their website? and (4) What keeps them up at night? (5) What are their greatest challenges? and (6) Do they know what they want to say, what their story is, what their creative approach is? If a prospect is truly interested, go as far forward to a final sale as you can, but do not close a deal on the first call. At the very least say something like, "I need to go back to the office, see what's available, do some research on what will work best for you, and come up with some ideas for an approach for your copy, because I to want make sure you stand out and are differentiated from your competitors. I can come back first thing in the morning."

Cold calls by phone

Prospecting by phone is not as effective as it was 10 years ago because of the vast increase in the number of media outlets, digital agencies, and digital marketing partners that are vying for the attention of advertisers and potential advertisers. If you do not have an established relationship or do not represent a high-profile media outlet, it is extremely difficult to get a response on the phone from a prospect. But that does not mean you should not use the phone to make prospecting phone calls; just be aware that it is not an easy method of prospecting. If you do make cold calls by phone, the script structure remains mostly the same as with in-person cold calls, but the objectives are a little different:

Objectives of phone cold calls   The objectives are (1) to pique curiosity and interest, (2) to establish your credibility and expertise, (3) to establish trust, and (4) to get a discovery/proposal meeting.

It is not as easy to establish rapport on the phone as it is in person because you are not face-to-face, you cannot shake hands, and you cannot observe body language. Therefore, you have to attempt to pique a prospect's curiosity and interest right off the bat. Furthermore, even though you will be using a script for phone prospecting calls, these calls rarely go as planned or as scripted. On the phone, you must remain flexible and go where the prospect takes you and not stick to the script; you need to be able to ad lib.

Exhibit 9.3 is a sample phone prospecting script.

Exhibit 9.3   Sample script for initial phone contact

Introduction
"Hi, Mike?"
"I'm Jane Doe, and I'm with Zimmer Radio and Marketing Group. You might know our radio stations: KTGR, which broadcasts Missouri basketball and football; The Eagle, an ESPN sports station that carries Cardinal baseball; and Y107, the most popular radio station in town. Let me steal a minute." (Pause)

Referral
"Tami Benus suggested I call you because she thought you'd like to hear about how we helped her start her CPA practice."

Prospect/industry knowledge and challenge
"I read that you just opened your practice and that you're going to be specializing in personal injury and liability cases. I think it's certainly a good time to open an office because the number of fatal accidents in Missouri is up eight percent so far this year."

Case study
"When Tami Benus opened her CPA practice, she said the Zimmer Radio and Marketing Group was great with helping find the correct radio station for her target clients. She told me, 'They allowed me to reach my goals faster than I ever dreamed.'"

Directed questions
"Have you thought about the best way to get your name out to the public? Do you have a website yet? And is advertising in sports something you like and think might work for you?"

New information
"Are you a Mizzou sports fan?" (Pause)
"Then you know coach Cuonzo Martin just recruited a point guard who was ranked number seven among high school prospects."

Close
"I'd like to set up a time when I can visit you and show you how we hit it out of the park for Tami Benus's opening and then see if we can help you."

A closer look at the script sections

Introduction   On the initial phone call the first objective is to pique curiosity and interest. Use the prospect's first name because it is less formal, more conversational, just as you did on the in-person call.

Pacing is key when you are talking on the phone. You want to get to the point quickly and pause often to get responses and make the call as interactive as possible. Synchronize with a prospect's speech patterns and pace – fast in New York, slower in the South, for example.

If you are using an office phone or a cell phone for your calls, make sure to use headphones, ear buds, or Air Pods so you can keep your hands free to take notes. Sit in front of your computer screen with the script clearly visible. On a regular basis stand up and talk as you walk around. Not only is the exercise good for your health, but also when you stand up and talk you sound livelier, more energetic.

In the next sentence after the greeting, introduce yourself and your product. If you represent a well-known media outlet, that in itself will tend to pique interest.

Some experts recommend *not* opening with "Can I have a minute of your time," or "Did I catch you at a good time?" These questions can be answered with a "no" too easily. Mike Weinberg recommends the question "May I steal a minute?" because it's "Acknowledging on the front end that I'm an unexpected intrusion. It's human and real. In a subtle way, it lets the prospect know that I get it."[12] If the answer is "yes" to this question, you have permission to proceed. If the answer is "no," you have the opportunity to tell (do not ask) the prospect that you will call back. The second call will be easier because the prospect will more than likely remember that you were sensitive to the situation on the first call.

On the other hand, Ross and Tyler in *Predictable Revenue* recommend using the opening question "Did I catch you at a bad time?",[13] the same question they recommend for the opening of an in-person cold call. I tend to prefer Weinberg's "May I steal a minute?" which is a little more unusual and not trite. A/B test both or use another opening introduction line that seems authentic to your style, but A/B test this opening line often because people's tastes and perceptions change, and you have to feel comfortable with your approach wording. See below for more about A/B testing.

Referral   Use a referral if you have one.

Prospect/Industry knowledge and challenge   This establishes your credibility and expertise.

Case study   Use case studies ("performance stories") to enhance your credibility. See "How to Write an Advertising Success Case Study" in the Downloads section of http://www.mediaselling.us for instructions on how to write a case study.

Directed questions   You are building trust by not attempting to sell something or talking about your product, you are getting information about a prospect's problems, competitive challenges, and pain points.

New information   You need to be flexible with the new information element, which, of all the elements in the structure of a script, is the easiest to drop. However, if you use Google Alert or have an AI application that gathers sentiment analysis or information about an account, you will almost always have some new information you can introduce.

Close   In the close section, you are attempting to meet the fourth objective, to get a discovery/proposal meeting in-person or online. Note that the script does not use the term "meeting" or "appointment" and uses "visit" instead because, as Mike Weinberg recommends, no one likes meetings and appointments, they remind people of unpleasant appointments with a doctor or dentist. Visits are more informal, more fun, and are likely to produce less anxiety. For an online meeting, there are a number of options for sales enablement software such as Clear Slide, Show Pad, Slide Share, or HubSpot. Or there are video call and meeting platforms such as Skype, Zoom, and Join.me that you can use if you cannot get an in-person visit.

Voicemail

If you do not get an answer to a prospecting phone call, which happens most of the time, make sure you use voicemail effectively so that you increase the odds of getting a call back. Think of a voicemail as being an audio version of an email because many people use phone-answering apps such as Google Voice, You Mail, Pinger Text File, Line 2, or Instavoice that translate voice messages into email texts that are read rather than listened to.

A message that you leave on voicemail should last no longer than a minute and should communicate that you respect the time the prospect's time and, so, will not take up too much time on a call back. Do not mention sales or selling but emphasize you are interested in showing how you might be able to help a prospect. Exhibit 9.4 is a sample voicemail script.

Exhibit 9.4   Sample script for voicemail

Introduction
"Mike, I'm Jane Doe, with Zimmer Radio and Marketing Group. You might know our radio stations KTGR which broadcasts Missouri basketball and football; The Eagle which carries Cardinal Baseball; and Y107, the most popular radio station in town.

Prospect/industry knowledge and challenge
"The reason I called you is because I read that you just opened your practice and that you're going to be specializing in personal injury and liability cases. I think it's certainly a good time to open an office because the number of fatal accidents in Missouri is up eight percent so far this year."

Case study
"When Tami Benus opened her CPA practice, she said the Zimmer Radio and Marketing Group was great with helping find the correct radio station for her target clients. She told me, 'They allowed me to reach my goals faster than I ever dreamed.'"

Close
"I'd like to talk to you about how the Zimmer Radio and Marketing Group can get similar results for you. Please call me back at 573-875-1099, that's Jane Doe at 5…7…3…8…7…5…1…0…9…9."

A closer look at the script sections

Introduction   Use the decision-maker's first name. Be informal and conversational, not pushy or aggressive.

Referral   Generally, don't use a referral when leaving a voicemail because it takes up too much time. If you have one, you can integrate it into the case study section.

Prospect/industry knowledge and challenge   Note the line "the reason I called." This is a good phrase to use when leaving a voicemail because it defines the purpose of the call.

Case study   The case study section of the script must be short, but it is a necessary proof of performance that must be included in a voicemail.

Close   In a voicemail you are trying to get a call back and you will increase your chances if you ask a provocative question. The last thing you utter on a voicemail is your phone number. Say it twice, and the second time say it slowly as though you are waiting for the person who is listening to the voicemail to write down each number. Remember from Chapter 6 that primacy and recency are the two elements in a communication that people tend to remember most. You want your phone number to be the last thing people hear (recency).

Voicemail Don'ts

Jack Loechner in a Media Post article quotes Jeff Hoffman of HubSpot who shares some common mistakes that salespeople tend to make when leaving voicemail messages:

- One mistake is leaving the "just following up" voicemail. These too-casual calls do not give the recipient a reason to call back, says Hoffman. Closing with phrases like "get back to me when you can" or "just wanted to follow up" does not clearly define a purpose for the call. Instead, Hoffman suggests ending the voicemail with a call to action…ask a question before ending with your phone number, enticing the other person to call back (and in a timely manner).
- Another mistake is rambling. "When leaving a voicemail, be conscious of the time spent doing so. In general the sweet spot for voicemails is 25–40 seconds. As Hoffman explains, "under 25 seconds looks like you dialed and hung up. Over 40 seconds looks too long."
- And *always* leave a voicemail; do not let concerns over mistakes stop you. As Hoffman writes, "If you don't leave a voicemail, you've set the precedent your messages aren't important to listen to or respond to."[14]

Email prospecting

In recent years, email has become the primary prospecting tool for many media companies, especially for websites and apps that are not well-known, are not established brands, or are not high-profile media outlets without the massive reach that Google, Facebook,

ABC, NBC, CBS, ESPN, Fox News, and iHeart Media have. Some of the reasons email is a primary prospecting tool are: (1) time constraints on advertising and marketing decision-makers have tightened with the fragmentation of media, which has meant that there are vastly more media options to consider and evaluate, (2) media placement decisions have become a more collaborative effort because of the perceived risk involved due to concerns about digital advertising and online content that heightened after the 2016 presidential election, (3) finding decision-makers' phone numbers has become much more difficult with the virtually universal switch from corporate business phone numbers to individual smartphone numbers, and (4) the rapid adoption of voicemail apps such as Google Voice and YouMail that use algorithms to screen, answer, and translate calls to text.

Another reason email prospecting has proliferated is because of the facility email provides for A/B testing subject lines, script template structure, offers, and content, all of which can now be facilitated by AI applications such as Salesforce, Efficio, Matrix, HubSpot, Conversica, a virtual sales assistant, and the Gmail plug-in, Boomerang, and its feature, Respondable, which uses AI to help improve email wording as you compose an email.

The script structure for email prospecting is similar to that for in-person and phone prospecting, as are the objectives.

Objectives of a prospecting email   The objectives are (1) to pique curiosity and interest, (2) to establish your credibility and expertise, and (3) to get a discovery/proposal meeting online or offline.

It is virtually impossible to establish rapport in an email. Therefore, you have to attempt to pique a prospect's curiosity and interest right off the bat. Exhibit 9.5 is a sample email script, which makes the same assumptions as the scripts above do.

Exhibit 9.5   Sample script for prospecting email

Subject line
Hey, Mike, Columbia and Jefferson City's Most Popular Radio Stations Helped Tami Benus

Introduction
I'm Jane Doe with the Zimmer Radio and Marketing Group. You might know our radio stations: KTGR, which broadcasts Missouri basketball and football; The Eagle, an ESPN sports station that carries Cardinal baseball; and Y107, the most popular radio station in town.

Referral
Tami Benus suggested I contact you because she thought you'd like to hear about how we helped her start her CPA practice.

Prospect/industry knowledge and challenge
I read that you just opened your practice and that you're going to be specializing in personal injury and liability cases. I think it's certainly a good time to open an office because the number of fatal accidents in Missouri is up eight percent so far this year.

Case study
When Tami Benus opened her CPA practice, she said the Zimmer Radio and Marketing Group was great with helping find the correct radio station for her target clients. She told me, "They allowed me to reach my goals faster than I ever dreamed."

Exhibit 9.5 Sample script for prospecting email (cont'd)

To learn more about how we helped Tami and about all the services we provide to help our partner get results, please go to http://zimmercommunications.com. Check out our free marketing guides like"6 Steps to Converting Your Marketing Leads" and download them.

Directed questions
Have you thought about the best way to get your name out to the public? Do you have a website yet? And is advertising in sports something you like and think might work for you?

Close
I'd like to set up a time when I can visit you and show you how we hit it out of the park for Tami Benus's opening and then see if we can help you. Do you have 20 minutes next Tuesday or Wednesday? What times work for you? Feel free to reply to this email, or you can ring me directly at 573-875-1099.

Thanks,
Signature
Jane Doe
Certified Radio Marketing Consultant
Zimmer Radio Marketing Group
573-875-1099

A closer look at the email script sections

Subject line An email's most important element is the subject line, and it must be customized. A report by author Ryan Myers from *Sales and Marketing Management* was quoted in a May 22, 2018 Media Post "Research Brief" and it read in part:

> Landing sales meetings from a cold email exchange takes persistence and a data-driven approach to crafting the right messages and responses. For example, simply personalizing cold emails can increase open rates by as much as 100%…If you send out 1,000 carbon-copied emails to random businesses, you shouldn't be surprised when most go unopened… On average, canned business emails are opened only between 15 and 29% of the time, depending on the industry. Yet when [we] sent 1,000 customized emails to the busiest people [we] could find, about 700 emails successfully were sent through. Of those, the open rate was a whopping 45%.[15]

An informal customized subject line ("Hey, Mike") demonstrates to decision-makers that the message was specifically designed for them. Referrals, if you have them, are the most effective element you can put in a subject line because they are almost certain to pique interest and curiosity and increase the odds that the email will be opened.

If you do not have a referral, drop a hint about a case study for a similar business, organization, or candidate. For example, "Hey, Mike, We Hit A Grand Slam For A CPA's Business Launch." Or how about, "Hey, Mike, Worried About A Weak Launch Of Your Practice?"

Think long and hard about a prospecting email's subject line, try dozens of them, keep them informal, seemingly casual, and always try to address directly or by implication a prospect's problem, pain point, or challenge.

Introduction   An introduction should inform a prospect who you are and who you work for. In an email use 14- or 16-point type, do not use a smaller font size because emails with less than 14-point type are hard to read, and look unimportant.

Referral   Repeat the referral that you used in the subject line if you have a referral, if not, go to the next section.

Prospect/industry knowledge and challenge   Always talk about the prospect's business before you talk about your business. By writing that you know something about their business you establish your credibility and customer focus.

Case study   In a prospecting email always refer to a case study that details how your media outlet has helped a similar business, organization, or political candidate get results. Also include in the case study section a link to your website where prospects can learn more about how your medium solves marketing and advertising problems and about the variety of services or products you offer.

Directed questions   Ask directed questions that link a prospect's problems to your solutions.

Close   The close in an email is a call for action; it asks for a visit (or appointment) to see if there is a fit. You are not selling yet; you have not given details about your features or advantages. You are writing from the prospect's, the decision-maker's, point of view. You are taking a helping approach.

Signature   Include your name, title, business name, and phone number. Having a well-designed, professional-looking signature lends gravitas and importance to your name and title. If you have been certified by the IAB, RAB, Salesforce or other professional organizations, do not fail to let prospects know because it enhances your credibility and perception of expertise, thus increasing your chances of getting an appointment. If you have a small image of your organization's logo, use it in the signature.

Script templates

Templates for all scripts should be kept in some kind of source repository such as Google Docs, Dropbox, or a sales enablement software or CRM platform such as Salesforce, Matrix, Efficio, Yesware, SalesLoft, or Hubspot so that salespeople can easily access them and then log their use of them.

The scripts in Exhibits 9.2, 9.3, 9.4, and 9.5 can be downloaded from www.mediaselling. us in the Downloads section.

A/B testing scripts

One of the advantages of using scripts is that you can test and then optimize the wording. In order to do A/B testing you must label each script and keep an accurate log on which scripts you used on each call you make or email you send. For the testing to be reliable, you need to have a reasonable number of incidences – a sample of at least 40 or more calls or emails. So, test Script A one week and Script B the next week, then you will have a reasonable sample to analyze and see which wording works best.

For example, in phone scripts you might change the order of the new information and the directed question section. Label as Script A the one that has the directed question after the case study section and label as Script B the one that has new information following the case study. Or, on the phone one week you could test the line in the introduction that reads, "Let me steal a minute," and replace it the next week with, "Is this a bad time?" Mike Weinberg's advice about "stealing a minute" might be wrong, and the only way you will know is to A/B test various wording.

For emails, continually A/B test a wide variety of subject lines – formal vs. informal, statements vs. questions, for example. A/B test the position of the directed question and the new information section. A/B test leaving out the new information and case study sections and, thus, make a test email short with just a question in it.

To learn more about how to conduct valid and reliable A/B testing, read *HBR Guide To Data Analytics Basics for Managers*.

Also, when you use a sales enablement platform such as Salesforce, Matrix, or Efficio or an email platform such as Mail Chimp or Boomerang, it allows you to see which prospects are opening your emails and which are clicking to go to your website and, thus, demonstrating interest in your solutions. This information gives you an excellent reason to follow up with a phone call or another email.

Organizing email prospecting

Response rates for prospecting emails range from 10 to 30 percent, sometimes higher – up to 50 percent – if the emails are customized and particularly effective. Therefore, email prospecting efforts should be organized in such a way as to take into consideration the response rates that an organization has tracked over time and fit the response rate to the size of a sales staff. For example, if a sales staff has two development salespeople and if typical response rates are 18 percent, then if a sales staff sends out 100 emails one week, 18 responses will turn 18 prospects into 18 leads. Eighteen leads divided evenly by two salespeople means each salesperson has nine leads to follow-up on.

Organizing a prospecting system will be different for each sales team, so figure out through trial and error what works best for your situation and then stick to the system you develop.

Social media prospecting

LinkedIn is the best overall social-media prospecting tool. Use it to discover information about the people you are going to contact, because it helps you know them better and, therefore, aids you in determining what new information might appeal to a prospect. Follow target account prospects on Instagram and Twitter. Often when you follow someone, they will follow you, which gives you an excellent potential opening opportunity. If you follow prospects on Twitter, make sure you occasionally retweet some of their Tweets, as they will generally appreciate it, which gives you another opening for contacting them. Most companies have a Facebook page, so make sure you become familiar with prospects' pages if they have one. Again, it gives you the opportunity to give them a compliment on their page in an introduction.

Also make sure that you regularly post on Instagram and Twitter so if prospects know that you follow them, they might follow you. And keep your LinkedIn profile up to date and interesting for the same reason.

The top six prospecting mistakes development salespeople make

In *Predictable Revenue*, the Aaron Ross and Marylou Tyler list the top six mistakes that they believe salespeople make when prospecting:

1 *Expecting instant results*. It often takes weeks, even months, to close a deal with a larger company that has several decision-making levels, or, perhaps, it is not the right season. There are many legitimate reasons why an opportunity doesn't close quickly. Be patient and keep in mind that marketers will buy on their schedule, not yours, and pressing to close too hard can kill a deal. Persistence is the key.
2 *Writing long emails*. Long emails can be hard to process, especially when so many people read them on their cell phones. Keep emails as concise as possible; use Boomerang's Respondable feature.
3 *Going wide, not deep*. Hitting 100 accounts once instead of 10 accounts 10 times each. Focus on the accounts with the best fit.
4 *Giving up too quickly at ideal targets*. If an account is the right fit, stay on it until you get an absolute no from the decision-maker. Be "pleasantly persistent."[16]
5 *Not giving up quickly enough on non-ideal targets*. Persistence is valuable, but is also a double-edged sword. Being persistent with an account that is not a good fit is a waste of time.
6 *Depending on activity metrics rather than a proven process*. Throwing lots of activity at an objective such as calls placed is not as good as tracking call conversations per day or appointments per week. Focus on results – appointments – not merely how many calls were made or how many emails were sent out.

Inbound Prospecting

In-person cold calls, cold calls by phone, and cold-call emails are all outbound prospecting – identifying target accounts that have a logical fit with your medium and contacting them. However, it is virtually impossible to identify every possible business, organization, political candidate, or advocacy group that could possibly need help in reaching its target audience. Therefore, in order to generate inbound leads a well-planned marketing program is required. Marketing tools such as a website, webinars, blogs, podcasts, articles in business-oriented publications, booths at trade shows and conferences, and ads in your own medium can bring in leads.

A well-designed, interactive website on which someone can get information about your medium, your product, your services, how you help get results, what your customers say about you, and how to contact you is an essential tool for generating leads. The Zimmer Radio and Marketing Group website at https://zimmercommunications.com is an excellent example of a well-designed, interactive website for a group of small-market radio stations. ESPN's Customer Marketing and Sales website at http://espncms.com/advertise-on-espn.html is a great example of a national media website on which an interested marketer can not only get detailed information in the form of tool kits, information about the creative services ESPN offers, and information about ESPN's different products (sports, TV, digital, audio, and ESPN Desportes) but also anyone can actually create a campaign and buy advertising on ESPN via the website. Verizon Media's website at https://www.verizonmedia.com/insights is also effective in providing the type of information and case studies that might interest marketers and generate leads.

Information-based webinars, blogs, podcasts, and articles in business publications are other elements in a marketing toolkit that can create curiosity and interest and, thus, generate incoming leads. Ross and Tyler call these tools "marketing as teaching," a concept that is in harmony with one of the main precepts of this book, which considers selling as educating.[17] Make sure that if you use any of these tools, they are not a sales pitch; they must be educational, informative, and useful. See the Zimmer Radio and Marketing Group blog at https://info.zimmercommunications.com/blog as an example of providing useful information. Booths at trade shows and conferences can create interest in your company, product, or medium, as can running ads in your own medium that are directed to potential advertisers. Such ads should be written so that they drive traffic to your website.

Many companies depend on a multifaceted marketing campaign to produce leads rather than hiring and depending on a staff of missionary/development salespeople, because sales management feels that getting inbound leads through marketing is more efficient than having salespeople do the digging. The authors of *Predictable Revenue* suggest one reason that marketing is more efficient is because experienced salespeople "hate to prospect."[18] My experience in media sales leads me to agree, and, therefore, if a media company is going to have a development sales staff, it is often better to hire inexperienced people to do it, because newly hired salespeople often do not have preconceived notions or a negative attitude about prospecting.

How to handle inbound leads

In pre-Internet days non-solicited inquiries were referred to as *coming in over the transom*, but now they are most often referred to as being inbound. Many larger companies that receive lots of incoming leads have a market-response salesperson or team or even an AI virtual assistant such as IPsoft's Amelia to deal with inbound leads. In smaller organizations that do not have a market-response team or virtual assistant, sales management must figure out the best way to deal with incoming leads. If accounts in a sales department are assigned by category, or vertical, which I strongly recommend, then inbound leads should be distributed based on which category they are in.

If a sales department is not organized by category, then it is best to distribute inbound leads on a rotating basis, which is the fairest way to distribute accounts. Or, some sales managers give inbound leads to the last-hired salesperson in an attempt to build that person's confidence and account list. Whatever system is ultimately used, it is imperative that it be perceived as fair by the entire sales staff. One way *not* to deal with inbound leads is for sales management to handle them and then put them in a house account, or an account on which no commissions or bonuses are paid.

Sales Management Tips to Improve Prospecting

It is vital that media salespeople have a variety of tools for prospecting and qualifying because as Peter Kazanjy, co-founder of TalentBin, writes in his article on prospecting, "Here are the scripts for sales success – emails, calls and demos that close deals," "you can't build a house with just a hammer. You need the right tools for each part of the job."[19]

Tools such as a sales narrative and scripts for different types of prospecting cold calls are important, but so are management coaching, training, and involvement. Below are 18 sales management tips cherry picked from "The 39 best pieces of sales advice you'll hear this year" articulated by Wiley Cerilli in an interview in First Round Review.[20] Even though Cerilli is a tech startup entrepreneur, his advice is excellent for media sales managers whose salespeople have to prospect for new business. Too many media sales managers, especially in traditional media such as newspapers, magazines, radio, and television manage the same way they always have – by fear and "kicking ass," which no longer works with millennials.

Here are Cerilli's tips:

- *You need a scripted sales pitch designed to hit your metrics*. "It takes months and months of testing to come up with the right formula" to see what resonates.[21]
- *Test in a weekly schedule*. "All of the tests you're running can be affected by a lot of things – people's personal lives, how many closes they've had recently, a string of particularly hard targets, etc."[22] You want to end up with scripts that work best under most conditions. Do not test more than one or two changes per repetition or you will not know what works.
- *Adopt a buyer's mentality*. What do buyers want to buy? Always keep in mind WIIFM (What's in it for me?).
- *Don't oversell*. One major way people oversell is offering too many features. Keep it simple.
- *Put new recruits through bootcamp*. Train all new hires for a week before making sales. Training includes everything from breaking down personality tests so they know what kind of prospect they are talking to, to written tests, and to listening in on hours and hours of live sales calls. This last phase includes making simulated calls to their manager and other salespeople in the company to see if they can sell to the toughest audience.
- *Immerse hires in success*. Play recordings of successful calls on a weekly basis. "When you play them calls that were made by people they work with who got the sale, people start assuming that they are going to make the sale too."[23] Statistics show that when you make a sale, the probability of you making a sale on the next call is way

higher. When people assume success, they go in with the confidence necessary to make it a self-fulfilling prophecy.

- *Give people goals they can hit.* As you learned in Chapter 4, goal setting is an art, and a big part of that art is setting achievable goals that are challenging (moderately difficult) but doable.
- *Have a script in front of people at all times.* This goes for new and old hires. You want people to stick to what has been tested and that works. Print out a new version of the scripts every week, and do not have more than one script change a week.
- *Teach hires to sell with customer stories.* You don't want salespeople using words like "I" or "we" when they are selling on the phone. No one cares why someone they don't know thinks a product is awesome. You want salespeople to communicate why customers think the product is awesome.
- *Make constant coaching practical.* Make it possible for managers to monitor and help their salespeople by using a phone system such as ShoreTel's M5 system. This allows managers to not only listen in on calls, but also provide real-time feedback such as, "Hey, it sounds like they're still worried about X. Why not try Y?"[24]
- *Kick off Mondays on the right note.* Begin every week with a sales meeting where the focus is on positive motivation. Account managers read a "wow" customer success story so salespeople can hear the impact they are making for the people they call. Also, play a recording of a particularly good call and crown that person King or Queen for the week, and have a crown to give them.
- *Motivate with group competition.* Run all kind of competitions for teams: Who spent the most minutes on the phone? Who had the most meetings? Who has the longest winning streak?
- *Make it fun.* Have themes like March Madness or Battle of the Sexes. Give silly awards such as Legos. People will build Lego towers and have a ball.
- *Celebrate victories everywhere you can.* Communicate wins every time you can. Send out emails to the whole team about the biggest sale of the week or of the month. Award actual prizes, whether it's cookies or doughnuts or a day of go-karting.
- *Celebrate the Nos, too.* When people hit their first 10 Nos, ring a bell or a gong and celebrate that too; it helps people get past the fear of rejection.
- *Bring customers in as much as possible.* People are typically fascinated with the media, so when it is feasible, bring customers to the office, station, or studio and have them tell their success story. Both customers and salespeople love it.
- *Start a meaningful speaker series.* Often speaker series are not well attended, but they will be if you invite CEOs or top executives of other sales-oriented companies to talk about their sales struggles and how they handled them.
- *Run product demos early and often.* Bring in people from the content team to talk about features of your product or medium – editorial decision-makers, producers, writers, editors, actors, for example. Get the salespeople to feel like they own the product/content and love it.

Because in the process of prospecting salespeople get at least 10 nos for every yes, keeping a positive attitude is imperative, and doing so is really hard in the face of continual rejection. Therefore, creating a fun, positive, upbeat sales culture as outlined above is vital. One thing to emphasize with development salespeople when they get rejected and think they have failed is, "'Failure' is just your judgment on an experience, because there are no failures, just learning opportunities."[25] This aphorism reinforces the importance of the first and last letters in the AESKOPP system selling – A and P – attitude and persistence.

But if you maintain a positive attitude and are persistent, you will see a satisfying number of yeses for a meeting in which you can scope out the prospect and see if there is a good fit with what you have to offer. Preparing for that second meeting is the subject of Chapter 10.

Test Yourself

1. What are the nine ways to organize a search for target accounts?
2. What are the six steps for prospecting and qualifying?
3. What two factors determine if an account is a good fit with what you are selling?
4. What are the three types of prospecting cold calls?
5. What are the five objectives of an in-person cold call?
6. What is another name for a case study?
7. What is the Trust Equation?
8. What are the four objectives of a cold call by phone?
9. What are two mistakes salespeople tend to make when leaving voicemails?
10. What are the three objectives of email prospecting?
11. What is A/B testing?
12. What are at least three platforms for in-bound prospecting?
13. What are at least five tips for sales management to improve prospecting?

Project

Assume you are a salesperson for a local news website. Write a script for a prospecting phone call. Assume the prospect you are calling answers yes to all of your questions. Rehearse reading your script several times, and then record yourself. Play back the recording. Did you sound friendly and confident? Would you give you an appointment? Make notes on how you could improve your telephone technique and try again. Repeat this exercise until you are satisfied that you sound natural, friendly, authentic, and confident.

References

Antonio, Victor and Glenn-Anderson, James. 2018. *Sales Ex-Machina: How Artificial Intelligence Is Changing the World of Selling*. Alpharetta, GA: Sellinger Group.

HBR Guide To Data Analytics Basics for Managers. 2018. Boston, MA: Harvard Business Review Press.

"Here are the scripts for sales success – emails, calls, and demos that close deals." Retrieved fromhttp://firstround.com/review/here-are-the-scripts-for-sales-success-emails-calls-and-demos-that-close-deals/.

Ross, Aaron and Tyler, Marylou. 2011. *Predictable Revenue: Turn Your Business Into a Sales Machine*

With the *$100 Million Best Practices of Salesforce. com*. Hoboken, NJ: PebbleStorm.

"The 39 best pieces of sales advice you'll hear this year." Retrieved from http://firstround.com/review/The-39-Best-Pieces-of-Sales-Advice-Youll-Hear-This-Year/.

Weinberg, Mike. 2013. *New Sales Simplified: the Essential Handbook for Prospecting and New Business Development*. New York: AMACOM.

Zoltners, Andris A., Sinha, Prabhakant, and Lorimer, Sally E. 2014. *The Power of Sales Analytics*. Evanston, IL: ZS Associates.

Resources

Ad Age data center (www.adage.com/datacenter)

Amelia (www.ipsoft.com/amelia)

American Beverage Association (www.ameribev.org)

American Cities Business Journals (www.acbj.com)

Conversica (www.conversica.com/)

Dun & Bradstreet (https://www.dnb.com)

Efficio Media Sales CRM (www.efficiosolutions.com/solutions/media-sales-crm)

ESPN Performance Stories (www.espncms.com)

Google Alerts (www.google.com/alerts)

Google Boomerang add-on to organize emails (www.boomeranggmail.com)

HubSpot (www.hubspot.com)

IBM's Watson Tone Analyzer (www.ibm.com/watson/services/tone-analyzer)

Kantar Media (www.kantarmedia.com/us/our-solutions)

LinkedIn (www.linkedin.com)

The List (www.winmo.com/thelistonline)

Matrix Media Sales CRM (www.matrixformedia.com)

Moat creative execution website (www.moat.com)

Mobile Marketing Association (MMA) (www.mmaglobal.com)

National Automobile Dealer's Association. (www.nada.org)

National Newspapers Organization (https://www.nna.org)

Papers and articles by Charles Warner (http://charleswarner.us/publications/)

Radio Advertising Bureau (https://www.rab.com)

Red Books agency database (www.redbooks.com)

Salesforce (www.salesforce.com)

Sales Enablement Software aggregator (/www.capterra.com)

Television Bureau of Advertising (www.tvb.org)

The Video Advertising Bureau (www.thevab.com)

Zimmer Radio Group (www.zimmercommunications.com)

Notes

1   Weinberg, Mike. 2013. *New Sales Simplified: The Essential Handbook for Prospecting and New Business Development*. New York: AMACOM.

2   Dixon, Matthew and Adamson, Brent. 2011. *The Challenger Sale: Taking Control of the Customer Conversation*. New York: Portfolio/Penguin.

3   Zoltners, Andris A., Sinha, Prabhakant, and Lorimer, Sally E. 2015. *The Power of Sales Analytics*. Evanston, IL: ZS Associates.

4   Ross, Aaron and Tyler, Marylou. 2011. *Predictable Revenue: Turn Your Business Into a Sales Machine*. Hoboken, NJ: PebbleStorm.

5   McCurdy, Bob. 2018. "How to get face time with 'economic buyers,'" November 18. Retrieved from https://radioink.com/2018/11/18/tactics-for-getting-face-time-with-economic-buyers.

6   Ibid.

7   Ibid.

8   Ibid.

9   "Here are the scripts for sales success – emails, calls, and demos that close deals." Retrieved from http://firstround.com/review/here-are-the-scripts-for-sales-success-emails-calls-and-demos-that-close-deals. WAS 8

10 McCurdy, Bob. "An educated client is a more valuable client." Retrieved from

11 "Use this equation to determine, diagnose, and repair trust." Retrieved from https://firstround.com/review/use-this-equation-to-determine-diagnose-and-repair-trust.

12 Weinberg, Mike. 2013. *New Sales Simplified: the Essential Handbook for Prospecting and New Business Development*. New York: AMACOM

13 Ross, Aaron and Tyler, Marylou. 2011. *Predictable Revenue: Turn Your Business Into a Sales Machine*. Hoboken, NJ: PebbleStorm.

14 Loechner, Jack. 2018. "Cold sales calls can be productive." Retrieved from https://www.mediapost.com/publications/article/312592/cold-sales-calls-can-be-productive.html.

15 Loechner, Jack. 2018. "Heat up cold mail." Retrieved from https://www.mediapost.com/publications/article/319501.

16 Ross, Aaron and Tyler, Marylou. 2011. *Predictable Revenue: Turn Your Business Into a Sales Machine*. Hoboken, NJ: PebbleStorm.

17 Ibid.

18 Ibid.

19 "Here are the scripts for sales success – emails, calls, and demos that close deals." 2018. Retrieved from http://firstround.com/review/here-are-the-scripts-for-sales-success-emails-calls-and-demos-that-close-deals/.

20 "The 39 best pieces of sales advice you'll hear this year." 2018. Retrieved from http://firstround.com/review/The-39-Best-Pieces-of-Sales-Advice-Youll-Hear-This-Year.

21 Ibid.

22 Ibid.

23 Ibid.

24 Ibid.

25 Ross, Aaron and Tyler, Marylou. 2011. *Predictable Revenue: Turn Your Business Into a Sales Machine*. Hoboken, NJ: PebbleStorm.

10

Researching Insights and Solutions

Brian Moroz

In both types of selling – missionary, development selling, and service, agency selling – the second step is researching insights and solutions, and you learned in Chapter 8 that the objective for this second step of selling is to find insights or a Big Idea that will help solve marketing and advertising problems. In the case of missionary selling the researching insights and solutions step of selling comes between an initial contact with a prospect and the second contact or meeting in which you scope out a prospect and see if there is a good fit with what you have to offer. In the case of service selling this step comes after an agency or customer has indicated some interest in learning more about what you have to offer, perhaps even has requested a proposal.

Because of the explosion of Big Data and artificial intelligence (AI), salespeople must be well versed in how to use and analyze data in order to make a compelling case for their product; to give prospects, customers, and partners insights that will make their advertising more effective; and to lend credibility and weight to proposed solutions.

Media Selling: Digital, Television, Audio, Print and Cross-Platform, Fifth Edition.
Charles Warner, William A. Lederer, and Brian Moroz.
© 2020 John Wiley & Sons, Inc. Published 2020 by John Wiley & Sons, Inc.

Introduction

Every business in the current media landscape attempts to make decisions based on data. Data from the users that the business itself owns, publically available data, and at times paid-for third-party data. As we become an increasingly digital global society, the amount of data has skyrocketed, and navigating these vast and complex resources has become an ever more important challenge for brands, agencies, and platforms.

Big Data has upended traditional media planning and creative work, but rather than easily solve formerly difficult questions about what users want, what brands mean, and what products work best, it has led to as many new questions as it answers. To understand the context businesses are working within, consider this:

- Ninety percent of the world's data has been produced in the last two years.
- YouTube alone sees around 300 hours of video uploaded every minute.
- Around 350,000 Tweets occur every minute.

Of course these numbers are only increasing. How are we to make sense of, and more importantly, to strategically use, all of this information?

Data, Observations, and Insights

The first step in harnessing data for your business or for your clients is to understand the distinction between three categories of information that are often conflated. These are data, observations, and insights.

Data

Data is the raw numbers, the spreadsheets, charts, and graphs that give you the tools to develop insights. They are not insights in and of themselves, a common mistake made by sellers in the media industry. A pie chart of how much time people spend on specific devices per day is data. A Google Trends graph is data. A number of retweets is data. None of these are directly useful or actionable for your clients. Knowing that Netflix streams 250 million hours of video a day is interesting, but what does it mean for your clients?

Data is the cornerstone of insights – without data you are left to gut feeling, guesses, and anecdotal observations. This is not to say that those categories are useless – you will have to combine all of the information you have to build a truly useful insight, but without hard data they have no provable basis.

An example of data would be: As of 2017, millennials check their cell phone 157 times per day on average.

Observations

Observations are experiences drawn from real behavior that take one step further than raw data. While observations are by necessity somewhat subjective, they are defensible when they derive from a base of hard data. Some observations are self-evident, some require focus groups or research, but all observations begin to point to human behavior beyond the numbers.

Observations begin to put the data into context so that you can build a useful, inspiring and action-oriented insight for your client. They are a springboard to the insight you will develop, but like data, are not the insight itself.

An example of an observation would be: Millennials frequently check their phone while at meals with friends.

Insights

Insights are a distillation of data points and observations that an agency or client can use to build powerful solutions for their users. They are human truths that can drive everything from a single campaign to an entire new product line or business model.

An insight not only outlines a data-founded truth but also offers a path to connecting with your client's users in an effective manner.

An example of an Insight would be: The very device we once used to keep in touch with loved ones is now a barrier to maintaining close relationships with the ones we love.

The remainder of the chapter will illustrate how to perform the research you will need to gather useful data, how to interpret that data to develop insights, and how to use that ability to become indispensable to your clients.

Research

The first step on the path to developing insights for your clients begins with research. This is rarely a linear process and often leads to some false starts, some dead ends, and some information that is interesting but not actionable. All of this is to be expected and does not mean that your research is going poorly. To the contrary, in order to cast a wide enough net to develop great insights you will have to be comfortable with initial ambiguity as to what is and is not relevant to the client problem you are trying to solve.

Common research mistakes

There are some guidelines that will help you quickly focus and save you time and effort as you develop your insights. Unlike much scientific research, your research has a very narrow goal. That goal is to help your client succeed, to get results. It is not uncommon to discover fascinating sociological patterns, new digital trends, or unexpected behaviors during the course of your research, but in this case your only goal is to advance your client in the marketplace. Anything you discover that does not help solve that problem should be remembered, perhaps filed away for use another time, but left behind as you search for insights that solve for your client's problems.

In most cases in the media industry you will have a client brief or a specific challenge that your client wants to solve for. Always interrogate your brief to understand what the client needs from you. This means looking at what your client wants to solve, framing it in human terms, and researching for that problem. Do not jump into your available data sets immediately. Instead, read through the brief or the challenge and ask yourself what the client is really asking. This can save you a great deal of time during your research phase.

Here is an example brief or RFP that a client might send you:

Assignment: Build an integrated top-layer marketing program that creates purchase intent for our detachable and convertible PCs while further developing our Next Generation platform.

Marketing Objectives:
• Drive continued awareness for our detachable portfolio
• Drive mass market awareness for our convertible portfolio
• Drive preference for our lineup by showcasing the usefulness of the form factors
• Create authentic opportunities for interaction with Millennials.

Before you begin to look into data for this brief, ask yourself what your client really wants. Briefs can be jargon-laden and unclear. Interrogating your brief by looking at it from a human perspective can help to clarify what your client needs to accomplish. In the above case, after carefully reading a complex and hard to understand challenge, one could translate that to: "People (especially younger ones) don't know about and aren't buying our tablets. How can we get them to do that?"

Once you have converted the brief or assignment into clear language, you can begin to research. Always interrogate your brief or challenge and make sure it makes sense before you start your work.

What is and is not useful to your client's needs

As you delve into the research options available, it can be easy to focus on what seems interesting, instead of focusing on what your client requires to succeed. In the above example, the client seeks awareness and purchase of their tablet product. It is likely that there is data that shows interesting behaviors using tablets, articles on how the technology is advancing, whitepapers on tablets and young children, etc. If those data points do not show a path to growing awareness and sales of your client's tablet line, they are not useful to your insights. Remember to focus on the needs of your client as you collect data.

How to manage the data you find

It can be overwhelming to see just how much data you can pull from the many tools and resources available. It is helpful to use a document- or slide-making software such as Keynote, PowerPoint, Google Docs, or Word, and to learn to screenshot anything that seems potentially useful. As you begin to pull data it is often most effective to screenshot or copy and paste anything that has relevance to your client's needs. At this stage of the process anything that might be useful should be included. This is analogous to a brain-storming session where any idea is on the table at first, before you begin to filter ideas. At this point, find all of the data you can, then place it into the groupings below which you can parse for valuable information.

Data should be researched and stored in broad categories: user, industry, product, and culture.

User   This is research that teaches you about how people who already use the brand's products behave, and how people who might one day use the brand behave. In the case of Nike for example, how do athletes search, what videos do they watch, what comments do they make and what content do they share? What is important online to someone searching about running their first marathon? What do people who wear sneakers for fashion purposes care about?

Industry   What are the trends in the data on your client's industry? Do consumers find your client's industry positive to engage with or negative? Is the industry in deep competition, like cable networks vs. Netflix, or trying to convince users to try them as a new service, like Blue Apron or Casper Mattresses? When you look for industry data, be sure to look beyond industry publications and seek out data and opinions from the general public.

Product   What are the search and content trends around the specific product? Are there reviews, unboxing videos, hashtags, or questions that come up often? Is search around the product seasonal or has there been a big spike in the past? What products are competing with your client's? Do you see a general tone of online discourse regarding the product?

Culture   Where does your brand fit culturally? Is it seen as futuristic, dependable, edgy, funny, antiquated – what is the cultural sense of your brand? Old Spice, for example, realized the brand was seen as your grandfather's brand several years ago, and decided to completely reinvent itself. Brands shift over time – JetBlue when launched was a major disruptor in the airline industry, but currently consumer studies show it has become a standard, low-fare option (at least in the minds of the general public). Where does your brand fit? Keep in mind that the client may have a skewed perspective and it is part of your role to bring them facts. Your role as a media seller is to guide the client to what they need to do, impartially and with the confidence that data-based insights provide.

Data

A theory of data

Data will be the bedrock on which your insights will be built. Data here is defined as any credible, numeric source of consumer behavior. This means hard data such as Google Trends or Instagram Analytics or Nielsen ratings. It may include more qualitative data such as sentiment analysis or survey results as long as the sample set is large and the origin of the data is neutral to outcome. Data is a more rigorous form of information than anecdotal evidence, which can suffer from very small sample sets, cognitive bias, and other potential weaknesses.

An important element of any data collection is to cross reference data between tools. If you see a spike in interest in your brand in search every Sunday, look at comments or video shares as well. Do they show the same pattern? If not, can you determine why search intent is high at one time but sharing is high another?

Data without analysis and interpretation is not useful to your client. To say that searches for yogurt drop every December does not help drive marketing and sales efforts. Ask yourself "why does this happen?" and "what does this mean for my client?" All too often media salespeople present data as marketing insights. It is no surprise that searches for "super bowl" explode the first week in February. What does that mean for a client who has spent millions on a Super Bowl ad? What does it mean for a client that is not advertising in the Super Bowl? Your interpretation of the data is where you add value and become a true partner of the client.

Data will be the source of every insight you bring, but the data is the beginning of the road, not the end point.

Big Data

Big Data is a term used to describe massive data sets now available along the lines of Facebook's data on its users, Google's data on search behavior, *The New York Times* data on trending article topics, or Apple's data on Apple Pay transactions. These are generally data sets involving millions or more users, usually nationally or globally, but easily filtered for demographic variables such as geography, age, and so on.

For several years during the advent of Big Data, it was assumed that these huge data sets would tell a marketer the truth about consumer behavior, brands, purchase intent, and social engagement. While some of that promise has come to pass, much is lost in the sea of information and many brands are unsure how to interpret all of the data that are available. Consumers are also reacting to what they see as invasive behavior on the part of marketers who have access to this data. Retargeted ads that show up for weeks after a consumer searches for a specific item are seen as creepy and annoying. Elections that seemed fully predictable via Big Data turned out to surprise the researchers. Films that seemed likely to become blockbusters faded on opening. Big Data is useful, but only via the interpretation of skilled humans who understand what human drives or behaviors underlie the numbers for their specific client needs.

Big Data as an information set is generally confined to a handful of resources. Proprietary data sets, such as those owned by Internet platforms, massive retailers, or the government, are not always possible to access. That said, many of these sources have provided some access. Google Trends, Facebook Research, Twitter Search, Census data, and many other publically available tools will give you access to truly astounding data sets. These are incredibly useful starting points for you to develop useful insights for your clients. They provide a macroscopic view of what people are interested in, concerned about, and researching.

Your role with Big Data as a media seller is twofold: (1) Know and understand the private Big Data collections that you have access to. If you work at an organization that allows you access to a proprietary set of Big Data, as most digital platforms or media companies do, then you have an advantage when working with your clients. Alternately, if your organization has subscriptions to private data sets, use that to your advantage. (2) Know the public data sets available to everyone and be expert in using them.

If you can master these two skills, you will be far ahead of most of your competitors in the media selling space. Few media sellers make use of these powerful tools. The tools can seem complex, or time-consuming to learn, or beyond the role-scope of a seller. While it may take you some time to learn how to access and use large data sets, it will be a tremendous differentiator for you in the marketplace. It is well worth the investment.

Current marketing challenges and data

Given the increasing number of data sets, brands struggle to master and incorporate all of the available information while juggling their own complex business needs. Sophisticated brands will have internal departments that do look closely at data, but an external eye from a dedicated media seller is always incredibly welcome. Brands generally do not have access to every data set, and they also suffer from internal bias, whereby corporate goals, executive personalities, and often long-held assumptions about the brand color their perception of the data they see. You, as a skilled, impartial and honest media seller become an enormous asset to your clients.

Insights

What is an insight?

You will know you have an insight that is useful, inspiring and engaging to your client when: (1) it is based on real data and behavior, (2) it reveals something about the consumer or user, (3) it makes you say, "Yes! that is true!" and (4) it provides the platform from which you can solve your client's specific problem.

This is not an insight: Drunk drivers are largely men between the ages of 18 and 25. They like beer and are social.

This is an insight: Men from 18 to 25 years old are the most likely people to drive drunk, but they also love video games and social status. We can combine social media, games, and getting home without driving drunk to give status to those young men who make the right call.

For this insight example there are several brands that could benefit: a spirits brand, a government brand such as the National Highway Traffic Safety Administration (NHTSA), or a bar/restaurant brand. Each has opportunities to acknowledge real data, see what it reveals about their consumers, agree that it is true, and create something that solves the problem using media.

Insights are powerful tools for selling media because they are based on a human articulation of your client's need and are inarguably useful to them. An opinion, or a sales pitch, or an uninterpreted data point are not interesting or actionable, but an insight is always both interesting and actionable. It is not an exaggeration to say that if you, as a sophisticated media seller, bring real insights to your client you will be seen as part of their team.

How do insights drive success?

Insights allow your clients to accomplish several goals at once. Marketing and media based on insights have a head start when launched because of the basis in factual data and human truths, not a clever but unfounded idea or a solution seeking a problem. Insights also help your clients look at their business from a new perspective, possibly opening up new lines of product or consumers (which leads to new lines of media buying for you). Insight-based marketing shows the brand's audience that the brand understands them, creating brand lift and improved sentiment. Insights bring focus to brands that have several campaigns currently in market, acting as a kind of North Star that can pull together disparate messages.

Human beings vs. algorithms in the insights game

Algorithms have replaced human decision-making across large swaths of life in recent years. They are used for everything from planning traffic light timing to serving you social media posts. And in many cases they do a much more efficient and rational job than a team of human beings trying to accomplish the same task would. Algorithms can process and organize vastly more data than any human possibly could, and do so almost instantaneously. An algorithm is what serves you your Google search results in less than a second after sorting through millions and millions of webpages, for example.

The down side to algorithms is that, by and large, they lack the context that a human mind brings to a data set. We have seen this in recent years as many Internet platforms like Facebook and Google try to build sentiment analysis algorithms that can tell if a social media comment or news story is positive or negative. What may seem like a relatively simple problem turns out to be deeply complex for a computer, while it is trivial for a human. Similar difficulties arise with automated translation software, which can deliver results from the accurate to the outright comical.

While algorithms bring you the data, if you are seeking to build useful insights, it is you who must interpret it. There are three key elements that you bring to the table when you interpret a data set looking for insights.

Personal inputs   Your lived experience is key to understanding how to build insights for your client from the data you collect. When you see that searches for ice cream peak every July, you know that it's because it is hot in the Northern Hemisphere every summer, and that ice cream is a primarily a summertime treat.

You are aware of the news cycle so understand why certain videos or memes may be being shared broadly at a moment in time. You understand human emotion and can apply that understanding to the data you collect.

Cultural inputs   When you enter "yogurt" into Google Trends and see that searches for it drop tremendously every December, it is your cultural knowledge that tells you that this is due to the holidays, a time traditionally associated with celebration, treats, and loosening of dietary restriction. To an algorithm, December is an arbitrary month, simply a number.

When the Oscars or the Olympics come around, it is your cultural knowledge of major events and how people engage with them that you can apply to the behavioral data to craft insights for your client's needs.

Thinking broadly and thinking deeply   You are able to think beyond the specific data and into similar or overlapping categories. If you see that there is big interest in grilled salmon one summer, you might think broadly and wonder if something similar is happening for white wine or watermelon. This lateral thinking brings breadth to your insights and can sometimes uncover useful and unexplored opportunities for your client. Always feel free to think beyond the specific product or brand. Given the same example, you might think more deeply about why grilled salmon is so popular. Has the price changed? Has the media been focusing on health benefits of salmon? Are other fish similarly popular this summer? These kinds of question bring depth to your understanding of the data.

The power of insights for a salesperson

Learning to build strong, data-backed media and creative insights is an incredible tool for any media salesperson. There are four key advantages this skill will bring you, though these are by no means the only benefits to learning and using this process.

Persuasion   It is one thing to go to a client meeting and present them with a pitch, saying "This is my opinion of what your best media plan looks like." It is quite another to show your client one or more insights, with the data that drove the insights and the thought process behind them, then say "And here is how we can take advantage of these insights with a media plan."

When you present a media plan or other product backed by solid insights, it becomes unassailable. That doesn't mean that your client will automatically buy it of course – it may not be what they want right now, or they may have a different focus, but they cannot say that what you are pitching is wrong or not well thought out. Well-crafted insights are tremendously powerful persuasion tools.

Market differentiation   Few of your colleagues or competitors will have this skill set available to them when they develop pitches and deliver them to their clients. The majority of sellers leave the research and data work to other departments within their company, using what is delivered to them to bolster a pitch. Generalized pitch assets are of course useful, but nothing is more convincing to your client than custom insights about their specific, immediate business needs. The media salesperson is the best-positioned person to deliver insights and solutions and present a plan to act on them.

These insights will set you apart from competing sellers and will also set you apart when you seek employment or promotion in a current role. Mastering insight development places you in an elite category of salespeople, a category that goes far beyond the day-to-day needs of the role.

Client retention and growth   When you bring data and insights to your clients during pitches or regular meetings, you become a resource for them. You need not bring insights every time you meet, but when you do, you will become a de facto extension of their own marketing team, not a salesperson looking to close a deal. This shift in perception is a powerful tool to both keeping the clients you have and growing your business with them.

Career path   Understanding how to collect and interpret data into insights opens several career paths that are not traditionally open to a media salesperson. If, after some time in the sales department, you may determine that you would like to explore product development, user experience design, marketing, or many other specialty areas. An insight development skill set is highly beneficial to many roles both at brands and agencies. You expand your future options when you develop this knowledge.

Data: Tools and Processes for Insight

Where is the data?

Public tools: an introduction   Public tools are those tools based on massive data sets that have filters and research options available to the general public. Many data sets are inaccessible to the average user. For example, National Security Agency (NSA) data, corporate data, and so on are all off the table for obvious reasons. However, there are a surprising amount of open data sets with easy to use front-end tools that allow you to learn about human behavior across a broad range of topics.

A selection of these tools is presented here but this is by no means a complete list, and new data tools come online all the time. This list is intended to get you started exploring the world of public data tools. It is not a complete guide to these tools – you will have to master them from the training provided by each tool. Most have frequently asked questions (FAQ) sections, introductions, and other aides. For those that do not, a quick Internet search on "how to use" the tool will usually provide a wealth of information.

Major digital platform tools   Most large digital platforms such as Google, Facebook, and Twitter have some kind of data tool that is open and free to use. These tools vary in depth and complexity. You should have a base understanding of what tools are available to you from every major digital platform that could benefit your clients. The tools listed should be of use for developing insights for most brands you will work with, so it is helpful to explore each and learn what they can provide.

Search

Google Trends   Google Trends is one of the most robust tools available for big data research. It also happens to be one of the most useful for developing insights. This tool allows you to see the relative search volume over time of any keyword you would like to put in. You can compare up to five keywords or terms at once. If you would like to see how this can be useful, try comparing searches for "yogurt" to "pudding" over the last five years. See anything interesting? Why do you think the graph looks like that?

Video

YouTube Trends   This tool is not searchable or as customizable as some other tools, but it does give you categories like Culture, Holidays, and Sports to narrow down your data set. You can learn what videos or types of content have been trending in that category, often with editorial content explaining why. Some of the content is unfortunately outdated, which is why the next tool is useful.

YouTube Trending Videos   On the left hand side of the YouTube home page you will find a "Trending" link. Click that to see what videos are most popular currently. You can also use YouTube to search for videos via your brand's name or the product or category, then filter by "view count," "rating," and other variables.

Collecting and Categorizing: A Process Plan

Handling large data sets

Large data sets can be incredibly useful but can also lead to a paralysis when the information gathered is overwhelming. The first thing to do as you collect data to build insights is to filter out anything that won't help your client meet their business objectives. If you are looking at search trends, look for either repeating patterns (i.e., the search volume goes up every summer, or every Tuesday), or for major one-time spikes or drops. If the reasons for those patterns or spikes are obvious, like ice cream sees a search boost in the hot months, you probably don't need that data. But in that example, take a look at related searches, or perhaps flavors that have trended up recently. You want to bring new insights to your client, not tell them what they already know. Filtering out the very obvious data will reduce some of the filtering work you must do after the collection process.

Screen captures are a useful and easy tool for grabbing images, graphs, or other visually presented data. Learn how to do a screen capture on your computer before you set out to work with big data.

Create a folder where you will store all the URL links, screen shots, and copied data tables for your project. Keeping all the data in one place seems obvious but it can be easy to end up with a desktop screen full of images.

Always retain the source of any data you use. You should cite the source of any data you present to a client, so make sure as you move through the data tools you keep track of what data you found where.

Defining data categories

Once you have explored all the tools that you are going to use for an insights project, your next step is to create categories or buckets to begin to sort all of that data. There is no set group of categories to use, instead your data will indicate how to break it out. If you look at data for an automotive client, for example, you might find the data could be bucketed like this:

- Make/model data
- Family driving data
- Auto industry data
- Video content data for this model
- Auto buying concerns (gas mileage, etc.)

For a breakfast cereal client, it may look like this:

- Brand sentiment
- Health concerns
- Breakfast trends
- Moms and kids

Each project will have its own set of categories that the data breaks down into, and that is already the start of developing insights. What kind of questions, searches, video content, and social content are users engaged with, just by looking across the data you've gathered?

There will be some data that does not fit into any bucket, and that is fine. There will always be an "other" category. Sometimes the most useful insights come from this "other" bucket, so don't necessarily discard data that doesn't sit clearly in any of the categories you've developed.

Discarding data

There are three major reasons to discard data, and it will be necessary to do so in order to narrow down useful, actionable data to craft into one or several insights.

The data is obvious　Per the above example, telling an ice cream client that they are more popular in summer than in winter is not particularly useful.

The data is peripheral to the client's needs　You may come across data that is interesting, but does not help to address for the client's business goals. If the client is focused on a particular demographic, for example, and you find data on a completely different demographic, that isn't useful for building an insight right now. It may be of use later, but it should be discarded for the current project.

The data is too broad　If, using a research tool, you find that people who like to surf also like *Star Wars*, but then see that people who like to cook, people who like to dance, and people who like to paint also like *Star Wars*, it is probably not useful data.

Seeing the negative space

Often what is not there is as important as what is there. If, for example, you are researching a brand of electric toothbrush, and see many searches for how to use it properly, look at video content. Is the brand (or a competitor) there with how-to videos? If not, are users filling in that need with user-generated content?

If an auto brand is trying to highlight a key new feature on their cars, is there any search interest in it? Do people even know to ask about it?

This is a bit of an advanced technique when collecting data, but as you learn to do so you will start to notice when the data shows a lack of knowledge, interest, or content where you might have expected to see the opposite. These empty spaces are golden opportunities for brands to move in and own that part of the message.

Building Insights

Once you have all of your data collected, categorized it into buckets, and have discarded the unnecessary data, you are ready to build out insights. Here is where your human brain crafts the raw numbers into human truths that will help your client succeed. Crafting insights is both an art and a science. The process is elucidated below, but it does take some practice and some feedback to become skilled at insights development. Try building a few insights on brands you like and share them with your friends, colleagues, or classmates if you would like to learn the process in a risk-free environment.

Data does not equal insights

As mentioned earlier in this chapter, data is the foundation for your insights, not the insights themselves. Never present a number or a statistic as an insight. It is fine to use raw data as part of a sales pitch, and most salespeople do so. Insights are a different category of information and should be treated as such. Insights are a gift to your client.

Common mistakes

There are some common mistakes made when building and delivering insights. They are easy to avoid if you remain aware of them as you work.

Insights should be expressible in just a sentence or two   If your insight takes a paragraph to describe, you have more distilling to do. Fully explaining the thought behind the insight, the data used, may of course require a longer explanation but the core insights should be clearly articulated in at most two sentences.

Keep the data you show to a relative minimum   You may have used many data points and sources to develop your insight, but when presenting to your clients stick to one or two particularly interesting data points to bolster your insight. Keep the remaining data in an appendix for those clients who wish to do a deep dive, but do not get bogged down in presenting data – the insight is the actionable information.

Follow the insight with an implication   The implication can be a specific recommendation for how your client can act on the insight via the products you are selling, or it can be a provocative question that starts with "How can your brand…" with a general direction for you and your client to brainstorm around. This insight is the "Aha!" moment, but it needs a follow-up prompt to help you make a sale.

The human lens

Don't be afraid to move out of the realm of business-speak when you present your insights. Your clients are business people looking for solutions and return on investment (ROI), but they are also human beings. Humans respond to narratives, and your insights and implications are just that. Of course, they are backed by hard data and lead to business solutions, but good insights speak to human truths and are best presented as such. If your insights are strong, they will feel real and inspiring to your clients, so do not be afraid to treat them as powerful stories that can drive business forward.

The four questions

When building your insights, keep in mind the following four questions:

What are you trying to do?   If you have properly interrogated your brief or request for proposal (RFP), you will have a clear idea of how to answer this question.

Who are you trying to motivate?   What demographic, audience, or user base are you focused on? An insight for a brand based on behavior of teens will likely be different than one based on Baby Boomers.

How do you want people to react?   What action does your client want to see from its target users? Is it brand awareness, product purchases, social media sharing, subscriptions, or any of a variety of other outcomes? All marketing is in service to some desired outcome. Your insights should reflect the outcome that your client is seeking.

Why should people care?   This is a particularly important question. Given the glut of information, content, and digital noise that the average person encounters on a daily basis, your insights need a reason to engage with them. The ALS Ice Bucket challenge, for example, provided a reason to care by giving users a funny, shareable video format that was both entertaining for their friends to watch while signaling that they are people who care about charity. That hook was quite different than simply asking for a donation.

Solutions, Not Campaigns

One of the key strengths of insights as compared to data or standard sales pitches is that they can inform far more than an advertising campaign. Certainly your insights should set up immediate campaigns that produce media sales for you, but strong insights can lead to new products, rebrands, or entire platforms that your client can develop to leverage your hard-earned knowledge of their users and the world at large.

As a seller you must of course focus on the bottom line and the quarter-to-quarter quotas you likely work with, and insights will help you succeed. You can also use them to suggest much broader opportunities to your clients with the goal of expanding your business relationship with them. Don't hesitate to suggest ways of leveraging your insights beyond the immediate needs of the current brief.

Examples of powerful insight-driven advertising

Nike: "Find Your Greatness"   In 2012, Nike ran an ad that received a great deal of press and commentary. Titled "Find Your Greatness," the ad shows a long stretch of asphalt road in the middle of fields. A figure comes into the frame, an overweight boy who is jogging along the road. The voice-over message is that greatness is inherent in every person, and your actions make you great, not the perceptions of others. This was followed with a broader campaign that included a Little League pitcher with one arm, children playing rugby in a dusty, barren field, and many other examples.

Nike realized that the majority of their marketing message used incredible athletes at the top of their game, possibly alienating people that didn't feel great. The insight they tapped into is that everyone has greatness inside of them, and Nike could help them find it with inspiring, real messages. This led to a full marketing strategy that ran across all forms of media.

Pinterest: "What If"   In 2017, Pinterest looked at some internal data and found that 84 percent of people on Pinterest say it helps them learn new things, and 70 percent of people search, save, or click through on Pins to learn more. Pinterest also found that the major barrier to trying new things or learning new skills was the very person who is interested in it – they described the "voice in your head" that tells you that you could never do that.

Armed with that insight, they built an outdoor, display, and social media campaign. In their own words:

> In every ad, we're showing real people, not models – Pinterest employees and close friends – to keep it feeling grounded, relatable, and true to the real-life spirit of 'what if.'
> You'll also notice that the focus intentionally is not on outcomes, since achieving a perfect end result is far less important than taking a chance and trying something new.

This focus on real people, learning or trying new things without concern if they succeed right away, became a cross-platform campaign that resonated deeply with current and new users alike.

Hinge: "Let's Be Real"   Hinge is a dating app billed as the app for people who want real relationships and deep connections. Looking at its own data in 2017, Hinge found that 81 percent of its users have never found a long-term relationship on any dating or swiping app. The company explored several other data points which they published, leading them to the following insight: "Humans make real connections through shared vulnerabilities – something most dating apps fail to recognize."

With this insight, Hinge developed a full marketing campaign by creating stories that real users allowed them to share, telling heartwarming and funny tales about dates they went on that were successful. The campaign was a success and differentiated Hinge from the many dating apps in the market, speaking directly to the kinds of users the company hoped to attract.

Building an insight from the ground up

The following is an example of how an insight is built. The yogurt data that was referenced earlier in this chapter will be used for this example. Here we will go step by step into the process, though the steps will be streamlined and abbreviated for brevity. To keep the example succinct, only a few data points will be used, but in practice you should seek to find as much relevant data as possible.

The brief   A yogurt company seeks to increase sales year over year, and wants to differentiate its brand from the many competitors in the yogurt marketplace. There is no specific demographic focus, and the campaign timeline is for a full year.

The data   Figure 10.1 shows that, looking at the last five years of search for *yogurt* in Google Trends, the lowest dip every year is in December, and it is a steep drop off. As data, this is interesting, but adding an observation moves it closer to an insight.

Observation   What happens in December? The holidays occur, which is traditionally a time of indulgence in treats and eating, and a time when people relax their health habits.

Thinking beyond our specific brand, and thinking observationally, what else is like yogurt, but more treat-like and related to holidays? Pudding comes to mind. It's a sugary treat that has a similar consistency and packaging to yogurt. Looking at the data (see Figure 10.2), we see that *pudding* does indeed spike in December every year (and in November during Thanksgiving as well).

We have data   (1) *Yogurt* searches, and presumably interest, drop deeply every December and (2) *Pudding* searches, and presumably interest, spike heavily every December.

We have an observation   People like to loosen up on dietary restrictions and enjoy treats with friends and family during the December holidays.

We used a cultural lens and we looked beyond our specific brand and product (yogurt) to the general food market to discover the pudding data. Now we need to craft an insight. Different media sellers might derive different but equally powerful insights from this same setup, depending on the specifics of their client, their industry background, or other factors.

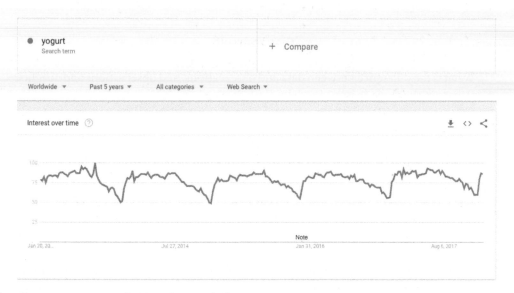

Figure 10.1   Google Trends: search for *yogurt*

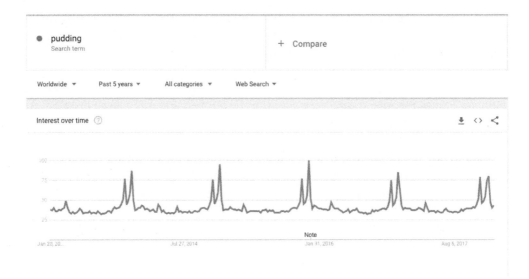

Figure 10.2   Google Trends: search for *pudding*

For this example, a broad insight might be   People want to relax about their eating during the holidays and yogurt feels like a restrictive, health-based food so they turn to more indulgent treats.

An implication might be framed as prescriptive, or as a question   (1) Your brand can partner with our media company on a campaign showing how yogurt can be a healthy ingredient in all kinds of indulgent, delicious dessert recipes, or (2) How can we work together to make your yogurt feel like a treat this holiday season?

Test Yourself

1.   What is the difference between data and observations, and observations and insights?
2.   What are the three reasons for discarding data?
3.   Why are negative spaces important when analyzing data?
4.   What are the four questions to ask when building insights?
5.   Why are solutions not necessarily campaigns?

Project

Select a common household product that you have seen advertised on television, such as laundry detergent, and then go to Google Trends, enter "laundry detergents" (or whatever product you choose), hit return, and look at the trend-over-time chart that comes up. When is the peak month and week of the year for the product you chose?

Then pick a brand name such as Tide or Lysol and make some comparisons. Are the patterns of interests the same or different? Are there any geographic patterns that you find interesting? Write down your observations and then see if you can come up with any insights.

References

HBR Guide to Data Analytics Basics for Managers. (2018). Boston, MA: Harvard Business Review Press.

Resources

Google Alerts (www.google.com/alerts)
Google Trends (trends.google.com/trends/?geo=US)

11

Educating

Charles Warner

In the first to fourth editions of *Media Selling*, this step of selling was called *Presenting*, which implied one-way presenting of selective information designed to persuade prospects or agencies to give the presenter an order for a medium that prospects or agencies were familiar with.

Pre-digital-era media that prospects and buyers were familiar with were primarily television, radio, newspapers, and magazines. Television and radio commercial inventory in this era was scarce, inelastic, and negotiable. Newspaper and magazine inventory was elastic (expandable), relatively expensive on a cost-per-thousand (CPM) basis, and generally not highly negotiable. Furthermore, all transactions involving these media had to go through a salesperson, which limited the number of advertisers that could be accommodated and which often required lengthy negotiations and lead times.

Google's introduction of a self-serve, online auction and cost-per-click model changed the media-buying process. Because advertisers no longer had to deal with a salesperson, all advertisers needed was a credit card, a way to connect to, and the know-how to use AdWords (renamed Google Ads on July 24, 2018). In order to encourage as many people as possible to participate, AdWords had to be easy to use, which it was and still is as Google Ads. Therefore, small and large advertisers flocked to self-serve AdWords to buy search terms based on a cost-per-click model. Millions of advertisers could invest in advertising for as little as $100, see if it worked, easily calculate a return on investment (ROI) by looking at Google Analytics, and increase their investment as long as the advertising paid off. Although Google does not reveal publicly the number of advertisers it accommodates, those knowledgeable about search advertising estimate that Google in

Media Selling: Digital, Television, Audio, Print and Cross-Platform, Fifth Edition.
Charles Warner, William A. Lederer, and Brian Moroz.
© 2020 John Wiley & Sons, Inc. Published 2020 by John Wiley & Sons, Inc.

2018 was able accommodate more than six million advertisers, because in 2018 Facebook announced that it had six million advertisers worldwide, and Google is perceived to certainly have as many, if not more, advertisers than Facebook has.

Google and Facebook are able to accommodate so many advertisers because their self-serve models mean that the vast majority of those advertisers did not have to deal with a salesperson. However, both Google and Facebook have sales forces, which Facebook calls its marketing solutions and global partnerships groups. Google has agency and partnership teams; internally Google refers to teams as pods. Both Google's and Facebook's sales or partnership teams' jobs are to (1) educate clients about the benefits of precisely targeting intended buyers and multidimensional behavioral and psychographic segments, and (2) to manage the accounts for large advertisers.

Neither Google nor Facebook will reveal what the minimum advertising investment is for them to agree to manage a partner's account, but according to some sources the amount is usually over $1,000,000 annually, and typically an account they agree to manage has the potential for a much larger investment. Therefore, if advertisers will invest, as an example, $8,5000 a month, or $1,020,000 a year, a team of Google or Facebook account executives, account managers, strategists, and analysts will manage the auction bidding process to meet dollar investment budgets, optimize the creative executions, and recommend additional opportunities.

When I conducted a search for monthly ad dollars invested in search advertising, the most relevant data I got was a 2016 Statista article titled "Leading online retailers in the United States in 2016 by average monthly paid search spending (in millions of US dollars." Exhibit 11.1 shows the top ten in retail search advertising.

Exhibit 11.1   2016 top retail investors in search (in $ millions)

	Average month	Year
Amazon.com	41.2	494.4
Target.com	10.3	123.6
Walmart	9.9	118.8
Macys	8.4	100.8
Wayfair.com	7.7	92.4
Sears.com	7.2	86.4
Home Depot	6.3	75.6
Lowes	6.2	74.4
Walgreens	5.1	61.2
Play.google.com	5.0	60.0
	107.3	1,287.6

Source: https://www.statista.com/statistics/685849/onlien-reatiler-paid-search-ad-spend.

As you can see in Exhibit 11.1, the number one online retail search advertiser in 2016, Amazon, invested almost half-a-billion dollars in search, and the top ten online retailers invested $1,287,600,000 in search advertising, about 92 percent of which went to Google.[1]

If you were a local television or radio station or a local newspaper salesperson assigned to the retail category and, thus, virtually all of your prospects were retailers, what would you think about the above numbers? Would you be worried that your prospects did not need your help to go Google Ads online and buy search terms and then only pay if someone clicked on their ads? Of course you would. A May 22, 2018, Axios Media Trends newsletter contained a chart titled "Big tech takes a bite out of local media advertising," which displayed the following numbers:

Change in local media ad revenue, 2010–2022		*2022, Est.*
All local media	−27%	$47.6b
Digital	+170%	$11.0b
Cable TV	+21%	$4.7b
Broadcast TV	−19%	$12.1b
Radio	−25%	$10.7b
Newspapers	−92%	$1.8b

Data: Pivotal Research Advertising Forecast May 2018.[2]

If you sold for a local television station and your account list contained mostly local retailers, considering the information above, how would you deal with the retailers on your account list? What do you think your chances would be of making a sale? How would you increase your chances of making a sale? You would most likely break down and examine each step in the old sales process and then see what steps needed to be changed or improved in light of Google's and Facebook's ease of use, relatively low cost, performance-based pricing, reducing by almost 20 percent the advertising dollars that used to go to television stations.

As a reminder, Exhibit 11.2 repeats Exhibit 8.1 to show the old, pre-Internet-era sales process and two new digital-era sales processes.

Exhibit 11.2   Sales process models

Old sales process steps of selling	*New missionary sales process steps of selling*	*New service sales process steps of selling*
1. Prospecting	1. Prospecting and qualifying	1. Finding decision makers
2. Identifying problems	2. Researching insights and solutions	2. Educating
3. Generating solutions	3. Educating	3. Researching insights and solutions
4. Presenting	4. Proposing	4. Proposing
5. Negotiating and closing	5. Negotiating and closing	5. Negotiating and closing
6. Servicing	6. Customer success	6. Customer success

The *educating* step replaces the *presenting* step because, as stated in Chapter 8:

A selling-as-educating approach is now required for a number of reasons, including self-serve auction buying models and programmatic buying and selling of media advertising. Buying digital and mobile advertising direct from a salesperson or buying programmatically is extremely complex, and buyers need to be thoroughly educated on the advantages, benefits, and technical requirements of the proposed solution. It is in the educating step that you create value for your eventual solution.

Furthermore, the concept of presenting implies a one-way presentation of facts and figures that congers up an image of a dreaded classroom lecture. Educating requires a two-way dialogue that is further enhanced by the power of asking questions and listening effectively. An educating approach is also in harmony with the teaching, tailoring, and taking control approach to selling discussed in Chapter 2.

Also, the concept of educating rather than presenting is cognitively consistent with the selling-as-serving approach and the notion that we tend to be happier when we get intrinsic value from our work than when we get extrinsic value from our work. Salespeople tend to *feel* better about helping others, helping customers be successful, and helping them get results rather than trying to manipulate or persuade them.

The above sentence reads in part, we *"feel* better." It is about feelings, emotion, not about data or numbers. In the age of Big Data, we too often make the mistake of relying too much on data and numbers. We too often behave as though we believe that prospects and customers are rational and make rational decisions based on data and logic. If we believe that people make rational decisions, we have not kept up on the research and literature of behavioral economists such as Daniel Kahneman, Amos Tversky, Richard Thaler, and Daniel Airely.

Behavioral economics has taught us that the theory of rational choice that had been assumed by economists for decades is a flawed theory. The rational choice theory assumes that people make rational decisions based on facts. However, this theory does not adequately describe human decision-making or human nature. Several behavioral economists dubbed the two decision-making systems of the human mind as the *Planner* and the *Doer*.

The Elephant and the Rider

Jonathan Haidt in his groundbreaking book, *The Happiness Hypothesis,* uses a visually appealing metaphor for the two decision-making systems of the mind: the Elephant is the Doer and the Rider is the Planner.[3] Daniel Kahneman in his best selling book, *Thinking, Fast and Slow* refers to the two mind functions as System I and System II, but the concept of the Elephant and the Rider is more vivid and understandable.

Visualize a massive elephant carrying a human rider as it lumbers along a path on the African savannah. The rider gives the elephant signals with a thin harness in order to keep the huge animal on the path, but the rider's control is precarious because the rider is so small compared to the elephant. When a six-ton elephant and the rider disagree about which direction to go, the rider is always going to lose. The rider is completely overmatched.[4] The elephant is the emotional and instinctive system, and is lazy and selfish, often looking for a quick payoff and instant gratification.[5] The rider's strength is being able to think long-term, to plan, to think beyond the moment, and to think rationally.[6]

Feelings and emotions are the elephant's turf – love, compassion, sympathy, and loyalty.[7] Rationality, facts, plans, and data are the rider's turf.[8] Therefore, if you want to influence or persuade people, you have to appeal to *both* the elephant and the rider, keeping in mind that the elephant, the emotional system, is much more powerful than the rider, the rational system.

Therefore, to influence the elephant, you have to engage its emotional side, make it feel something – loyalty, liking, connection, or kinship. To influence and persuade the rider, you have to provide crystal clear direction – facts, data, and logical arguments. For the rider, you must focus on the positives, follow a budget, specifications, and lay out a clear path.

Research conducted in 2018 by the *Financial Times* is published in a report titled "The Business Feeling Index: The Feelings That Move Businesses Forward." The report is published by Gyro, a business-to-business (B2B) advertising agency, and it indicates that there were three stages in a B2B relationship: (1) The pre-contact or research phase, (2) the initial conversation, and (3) working together.

In stage 1 (pre-contact) 86 percent of the respondents in the survey indicated that confidence is the "feeling that is most important for deepening consideration."[9] Customers "need credible proof that you own your expertise."

In stage 2 (initial conversation) active listening and alignment make customers feel understood. Seventy percent of respondents said "a clear understanding of my needs contributed most to selecting a partner." Lack of expertise was "the most likely trait to derail a…deal."[10]

In stage 3 (working together) respondents said, "feed my learning," which reinforces the importance of this step of selling being an educating step. Also, face-to-face meetings prove invaluable as the relationship continues and, according to 73 percent of the respondents, because face-to-face contacts are the most effective behaviors in maintaining a strong relationship. See Exhibit 11.3 for confidence builders and confidence killers in working together in a partnership according to the *Financial Times* survey.

In the list of *confidence builders* in Exhibit 11.3, take particular notice of numbers 3–5: Active listening and adaptability, Honesty/transparency, and Humility. These behaviors and traits reinforce the importance of active listening that you learned in Chapter 6, which included tips on effective listening, and in Chapter 3: Sales Ethics, in which you learned the importance of honesty and transparency. Although humility has not been covered specifically in this book up to this point, it is a vital trait to emphasize in this new era of post-Internet selling because prospects, customers, or buyers are not eager to partner with overconfident, aggressive salespeople who spout

Exhibit 11.3 Working together

Confidence builders

1 Being proactive
2 Frequent and candid communication
3 Active listening and adaptability
4 Honesty/transparency
5 Humility
6 Setting and abiding by clear goals
7 Demonstrating an "in-it-together" attitude
8 Showing empathy

Confidence killers

9 Apathy/disinterest
10 Failure to communicate
11 Incompetence
12 Inflexibility
13 Dishonesty (real or perceived)
14 Defensiveness
15 Legalism [technobabble]
16 Lack of accountability

Source: Financial Times/gyro/Russell Research. Used with permission.

technobabble jargon due to their in-depth knowledge of the technology that underlies what they are selling.

Nancy Duarte writes in her essential book, *Resonance: Visual Stories That Transform Audiences*, "Presenters think they can hide behind a wall of jargon, but what people are really looking for at a presentation is some kind of human connection."[11] Duarte also writes, "Embrace a stance of humility and deference to your audience's needs" and "Audience insights and resonance can only occur when a presenter takes a stance of humility."[12] Therefore, if you have expert technical knowledge, make sure you do not show it off, because showing off is a turnoff. Humbly educate rather than pontificate.

The *Financial Times*'s "Business Feeling Index" also reinforces the behavioral economists' research findings that people tend to make decisions based much more on feelings, on emotion, and on human connections rather than on rational, objective analysis of facts and data. What often happens when people make a decision is that they "are skilled at finding reasons to support their gut feelings" and conduct a one-sided search for supporting evidence only."[13]

Therefore, in order to educate prospects, customers, or buyers you have to (1) connect to them emotionally, to their elephant and (2) present the evidence consisting of facts, data, and numbers that can be used by the rider to rationalize and support where their gut feelings, the elephant, wants to go.

It is vital to learn how to connect emotionally with decision-makers because, as emphasized in Chapter 2, it is connecting emotionally that gives salespeople an advantage over speed-of-light algorithms that make incisive, but emotionless, media buying and selling decisions.

Connect emotionally with stories

Knowing that your education efforts have to appeal to the Elephant *and* Rider at your prospects, customers, and agency planners and buyers, what is the best way to make your message memorable?

Chip Heath and Dan Heath answer the above question in their practical and highly readable book, *Made to Stick*. The authors provide a checklist, based on the notion that "facts tell, but stories sell,"[14] of elements that make ideas memorable:

- Simple
- Unexpected
- Concrete
- Credible
- Emotional
- Stories

Simple   A simple story contains the essential core of an idea, a concise theme that summarizes the essence of your sales story.

Unexpected   Surprise people to get them to pay attention. You need to "violate people's expectations" and "be counterintuitive" to grab attention.[15]

Concrete   Facts that are specific to the situation makes your idea clear. "Trying to teach an abstract principle without concrete foundations is like trying to start a house by building a roof in the air."[16] Concrete ideas are easier to remember. "Experiments in human memory have shown that people are better at remembering concrete, easily visualized nouns ('bicycle' or 'avocado') than abstract ones ('justice' or 'personality')."[17] One way to help prospects remember the numbers that are inevitably included in a media sales presentation is to use *equivalencies*. An example of an equivalency would be to tell a prospect, "If the Cineplex movie theater in the mall sold out four showings of *Black Panther* every day for an entire year, not as many people would see the movie as would see just one commercial on my station's 'News 6 at 10:00 P.M.' on Sunday evening." Equivalencies dramatize numbers and make them understandable and concrete.

Another way to make a concept concrete is to humanize it. Rather than say the target audience for your receipt website and app is "busy women 25–49," say you are trying to help "Juggler Julia, a harried single mother of two pre-teen boys who is an Emergency Room nurse, who is slightly overweight, and who is trying to juggle both her desire for healthy, non-fattening foods with growing boys' finicky tastes in food."[18]

Credible   Data is dull, statistics are even duller, and dull is forgettable. One way to make numbers memorable is to use "the human-scale principle," as illustrated in *Made To Stick*. "Scientists recently computed an important physical constraint to an extraordinary accuracy. To put the accuracy in perspective, imagine throwing a rock from New York to Los Angeles and hitting the target within two-thirds of an inch of dead center."[19] Americans know roughly the distance for New York to Los Angeles, so the example is tangible to most people.

Emotional   To make people care about your ideas, you have to engage their feelings, use the power of association, appeal to their identity. We are wired to feel things for people, not abstractions, so personalize your presentations, emphasize your personalities if you sell for a television or radio network or station, for an influencer with a video channel, or for a podcast. Emphasize your star reporters, columnists, and writers if you sell for a magazine, newspaper, or a news and information website.[20] Mother Teresa once said, "If I look at the mass, I will never act. If I look at the one, I will."[21] The abstract "mass," is replaced by a connection to a single person, who is much easier to connect with emotionally and which is why you see photos of children, often with names, in ads for charities.

Stories   Chip and Dan Heath in *Made to Stick* make the point that it is not easy for experts in a particular discipline to tell simple, emotional stories because of what psychologists call the curse of knowledge. "Once we know something, we find it hard to imagine what it was like not to know it. Our knowledge has 'cursed' us. And it becomes difficult for us to share our knowledge with others, because we can't readily re-create our listener's state of mind."[22]

Therefore, in order to avoid the curse of knowledge, and to make your education efforts effective, you need to learn to tell simple, unexpected, concrete, credible, emotional stories.

Humans are wired to love stories. In fact, we are addicted to story. Even when the body goes to sleep, the mind stays up all night, telling itself stories."[23] All stories are almost always about people (or personified animals) with problems. "The people in stories want something badly – to survive, to win the girls or boy, to find a lost child. But big obstacles loom between the protagonists and what they want."[24] Thus, the formula for a story is:

$$\text{Story} = \text{Hero} + \text{Problem} + \text{Attempted Extrication}$$

The main character in a story is the Hero, or protagonist; the Problem is personified by an antagonist, or villain; and the Attempted Extrication is the process of solving the problem, typically by vanquishing the antagonist.

According to evolutionary thinkers "story is where people go to practice the key skills of human life."[25] Stories are "the flight simulators of human social life."[26] And "In Steven Pinker's groundbreaking book, *How the Mind Works,* he argues that stories equip us with a mental file of dilemmas we might someday face, along with workable solutions."[27]

If you examine the above formula and Pinker's quote, you will understand why every script in Chapter 9 included the use of a case study. Case studies are customer success *stories*. A customer (hero) has a problem and wants a solution (attempted extrication), which your medium provides. See "How to Write an Advertising Success Case Study" in the Downloads section of the *Media Selling* website (http://mediasellng.us/downloads/).

In the sections below, you will learn how to use stories and the story formula when educating one-on-one and groups.

Educating One-on-One

Your objective in the educating step in both missionary and service selling, as articulated in the Step Management Guide (see Chapter 8), is "To establish your credibility and expertise, to teach your product's benefit and advantages, and to move prospects (the agency) to active consideration." The assumption we make in this step is that you have made an initial prospecting contact with an account, or you have found the right strategy, planning, or buying decision-maker at an agency or client. We also assume that you have conducted research to find some insights and possible solutions if you are missionary selling, or that you have met with agency or client decision-makers if you are service selling, and that this educating step is the meeting in which you will educate yourself about the prospect's or agency's problems and challenges and educate your them about your medium. In this step you are not yet ready to make a specific proposal because you have get more details about what your decision-maker's specific problems and needs are.

In an educating meeting your major focus must be on connecting with decision makers emotionally, connecting to their elephant. Editions 1–4 of *Media Selling* recommended that calls be highly structured in six discrete phases: Greeting, New Information, Opening, Recap and Purpose, Discussion, and Summary and Close. However, this approach is too rigid for selling in the post-Internet, Big-Data, programmatic-dominated era because the biggest advantage people have over algorithms is their ability to connect emotionally to other people. Therefore, when selling in person, it is vital to leverage your human advantage and concentrate on connecting with decision-makers emotionally and gaining their trust.

Preparation

There are four steps in preparing for a one-on-one education meeting:

1   Conduct pre-meeting research.
2   Plan what peripheral material to use.
3   Plan to control the environment.
4   Rehearse mentally.

Conduct pre-meeting research   Before meeting with a decision-maker, conduct research on LinkedIn and on other social media (Instagram, Twitter, Snapchat, and Pinterest) to learn about the people you are meeting with. Where did they go to school, what associations to they belong to, what are their interests and hobbies, what jobs have they had? The information you gather will make it easier to kick-start a friendly conversation that will help you connect.

Plan what peripheral material to use   For a one-on-one meeting it is best not to give a PowerPoint presentation because a slide presentation is too formal and too impersonal. If your sales management insists or if it is appropriate that you show prospects and buyers a general presentation (GP) or a slickly produced video at your first meeting, it is best to put it on an iPad or tablet and then sit side-by-side to show it. I know of several companies that equip their salespeople with tablets on which to show a GP or videos, who then give the tablet to the prospect or buyer so they can review it on their own time. Tablets can be purchased for about $100, which is a reasonable investment for any order of $5,000 or more.

Instead of PowerPoint presentations or videos, use one-page brochures, or sell sheets, and one-page case studies that you can go over with your prospects or buyers. You can use a highlighter marker to emphasize important words or phrases on the sell sheets and case studies. You can then leave the highlighter with the prospect or buyer. Many companies put their logos on highlighters so salespeople can leave them as a branded gift.

Sell sheets and case studies should be kept to one page and also put up on the company's website. If you are selling a complicated product, then you will have several one-page sell sheets on a variety of topics such as benefits, advantages (numbers and statistics), and technical requirements (file sizes, ad sizes, tags, and so forth).

One-page case studies contain facts and numbers, but do not tell dramatic stories; therefore, when you get to an appropriate point in the meeting to talk about successes other advertisers have had (social proof), tell a simple, unexpected, credible, concise, emotional story, and then hand out the one-page case study. Do not pass out the case study before you tell the story because you do not want your prospect or buyer to be reading while you are telling your story.

Plan to control the environment   In preparation for your meeting think about the physical environment and attempt to control as much as you can so that you eliminate barriers that make developing rapport difficult. Sitting across a desk from someone is not personal because the desk acts as a barrier. Therefore, if you can work side by side on a table or on an office couch it is much more personal. In general, you should work as close as possible without violating the decision-maker's social space. Use emotional intelligence when evaluating the proper social space in which to work. By careful observation, you can find ways to connect with the person you are meeting with; you will see where their social space is and not invade it. Often invading someone's social space is a matter of inches, so get as close as you can, but never too close. Be very sensitive to gender differences as well as differences when evaluating the proper social space in which to work. If you get too close, some people can become offended or take it the wrong way. Always plan to work in *professional space*.

Rehearse mentally   Rehearse in your mind your opening, your presentation of new information, your case study stories, several trial closes, how you will deal with objections when they come up, and what decision criteria you want to agree on. You want to go over these elements several times in your head before a meeting so you are not winging it and are prepared to answer questions and some common objections.

One-on-one educating meeting

In your one-on-one educating meeting you want to implement your plan and accomplish the following:

1 Open to establish rapport.
2 Present new information to enhance your credibility.
3 Tell case study stories.
4 Assess the decision-maker's personality.
5 Attempt a trial close.
6 Deal with objections:
    a Probe to understand.
    b Compliment, restate the objection, and get agreement.
    c Empathize, reassure, and support.
7 Agree on decision criteria.
8 Summarize and close.

Open to establish rapport   Open the conversation with something you discovered in your pre-meeting research: "On LinkedIn I saw you went to University of Missouri. Great school. Were you in a sorority (fraternity)?"

This opening compliments the person you are meeting with because it demonstrates that you did your homework and, thus, begins to establish your credibility and likeableness and helps establish rapport. Also, appropriately phrased compliments are a good way to continue the conversation; notice the office decor, what books are on a bookshelf, and desk photographs, and say something complimentary.

On the other hand, some prospects dislike making polite conversation. You should have a sense of how business-like a prospect is after the telephone discussion or email exchange that set up the meeting. If your prospect takes a serious, business-is-business approach, limit small talk to one or two comments, such as, "How are you today?" or "Good to see you again." No matter what the circumstances, make your initial comments warm and sincere. Take your cues on the timing of when to move the conversation to a business focus from the person you are calling on.

Present new information to enhance your credibility   Give the person who you are meeting with some relevant new information that you discovered in your researching step – tell them "something they don't know." By giving relevant new information, you add to your source credibility and your prospects' or buyers' perception of your expertise. Examples of information you might give are: "I saw a new creative execution your competitor is using. Have you seen it? Do you like it?" Show the competitor's video ad to your prospect or buyer on your smartphone or tablet. When you give new information, you turn the conversation from a discussion about personal matters to a focus on business. A good way to keep up on digital advertising trends so you'll always have new information to pass on is to listen to eMarketer's daily "Behind the Numbers" podcast and read the relevant trade news websites such as Media Post, *Ad Age*, Digitday, and Radio Ink, for example.

Tell case study stories   Somewhere in the initial conversation, begin a discussion of one, two, or three case studies – each one a story that tells about how a customer (the hero) had a problem, got results (attempted extrication), which made them happy.

Remember to use case studies as opportunities to tell simple, unexpected, concrete, credible, emotional stories. After telling a story, ask some questions that will elicit more discussion or, hopefully bring out objections. You might say, "Isn't that terrific," or "Would that work for you?"

Assess the decision-maker's personality   As your prospects, customers, or buyers are talking and responding to you, make a mental note of their tone of voice, mannerisms, body language, pace of talking, attitude, and general demeanor. Do they continually talk about themselves and say "I," or do they talk about their team and say "we?" Are they smiling and being friendly and cooperative, or are they trying to dominate you by talking tough? You are collecting information about their personality traits so that you can do a preliminary Needs Portrait of them after meeting is over. Developing a Needs Portrait will help you create a Benefit Matrix so you can frame your offers effectively when you make a proposal in a subsequent meeting.

Attempt a trial close   The phrase "Would that work for you?" is, in essence, a trial close. A trial close is your attempt to see where you are in the process of moving a sale forward. A good result of a trial close is that you might well uncover some objections.

Deal with objections   Part of prospects' education process comes from them asking questions or bringing up objections. Bodybuilders use the expression "no pain, no gain." Salespeople should use the phrase "no objection, no sale." To the novice, objections might seem to be negatives and barriers. On the other hand, to the experienced professional, objections are a welcome and necessary part of the discussion process; they are not negatives, they are requests for more information, they are an integral part of the selling process. Decision-makers do not ask questions or raise objections if they are not interested in what you are offering.

Dealing with objections successfully is one of the most important skills a salesperson can learn. There are two types of objections: *figurative* and *literal*. A figurative objection is one that does not represent what prospects' words seem to indicate and should not be taken literally. They have no real meaning, but rather represent other, hidden objections, which are often quick initial responses that represent defense mechanisms rather than real reasons. Figurative objections are often used as a buying or negotiating tactic by prospects whose motives are to put salespeople on the defensive and to gain an upper hand.

Literal objections are real reasons why prospects are seriously questioning what you are presenting, and must be answered with additional information in order to move the sale forward. When you deal with literal objections, you should encourage prospects to answer their own objections, which is accomplished through the use of probing questions and restatements and the legitimate use of some of the principles of influence.

Following are some techniques for dealing with objections. You will notice that the following techniques for listening to objections are the same as the effective listening techniques you learned in Chapter 6, but another step has been added, a trial close. Here are examples of some appropriate responses:

Probe to understand. Used open- and closed-end questions to be sure that you hear the full objection or concern and that you and your prospect have the same understanding of it. Discover exactly what the objection is so that you can give a thorough, intelligent answer. Always listen rather than respond when prospects begin to express an objection and encourage them to continue. Never jump in with a counterargument. Sometimes a short response such as "Oh?" will provide additional information. For example:

PROSPECT:	"ESPN radio is pretty good, but it doesn't cover golf enough."
YOU:	"Oh?"
PROSPECT:	"Yeah, I like to watch golf and see the great players select their clubs."
YOU:	"Oh?"
PROSPECT:	"Yes, I know it's a personal preference. After all, I'm selling all sorts of sports equipment to everyone, not just to the upscale guys who play golf."
YOU:	"Oh?"
PROSPECT:	"Yeah, my audience prefers NFL football. ESPN does a lot of football coverage doesn't it?"
YOU:	"Yes. It's the most popular sport in the country" (Social proof).

Compliment, restate the objection, and get agreement. As you learned in the Effective Listening section of Chapter 6, compliment prospects for raising an objection, for having such good insight. By giving them a compliment, you put prospects in a receptive frame of mind, not on the defensive, and you trigger an obligation for them to reciprocate by listening to your answer. Next, restate the objection and then get their agreement that you understand it.

PROSPECT:	"I don't like your newspaper's editorials praising the mayor."
YOU:	"That's a very good point, Mark. I'm glad you brought that up. Let me make sure I understand your point; you don't like the mayor and don't think he's doing a good job. Right?"
PROSPECT:	"Yes, that's right."

Empathize, reassure, and support. Empathize with prospects' objections (how they feel), then reassure them that their objection is not out in left field somewhere (reassure them), and, finally, support your position.

YOU:	"I understand how you feel, Mark. A lot of my clients have felt the same way, but they have found that their ads still pull well no matter what stand our editorials take. By the way, why don't you write a letter to the editor; they'll probably print it. You express yourself very well and speak for a lot of people."
PROSPECT:	"That's a good idea. I think I will."

The best sales organizations spend a great deal of time practicing how to deal with objections and how to influence decision criteria. Write down the most common objections for your medium and product and then craft intelligent, concise answers.

Rehearse the answers repeatedly until you can deal with the most common objections in your sleep and with confidence. Find out from other salespeople in your organization how they answer these objections and how they influence decision criteria.

Agree on decision criteria   Depending on the type of customer you are calling on, getting agreement on decision criteria is a vital step in the sales process. Inexperienced generalists and many local clients will accept the advertising effectiveness criteria you suggest. Typically, the criteria for effectiveness are results, such as increased sales or store traffic. Experienced specialists such as agency media buyers have decision criteria dictated by a media plan, and it is very difficult, but not impossible, to change the decision criteria. However, by diligent work at the strategy and planning level at an agency, you might be able to get the decision criteria altered in in your favor. For example, if you were selling for a radio station or group, which the agency planners and strategists think of as a frequency medium, you might show them credible research that supports using radio as reach medium that is particularly effective in reaching younger demographics when used in conjunction with television, which has high reach in older demographics but has low reach in younger demographics.

Summarize and close   You have presented the decision-maker with at least one new idea, you have told at least one compelling case study story, you have used a trial close to see where you are in the process, you have answered the decision-maker's objections effectively, and you have agreed on the decision criteria. The next step is to *summarize* the three main points you have made and to *close*, which means to get a commitment to consider a specific, problem-solving proposal. You want to look for indications of conviction – body language such as leaning forward or more rapid head nodding; it is time to close and get a commitment on next steps, which include setting up a meeting with all those involved in making a final decision to consider a formal proposal.

Educating Groups

The primary objectives of educating a group of people are the same as educating one-on-one: "To establish your credibility and expertise, to teach your product's benefit and advantages, and to move prospects (the agency) to active consideration." The big difference between educating one-on-one and educating to a group is that with a larger group the education process typically has to be a presentation rather than a discussion. You should use a PowerPoint presentation to a group because this more formal approach focuses the group's attention on your content and limits discussion, which can get out of hand in a group, especially in a large group of over 25.

Preparation

There are six preparation steps for educating a group of people:

1   Conduct pre-meeting research.
2   Answer the Who, Where, When, and Why questions.
3   Create a presentation.
4   Plan handouts.
5   Plan to control the environment.
6   Rehearse the presentation.

Conduct pre-meeting research   Knowing your audience is critical to the success of any presentation. If you are in a missionary selling role and are educating a prospect's team on your medium or product, you must not only have in-depth knowledge of the prospect's business but also as much as is practical about the decision-maker, their personality (the Big Five personality traits plus their risk-taking profile), hobbies, interests, and perception of your company.

If you are a service role and educating an advertising agency group of strategists, planners, and buyers, you need to know what their biggest concerns are. If a large portion of your account list consists of advertising agencies, you should read two books that explain the current state of ad agencies: Ken Auletta's *Frenemies: The Disruption of the Ad Business (and Everything Else)* and Michael Farmer's *Madison Avenue Manslaughter: An Inside View of Fee-Cutting Clients, Profit-Hungry Owners and Declining Ad Agencies.* By understanding the challenges advertising agencies face, you can partner with them and make recommendations that will help them serve their clients better.

Nancy Duarte in *Resonate* writes, "Truly communicating effectively takes research" and "you need to define the audience in a way that's accurate and appropriate to the kind of presentation you will deliver." She continues:

> One way to get to know your audience is through a process called segmentation. By partitioning a large audience into smaller segments, you can target the segment that will bring the most additional supporters. Determine which group is most like to adopt your perspective – the group with which you can make the greatest impact with the least effort. It's tricky to appeal to the broader audience and simultaneously connect deeply with the subset that will play a key role in helping you.[28]

In *Resonate,* Duarte writes about a presentation that she gave to top executives of a major national beer manufacturer. Here is how she did her research:

> Several things helped me prepare for the presentation to the beer executives. I bought subscriptions to a couple of key marketing publications to see what was being said about their brands, solicited feedback from my social network, searched for articles about them, reviewed the conversations in the top beer blogs, found their own presentations on the Web, read their press releases, and read their company's annual report.
>
> The research helped me understand their challenges. Even though I used only a portion of the insights in the actual presentation, I felt I knew them and had empathy for what was on their minds. Those insights helped me feel connected to them.[29]

The above is a good guide for the type of pre-meeting research you need to do to deliver a memorable presentation.

Answer the Who, Where, When and Why questions   The second step in preparation is answering the Who, Where, When, and Why questions.

Who?.   Who in your organization should be the person to give a presentation? The rule of thumb is to try to match size and levels. In other words, have your CEO present to CEOs of large companies, your President (or equivalent) present to Presidents of large companies, your Senior VPs present to Senior VPs of large companies, and so forth.

Sometimes there will several people on your presentation team. It might include your CEO, a VP of Sales, yourself (a salesperson), and a marketing person. There should be no more than three, or, at most, four people from your organization on the presentation team, and everyone on the team should actively participate in the presentation and not merely be listeners. Too many people overwhelm and confuse your audience. If the leadoff person from your organization is a CEO, President, or Senior VP, then the primary salesperson on the account should be present and be introduced as the primary contact for the account in the future. The lead should deliver at least one-third of the presentation so prospects can get to know that person. In some situations, with an organization's largest accounts, a CEO might do the entire presentation talking to an account's CEO and promise the client their continued involvement in the account. Also, it is a good idea to give different areas of expertise to different members of your team. For example, assign ad operations to the person who is an expert, ad-serving to someone with that expertise, and research to an expert in that field. This arrangement not only relieves pressure on the main presenter, but also introduces other members of your team of experts. Make sure you rehearse transitions from one team member to the next in order to make them fast and smooth.

Who?.   The other "Who" is Who should receive a presentation? The first presentation to an account or agency should be to the most senior-level executives that you can gather so that you can introduce your organization and get agreement to pursue a relationship. You want to sell to VITO (Very Important Top Officers), as designated by Anthony Parinello in *Selling to VITO*, an excellent book that I strongly recommend.

Where?.   If possible, give presentations in your offices, because you get the home field advantage and can control the environment and timing. If you give a presentation at a prospect's location or at an agency, make sure you check beforehand to see if the there is an LCD projector or large-screen TV that will take input from your computer. Also, offer and arrange to have food or refreshments delivered. Serve coffee and food before or after a presentation, but never during. Always arrive at least half-an-hour early to give yourself plenty of time to set up.

When?.   You should give your presentation during prospects' advertising planning cycle. You must find this out during your qualifying process and give your presentation at the beginning of the process, as it is a waste of time to give a presentation a few months after a major account and its agency have planned their media expenditures for the coming year. If you have a choice, it is better to give presentations in the morning when people are fresh and can more easily stay awake than later in the afternoon when they are often drowsy.

Why?. Define your specific objectives, because when presenting to groups, there will be several presentations during the sales process and you must set objectives for each presentation. There are three general objectives that define why you give a presentation: (1) Introduce, (2) Inform/Educate, and (3) Persuade. The objective of the first presentation might be a customized general presentation designed to *introduce* a product or medium, if it is unfamiliar to the audience, or to update the audience to changes and improvements in a familiar product or medium. The objective of a second presentation might be to *inform/educate* an audience on a Big Idea about how to use your product or medium in the most effective way. A third presentation might be to *persuade* your audience to consider a specific solution that has been customized to help prospects' get the results they want and to get a firm commitment to invest in your medium. Initial presentations are not designed to close a deal and, typically, the second presentation is selling your overall benefits and advantages; the third presentation is designed to get a commitment. With bigger deals, a commitment often leads to further negotiations on deal terms, contract conditions, payment terms, and pricing structure.

Create a presentation   Guidelines for writing and designing a presentation are covered in the next section of this chapter, "Creating Presentations."

Plan handouts   Have plenty of handouts such as relevant articles, pictures of what you are offering and copies of the presentation. It is OK to hand out copies of your presentation beforehand along with reinforcing data and encourage people to take notes on the handouts if the audience is relatively small. There are some drawbacks to handing out copies of a presentation at the beginning – often people skip ahead to an area in which they are interested. However, the positives of people being able to follow at their own speed and take notes reinforces the points you make, and in most cases the positives outweigh the negatives.[30] If the audience is larger than 12 people, it is not a good idea to hand out copies of your presentation because, with that many people or more, it creates too much of a distraction and eliminates the element of surprise, or the unexpected.

Plan to control the environment   An effective presentation begins with an effective venue or room setup. In the annual television upfront presentations the TV networks make great efforts to have impressive venues, or locations, for their extravagant, star-studded presentations of their programs for the coming seasons because they understand that the perception of the quality of their programming can be enhanced by an impressive, lavish location. If the location of your presentation is in a room in which people sit around a conference table, plan in advance exactly how you want to arrange the seating. Do not have alternate seating – a member of your team, then a prospect, then a member of your team. Give those who are receiving the presentation the best seats and put them all together in a row or in a circle at the end of a table so they have the best view of the projection screen. Sit the main decision-makers in the middle so that they are always the center of your attention, although you will include others from time to time in your eye contacts. Have your team sit behind the audience or at the front of the table – your people do not need to have a good view of the presentation. The message you want to convey is that your focus and complete attention is on the audience. Assign members of your team to watch a member of the prospect's or agency's team and take notes unobtrusively of their assigned prospect's or agency person's reaction to different parts of the presentation so they can give you accurate feedback in a debriefing after the presentation.

Rehearse the presentation   Rehearsal is imperative, no matter the size of the audience or the amount of dollars involved. If the situation requires a presentation, then it requires that it be done professionally. In order to make certain that your presentation is better than those of your competitors, you must rehearse. While you do not need the months of rehearsal that a Broadway play does, you need to rehearse at least once or twice in front of your team. If possible, it is a good idea to try to rehearse in the room where you will give the presentation so you will feel comfortable in that venue. Rehearse walking around the room, asking questions to get involvement, and talking to empty chairs, especially to the chair in which you want the decision-maker to sit.

When you rehearse, keep a mental picture of the physical setup so you will be prepared and comfortable. You want to work in as intimate space as possible in order to develop rapport with your audience. Practice your movements in a space that is similar to the one in which you will be presenting. Rehearse everything in your script, including your stories, equivalencies, and questions. Rehearse your gestures, too. Time all your rehearsals so you know exactly how long your presentation and questions take. Use the same presentation aids, such as a laser pointer and a remote slide clicker that you will use in the actual presentation.

Presenting effectively is a skill that, like acting, requires rehearsal and feedback in order to perfect your technique. Also, like the best actors, the best presenters come across as natural and confident. "Their style is conversational, and they look completely at ease in front of any audience."[31] It is worth the time and effort you invest in rehearsal, because the success of your presentation depends to a great degree on how much you practice. As Timothy J. Koegel writes in *The Exceptional Presenter*, "Those who practice improve. Those who don't, don't."[32]

Furthermore, "Relentless preparation is the single best way to overcome stage fright," Carmine Gallo writes in *The Presentation Secrets of Steve Jobs*.[33]

Creating presentations

If you are going to create a presentation yourself or have significant input into a presentation that is created by another department, such as marketing, the first thing you should do is read carefully Nancy Duarte's book, *Resonate: Present Visual Stories That Transform Audiences*. Duarte's Silicon Valley firm has created some of the most memorable presentations of all time, including probably the most iconic presentation ever, Steve Jobs's introduction of the iPhone. The second thing you should do is to read Carmine

Gallo's book *The Presentation Secrets of Steve Jobs: How to Be Insanely Great In Front of Any Audience*. The third thing you should do is watch the video of Jobs's 2007 introduction of the iPhone at https://youtu.be/x7qPAY9JqE4.

The process of creating a presentation consists of four steps:

1   Writing
2   Editing
3   Sketching
4   Producing

Writing   When you write a presentation, you should begin with a list of all the points you want to make, then combine elements and narrow down the list to three key points. When writing, always keep in mind the "Rule of Three" and use it throughout your presentation, because people cannot and will not remember more than three points. The Rule of Three is used effectively in a number of great, documents, speeches, and presentations. As Gallo writes in *The Presentation Secrets of Steve Jobs,* perhaps one of the most notable use of the Rule of Three is in the second paragraph of the *Declaration of Independence,* which reads, "We hold these truths to be self-evident, that all men are created equal, that they are endowed by their Creator with certain unalienable rights, that among these are life, liberty and the pursuit of happiness." The Rule of Three is used in Vince Lombardi's famous admonition to his professional football players, "There are three important things: family, religion, and the Green Bay Packers."[34]

Next, make notes about how you want your audience to feel at various sections of your presentation. Outlining major points and how you want your audience to feel keeps the focus on connecting emotionally to your audience.

When you write, you want to write for the ear, not the eye.[35] You want to tell a good story that people want to listen to, because audiences want to be informed, educated, *and* entertained. You entertain people by telling stories, by appealing to their elephant, while at the same time giving them information to appeal to their rider. As you write, observe the following rules of creating presentations:

Writing Rule #1: The audience is the hero of your story, not you.   In this book we have emphasized the vital importance of focusing on the customer, of serving, of helping, and getting results for your prospects, customers, and agencies. Therefore, you must make them the hero of the overall story you are going to tell, and you need to identify the emotions and reactions you want from the audience.

Writing Rule #2: Follow the classic, familiar structure of a story.   Remember that you are going to tell a simple, unexpected, concrete, credible, emotional story that follows the familiar structure of Hero (the audience, the group you are presenting to) + Problem (antagonist) + Attempted Extrication (solution). Your audience is familiar with this story structure as they have been through the ages from early mythology, through Shakespeare's plays, and through movies. By following a story structure that is in the collective unconscious of your audience, you will reduce their resistance, get them on your side, and engage them (see, I used the Rule of Three).

Writing Rule #3: Introduce the antagonist early in the story.   The opening scene of the first *Star Wars* movie, *Episode IV: A New Hope* depicts Darth Vader capturing a rebel spaceship and trying to find the stolen plans of the Death Star, which Princess Leia has inserted into R2D2. The opening scene of the highest grossing movie ever, *Star Wars: Episode VIII: The Force Awakens*, depicts Kylo Ren killing San Tekka, a spiritual leader of a group of people who live on the planet Jakku. Both of these phenomenally successful movies introduce the antagonist – the villain, the Problem – before introducing the hero – Luke in *A New Hope* and Rey in *The Force Awakens*. Another reason for introducing the problem early in a presentation is that doing so clearly shows that you understand the prospect's or agency's business and problems, which immediately establishes your credibility and expertise. By stating the problem first, you focus on the customer, not on yourself or on your company.

Too many presentations I have seen over the years start out being all about the presenter's company, and include chest thumping and bragging about themselves. "We're number one!" or "We're the industry leader!" followed by number- and chart-heavy, boring slides that are not about prospects or customers, but are about narcissistic mirror gazing, and which, therefore, turn off audience members who want to know "what's in it for me" (WIIFM).

Writing Rule #4: Offer a solution to, an extrication from, the problem and tell the audience why you are best qualified to provide the solution.   When you offer a solution, you have to tell the audience first why your medium or company is best qualified to extricate them from the problem; therefore, in this section of a presentation, you can finally write about your medium or company.

When you mention your company, emphasize your organization's vision, or mission, and then show how that mission aligns with your prospect's or agency's mission. When you describe your company's mission, you are, in essence, telling the audience what the company does in simple clear language. Carmine Gallo in *The Presentation Secrets of Steve Jobs* recommends that your "what-you-do" statement be in 10 words or fewer. For example, when Larry Page and Sergei Brin first pitched Google to venture capitalists, they said, "Google provides access to the world's information in one click."[36] "Cisco changes the way we work, live, play and learn," is the way CEO John Chambers positions his company.[37] Howard Schultz believes "Starbucks creates a third place between work and home."[38] ESPN's mission statement is serve sports fans wherever they are."

All of these statements are simple and humble, not chest-thumping bragging. They do not boast that they are number one, or the leading provider, or the best. Remember from Chapter 2 that people are motivated by *autonomy, mastery,* and *purpose*. Audiences tend to connect to a company that has a meaningful purpose, or mission. Who would not understand what a company does or not like a company that provides access to the world's information in one click or that serves sports fans wherever they are?

Writing Rule #5: Insert case studies – advertiser success stories.   Personalize case studies in story form. Case studies validate, give social proof to your extrication, to your solution.

Writing Rule #6: Summarize. Most summaries are too long. I have seen presenters summarize 15 points at the end of a presentation. That is not a summary; it is a novelette. Use the Rule of Three and keep your summary to three points, because more than likely that is all your audience will remember.

Writing Rule #7: Conclude with a call to action. At the end of Steve Jobs's iconic iPhone introduction, his call to action was simple: "Now go buy one." However, your call to action will differ depending on the type of presentation you are giving. If it is an *introductory* presentation, a call to action might be, "What day next week can we meet so I can learn more about your biggest challenges?" If you are giving an *informational* presentation, your call to action might be, "What are the three next steps we can make to move things forward toward you getting better results, a better ROI on your advertising?" But, Nancy Duarte writes in *Resonate*, "Many presentations end with a call to action; however, ending a presentation with a to-do list for the audience is not inspirational. So it's important to follow up the call to action with a vivid picture of the potential reward."[39] "The call to action should leave the audience with a sense of what could be," writes Duarte.[40] If you are giving *persuading* presentation, your call to action might be, "May we go ahead and help you solve this problem and become more profitable?" In any case the call to action, should include a clear summation of what's in it for them (WIIFM) and leave them thinking of a better tomorrow.

Widely regarded as the greatest speech in the English language, Lincoln's Gettysburg Address opens memorably with "Four score and seven years ago," and ends unforgettably with "…and that government of the people, by the people, for the people shall not perish from the earth." (Lincoln used the Rule of Three.) I do not expect you will be able to write as moving, as unforgettable a finish as Abraham Lincoln did, but his stirring words are a good place to start when you think about writing your conclusion, your call to action.

Editing As you go back over what you have written, edit for meaning, clarity, and brevity.

Editing Rule #1: Edit on behalf of the audience. The audience does not want to know everything that you know. Ask yourself if the audience wants you to cram more information into your presentation. Have you ever heard someone say after listening to a presentation, "Gee, that presentation would have been much better if it were longer?" Also keep in mind the concept that you never want to give a presentation that you would not want to sit through.

Editing Rule #2: Edit ruthlessly and keep only simple, jargon-free words. Often presenters think they can hide behind a wall of jargon, so edit out all technobabble and jargon. Notice the simple language Steve Jobs uses in his introduction of the iPhone, which is a very technologically sophisticated and complicated product, yet he uses simple language and zippy phrases like, "Isn't that terrific!"

Sketching   After you have edited what you have written, it is time to sketch out the slides you will use and follow the sketching rules below. If you sketch on 3 in. x 3 in. PostIt Notes, you can stick them on a wall and move them around for an optimum arrangement.

Sketching Rule #1: Put only one idea on a slide.   You are creating a presentation, not a document; therefore, *do not use bullet points,* and put just one idea on a slide. Garr Reynolds, author of *Presentation Zen,* calls slides with lots of text and bullet points "sli-deuments," which is an attempt to merge documents with slides. On slides, do not put in text the same information that you will be talking about, because it confuses an audience, who cannot read and listen at the same time.[41] Keep it simple. As you will see if you watch Google's CEO, Sundar Pichai's presentation at the 2018 i/O Conference at https://www.youtube.com/watch?v=zxKCK1rTHCA, slides with images and videos act as a prompt or mere backdrop for Pichai's remarks. You do not want the slides to distract the audience's attention away from the speaker.

Sketching Rule #2: Turn words into pictures.   A single photo or screen shot is often all that is needed on a slide to communicate the single idea that is on the slide.

Producing   After you have sketched your slides on PostIt Notes, stuck them on a wall, and rearranged them to fit your written script, the next step is to produce them in PowerPoint or Keynote. Generally Power Point is preferred, because if you want to share your presentation, PowerPoint is virtually universal and, thus, it is more convenient for more people to open.

Producing Rule #1: Have lots of white space on your slides.   Have plenty of white space on your slides to "give them breathing room… clutter is a failure of design," as Nancy Duarte writes in *Slide:ology: The Art and Science of Creating Great Presentations.*[42]

Delivering presentations

Before you begin your PowerPoint presentation, make opening remarks that deal with questions such as, "Should I take notes?", "Can I ask questions?", and "How long will the presentation take?" Opening remarks should also deal with how to handle questions as they occur in a presentation. One way is to take questions at the end of the presentation, another is to take them at any time, another is to take them at specific times during the presentation, or to take only important questions during the presentation and others afterwards. Saving questions until the end will allow you to save time, but it creates a one-way presentation. While you maintain control, you limit interaction and leave some questions unanswered. Worst of all, it hurts the rapport you would like to build between you and the audience.

Taking questions any time during a presentation is very effective if you have relative loose time constraints, because it gets the audience involved. But keep close track of time. If people ask too many questions, you might not finish the entire presentation, so give the problem to them by saying, "Time is in your hands. Our presentation runs 25 minutes and I have built in 15 minutes for questions, but please feel free to ask as many questions as you like, and we can extend the time frame." In this way you alert them to the need to keep track but that you can extend the time if they want.

Taking important questions during the presentation and the rest later is another good tactic. By saying in your opening remarks, "we have allowed time at the end of the presentation for questions, but, of course, feel free to ask any questions that help clarify our presentation," you encourage you audience to save questions while not muzzling them.

Delivery Rules #1, #2, and #3: Never, never, never read the slides to the audience.   Reading text from slides is a sleep-inducing practice that is repeated in too many presentations. Do not do it.

Dos and Don'ts of delivering a presentation   Nick Morgan in an article titled "The kinesthetic speaker: Putting action into words" in the *Harvard Business Review*, writes, "Sure, presentations are about what a speaker says. But they're also about how a speaker moves. By making adroit use of your body and the space around you, you can create a physical connection with the audience that will earn trust and inspire action."[43] In the article Morgan writes the Dos and Don'ts of kinesthetic speaking, as seen in Exhibit 11.4.

Exhibit 11.4   The Dos and Don'ts of kinesthetic speaking

Do...
– identify individuals who can serve as proxies for the whole audience.
– vary the distance between yourself and the audience, moving into the personal space of proxies to recount an anecdote or to make a plea.
– ensure that your physical moves are in harmony with your verbal message.
– prepare your own presentations so your physical moves don't betray inauthentic content.
– read and respond to the nonverbal cues of audience members.

Don't...
– speak generally to the entire audience for long periods.
– repeatedly move back and forth between podium or slide projector and the screen.
– turn away from the audience to cue up your next slide while speaking.
– fidget away your nervous energy.
– count on the audience remembering more than one or two of your main points.

Source: Morgan, Nick. 2001 "The kinesthetic speaker: putting action into words." *Harvard Business Review*. Used with permission.

Delivery tips   For helpful tips on how to deliver a presentation see Exhibit 11.5, which is based in part on a 1998 article in the *Harvard Business Review* by Jay Conger.

Exhibit 11.5   Delivery tips

Tip		Description
1	Audience expectations	You should have a sense of your audiences' expectations and their preferred style: for example, conservative, formal, and straightforward or informal, humorous, and glitzy.
2	Involve the audience.	People learn better when they participate than they do when they just listen, so ask questions such as "What is the biggest challenge facing you industry in the next five years?" or ask them to write down the five most important people in their company, and then ask how many wrote down "the customer."
3	Poise and confidence	Having poise and demonstrating a sense of confidence are critical for delivering a successful presentation.
4	Love your product.	Be passionate about it and convey that passion to your audience with your physical movements, gestures, and use of common expressions such as, "Isn't that terrific!" like Steve Jobs does in his iPhone introduction.
5	Be concise.	Don't ramble. Stick to your script and stay within the allotted time. Remember that the ideal length of time for a presentation is 20 minutes. The average length of the time of TED Talks is 18 minutes.
6	"We're number one" never sold anything.	What prospects and buyers want are solutions, not chest-thumping numbers. Use equivalencies for numbers whenever you can and make sure the numbers you use are relevant to the solutions you are proposing. No one cares if you are number one if you cannot solve their problems.
7	Don't be defensive.	If you get a question, even a hostile one, do not panic. Repeat the question, say something like "good point," and answer it concisely, honestly, and directly or put it off until later in your presentation when you have an answer for it. Do not waffle or lose your confidence.
8	Smile	Inexperienced speakers are often frightened when they present in front of a group and forget to smile. Do not make that mistake; smile as appropriate and authentically throughout the presentation.
9	Establish eye contact with everyone.	Move around and try to establish some eye contact with everyone, even though you will be concentrating most often on the decision-maker.
10	Vary your voice.	Vary your tone of voice, your pitch, and your volume. Modulate well; you do not want to lull people to sleep with a monotone.
11	Use people's names.	Direct your points to specific people and use their names: "Isn't this the solution you asked for, Jane?", for example.
12	Be careful about injecting humor.	Unless you are funny and have a knack for telling jokes and for humor, do not use it. Nothing falls flatter than a poor joke. Never insert off-color or inappropriate humor.
13	Keep going.	It takes listeners a long time to catch up to the fact that you have lost your place or gone to the wrong slide. Pause, collect yourself, and keep going. Never say, "I'm sorry" or point out a mistake because your audience more than likely will not notice a mistake unless you point it out. Keep on trucking.

Exhibit 11.5	Delivery tips (cont'd)
Tip	*Description*
14 Laugh it off.	If something happens such as a projector breaks or a bulb burns out, so what? Keep on going. Your audience is with you and wants you to do well, so make them comfortable by handling a crisis with grace and humor without blaming someone – your assistant, the projector, or God. Laugh it off gracefully and keep on trucking.
15 Be yourself and have fun.	Relax and be natural; rehearsals will help a lot to give you confidence and to relax enough to be yourself. You must be authentic because people will know if you are trying too hard or are a phony trying to sell them snake oil.

Delivering your conclusion, your call to action   Richard B. Chase and Sriram Dasu stress the importance of finishing strong in an article titled "Want to perfect your company's service? Use behavioral science" in the *Harvard Business Review*. The authors indicate that of the two ordering effects – primacy and recency – recency, or the last experience people have in an encounter such as a presentation, is by far the most important.[44] Therefore, not only is it important to have a dramatic, attention-getting opening, but it is even more important that your conclusion, your call to action, is memorable.

Ratchet up your passion in your final comments. You want to make your appeal as emotional as you can for why a deal between your company and a prospect's or buyer's company is an ideal partnership.

Debriefing

In the first few days after a presentation, the team that presented it should have a debriefing meeting. Go over your script and each slide in the presentation and ask if your preparation was on target and if your audience accepted your ideas and solutions.

You cannot learn by your mistakes unless you analyze them objectively. After every presentation, be paranoid about not meeting your objective for the presentation and then debrief thoroughly. This debriefing process puts into practice the Japanese manufacturing concept of *kaizen*, or continuous improvement.

Test Yourself

1. In 2016, how much did Amazon invest in search advertising?
2. What step in this fifth edition of *Media Selling* replaced the *presenting* step in the fourth edition of *Media Selling*? Why?
3. Explain the Elephant and the Rider.
4. What is item number five in the Confidence Builders list from the *Financial Times* research study?
5. What are the six elements from *Made to Stick* that make ideas memorable?

6. What are the four steps of preparation for a one-on-one meeting?
7. What are the eight things you need to accomplish in a one-on-one meeting?
8. What are the six steps of preparation for a presentation to a group?
9. What are the four steps of creating a presentation?
10. What are the seven rules for writing a presentation?
11. What are the two editing rules?
12. What are the two sketching rules?
13. What is the producing rule?
14. What are delivery rules #1, #2, and #3?
15. Why is debriefing important?

Project

Choose a local advertiser such as an electronics and appliance store as a prospect and create a presentation to educate this advertiser. Assume you are selling for the Zimmer Radio and Marketing Group (see zimmercommunications.com/). Use the rules in this chapter for creating a presentation: (1) write a script, (2) following the *delivery tips* in this chapter, rehearse delivering the presentation in front of a full-length mirror, and (3) ask a friend or a colleague to play the part of the electronics-and-appliance-store prospect and give the presentation to them. After you have made the presentation, debrief with your friend or colleague and get feedback on how you did. What did you remember to do and what did you forget to do?

References

Agrawal, Ajay, Gans, Jonathan, and Goldfarb, Avi. 2018. *Prediction Machines: The Simple Economics of Artificial Intelligence*. Boston, MA: Harvard Business School Press.

Auletta, Ken. *Frenemies: The Disruption of the Ad Business (and Everything Else)*. New York: Penguin Books.

Conger, Jay. 1998. "The necessary art of persuasion." *Harvard Business Review*, May–June.

Chase, Richard B. and Sriram Dasu. 2001. "Want to perfect your company's service? Use behavioral science." *Harvard Business Review*, June.

Duarte, Nancy. 2010. *Resonate: Visual Stories That Transform Audiences*. Hoboken, NJ: Wiley.

Duarte, Nancy. 2008. *Slide:ology: The Art and Science of Creating Great Presentations*. Sebastopol, CA: O'Reilly Media.

Farmer, Michael. 2017. *Madison Avenue Manslaughter: An Inside View of Fee-Cutting Clients, Profit-Hungry Owners and Declining Ad Agencies*. New York: LID Publishing.

Gallo, Carmine. 2010. *The Presentation Secrets of Steve Jobs: How to Be Insanely Great in Front of Any Audience*. New York: McGraw-Hill.

Haidt, Jonathan. 2006. *The Happiness Hypothesis: Finding Modern Truth in Ancient Wisdom From Ancient Wisdom*. New York: Basic Books.

Heath, Chip and Heath, Dan. 2007. *Made to Stick: Why Some Stories Survive and Others Die*. New York: Random House.

Heath, Chip and Heath, Dan. 2010. *Switch: How to Change Things When Change Is Hard*. New York: Crown Business.

Koegel, Timothy J. 2007. *The Exceptional Presenter.* Austin, TX: Greenleaf Book Group Press.

Morgan, Nick. 2001. "The kinesthetic speaker: Putting action into words." *Harvard Business Review,* April.

Parinello, Anthony. 1999. *Selling to Vito: The Very Important Top Officer.* Holbrook, MA: Adams Media Corp.

Rackham, Neil. 1989. *Major Account Sales Strategy.* New York: McGraw-Hill Education.

Reynolds, Garr. 2008. *Presentation Zen: Simple Ideas on Presentation Design and Delivery (Voices That Matter),* 2nd ed. Berkeley, CA: New Riders.

Tufte, Edward R. 2006. *The Cognitive Style of PowerPoint: Pitching Out Corrupts Within.* Cheshire, CT: Graphics Press.

Underhill, Roy. 2000. *Khrushchev's Shoe.* Cambridge, MA: Perseus Publishing.

Resources

eMarketer "Behind the Numbers" podcast (www.emarketer.com/Article/Behind-Numbers-eMarketer-Podcast)

Notes

1   Galloway, Scott. Interview retrieved from https://youtu.be/pTzCGV1w-ng.

2   Fischer, Sara. 2018. Axios Media Trends. Retrieved from http://www.axios.com/newsletters/axios-medi-trends-0f657410-6347-41f5-a829-4b327da57f54.html.

3   Haidt, Jonathan. 2006. *The Happiness Hypothesis: Finding Modern Truth in Ancient Wisdom From Ancient Wisdom.* New York: Basic Books.

4   Heath, Chip and Heath, Dan. 2010. *Switch: How to Change Things When Change Is Hard.* New York: Crown Business.

5   Ibid.

6   Ibid.

7   Ibid.

8   Ibid.

9   Financial Times. "The Business Feeling Index." Retrieved from https://gyro.com/wp-content/uploads/The-Business-Feeling-Index.pdf.

10 Ibid.

11 Duarte, Nancy. 2010. *Resonate: Present Visual Stories That Transform Audiences.* Hoboken, NJ: Wiley.

12 Ibid.

13 Haidt, Jonathan. 2006. *The Happiness Hypothesis: Finding Modern truth in Ancient Wisdom from Ancient Wisdom.* New York: Basic Books.

14 Heath, Chip and Heath, Dan. 2007. *Made to Stick: Why Some Stories Survive and Others Die.* New York: Random House.

15 Ibid.

16 Ibid.

17 Ibid.

18 Ibid.

19 Ibid.

20 Ibid.

21 Ibid.

22 Ibid.

23 Gottschall, Jonathan. 2012. *The Storytelling Animal: How Stories Make Us Human.* New York: Houghton Mifflin.

24 Ibid.

25 Ibid.

26 Ibid.

27 Ibid.

28 Duarte, Nancy. 2010. *Resonate: Present Visual Stories that Transform Audiences.* Hoboken, NJ: Wiley.

29 Ibid.

30 Tufte, Edward R.2006. *The Cogn-
    itive Style of PowerPoint: Pitching Out
    Corrupts Within.* Cheshire, CT:
    Graphics Press.

31 Koegel, Timothy J. 2007. *The Exceptional
    Presenter.* Austin, TX: Greenleaf Book
    Group Press.

32 Ibid.

33 Gallo, Carmine. 2010. *The Presentation
    Secrets of Steve Jobs: How to Be Insanely
    Great in Front of Any Audience.* New York:
    McGraw-Hill.

34 Ibid.

35 Ibid.

36 Ibid.

37 Ibid.

38 Ibid.

39 Duarte, Nancy. 2010. *Resonate: Present
    Visual Stories that Transform Audiences.*
    Hoboken, NJ: Wiley.

40 Ibid.

41 Gallo, Carmine. 2010. *The Presentation
    Secrets of Steve Jobs: How to Be Insanely
    Great in Front of Any Audience.* New York:
    McGraw-Hill.

42 Duarte, Nancy. 2008. *Slide:ology: The Art
    and Science of Producing Great Presentations.*
    Sebastopol, CA: O'Reilly Media.

43 Morgan, Nick. 2001. "The kinesthetic
    speaker: Putting action into words."
    Harvard Business Review, April.

44 Chase, Richard B. and Dasu, Sriram. 2001.
    "Want to perfect your company's service?
    Use behavioral science." *Harvard Business
    Review*, June.

12

Proposing

Charles Warner

The fourth step of both missionary and service selling is *proposing*, or putting a specific proposal, or offer, on the table. "On the table" is a concept that is used in formal negotiations, and it means that an offer is firm, or an offer that, if accepted by the other side, obligates the proposing side to accept the proposal as presented.

In today's non-programmatic media advertising marketplace, a typical proposal contains at a minimum, available inventory, prices, terms, and conditions. Generally, the prices, terms, and conditions are negotiable, depending on a number of conditions, especially the size of the order – the larger the schedule and the longer the schedule runs, the more negotiable prices, terms, and conditions there generally are.

In missionary selling, proposals for a four-week advertising campaign on a medium-size market radio station and its website might be relatively simple and consist of an overall weekly package price for a stated number of spots and impressions, terms, and conditions. The terms and conditions are typically the standard ones detailed in the 4A's/IAB Standard Terms and Conditions for Internet Advertising for Media Buys One Year or Less that can be found at https://www.iab.com/guidelines/standard-terms-conditions-internet-advertising-media-buys-one-year-less/. Go to this link and click on the Education Guide link. Download the 22-page Education Guide and read it. Reading the Guide is a slog – it is not a Stephen King thriller – but it is vital for you to read carefully and understand the terms and conditions that apply to the advertising that you will be selling, and it is just as important for you to know if your company's terms and conditions are different in any way from the 4A's/IAB standards, and if so, exactly how they differ.

If you are doing missionary selling to local businesses people who are inexperienced generalists, you will need to explain the terms and conditions to them so they

Media Selling: Digital, Television, Audio, Print and Cross-Platform, Fifth Edition.
Charles Warner, William A. Lederer, and Brian Moroz.
© 2020 John Wiley & Sons, Inc. Published 2020 by John Wiley & Sons, Inc.

fully understand, in a sense, what they are agreeing to when they give you an order. If you are making a proposal to experienced specialists at an advertising agency, they assume that the 4As/IAB Standard Terms and Conditions apply to what you are selling, so you do not need to mention them unless your organization has different terms and conditions; if this is the case, you must clearly point out how the terms and conditions on your contract or insertion order (IO) differ from the standard 4A's/IAB terms and conditions.

Terms and conditions for television and radio station, newspaper, magazine, and out-of-home advertising will differ, of course, depending on the medium, but many of the Payment and Liability and Cancellation and Termination terms and conditions will be similar or the same, especially for television and radio stations.

There is a virtually infinite number of possible variations in types of proposals and proposal strategies and tactics for different media, so they cannot all be covered in this book. Therefore, below are some general guidelines for making proposals in both missionary and service selling.

Proposals

The topic of proposals brings up several questions:

1   What is the ultimate purpose of a proposal?
2   To whom should a proposal appeal?
3   What is the best way to format a proposal?
4   How detailed and how long should a proposal be?
5   What are the ordering tactics for proposals?

Answers to the five proposal questions

The purpose of a proposal is to open a negotiation that will result in a favorable outcome   In situations that are not complicated and are pretty straightforward, such as with a campaign on a medium-sized market radio station and website, a proposal might be accepted as offered and require no further negotiation. However, in larger, more complicated deals, the purpose of a proposal is to set the stage favorably for additional negotiations.

A proposal should appeal to the decision-maker's Rider   In previous meetings you have established your credibility, gained the decision-maker's trust, and made an emotional connection. In the initial steps of selling you have appealed primarily to the decision-maker's Elephant, but in the *proposing* step you should appeal to the decision-maker's Rider with numbers, data, and statistics based on agreed-upon decision criteria and that are properly referenced and sourced.

A proposal should be formatted the way a prospect, client, or an agency wants Over the years I have seen too many media proposals done the way a company's marketing or design department wants them done, typically on PowerPoint with lots of pretty graphics and pictures of logos, headquarters buildings, founders, and CEOs – stuff that has nothing to do with what a prospect, client, or agency is looking for. Keep in mind that *educating* presentations live in the Land of PowerPoint and that *proposing* documents live in the Land of Excel or Google Sheets.

Here is a list of Dos and Don'ts for formatting proposal documents:

Dos for formatting proposals.

- Do check with your prospect, client, or agency about what format they prefer. If they don't have a preference, use Excel or Google Sheets, because you want to focus on the prospect's, client's, or agency buyer's rider and not on yourself. You do not necessarily want your proposal to look pretty; you want it to be data based and credible.
- Do remember that proposal documents will probably be shared with people who were not at your educating presentation and who may not be familiar with your benefits and advantages. Therefore, you need to attach clarifying documents in an Appendix in a Word or Google Docs format. The clarifying documents should expand on the benefits and advantages that you have highlighted in your proposal document and that you support with credible sources such as Nielsen ratings or comScore numbers. You will learn more about credible sources and Nielsen and comScore in the Chapter 18: Measuring Advertising.
- Keep the proposal worksheet file size small enough to attach to an email, so you do not have to FTP the files to a third-party platform such as SlideShare.

Don'ts for formatting proposals.

- Don't ever submit just one proposal.
- Don't impose your company's preferred presentation or proposal design or template on prospects, clients, or agencies.
- Don't ever submit a software- or AI-generated proposal in its original form.

A proposal should be as detailed and as long as needed to win Although you should try to avoid creating a large file that needs to be sent via FTP, the amount of detail in and the length of a proposal depends on two factors: (1) how much money is involved, and (2) what the definition of *a win* is. Figure 12.1 shows, in very general terms, how detailed and long a proposal should be based on how much money is involved.

Figure 12.1 simply means that the more money that is involved, the longer a proposal should be. It also emphasizes the concept that you do not want to overwhelm prospects, clients, or agencies, instead you want to give them what they have agreed to consider, which is a straightforward proposal. They do not need or necessarily want nice graphics, pretty pictures, or you patting yourself on the back about your company or medium.

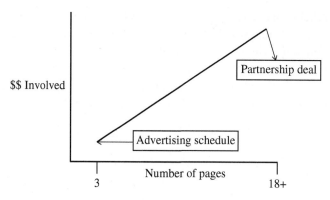

Figure 12.1   Proposals

The definition of a win is more nuanced. First, the concept of winning assumes that there is competition – more than one person or company are making proposals and competing for the business. When an advertiser goes to Google Ads or to Facebook to buy advertising, the competition is not other media companies, the competition is among advertisers who are bidding in an online, automated auction based primarily on price. Therefore, a win for advertisers who are bidding would be investing in ads based on what they are willing to pay – pretty straightforward. However, when an agency sends out an RFP to publishers, the competition is among other publishers, and those publishers are competing on a number of dimensions that include price, terms and conditions, demographics, psychographics, safe content, and more. With multiple competitors, the strategy and tactics for competitive moves are governed by game theory.

Game theory. Game theory is often applied to competitive situations in economics, investing, politics, sports, and international relations. The mathematical genius John von Neumann first developed game theory in 1928.[1] Watching players bluff in a poker game in 1928 inspired von Neumann – godfather of the modern computer and one of the sharpest minds in the twentieth century – to construct game theory, a mathematical study of deception and competitive strategies.

At its most basic level, game theory posits that players of any game, or competitive situation, such as Monopoly, poker, sports, business, war, negotiating, or selling, should make tactical moves not only based on the probability of success, but also based on the moves of their competitors. So, when you play poker, you do not only consider the odds of drawing a particular card or hand, but you also consider what the other players' tendencies and moves are. In other words, you base your tactical moves on what your competitors' moves are.

I used a good example of the use of game theory principles in the fourth edition of *Media Selling*. The example was in Super Bowl XXXVII when Jon Gruden's Tampa Bay Buccaneers whomped the Oakland Raiders. Gruden had been the coach of the Raiders the previous year and knew the team's tendencies. He knew that Raider quarterback, Rich Gannon, usually pumped one way and then threw the other way. Because the

Buccaneers' defensive backs knew Gannon's tendencies, the Tampa Bay secondary grabbed a record five interceptions. The Bucs played the game according to what moves they knew their competitor would make.

Game theory also defines different types of games. One type of game is a zero-sum game such as a soccer match or a political race in which there are just two competitors and only one winner (+1) and one loser (−1), thus, the sum of the two is zero. There are also multiplayer games in which the definition of a win depends on the expectations of the competitors. If a top-ranked marathon runner expects to win a race but comes in third, it is not a win. If an unranked runner expects to finish in the top 25 in a Marathon race in which there are 400 competitors and that runner comes in 24th, it is a win.

Therefore, winning in a multiplayer competition for an advertising campaign is not an absolute concept, it is a comparative concept that measures (1) how you do against other media company competition, and (2) what your expectations are.

How to beat other media competition. In order to measure how you do against your other media company competitors, you must know what kind of proposals they make, and the best way to discover what their proposals look like is to do some detective work and ask prospects, clients, and agencies, "How do you want to get proposals? Please show me a few of the best proposals and a few of the worst proposals you've received so I can tailor mine to the way you like them." You may not always get cooperation, but, as you will learn in the next chapter on negotiating and closing, you never get anything you don't ask for. So, ask.

How to set your expectations. In the Chapter 13, which includes negotiating tactics, you will learn more about highest legitimate expectations (HLE), a term with obvious implications. Your expectations should be set high, but legitimately high. You can call them "Goldilocks expectations," not too high and not too low, but just right.

Let's assume that you are selling for an NBC-affiliated television station in a three-station, medium-sized market and are responding to a request for proposal (RFP) sent out by a local advertising agency that wants a proposal for a six-week campaign that reaches women 25–49, and has a total budget of $100,000. Let's also assume that the latest Nielsen ratings show that your station reaches 33 percent of all 25–49-year-old women in the market each week. That means that if the buyer at the agency gave you 33 percent of the budget, or $33,000, it would be a fair share of the campaign's budget.

However, if you remember the answer to the first question about proposals, that the purpose of a proposal is to open a negotiation that will result in a favorable outcome, a favorable outcome is not getting a fair share of the budget, a favorable outcome is getting more than your fair share. Salespeople are not hired to just get a fair share – algorithms and auctions can get a fair share, or a fair market price. If 33 percent of the budget is a fair share, what is the highest legitimate expectation (HLE)? The HLE is probably somewhere in the neighborhood of 37–40 percent. How are you going to get 37–40 percent of the budget, which brings us to the fifth and final question about proposals, "What are the ordering tactics for proposals?"

There are two ordering tactics for proposals   The cardinal rule for proposals brings us back to the familiar Rule of Three. Always submit three proposals ordered in one of two ways: (1) small, medium, and large or (2) large, medium, and small. The first ordering option employs a foot-in-the-door tactic, as detailed in Chapter 7: Influence and Creating Value. The second ordering option employs a door-in-the-face tactic, defined in the same chapter.

Foot-in-the-door ordering tactic – small, medium, large. If you use this tactic when submitting proposals based on the medium-sized market television station scenario used above, your three proposals would look something like this:

- *Small proposal* for $33,000, or $5,500 per week for 25 spots at an average rate of $220 per spot. The small proposal also has three concise benefits statements and three concise advantages statements.
    - ° *Benefits statements* are positioned according to your Benefits Matrix for the decision-maker. For example, a benefit to an anxious buyers would be that your NBC station is a "safe buy" because ratings in all time periods have either held steady or gone up over the last year.
    - ° *Advantages statements* are also positioned according to your Benefits Matrix. For example, an advantage would be that your NBC station guarantees rating levels and will offer makegoods if future rating information indicates that the average rating level of the schedule falls below 10 percent of the guaranteed levels, which is guarantee that other stations in the market do not offer.
- *Medium proposal* for $36,000, or $6,000 per week for 30 spots at an average rate of $200 per spot. The medium proposal also has five concise benefits statements and five concise advantages statements. For example, one of the benefits would be that the 30-spot schedule has 20 percent more spots than the small proposal for a nine-percent discount on the small-proposal average cost per spot – more for less.
- *Large proposal* for $40,000, or $6,667 per week for 40 spots at an average rate of $166.67 per spot. The large proposal also has seven concise benefits statements and seven concise advantages statements. For example, one of the benefits would be that the proposed schedule has 33 percent more spots than the proposed medium schedule and 60 percent more spots than the small schedule for a whopping 17 percent discount on the medium-proposal average cost per spot – even more for even less. Further benefits could be increased social media support for a larger order, or sponsorship billboards (opening and closing audio and visual mentions), event promotions, or a host of other added-value features.

Notice that the above examples offer increasing rewards to the buyer for investing more. Also notice that the small proposal is for a fair share of the budget, a share that would be appropriate based on your station's share of the target audience ratings. This foot-in-the-door tactic clearly gives incentives and more benefits and more advantages for giving you a higher share of the buyer's budget. Also notice that in the large proposal the use of the zippy word "whopping."[2] Using such informal, non-technical, zippy words makes the proposal less formal, less technobabbly, and less boring, and, thus, more likely to be understood and to seem more friendly.

Furthermore, giving the buyer three options sets up the Choice Close (details in the Chapter 13), which gives buyers the perception that they are in charge and in control, and that they have options.

Door-in-the-face ordering tactic – large, medium, small. You will only use this tactic in a few rare situations, such as when you are asked to make a proposal to someone or to some agency that you have little or no knowledge of, or to someone or to some agency that has a reputation as a low-baller, or bottom feeder – always looking for the lowest possible price. In such a situation the purpose of your first, large proposal would be unrealistically large so that it makes the second and third proposals seem reasonable.

If we use the above scenario of an NBC television affiliate submitting a proposal to an agency that has a six-week, $100,000 budget and also has a reputation for being a low-balling bottom feeder, you might structure your proposals as follows:

- *Large proposal* for $100,000, or $16,667 per week for 110 spots at an average rate of $151.52 per spot. This large proposal has three concise benefits statements and three concise advantages statements. If you use the door-in-face tactic for a proposal to a bottom feeder, you do not want to include any value-added benefits such as sponsorship billboards, social media support, or event promotions, because a tough, competitive negotiator will demand any added-value extras for a smaller schedule. You want to save these extras so that you can use them as Clincher Closes (see Chapter 13) and give them up as needed to hold your price, but give reasonable concessions on terms, conditions, and added-value extras if you need to.
- *Medium proposal* for $60,000, or $10,000 per week for 62 spots at an average of $161.29 per spot. As with the large proposal, only give three concise benefits and advantages statements and save added-value items as concessions in a negotiation.
- *Small proposal* for $40,000, or $6,667 per week for 40 spots at an average rate of $166.67 per spot. The small proposal should also have just three benefits and advantages statements.

You can see that you wind up with the door-in-the-face ordering tactic at the same place that you did with the foot-in-the-door tactic, with 40 percent of the budget. By using this large-medium-small tactic, you also give the message that if the buyer wants the lowest possible price, they will have to give you the entire budget, plus you control the pending negotiation because you can concede added-value elements as needed and, thus, do not have to move on price.

AI and Proposals

Artificial intelligence (AI) is transforming sales, as discussed in Chapters 8 and 9, and it is also transforming the way proposals are generated. Most media sales organizations use some sort of customer relationship management (CRM), sales process, or sales administration software or platforms, most notably Salesforce, Matrix, and Efficio. Most of these platforms have proposal-generating capabilities, such as Salesforce's CPQ package. CPQ stands for configure, price, and quote, and the Salesforce CPQ application generates proposals that fit strict company guidelines and legal and financial rules.

Also, automating proposal generation stops costly pricing and quoting errors, ensures compliance with sales processes, and saves salespeople's time in constructing complex packages and offerings.[3] However, as emphasized in the *Harvard Business Review* article "Algorithms need managers, too," automated AI application such as Salesforce's CPQ need managing in the sense that they need guidelines. "All algorithms share two characteristics: They're literal, meaning that they'll do exactly what you ask them to do. And they're black boxes, meaning that they don't explain why they offer particular recommendations."[4] Therefore, when giving instructions to algorithms, be explicit about all your goals and strategies, such as low, medium, high, or high, medium low, and make sure you choose the right data inputs.[5]

I hope that now you understand that crafting a tactically sophisticated set of three proposals is not an easy task, but one that requires a great deal of thought, preparation, insight, and, hopefully, automation. I also hope you understand that the effort is worthwhile and that you can design a series of three proposals that accomplishes the purpose of proposals, which is to open a negotiation that will result in a favorable outcome.

Test Yourself

1. In the 4A's/IAB Standard Terms and Conditions what are CPA Deliverables?
2. In the Standard Terms and Conditions, is email considered written communication?
3. Can advertisers restrict having their ads adjacent to content that promotes violence?
4. How many days written notice are required to cancel a schedule before it starts?
5. How many days do agencies have to make payments to media companies after they receive an invoice?
6. Explain a sequential liability clause.
7. What is a short rate?
8. What are the four proposal questions?
9. What are the answers to the four proposal questions?
10. Explain briefly the tenets of game theory?
11. What are the two ordering tactics for proposals?
12. Why in the door-in-the-face tactic do you not include more than three benefits and three advantages for the large proposal?

Project

Visit a local television or radio station, ask to see a sales manager, and then tell the sales manager you are working on a project for a course in media sales. Tell the sales manager that your project is to come up with three proposals for a local advertising agency that has a budget of $100,000 for a six-weeks campaign to reach women 25–49. Ask if that budget is a reasonable amount and if not, adjust the budget to a reasonable level. Then ask what the station's weekly rating share is of women 25–49. Then ask what the station's average spot rate would be for a small, a medium, and a large schedule. With this information, create small, medium, and large proposals with concomitant benefits and advantages statements that will help you get more than your fair share of the budget.

Resources

4A's/IAB Standard Terms and Conditions For Internet Advertising For Media Buys One Year or Less. https://www.iab.com/guidelines/standard-terms-conditions-internet-advertising-media-buys-one-year-less.

Notes

1 Poundstone, William. 1992. *Prisoner's Dilemma*. New York: Doubleday.

2 Gallo, Carmine. 2010. *The Presentation Secrets of Steve Jobs: How to Be Insanely Great in Front of Any Audience*. New York: McGraw-Hill.

3 "CPQ for sales leaders." Retrieved from http://salesforce.com/form/conf/steelbrick/ebook-cpq-sales-leaders.

4 Luca, Michael, Kleinberg, Jon, and Mullainathan, Sendhil. 2018. "Algorithms need managers, too." *Harvard Business Review*, January–February.

5 Ibid.

13

Negotiating and Closing

Charles Warner

Negotiating

Negotiating is one of the most researched and studied topics in business, law, politics, and international affairs; therefore, you must assume that your prospects, customers, and buyers possess varying degrees of negotiating knowledge and expertise. To assume otherwise is foolhardy because an uninformed and unprepared salesperson will lose badly when up against a knowledgeable and prepared negotiator. If you are calling on retailers, you must assume they are experts in negotiating because they negotiate every day with their vendors and customers. If you are calling on media buyers, you must also assume that they are trained in negotiating.

The majority of negotiating books are about how to negotiate in one-time situations in which long-term relationships are not important and about how to negotiate for tangible goods, such as real estate. Negotiating in the media is different from most other types of negotiating and requires special skills for two reasons. First, media negotiating is not about winning at all costs in hard-nosed competitive battles over price and terms. The media do the vast majority of their business with long-term customers and agency buyers, and maintaining relationships with these customers and buyers is vital. Second, the media sell perishable inventory that if not sold, goes to waste and becomes worthless.

All media in-person, non-programmatic selling involves negotiating. A negotiation might be a simple three-step process such as, "My price is $100," "I'll give you $90," and "I'll take it." Or an advertiser might negotiate over the position of an ad with a newspaper

Media Selling: Digital, Television, Audio, Print and Cross-Platform, Fifth Edition.
Charles Warner, William A. Lederer, and Brian Moroz.
© 2020 John Wiley & Sons, Inc. Published 2020 by John Wiley & Sons, Inc.

that will not budge on rates. Or television network executives and advertising agency negotiators might negotiate for a $100 million upfront deal. Or a major media conglomerate might negotiate with a major advertiser for a multi-million-dollar cross-platform deal on all of its media properties. But whatever the size of the deal, if you do not learn to be an effective negotiator, your chances of having a successful career in media selling are small.

Negotiating and *closing* are included in the same step of selling because the ultimate goal of negotiating is to reach a satisfactory agreement, to close a deal. Therefore, you should look forward to negotiating and not be apprehensive. Why? Because, when you enter into negotiations, prospects, customers, and buyers have shown interest, have been educated, and have seen proposals; and they want to make a deal. They are ready to take the next step and make a commitment if they can get what they perceive to be a good deal. It is your task in negotiating to see that customers perceive that they get a good deal, which should be good for both sides. An "exchange of satisfactions" best describes negotiating. In his classic book, *The Fundamentals of Negotiating*, Gerard Nierenberg writes, "All parties to a negotiation should come out with some needs satisfied."[1]

The Negotiating and Closing Process

The process of negotiating and closing is quite complex – it is full of a wide variety of rules, tactics, and choices. The 53 rules that follow will help you successfully navigate the negotiating process and arrive at a favorable outcome.

> **Rule #1:** Do not negotiate until you've created value and created a differential competitive advantage for your product in the mind of a prospect, customer, or buyer.

> **Rule #2:** Do not discuss price until you are ready to negotiate and to close.

Many inexperienced salespeople make the mistake of negotiating too soon, before they have created value. The first question both inexperienced prospects and experienced media buyers often ask is, "What's the price?" For example, a prospect new to your medium might innocently ask, "How much does an ad on your website cost?" Your response should be, "Well, that's like asking how much a car costs. Are you talking about a Kia or a Lamborghini? The answer is, it depends. Let's find out what your needs are and then we'll see what the best type of ad for you would be." If an experienced media buyer whom you have dealt with frequently asks, "What is your cost-per-thousand?", you should delay the answer until you have had a discussion about the value, benefits, and supply-and-demand issues concerning your product. Even with experienced buyers, always follow the first two rules above.

Some negotiations are not complicated and require minimal preparation. However, because 80 percent of your business will likely come from 20 percent of your customers, you will find that the majority of your business might involve complex negotiating with the 20 percent of your more important customers and agency media buyers. In large markets and in national media such as network television, virtually all business involves complex negotiating, which requires thorough preparation, as outlined below.

The five steps in the negotiating and closing process are:

1   Your negotiating approach
2   Preparation
3   Maneuvering for dominance and control
4   Bargaining
5   Closing and getting commitment

See the Negotiating and Closing Outline in the Downloads section of *Media Selling*'s website (http://www.mediaselling.us/downloads) for a summary of the rules of negotiating as applied to each of the five steps above. Also, download and print out a Negotiating and Closing Planner at http://www.mediaselling.us/downloads and fill it out as you continue to read this chapter.

Your negotiating approach

Your approach to negotiating should be information-based, relationship-based, ethical, and flexible.

Information based   It is often said that information is power, and in no situation is information more powerful than in negotiating. You should conduct research and gather information about the other side and their competitors, about your competitors, about the other side's cultural background, and about the other side's attitudes and bargaining tactics. Also, by this step in the selling process, you should have created a Benefits Matrix, which will be of immeasurable help in framing your offers, asks, and concessions.

Information about the other side's business. The more information you can gather about your prospects', clients', and agencies' business goals, strategies, and challenges, the better chance you have to achieve your objectives in a negotiation.

Information about the other side's competitors. It is also important to gather information about the other side's competitors, their marketing and advertising strategies, their market position, their value proposition, their image, and their reputation. As we learned in game theory, your customers' strategies will be determined by their competitors' strategic and tactical moves, so you must have competitive information in order for you to position your offers in a way that helps your customers beat their competitors.

Information about your competitors. In the book, *The Art of War*, by Sun Tzu, the legendary Chinese general, writes: "Spies are a most important element in war, because upon them depends an army's ability to move."[2] For "spies" substitute the modern concept of *competitive intelligence*, for "war" substitute *negotiating*, and for "army" substitute the word *negotiator*. The sentence now reads: Competitive intelligence is the most important element in negotiating, because a negotiator's ability to move depends on it. Another lesson from Sun Tzu that we must not forget is that the "the true object of war is peace."[3] Likewise, the true object of negotiating must be agreement, not victory.

Intelligence about your competitors in three areas is critical to your negotiating planning and to reaching a final agreement: (1) intelligence about what prices your competitors will offer, (2) intelligence about what concessions your competitors are most likely to make, and (3) intelligence about what tactics they have traditionally used in past negotiations. Using game theory as a guide, having this information will help you determine your prices, your offers, and your tactics.

Information about the other side's cultural background. The way people approach negotiating and their negotiating style is primarily based on their cultural background. For example, many people from the Middle East conduct business based on haggling over price and, also, some people in America believe in negotiating at every opportunity. On the other hand, others believe that negotiating communicates to others that they cannot afford something and, thus, they do not negotiate to avoid being perceived as not having much money.

I gave a negotiating seminar to a group of magazine salespeople in New York several years ago and made the point that negotiating approaches are culturally based. A woman in the audience said, "Yes, I agree. My family never negotiated for anything." A salesperson sitting next to her said, "Wendy, you grew up in Greenwich, Connecticut. I grew up in the Bronx. My father sold garments on Seventh Avenue and the first two things he taught me were 'do not eat ham' and 'do not pay retail.'" Neither approach is right or wrong; both are perfectly valid approaches. It is important for you to acquire information about the other side's approach so you can plan your negotiating tactics accordingly.

Information about the other side's tactical tendencies. You might discover in your competitive intelligence research that the person you will be negotiating with tends to be an overconfident braggart who takes great pleasure in belittling others. Bob Woolf, in his book, *Friendly Persuasion,* recommends adopting an attitude of being self-effacing and non-blustering, especially when you have an advantage, or leverage. Woolf suggests that confidence in yourself, your plan, and your offer is vital, but he also recommends that you maintain a humble, agreeable, attitude to keep the other side off guard, especially if the other side is overconfident.

Or, you might discover that the other side's lead negotiator has a habit of keeping people waiting for an hour or so before arriving at a negotiating session in order to get the other side angry. Many unethical negotiators will use various bargaining tactics to get the other side angry because they know that when people become angry, their emotional intensity rises and they will make irrational, emotional decisions instead of rational ones. Richard Shell writes in *Bargaining for Advantage* that, "You must learn to recognize the hidden psychological strategies that play such an important role in negotiation."[4]

The "Psychology of Influence" section of Chapter 7: Influence and Creating Value covers many of these psychological tactics. Some negotiators will try to use the reciprocity principle against you by giving you a small concession and then asking for a big one in return. Sometimes clever negotiators will try to get you overcommitted by threatening to buy from your competition in the hope that such a threat will create competitive bidding and, thus, lower prices substantially, which has happened in the advertising agency industry.[5] If you do your research on the other side's typical attitudes and its tendency to use various tactics, you can plan your approach to respond accordingly and, therefore, gain an advantage.

Relationship based   Successful negotiating is based on trust. And because media salespeople are selling an intangible service in which they become the surrogate for their product, media selling is all about relationships – remember it is relationships that distinguish you from algorithms. Furthermore, as discussed earlier in the book, to get trust, you must first give trust. However, do not give your trust unconditionally. The first time you negotiate with someone be skeptical. Being skeptical means delaying judgment about people until you learn from their behavior that they can be trusted. Initial wariness is important because you might discover eventually that you are dealing with highly competitive, unethical negotiators. However, in media selling you will find that the majority of the people you deal with take pride in being fair and honest, especially at large, reputable advertising agencies and clients. But you must establish a bond of mutual trust with these people. Once this trusting relationship occurs, you will find that negotiating is not necessarily contentious and competitive, but can be cooperative, challenging, and enjoyable.

Ethical   No matter what approach the other side takes, you must retain your integrity, be true to your convictions, and always act ethically – follow the ethical guidelines in Chapter 3.

Flexible   There is no one best way to negotiate. You must remain adaptable and be able to adjust to the demands of maintaining a relationship, to the urgency of the situation, to the complexities of a deal, and to whether you are negotiating with a team or an individual. If you negotiate with people on a frequent basis, the rules and patterns of negotiating often become implicit, unstated, and comfortable. But always be alert, because they might take advantage of your comfort and change their mood, attitudes, style, and bargaining tactics in order to catch you off guard and gain an edge. You must be flexible in your approach, and you must deal with each negotiation based on the situation at the moment and not based on past patterns.

Preparation

The side that is best prepared and has the most well-thought-out plan, comes out ahead in virtually every negotiation.

There are 10 preparation steps in negotiating:

1   Assess the situation.
2   Assess negotiating styles.

3   Identify interests, set objectives, and determine targets.
4   Assess leverage.
5   Estimate the ballpark, commit to walk-aways, and set anchors.
6   Determine bargaining tactics.
7   Decide when and how to open.
8   Determine frames.
9   Determine concessions and trade goals.
10 Plan your closes

Assess the situation   The first step in planning is to assess the negotiating situation. One of the elements that distinguishes Richard Shell's *Bargaining for Advantage* from other books and seminars on negotiating and makes the book applicable to media negotiating is his concept that there are four basic situations that require different strategies, as shown in Exhibit 13.1.

- *I. Balanced concerns*. In media selling you will run into all four types of situations, but the majority of your negotiating will be in a balanced concerns situation in which both stakes, such as price and deal terms, and conditions, such as social media support or position in a publication, are as important as maintaining a relationship. Because media negotiating is typically conducted with regular customers or buyers who will give you repeat business, you must not negotiate so

Exhibit 13.1   The situation matrix

		Perceived Conflict Over Stakes	
		High	*Low*
Perceived Importance of Future Relationship Between Sides	*High*	**I. Balanced Concerns** (Business partnership, joint venture, or merger) *Best Strategies*: Problem solving or compromise	**II. Relationships** (Marriage, friendship, or work team) *Best Strategies:* Accommodation, problem solving, or compromise
	Low	**III. Transactions** (Divorce, house sale, or market transaction) *Best Strategies:* Competition, problem solving, or compromise	**IV. Tacit Coordination** (Highway intersection or airplane seating) *Best Strategies*: Avoidance, accommodation, or compromise

Source: Shell, G. Richard. 1999. Bargaining for Advantage. Penguin Books. Used with permission.

aggressively and competitively that you win and your customers lose. You must have a balance between getting favorable prices and terms and maintaining a trusting relationship.

- *II. Relationship*. You will rarely encounter a relationship situation in media selling in which maintaining future relationships is such an overriding concern that you will accommodate advertisers with large discounts or overly generous terms and conditions. Because the stakes in a media deal are often public knowledge, as they are in the upfront market or when large contracts between public companies are posted on the Internet, media companies are usually unwilling to give one advertiser a significantly better deal than they would give to another advertiser for the same size order and similar terms and conditions. On the other hand, many media deals and contracts include a favored-nation clause in which a media company agrees to give an advertiser the same low price if the media company ever charges another advertiser a lower price. In businesses in which most advertisers have many competitors, advertisers and their agencies trust media companies not to give better deals to competitors. Most media companies maintain their integrity and attempt to treat advertisers fairly.

  Furthermore, by overemphasizing a relationship, media companies are subject to relationship blackmail. In an article in the *Harvard Business Review* titled "Negotiation as a corporate capability," author Danny Ertel writes:

  > Over the years, I have asked hundreds of executives to reflect on their business relationships and to ask themselves which kinds of customers they make the most concessions to, do more costly favors for, and generally give away more value to. Is it their good customers or their bad customers? The vast majority respond, with some chagrin, "The difficult ones, of course. I'm hoping to improve the relationship." But that hope is almost always in vain: once customers find they can get discounts and favors by holding a relationship hostage, why should they change? Without realizing it, many companies have systematically taught their customers the art of blackmail.[6]

  It is important not to allow advertisers to blackmail you by threatening to take their business elsewhere if they do not get more than other advertisers get. Be firm and do not cave in; it is vitally important to treat everyone fairly.

- *III. Transaction*. In media selling you will occasionally run into a transaction situation in which stakes are much more important than relationships. These situations sometimes occur with new customers who try to make a large one-time deal and negotiate a very low price. But beware of someone who is not a regular customer, whose reputation you do not know, who makes big promises, and who asks for big discounts in return. Always remember that your regular customers are your best customers and vow never to make a one-time deal, no matter how big a promise, that you would not make with your regular customers.

- *IV. Tacit coordination*. You will also find that you will often be in tacit coordination situations. Tacit coordination occurs when two people pull up to a Stop sign at the same time or when two people simultaneously try to sit in a seat on an airplane. Negotiation is typically quick and unspoken; one person or the other will nod and accommodate the other and move on. Remember the 80/20 rule applies. Twenty percent of your customers who give you 80 percent of your business will typically be repeat ones who are familiar with your pricing, your terms, conditions, and the added value you offer, if any. They will typically renew with little or no negotiating involved. In these situations, trust is the key factor. If your clients have learned to trust you to give them the best deal available at the time of the negotiation, they will not haggle – a tacit coordination situation.

In broadcast and cable where inventory is limited and, thus, pricing is based on supply and demand, customers and buyers will usually negotiate to get the best prices available at the time they are making a buy. Some agencies will buy for an account on a weekly or monthly basis and those negotiations will be short and to the point. In these situations your goal should be to develop strong relationships with your customers so they trust you to bring them the best available deals at all times. Mutual trust keeps negotiating to a minimum and makes tacit coordination possible.

Another example of tacit coordination would be when customers indicate they do not want to negotiate. They might say, "Bring me your best deal and if I like it, I'll buy it," and mean what they say. In such cases, it is imperative that you know the attitudes of your customers before you enter a negotiation and bring these customers reasonable, fair prices and offers.

Assess negotiating styles   The next step in preparation and planning is to assess the negotiating style of the other side and to recognize your own negotiating style. Research on negotiating indicates that there are two primary negotiating styles: competitive and cooperative. Author Richard Shell reports that in one study of lawyer-negotiators, who one might expect to be competitive, instead he found that "65 percent of the sample of attorneys exhibited a consistently cooperative style of negotiation, whereas only 24 percent were truly competitive in their orientation. (11 percent defied categorization using these two labels)."[7]

Some of the people Shell uses as examples of highly competitive negotiators in *Bargaining for Advantage* are Donald Trump, Wayne Huizenga, and Henry Kravis. In 1999 these famous businessmen appeared to fit the personality classification of narcissist, as described by Michael Maccoby in his *Harvard Business Review* article, "Narcissistic leaders: The incredible pros, the inevitable cons." From my 45 years in the media business, I have come to believe that many of the top executives in the media fit Maccoby's narcissistic label. I have included narcissist in the description of Negotiating Types in Exhibit 13.2 because I believe many of the 11 percent that defied classification in the study mentioned by Shell probably fall into the narcissist category, particularly in the media business.

Just as it is vital to know yourself if you are to acquire emotional intelligence in order to be effective at establishing and maintaining relationships, it is equally important to know your negotiating style if you are to be an effective negotiator. You must also be flexible and change your negotiating style to match the other side's style. Because changing styles is extremely difficult for many people, if you find it difficult to change your style, select a colleague who has a style that matches the other side's style and ask that person do the negotiating.

Rule #3: Match the other side's style (cooperative or competitive).

Exhibit 13.2 Negotiating types

Competitors. Favored outcome: "I win, you lose." These people are highly competitive; they focus on winning – often at any cost. They usually put winning in personal terms; they want to beat you. They typically pay close attention to the size of their piece of the pie. They are unconcerned about being fair; they want the biggest slice. Winning (and not getting a worse deal than someone else) is everything to them. They often see negotiating as a game and enjoy the process as long as they think they can win.

Accommodators. Favored outcome: "I lose, you win." Accommodators want to maximize the other side's gain; they want the other side to have the biggest piece of the pie. They want you to think they are fair at almost any cost to them. They want you to get the best deal for you – the relationship is the most important thing to them. They are rarely seen in media negotiations.

Narcissists. High probability of an "I lose, you lose" (no deal) outcome. Narcissists do not care about any outcome that does not give them what they want, and they typically want the whole pie. Driven by ego, pride, greed, and selfishness, narcissists are only interested in their own outcomes. They hate to compromise, which means they make threats and demands and then will not negotiate. When others refuse to deal on their terms, which is often the case, narcissists usually turn into fierce, ruthless competitors. This switch is progress because they can be bargained with, although with great difficulty because they tend to use unethical tactics.

Cooperators. Favored outcome: "I win, you win." Cooperators try to maximize joint gain, build trust, and enhance the relationship. They are concerned about being fair. Cooperators are often problem-solvers who can increase the size of the pie.

One of your objectives in negotiations is to train the other side to cooperate by demonstrating that both sides can win, to show them that negotiating fairly and in good faith can produce an outcome that is beneficial for both sides.

Patterns of Negotiations

Cooperators versus Cooperators: A good combination. If a problem can be solved and an agreement reached, it will be. Often increases the gain for both sides – the pie gets bigger.

Competitors versus Competitors: They understand each other, although there is a higher risk of a breakdown and it consumes more time and resources, it is not a bad combination. Rarely is there an increase in the size of the pie; in fact, when competitors try to maximize their own gain or share, the amount of the settlement usually decreases.

Cooperators versus Competitors: A dangerous combination. Most negotiating problems occur with this combination. The two sides do not speak the same language, do not have the same goals, and do not understand each other. Invariably the competitor takes advantage of the cooperator, who winds up with a small piece of the pie, even though there is some research that suggests with training and prompts, a cooperator can learn to be more competitive.

Cooperators' objectives	*Competitors' objectives*
1. Conduct self ethically	1. Maximize gain
2. Get a fair agreement	2. Win by outmaneuvering
3. Build trust	3. Relationships not important

Cooperator traits Competitor traits

1. Trustworthy, ethical, fair	1. Dominate, forceful, attacking
2. Courteous, tactful, sincere	2. Crafty, rigid, strategic, uncooperative
3. Fair minded	3. Carefully observes opponent to gain an edge
4. Realistic opening position	4. Unrealistic opening position

Exhibit 13.2   Negotiating types (cont'd)

5. Does not use threats	5. Uses threats
6. Willing to share information	6. Reveals information only strategically, gradually
7. Probes opponent's position	7. Willing to stretch facts

Thompson, Leigh. 2018. "Research: Simple prompts can get women to negotiate more like men, and vice versa." Harvard Business Review. https://hbr.org/2018/09/research-simple-prompts-can-get-women-to-negotiate-more-like-men-and-vice-versa.

Cooperators are quintessential win–win negotiators because they can increase the size of the pie. On the other hand, competitors are win–lose negotiators because they do not care if the pie shrinks, as long as they get the biggest piece. Neither cooperators nor competitors are wrong, they just see the world differently. If you trust a competitor, you will be easily exploited. If you try to be pleasant and get along with or be well liked by a competitor, you will be seen as naive and weak and be taken advantage of. It is imperative to match the style of the other side. When in doubt, be skeptical and assume the other side is a competitor until proven wrong.

Identify interests, set objectives, and determine targets

Identify interests   In your negotiating planning process, you must identify both sides' interests before you can set your negotiating objectives, because the ideal outcome of a negotiation is an agreement that satisfies most of both sides' interests. For example, one advertiser may want the lowest price on digital video, regardless of targeting demographics. To another advertiser, specific demographic targeting might take precedent over price. Once you have determined what both side's interests are, write them down in your Negotiating and Closing Planner.

Set objectives. Next, you should set your objectives based on your understanding of both sides' interests. Set MADCUD objectives (see Chapter 4) for each negotiating opportunity you have:

- *Measurable.* An example of measurable objectives for a negotiation would be: To get a minimum of a 13-week insertion order for at least three banner ads a week and to get a no-cancellation contract term.
- *Attainable.* The measurable objectives must be realistic and reasonable for the advertiser in question and, thus, reasonably attainable, or not too much of a stretch.
- *Demanding.* Richard Shell suggests you should set objectives based on your highest legitimate expectations (HLE). Research indicates that those who expect more, get more. As we learned in Chapter 4, reasonable but challenging objectives have the greatest motivating effect. Therefore, how you define the concept of *more* is critical to your success. If by *more*, you mean your highest legitimate expectations (HLE), your chances of being successful will be much greater.
- *Consistent with company goals.* Too often media salespeople set objectives that meet their own selfish needs and are not consistent with the overall long-term goals and strategies of their companies. For instance, salespeople might set an objective of making a sale regardless of price in order to make the commission on the sale or make their quota.

Or they might set an objective of getting a sizable order by promising exceptionally favorable positions in a magazine contrary to the magazine's policy guidelines of offering desirable positions only to the largest advertisers. When you set negotiating objectives, always keep in mind that your company's interests, not yours, come first.

- *Under control of the individual.* In a negotiation, you cannot control the other side's attitude or behavior, but you can control your own. As in sports, the mental game in negotiating is as, if not more, important as the physical game. Often the strategy of the other side is to get you to lower your confidence and expectations. If you allow this to happen, you will be inclined to lower your prices, give away too much, and settle for much less than you deserve. Control your confidence and expectation during a negotiation and keep them both high.
- *Deadlined.* Deadlines in negotiating are based on the scarcity principle – the scarcity of time. When you are selling a non-perishable product such as a house, do not set a deadline for a settlement because having no deadline puts pressure on the other side to settle and increases the fear of losing, which gets more intense over time, thus giving an advantage to the seller. The opposite is true when you are selling a perishable product such as seats on an airplane, hotel rooms, broadcast or cable time, a position on a website or mobile phone, or a special issue or section of a publication that has a firm closing date. Set a deadline for settlement, because without a deadline there is no pressure on the other side to settle before the product perishes. Without a deadline, crafty buyers will wait until the very last possible moment in hopes that sellers will reduce prices significantly rather than see what they are selling go to waste, thus giving an advantage to the buyer.

Setting deadlines on all of your offers counters delaying tactics by the other side. So, when you present prices in proposals, include a comment that that reads something like this: "These rates are good until December 1," when you know the schedule is planned to start December 7, for example.

> **Rule #4**: When selling a perishable product, always set a deadline on your offers.

Determine targets. There are four basic types of targets: (1) a specific opportunity, such as a sponsorship, (2) price, (3) size of order, and (4) share of budget. Determine your targets for a negotiation and then write them down in the Negotiating and Closing Planner. Furthermore, once you set your targets based on your highest legitimate expectations, you must commit to them. The best way to increase your commitment is to write down your targets and then tell someone about them. For example, send an email to your boss, "I'm convinced I can get a 40 percent share of budget from this account, and here are the prices, terms, and conditions I'm going to get to achieve that target."

> **Rule #5**: Make a commitment to your objectives and targets, write them down, and tell someone about them.

Assess leverage   The next step in the planning process is to assess your and the other side's leverage situation to determine who has the stronger and weaker position. Leverage is based on how badly people want something and how fearful they are of losing it. As Bob Woolf writes in *Friendly Persuasion*, "Every reason that the other side wants or needs an agreement is my leverage – provided that I know those reasons."[8]

There are two kinds of leverage: positive and negative. You have *positive leverage* when you have something that the other side wants much more than you want to hold on to it. You have *negative leverage* when the other side is afraid of losing something you have. Both are powerful, but negative leverage is more powerful, as shown in a great deal of research of behavioral economists that indicates that the negative feelings caused by losses loom much larger with most people than the positive feelings from gains do. Competition for a scarce resource increases negative leverage and often leads to overcommitment, which occurs when people invest their egos and a lot of time in negotiating. Their fear of losing after they have invested so much time in a negotiation escalates to the point that they often become overcommitted and make unrealistically high offers.

Media salespeople, especially inexperienced salespeople, usually have more leverage than they realize. Most businesses, except for very small ones, must advertise in order to attract customers, survive, and grow. If a business has competitors, it must advertise more than its competitors if it hopes to gain market share. Also, advertising agencies have to invest all the money their clients allocate to advertising because advertising budgets reflect the sales levels that advertisers hope to achieve. Their ultimate goal is not to save money, but to get the optimum reach, frequency, and engagement with ads for the money they have allocated. This necessity to advertise gives media salespeople leverage if they are selling a medium or a product that is in demand or can provide a viable solution to an advertising problem.

Assessing both sides' leverage is critical in deciding your overall negotiating strategy and tactics. Once you have a sense of which side has the stronger leverage, there are several tactics you can use to strengthen your leverage or weaken the other side's leverage.

Strengthen leverage. Below are four tactics for strengthening your leverage:

- *BATNA.* A BATNA is the *best alternative to a negotiated agreement.* Fisher and Ury first introduced the concept of a BATNA in their best-selling book, *Getting to Yes.* The purpose of a BATNA is to have at least one viable alternative when you enter into a negotiation. For example, when people ask me how they should ask for a raise, I tell them to get an offer in writing from another company for a job that pays more money than they are currently making. This offer is a BATNA and it provides leverage. Without a competing offer, people who ask for a raise have little leverage and their employer has most of the leverage, and this is especially true if there are many people who are able and willing to replace you.

  In media selling, an example of how to acquire a BATNA would be for KAAA-AM, being aware of the strong interest of beer advertiser X in sponsoring its baseball broadcasts, to offer sponsorships to several other beer advertisers in order to generate interest in baseball before talking to the beer company X. If KAAA-AM drums up sufficient interest to be certain of an order from another beer advertiser, the station has a BATNA, which increases its leverage considerably with beer company X.

  Rule #6: Always go into a negotiation with a BATNA, if at all possible.

- *The tit-for-tat tactic.* This means that you reciprocate the tactics, behavior, and style of the other side by matching them with your tactics, behavior, and style. For example, if the other side pounds the table and threatens to walk out, you pound the table and threaten to walk out. In order to understand the power of tit-for-tat, warnings, and bluffs, let's return to game theory that was introduced in Chapter 12.

   You will recall that John von Neumann invented game theory in 1928 after watching a bluff in a poker game. He reasoned that in order to win in poker it was important not to play according to the probabilities of a certain card being dealt, but to play according to the moves of competitors. Twenty-two years later in a program that was funded by the US Government at the Rand Institute in California, mathematicians, physicists, and other scientists studied, within the context of game theory, the strategic implications of two major world powers, the United States and the Soviet Union, each possessing the horrible destructive power of the atomic bomb.

   One of the scientists invented a game called the Prisoner's Dilemma. The game was set up so that the punishments the two prisoners, who were isolated from each other, would receive were a great deal less if they turned in evidence that the other prisoner broke the law (whether the evidence was true or not). The scientists called turning in evidence *defecting*. The temptation to defect was so strong because of the way the punishments were weighted. Each turned in evidence that the other broke the law and, thus, both prisoners wound up in jail for 10 years. While in jail, the prisoners met and realized that if they had not defected and had said nothing, in other words if they had silently cooperated, they would have each received a minor punishment.[9]

   When two scientists played a computerized version of the game repeatedly, they found that the best strategy was for each player to cooperate and settle for a smaller reward rather than being greedy (defecting) and going for a big reward. However, occasionally, one of the players would get greedy, and get a bigger reward. The players learned that when this defection happened the best strategy on the next move was to defect, or, to use the tit-for-tat tactic, which taught the other player to cooperate again on subsequent moves and settle for smaller, but dependable, rewards. The US Government adopted the tit-for-tat tactic as the basis for its policy of deterrence based on the credibility of massive retaliation. In other words, if the Soviet Union built an ICBM (intercontinental ballistic missile) with a nuclear warhead, the US would do the same – tit-for-tat.

   Eventually, the tit-for-tat policy worked and the Soviet Union, virtually bankrupt from spending on a massive nuclear war machine, agreed to a program of mutual disarmament – cooperation. And in his book *The Happiness Hypothesis* Jonathan Haidt writes that in computer games designed to test cooperation and altruism, "no strategy ever beats tit-for-tat."[10] These lessons from the Cold War, from game theory, and from computer games are the foundation for another fundamental rule of negotiating.

Rule #7: Use tit-for-tat to teach the other side to cooperate.

- *Warnings.* A warning is an implied threat. The difference between a threat and a warning is that a warning is a relatively polite statement about what might happen. A threat is a more aggressive statement that communicates, "If you do X, I will retaliate by doing Y."

Warnings and threats are effective only if they are credible. The other side must share your assumption that carrying out the warning or threat will make them worse off and believe it is not a bluff. President Bush's threat of war against Iraq became credible when the United Nations passed a motion to support a war, when Great Britain's Tony Blair strongly supported the war, and when 150,000 troops were mobilized and put on alert in the Middle East. Unfortunately, Bush's credible threat did not accomplish its purported purpose of motivating Saddam Hussein to disarm; rather it backfired and caused Iraq to intensify its resolve to resist. The war in Iraq is an excellent example of the danger of making credible threats: they often lead to destructive escalation.

People usually respond with hostility and anger when threatened. In business negotiations, warnings are much more effective than threats. Author Richard Shell writes that, "Using threats in most negotiations is "like playing with fire – dangerous for everyone involved."[11] If you have a strong leverage position, your confident demands can become implied warnings. As an example, station KAAA-AM can tell beer sponsor X, "This is our price. We have several offers on the table. The decision is up to you if you want to pay our price and agree to our terms. We'd really prefer to do business with you, but in fairness to everyone, we can't turn down the highest offer." When you warn that you might use your BATNA, be extremely careful and do so politely, self-effacingly, and almost apologetically in order to avoid unintended consequences and escalation.

Rule #8: Never threaten; politely warn instead.

- *Bluffs.* A bluff is when you act as though you have a strong position when, in fact, you have a weak position. It takes a great deal of confidence to pull off a successful bluff. Beginners should not bluff. However, in negotiating, just like when you play poker or like when you play a team sport such as football, a bluff, or a fake, is an acceptable and sometimes effective tactic. But to pull it off, you must understand the subtleties and proper timing of a winning bluff. We must once again turn to game theory for answers on how to bluff successfully.

  Game theory researchers discovered that the best strategy in playing many games, including the Prisoner's Dilemma, is a mixed strategy of bluffing or defecting occasionally and on a random basis. The logic of this strategy is that if you never bluff, you are too predictable and the other side will take advantage of you because it knows you will be consistent and never retaliate. On the other hand, if you bluff on a regular, predictable basis, the other side will eventually figure out your bluffing pattern and your bluffs become as predictable as Rich Gannon's fakes were in Super Bowl XXXVII. Therefore, the best way to keep the other side on the defensive is to bluff occasionally on a purely random basis so the other side never knows what to expect.

  An example of a bluff in a media selling situation would be to set your initial offer higher than you are actually willing to accept. If you are dealing with a buyer with whom you regularly negotiate, you must have walked away from business in the past. By doing so, your current bluff becomes credible. Two things can happen in this bluffing situation: either the buyer pays the highball rate or the buyer may call your bluff and say that your price is too high. In which case, you can back down, lower your price and get the business. However, you can only back down on rare occasions, because the buyer will learn that your bluffs are just that, bluffs, and will not believe them.

Rule #9: If you bluff, use a mixed strategy and occasionally bluff on a random basis.

If you bluff on an occasional random basis, a buyer will never be certain whether or not you are bluffing. And remember, bluffs are only for experienced negotiators, not for rookies.

Estimate the ballpark, commit to walk-aways, and set anchors

Estimate the ballpark. A ballpark is the difference between a buyer's initial offer and your highest legitimate expectations (HLE). Your HLE includes not only price but also terms and conditions. Rarely are media negotiations about price alone; they include many other elements such as contract terms, non-cancellation clauses, added value, favorable ad positions, options for renewals, favored-nation clauses, or competitive ad separation. Some of these conditions are often more important than price, and one or more of these elements might be deal breakers for both sides. It is important to know what your deal breakers are and estimate what the other side's deal breakers might be, and then to plan accordingly.

Just as in Major League Baseball, negotiating ballparks come in different sizes. You want to negotiate in the smallest ballpark possible because it is easier and quicker to reach agreement. The size of the ballpark is determined by the other side's initial offer. Exhibit 13.3 shows an example of how a ballpark estimate works.

One end of the ballpark is your walk-away ($200 in Exhibit 13.3) and the other end is the buyer's walk-away ($300 in Exhibit 13.3). Note that the mid-point of the ballpark is $250, which is the potential agreement point – one that would satisfy both sides.

Rule #10: Most settlements are close to the mid-point.

You can gain knowledge of the other side's probable initial offer through careful research or by an understanding of the other side's past tendencies and approaches. For example, in Exhibit 13.3 we will assume the buyer has paid $250 in the past after making a lowest

Exhibit 13.3 Ballpark

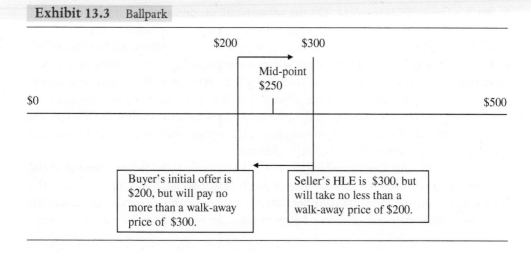

legitimate expectation (LLE) initial offer of $200, so you can assume that the buyer will open again with $200, but will pay more as in the past. Therefore, you should set your HLE at $300 to make sure you arrive at the $250 mid-point, at the minimum.

You will not always find that a buyer's initial offer is a reasonable, legitimate LLE, but is a lowball offer. Many buyers have a rule of negotiating that states: The lower price you initially ask for, the lower price you will wind up with. Therefore, many buyers open with an unreasonable lowball offer rather than with an LLE, and the lowball is way below your walk-away. No matter what the other side's initial offer is, you must clearly define and stick to your walk-aways.

Commit to walk-aways.   Without a walk-away, or a firm downside position, you will be nibbled away at by clever negotiators, which is like getting pecked to death by ducks; it takes a long time and is very painful. Walk-away means just that – you will walk away from a negotiation rather than settle for anything less. Your walk-aways must be absolutely firm; you must be committed to them, because having a soft downside position is a prescription for disaster.

Rule #11: Always go into every negotiation with a commitment to your walk-aways.

Even though it is vital to have walk-aways, do not focus on them during negotiations. Research shows that inexperienced negotiators have a tendency to focus on their low-end walk-away rather than their high-end HLE because of their aversion to loss. This tendency brings us to another rule of negotiating:

Rule #12: During negotiations, you must focus on your highest legitimate expectations (HLE), not on your walk-away.

Set your anchor.   Your HLE, which in Exhibit 13.3 is $300, should not only be what you must focus on and expect to get, but also should be the starting point in determining your opening offer. Your opening offer is your *anchor*. In negotiating, when buyers first hear a high or low number, they unconsciously adjust their expectations accordingly. Therefore, it is vital that you open reasonably high and thus have room to come down to reach a favorable agreement. On the other hand, an unreasonably high initial offer can easily kill a deal or destroy your credibility if you drastically reduce your offer later.

It is crucial that you invest time in determining what your optimal anchor should be, as it is the most significant decision you will make in preparing for a negotiation and will be critical to a successful outcome. Anchors include price as well as terms and conditions, so your anchor should include a price that is high enough to give you room to come down to your HLE and include givebacks of terms and conditions that you are willing to concede. By carefully planning your price concessions and givebacks, you can decide effective concession and closing techniques.

Since the other side's suspected initial offer is the basis for your anchor, a lowball initial offer by the other side increases the size of the ballpark because you must increase the relative size of your anchor. Lowball offers often come from inexperienced or unreasonable negotiators or from new customers who are not familiar with your regular pricing, terms, and conditions. In such situations, let the other side open first, remain calm and polite, and set your anchor to move the mid-point close to your HLE.

On the other hand, initial offers from experienced negotiators and regular customers who are familiar with your pricing, terms, and conditions will often be reasonable and be close to current market prices and conditions – a tacit coordination situation.

Rule #13: Always have a well-thought-out anchor.

Determine bargaining tactics   The literature on negotiating identifies a number of bargaining tactics that negotiators can use to their advantage. Some are reasonable, and acceptable; others are unfair, unreasonable, and unacceptable. Never use the unacceptable ones and learn to recognize them.

Rule #14: Never split the difference when it is in the other side's favor or is not close to your HLE; have patience and continue negotiating.

Rule #15: When faced with unacceptable and unethical bargaining tactics, name them and tell the other side the names so the other side knows you are not fooled.

Rule #16: Never respond emotionally; respond calmly, politely, and firmly.

After you have done the following: (1) assessed the situation, (2) assessed both side's negotiating styles, (3) identified interests, set objectives, and determined your targets, (4) assessed both side's leverage, (5) estimated the ballpark and committed to your walk-aways, and set your anchors; the next step, number 6, in the planning process is to determine the most appropriate bargaining tactics from the list of acceptable tactics in Exhibit 13.4.

We have now covered six of the 10 preparation steps. We will pause for a while in the discussion of the negotiating planning process so you can acquire an understanding of how to maneuver for dominance and control, and then move on later in the chapter to the last four steps of preparation: (7) decide when and how to open, (8) determine frames, (9) determine concessions and trade goals, and (10) plan your closes.

Maneuvering for dominance and control

Maneuvering for dominance and control is third step in the negotiating and closing planning process. Each side wants to gain a perceived power advantage so as to be perceived as dominant, and often maneuvers accordingly – the objective is to make the other side submissive. The most common maneuver is for one side to use the authority principle to impress the other with its status, authority, power, titles, and overall importance. Because most people tend to defer to authority and are impressed with status, if one negotiator is perceived to have more status, a more impressive title, or more power, that negotiator has an edge and becomes dominant.

Rule #17: The other side only has the power you give it.

Exhibit 13.4   Bargaining tactics

Acceptable bargaining tactics

Tactic	Description/ purpose	When to use	When used against you, your best response
Auction	Create an auction of competitive bids for a scarce resource – either a buyer for an advertising budget or a seller for a high-demand product.	When you have strong leverage – inventory or a product in high demand. Create a fear of losing in the other side.	Focus on your HLE, never go lower than your walk-away, and signal to the other side that you will walk away and not get into a competitive auction.
Cherry-pick	Pick only the best, most desirable elements of a product or package.	To pick apart a package offering; to negotiate for the most desirable individual elements separately, not as a whole.	When a buyer tries to cherry-pick you, show high prices for the individual units and a lower price for the overall package.
Crunch	Respond to an offer by saying, "It's not good enough," but do not give a number. The objective is to get the other side to respond with a number that is lower than you hoped for because of the other side's fear of losing.	In response to a low offer. The rule is, "Whoever gives a number first, loses."	Don't give a number. If a buyer says, "You're too high," without giving a number, you respond with, "What number do you have in mind?"
Flinch	A sudden, physical reaction that tries to elicit a feeling of guilt, like, "You've got to be kidding!" response to an offer.	In response to a lowball offer. Only use occasionally.	Remain calm. Do not react. The other side is trying to get a rise, to shock you. Do not respond.
Good guy/ bad guy (Good cop/ bad cop)	The bad guy makes highly unreasonable demands and threats; the good guy's low requests seem reasonable in comparison – the contract principle at work.	In major, complex negotiations. Use your lawyers or management as bad guys (that is what they get paid for); as a salesperson, you be the good guy and offer a reasonable solution.	Make the right comparison. Don't compare the good guy's offer to the bad guy's offer; compare the good guy's offer to your HLE. Keep focused on your HLE.

Exhibit 13.4   Bargaining tactics (cont'd)

Acceptable bargaining tactics

Tactic	Description/ purpose	When to use	When used against you, your best response
Limited authority	To indicate that a negotiator has limited authority, cannot make a final decision, and has to check with a higher authority – a hint of a pullback in order to gain further concessions.	Use to stall for time, to think over an offer, and craft a counteroffer, even if you have the final authority.	Agree to a break in the negotiating process while the other side checks with their higher authority and say, "That's a good idea. I have to check with my boss, too, because I may have gone too far." Hint at a pullback.
Nibble	A negotiator will indicate a strong readiness to settle, but will ask for just one more very small concession…then another, then another.	In the last stages of negotiations after many agreements and the other side is overcommitted, nibble at the last remaining issues, "Can you give me just a dollar more?"	Stop the nibbling with a pin-down close. "I can't give you an additional 2% discount, but I will give you a half-percent discount if you give me the order right now with no further requests or changes." Give a small concession you were willing to give anyway to pin down a close.
Price tag	To set a price limit. A buyer might say, "I like your proposal, but I only have $10,000, not the $15,000 you're asking for."	Price tags are buyers' LLE, not their walk-aways. Based on the rule that you never get anything you don't ask for, why not ask for an LLE?	A price tag is a starting point, not a walk-away. Always challenge a price tag and treat it as an opening offer, not a final, walk-away.
Red herring	To negotiate hard on an unimportant issue, get concessions, and then ask for reciprocal concessions on an important issue.	With multiple issues, feign the importance of a minor issue to you, receive concessions and then transfer those concessions to an important issue. Set a reciprocity trap.	Do not fall into reciprocity traps. Don't transfer concessions. Compare apples to apples – concessions on one issue do not apply to concessions on another issue. Commonly used tactic by media buyers.

Exhibit 13.4   Bargaining tactics (cont'd)

Acceptable bargaining tactics

Tactic	Description/ purpose	When to use	When used against you, your best response
Silence	To respond to an offer with silence.	Silence, like a crunch, is an attempt to get the other side to respond with concessions – bigger ones than you might have asked for.	The rule is: The first one to talk loses. Respond to silence with silence.
Split the difference	To offer to settle at the mid-point.	To get a quick settlement when the two sides are not far apart. Split the difference sounds like a fair offer, even if it is not.	Often buyers will make a lowball offer and then offer to split the difference. Never split the difference when it is in the other side's favor or is not close to your HLE. Have patience and keep negotiating.
Take-it-or-leave-it	An ultimatum and refusal to continue negotiations. forces the other side to make a yes/no decision.	To signal a final offer; often used with the phrase, "A fair, final offer. Take it or leave it."	Leave it unless it is above your walk-away, which it usually is not. Often a take-it-or leave-it offer is a bluff, so always call the bluff.
Throw-aways	Issues, terms, conditions, and added value that are part of an initial offer but are intended as concessions later in a negotiation.	Always have throw-aways in complex negotiations. Throw-aways should be issues, terms, conditions, and added value that are of relatively low importance – elements that you would normally give up. By including them in your initial offer, you set them up as concessions later to get the other side to give you concessions you want – the reciprocity principle at work.	Do not fall into reciprocity traps and give away something important to you when the other side makes a concession of minor importance to you. Always work on the fairness principle – trade concessions of similar value or importance.

Exhibit 13.4   Bargaining tactics (cont'd)

Unacceptable bargaining tactics

Tactic	Description/ purpose	When to use	When used against you, your best response
Big bait	Make a large initial offer in an attempt to find your bottom and walk-aways.	Never, because it is a hollow bluff or a lie. Users of big bait have no intention of making good on their initial, implied promise, but are just looking for the other side's rock bottom.	Recognize the tactic and name it. Call the other side's bluff. Say, "This sounds like a big bait to me. Are you willing to sign a firm, non-cancelable contract for the full amount?"
Blackmail	A threat meant to instill fear of loss. Usually a bluff.	Never, because it is unethical.	Recognize the tactic and name it. Call the bluff. Never give in, because it will make you vulnerable to future blackmail and larger and larger demands. Blackmail will continue regardless of what the other side promises. By giving in, you train the other side to blackmail you.
Change of pace	Bring someone close to an agreement with a false promise, then back off, then promise again and to get the other side so frustrated it will say yes to anything just to get closure.	Never, because it is unethical.	Recognize the tactic and name it. Have patience. Remain confident in the fairness of your proposal and in your HLE. Never respond with anger.
Deliver garbage	Insult the other side, its product, its management, and everything to instill a fear of losing on the other side. This lowers confidence and expectations.	Never, because it is too competitive and destroys relationships.	Do not catch the garbage. Pay no attention to it. Do not respond, and most important, do not lower your confidence or HLE. Smile and remain silent.
Renege	To take back a previously agreed-upon element in a negotiation. The objective is to instill fear of losing even more.	Never, because it breaks a promise, destroys trust, and leads to escalation – tit-for-tat reneging.	Recognize the tactic and name it. Flinch and say, "That's not fair! I have been negotiating in good faith and now you're taking something back." Never agree to reneging by the other side.

Exhibit 13.4	Bargaining tactics (cont'd)		

Unacceptable bargaining tactics

Tactic	Description/ purpose	When to use	When used against you, your best response
Starvation	Keeping food and water away from the other side in a lengthy negotiation in order to try to force a favorable settlement. The side that controls the turf (location) will eat and drink before a negotiating session that begins at 11:00 am, for example, and that will last for several hours and then doesn't provide food or water to the other side.	Never, because it destroys trust and shows lack of respect for the other side. It's manipulative.	Name the tactic. Say, "I think you're trying to starve me, so I'm taking a break for an hour to go get something to eat and drink." If the other side objects, say, "Then order in some food. I'm much more agreeable on a full stomach."
Threats	To threaten to take a competitor's offer or to walk out of the negotiating. A threat is like blackmail, often a bluff.	Never, because it destroys trust and discontinues fair negotiations.	Recognize the tactic and name it. Call the bluff and never give in because it will lead to more, larger threats.
Walk-out	To walk out of a negotiation before an agreement is reached; to refuse to negotiate further. Usually accompanied with an accusation of not being fair. Used to instill fear of losing. It is invariably a bluff.	Never, because it destroys trust and prolongs negotiations unnecessarily.	Recognize the tactic and name it. Call the bluff. Let the other side walk out. Do not respond emotionally. The other side would not resort to this tactic if it did not want a deal; therefore, increase your HLE after a walk-out with confidence.

Because experienced negotiators, especially agency media buyers, will usually try to lower your confidence and expectations in order to gain an advantage, confidence is vital in negotiating: confidence in yourself, your proposal, your company, and your medium. Experienced negotiators will often try to get you to fall for an authority trap and indicate that they have the power to give you an order (and, therefore, affect your income). Other authority traps occur when buyers try to lower your expectations and remind you that their media plans and instructions from their clients will not allow them to pay your asking price. Buyers will also try to instill in you a fear of losing by reminding you that they can get lower prices from competitors or that they can buy another medium. In the face of these maneuvers, you must maintain your confidence and never lower your expectations; always keep your focus on your HLE.

Other maneuvers that crafty buyers often use to lower your confidence, reduce your expectations, and get you frustrated and angry (so you will make an emotional, not rational, decision) are: interruptions, hurry-up, delay, keep-you-waiting, and bring-in-the-boss.

Interruptions. Some buyers will continually interrupt a sales discussion or negotiation by taking phone calls, going for coffee, or even making quick calls. Buyers make these maneuvers in order to get you flustered, frustrated, and furious. Buyers know that if you let your ego and your emotions highjack your rationality, you will try to settle too fast just to get it over with and make a bad deal (for you).

Hurry-up. When buyers call for avails or give you a request for a proposal (RFP) or request for information (RFI), they will often indicate they need it "immediately, if not sooner" in an attempt to hurry you up. Such a request is often followed by, "E-mail me the information by 1:00 p.m. I don't have time to see you," or something similar. This maneuver is often to hurry you up so that you do not have time to prepare adequately and to instill in you fear of losing if you do not meet their timetable. Of course, if you meet a hurry-up deadline, a buyer will rarely make the buy immediately. They typically use the delay maneuver.

Delay. Once you have made a presentation or responded to an RFP, buyers often delay making a buy for as long as possible. They often use this delay maneuver to make you worry about losing the order, hoping you will lower your prices to avoid a loss. It is to counter this delay tactic that you should always put a deadline on your offers. Another way to counter the delay maneuver is to call or email the buyer who uses it and say something like, "I just wanted to let you know that we're filling up fast and those positions you wanted may not be available after today. Please give me an order ASAP, because I'd hate to see your client miss out on this opportunity and not be able to run its advertising."

Keep-you-waiting. Often buyers will keep you waiting, knowing that you will become frustrated and angry. Sometimes they will schedule appointments early and make you wait in a reception area with competing salespeople. Buyers use this maneuver because they know that salespeople often put competition on a personal level and, therefore, will lower their expectations and prices in order to avoid losing to a competitor waiting in the reception area. Remember that fear of losing can be a powerful influence, so do not let fear overcome you when you see a competitor. Be friendly, and increase your resolve to achieve your HLE.

Bring-in-the-boss. In the middle of a negotiation, sometimes buyers call in their boss and say, "We're getting nowhere; I'm calling in my media director who will make sure you know that you will lose the business if you don't accede to our demands." This is an authority trap; do not fall for it. Do not lower you confidence or expectations. This is a good guy/bad guy tactic designed to intimidate you. Focus on your HLE and keep in mind that the buyer is admitting a desire for the deal by calling in the boss to help.

> **Rule #18:** Check your ego at the door and do not let your fear or emotions get the better of you. Patience wins.

It will help you maintain your confidence and keep your expectations high if you realize that the other side's maneuvering for dominance and trying to appear to have a power advantage is nothing more than a thinly disguised bluff. After all, who has the power in today's media-dominated world: advertising agencies and their clients or the media? The media are the most powerful communication force in the world. Without advertising carried by the media, companies trying to sell their products and services to mass audiences would have to sell them one-on-one to individual consumers. Without advertising, there would be no mass distribution and no mass consumption of products. Modern marketing warfare is conducted by the forces of advertising on the battlefield of the media; this central position gives the media enormous power. As mentioned previously, companies must advertise and agencies must invest their clients' money in advertising, and the media provide advertisers access to audiences. Therefore, as a media salesperson, never forget who has the power – you – and use this knowledge to boost your confidence in the face of threats and bluffs.

Experienced negotiators will also try to control the negotiating agenda. They will often come to the negotiating table with a printed agenda and demand sticking to it. The reason for this is simple, and is expressed by the following rule:

> **Rule #19:** Whoever controls the negotiating agenda controls the outcome.

The concept is straightforward. If you can control the items you will negotiate about, you can control the shape of subsequent agreements. For example, a media-buyer's one-sided agenda might be as follows:

1 Discussion of price
2 Discussion of discounts
3 Discussion of added value
4 Discussion of viewability
5 Discussion of terms and conditions

The above agenda will not lead to a discussion, but to a series of demands, beginning with demands for reduced or discounted prices. Once a buyer gets a discounted price, demands for add-ons at no cost will follow. When faced with such a lopsided agenda, do not begin negotiating. Instead, discuss the agenda and do not start negotiating until you have reached consensus on a fair, balanced agenda. It is best to hammer out an agreement on an agenda several days before a major negotiation begins.

Or, you can anticipate an agenda similar to the above, especially if you have previously negotiated with someone. You can anticipate that price will be the first item on their agenda. The first question will be, "What does it cost?" You can reply by saying, "In my price, I factored in the schedule of advertising you requested, our standard terms and conditions, the viewability percentage you asked for, and the total, packaged price is $125,000." If the buyer asks for individual cost breakdowns, make sure that you have priced them so that they add up individually to more than $125,000, otherwise the buyer will try to negotiate on each item in the hope of lowering the overall price. By packaging in this way, you take away much of a buyer's negotiating power.

Therefore, as opposed to the buyer's agenda above, an agenda that would be favorable to you would be as follows:

1   Discussion of terms and conditions
2   Discussion of position
3   Discussion of viewability issues
4   Discussion of price

The above agenda is better because the final element, price, will depend on agreements on the preceding items. For instance, if a buyer wants a favorable position or 100 percent viewability, then the price should go up. Price is not a single element, but is inextricably linked to the other parts of a deal – the more extras, the higher the price. Just like when you buy a car, the final price you pay depends on many factors such as terms (loan), conditions (insurance), and extras (trim, radio, undercoating, and so forth).

> **Rule #20:** In order to avoid negotiating on each element individually, package all the elements in a deal so that the prices of the individual elements always add up to more than the packaged price.

Following are several more rules that apply to the pre-bargaining maneuvering for dominance control phase of negotiating.

> **Rule #21:** Negotiate only after you have created value, early in customer's planning cycle, and well before your imposed deadline.

> **Rule #22:** Negotiate at the highest level possible – only with the buying decision-maker.

The bigger the deal, the higher in an organization you should go, because as deals get bigger the decision-making authority level increases and you always want to negotiate with the final decision-maker if at all possible – with the boss. The converse of this rule applies to you.

> **Rule #23:** Don't negotiate with your boss present if you can avoid it.

If your boss is present when you negotiate, the buyer will not talk to you, but to your boss, and you not only lose control of the discussion, but you will also lose control of the account, because the buyer will want to continue to deal with the boss. Furthermore, when bosses are present at a negotiation with a salesperson, too often they – the bosses – do not want to look bad or lose the business and will make a bad deal. Some of the worst deals in the media are made by bosses who want to show off to salespeople that they can close and demonstrate to clients to that they have the authority to change terms and lower prices – it is a power trip.

On the other hand, there are times when it is desirable to have a boss present in a negotiation. For example, often on a big deal, the other side will want to negotiate at high levels in an organization. Sometimes, you might want to use the boss as the bad guy so you can play the good guy in a negotiation. Often, the boss can impress the buyer and put the buyer in an authority trap.

However, whenever the boss is involved in a negotiation, it is critical to come to an agreement beforehand as to the exact role the boss will play. When you negotiate with an account that is assigned to you, you should take the lead in recommending a negotiating strategy. For example, if a boss wants to accompany you on a call on a buyer and you understand the buyer well enough to know such a call is not appropriate, you might say, "I don't think it's a good idea for you to come on this call. The buyer is very defensive and is intimidated by managers; she thinks they put too much pressure on her. We have a great relationship and she might think you don't trust me. I'll take you on a call next week on a buyer with whom you can be a great help."

An effective use of bosses is to ask them to make a call with you on a buyer or customer to create value and not to discuss price. Managers can talk effectively about a company's mission, culture, or new content – things that enhance your company's image and create value. When the buyer asks about price, your boss should say, "I'm not the person to talk about price. I think our product is so terrific that I'll ask for a high price. You deal with Jane. She will look after your best interests and get you the best deal we can offer. Also, she knows your needs better than I do." This is an ideal one–two approach that uses a boss effectively and keeps the negotiation under the control of the salesperson.

Rule #24: Negotiate on your own turf if possible.

As professional football, basketball, and baseball teams know, it is always better to have a home-field advantage. If you negotiate in your offices, you control the environment and the room set-up, you can be sure that you have the right equipment, and you have access to your management, to experts, and to information that can help you. Also, there is a subtle advantage to negotiating on your turf – it is your meeting and your chances of controlling the agenda are better. This rule particularly applies if you have nice turf, if your offices are attractive and reek of glamour (people love the glamour of the media), power, and authority. If you have shabby, unglamorous offices, go to customers' offices.

If customers prefer to negotiate on their turf, which is usually the case with media buyers at ad agencies, do not hesitate to go to their offices. If you go to a buyer's office, take advantage of the opportunity to read the room and learn as much as you can about the buyer's personality, needs, tastes, and preferences.

Rule #25: Negotiate face-to- face whenever possible.

A lot of media business is conducted on the phone or by email. But when you negotiate on the phone or email, you are at a disadvantage. You cannot see the body language or non-verbal behavior of the prospect, thus substantial communication goes unnoticed and is lost. It is easier to be tough, mean, and competitive on the phone or in emails (or on Twitter) than face-to-face where a buyer has to look you in the eye and deal in person with your potential for retaliation (tit-for-tat). Also, it is more difficult to establish rapport and empathy and build a solid relationship with a buyer on the phone or in emails than it is in person. Negotiating face to face gives you an advantage over competitors who do business on the phone or by email.

If you have to deal with a distant buyer on the phone, always be the caller so that you are prepared. And if a buyer calls and wants to place an order, tell the buyer that you will call back. Do not sell or negotiate on an initial call or inquiry. Return the call as promptly as possible, but not before you are thoroughly prepared.

Rule #26: If you have to negotiate on the phone, you be the caller.

Bargaining

Bargaining is the hand-to-hand combat of the negotiating process; it is where the final agreement or settlement is determined. There are five steps in the bargaining process:

1 Warm-up
2 Open and frames
3 Signaling leverage
4 Making concessions
5 Building agreement

Warm-up The warm-up is the opening skirmish in which you test your assumptions about the other side's style, strategy, and tactics. During the warm-up, you listen and observe carefully and do not give away any information that could be useful to the other side.

Rule #27: Listen and get information 66 percent of the time, give information only 33 percent of the time.

While you are listening, look for gestures, body, language, and grooming that indicate low self-esteem and lack of confidence. Look and listen for clues as to whether the other side is competitive or cooperative. During the warm-up conversation, start with a positive, complimentary approach. Compliment the other side, its organization, and its advertising, but do not go overboard and be wildly enthusiastic. For example, after listening to opening remarks, you might say, "Because you are a reputable company, we look forward to doing business with you. We would like to have your advertising on our website because it makes us look better, and I always enjoy negotiating with you because

I learn so much." Do not go overboard, but be positive, complimentary, and sincere to set the tone for cooperation and an amicable bargaining process.

This approach works particularly well with cooperative negotiators because it signals a desire to be cooperative and to improve the relationship. Use this approach even with highly competitive people because it will put them off guard and make them overconfident. They will learn how tough you are when they make their first bombastic, outrageous, threatening demand and you use tit-for-tat and counterattack with equal force. When competitors discover that their initial assumptions about you were incorrect, they often become confused and make mistakes. When bullies are challenged, they often give in easily.

Also, before you begin bargaining and during the warm-up, you should have a discussion to verify what you are negotiating about, to get all of the issues on the table. It is important that you observe the following rule:

> **Rule #28:** Get the other side to state what they want at the beginning, and you tell them what your issues are in order to put the most relevant issues on the table.

When the other side tells you what it wants, repeat the requests (or demands) and get agreement. For example, "You would like to run a 52-week schedule of ads in my newspaper at the bulk rate of 30,000 inches and would like to top left position on page two and top right position on page three. Is that correct?" If you get agreement, then you tell them what your issues are. For example, "We'd like your business very much, but those positions you ask for will be difficult to deliver. So, let's see if we can work something out." It is vital to put important (to you) terms and conditions that are different from standard media contract terms that advertisers are used to in your proposal and sell them aggressively, because you want prospects to know what your terms and conditions are before you get into negotiations. By selling in deal terms and conditions in your proposals, you can set up this discussion about issues at the beginning of a negotiation.

In larger, more complex deals there might be some terms and conditions that are so vital to you that they are deal breakers. In these situations, it is important to tell the other side what issues are important to you. When you do so, it is best to include, in addition to the important terms, several throw-away terms you can use as concessions later in the negotiation. If you do not have throw-away deal terms and corresponding price concessions, you will appear to be inflexible and the deal terms will be seen as unreasonable demands, which could stall and even sink a negotiation.

The other reason for this rule is that you will negotiate based on the other's side's initial requests. If the other side puts additional requests or demands on the table later in the process, it is unfair to you because you have been negotiating in good faith based on the assumption that all of the issues were on the table. You have been hoodwinked if the other side asks for more later on. If this should happen, your response should be, "Oh, I'm sorry. I didn't know you wanted 50 percent bonus ads every month. You didn't tell me that up front. I was basing my negotiating based on what you originally put on the table. Now we'll have to start all over again based on this new request."

Before you make an opening offer it is vital to get all the issues on the table so you know the size of the pie you are trying to get a piece of.

Open and frames   We will return now to the 10 steps in preparing for a negotiation. Step seven was to determine when and how to open. When you plan your opening strategy, there are two initial questions you have to ask yourself, "Should I open first?" and "Should I open optimistically or realistically?"

Open first?   Yes. In almost every situation in media selling, you should know what the other side's offer will be. In the *identifying problems and qualifying* step of selling, you have discovered customers' advertising budgets and have some sense of what they will pay and what terms they want. In the case of selling to agencies, buyers typically send an RFP or call for avails that list the parameters of a buy: price, ratings, demos, dayparts, and so forth.

The only occasions in which you should let the other side open are: (1) those in which you are not familiar with the style or demands of the other side or when you do not know them at all, and (2) when the other side are novices and are unfamiliar with media prices.

> **Rule #29:** Open first to set an anchor except when you do not know anything about the other side.

Open optimistically or realistically?   In general, open optimistically. In the majority of situations you should open optimistically with the highest price and terms for which there is a supporting standard or explanation that would allow you to make a plausible case for it. In words, if you can reasonably justify prices and terms, such as basing it on high demand, ask for it. A good rule of thumb is to open at least 15 percent above your HLE price, which gives you room to give concessions and still have the potential for getting your HLE. Also, include at least three throw-away terms in your initial offer for the same reason.

In some situations where you are not dealing with an experienced media buyer or regular customer, you can use the contrast principle and open for up to 50 percent higher and then come down to your HLE, which will seem low in contrast (door-in-the-face strategy). This tactic works best when you are making a presentation that has three proposals, as covered in Chapter 12. For example, if the largest of your proposals is for $75,000, then the second proposal for $50,000 seems much lower than if you opened with the $50,000 proposal.

Jonathan Haidt writes in *The Happiness Hypothesis* that:

> In financial bargaining, too, people who stake out an extreme first position and then move toward the middle end up doing better than those who stake a more reasonable position and then hold fast. And the extreme offers followed by a concession doesn't just get a better price, it gets you a happier partner...she is more likely to honor the agreement because she feels she had more influence on the outcome.[12]

Opening optimistically brings us to two more fundamental rules of negotiating:

Rule #30: When in doubt, open optimistically and have room to come down.

Rule #31: You never get anything you don't ask for, so ask for more than you hope to get.

Optimistic openings work best in transaction negotiating and when you do not know much about the other side.

There are several situations when optimistic openings are not a good tactic and realistic openings are better, which leads to the following rule and three corollaries:

> **Rule #32:** When you know the buyer well, open realistically. Also, open realistically when you have no leverage, when in a tacit coordination situation, and when people say they will not negotiate and mean it.

When you have no leverage, an optimistic opening does not work. When you have a weak position, an overly optimistic open leads buyers to conclusions that you are either bluffing or not too smart – both bad signals to give. When dealing in a tacit coordination situation, you should be realistically optimistic, or close to your highest legitimate expectation. When you are dealing with a person who says, "I won't negotiate, bring me your best price," and you know from experience that the person is telling you the truth, it is best to open realistically with a fair initial offer just above the mid-point in your settlement range.

Experienced media buyers and negotiators, who have read books and attended seminars on negotiating, know the fundamental rules and understand the power of high expectations. Therefore, experienced agency and client negotiators, especially when negotiating for broadcast and cable, will try to lower your expectations every chance they get. They will lower your expectations when they call for avails or send out RFPs. They will say, "I'm in a hurry and have to make the buy today, email me your avails and give me your lowest rates. You have only one shot." In such cases, if you do as instructed, buyers will call back and say something like, "You're too high, lower your rates or you won't get the business." So they lied, in a sense, and are in fact giving you a second shot. Therefore, it is imperative to know your buyers, know what their negotiating tendencies are, and respond accordingly with you opening offers.

When you open, remember the following two rules:

> **Rule #33:** Get the bad news out of the way early.

> **Rule #34:** Don't include most of the other side's requests in your initial offer.

Rule #33 comes from the advice of Richard Chase and Sriram Dasu in their *Harvard Business Review* article, "Want to perfect your company's service? Use behavioral science." The authors write: "Behavioral Science tells us that, in a sequence of events involving good and bad outcomes, people prefer to have undesirable events come first – so they can avoid the dread – and to have desirable events come at the end of a sequence – so they can savor them."[13] Recency effects indicate that people tend to remember the last events or experiences in a series of events, so it is effective practice to save the best, most favorable experiences until last. For example, if your company requires unusual or onerous terms and conditions, such as asking for cash up front, it is best to introduce these items at the beginning of the bargaining process and get them out of the way.

Rule #34 about not including most of the other side's requests or demands in your opening offer is based on the notion that you want the other side to ask for them so you can bargain and ask for something in return for each request. If you give the other side all they ask for initially, you lose the opportunity to get something in return during the subsequent bargaining and concession-making process, but include a few of their requests in your initial offer to signal some degree of cooperation. Make the other side ask for most of their demands and requests because in that way you control your give-backs and concessions.

The eighth step in the planning process was to determine frames. When you open, frame your initial offer positively, as you learned in Chapter 4 ("Free throws win ball games"), and during the bargaining process continue to frame all of your offers positively. Emphasize the value of your offers and their benefits that give the other side a good deal. For example, "The $125,000 package is the best deal we are offering currently. It is a 25 percent discount on the individual elements in the package if purchased separately." Positive framing provides the other side with justifications for making concessions. If you have prepared properly and have a needs portrait of your buyer and a Benefit Matrix, you will know the best way to frame your offers. With competitive negotiators who want victory, frame your offers as gains and wins for them – really good deals. With negotiators who fear losing, frame your offers as a way to avoid a loss and emphasize the pain and shame of losing.

Rule #35: Always frame all of your offers appropriately.

Signaling leverage   After you frame and present your initial offer and before you begin trading concessions in the bargaining process, you want to signal your leverage, if you have leverage. Exhibit 13.5 shows how you should act when your leverage is strong and when it is weak.

As you can see in Exhibit 13.5, when your leverage is strong and you want to act firm, make confident demands, lay out your BATNAs, and leave the decision up to the other side. A particularly strong BATNA will communicate that you have buyers who will pay higher prices for smaller chunks of a package you are offering and want to buy soon in order to get first-mover advantage. If you want to be flexible, show the other side that you are willing to invest in the relationship and be reasonably generous and cooperative.

If you see yourself as having a weak leverage position and want to be firm, emphasize the uncertain future – that someone else, even a competitor, could buy your offering and the rates might go up. In this situation, making an early, small concession might be advisable to show your willingness to do a deal. If you want to be flexible when you have a weak leverage position, acknowledge the other side's advantage and frame your offers positively. Appeal to the other side's sympathy and call in some relationship chits. Ask what they would do in your position, and, in effect, throw yourself to the mercy of the court, as lawyers say.

The best way to signal leverage is to show and maintain a high level of confidence. At no time in negotiating can you communicate a fear of losing or a need to close fast. You must be calm, patient, and, most of all, confident. As in a gunfight in the old Western movies, the following rule applies:

Rule #36: Confidence is everything; whoever blinks first, loses.

Exhibit 13.5   Signaling leverage

Signaling Leverage

Your actual leverage situation (as you see it)

	Strong	*Weak*
Firm	Make confident demands and credible threats. Display your alternatives and leave the decision up to the other party.	Emphasize the uncertain future Bluff (act strong when you are not).
Flexible	Show the other party you are investing in the relationship. Be generous	Acknowledge the other party's power and stress the potential gains from future cooperation. Appeal to the other party's sympathy. What would they do in your position?

How You Want to Act

Source: Shell, G. Richard. 1999. *Bargaining for Advantage*. Penguin Books. Used with permission.

Making concessions   Step nine in the preparation process is to determine concessions and trade goals. After you open and set an anchor, after you frame your initial offers to appeal either to their desire for a win or to increase their fear of losing, and after you have signaled your leverage and firmness or flexibility, you are ready to make concessions, or, better, to make trades. The first three rules of making concessions in the bargaining process are as follows:

Rule #37: Never begin with a major concession.

Rule #38: Don't just concede, try to trade; if you give up something, always try to get something in return.

Rule #39: Give the first concession on an unimportant issue, and then get a concession from the other side.

These rules are important because they remind you to begin with a small concession; they also indicate that it is acceptable to give the first concession in order to break the ice and get things started, but give a small, unimportant concession. The second rule also reminds you that when you give a concession, always try to get a reciprocal concession before you move on. Sometimes you have to ask for reciprocation by asking, "I gave up on my request for a thirteen-week commitment. Can you give me a little higher price?"

Rule #39 is important to remember because it gives you a clue as to what is important to the other side. Your first concession will be on an unimportant issue, so you must assume the other side's first concession will be on an issue that is not important. Trading concessions at the beginning of the bargaining process is like bidding in the game of bridge, you are giving the other side signals as to what cards you hold and how strong your position is. Your goal in bargaining is not just to concede, but to trade – to get something in return for the concessions you make. If you plan your concessions properly, you can trade small, unimportant concessions for ones that are more important to you. Remember that media buyers usually have to invest all of their client's money, so even though they ask for a lower price initially, low price is often not their most important issue.

As you proceed in the process of trading concessions, follow the next two rules:

Rule #40: Make small concessions and give them slowly.

Rule #41: Make the other side work hard for everything; they will appreciate it more.

These rules are based on the principle, "What we obtain too cheaply, we esteem lightly."[14] For example, if you open with a price of $100 in the demographic a buyer requested and the buyer says, "That's a little high, but can you give me some added bonus impressions?" you know price is not the most important issue. The buyer virtually conceded on price and you know added bonus impressions are more valuable. In this situation, switch from discussing price to making concessions for how many bonus impressions, starting small and working up slowly to a *clincher close*, which I will discuss later in the chapter.

As you go through the exchanging of concessions, make sure to continually invoke the principle of reciprocity. For example, "OK, I gave you the social media support you wanted, will you give me the price I originally asked for?" Use the reciprocity principle as often as you can. If you feel what you are getting in return for a concession is not fair, say so. As in, "I gave you a valuable social media support and you are not going to give me the price I asked for. That's not fair!" A little outrage in the right places can be quite effective.

As you proceed with bargaining and trading concessions, use an effective concession pattern, which you have planned in advance. Exhibit 13.6 shows six concession patterns.

Look at Exhibit 13.6 and let's assume you have planned to give a series of discounts in four steps that add up to a total of a 15 percent discount. Therefore, just considering price and not terms and conditions, Pattern #1 is ineffective because all the concessions are of equal value, so buyers expect the pattern to continue because you have given no signal that you are close to your walk-away and they will continue to push for more.

Pattern # 2 is equally ineffective because you say no, then give a big concession, so your buyers expect this pattern to continue and will not believe your no after the fourth concession.

Pattern #3 is ineffective because you say no several times, and then give a huge concession; therefore, buyers will extend the negotiating interminably because they expect another large concession after several nos.

Pattern #4 is also ineffective because you give a huge first concession and then stonewall, so buyers will extend the negotiation and insist on more concessions equally as large.

Exhibit 13.6   Concession tactics

Which tactic is most effective?

	First concession offered	Second concession offered	Third concession offered	Fourth concession offered
Pattern #1*	3.75%	3.75%	3.75%	3.75%
Price**	$96.25	$92.64	$89.17	$85.83
Pattern #2	0	7.5%	0	7.5%
Price	$100	$92.50	$92.50	$85.86
Pattern #3	0	0	0	15%
Price	$100	$100	$100	$85
Pattern #4	15%	0	0	0
Price	$85	$85	$85	$85
Pattern #5	1.5%	3%	4.5%	6%
Price	$98.50	$95.5	$91.20	$85.73
Pattern #6	6%	5%	3%	1%
Price	$94	$89.30	$86.63	$85.76

*15% total discount offered; ¼ of 15%=3.75%
**Assume an average price of $100

Pattern #5 is ineffective because with each larger concession you raise buyers' expectations, which extends negotiating.

Pattern #6 is obviously the most effective one. Because you are willing to give a total discount of 15 percent, your concessions get smaller each time with Pattern #6, which signals you are approaching your walk-away. In Pattern #6 when you get to the third concession, you could say something such as, "Well, I can lower my price by $1 but you will have to give me another two weeks on the schedule" (assuming a price of $86.63). If the buyer cannot give you another two weeks, probe until you get something, a larger share of their budget, for example.

As you go through the bargaining process of trading concessions, get small, easy issues out of the way first. If you run into a big issue, set it aside by saying you will come back to it later and move on to get agreement on smaller issues. This tactic uses the commitment principle. As the other side invests increasingly significant amounts of time, energy, and other resources in the negotiating process, they become more and more committed to closing the deal for fear of losing it and wasting their time and energy. As an example, "OK, we've agreed on a promotion and on the last position in a commercial pod, but we're still a little bit apart on price. Let's put the price issue aside for now and see if we can't reach agreement on how long your promotion will run."

Finally, as you progress through bargaining, keep your eye out for what tactics the other side is using. Be aware of all of the tactics in Exhibit 13.4. As Sun Tzu writes, "Do not swallow bait offered by the enemy."[15] Of course your customers are not your enemy, but they will often use tactics, or bait, to try to get an advantage. When you recognize a tactic, name it, do not fall for it, keep your confidence up, and move on.

When you determine the most effective concession pattern for an upcoming negotiation and determined your trade goals, fill out that section in the Negotiating and Closing Planner.

> **Rule #42:** Develop an effective concession pattern that signals when you get close to your walk-away.

Building Agreement   Finally, as you go through the process of bargaining, follow the next rule:

> **Rule #43:** Summarize agreements and restate the other side's position on a regular basis.

Frequently restate the other side's positions during bargaining because, "if they understand you're hearing what they're saying, it reduces stress levels," according to Victoria Ruttenberg, a successful Washington, DC lawyer and mediator.[16] You are trying to build agreement brick by small brick; you are trying get the other side to invest time and effort on a series of small agreements so their commitment to the process increases. Perhaps you have put off major issues earlier in the bargaining process, come back to them after you have reached a number of smaller agreements. You will find that large issues are easier to settle after smaller agreements have been reached – the other side's commitment is at its height. During this final stage of the bargaining process, do not get impatient:

> **Rule #44:** Be patient – with patience and hard work in exploring alternatives, you can make the deal better for both sides.

When you finally deal with the remaining major issues on the table that you have put aside to get agreement on smaller issues, have patience and explore alternatives – be creative in finding solutions. As soon as you have reached agreement on all of the major issues, transition smoothly and calmly into your close – stay cool.

Closing and getting commitment

A *Harvard Business Review* article by Steve Martin discussed the results of a survey of business-to-business (B2B) buyers that illustrated seven important lessons about the mistakes salespeople make when they lose business.[17]

1 *They are not trusted or respected.* Just 18 percent of the salespeople that buyers in the survey met over the past year would be classified as trusted advisors.
2 *They can't converse effectively with the senior executives.* It is imperative for salespeople know how C-level executives think and to communicate with them in the language they use.
3 *They can't clearly explain how their solution helps the buyer's business.* Only 54 percent of salespeople could clearly explain how their offer impacted a client's business.
4 *They are too self-centered.* Buyers perceived the majority of salespeople as serving their own agenda or care only about making a sale, not helping the buyers.

5   *They use the wrong closing strategy.* Hard closes such as "last time we'll make this offer" didn't work. Soft closes such as "invest another $100,000 and I can offer an additional 10 percent discount" worked much better. Buyers don't like to be pushed.

6   *They don't alleviate the risk of buying their solution.* Salespeople don't make it safe to buy their solution.

7   *They can't establish a personal connection with the buyer.* Buyers cited five key reasons why there isn't a personal connection:

  a   The salesperson was too pushy.
  b   There was a difference in communication styles.
  c   The salesperson's personality was much different from mine.
  d   The salesperson was too eager to befriend me.
  e   There was a difference in age.

So far in this book we have covered all of the mistakes in the above list except number five: "They use the wrong closing strategy." The final step in the negotiating process is *closing*, and this next section will teach you how to use the right closing strategy.

The first rule of closing is:

Rule #45: Expect to close.

You have planned well, you have bargained intelligently, and your confidence should now be at its peak. You must act as though you deserve the order, as though there is no doubt in your mind that you have the best offer, so ask for a decision. Close.

Closing can be smooth or a time of high anxiety. It is important to remain cool and confident when you close and not show any worry or anxiety, regardless of the circumstances. Often experienced negotiators save their most powerful tactics for closing. You may think you have reached agreement on all of issues under discussion and have asked for the order, but buyers might introduce tactics they have not used before – a crunch or a nibble (see Exhibit 13.4).

Sellers might use the limited-number approach, the act-now-before-a-competitor-buys-it approach, or the get-in-before-the-deadline approach. Buyers might use the your-competitors-want-a-big-share-and-are-offering-much-lower-prices approach and attempt once more to get you to lower your price. This threat may be a bluff or it may be true. According to Richard Shell in *Bargaining for Advantage*, scarcity is an emotional issue; both sides use it to attempt to create the fear of losing in the other side. One side can increase the other side's fear by warning that others are competing for a scarce resource (the seller's offering or the buyer's money). It is always a matter of judgment whether to hold firm or yield. Your judgment will be informed by your understanding of the leverage situation at the moment when you must decide.[18] If you know your buyer's tendencies, you will know if they tend to bluff or not and, therefore, whether to hold firm or yield. However, in no circumstances should you go below your walk-away.

If a buyer's apparent final offer is below your walk-away, then always walk away, but do so nicely and not in anger. Say, "I'm sorry I can't go any lower. I'll take your offer back to my management, but I'm not sanguine about their agreeing," which leads to the next rule:

Rule #46: When you walk away, always leave the door open.

When such a walk-away occurs, you and your management can decide outside the heat of battle, whether to go back with another offer. But make sure you wait at least a day – the buyer may call or email you and meet your terms during that day.

In many situations the close will go smoothly, especially if you have used trial closes throughout the bargaining phase.

There are five types of closes:

1   Trial closes
2   Choice closes
3   Clincher closes
4   Last-resort closes
5   Bad, never-use closes

Trial closes   There is on old saying in selling, "ABC, always be closing." The phrase comes from the old-fashioned, hard-sell school of selling, but as in many rules of thumb, there is a kernel of wisdom in the phrase. In post-internt selling and negotiating techniques, the always-be-closing concept translates into "use trail closes throughout your selling and negotiating process." Trail closes are an indirect method of testing buyers' temperature. Are buyers cold and need more information, or are they warm and ready to buy? The only way to know for certain is to ask. The worst that can happen is that you discover that they are not ready and they raise another objection. Actually, the main purpose of a trial close is to bring objections to the surface so you can deal with them. If there are no more objections, then you have a deal. Following are several trial closes you can use throughout your presentations and negotiations to test the water.

*   *The direct close.* Simply ask for the green light. Always avoid using the words *buy* or *order*. Do not ask, "Will you buy this?" Do not say, "How about it? Could I have the order?" Those words may frighten buyers. "I'll book this right away so you can get on the website by Monday, OK?" or "We'll agree on this price, then. Isn't that fair enough?" are better direct closes.

    The phrase "Isn't that fair enough?" is one of the strongest closing phrases you can use. Nobody wants to be accused of implying that someone else is unfair and so will often go to great lengths to answer this question positively.

    If a buyer says no to your direct close, then you can say something like, "OK, where are we hung up? What can we do to wrap this up?"
*   *The assumption close.* This close is particularly powerful because it is so painless for both a buyer and a salesperson. When you sense that the time has come, that a buyer has shifted gears from desire to conviction, you simply assume that the buyer has made the decision to buy and proceed accordingly. Talk and act as though the buyer has given you the green light. You can say something such as, "I'll put this order through and you'll start next Monday." If you are correct in your assumption, the buyer will not stop you, in which case you have the order. If the buyer says, "Hold on. I haven't bought anything yet," then proceed with some probes to find out why the buyer is not ready.

- *The summary close.* This close is an excellent trial close and should be used often. On a regular basis, summarize all the benefits to which a buyer has agreed. Emphasize those benefits in which a buyer has shown the most interest. Present an overwhelming weight of accepted evidence of superiority in your summary. Follow your summary with a statement such as "Can we go ahead with this plan?"
- *The pin-down close.* This closing technique should be used judiciously. After prospects have expressed an objection, pin them down by asking if you can have the go-ahead if you can overcome their objection. For example, if a prospect says, "I don't like those early news spots," your response would be, "If I can get my manager to agree to move them to the late news, may I book the schedule?" You have used a pin-down close. Be careful, though; avoid using this close too often or too early because a prospect might understand what you are doing and use the same tactic against you to get a string of concessions. If a prospect tries to extract another concession from you after a pin-down close, a good tactic is to say, "Hey, let's be fair. You said we could go ahead if I moved those spots."

  A good time to use the pin-down close is when prospects try to put off a decision. When prospects say they want to think it over or that they will call or email you later, quickly isolate their reasons for the stall and use a pin-down close. The let-me-think-about-it excuse is probably the most common one you will encounter, and you must learn to overcome it quickly or you will lose sales. When you get this excuse, pin down the reasons for the excuse, narrow the objection, and then try a pin-down close or a clincher close (which you will learn about a little later in this section).

  Another time when pin-down closes work well is when buyers try to nibble you (see Exhibit 13.4). A pin-down close stops a nibble by saying, "OK, if I can get half of your spots moved to the late news, do we have a deal – no further changes?" After a nibble, do not give the other side their full demand, cut it in half, then if you want to, you can go all the way on their demand if half does not work and you are still above your walk-away.
- *The T-account close.* Use a lined tablet or any sheet of standard-sized paper and draw a line down the middle of the paper and then cross the T across the paper near the top. Next, at the top of the left column, write down a buyer's objections and in the area underneath write a list of all the reasons supporting the buyer's objections. Next, write in right column your offsetting benefits. Your list should be longer than a buyer's; if it's not, do not use this technique.

  For example, if a buyer wants to put off making a final commitment until next month, put "Start Next Month" on top of one column and "Start Now" on top of the other column. With a prospect's help, write all of the objections in the left column and then you write all of the reasons to start now in the right column. This technique is dramatic and graphic; it is particularly effective with precise, fact-oriented people. It also gives buyers the perception that you are being objective and fair ("Isn't that a fair list?").

Rule #47: Use trial closes throughout the negotiating process.

Choice closes   Choice closes are especially powerful because they build commitment through choice. Chase and Dasu report on an interesting study that found that blood donors perceived significantly less discomfort when they were allowed to select the arm from which their blood would be drawn. The authors write that the lesson from this study is clear: people are happier and more comfortable when they believe they have some control over a process, particularly an uncomfortable one such as giving a salesperson an order. In some cases, the control given over is largely symbolic (as in the choice of arm), or it can be a meaningful, high-stakes decision. The medical profession has long recognized the value of allowing patients to make an informed choice about alternative treatments for cancer and heart disease. Doctors realize there is enormous value in involving the patient in these important decisions. Patients feel less helpless, less hopeless, and, most important, more committed to making the process work.[19] For this reason, increase commitment through choice by offering not just one proposal but three proposals and let the other side choose.

- *The choice close.* The choice close is one of the easiest closes to use. It is probably used more than any other close, and should be. You have already set up this close by providing three proposals, and then, you can simply ask prospects which of the three options they prefer. When you have the answer, you have the order. "Do you prefer the first, second, or third proposal I offered, Mr. Franklin?" "The third." "Great, an excellent choice! Thank you. I'll run right back to the office and get this scheduled and email you the confirmation." The buyer might never say yes or "I'll buy it," but the buyer has given assent by making a choice.

    When buyers are given a choice, they can make a decision without feeling forced into a corner. Buyers have the reassurance and confidence of asserting their free will and of expressing themselves. Furthermore, after they make the choice, you have the opportunity to reinforce their final decision. Always compliment prospects on their wise judgment.

- *The minor-point close.* This is another popular, effective, and easy close. With the minor-point close, you attempt to get buyers to choose and approve one or more minor details in an offer; if they agree, you have made a sale. The more minor points on which you can get agreement, the better. "We'll start the schedule next Tuesday so we have time to get the creative in, OK?" or "Instead of billing this to you the first week of the month, we'll send the bill to you a week early so you can be reimbursed more quickly from your client, OK?" When buyers agree to a minor point, they are saying yes the easy way. For example, a buyer who might hesitate if you ask whether you can go ahead with the $200,000 order for sponsoring baseball broadcasts will probably find it a snap to agree to provide you with artwork for a sponsorship ad in the stadium program booklet.

Clincher closes   A clincher close is a well-planned close in which you make a final concession on a major request, on an important issue, or on substantial added value – you hold it back until the end and offer it to clinch the deal. From the beginning, you have your concession or improved offer in your back pocket but bring it out at the end only if you need it to close the deal. For example, you might be negotiating for a major 52-week buy on your website. The agency, on behalf of its client, has requested a low rate in return for giving you a firm 52-week commitment, wants four event promotions (one each quarter), as well as merchandising support for the client's sales force (prizes such as golf clubs and golf balls for sales contest winners). As you have progressed through the negotiation, you have agreed to the merchandising but are 10 percent apart on prices. The agency's final offer has been $50,000 and they are not budging. You are holding out for $55,000. However, you have not offered the four event promotions even though the other side has continually asked for them, and even though you have been prepared to give the promotions. The clincher close would be to say, "OK, we seem to be stalled. What if I give you the four event promotions, which will cost us a great deal, and you give me my price of $55,000? That seems like a win–win, fair agreement, doesn't it?"

Using clincher closes requires detailed planning before the negotiation and great discipline during the process because you lose the power of a clincher close if you introduce it too early in the process. Also, use clincher closes the first time you negotiate with someone, but not the second time. If you consistently use clincher closes with people with whom you regularly negotiate, they will expect them, always hold out for a major concession at the end, and when they receive the concession, they will not appreciate it but instead feel it is their due. With people with whom you regularly negotiate, use clincher closes only on an occasional, random basis. Use the same mixed strategy as discussed earlier in regard to bluffing.

Last-resort closes   When the above closing maneuvers do not work, try some of the following closes.

- *The "make-me-an-offer" close*. Real estate and automobile salespeople fully understand the power of this closing technique because it gets prospects to express verbally their commitment to buy. When buyers make an offer, they are not only committing to buy but they are also giving you the parameters of the final barriers to a sale. This is one of the last techniques you should employ because it typically results in a major concession. Even though it is somewhat tricky to do, the best way to handle this close is to get buyers to make you an offer on terms other than price alone. You might say: "I know that you want to advertise with us and that what I am offering is right for you. Make me an offer that contains an adjustment on something other than price and I'll see what I can do."
- *The "what-will-it-take?" close*. This is a more desperate version of the "make-me-an-offer" close. With this close you are vulnerable to lowballing, but often, as a last resort, you can see if the other side goes below your walk-away and how much lower, which is information you can use in your next negotiation, after you walk away. Sometimes you might use this close on a small piece of business when the offer is low and you can walk away to give the other side a clear signal that you will walk away from low offers; it makes your anchor in subsequent negotiations credible.

Bad, never-use closes   The following are some closes not to use because they will ruin relationships.

- *The poor-me close.* Salespeople have been known to beg for orders by saying that they will lose their job if they do not get an order or that they must have the money to pay for their child's organ transplant. Do not try to heap guilt on buyers and do not beg to get an order; do not lower yourself or diminish your own dignity. Confidence and self-esteem are vitally important in the selling and negotiating process; do nothing to lessen yourself in the eyes of prospects. Customers admire strength. Begging also puts you in an awful negotiating position at the time and in the future. Buyers will never want to see you again.
- *The now-you-have-it-now-you-don't close.* Some unscrupulous salespeople will promise anything just to get an order, knowing full well that they cannot deliver what has been sold. Their strategy is to take an order and then go back to buyers later and say they cannot deliver. This maneuver has a narcotic temptation because it can shut out competitors; however, buyers are not dumb enough to let this work more than once. Nothing destroys your credibility faster than this bait-and-switch technique.
- *The for-you-only close.* Some weak salespeople try only one close and then immediately rely on giving big concessions to make a sale. They promise prospects, "If you give me an order right now, I'll give you the lowest price possible, lower than anyone else." Salespeople who use this approach sound as though they just came in from an alley where they were peddling pornographic postcards, and buyers tend to show them about that much respect.

Whichever appropriate close you decide to use, do not close too aggressively, especially on bigger deals. You can create a sense of urgency with deadlines and limited-supply maneuvers, but the timetable has to be the other side's. Too much pressure can kill a prospective deal. Pressure on your part to close will make the other side suspicious – you will appear too eager for a deal and cause the other side to push for more concessions. As indicated earlier in this chapter, when people buy, they want to make a choice. People do not like to be sold or pressured; they are much more comfortable in choosing and controlling the timing of their buying decision. Also, pressure to close often strains a relationship, so you must be particularly careful in pressuring people with whom you regularly negotiate.

Rule #48: Do not close too aggressively; always keep the relationship in mind.

Sales managers, sales trainers, and many sales textbooks often overemphasize closing. You should close only when you are convinced that your customers are committed to your proposed solution and negotiated agreement and that you are convinced it is a fair deal that is right for the other side. Never push people into buying. Remember, you are managing a relationship for the long haul, and it would be counterproductive to close too aggressively and jeopardize a relationship. Also remember that your biggest competition is not other salespeople or other media, it is algorithms, and the only advantage you have over algorithms is your ability to forge relationships. Do not jeopardize relationships.

However, people have a natural tendency to avoid saying yes, either from fear of losing or fear of not getting a good deal, so you must maintain your confidence that your deal is the right one for them and not signal anything that would give them pause or give them an excuse to hesitate.

> **Rule #49:** When closing, confidence is vital; you cannot signal in any way your fear of losing or need to close fast.

Confidence is vital throughout the negotiating process, but even more so in the closing phase. Here are several things to keep in mind that will enhance your confidence.

Give the other side a "good deal"   People have their own unique definition of a good deal – it is an individualized perception. Your task before or during a negotiation is to discover your customers' personal definition of a good deal and then see that they get it.

Exhibit 13.7 shows a list of some customers' definitions of a good deal and how to respond.

Exhibit 13.7   Types of good deals

Definition	Description	Tactic
Got a low price.	The perception of a low price is always relative. Remember the salesperson's father's advice, "never pay retail?" Some people will go to enormous lengths in time and effort to get what they perceive to be a lower price. Often such bargain hunters are called bottom feeders. They will take risks on quality and preemptability (not running an ad and replacing it with another, higher priced one).	Offer bottom feeders low-priced packages of less-desirable, remnant, or pre-emptible inventory. Identify and keep a list of bargain hunters and call them when you have last-minute, reduced-price inventory. These are people who often know the price of everything and the value of nothing and, thus, might buy hard-to-move inventory. Make sure you emphasize the bargain, low-priced nature of your offering. When you get the order, compliment them on getting such a good bargain.
Got something someone else wanted.	The scarcity principle at work. Competition for scarce resources often gets people overcommitted and makes inventory more desirable. Price, discounts, quality are not important, all that counts is that someone else wants it – especially if a hated competitor wants it. Fear of loss and envy are involved.	During negotiations, make sure people that have a tendency to be envious are aware of your BATNAs and know that their competitors are interested or have made an offer. Be honest, but on the other hand, do not fail to communicate such information. When you make the sale, compliment them for snatching it away from their competitors.

Exhibit 13.7 Types of good deals (cont'd)

Definition	Description	Tactic
Got high quality at a reasonable price.	Many buyers are concerned with quality and service, and do not mind paying for it. For example, many people pay much more for a Mercedes or a Lexus than for a Ford or Chevrolet because of their perception of quality.	Create value from the beginning for these people and continually mention the word *quality*. When you reach agreement, compliment them for having the excellent judgment to recognize quality.
Got the last one.	The scarcity principle at work again. Fear of loss of a scarce and valuable resource is involved.	The limited-supply maneuver works well here. Be honest when you let buyers know that there is only one left and create a sense of urgency due to the competition for it. Price is never the issue, so raise the price for the last one. When you close the deal, compliment them on their ability to make a fast decision.
Got a warranty or guarantee: low risk of dissatisfaction	Some people with low self-confidence, who are risk-averse, and, especially, those who fear making a mistake, feel much more comfortable with guarantees or warranties. Ratings for upfront buys on network television and impressions on interactive buys are typically guaranteed.	Emphasize the safe, low-risk nature of guarantees. Because guarantees are more important than price, buyers will generally pay more for guarantees. When you get agreement on a deal, compliment them on being such good, smart negotiators.
Got a discount.	To people who crave discounts, the actual price is not as important as the perception that they got a discount. Goods on sale appeal to these people; they will buy more than they need because they cannot resist a "50 percent discount."	Going in to a negotiation, raise the price on your initial offer by 20 percent, negotiate, and then as a clincher close, offer a 20 percent discount. When you make the sale, compliment them on being such a good negotiator and being able to get such a large discount.
Got something else free thrown in.	There are some people who love to get something for nothing, something free. They will pass up a "50 percent discount" offer, often feeling that is damaged or undesirable goods, and snap up an offer of "buy one and get one free." Same price, different frame.	With people who you have identified as those who like something else free thrown in, as with those who crave discounts, planning is the key. During negotiations, do not concede on price, even though you are willing to come down 15 percent but as a clincher close, say, "OK, if you'll give me my price, I'll give you 15 percent more inventory – a bonus of 15 percent." When you reach an agreement, compliment them for getting something free.

Exhibit 13.7   Types of good deals (cont'd)

Definition	Description	Tactic
Got a win; feel like they won something important to them.	Many competitive buyers and negotiators care more about winning than anything else. In fact, they will not make a deal unless they feel like they have won.	Good planning will do the trick. Use a red herring, such as an event promotion that the other side insists on. Say no repeatedly, then as a clincher close, say, "OK you win, I'll give you the promotion if you'll give me the order now – before I change my mind." When you get the order, compliment them on winning. Make sure you tell them they have won.
Got good results from advertising.	Many experienced advertisers view advertising as an investment, so it is not how much it costs that matters, but what their return on investment is. Digital advertising is especially good at showing return on investment (ROI).	With people who care most about results and ROI, it is vital that you control their expectations from the beginning and always underpromise and overdeliver. By lowering their expectations from the start, you can help ensure results. When you make the sale, compliment them for their sophisticated approach and deep understanding of the ultimate purpose of advertising, and reassure them that your primary objective as a salesperson is to get results for your customers.
Got a good deal compared to other media.	In today's media-saturated environment, buyers have a multitude of choices for placing advertising. If they select one over another or in combination with another medium, they typically want to feel that they got a good deal.	When you are in a selling or negotiating situation in which other media are being considered, stress the benefits of your medium – not based solely on price – but based on a wide variety of dimensions. A T-account close works well in these situations, where you compare the benefits of your medium to other media. When you reach agreement, compliment buyers on their insight and professionalism.

Note in 13.7 that all of the tactics involve complimenting people on their ability to get a good deal and to reinforce their perception of a good deal. Therefore, you have the power when you negotiate to give people a good deal, only if you know what their definition of a good deal is and you can plan your tactics in advance to make sure you give them a good deal as they define it.

Rule #50: Have confidence that you can give the other side a "good deal" – their definition of a good deal.

Finally, it will give you confidence and power in a negotiation if you have no fear of walking away. Good BATNAs vastly increase your confidence to walk away. If you have the confidence to leave if you do not achieve your walk-away, it does you no good unless you signal your confidence by how you act, walk, sit, and talk. Confidence does not mean arrogance, bluster, or threats, but it reflects a firm resolve to make a deal that is fair to both sides.

Get commitment   When you call on media buyers who are examining a number of competitive proposals, it is sometimes difficult to close a deal on a call or with an exchange of emails. If you find that one of the many closes above is not appropriate because the buyer has to evaluate more proposals, then it is important that you get some kind of commitment from the buyer (1) to recommend your proposal to a client or (2) to let you know where you stand so you can adjust your proposal if necessary. It is in these types of situations that having a strong personal relationship with a buyer is vitally important. If buyers know you and trust you, then they are more likely to give you some kind of verbal commitment. So, if you can't close, push for a verbal commitment of some kind.

On the other hand, when one of your closes is successful and you get an agreement, do not be satisfied with just a verbal agreement – get a formal commitment such as an insertion order (IO) sent by email, or a signed contract for very large complicated deals. The objective of every negotiation is to secure commitment, not merely agreement. Commitment in closing a deal gives you a deal that sticks and that has incentives or penalties to insure that both sides perform. Different kinds of negotiating situations call for different types of commitments, and IO being the most common one.

Whichever form of commitment you use, always follow this rule:

Rule #51: Once you get commitment, say "thank you," shut up, and leave quickly.

Buyer's remorse usually sets in after someone buys something. You do not want to be present when buyer's remorse occurs. One of the biggest mistakes inexperienced salespeople make is to hang around and chat after they have made a sale or reached an agreement. They are afraid of being considered impolite and ungrateful by rushing off. Forget about being impolite; leave fast. You might want to make an excuse for your quick exit and say, "You've got an excellent deal. Thank you so much for the business. Now I have to run back to the office and book this order before someone else buys the great inventory you just invested in. Goodbye." There is an old saying in sales that the jaw-bone of an ass slew a thousand Philistines and as many sales have been lost for the same reason because salespeople talk too much after making a sale.

Putting It All Together: Create a Negotiating and Closing Plan

You should fill out the Negotiating and Closing Planner, available on www.mediaselling. com/downloads whenever you are going into a major negotiation. Also, download the Negotiating and Closing Outline that summarizes all of the rules, strategies, and tactics in this chapter so you can review them and use them to help you fill out your Negotiating and Closing Planner.

Once you have created a thorough negotiating and closing plan, and before you enter into a major negotiation, rehearse. An excellent way to rehearse is to get a colleague (salesperson or sales manager) to rehearse with you and to play the other side's role. Rehearsing in this manner is the best way to refine and perfect your plan.

Rule #52: Always rehearse your negotiating and closing plan.

After you have rehearsed your plan, commit to it. Carry it out just as you have rehearsed it because rehearsal will give you confidence and increase your commitment.

Finally, just as when you make major presentations, debrief after negotiating, which leads to the final negotiating rule:

Rule #53: After every negotiation, debrief.

Many of the concepts and the strategies used in this chapter are those recommended by Richard Shell in *Bargaining for Advantage*, an excellent book that is applicable to media negotiating and one I recommend you read and study.

Test Yourself

1. What are the five elements in the negotiating process?
2. Why is knowing the other side's cultural background important?
3. What are the 10 *preparation* steps in negotiating?
4. What are the four negotiating situations?
5. What are the two basic negotiating styles?
6. What is a BATNA?
7. What is the purpose of the tit-for-tat tactic?
8. What is negative leverage?
9. What is an HLE?
10. What is a ballpark?
11. Name six acceptable bargaining tactics.
12. How can you avoid negotiating on each element in a package individually?
13. What are the five steps in the bargaining process?
14. Should you open first?
15. Should you open optimistically?
16. Give an example of a frame.
17. How should you give concessions?
18. Name three trial closes.
19. Give an example of a clincher close.

Project

Go to the Downloads section of the *Media Selling* website at (http://mediaselling.us/downloads/) and download "A Salesperson's Dilemma" and "Janet Negotiates." Read "A

Salesperson's Dilemma" carefully, read "Janet Negotiates," and then complete the Assignment at the bottom of "Janet Negotiates."

References

Chase, Richard B. and Dasu, Sriram. 2001. *"Want to perfect your company's service? Use behavioral science." Harvard Business Review,* June.

Conger, Jay. 1998. *"The necessary art of persuasion." Harvard Business Review,* May–June.

Ertel, Danny. 1999. *"Negotiation as a corporate capability." Harvard Business Review,* May–June.

Fisher, Roger and Ury, William with Patton, Bruce. 1991. *Getting to Yes,* 2nd ed. New York: Penguin Books.

Maccoby, Michael. 2000. *"Narcissistic leaders: The incredible pros, the inevitable cons." Harvard Business Review,* January–February.

Mérö, Lászlo. 1998. *Moral Calculations: Game Theory, Logic, and Human Frailty.* New York: Copernicus.

Nierenberg, Gerard I. 1973. *Fundamentals of Negotiating.* New York: Hawthorne Books.

Poundstone, William. 1992. *Prisoner's Dilemma.* New York: Doubleday.

Putnam, Linda L. and Roloff, Michael. 1992. *Communication and Negotiation.* Newbury Park, CA: Sage Publications.

Raiffa, Howard. 1982. *The Art & Science of Negotiation.* Cambridge, MA: Harvard University Press.

Schelling, Thomas C. 1980. *The Strategy of Conflict.* Cambridge, MA: Harvard University Press.

Sebenius, James K. 2001. *"Six Habits of Merely Effective Negotiators." Harvard Business Review.* April.

Shell, G. Richard. 1999. *Bargaining for Advantage.* New York: Penguin Books.

Tzu, Sun. Edited by James Clavell. 1983. *The Art of War.* New York: Dell Publishing

Woolf, Bob. 1990. *Friendly Persuasion.* New York: Berkley Books.

Notes

1   Nierenberg, Gerard I. 1973. *Fundamentals of Negotiating.* New York: Hawthorne Books.

2   Tzu, Sun. Edited by James Clavell. 1983. *The Art of War.* New York: Dell Publishing.

3   Ibid.

4   Shell, G. Richard. 1999. *Bargaining for Advantage.* New York: Penguin Books.

5   Auletta, Ken. 2018. *Frenemies: The Epic Disruption of the Ad Business (and Everything Else).* New York: Penguin Books.

6   Ertel, Danny. 1999. *"Negotiation as a corporate capability." Harvard Business Review.* May–June.

7   Shell, G. Richard. 1999. *Bargaining for Advantage.* New York: Penguin Books.

8   Woolf, Bob. 1990. *Friendly Persuasion.* New York: Berkley Books.

9   Poundstone, William. 1992. *Prisoner's Dilemma.* New York: Doubleday.

10 Haidt, Jonathan. 2006. *The Happiness Hypothesis: Finding Hidden truth in Ancient Wisdom.* Basic Books.

11 Shell, G. Richard. 1999. *Bargaining for Advantage.* New York: Penguin Books.

12 Haidt, Jonathan. 2006. *The Happiness Hypothesis: Finding Hidden Truth in Ancient Wisdom.* New York: Basic Books.

13 Chase, Richard B. and Sriram, Dasu. 2001. *"Want to perfect your company's service? Use behavioral science." Harvard Business Review.* June.

14   Shell, G. Richard. 1999. *Bargaining for Advantage*. New York: Penguin Books.

15   Tzu, Sun. Edited by James Clavell. 1983. *The Art of War*. New York: Dell Publishing.

16   Lancaster, Hal. 1998. "Most things are negotiable: Here's how to get good at it." *The Wall Street Journal*. January 27.

17   Martin, Steve. 2017. "7 reasons salespeople don't close the deal." *Harvard Business Review*. Retrieved from https://hbr.org/2017/08/7-reasons-salespeople-dont-close-the-deal.

18   Shell, G. Richard.1999. *Bargaining for Advantage*. New York: Penguin Books.

19   Chase, Richard B. and Dasu, Sriram. 2001. "Want to perfect your company's service? Use behavioral science." *Harvard Business Review*, June.

14

Customer Success

Charles Warner

As you learned in Chapter 2, the mission of a media sales organization is t*o get customers and keep them*, and the number one objective is *to get results for customers*, or to make sure they are successful, which, of course, is the best way to keep them. The first five steps of missionary selling and the first four steps of service selling are focused on getting customers and only one step is focused on keeping them, and that step is customer success.

In the first four editions of *Media Selling* the final step in the selling process was referred to as *servicing*, but just as the Internet and automation has disrupted and transformed other steps of selling, it has transformed the final step, too. The last step in both missionary and service selling is now called *customer success* because it parallels the name of the function or department in many forward-thinking companies, especially digital-era companies such as Apple and Amazon that are dedicated not to just satisfying customers, but to delighting them. It is no accident that Apple and Amazon, the two companies that by all accounts are the major companies most dedicated to putting customers first and delighting them, are the two most valuable companies in the world – the only two with market caps that have reached at one time or another in the last year and half of over $1 trillion.

Media Selling: Digital, Television, Audio, Print and Cross-Platform, Fifth Edition.
Charles Warner, William A. Lederer, and Brian Moroz.
© 2020 John Wiley & Sons, Inc. Published 2020 by John Wiley & Sons, Inc.

Pre-Digital-Era Selling

In the pre-digital era many media salespeople, especially in local media, were expected to both sell *and* service their accounts. The vast majority of media sales organizations, such as in local broadcasting and cable systems, were modeled after manufacturing companies. Their organization charts, processes, and operating models were adopted from industrial-era companies in which performance measures were based on quantity and quality of output.[1] Therefore, salespeople in manufacturing companies and in broadcasting, cable systems, and most magazines were paid commissions that rewarded them for getting accounts, but not for keeping them. Because salespeople, not illogically, do what they are paid to do, it was usually not a priority to service accounts, or make sure they got results and were successful.

In the pre-digital era, advertisers negotiated and paid for available inventory on television networks, television stations, and top-rated radio stations based on the relative scarcity of that inventory. Advertisers paid high cost-per-thousands in major-market newspapers because in most cities, the newspapers had a monopoly and, thus, could charge, on a cost-per-thousand (CPM) basis, high premiums for ads, as could mass-market and upscale magazines. As Ken Auletta wrote in his book, *Googled*, in 2003, when Mel Karmazin was Chief Executive Officer (CEO) of CBS, he said that advertisers "paid their money and took their chances."[2]

But when Google, then Facebook, and most digital advertising-supported platforms and publishers began taking responsibility for the success of their customers, it raised advertisers' expectations. Legacy media such as television, radio, and cable systems, in order to survive needed to raise the level of their servicing to meet a much higher bar of customer expectations. Advertisers were no longer willing to "take their chances" when they invested in advertising. Advertisers wanted a clearly demonstrable return on their investment; they wanted results they could measure.

Selling an Intangible Service

Selling media advertising is not like selling widgets made in a factory, even though many pre-digital era media companies were organizationally modeled after manufacturing companies. The media offer a service – entertainment and information – not a product such as clothing or cars and, as described in Chapter 2, services that are intangible require a different pre- and post-sale approach. Services differ in four fundamental ways from tangible products:

1 *Services are like handshakes, because for a service to work, both the service provider and the consumer/customer have to participate.*[3] In the media, a medium creates content and the audience must participate in consuming that content, just as advertisers have to participate in the creation of the advertising.

2 *Most services involve many interactions between buyer and seller.* For example, when an ad agency or a medium creates an ad, both the agency/media and the client have to participate in the ad-creation process.[4]

3 *With services it is hard for customers to know in advance exactly what they are getting.* For example, when investing in a search term purchase on Google, an advertiser does not know how many clicks it will get, or when paying for a visit to a doctor's office, you do not know that the doctor can cure your cold.[5]

4 *Customers of a service do not own what they paid for; they experience it.* Customers cannot return a service in the same way they can return a tangible product if it is defective. There is no market for used experiences.[6]

Because of the above four differences between intangible services and tangible products, the benefits of services after they have been purchased must be tangibilized. Customers of services such as media, advertising, or insurance are typically not fully aware of all of the benefits these services provide and need to be reminded in the form of stewardship reports of some kind. For example, a General Manager of a television station might make a stewardship report at the end of a year to the CEO of a local bank that is the station's largest advertiser. The stewardship report might include the number of commercials the bank ran, the number of contacts the station initiated with the bank that resulted in schedule improvements, copy improvements, content creation, and social media posts. The stewardship report might also contain the number of contacts the station initiated with the bank that included an analysis of social media likes, comments, and reviews that might also suggest a new approach or a new product that the bank might offer.

Digital-Era Service

Because of the popularity of the Internet, as more and more data became available about consumers and their preferences, those consumers began to expect a seamless, personalized experience from the start of the sales process to the finish of the process like they get from Apple or Amazon. Also, advertisers expected the sales, service, and marketing functions in a media organization to be engaged with them and not only to help them get results, to be successful, but also to give them insights into new product and selling opportunities that came from analyzing the mountains of data available about consumer behavior, attitudes, passions, and unmet wants.

Furthermore, because most media selling today now includes some element of digital advertising, ensuring that an advertising schedule gets results is complicated and time consuming, especially in regards to advertising creative executions. For example, during the 2016 presidential campaign, the psychometric consulting firm Cambridge Analytica handled a portion of Donald Trump's digital advertising campaign on Facebook. "Pretty much every message that Trump put out was data driven," Cambridge Analytica CEO Alexander Nix was quoted as saying in a January 28, 2017 article in online news site, Motherboard.[7] "On the day of third presidential debate between Trump and Clinton,

Trump's team tested 175,000 different ad variations for his arguments in order to find the right version, above all on Facebook," the authors of the Motherboard article write.[i]

One person or even 1,000 people could not test 175,000 different ad variations in a single day. The testing could only be done by automation, by sophisticated algorithms.

Digital-era pre-and post-sale processes

What is needed to automate the complex pre- and post-sale process in the digital era?

First, management has to clearly define every step in the sales process for their media company. The pre-sale process is outlined in general terms in Chapter 8 in Exhibits 8.2 and 8.3, the Step Management process for missionary and service selling. The post-sale process must be similarly defined on a step-by-step basis so that it fits the unique needs of each media organization and each individual customer. For example, the post-sale process for a mid-sized market radio station might look something like that shown in Exhibit 14.1.

Exhibit 14.1   Radio station customer success checklist

- Read contract or insertion order (IO) carefully to make sure all terms and conditions in the contract are understood and followed, including start and end dates clearly noted.
- Check to see that the traffic department has received advertising copy and copy rotation instructions from advertiser or agency.
- Check to make sure that the ad copy has been cleared as safe and acceptable.
- Check to make sure that the proper copy is inserted into the station's commercial log in the positions indicated in the IO.
- If the ad copy is to be read live, listen to each host's or personality's delivery of the copy. Is the copy being read with product understanding, sincerity, and enthusiasm?
- At the end of each week the schedule runs, check to see that the promised level of impressions was delivered.
- At the end of each week that the schedule runs, check to see that it ran in the times put forth in the contract, and suggest changes in the scheduling if a change is appropriate and reasonable.
- Contact the customer's representative in person or via email to see about results. Did results meet expectations?
- If a live read, did the customer hear the commercial, and, if so, any comments or suggestions.
- Is the customer delighted with the wording of their commercials? If they are, make some suggestions on ways to improve the copy or delivery. If they're not, make even more suggestions on ways to improve the copy and the delivery. Does the copy need different wording, different positioning, or different offers?
- Explore opportunities for improvement in the ad schedule's placement and frequency level. Explore opportunities for sponsorships, events, and promotions that might improve customer's visibility, image, and success.
- Two weeks before the end of a schedule contact the customer and ask for a renewal and propose new opportunities to improve results, visibility, image, engagement, and success.

---

[i] Due to revelations that Cambridge Analytics harvested the data of an estimated 87 million people on Facebook and violated Facebook's privacy policies, the company closed on May 2, 2018 and started insolvency proceedings.

A customer-success checklist for a schedule of digital advertising, for example, on ESPN.com, might be four times as long as the checklist in Exhibit 14.1, and would not only include constant vigilance in order to optimize multiple ad creative executions but also might include postings on social media such as Facebook, Twitter, and Instagram.

If you are curious why ESPN would post on social media on behalf of its clients, you need to understand that there are three types of media: paid, owned, and earned. *Paid media* is the same as advertising – an advertiser pays for media exposure such as ads on Google search results pages. *Owned media* refers to a company's web properties such as a website, a mobile site, an app, a blog, or a page on Facebook or other social media platforms. *Earned media* refers to media that is shared, liked, reposted or retweeted, or reviewed online.[8] For example, an advertiser such as Budweiser might invest in a sponsorship of an NFL Fantasy League on ESPN.com and run a commercial of a Clydesdale horse and a puppy on the Fantasy League site; it would also post the commercial on its company website, and put the commercial on YouTube for people to watch, share, like, and comment on – in other words, earn additional distribution for the commercial. To help make the commercial successful and gain as wide an audience as possible, the ESPN customer success department might post the commercial on ESPN's Facebook page and in the Twitter feed for the Fantasy League. In other words, ESPN would try to boost the commercial's distribution and popularity in earned media. ESPN would be making an effort to ensure customer success.

If you post on social media to increase earned media exposure for an advertiser, you have to make sure you inform your client about your effort and also tell them how many likes, comments, and reviews they got from your posts. It also reinforces your case if you can put an approximate monetary value on the earned media that was generated. This type of effort clearly tangilbilizes your service and your commitment to customer success.

Service Design

Because of the complexity of selling and servicing digital advertising and the necessity of deliberately designing the pre- and post-sales process, the importance of service design has increased geometrically in the digital era. Tom Stewart and Patricia O'Connell write in their book, *Woo, Wow, and Win: Service Design, Strategy, and the Art of Customer Delight*:

> Service design and delivery involve reimaging, recreating, and rethinking the execution of every stage and aspect of the customer and company interaction, regardless of what is being sold and regardless of whether a transaction actually occurs, to satisfy that customer and advance your strategic goals.[9]

They also write that service design must be proactive, not reactive, and that it involves choices, actions, and consequences. It is about delivering on your promises to customers in accordance with your strategy, not about acceding to everything a customer requests. And "service design creates consistency, and consistency is no accident."[10] Thus, the first rule of service design:

Rule #1: Consistency, consistency, and consistency.

Consistency means that your customers can expect the same experience every time they interact with you. Consistency molds customers' expectations, and consistency also means not surprising your customers, because surprising them too often confuses them. For example, think how you feel when you get an automated voice response when you call your doctor's office, "Listen carefully because our options have changed." You might feel confused and frustrated. A consistent experience keeps frustrations to a minimum.

Also, computers, algorithms, and artificial intelligence (AI) are infinitely more consistent than human beings, which is why virtually all sales organizations use customer-relationship-management (CRM) software or platforms such as Salesforce, Matrix (the dominant CRM platform in media), or Efficio (used by many media organizations), or HubSpot, or many other CRM or sales productivity platforms. Automating repetitive tasks such as notifications of schedule changes or delivered impression levels can free salespeople for more important tasks that require a personal connection.

Rule #2: Automate everything but the hugs.

Automation and AI are much faster and better at doing repetitive, transactional work than humans are, so automate as much as possible, which will leave those responsible for customer success the time to make personal, emotional connections to customers. "Hugs" refers to empathetic, personalized responses to customers' problems, complaints, and pain points, not necessarily physical hugs, although they might be appropriate in certain, rare situations.

Organizations have to be careful and not automate too many customer contacts and servicing tasks and, rather than using too much AI, they need to use collaborative intelligence.[11] Collaborative intelligence occurs when AI augments human workers instead of replacing them.

> Companies see the biggest performance gains when humans and smart machines collaborate. People are needed to train machines, explain their output, and ensure their responsible use. AI, in turn, can enhance humans' cognitive skills and creativity, free workers from low-level tasks, and extend their physical capabilities.[12]

AI and automation also improve the consistency and reliability of customer service and allow for more personalized, empathetic responses. Thus, excellent, consistent service design can differentiate a company from its competitors, and *profitably* wow and win not just any customers, but the *right* customers, as defined by your company's strategy, which leads us to the third rule of service design:

Rule #3: The customer is always right, if they are the right customer.[13]

The right customer is a profitable customer and a customer you are prepared to service in every sense – it is the customer you are targeting, not the other way around.[14] The right customer is also the customer you want to retain, because retaining customers is more profitable than getting them. Increasing customer retention rates by five percent "increases profits by 25 percent to 95 percent," according the authors of *Woo, Wow, and Win*.[15]

Designing the customer journey

Whether you are providing a low-cost solution such as programmatic buying on an open exchange, a middle-cost solution such as buying advertising programmatically on a private exchange, or a high-end solution of buying guaranteed placements through a salesperson, study after study has shown that the nature of the customer's *experience* with a company is a key deciding factor in whether or not they choose to buy. As Stewart and O'Connell write in *Woo, Wow, and Win,* "Experiences matter. Experiences are journeys. Journeys are designed."[16] An experience covers every touchpoint with a customer from the first contact in person or via email, to educating a prospect or agency, to negotiating and closing, to the purchase, to ensuring customer success, and to the renewal process. Every touchpoint must be designed so that it aligns with all other touchpoints and so that there is a seamless, integrated experience. Touchpoints must be also aligned among all of your organization's strategic goals, your customers' wants and needs, and what happens between you and your customer. The alignment is a function of 10 elements:[17]

1 *Empathy.* Did you develop a customer's journey from the customer's point of view? Did you put yourself in your customer's shoes? Do you know how they walk?
2 *Expectation.* Do you know what your customers expect from you? If you are not sure, ask.
3 *Emotion.* Do you understand the emotions customers bring to the relationship? Are they fearful, anxious, or uncertain? Are they confident and happy to be a partner?
4 *Elegance.* Is your service process simple and easy to navigate and thorough?
5 *Engagement.* Do you communicate effectively at every touchpoint and understand your customer's experience and how to improve it?
6 *Execution.* Do you reliably meet all expectations?
7 *Engineering.* Are your touchpoints technically excellent, up to date, and equal to or better than what all of your competitors offer?
8 *Economics.* Do your customers get the service they expect *and* do you get the profits your company expects?
9 *Experimentation.* Do you build a process for improvement and innovation into all of your interactions so that you can develop new and improved capabilities?
10 *Equivalence.* Are you satisfied with the relationship? Both partners must continue to be satisfied and happy with the relationship.

The above 10 points are adopted from SD² Report Card in *Woo, Wow, and Win,* and emphasize that service design includes all of the touchpoints from start to finish of the sales process, and that service thinking must be holistic.[18]

Rule #4: Design the entire customer journey, not just parts of it, to delight customers.

Delighting customers means ensuring that they get results, that there are solutions to their marketing and advertising problems, and that they were delighted with the experience of dealing with you. Delight matters because, as Steward and O'Connell write in *Woo, Wow, and Win:*

1   Delight creates goodwill between you and your customer.
2   Delight improves retention and customer value.
3   Delight generates good word of mouth.
4   Delight buys you a break.[19]

The last point is an important one. Think back to your experience as a customer. Has someone you regularly buy from, such as Amazon, ever made an error? Did you forgive them because you had been delighted with all of your previous transactions? Giving a vendor a break because of past excellent service almost always leads to a repurchase, to a renewal.

And a fifth point about the importance of delighting customers comes from Brian Halligan, co-founder and CEO of HubSpot, a marketing and sales software company. He writes that, "Today...delighted customers are the biggest new driver of growth."[20]

In today's marketplace where both good and bad news about a product or service travels at the speed of light on social media and throughout the Internet, a business must make sure that the news about it is good, that people are loyal fans, and are advocating for it. If the good news spreads via digital word-of-mouth (social media) and that news is generated by delighted customers, not by the company itself, the advocacy has more credibility than a company advertising or a company patting itself on the back does, and, therefore, tends to generate both business growth and loyalty.

What are some of the elements that generate loyalty? In eMarketer's "Behind the Numbers" podcast, digital strategist Chris Lundquist reported on an analysis he did of a collection of consumer surveys. Lundquist looked for data in the surveys that could answer the questions, "What really drives loyalty?", "What really makes customers come back?", and "What drives emotional connection to a product or service?"[21] The data showed that 85 percent of shoppers came back to a store, a product, or a service because of habit, and their habits were built on a trust that the product provided a solution that met their individual needs. This trust in a product's solution is referred to as a *solution premium*, and a solution premium consists of five factors, according to Lundquist. Three of those factors apply to the customer success process in media selling:

1   *Personalization.* When a customer feels like a solution fits their individual needs, when they feel like a solution is relevant, or that an offer is just for them, it feels personal. Collaborative intelligence between AI and humans can be a big help in personalizing service and making customers feel like the solution and the service is uniquely for them.
2   *Simplicity.* Designing a service experience that is simple, convenient, and easy to navigate is essential in building loyalty and customer delight.
3   *Immediacy.* When customers buy something, they want it *now*, or as close to now as possible. Google AdWords (now Google Ads) allowed advertisers to get an ad up in minutes, and change copy as quickly; it therefore raised customers' expectations accordingly. Your service response times need to speed up to meet your customers' expectations.

Manage your whales

Just as whales are the largest creatures in the world's oceans, often the largest advertising accounts are called whales. As a general rule of thumb, the Pareto Principle applies to clients of the media – 20 percent of the clients account for 80 percent of the advertising revenue. The good side of this revenue coin is that a media organization can focus its attention on super-serving 20 percent of their most profitable clients, their whales, and not devoting too many resources to 80 percent of their less profitable accounts, thus being more efficient.

There are two parts of the bad side of the revenue coin. One is that losing a large account in the 20 percent group can be devastating to the financial health of a media organization. Many sales managers prefer to have a large number of mid-sized clients rather than a few very large ones, because the inevitable loss of a medium-sized account does not hurt as much as the loss of a large one, and a medium-sized account can be replaced more easily than a large one.

Note that small accounts are not mentioned. Each media organization must have its own definition of a small account, but typically a small account is one that costs more to sell and service than the revenue it generates, or, in other words, is unprofitable.

The other part of the bad side of the revenue coin is that because whales are so vital to revenue, there is too often a tendency to do whatever it takes to keep these very large clients happy. Efforts to placate a whale can lead to disastrous price cuts and onerous concessions on terms and conditions. Very large clients are more than aware of their power and leverage, and often use their leverage to make unreasonable (and, of course, unprofitable) demands on price, conditions, and service requirements. This situation leads to the fifth rule of servicing:

Rule #5: Be careful about overfeeding the whales.

A partnership means that both partners want the other to be successful *and* profitable, which is the reason that you want to make all of your clients partners – you will look after their success and profitability and they will do likewise. If advertisers are not successful, they will not renew. If your media company is not profitable in the long term, it will not survive, which means that advertisers will have less choice and fewer selections for how to reach their customers.

It is vital to enter into partnerships with your clients and to delight them with superior service, because, as mentioned above, delighted partners are: (1) more than likely give you break when you inevitably make a mistake and (2) lead to growth because of recommendations to other clients, which leads us to the last servicing rule:

Rule #6: Handle mistakes and complaints immediately and honestly.

When mistakes happen, it is vital to contact a customer immediately, before the customer contacts you to complain about a missed ad, an undelivered sponsorship, or running the wrong copy. And when you notify a customer about an error or mistake, you should also tell them what you are doing to correct the mistake. Always offer a solution – a generous solution that aligns with your company's overall customer-success strategy.

Feedback

You are not finished with the customer-success process when you deliver on your promise to delight customers by giving them extraordinary service; you must continue the spiral of success by giving extraordinary service time and again, over and over, at every touchpoint of the sales and service cycle. In order to maintain consistency and to continually improve – what the Japanese refer to as *kaizen* – you must have honest feedback so you can refine and improve your customer success checklist.

Ed Koch was the mayor of New York City from 1978 to 1989, and was famous and beloved for continually asking, "How am I doing?" He wanted feedback, and not just positive feedback. I know because when I was VP and General Manager of WNBC-AM, NBC's owned station in New York, one day in 1979 I was in my office and was shocked when my assistant came into my office with a wide-eyed, flustered expression and uttered, "Mayor Koch is here and would like to see you." Of course, I jumped up as he came into my office, shook hands and motioned for him to sit down, which he did. The first words out of the mayor's mouth were, "How am I doing?" I'm sure I stammered and said some positive things, but I also mentioned how tacky and messy 42nd Street near Times Square was. The mayor's response was classic good listening. He said, "I'm glad you brought that up. A lot of people have told me they, too, are concerned about the environment around Times Square. And here's what I'm going to do to fix it." Mayor Koch was not defensive; he listened, understood my concern, and said he was working on a solution. He got feedback and handled it positively, not defensively.

And in the act of receiving my feedback, he delighted me. I was honored that the mayor wanted my input, was interested in my opinion, and just by asking for feedback, he boosted my opinion of him enormously. By asking your customers for feedback, you not only honor them and increase their positive attitude about you and your company, but you also get input into your sales and customer-success process and can improve it.

Rule #7: Always get feedback from clients.

There are many ways of getting feedback, such as formalized customer success surveys conducted by independent research organizations or by your own company via email or an online survey platform such as Survey Monkey. Customer success surveys can be done yearly, quarterly, or directly after a major transaction, as is done when you interact with Apple customer support, for example.

As a general rule, you do not want to bother customers or buyers with too many surveys. Therefore, for most established media organizations, a yearly survey is sufficient, but for a startup, perhaps monthly would be better so adjustments can be made on a more timely basis. You can find an example of a Customer Success Survey in the Downloads section of www.mediaselling.us.

Some media companies get customer feedback by having a top executive such as the CEO, Chief Revenue Officer, or head of sales contact major customers and ask the Ed Koch question, "How are we doing?" I prefer this informal, personal approach because: (1) it gives senior executives the opportunity to listen to customers and (2) it lets customers know that the company cares about their opinion concerning the kind of service they are getting. Too many top media executives do not have a clear sense of how their companies are perceived by those customers and buyers who deal on an everyday basis with salespeople.

But whatever the timing, whatever the format, and no matter who does the customer satisfaction surveys, some sort of customer feedback is vital for every organization so they have a strategic, effective, ever-improving customer service design that looks after their customers' success.

Test Yourself

1. What are the four ways that intangible services differ from tangible products?
2. What are three types of media?
3. What are the reasons why delighting customers matter?
4. What is the rule about managing whales?
5. What are the three factors of a solution premium?
6. What is the Ed Koch question?

Project

The next time you go into a retail store – a Best Buy, a department store, a Staples, or any store that is not self-serve and that has salespeople – ask a salesperson on the floor a simple question such as, "Where do I find flash drives?" Pay attention to the answer you get and to the person's attitude, demeanor, friendliness, and helpfulness. Were you delighted with the treatment you received? Would you recommend to your friends that they shop at the retailer because of the wonderful service you received? If the answer to these questions is "no," write down some notes about how you would improve the store's service design.

References

Stewart, Thomas A. and O'Connell, Patricia. 2016. *Woo, Wow, and Win: Service Design,* *Strategy, and the Art of Customer Delight.* New York: Harper Business.

Resources

Efficio, Media Sales Management software (www.efficiosolutions.com) eMarketer's "Behind the Numbers" podcast (www.stitcher.com/podcast/behind-the-numbers/e) Salesforce (www.salesforce.com) Hubspot (www.hubspot.com) Matrix, Media Sales Management software (www.matrixformedia.com/) Survey Monkey (www.surveymonkey.com)

Notes

1 Stewart, Thomas A. and O'Connell, Patricia. 2016. *Woo, Wow, and Win: Service Design, Strategy, and the Art of Customer Delight*. New York: Harper Business.

2 Auletta, Ken. 2009. *Googled: The End of the World As We Know It*. New York: Penguin Press.

3 Ibid.

4 Ibid.

5 Ibid.

6 Ibid.

7 Grassegger, Hannes and Krogerus, Mikahel. 2017. "The data that turned the word upside down." Retrieved from https://motherboard.vice.com/en_us/article/mg9vvn/how-our-like-helped-trump-win.

8 Garman, Erica. 2018. "What Is earned, owned, and paid media? The difference explained." Retrieved from https://www.titangrowth.com/what-is-earned-owned-paid-media-the-difference-explained.

9 Stewart, Thomas A. and O'Connell, Patricia. 2016. *Woo, Wow, and Win: Service Design, Strategy, and the Art of Customer Delight*. New York: Harper Business.

10 Ibid.

11 Wilson, James and Dugherty, Paul R. 2018. "Collaborative intelligence: Humans and AI are joining forces." *Harvard Business Review*, July–August.

12 Ibid.

13 Stewart, Thomas A. and O'Connell, Patricia. 2016. *Woo, Wow, and Win: Service Design, Strategy, and the Art of Customer Delight*. New York: Harper Business.

14 Ibid.

15 Ibid.

16 Ibid.

17 Ibid.

18 Ibid.

19 Ibid.

20 Halligan, Brian. 2018. "Replacing the sales funnel with the sales flywheel." Retrieved from https://hbr.org/2018/11/replacing-the-sales-funnel-with-the-sales-flywheel.

21 eMarketer. "Behind the numbers" podcast. "What truly motivates customer loyalty? An interview with digital strategist Chris Lundquist." Retrieved from https://www.emarketer.com/content/what-truly-motivates-customer-loyalty.

15

Marketing

Charles Warner

Marketing is the process of getting consumers to be aware of, to be interested in, and to purchase a product; and it includes all of the steps of getting that product into the hands of customers, from product development and design, to pricing, to distribution, to advertising, to the transaction of a sale.[i]

In Chapter 1 you learned that a production-focused business first produces products and then tries to sell them. Production-focus was the approach manufacturing-oriented businesses took in the 1950s and 1960s. In the book *Marketing 3.0: From Products to Customers To Human Spirit*, Philip Kotler and his two co-authors refer to a product-focused approach as *Marketing 1.0*.[1] In the 1970s businesses generally began to adopt a customer-focused business approach that produced products that it knew would sell based on market research that revealed customers' aspirations, wants, needs, tastes, and preferences. Philip Kotler, who is often referred to as "the father of modern marketing," refers to a customer-focused approach as *Marketing 2.0*.[2]

Marketing 1.0 and Marketing 2.0 focused on the Four Ps of marketing: product, price, place, and promotion:

Product included coming up with new products based on thorough market research about market demand – was there enough demand for a product to be produced and sold at a profit?

---

[i] Remember from Chapter 2, that when a "product" is referred to, it covers both a product and a service.

Media Selling: Digital, Television, Audio, Print and Cross-Platform, Fifth Edition.
Charles Warner, William A. Lederer, and Brian Moroz.
© 2020 John Wiley & Sons, Inc. Published 2020 by John Wiley & Sons, Inc.

Price was often determined by what it cost to produce a product, adding a profit margin, and then adjusting the price based on the pricing of competitive products. Demand, scarcity, and brand image were also factored into pricing decisions.

Place was about where a product was sold, such as in a retail store, or to wholesalers, or by a sales staff directly to consumers (Avon, e.g.). Place was also referred to as distribution – how a product got to a customer.

Promotion was primarily advertising, or paid placement of ads in various media. Promotion also included incentives to buy a product such as contests, sales, volume discounts, and in-store signage.

In the fourth edition of *Media Selling,* a fifth P, post-sale service, was added to the classic Four Ps of marketing. At the time the fourth edition was published in 2009, marketing departments in most companies had also taken over responsibility for post-sale service, commonly referred as customer-relationship management (CRM). However, even Five Ps were not enough to cover the multitude of changes in marketing that occurred in the post-Internet, Big-Data digital era.

The digital era has required that a dozen or more Ps be added to the Five Ps of marketing. Seth Godin, in his best-selling book, *Purple Cow,* writes that there are "not enough Ps."[3] Godin adds positioning, publicity, packaging, pass-along, permission, and purple cow. The purple cow stands for a truly remarkable product, because in the digital era there are way too many products being promoted on way too many media so that an ordinary product gets totally lost. Also, today's consumers are so well informed that they can compare with ease many different products and offerings, which means that in the current marketplace, consumers, not the company, defines a product's value. For instance, using an example from Chapter 1, a consumer wants a quarter-inch hole, not a quarter-inch drill. And it is the consumer who defines the value of a quarter-inch hole.

The Era of Marketing that Provided Meaning

With the current dominance of digital advertising, not only does a product have to be remarkable – a purple cow – to stand out, but just as important, it also needs to appeal to people's values. In *Marketing 3.0: From Products to Customers to Human Spirit,* Philip Kotler and his co-authors write that they see "marketing transforming once again in response to the dynamics of the environment. We see companies expanding their focus from products to consumers to humankind issues."[4] Future-focused companies balance profitability with corporate responsibility.[5]

In order to achieve its goals in a digital economy, a company must share its mission, vision, and values with a "loyal network of partners" – employees, distributors, dealers, and suppliers.[6] If a company chooses its network of partners well, if their goals are all aligned, and if the rewards to their partners are equitable and motivating, a company can become a powerful competitor.[7]

In the values-driven marketing era, instead of treating people simply as consumers, or targets of their advertising pitches, marketers are more and more approaching people as whole human beings with minds, hearts, and values. In an ever more confusing and complicated world, people seek out companies that address their deeper personal needs for social, economic, and environmental justice as articulated in a company's mission, vision, and values statements.[8] For example, TOMS shoes promises "With every product you purchase, TOMS will help a person in need. One for One." The online eyeglass company, Warby Parker also uses a buy-one, give-one model, in which for each pair of glasses purchased, the company pays for the production of another pair of eyeglasses for the non-profit organization VisionSpring. VisionSpring in turn sells the glasses at a low cost to consumers or companies in developing countries as a way to encourage entrepreneurship. Amazon encourages online shoppers to sign up for AmazonSmile, select a charity such as Charity:Water to support, and then a small percentage of each Amazon order goes to the selected charity. When people buy from TOMS or Warby Parker, or sign up for AmazonSmile, they not only get functional fulfillment but also get emotional and values-driven fulfillment. People feel good because they are making a small contribution to help address problems in society.

By emphasizing social responsibility such as protecting the environment, distributing sustainable products, or supporting charities, companies can do well by doing good. By being socially responsible, companies appeal to people's sense of purpose. As you learned in Chapter 2, Daniel Pink writes that psychological research shows that there are three drivers of people's motivation: autonomy, mastery, and purpose.[9] Purpose motivates people because having a sense of purpose gives people's lives meaning, which is especially important to younger people such as millennials (those born between 1980 and 1995) and Generation Zs (those born between 1996 and 2010). A 2018 study by the marketing firm Do Something Strategic titled "Dollars and change: Young people tap brands as agents of social change" revealed that more than 76 percent of Generation Z has purchased, or is open to purchasing, a brand or product to support the issues that a brand stands for.[10] Furthermore, the study also reported that 40 percent of the Generation Z respondents stopped purchasing or boycotted a brand or company because they stood for something or behaved in a way that did not align with their values.[11]

Also, a November, 2018, study by CGS showed that shoppers were increasingly considering sustainability when making purchases. The study found that 68 percent of US Internet users deemed product sustainability as an important factor in making a purchase.[12]

Because of the inclusion of human values that many companies added to their marketing efforts, in 2013 the American Marketing Association articulated a new definition of marketing to include an element of social responsibility: "Marketing is the activity, set of institutions, and processes for creating, communicating, delivering, and exchanging offerings that have value for consumers, clients, partners, and society at large."[13]

Salespeople for local media, such as television and radio stations or newspapers, who call on companies that have some element of social responsibility in their mission and/or purpose statement should view such a commitment as an opportunity to create value not only for a prospect or customer but also for their community and for their medium. For example, the largest bank in the United States is Bank of America, and its mission statement is: "At Bank of America, we have a clear purpose to help make financial lives better through the power of every connection. We fulfill this purpose through a strategy of responsible growth, which includes a focus on environmental, social and governance leadership."[14] The first element in the "focus on" phrase is "environmental." If you are selling for a local television station in a city such as San Francisco or Boston and your station's news department is producing a week-long series titled "Save the Bay" that is about creating public awareness of the environmental degradation of the nearby bay, you could call on the heads of the Bank of America branches in the area, remind them of their corporate commitment to environmental leadership, and educate them on the value of sponsoring the "Save the Bay" series and boosting their image in the community. This type of sale must be made at the highest level of the client, not at the client's advertising agency because agencies are interested in, and often remunerated according to, efficiency (low cost-per-thousand (CPM) impressions, basically) and not necessarily based on a company's overall image in a community.

The Era of Participation and Collaboration Marketing

In the 1970s, 1980s, and early 1990s Marketing 2.0 and Marketing 3.0 for a major consumer package goods (CPG) company was relatively straightforward: (1) do market research on what consumers liked and wanted, (2) design a product that matched those likes and wants and throw in a little social responsibility, (3) advertise heavily on television with a well-produced, expensive commercial that made an emotional connection to a targeted consumer segment and, therefore, created demand for the product, (4) contact wholesalers and retailers and ask them how much of the product for which there was now demand – demand that the television commercials created – they wanted to buy, and (5) ship the product by truck, train, boat, or airplane to a retailer (or to a wholesaler that then shipped it to a retailer) and then let the retailer worry about and pay the expenses for stocking the product and transacting a final sale.

But by 1998, old marketing models were disrupted, primarily by AOL and Yahoo. On AOL, consumers could discover a product, get information about it, and buy it without leaving their home or office. The product would then be shipped directly to the purchaser. Nothing would ever be the same again for companies that made products, that distributed products, or that sold products.

Not only did the Internet allow companies to give information about products, distribute digital products, and sell products online, but it also allowed people and communities to connect with each other and to collaborate via chat rooms, instant messaging, and email. Word-of-mouth has always been the most effective form of advertising and promotion, but before the Internet, word-of-mouth was essentially one-to-one or one-to-several communication via a conversation, via letter, or via telephone. For example, you recommend a movie to your mother in a letter, then to a couple of friends in person, then those friends recommend the movie to several of their friends on the telephone, and so forth until the recommendation reaches, maybe, 150 people. On the Internet, you might rave about a movie in a chat room, and it might be seen by thousands, or you might post a positive review on Rotten Tomatoes and it might be seen by millions. The Internet allowed people and groups to communicate one to many and, thus, word-of-mouth grew exponentially and became an even more important element in the marketing mix.

The burst of technological advancement and innovation, fueled by dramatically lower storage costs via cloud computing, by faster processors, by smartphones, by Big Data, by algorithms and artificial intelligence, and, especially by social media facilitated billions of people being able to connect, participate, and collaborate.

In his 2008 book, *Here Comes Everybody,* Clay Shirky writes that "human beings are social creatures – not occasionally or by accident but always."[15] Shirky believes, "We have always relied on group effort for survival" even before agriculture was invented. He continues:

> We act in concert everywhere, from simple tasks like organizing a birthday party … to running an organization with a thousand or even a million members. This skill allows groups to tackle tasks that are bigger, more complex, more dispersed, and of longer duration than any person could tackle alone. Building an airplane or a cathedral, performing a symphony or heart surgery, raising a barn…all require the distribution, specialization, and coordination of many tasks among many individuals, sometimes unfolding over years or decades and sometimes spanning continents.[16]

Humans are good at cooperating and making a coordinated, collaborative effort in groups; and new technologies, especially social media, enable new kinds of groups to form. Shirky believes that social media is built on an instinct for participation, which has enabled the transfer of group capabilities from expert individuals and various professional classes to the general public. He writes that "When we change the way we communicate, we change society."[17] Social media has made forming groups much easier and much less expensive because we now have communication tools that are flexible enough to match our group-making instincts. "We are living in the middle of a remarkable increase in our ability to share, to cooperate with one another, and to take collective action, all outside the framework of traditional institutions and organizations," Shirky believes.[18]

Furthermore, groups now have as much, if not more, influence and power than powerful individuals such as kings, presidents, and Chief Executive Officers do. For example, in 2014 the *Time* magazine person of the year was a group of Ebola fighters, and in 2018 the *Time* person of the year was a group labeled as The Silence Breakers, consisting of women who spoke out about sexual harassment and launched the #MeToo movement.

Also, because of these new communications tools, especially social media, consumers and groups of consumers can give instant feedback to companies about their products. In addition, companies can manage a relationship directly with their customers via social media, online support forums, or chats, email, and text. This means that customers and consumer groups can participate and collaborate with their favorite brands in creating new, personalized products, and, most important, they can recommend and advocate for those brands effortlessly and do it at no cost by using social media such as Facebook Groups, Instagram, Twitter, YouTube, Pinterest, or LinkedIn. Customers can also advocate for brands by posting positive reviews on Amazon, Yelp, Trip Advisor, or hundreds of other similar review platforms.

Marketing 4.0

In the book *Marketing 4.0: Moving from Traditional to Digital,* marketing guru Philip Kotler and his co-authors write that: "The major premise of this book is that marketing should adapt to the changing nature of customer paths in the digital economy. The role of marketers is to guide customers throughout their journey from awareness and ultimately to advocacy."[19]

Kotler and his co-authors write that power has shifted to connected customers, because "Today we are living in a whole new world. The power structure we have come to know is experiencing drastic changes. The Internet, which brought connectivity and transparency to our lives, has been largely responsible for these power shifts."[20] They point out that with a population of over 2.2 billion people, if "the United States of Facebook, were a country, it would be the largest one in the world.[21] They also write that now people go to Twitter for breaking news "from citizen journalists," whereas in the past they would go to a cable news network such as CNN or Fox News to get their news.[22] "Even YouTube has taken Hollywood by storm. A survey by *Variety* revealed that for 13–18-year-olds, YouTube celebrities are more popular than Hollywood stars," according to the authors.[23]

Kotler and the authors of *Marketing* 4.0 also believe that the power shift has given connected groups more power than individual consumers have. "Random conversations about brands by groups are now more credible than targeted advertising campaigns," they write.[24] Social circles have become the main source of consumer influence, overtaking advertising and marketing communications. "Customers now tend to follow the lead of their peers when deciding which brand to choose," according to Kotler and his co-authors.[25]

They also write that "recent research across industries shows that most customers believe more in the F-Factor (friends, families, Facebook fans, and Twitter followers) than in marketing communications.[26] They write that many people will go online and ask strangers on social media for advice about brands and trust them more than they do advertising and expert opinion.[27]

As replace *Ps* as the elements of marketing

Because of the belief in the wisdom of the crowd, or of their F-Factor groups, many consumers are guarding themselves against brands that target advertising at them and are relying on trusted groups for advice. The market segments that are particularly guarded against advertising are youth, women, and netizens (YWN), according to the authors of *Marketing 4.0*.[28] *Youth* are defined as millennials and Generation Zs. *Women* are important because they often control household purse strings. *Netizens* are committed citizens of the web who embrace openness and sharing with others, with no geographical boundaries. They are social connectors.[29] In order to get these vitally important market segments to be aware of and ultimately to advocate for a brand, marketers need to engage them differently than in the past. Well-produced, expensive commercials on television do not have the same impact as they used to. The Four Ps have been replaced by the Five As: aware, appeal, ask, act, and advocate, as seen in Figure 15.1 which compares traditional marketing with digital marketing.

The customer path begins with consumers being *aware* of a product; then moves to the product having some sort of *appeal*; then moves to a consumer *ask* for more information – often on price-and-feature comparison websites; and then moves to

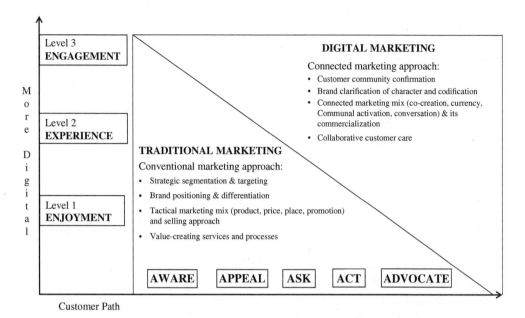

Figure 15.1 The Interchanging roles of traditional and digital marketing. Adapted from Kotler, Philip, Kartajaya, Hermawan, and Setiawan, Iwan. 2016. *Marketing 4.0:Moving From Traditional to Digital*. Hoboken, NJ, Wiley. Used with permission.

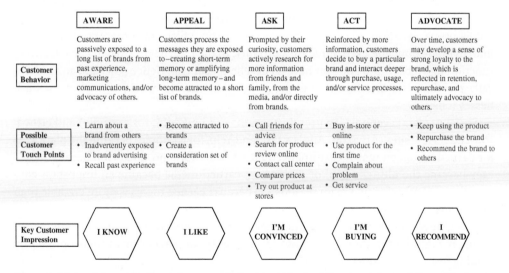

Figure 15.2 Mapping the customer path through the Five As. Adapted from Kotler, Philip, Kartajaya, Hermawan, and Setiawan, Iwan. 2016. *Marketing 4.0: Moving From Traditional to Digital*. Hoboken, NJ: Wiley. Used with permission.

consumers who *act* to purchase the product and become a customer; and, finally, the ultimate goal of marketing in the digital era, the customer becomes an *advocate* for the product and promotes it via word-of-mouth both online and offline. Figure 15.2 maps the customer path through the Five As.

The stages in the Five As are not necessarily always straightforward.[30] Customers sometimes skip a stage or two in the process of moving from aware to advocate. For example, someone might skip from aware to advocate without acting (buying), and someone might not only be aware of a Tesla automobile but also love it and advocate for it by praising the car on social media even if that person cannot afford to buy a Tesla. The Five As framework is a flexible tool that is applicable to virtually all industries, and can provide insights into a company's relationship with customers and how, when, and were to appeal to them.[31]

Marketing 4.0: The Increased Importance of Owned and Earned Media

As you learned in Chapter 14, there are three types of media: *paid, owned, and earned*. As indicated above, in the pre-Internet, Marketing 2.0 era, paid media were the dominant driver of demand by making people aware of products and creating appeal for those products. In the 1980s and 1990s national advertisers used broadcast and cable network television and large circulation magazines as the predominant paid media. In that era the favorite media for local advertisers were newspapers and local radio; owned media consisted primarily of company newsletters, which were rarely read by the average consumer; and earned media were generated primarily by publicity and public relations (PR) that drove free mentions in newspapers and magazines.

With the advent of the Internet and the growth of social media, owned and earned media became much more important in the marketing mix. In the digital era, owned media primarily consisted of a company's website on which consumers could get more information about and even purchase a product. In the Internet era, having an effectively functioning website and app that have an excellent user experience (UX) and an aesthetically pleasing user interface (UI) is the primary marketing touchpoint for most businesses today.

Social media (Facebook, Twitter, Instagram, and LinkedIn, for example) and crowd-sourced review sites (Amazon, Angie's List, and Yelp, for example) became the platforms for earned media on which customers could advocate for a product. And because advocacy became the ultimate goal of marketing, earned media became an important concern for marketers for two main reasons: (1) because earned media is more credible than advertising, and (2) because, by definition, earned media are free. Social media and online review sites are vitally important because up to 90 percent of all consumers read online reviews before they buy a product and up to 40 percent form their opinion by reading just three product reviews.[32]

Therefore, with paid, owned, and earned media all being important marketing channels, marketing strategy must consist of a multichannel approach once decisions have been made as to what kind of business a company wants to be in and what marketing approach is most effective for that business. Figure 15.3 shows a marketing decision tree that consists of the five decisions a business must make before crafting a marketing strategy.

If media salespeople are going to help their customers get results and be successful, they should be familiar with the business decisions that a company must make: (1) which

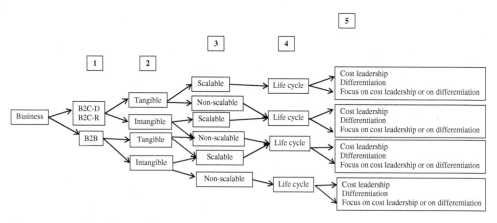

Figure 15.3 Marketing decision tree

types of customers to target, (2) what type of product they are selling, (3) whether a company's business model is scalable, (4) which stage in the business cycle a company is in, and (5) what generic competitive strategy a company decides to employ.

B2C-D, B2C-R or B2B The first decision that a business must make is if it is going to sell to consumers (B2C) or to other businesses (B2B). If a company decides to sell to consumers, it should then decide whether to sell to consumers directly (B2C-D) or through a middleman such as a retailer (B2C-R). B2C-Direct is also commonly known as *direct-to-consumer* (DTC) marketing. Answering this initial question starts a business on a path to determine what marketing channels are most effective for its key performance indicators (KPIs). The Shave Club is an example of a B2C-D company that sells razors and personal grooming products directly to consumers online and then delivers them by mail to customers' homes. Coca-Cola is a B2C-R company because consumers typically do not buy Coca-Cola online to be shipped directly to them, they buy from a middleman such as a retail store or street vendor. Salesforce is an example of a B2B company.

Tangible or intangible The next decision a business must make is to define the type of product it is selling. As discussed in Chapter 2, the approach for selling tangible products is different from selling intangible products. Coca-Cola is a low-cost, frequently purchased, tangible product that people can see, feel, and drink, and it is a product that virtually all consumers are aware of. Therefore, the primary marketing objective of Coke is for the product to appeal to the largest possible audience of soft-drink consumers, and the best way to accomplish this objective is to make an emotional connection to those consumers and to the consumers' peer group, as Coca-Cola did with its "Taste the feeling" campaign. Also, not only are the vast majority of consumers aware of Coke, they have also more than likely purchased a Coke at some time, and they might even be a loyal advocate of the brand. Thus, a secondary marketing objective is to remind people to buy a Coke next time they are thirsty and to reinforce their loyalty to the brand.

On the other hand, Salesforce sells an expensive, intangible software-as-a-service (SaaS) product to businesses that is purchased once, typically by a high-level committee over a long purchase cycle. Consulting companies, lawyers, doctors, advertising agencies, the media, and insurance companies all sell an intangible product, or a service. You can demonstrate a tangible product, show how it works, describe how it tastes, and make an emotional connection to the product. An intangible product is more difficult to sell, and many marketers find a way to tangiblize their services and make an emotional connection, such as GEICO, a B2C business, does with its gecko and the use of humor in its advertising. Salesforce, a B2B business, does not try to tangiblize its service or make an emotional connection, but instead uses a rational, social-proof approach to tout its "#1 customer-success platform." Its primary marketing objective is to get business to ask for more information about its products so a salesperson can educate it on Salesforce's many solutions.

Scalable or non-scalable   The third decision a businesses should consider is whether their business is scalable or not. The concept of scalability is often lost on many businesses and on many salespeople. A business is scalable if what it sells can be created once and sold over and over again at a very low increased marginal cost. An example of a service that is scalable is Salesforce, whose big expense is writing CRM software once, storing it in the cloud, and then selling virtually the same software application to hundreds of thousands of customers. When Salesforce adds a customer, it does not have to write the software again and, thus, it adds revenue faster than it adds expenses. Scalable businesses can be exceptionally profitable if they can amass a large number of customers.

Another way to look at scale is that a business that scales adds revenue at a faster pace than it adds expenses, as shown in Figure 15.4. Because scalable businesses can be quite profitable, the return on marketing investment can be considerable. Therefore,

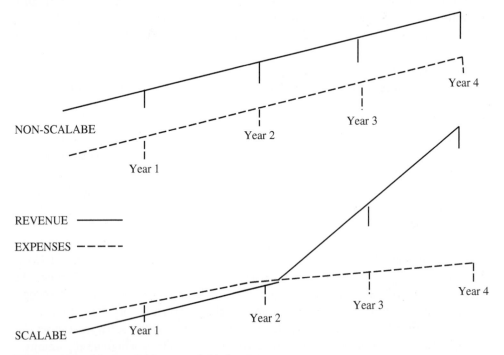

Figure 15.4   Non-scalable vs. scalable businesses

reaching as many potential customers as possible is the right marketing objective for a scalable business.

A business is not scalable if it prices its service based on time spent with a customer. Therefore, consultants, lawyers, doctors, advertising agencies, and audio and video production companies are not scalable businesses. Because there are only 24 hours in a day, these businesses cannot add hours to a day, so they only way they can generate more revenue is to charge more per hour or service more people in an hour. For example, most of us are familiar with having a 20-minute, hello–goodbye unsatisfying doctor's appointment. Because profit margins tend to be low in non-scalable businesses, marketing dollars are usually scarce; therefore, owned and earned media are typically the primary marketing channels for non-scalable businesses.

A media salesperson selling to non-scalable businesses should help them implement and improve their owned and earned media. For example, the Zimmer Radio and Marketing Group owns nine radio stations and three magazines in the Columbia-Jefferson City market in Missouri and provides a number of services to local advertisers, such as website design and ad creation and production. The Zimmer Group will also execute Google and Facebook advertising for their clients. In other words, it acts as a full-service marketing and advertising agency for its local clients for a reasonable fee. Another example of a medium helping its clients on a national level is ESPN. When ESPN signs a sizable deal for advertising on its cable television network or on its websites, it will typically support its advertisers by helping them get earned media by posting comments or videos for the advertiser on Facebook, Twitter, Instagram, and other social media sites.

Life cycle   The fourth business variable that needs to be examined is where a company is in its business life cycle. Figure 15.5 shows the five stages in the business cycle.

DEVELOPMENT	INTRODUCTION	GROWTH	MATURITY	DECLINE
Product	Promotion	Advertising	Marketing	Service
Drivers of Growth	• Free giveaway • Free trial • Freemium • Publicity • Public relations		**Sustaining Strategies**	
• Product features • Product features		• Mass media • Personalized media • Search • Social media • Events and Experiences	• Personalized media • Innovation • Brand extensions • Social media • Search • Events and Experiences	• Customer success management • Less advertising • Personal Selling

Figure 15.5   The life cycle of a business

Development.   At this initial stage of a business, marketing money is typically not available, so the drivers of growth are product features and benefits, and earned media are the primary focus.

Introduction.   Publicity, PR, and promotion drive growth in the introduction stage of the business cycle as a company attempts to make people aware of and interested in its product.

Growth.   Advertising in the mass media (television, radio) and in personalized media (digital programmatic), search, social media, and event sponsorships are all used to generate sales and to grow as rapidly as possible.

Maturity.   When a business reaches maturity, its marketing efforts should be in media channels that can target customers with personalized messages that are designed to retain them and so they purchase products more often. Marketing should also include social media and search to remind customers and reinforce their loyalty to the product. Sponsoring events and experiences such as concerts is also a way to reward customers for being loyal.

Decline.   Customer success management is critical when a business is in the decline stage. Businesses in this stage must super-serve their declining customer base. CRM software such as Matrix or Efficio is a necessity to keep in touch with customers. A business should consider personal selling to establish and maintain a humanized, emotional connection with its best customers.

Cost leadership, differentiation, or focus   There are three generic competitive strategies that a business must choose based on the competitive advantage it wants to pursue and the scope of the business it wants to be in: (1) cost leadership, (2) differentiation, or (3a) focus on cost or (3b) focus on differentiation. A business must decide which one of these strategies to pursue, because a business cannot be all things to all people. The three generic strategies were first articulated by Michael Porter in 1985 in his book *Competitive Advantage* and still hold up today in the digital era, as you can see in Figure 15.6.[33]

Cost leadership.   According to Porter, cost leadership is the clearest of the three generic strategies, and requires that companies have lower costs of producing a product, lower costs of distributing that product, and lower costs of selling it than competitors do.[34] Also, cost leadership does *not* mean advertising the lowest price, because unless a company can execute and maintain leadership in the cost of doing business, it cannot be profitable selling at the lowest prices. Porter writes, "A low cost producer must find and exploit all sources of cost advantage. Low cost producers typically sell a standard, or no frills, product and place considerable emphasis on reaping scale or absolute cost advantages from all sources."[35] In the retail category, WalMart developed the lowest cost information systems and the lowest cost of distribution to its stores, and it kept the wages of its store employees as low as possible so that it could fulfill its promise to consumers of "everyday low prices."

COMPETITIVE ADVANTAGE

COMPETITIVE SCOPE		Low Cost	Differentiation
	Broad Target	1 Cost Leadership	2 Differentiation
	Narrow Target	3a Focus on cost	3b Focus on differentiation

Figure 15.6 Generic competitive strategies. Adapted from "Porter's Generic Strategies." http://www.mindtools.com/article/newSTR_82.htm.

Differentiation. "In a differentiation strategy, a firm seeks to be unique in its industry along some dimensions that are widely valued by buyers," according to Porter.[36] Also, Porter states that "a firm differentiates itself from its competitors when it provides something unique that is valuable to buyers beyond simply offering a low price."[37] Differentiation is the strategy used by most mass-appeal consumer products such as cars, beverages, and cosmetics, and advertising often creates the differentiation more than the products themselves do because the products are often indistinguishable or easily substituted. An example of differentiation can be seen in the video produced by *Vanity Fair*, "Coke vs. Pepsi: Experts analyze 50 years of commercials" (available at https://youtu.be/Mo8pCkQWR00).

Focus. This generic strategy is different from the first two because it depends on "the choice of a narrow competitive scope within an industry" Porter indicates.[38] A business employing a focus strategy attempts to find a market niche that is being poorly served by competitors or in which there are no competitors and then attempts to super-serve customers. The focus strategy has two variants: (3a) *focus on cost*, in which a business seeks a cost advantage in its niche, and (3b) *focus on differentiation*, in which a business seeks differentiation in its niche. The niches must either have buyers with unusual needs and preferences, or else the production and distribution systems that serve the niche must differ from the systems of other, broader market segments.[39]

Big Data

When Marketing 2.0 (consumer focus) morphed into Marketing 3.0 (social responsibility included in a company's mission) in the 1980s and 1990s, many businesses changed their marketing messaging, but the marketing channels that businesses used did not change much in that time frame. In the era of Marketing 3.0, broadcast and cable television was the number-one medium for large national advertisers, followed by large-circulation magazines. Newspapers and radio were the favorite media for local advertisers. In all of these mass media, marketers targeted their advertising to specific market segments, depending on the profile of their customers. For example, Coca-Cola might target teens and adults aged 18–34. In order to reach their target audiences, Coke's advertising agency would buy media based on two basic criteria: (1) did a medium's content appeal to Coke's target audience segment, and (2) did a medium's audience have a concentration of viewers, listeners, or readers in the desired target audience segment? In other words, which medium had the least waste in terms of Coke's target audience? For example, Coca-Cola's agency might buy "Family Ties" on the NBC television network, MTV on cable television, and Top-40 and Urban Music radio stations.

By the late 1990s, marketers began to test the effectiveness of online advertising, primarily on AOL and Yahoo. Even though online advertising provided some new benefits to marketers such as consumers being able to get more information about a product, consumers being able to purchase a product online, and marketers being able to attribute a sale directly to an ad that was served to a user if a purchase was made, online advertising was still purchased based on the content's perceived appeal to a target audience segment.

In the late 1990s and early 2000s, as consumers began using the Internet more and more, doing more searches, browsing the web more, purchasing more products online, marketers entered the era of Big Data. Everybody's searches, browsing, and purchases on the Internet were recorded and saved by the sites they visited. Marketers now had access to a massive amount of data, including to their own data on consumers who bought their products online (first-party data), or bought from a retailer (second-party data), or whose data was aggregated by data management platforms (DMPs) by means of cookies on people's browsers (third-party data).[ii]

With so much data available, marketers aided by data analytic experts and data scientists were able to analyze huge amounts of data to define their market segments more precisely and gain valuable insights into the browsing, information-seeking, purchasing behavior, and content preferences of consumers in their target market segments.

From audience segments to individuals

Before 2007, marketers had to target market segments based primarily on age, sex, income, content preference, and geography. But in 2007 two innovations transformed marketing: (1) the introduction of programmatic buying and selling of digital ad

---

[ii] See Chapter 17: Programmatic Marketing and Advertising for more details about types of data.

inventory and (2) Apple's introduction of the iPhone. Programmatic revolutionized marketing from targeting broad market segments to being able to target individuals – in essence, an audience of one – and the iPhone and subsequent smartphone knockoffs (primarily Android phones) allowed marketers to target individuals by their location. A Silicon Valley Porsche dealer no longer had to hope that by placing an ad on ESPN's Fantasy Football site it would reach a 27-year-old male, college graduate who lived in Silicon Valley and who recently visited the websites of several luxury cars. By using programmatic technology, the Porsche dealer could bid, purchase, and serve a banner ad to the 27-year-old male with a personalized offer on his mobile phone at the moment he visited the ESPN Fantasy Football app or was within a mile of the Porsche dealership.

Programmatic buying and smartphones allowed marketers to target individuals, not broad audience segments, based on their location with a relevant, personalized offer. The ability to serve relevant ads to individual consumers with personalized messages not only led to an explosion of digital advertising because of the possibility of precise, one-to-one marketing, but also led to marketers switching their ad dollars from legacy media such as newspapers and magazines to digital. Television's revenue suffered to a lesser degree because of its massive reach and because highly produced video commercials still had impact. Radio's revenue did not suffer as much as print revenue because the vast majority of radio's revenue is local, and local advertisers are generally not as digitally sophisticated as national advertisers are. See Figure 15.7 for the relative strength of various marketing channels to influence consumers on their path from awareness to advocacy.

As you can see by the thickness of the lines in Figure 15.7, personalized, targeted digital advertising, search advertising, and personal selling are the most effective marketing channels overall. Search and personal selling are effective in moving consumers from being

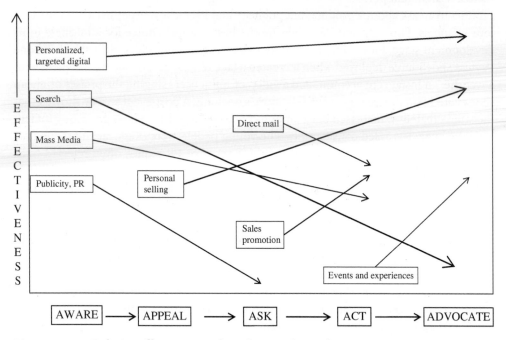

Figure 15.7   Relative effectiveness of marketing channels

aware of a product to getting them to act (buy a product). Search is relatively inexpensive, especially because it is generally sold on a cost-per-click basis. Personal selling is effective to get people to act, but it is also by far the most expensive channel. Therefore, personal selling is most typically utilized by businesses that sell products with a high price tag, such as airplanes and commercial real estate. What this means for media sales is that automated programmatic buying will disintermediate buyers and sellers in situations in which the typical sales transaction does not involve a lot of money, less than, say, $10,000. But personal selling in media such as network television in which deals are made in the millions of dollars will not be threatened in the short-term by programmatic automation. Local media selling, such as at radio and television stations, especially in mid-sized and small markets, will not be affected in the very near future by automation because salespeople in such local media mostly call on advertisers who are typically not technologically sophisticated and more than likely do not understand programmatic buying, although they might know how to buy advertising on Google or even Facebook on a self-serve basis.

Mass media, such as television and radio, are a little less effective in moving consumers from being aware to act because at the current stage of its development, programmatic which targets individuals with personalized messaging instead of targeting households is not widely available in television and radio, although predictions are that programmatic buying will be implemented in those media by 2020. Programmatic is not possible in printed newspapers or magazines, but is available in these media's digital versions, and all indications are that within a few years newspapers and magazines will be available in only digital versions, which means that they can be purchased programmatically and, thus, advertising can be targeted to individuals.

Publicity and PR are less effective than personalized, targeted digital advertising, mass media, search, and personal selling in transitioning consumers from being aware of a product to an ask about a product, but publicity and PR are less expensive than the other four channels. Publicity and PR might be the best channel choice for a business in its development stage. However, brands have to be careful about PR stunts such as the one Payless ShoeSource deployed when it created a fake retailer called Palessi, complete with a website, an Instagram account, and a video of influencers singing the praises of cheap shoes with luxury price tags at the fake store's opening. A post-event survey showed that the stunt created an increased buzz among consumers aged 35–49, while among millennials the buzz decreased considerably. The young people were skeptical and turned off by the publicity stunt.[40] The objective of these types of PR stunts, often referred to as *guerilla marketing*, is to be outrageous just to try to get noticed and generate publicity.

Direct mail is expensive on a CPM basis, but if targeted to the right ZIP codes, can get consumers who are looking for a particular product to make a purchase, to move people from ask to act.

Sales promotion typically tells consumers when to buy a product, as discussed in Chapter 7, and it can be effective in moving people from asking about a product to buying it. Therefore sales promotion can be an integral element in the marketing mix for consumer package goods or other relatively low-cost products for which an in-store nudge, a coupon, or a percent-off sale can trigger a purchase, but, on the other hand, marketers need to be aware of the downside of promotions, as detailed in Exhibit 7.2 in Chapter 7.

Sponsorship of events and creating experiences are effective for rewarding loyal customers who love a product and can be motivated to advocate for it on Twitter, Facebook,

Instagram, Pinterest, YouTube, or Snapchat, for example. Consumers seem to appreciate the effort brands go to in sponsoring events and creating *experiential marketing*.

But note that at the top of Figure 15.7 that the most effective marketing channel for the entire customer path, from aware to advocate, is personalized, individually targeted digital advertising. On the one hand, not only can digital ads be personalized by serving different offers and pricing to different people, but also creative approaches can be personalized as well. For example, on Facebook, an ad for Hubble contact lenses can make a special discounted offer to a young woman who attends the University of Alabama. The background color for the ad can be in Alabama Crimson Tide red, and the copy can read something like, "See the Crimson Tide win its next football game more clearly than ever before." This type of personalization is not only possible because of automated, programmatic ad buying but also because artificial intelligence (AI) can create hundreds of thousands of different message variations, as mentioned in Chapter 14 when the Trump campaign team tested 175,000 different variations of messaging in just two days.

On the other hand, the more slices of targeting information that are added and the more personalized creative executions that are produced, the more expensive a personalized digital campaign becomes. The more expensive an advertising campaign is, the higher the life-time value of a customer must be to justify the campaign. Therefore, highly targeted, personalized ads for lost-cost, short-life-cycle commodities such as paper towels, laundry detergents, or toothpaste do not make a lot of sense because of their expense, but targeted, personalized ads do make sense to a Porsche dealer.

A multichannel marketing approach

Once media salespeople understand a prospect's or customer's business decisions and the relative strengths of various marketing channels, they can make recommendations based on what channels are most effective for: (1) B2C or B2B businesses, (2) tangible or intangible products, (3) scalable or non-scalable business models, (4) a business's life cycle stage, and (5) a cost-leadership, differentiation, or focus generic competitive strategy.

If you are selling a national medium to Coca-Cola's advertising agency, you know that the company is in a B2C business, has a tangible product that is not scalable, that is in a mature life cycle, and that differentiation is its competitive strategy. Therefore, emphasizing how your medium is right for differentiation and connecting emotionally to Coca-Cola's targeted consumers is your best approach. Television, radio, and video on digital platforms such as YouTube, Facebook, or Snapchat are effective channels. You want to educate your agency buyer on how your medium helps Coca-Cola's customers think of Coke as an "extension of themselves."[41] When customers feel so invested in a product that it becomes an extension of themselves, it is called *psychological ownership*. One way to accomplish psychological ownership is to make the product or extensions of the product customizable. "When consumers can personalize products, they buy more and are happy to recommend those products to friends."[42] Coca-Cola's 2014 "Share a Coke" campaign reminded consumers that they could buy their own customized bottles or cans. Coke created bottles and cans of cola labeled with hundreds of common names. As a result of the campaign, Coca-Cola sales rose 2.5 percent in just 12 weeks.[43]

If you are selling a group of local radio stations to the chief marketing officer (CMO) of a hospital, you need to understand that the hospital is attempting to create an image of medical expertise and wellness. Therefore, you should educate the CMO about how radio can make an emotional connection between the hospital and its target customers and emphasize that radio is the most intimate medium because it connects to its audience with the warm sound of a human voice. You would also emphasize that radio allows listeners, through the concept of the theater of the mind, to create their own, personal, positive mental image of the hospital.

Every medium has its strengths, benefits, and advantages, and these can be positioned according to the business model, the marketing strategies, and the personality of any prospect or customer. See Exhibit 15.1 for a list of the various marketing channels available in paid, owned, and earned media.

Exhibit 15.1   Marketing communication channels

Paid media	Owned media	Earned media
Internet	*Website*	*Word-of-mouth*
• Mobile	*Blog*	*Social media*
• Search	*Social media pages*	• Facebook ratings and reviews
• Display	*Brochures*	• Instagram
• Social media	*Catalogs*	• Twitter
• Video	*In-store signage*	• LinkedIn
• Native	*Webinars*	• Pinterest
• Influencers	*Podcasts*	• Snapchat
	Case studies	
Television	*Videos*	*Online review sites*
• Broadcast network	*Telemarketing*	• Amazon customer reviews
• Cable network		• Angie's List
• Spot TV		• Yelp
• Spot cable		• Trip Advisor
		• Quora
Audio		• Captella
• Local radio		• CNET
• Network radio		• Consumer reports
• Podcasts		• Glassdoor
Newspapers		*Email forwards*
• National		
• Local		
Magazines		
• Trade		
• Business		
Direct mail		
Out of home (OOH)		
Sales promotion		
Events and experiences		
Email		
Text messaging		

As you can see in Exhibit 15.1, there are so many paid, owned, and earned media opportunities that the jobs of CMOs and ad agencies have become infinitely more complex in the era of Marketing 4.0 than in the eras of Marketing 1.0, 2.0, and 3.0.

Explosion of marketing complexity and workloads

The advent of the Internet, Big Data, digital advertising, programmatic buying and selling, mobile advertising, and AI's ability to personalize messaging all contribute to making marketing much more complicated and workloads much heavier than ever before for those who sell, create, and place ads. Figure 15.8 shows how marketing has become more complex.

So, how do marketers deal with the increased complexity and workloads in marketing? AI, automation, and programmatic can provide an automated buying and selling process so that buyers and sellers can concentrate on high-level strategy and to be more creative in finding new solutions to marketing challenges. For example, iHeart Media President of Strategic Partnerships, Michele Laven, tells how her team partnered with 20th Century Fox to develop a plan for a blockbuster opening of *Bohemian Rhapsody*, the movie about the rock group Queen and its charismatic lead singer, Freddy Mercury. In addition to buying commercials on many of iHeart's 880+ radio stations, 650 iHeart radio stations simultaneously played the six-minute version of Queen's hit song "Bohemian Rhapsody" at 9:00 a.m. the day before the movie opened on Thursday, November 1, 2018. Simultaneously playing a song or running an ad at the same time on radio stations, TV stations, or on all pages of a website is a scheduling strategy called a

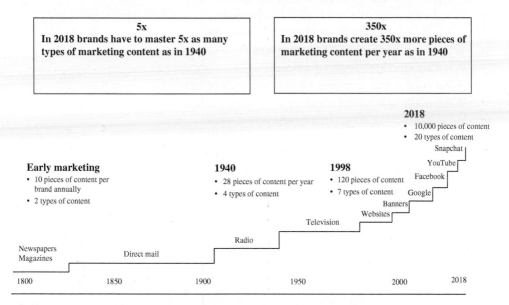

Figure 15.8   Explosion in complexity and workload Adapted from Cortex, "The CMO guide to artificial intelligence." http://www.meetcortex.com/the-definitive-cmo-guide-to-artificial-intelligence.

roadblock. When the song was playing simultaneously on iHeart's 650 radio stations, iHeart Radio posted on its Twitter feed, "It's undeniable. Queen's "Bohemian Rhapsody" is THE most epic track of all times. Listen to it playing right now across 650 iHeart Radio stations right now! Tune in…Great version of this iconic song!"

Automation and AI cannot create this type of multichannel marketing campaign that iHeart Radio did for *Bohemian Rhapsody* – it takes a team of knowledgeable people – but automation and AI can execute the routine details of buying and selling in order to allow for creative marketing solutions like iHeart Radio's *Bohemian Rhapsody* campaign to blossom.

Summary

Media salespeople should be familiar with the variety of decisions businesses have to make and the various marketing approaches those businesses use so the salespeople can: (1) recommend appropriate marketing strategies and solutions, (2) suggest what marketing channels are most effective for a given situation, and (3) come up with big ideas that will help customers and partners get results and be successful.

Test Yourself

1. Describe the progression from Marketing 1.0, to Marketing 2.0, to Marketing 3.0, and to Marketing 4.0 and what each means.
2. Give an example of a Marketing 3.0 company.
3. What are the four Ps of Marketing 2.0 and 3.0?
4. What are the five As of Marketing 4.0?
5. What are the three types of media?
6. What are the five decisions a business has to make?
7. What makes a business scalable?
8. What are the five stages in a business's life cycle?
9. What are the three generic competitive strategies?
10. What two innovations in 2007 changed marketing?
11. Is a company's website paid, owned, or earned media?
12. What is a roadblock?

Project

Assume you are a salesperson for a group of six local radio stations in a market ranked number 125. You have been assigned four businesses to call on: (1) a local Ford dealer that has been in the market 50 years, (2) a newly opened law office that practices family law, (3) an upscale, well established women's apparel store, and (4) a three-year old company that sells appointment-scheduling software to doctor's offices. Using Figure 15.4, for each business, decide: (1) what type of business are they in (B2C or B2B), (2) what type of product are they selling, tangible or intangible, (3) what type of business are they in, scalable or non-scalable, (4) what stage in the business life cycle are they in, and (5) what is their generic competitive strategy? When you have made the five decisions for the four businesses, come up with a Big Idea for each business.

References

Godin, Seth. 2003. *Purple Cow: Transform Your Business By Being Remarkable*. New York: Portfolio.

Kotler, Philip, Kartajaya, Hermawan, and Setiawan, Iwan. 2010. *Marketing 3:0: From Products to Customers to Human Spirit*. Hoboken, NJ: Wiley.

Kotler, Philip, Kartajaya, Hermawan, and Setiawan, Iwan. 2016. *Marketing 4:0: Moving From Traditional to Digital*. Hoboken, NJ: Wiley.

Kotler, Philip and Keller, Kevin. 2015. *A Framework for Marketing Management*, 6th ed. New York: Pearson.

Pink, Daniel. 2009. *Drive: The Surprising Truth About What Motivates Us*. New York: Riverhead Books.

Porter, Michael. 1985. *Competitive Advantage: Creating and Sustaining Superior Performance*. New York: Free Press.

Resources

American Marketing Association (www.ama.org)

Zimmer Radio Group (www.zimmercommunications.com)

Direct Marketing Association (www.thedma.org/marketing-insights/marketing-statistics/direct-mail-statistics)

iSocrates's Academy (www.isocrates.com/academy)

Notes

1. Kotler, Philip, Kartajaya, Hermawan, and Setiawan, Iwan. 2010. *Marketing 3:0: From Products to Customers to Human Spirit*. Hoboken, NJ: Wiley.
2. Ibid.
3. Godin, Seth. 2003. *Purple Cow: Transform Your Business By Being Remarkable*. New York: Portfolio.
4. Kotler, Philip, Kartajaya, Hermawan, and Setiawan, Iwan. 2010. *Marketing 3:0: From Products to Customers to Human Spirit*. Hoboken, NJ: Wiley.
5. Ibid.
6. Ibid.
7. Ibid.
8. Ibid.
9. Pink, Daniel. 2009. *Drive: The Surprising Truth About What Motivates Us*. New York: Riverhead Books.
10. Loechner, Jack. 2018. MediaPost. "What's it worth?" Retrieved from https://www.mediapost.com/publications/article/319847/whats-it-worth.html.
11. Ibid.

12 eMarketer. 2019. "Sustainability is driving consumer purchase decisions." Retrieved from https://retail.emarketer.com/article/sustainability-driving-consumers-purchase-decisions/5c3f9ad5b979f108148b2353.

13 American Marketing Association. Retrieved from https://www.ama.org/AboutAMA/Pages/Definition-of-Marketing.aspx.

14 "Who we are." Retrieved from https://about.bankofamerica.com/en-us/who-we-are.html.

15 Shirky, Clay. 2008. *Here Comes Everybody: the Power of Organizing Without Organizations.* New York: The Penguin Press.

16 Ibid.

17 Ibid.

18 Ibid.

19 Kotler, Philip, Kartajaya, Hermawan, and Setiawan, Iwan. 2016. *Marketing 4:0: Moving From Traditional to Digital.* Hoboken, NJ: Wiley.

20 Ibid.

21 Ibid.

22 Ibid.

23 Ibid.

24 Ibid.

25 Ibid.

26 Ibid.

27 Ibid.

28 Ibid.

29 Ibid.

30 Ibid.

31 Ibid.

32 Perzynska, Kasia. "Top 28 product review websites." Retrieved from http://partners.livechatinc.com/blog/best-product-reviews-websites.

33 Porter, Michael. 1985. *Competitive Advantage: Creating and Sustaining Superior Performance.* New York: Free Press.

34 Ibid.

35 Ibid.

36 Ibid.

37 Ibid.

38 Ibid.

39 Ibid.

40 Garcia, Krista. 2018. "Do PR stunts boost brand perception?" Retrieved from https://www.emarketer.com/content/do-pr-stunts-boost-brand-perception.

41 Kirk, Colleen P. 2018. "How customers come to think of a product as an extension of themselves." Retrieved from https://hbr.org/2018/09/how-customers-come-to-think-of-a-product-as-an-extension-of-themselves.

42 Ibid.

43 Ibid.

16

Advertising

Charles Warner

What is Advertising?

Advertising is selling, and it has similar steps on the way to a sale that personal selling does: (1) target the right prospects, (2) conduct research to gain insights into why and how they buy, (3) educate them, (4) make an offer, (5) make a sale, and (6) delight them with post-sale service so they will give referrals and advocate for what you are selling. The ideal advertising reaches the right customer, at the right time, in the right channel, in the right location, with the right message, and makes a sale.

Advertising is carried in the paid media, as seen in Exhibit 16.1, which contains the same marketing channels as Exhibit 15.1 in the previous chapter, but those media which carry advertising have been labeled as such. Descriptions of the various advertising media appear in sections below or in subsequent chapters, as indicated.

Internet advertising   *Mobile, display,* and *video* will be covered in more detail in Chapter 19, *search* will be covered in Chapter 20, and *social media* in Chapter 21.

Native.   This is paid advertising that typically uses written content that is partially disguised as original content, such as a cost-per-click ad on a Google search results page. Although these search ads are marked with a small "Ad" label, they are often hard to distinguish from non-ad search results on the rest of the page. Native advertising takes the same approach as these search results ads and inserts them contextually into content

Media Selling: Digital, Television, Audio, Print and Cross-Platform, Fifth Edition.
Charles Warner, William A. Lederer, and Brian Moroz.
© 2020 John Wiley & Sons, Inc. Published 2020 by John Wiley & Sons, Inc.

Exhibit 16.1   Marketing communication channels

Paid media	Owned media	Earned media
*Internet **advertising***	Website	Word-of-mouth
• Mobile	Blog	Social media
• Search	Social media pages	• Facebook ratings and reviews
• Display	Brochures	• Instagram
• Social media	Catalogs	• Twitter
• Video	In-store signage	• LinkedIn
• Native	Webinars	• Pinterest
• Influencers	Podcasts	• Snapchat
*Television **advertising***	Case studies	*Online review sites*
• Broadcast network	Videos	• Amazon customer reviews
• Cable network	Telemarketing	• Angie's List
• Spot TV		• Yelp
• Spot cable		• Trip Advisor
		• Quora
*Audio **advertising***		• Captella
• Local radio		• CNET
• Network radio		• Consumer reports
• Podcasts		• Glassdoor
*Newspaper **advertising***		*Email forwards*
• National		
• Local		
*Magazine **advertising***		
• Trade		
• Business		
*Direct mail **advertising***		
*Out of home (OOH) **advertising***		
Sales promotion		
Events and experiences		
Email		
Text messaging		

on other sites. On a magazine digital site, for example, native advertising might appear as sidebar written as though it were another article in the magazine, but marked with a label such as "sponsored" or "branded" in small, often light-gray type. The native ad is designed to fit seamlessly into the content that surrounds it, which is why it is often mistaken for actual content. In 2018, native ads were estimated by the research firm eMarketer to make up about 60 percent of digital display advertising, with mobile, social media, and Amazon being the major growth drivers.[1] Native advertising can be effective for both B2C and B2B businesses, but especially for those doing B2B for which a well-written native ad can be informative and lead to engagement by high-level prospects.[2]

Influencers.   Joel Mathew wrote an excellent definition of influencer marketing in *Forbes*:

> Influencer marketing is a relationship between a brand and an influencer. The influencer promotes the brand's products or services through various media outlets such as Instagram and YouTube. Not to be confused with celebrity endorsements, influencer marketing does more than just attach a well-known celebrity to a brand. Influencers must be trusted figures within a niche community and retain a loyal following. In addition, they typically possess knowledge or experience about what they are advertising.
>
> For example, a popular fitness vlogger on YouTube with extensive knowledge in weight training and proper nutrition may be asked to do advertising for sportswear or a supplement company. On occasion, an influencer may not have experience relevant to the product they are advertising. In this situation, they rely on the trust and loyalty they have built within their community to influence their followers. Common influencer categories include adventurists, photographers, food enthusiasts, how-to experts, beauticians, artists, models and comedians to name a few.[3]

Television; Newspapers, Magazines, and Out-of-Home; and Audio   Television, newspapers, magazines, and out-of-home, and audio will be covered in subsequent chapters: Television in Chapter 22, Print and Out-of-home in Chapter 23, and Audio (radio and podcasts) in Chapter 24.

Sales promotion   The major advantage of sales promotion is that it can inform consumers about *when* to buy. Contests, coupons, percent-off sales, shelf talkers, and end-aisle displays at retailers, volume discounts, supermarket slotting fees, and "Recommended for You" and "Last-Minute Deals" ads on Amazon can nudge people to buy *now*. A leading media agency, Zenith Media, forecast that in 2018 marketers in the USA. would spend $82.7 billion in sales promotion, or $4.4 billion more than they would spend on Internet advertising.[4] Even though sales promotion is the number one marketing expenditure, it has some disadvantages that were covered in Exhibit 7.2, which is included below as Exhibit 16.2 because, as I wrote in Chapter 7, one of the steps media salespeople should take in creating value is to reinforce the value of advertising and, therefore, to diminish the value of spending on promotion.

Events and experiences   Experiential marketing, or engagement marketing, has increased in importance, especially among affluent millennials (Generation Y – born between 1985 and 1995) and Generation Zs (born between 1996 and 2005). Experiential marketing is a growing trend which involves marketing a product through experiences that engage customers and create emotional attachment to the product, often with events such as concerts, music festivals such as iHeart Media's Music Festivals, exotic trips, and parades such as Macy's Thanksgiving Day Parade. Zenith Media, forecast that in 2018 marketers in the USA would spend $39.9 billion on event sponsorships and experiences, or more than twice as much than they would spend on radio advertising.[5] These experiences or events represent a way that a company can advance its corporate image, express commitment to a community or social issue, and gain competitive advantage by differentiating itself from competitors by identifying with a particular target market or

Exhibit 16.2   The seven problems with promotions

1   *Short-term effects.* There is overwhelming evidence that "the consumer sales effect is limited to the time period of the promotion itself." Contrary to some marketers' belief, there is no residual effect of a promotion. Consumers do not turn into long-term customers. "When the bribe stops, the extra sales also stop."

2   *Promotions mortgage future sales.* By encouraging consumers to take action immediately, a promotion brings forward sales from a future period and, therefore, future sales are lower than forecast because of problem #1 above.

3   *Promotions encourage stockpiling.* Savvy consumers stock up on low-priced promotion items, which cannibalizes future full-price sales, which lower margins.

4   *Promotions train consumers not to pay full price.* Price-conscious consumers are aware of continual promotions and wait for them – they become trained never to pay full price – which lowers profit margins.

5   *Promotions devalue a brand's image.* Continual promotions create a low-price, even "cheap," image and often appear to be desperate measures of a sinking brand in trouble. If consumers believe price cuts come from an oversupply, they will often wait for an even lower price.

6   *Promotions are addictive.* Marketers become dependent on more and more quick fixes in a vicious circle of more and more promotions at lower and lower prices at shorter and shorter intervals. Unilever describes this circle as "promotion, commotion, and demotion."[i]

7   *Continual use of promotions leads to retaliation.* Promotions "fuel the flames of competitive retaliation far more than other marketing activities."[ii] Competitors join the price war to defend their position. The long-term result of price wars can lead to the elimination of both retailers' and an entire industry's profit margins.[iii]

[i] John Phillip Jones. 1990. "The double jeopardy of sales promotions." *Harvard Business Review*. September–October.
[ii] Ibid.
[iii] Shuba Srinivasan, Koen Pauwels, Dominique Hansses, and Marnik Dekimpe. 2002. "Who *Benefits from Price Promotions?*" *Harvard Business Review*. September–October.

lifestyle. To achieve success, an experience should be engaging, compelling and able to touch the customer's senses and reinforce their loyalty. When customers are invested in an experience, their willingness to advocate for a brand is greater because they typically appreciate the soft-sell approach.[6]

Direct mail   Is a form of advertising sent through the mail, usually through the US Postal Service (USPS) and meant to attract new business or pass along relevant information to previous or existing customers. Zenith Media estimated that in 2018 marketers would spend $45.8 billion in direct mail, or three times what they would invest in newspaper advertising.[7] A direct mail piece such as a catalog usually includes an offer to entice recipients to respond either by calling an 800 number or visiting a website and placing an order. There are two types of direct mail: shared and standalone. Shared direct-mail pieces are also referred to as *marriage mail*, and consist of a packet of mail that contains messaging from multiple marketers. Examples of shared, or marriage, mail are coupon envelopes such as Valpac or magazines such as *Clipper*

Magazine. According to the Direct Marketing Association, direct mail has declined in volume over the past 10 years. "However, more marketers are adding mail to their array of integrated marketing tactics, because the engagement is growing as the clutter declines. Personalization and relevance is key. Costs are high but scale and return on investment (ROI) remain strong when direct mail is delivered to a well-targeted audience.[8] Direct mail is very expensive on a cost-per-thousand (CPM) basis, reaching CPMs as high as $3,000 for a multipage, four-color catalog. However, a well-produced catalog can show profitable returns even at a high CPM if it is sent to upscale ZIP codes such as 10121 in New York's Upper East Side where the average household income is over $180,000.

Email   Note in Exhibit 16.1 that even though email is listed under paid media, it is not labeled as advertising. In the book *Email Marketing Rules*, Chad White refers to email as granted media, and suggests that a POGLE (paid, owned, granted, leased, and earned) media model best describes the current types of media.[9] Paid media in White's view are essentially the same as the paid media listed in Exhibit 16.1 with the exception of email and text messaging. White's definition of paid media is "content created by the brand that's distributed to an audience developed by a third party via closed platform controlled by a third party."[10] He defines owned media as "content created by the brand that's distributed to an audience developed by the brand via a closed platform controlled by the brand."[11] Earned media is "content created by others that's distributed to an audience developed by anyone via any platform."[12]

According to White, email does not fit easily into any of the three above definitions. Email is granted media, and is "content developed by the brand that's distributed to an audience developed by the brand via a platform controlled by multiple third parties, such as email and SMS."[13] White describes email as *granted media* because consumers have to grant brands permission to send them emails. Seth Godin refers to this type of marketing as permission marketing in his book of the same title.[14] White refers to brand pages on social media as *leased media* because "brand content resides on a closed platform that is controlled by a single third party, such as Facebook, Twitter, and mobile app platforms."[15]

The concept of getting permission from consumers to send them emails is not just good practice, it is also required by law in the Controlling the Assault of No-Solicited Pornography and Marketing Act of 2003 (CAN-SPAM). According to the CAN-SPAM act, marketers not only have to get opt-in permission to send emails, but they also must include an unsubscribe link in all marketing emails. Furthermore, marketers cannot make consumers follow them on social media platforms, and they cannot push their apps onto consumers' smartphones without permission. Opt-in permission is a fundamental requirement and can be given and taken away at a consumer's whim "with no recourse for the marketer."[16] The CAN-SPAM law and the low open rates of marketing emails have led to relatively slow growth of email as a marketing tool in recent years.

Text messaging   The CAN-SPAM act also applies to text messaging (SMS), and unsolicited, non-granted marketing texts are considered toxic, especially by millennials and Generation Xers (born 1981–1996).

Advertising expenditures by medium

To get a sense of how marketers divide up their advertising budgets among the various media, Exhibit 16.3 shows estimated 2018 advertising spend by medium.[iv]

Exhibit 16.3   Zenith US media spend

	Spending (billions) 2017	Spending (billions) 2018	2018 vs. 2017	2018 Percent of Total
Media				
Internet	$69.2	$78.3	13.1%	38.4%
TV	$68.5	$68.2	-0.4%	33.5%
Radio	$17.6	$17.6	0.00%	8.6%
Newspapers	$16.6	$15.1	-9.0%	7.4%
Magazines	$15.4	$14.1	-8.2%	6.9%
Outdoor and cinema	$10.2	$10.5	3.2%	5.2%
TOTAL	$197.5	$203.8	3.2%	

Adapted from *Ad Age* Marketing Fact Pack 2019.

Note in Exhibit 16.3 that Internet advertising in 2018 grew at a healthy 13.07 percent increase over 2017, according to the Zenith Media estimates, while TV advertising declined 0.35 percent. The slow decline of television advertising is a trend that is not likely to turn around as marketers switch their marketing dollars to individually targeted, personalized ads on the Internet. Also note the 9.04 percent and 8.44 percent precipitous declines of newspaper and magazine advertising in just one year, which is another trend that is not only not likely to turn around, but is also liable to increase in percentage of decline even as these print media transition to digital versions on the Internet, where prices for digital ads are lower than prices for ads in print. In other words, digital dimes replace print dollars.

In light of these trends in advertising expenditures, let's take a look at some of the approaches, objectives, and types of advertising that will assist media salespeople to understand how advertising works so they can help their customers get better results, be more effective, be more efficient, and, ultimately be more successful.

Direct response vs. branding advertising

There are two broad approaches to advertising: (1) Direct-response and (2) branding.

[iv] In the standard advertising and media industry lexicon, expenditures in advertising are usually referred to as "ad spend." I prefer that salespeople refer to this as "investments" because I believe advertising should be considered an investment that returns future sales and profits.

Direct-response   Direct-response is an approach to advertising in which businesses communicate directly to consumers through a variety of channels such as search, email, catalogs, television, or magazines, and the message contains a call to action such as "50% off! Buy now!" A direct-response Internet ad allows marketers to gauge the performance of their advertising in real time, a much faster response rate than an advertiser can get from legacy media channels such as a television infomercial or a magazine or newspaper ad with a coupon. Also, direct-response advertising can easily be A/B tested to see which copy approaches, offers, or pricing work best with different individuals that the advertising targets. Search advertising on Google is the largest single type of direct-response advertising. Direct-response advertisers are also known as *direct-to-consumer* (DTC) brands, and Internet-only brands are sometimes referred to as *digital native vertical brands* (DNVBs).[17]

Branding   Branding is a form of advertising in which businesses, non-profits, and politicians try to create a positive image in the minds of consumers. It is "the process of giving meaning to specific companies, products, or services by creating, shaping, and positioning a brand in consumers' minds. It is a strategy designed by companies to help consumers quickly identify their products and to give people a reason to prefer their products over the competition's by clarifying what a particular brand is and is not."[18]

Branding typically contains a direct or implied promise about the benefits of a product, and typically positions the product with an emotional appeal directed at its target audience that will create brand awareness, brand appeal, curiosity about the brand, and consideration of the brand when a consumer is in the market to buy a product. There can also be a call to action in a branding ad, such as "Ask your doctor about Flomax" or "Go to our website for more information," but the overall purpose of branding is to create a positive perception, or image, of a brand in a consumer's mind.

Many large marketers do both branding and direct-response advertising if the product or service they sell is appropriate for buying or signing up for online. However, branding and direct-response advertising have different goals which are often in conflict. For example, branding can have a goal of awareness, which might possibly help in producing a sale, but brand advertising does not necessarily produce a sale; it typically is not meant to. Branding can have the goal of reputation management, customer service, community engagement, or consumer advocacy. On the other hand, direct-response advertising has one goal: Make a sale.[19]

Think of the two types of brand communication as follows: Direct-response advertising helps people buy; brand advertising helps people choose.[20]

If consumers are aware of and think positively about a brand and have had a previous interaction or relationship with it, they are more like to choose to buy that brand when they find themselves in a buying mode. Therefore, direct-response advertising without brand advertising is "less than efficient."[21]

New products or services need to take a branding approach in order to create a positive perception in consumers' minds, and advertising for new products works best when it appears in passive media such as television or radio. A passive medium is one in which the media content, including advertising, flows just one way, from the medium to the audience; thus, a viewer, listener, or reader has to make an effort to avoid an ad by fast-forwarding through commercials in a recorded television program or changing radio stations. Therefore, advertising on a passive medium tends to be interruptive because it requires an action to evade it, and as a result, the majority of advertising on passive media is noticed or heard, which gives a new product the opportunity to penetrate into a consumer's awareness.

An active medium is one in which the audience has to make an effort to interact with advertising, such as clicking on a link provided in a Google search ad. Direct-response advertising works best in active media such as in search or social media.

Advertising objectives

Advertising has one of four separate objectives: (1) to inform, (2) to persuade, (3) to remind, and (4) to reinforce.

Informative advertising   Informative advertising aims to create brand awareness and knowledge about a product or to inform customers about a new feature or new offer of a product they have previously purchased.

Persuasive advertising   Persuasive advertising aims to create liking, preference, conviction, and purchase of a product. Persuasive advertising at times compares the attributes of two or more products. A comparative approach works best on television and radio by making emotional appeals and best online with rational appeals, such as checklists that contain lists of comparative features. Persuasive ads can also operate as a subconscious dream machine that reinforces the concept that "people don't buy products; they buy better versions of themselves."[22]

Reminder advertising   Reminder advertising aims to stimulate repeat purchases. The majority of television advertising for inexpensive, frequently purchased, and impulse-purchased products, such as soft drinks or candy bars, is meant to remind consumers to act, to buy a product. Retargeted display ads and search ads are good, efficient reminder advertising. Research shows the success rate of selling to an existing customer is between 60 and 70 percent, while the success rate of selling to a new customer is between 5 and 20 percent. Also, returning customers contribute up to two-thirds of a brand's profits.[23] Thus, reminder advertising can be quite effective and profitable.

Reinforcement advertising   Reinforcement advertising aims to convince current customers they made the right decision. Automobile advertising often shows satisfied customers enjoying or praising special features of a new car. Reinforcement advertising works best with high-priced and luxury products as it attempts to lower "buyer remorse" and embed the perceived value of a brand with social proof ("Other people like me buy and love this product.") Extravagantly produced TV and video ads work well for reinforcement advertising, as do display ads on Amazon.

An advertising objective should emerge after a thorough analysis of the five business model decisions a company must make. You will learn about how to conduct an in-depth analysis of advertising messaging and media objectives in the section on local advertising later in this chapter.

National Advertising

Salespeople who sell national advertising are primarily reactive and are typically the embodiment of service selling. They call on advertising and media agencies that purchase advertising for leading national advertisers whose brands are widely available to the entire population of the United States. For example, According to *Ad Age's* 2019 *Marketing Fact Pack*, in 2017 the 10 most-advertised brands were: GEICO, Verizon, Ford, Chevrolet, T-Mobile, Apple, Samsung, McDonald's, ATT, and Progressive Insurance.[24]

National, service selling to agencies that buy for these leading national advertisers involves responding to response for proposals (RFPs) emailed by agencies to salespeople who represent large, mass-appeal broadcast and cable networks such as ABC, CBS, NBC, FOX, ESPN, Discovery, and A&E and digital platforms or websites such as Google, Facebook, Amazon, YouTube, Yahoo, MSN, Twitter, Instagram, ESPN.com, CNN.com, NYTimes.com, and the HuffPost.

See Exhibit 16.4 for an example of an RFP for an automotive client. The Automotive Client RFP, a Telecom Client RFP, and a Tire Client RFP can also be downloaded from the Downloads section of *Media Selling* website (http://mediaselling.us/downloads/).

Exhibit 16.4   Automotive client RFP

Automotive Digital Upfront
CLIENT: Automotive
DUE DATE FOR RFP SUBMISSION: 9/3/2018

[Agency] is approaching the digital media market for 2018 on behalf of our automotive client. Our goal is to demonstrate industry leadership through online advertising innovation. We want you to help us do that! This is a great opportunity to provide our automotive client with the strongest digital media placements that achieve brand objectives while also getting our client team excited about the endemic auto research space.

The proposals submitted will be assessed based on (in priority order):

1. Innovation across digital platforms	6. Cost/Value
2. First to Market Opportunities	7. Historical Performance
3. Strategic Fit	8. Cross-brand Opportunities
4. Unique and/or Exclusive Opportunities	9. Management/Service
5. Audience and Content	10. Flexibility

===

Exhibit 16.4   Automotive client RFP (cont'd)

The RFP below outlines the Automotive client's overall parameters as well as Brand details.

Project Descriptions:
In the past few years, our automotive client has reasserted itself through compelling advertising and a strong line of vehicles. As a result, the brand is strong and rising. In 2018, our Automotive client will continue to further enhance that reputation and become THE LEADER IN LUXURY AUTO DIGITAL MARKETING.

This goal will be achieved by a strong and deliberate focus on innovation, successfully launching two models (B7 & B6), gaining market share (Conquesting) and building awareness among prospects and current/lapsed owners (Auto Research). Please tailor your proposal by the following tactics (in priority order):

1   Innovation: In 2018, our Automotive client will surpass the efforts of their competition by demonstrating technology innovation in all advertising communications. To achieve this goal we need creative approaches to drive awareness, consideration and sales beyond standard banners and sponsorships. This objective is to develop unique opportunities never been done before within the endemic space that strengthens brand presence and meets our Automotive client's KPIs. We are looking to innovate the way the endemic category does business and want to take key site partners along for the ride.

2   B7 & B6 Launches: In April/May of 2018, our automotive client will launch the completely new B7 model. The B7 will be positioned as the power of pure attraction with its revolutionary design, exterior styling and power/pickup. In Sept/Oct of 2018, the completely revamped B6 will be released. The new B6 will become the leader in C-segment with revolutionary aluminum technology and 3.0 supercharged/4.2 V8 models. For both of these launches, we are interested in upper funnel, high impact tactics that aid in building awareness. We need to maintain our momentum in moving branding metrics.

3   Auto Research: Ensure that our Automotive client is relevant and accessible when consumers are researching luxury automotive purchases. We want to move prospects through the purchase funnel and protect potential car shoppers from being conquested by competitors. To achieve this, we are interested in purchasing 100% share of voice (SOV) on all of the client's make/model pages within your site. Please break out your proposal by model in the event that not all models can be afforded. Additionally, we are looking for creative approaches to drive awareness, consideration and sales beyond standard banners and sponsorships. We want to give luxury auto intenders a different experience than searchers who are looking outside C/D makes and models. Our Automotive client is the brand that can bring that to the luxury car shoppers. Your site will benefit from the innovative ideas we create together. We are expecting extensive collaboration and involvement with key senior leadership from your site.

4   Conquesting: The goal of conquesting in 2018 is to capture market share from key competitors of the newly launching B7 & B6 models. For this tactic, our Automotive client is interested in employing cutting edge tactics that will enable them to reach the consumer aggressively and subliminally. Examples include:
    a   Secure make/model pages of competitive set
    b   Upper funnel awareness tools that reach consumers that have not decided on vehicle make
    c   Utilize cookie profiles to reach individuals who have shown interest in competitive make/models
    d   Insert vehicle content not originally chosen by user into comparison set
    e   Any newly developed conquesting tactics utilizing new technology (i.e. Experian)

The chart below outlines our Automotive client's Objectives and Success Measures/KPIs with the associated tactics.

Exhibit 16.4   Automotive client RFP (cont'd)

Project	Objective	Success Measure/KPI	Thought Starters
Innovation	Demonstrate Technology Innovation in marketing communications that reflect our technologically advanced manufacturing positioning	• First Ever • New Technology and/or platform/device • Creative approach • Conversion Rate • Buzz/Press Worthy	• Display/Video Unique • Luxury Ownership • Mobile/Tablet Devices • High Impact • Data Matching • Cross Platform • Other never been done before concepts
B7/B6 Launches	Successfully Launch 2 Models	• Site Traffic / Activities • SOV • Brand Study Lift • Conversion Rate	• Display Banners • Video • Luxury Sponsorships • Ownership Sections
Auto Research	Build Awareness of Prospects & Current/Lapsed Owners	• Brand/Product Awareness • Site Traffic • Registration/Lead • Conversion Rate • Proprietary Data • SOV • Lower funnel activities	• Display Banners • Video • Links
Conquesting	Gain Market Share	• Site Traffic / Activities • Registration/Lead • Conversion Rate • Cross Shopping • Proprietary Data • Lower funnel activities	• Display Banners • Video • Comparison Tools • Contextual / Behavioral Targeting • Data Matching

Our Automotive client's Requirements (Priority Order)

We want to ensure that the partnership proposals include the following:

1   Opportunity to offer our Automotive client "first evers" and "unique opportunities" (e.g. First Auto to do X, new ad models, etc.)
2   Brand Integration with key pages/channels
3   Reduction in CPMs from 2017 to show value and savings for client
4   Added Value (including impressions/research studies)
5   Creative Flexibility based on client's Guidelines
6   Competitive Separation (brand level)
7   Inclusion of custom research
8   Creative assistance/mock-ups for custom offerings
9   Coverage of ad serving rich media fees, if applicable

Media and Creative Considerations:

• Targeting: US Only, Contextual, Demographic, Psychographic, Behavioral, etc.

Exhibit 16.4   Automotive client RFP (cont'd)

- Placements: Above the fold placements, high trafficked channels, homepage roadblocks, high SOV, etc.
- Custom Sponsorships: Inclusion of Distributed Content, Content Integration, Sweepstakes, Editorial Destinations, Creation of new navigation experiences, New ad formats not previously used on Auto Research Sites, etc.,
- Email/Newsletters: Inclusion of Custom Newsletter Series, Sponsorships, Media Ownerships, etc.
- Creative focus: Heavy emphasis to larger ad sizes and in-stream video
- Desired ad units: IAB Standard pixel sizes
  - Rectangles
  - Leaderboards
  - Skyscrapers
  - Fixed Panel
  - XXL Box (468 wide x 648)
  - Pushdown (970 wide x 418 ~opens to display the ad and then rolls up to the top of the page)
- As we expect our creative executions to be highly engaging and interactive, we require at least 50K file size for initial loads of all creative. Please let us know your ability to accommodate in your RFP response.

Technologies:

- Flash and/or Rich Media (Motif or PointRoll~ Expandable, Interact within, Video, etc.)
- Video (e.g. Pre/Mid Rolls w/companions - :15, :30, :60, etc.)

Tactic Summaries
Below outlines the objective, targets, flighting and proposed budget amount per tactic

Tactic	Objective	Target	Flight	Budget
Innovation	Demonstrate Technology Innovation	• Adults 25–54 $150K+ HHI who intend on purchasing a new luxury vehicle	1/1/2018 – 12/31/18	Please submit all innovative concepts without budget limitation
B7 Launch	Build awareness of the All-New B7	• Adults 25–54 $150K+ HHI who intend on purchasing a new luxury vehicle in the C Segment • Management, Business, Financial Occupations • Passionate about Design and Technology	4/1/2018 – 5/31/18	$250K

Exhibit 16.4   Automotive client RFP (cont'd)

Tactic	Objective	Target	Flight	Budget
B6 Launch	Build awareness of the new B6	• Adults 25–54 $150K+ HHI who intend on purchasing a new luxury vehicle in the C Segment • Management, Business, Financial Occupations	9/1/2018 – 10/31/18	$250K

Auto Research	• Drive qualified traffic & leads to audiusa.com
	• Popularize client brand by driving gains in:
	  ○ Awareness
	  ○ Consideration
	  ○ Image
	• Increase conversion
		• Adults 25–54 $150K+ HHI who intend on purchasing a new luxury vehicle
		• Impassioned, Influential, Innovative
			1/1/2018 – 12/31/18	Please submit all available inventory for new client Make/Models

B7 Conquesting	Gain market share among competitive set	• Adults intending on purchasing a new luxury vehicle from the below competitive set:
		  ○ Mercedes CLS
		  ○ BMW 5-Series
		  ○ Jaguar XF
			4/1/2018 – 5/31/18	$300K

B6 Conquesting	Gain market share among competitive set	• Adults intending on purchasing a new luxury vehicle from the below competitive set
		  ○ Mercedes E-Class
		  ○ BMW 5 – Series
		  ○ Infiniti M
		  ○ Jaguar XF
			9/1/2018 – 10/31/18	$300k

Please be sure to fill out our Excel spreadsheet thoroughly and send screenshots with brief notes about special placements and other considerations. When submitting your proposals, please consider [Agency] and client's online spending and marketplace conditions as we are seeking CPM reductions year-over-year (YOY) as well as increased proposal value for our Automotive client.

Exhibit 16.4 Automotive client RFP (cont'd)

Please feel free to contact us below with any questions. We will do our best to be readily available.

Primary Contacts

John Doe   212-xxx-xxxx John.Doe@bigpumkin.com
Jane Doe   212-yyy-yyyy Jane.Doe@bigpumkin.com
Mary Dough   212-zzz-zzzz Mary.Dough@bigpumkin.com

Additional Contacts

Tom Dick   212-xxx-xxxx Tom.Dick@bigpumkin.com
Amy Harry   212-xxx-xxxx Amy.Harry@bigpumkin.com

Thanks so much for participating in the 2018 Automotive client's Digital RFP process. We are really excited about seeing your innovative ideas!

If you were an account executive for ESPN.com, for example, and received the Automotive Client RFP, you would be the quarterback of a team at ESPN that goes through a prescribed, disciplined RFP response process. Your first step would be to create a timeline and set deadlines for both internal ESPN responses to the information requested in the RFP and for an external response to the agency. Next, you would set up ideation meetings with sports-specific teams at ESPN that specialize in specific sports such as NFL Football, Major League Baseball, NBA Basketball, for example, the Ad Operations team, the Research team, and the Creative Works team to brainstorm about sponsorship opportunities and ideas about creating custom-built digital opportunities such as sponsored scoreboards or sponsored team roster sites. Finally, once you had several ideas that addressed the challenges put forward in the RFP, you would set up a meeting with the Revenue and Asset Management teams to discuss impression and inventory levels that are needed, pricing, and CPM levels for the ideas the brainstorming came up with.

Once the internal work with the various teams was completed, you would work with the Marketing Services and Planning teams to create a PowerPoint presentation and Excel spreadsheets to present to the agency, which you would deliver by email on or before the due date in the RFP.

Marketers bring media chores in-house

In a March, 2018 "Media Village" article, Bill Duggan wrote that a frequent topic in the annual American Association of Advertisers (ANA) Media Conference was the continued growth of in-house media planning, analytics, and buying by marketers that was formerly managed by advertising and media agencies. Marketers such as P&G, Anheuser-Busch InBev, Target stores, American Eagle, and Nationwide Insurance expanded in-house capabilities and brought some media planning and programmatic buying in-house.[25]

This trend means that salespeople selling national advertising are calling directly on brands more often than previously and that marketers are initiating the RFPs.

Another trend is that more and more national advertisers are bypassing their agencies and working directly with major digital media platforms, especially Google and Facebook. Leading national advertisers such as P&G and Deutsche Telekom (T-Mobile) are openly questioning why they should continue spending so much with agencies when they work directly with Google, Facebook, and Amazon.[26] Advertisers also want to get closer to media owners, "especially for programmatic campaigns mired in transparency concerns."[27]

These trends of agency disintermediation will more than likely continue, which means that salespeople selling national advertising will not only have to navigate the complicated, technologically challenging RFP response process from agencies but also directly from brands, which makes both the process and maintaining multiple relationships more challenging than in the past when primarily advertising agencies did the vast majority of media buying.

Local Advertising

Salespeople who sell local advertising are primarily proactive and are typically the embodiment of missionary selling. They typically call on local businesses that tend to purchase advertising for themselves without using an advertising agency, or if they use an agency, it is usually a small local agency that is sometimes relatively unsophisticated in digital advertising and a multichannel marketing approach.

Let's assume that you are a salesperson for a local television station in a mid-sized market and that you have, like a good missionary salesperson, made a prospecting call on a local university-owned healthcare system's chief marketing officer (CMO). Your research has indicated that the four hospitals in the system have total patient service revenue of approximately $750,000,000, and that in the past three year the university hospitals' dominance in the area has been challenged by a privately owned hospital that has been advertising its cyber knife innovative prostate cancer technology aggressively on television, radio, Google, Facebook, and in the local newspaper. You have asked the CMO the four prospecting and qualifying questions shown in Exhibit 16.5 (as shown in Exhibit 8.2, the Step Management Guide for missionary selling). Those questions are based on the assumption that virtually every business or every entity that has customers, members, clients, or patients advertises, so you naturally ask the prospecting and qualifying questions. However, in the case of the hospital, you do not get answers that you expected.

The answers you got were, "We don't do any advertising other than occasionally sponsoring a boys and girls Little League baseball team and having our name on the uniforms. The hospitals also send out monthly newsletters and have websites. I'm not sure where we would start to develop an overall advertising campaign."

Where do you start in order to answer the question of how to develop an advertising campaign?

You start with an Advertising Planner (See Exhibit 16.8 at the end of this chapter) that prepares you to substitute for an advertising agency, which means that you can help prospects create and place advertising. In other words, you need to become a marketing and advertising consultant.

Exhibit 16.5   Prospecting and qualifying questions

STEP	*Prospecting & qualifying*	*Researching insights & solutions*
Objective	To establish your credibility and expertise and to move prospects from attention to interest.	To find insights or a Big Idea that will help solve marketing and advertising problems.
Key questions	"Are you satisfied with your current ads?" "Would you like to get better results?" "What keeps you up at night?" "What criteria do you use to make a decision on what media to invest in?"	(Conduct research so you understand prospect's industry, business, competitors, and advertising strategy and objectives.)
Key gives	Give some new information and a success story in prospect's category.	
Key gets	Get appointment to present insights, solutions, or a Big Idea.	
Next steps	Schedule appointment.	(Prepare customized presentation.)

Advertising planning

The first thing local salespeople need to do in planning an advertising campaign for their prospect is to define a business model by making the five decisions in the marketing decision tree in Figure 15.4 and outlined a the top of Exhibit 16.8 at the end of this chapter. Those decisions are: (1) B2B, B2C-Direct, or B2B-Retail, (2) tangible or intangible product, (3) scalable or non-scalable, (4) life-cycle stage (development, introduction, growth, maturity, or decline), and (5) cost leadership, differentiation, or focus (focus on cost leadership or focus on differentiation with a market niche).

Having defined the business model, local salespeople should then be prepared to help a prospect through the 10 steps of advertising planning:

1 *Understand applicable laws, regulations, and restrictions* that apply to a business or product. For example, beer advertisers and the advertising industry agree not to advertise to people under 21 and that no more than 28.4 percent of the audience of a beer ad audience can be underage. Thus, if a radio station's audience is 30 percent teenagers, a beer advertiser would not advertise on that radio station. Cannabis under Federal law is illegal, but even though its sale is legal in several states, advertising of cannabis is widely restricted in most states, and Google does not allow cannabis or any restricted substance to be advertised. Therefore, many cannabis retailers have pages on Facebook or Instagram as their only source of media exposure.

2 *State a value proposition* by answering the question, "If I am your ideal customer, why should I do business with you instead of your competitors?" When you craft a clear, appealing, exclusive, and credible answer to that question, you have a viable value proposition.

3 *Create a Unique Selling Proposition (USP)* aligned with the value proposition that clearly separates a local business from is competitors – what are the *different, unique* benefits to consumers that no other business can offer (or has not offered through advertising). Examples are: (1) "Steaks so good you'll want to pay more." (2) "The sports shop with the largest inventory in three states."[28]

4 *Define the ideal customer* or a target audience. It is best to define the ideal customer as a single person such as described in Chapter 11: "Juggler Julia, a harried single mother of two pre-teen boys who is an Emergency Room nurse, who is slightly overweight, and who is trying to juggle both her desire for healthy, non-fattening foods with growing boys' finicky tastes in food."[29] It is easier to visualize and create messaging for a single person than for an aggregation of people, which is what a target audience is.

5 *Define the desired results* of the advertising such as (1) awareness, (2) appeal (preference), (3) ask (seek more information by going to a website), (4) act (purchase, purchase more or purchase more often, or upsell), and (5) advocate (recommend).

6 *Select message objectives* such as (1) inform, (2) persuade, (3) remind, or (4) reinforce that will best accomplish the desired results.

7 *Define message appeal* such as (1) rational or (2) emotional that will best accomplish the message objectives. As a general rule, rational appeals work best with B2B and B2C-direct advertising, and emotional appeals work best with B2C-retail advertising. B2C-retail refers to sales situations in which a consumer does not purchase a product directly from an ad and has to go to a middleman such as Amazon or a retail store to buy.

8 *Define media objectives* such as (1) reach, (2) frequency, or (3) engagement. *Reach* is the number of *different* people that are exposed at least once to an advertising message during a specified time period.[30] The concept of different people is critical to understanding reach. In broadcasting reach is usually referred to as cumulative audience or cume. In digital, reach is referred to as unique visitors and is typically measured on a monthly basis by measurement firms such as comScore, Nielsen, Alexa, or Quantcast. At the beginning of 2019, the number one US reach website was Google; YouTube was second, and Facebook was third.[31] *Frequency* is the number of times within a specified time period that an average person is exposed to an advertising message.[32] *Engagement* is "a spectrum of consumer advertising activities and experiences – cognitive, emotional, and physical – that will have a positive impact on a brand." The more engaged people are with an ad, the more likely they are to recall the advertising messaging. Engagement incudes watching an entire pre-roll video ad, clicking on a banner display ad to learn more about an offer, clicking on a link in an ad and going to a website to get more information, clicking on a heart icon on Instagram or the Like icon on Facebook. Podcasts are a good engagement medium.

As a general rule of thumb, products with high awareness that are announcing a new offer or an introduction of a new, improved feature or model should go for as much reach as they can afford. Good reach media are broadcast and cable network television, Facebook, and large-circulation national magazines and the digital versions of national newspapers such as *The New York Times, Washington Post* or *Wall Street Journal.*

Another rule of thumb is that it takes a minimum average weekly frequency of three to break through the clutter of advertising to begin to make an impression on consumers. With new products, it can take up to an average weekly frequency of seven to get consumers to pay attention and act. Low-cost, impulse items and items that are bought frequently need relatively high levels of frequency to remind consumers to buy them. Good frequency media are local radio, Instagram, and Facebook.

9   *Craft media strategy* such as media vehicle dominance, consistency, flighting, and recency. *Dominance* of a local medium such as a popular local radio station, a radio time period such as overnight, a television station time period such as morning news, or a sports section of local newspaper can shut out competitors, build frequency, and allow for multiple messages to have impact. *Consistency* is an effective strategy for a local business to build an equity position in its community, and it means advertising consistently throughout the year because the business never knows when someone is in the market for what they sell.[33] *Flighting* means running advertising schedules occasionally at times when business is heavy such as for six weeks before Christmas or for four weeks before school starts in the fall. *Recency* refers to the fact that the most effective advertising is the last advertising (most recent) a consumer sees or hears before making a purchase. Good media for recency are Google search ads, radio, and out-of-home.

In today's highly fragmented media environment, investing in a single medium does not make sense. A multichannel approach is necessary to reach consumers who are watching multiple screens – mobile phones, television, and tablets– listening to podcasts and radio stations, and passing billboards and posters in airports, bus, and train stations. Therefore, a mix of media that achieves a desired level of reach, frequency, and engagement must be considered. See Exhibit 16.6 for further concepts in crafting an effective media strategy.

Exhibit 16.6   Concepts in crafting an effective media strategy

---

Last week WARC's (World Advertising Research Center) "Admap," its monthly thought leadership report, focused on frequency in a paper titled, "Frequency: How much is too much?"

This topic has been debated for decades but with the increase in multi-tasking and ad avoidance, commercial "exposure," the building block of frequency, might no longer be sufficient to count as an "impression." In other words in this ADD, fast is too slow world, it likely takes more than one commercial exposure to count as being exposed.

While the report was frequency focused, reach was also addressed. Report conclusions follow:

- **Responsible marketers should not get to the point where messaging becomes irritating. Instead, they should focus on the most efficient way to maximize reach.**
  Comment: Excessive frequency progresses in stages, accelerating from mere annoyance, to irritation, to distress, to anger and ultimately lost sales. Overdo frequency at your own or your client's risk. Some re-targeting borders on this [overdone frequency].
- **Plan for the first exposure to be the most effective, and then plan for ad decay which reduces waste and maximizes spend.**
  Comment: The Law of Satiation states that the first impression is more impactful than the second or third, etc. It's the same reason why the first bite of anything always tastes

best. Strive for as many first impressions as possible, which speaks to reach and a mix of media. Some ad decay is to be expected and welcomed, due to limited budgets and the fact that advertising does have a carry-over effect. Always schedule commercials such that that there is some time gap between exposures for maximum payback.

- **Byron Sharp's work has proved that reach is a critical measure. In his words, "Reach is more important than frequency of exposure; continuous advertising is more effective than bursts followed by long gaps.**

  Comment: Bursts [flighting] of commercial messaging followed by gaps in messaging leads to dangerous levels of ad decay, as without reinforcement (exposure), commercial impact eventually declines until any positive influence as a result a previous commercial exposure all but disappears. Long ad gaps limit sales.

- **It also becomes harder to deliver that reach in channels with declining mass audiences.**

  Comment: Speaks to the importance of a mix of media as every medium has its heavy and light users. Different media help insert a commercial message into a buyer's life in different contexts and locations. But radio's reach, unlike other media, is not declining.

- **Reach today is achieved through multiple media, and optimal platforms may change as a campaign progresses.**

  Comment: True. There does come a point when the next ad dollar could be better spent in another medium. For instance, use TV in the "introductory" phase then segue to radio during the "sustaining" phase. Several Ear vs Eye studies, conducted several years back, but still completely valid, confirm that there is indeed a point in many television campaigns when radio can deliver the same marketing wallop as a television commercial. The first study can be found at http://www.raisingthevolume.com/eyevsear/. The second at http://www.raisingthevolume.com/eyeearmomedition. Both are worth a few minutes of review.

- **If you focus on the most efficient way to maximize reach, then frequency becomes a data point to be understood in the context of diminishing returns for your brand.**

  Comment: Viewing reach and frequency instead through a reach and continuity lens transforms frequency into something more valuable – continuing brand presence/ visibility. Avoid ad bursts followed by ad darkness. Opt for consistency of advertising, even at smaller GRP levels. Products with extremely limited or no mental availability are rarely purchased.

- **When properly implemented frequency capping can bring long-term benefits such as better consumer engagement and brand loyalty.**

  Comment: Digital media can cap frequency more effectively than radio but there are still ways for us to address this issue:

  o Airing messaging across as many dayparts/days as possible will not only lead to a more consistent frequency of exposure, but also to maximize reach.

  o Lighter commercial loads across more stations rather than heavier across fewer prevents the piling up of excessive frequency.

- **The expected level of ad avoidance should have an influence on how each channel is planned.**

  Comment: Radio is not exempt from ad avoidance behavior, though a guerilla mindset can assist in minimizing it. "Guerilla" in terms of existing outside the normal rules of commercial engagement, working to seize listeners attention when and where they least expect it, via short- form messaging, multiple creative executions, bookends, and episodic creative executions can all assist in minimizing commercial avoidance. The most effective antidote to commercial avoidance though is better creative. The most expensive cost in advertising is running creative that doesn't work.

- **Keeping on top of insights into frequency of exposure, time decay between exposures, repetition, and wear-out across platforms enables a greater chance of optimal frequency being achieved.**

  Comment: Each ad impression costs the same, but close-together, repeat impressions return less revenue, so repeat impressions against the same individual within a short time frame generates fewer sales than reaching another new potential customer. Avoid clumping of exposures within dayparts, days, or listeners.

It's a jungle out there, and there's no single, one-size-fits-all frequency rule as so many factors impact the ideal amount: the complexity of messaging, ad decay, wear out, the quality of creative, micro- and macro-economic conditions, competitive ad spend, clutter, previous spending history, etc, but keeping the above in mind when discussing optimal scheduling with clients can assist us in making better recommendations that deliver a greater payback.

Source: McCurdy, Bob. 2019. "Breaking down ad frequency." https://radioink.com/2019/03/18/breaking-down-ad-frequency.

10 *Create a budget* using the *considerations* and the most appropriate of the *methods* outlined in Exhibit 16.8 at the end of this chapter. Craft a 12-month advertising budget that will achieve the message and media objectives you have set.

The *considerations* are: (1) stage in business life cycle, (2) brand market share and customer base, (3) competition and ad clutter, (4) share of voice (SOV), and (5) product substitutability.[34]

In the Development and Introduction stages in a business life cycle PR, publicity, and Google search ads are most effective and efficient. In the Growth stage mobile advertising, television, social media advertising, and radio are most effective and efficient. In the Mature stage personal selling and events and experiences tend to be the most effective and efficient. In the Decline stage, personal selling, sales promotion, and email are usually the most effective and efficient.

A business with a high market share has to invest less in advertising than one that is trying to gain market share. Advertising for high-market-share brands with a strong customer base tends to be defensive, and ad investment levels should be high enough to cause pain to market followers who must outspend them to catch up.

In a competitive ad environment in which there is a lot of advertising clutter such as there is with automotive advertising, in order to stand out, brands must keep up with the competition in terms of advertising investments and try to best their competitors with creative messaging rather than trying to outspend them.

In terms of SOV, brands need to have a general idea about the ad expenditures and frequency levels of competitors' advertising so they can estimate what share of voice SOV they need to achieve their messaging objectives with enough frequency to stand out and have impact.

Brands in less differentiated, easily substituted for, or "commodity-like product classes (beer, soft drinks, and banks) require heavy advertising to establish a unique image."[35]

The *methods* of budgeting are: (1) the affordable method, (2) the percentage-of-sales method, (3) the competitive parity method, and (4) the objective-and-task method.[36]

The *affordable method* is based on what a business owner thinks they can afford. The disadvantages of this method are that it does not take into consideration the reality of competitive advertising investments, and it is not related to a long-term growth plan.

The *percentage-of-sales method* is most commonly used. In this method an annual advertising budget is determined by allocating to advertising a percentage of a business's annual total sales. Various industries have average ad-to-sales ratios that most businesses use as a general guideline for the percentage of sales they allocate to advertising. The 2018 ad-to-sales ratios of 200 business categories are available in the Downloads section of *Media Selling's* website (http://www.mediaselling.us/downloads.html), and see Exhibit 16.7 for a list of ad-to-sales ratios in 15 selected industries so you can get sense of what these ratios look like.

Exhibit 16.7 Ad-to-sales ratios of selected industries

Industry Name	2018 Ad Spend ($Millions)	2019 Ad Spend ($Millions)	Annual Ad Growth Rate (%)	Annual Sales Growth Rate (%)	2019 Ad $ as % of Sales
AIR TRANSPORT, SCHEDULED	3,590.72	4,115.73	18.9	6.10	0.9
APPAREL & OTHER FINISHED PDS	2,588.98	2,811.62	7.9	6.4	4.6
AUTO DEALERS, GAS STATIONS	3,790.31	3,977.52	4.9	6.3	0.7
BEVERAGES	2,600.00	2,637.09	1.5	1.4	4
BOOKS: PUBG, PUBG &PRINTING	1,183.90	1,186.55	0.4	2.9	11.2
CABLE AND OTHER PAY TV SVCS	14,557.99	15,177.51	5.2	7.9	6.8
COMPUTER & OFFICE EQUIPMENT	979.567	957.615	−2.3	3.3	0.6
DEPARTMENT STORES	2,861.99	2,827.83	−1.1	−5.1	4
EATING PLACES	4,348.51	4,476.70	4.7	2.9	2.7
FURNITURE STORES	153.41	161.33	5	5.1	4.3
JEWELRY STORES	796.98	818.37	2.6	1.3	7.5
MEN'S, BOYS, FRNSH, WORK CLTHNG	1,748.31	1,824.34	4.4	5.5	6.1
PERFUME, COSMETIC, TOILET PREP	18,255.39	19,810.33	7.8	7.4	22
RUBBER AND PLASTIC FOOTWARE	3,832.28	3,959.62	3.3	4.9	9.3

Source: Schonfeld and Associates, "Advertising Ratios and Budgets." http://rab.com/research/10014.pdf.

The percent-of-sales budgeting method is the one I recommend you use in most cases when dealing with local businesses.

The *competitive parity method* is the method that is probably the most difficult to use in local sales situations because it is difficult and expensive to acquire the required competitive advertising investment information. Getting competitive information typically requires subscribing to national media monitoring services such as Kantar Media or Critical Mention.

The *objective-and-task method* is setting a budget by defining specific objectives, identifying the tasks that must be performed to achieve the objectives, and estimating the costs of performing them.[37]

See Exhibit 16.8 for an Advertising Planner that contains a summary of the 10 steps outlined above. You can use the planner to help your prospects set an advertising budget that will get the results that will make them successful. A blank Advertising Planner is available in the Downloads section of the *Media Selling* website (http://www.mediaselling.us/downloads.html).

Exhibit 16.8   Advertising planner

Advertising Planner

Advertiser _____

Business model (Check one)	B2B _____ B2C-D _____ B2C-R _____	Tangible _____ Intangible___	Scalable _____ Non-scalable___	Development_____ Introduction _____ Growth _____ Maturity _____ Decline _____	Cost leader ___ Differentiation ___ Focus: Cost___ Focus: Diff ___

Laws, regulations, restrictions		
Value proposition		
USP		
Ideal customer		
Desired results	Aware ___ Appeal___ Ask ___ Act _____ Advocate__	
Message objectives	Inform_____ Persuade___ Remind ___ Reinforce___	
Message appeal	Rational ___ Emotional _	
Media objectives	Reach _____ Frequency _ Engagement_	

Exhibit 16.8   Advertising planner (cont'd)

Media strategy	Vehicle dominance _ Consistency_ Flighting __ Recency ___	
Create budget	*Considerations*	*Methods*
	Life cycle stage	Affordable
	Market share	Percent of sales
	Competitive clutter	Competitive parity
	Share of voice	
	Substitutability	Objective-and-task

Test Yourself

1. What is native advertising?
2. What is influencer marketing?
3. In 2018 did marketers invest more in Internet advertising than in sales promotion? If so, how much more? If not, how much less?
4. In 2018 did marketers spend more in newspaper advertising or direct mail?
5. What is marriage mail?
6. Is email paid, owned, or earned media? If not, what is it?
7. Do marketers have to get permission to send text messages to consumers?
8. In 2018, how much more was invested in advertising on the Internet than on television?
9. What are two broad approaches to advertising?
10. What are the four advertising objectives?
11. Salespeople who sell national advertising do what type of selling – missionary or service selling? Reactive or proactive selling?
12. What is an RFP?
13. Give two reasons why marketers are bringing media chores in-house.
14. Salespeople who sell local advertising do what type of selling – missionary or service selling? Reactive or proactive selling?
15. What are the 10 steps of advertising planning?

Project

Go to the Downloads section of the *Media Selling* website (http://www.mediaselling.us/downloads.html) and download a blank Advertising Planner and then fill it out based on the university-affiliated hospitals described in the Local Advertising section in this chapter.

Once you have completed the Advertising Planner, write an Executive Summary that describes the hospitals': (1) business model, (2) value proposition, (3) unique selling proposition (USP), (4) ideal customer (patient), (5) desired results, (6) message objectives, (7) message appeal, (8) media objectives, (9) media strategy, and (10) twelve-month advertising budget, including the Consideration you thought about and Method you used to create the budget.

Next, download the Hospital Advertising Planner and compare your completed planner and Executive Summary to the Hospital Advertising Planner and Executive Summary. In that planer, the Ad/Sales ratio is only 0.05 percent (0.005). If the budget were 10 times larger (0.05 percent of revenue), what could the hospital do for the community?

References

Corbett, Michael. 2002. *The 33 Ruthless Rules of Local Advertising*. Hanover, MA: Pinnacle Books.

Kotler, Philip and Keller, Keith. 2015. *A Framework for Marketing Management*, 6th ed. New York: Pearson.

White, Chad S. 2017. Email Marketing Rules: Checklists, Frameworks, and 150 Best Practices for Business Success, 3rd ed. Amazon Digital Services.

Resources

Kantar Media (www.kantarmedia.com/us)
Critical Method media monitoring (www.criticalmention.com/media-monitoring)
iSocrates's Academy (www.isocrates.com/academy)

Notes

1   Sterling, Greg. 2018. "Native will dominate display spending in 2018." Retrieved fromhttps://marketingland.com/native-will-dominate-display-speninding-in-2018-238081.

2   Lochner, Jack. 2018. "Think about it." Retrieved from https://www.mediapost.com/publications/article/329061/think-about-it.html.

3   Mathew, Joel. 2018. "Understanding influencer marketing and why it is so effective." Retrieved from https://www.forbes.com/sites/theyec/2018/07/30/understanding-influencer-marketing-and-why-it-is-so-effective.

4   *Ad Age*. 2019. *Marketing Fact Pack*.

5   Ibid.

6   Kotler, Philip and Keller, Keith. 2015. *A Framework for Marketing Management*, 6th ed. New York: Pearson.

7   *Ad Age*. 2019. *Marketing Fact Pack*.

8   "Direct Mail Statistics." Retrieved from https://www.ana.net/mkc.

9   White, Chad S. 2017. *Email Marketing Rules: Checklists, Frameworks, and 150 Best Practices for Business Success*, 3rd ed. Amazon Digital Services.

10 Ibid.

11 Ibid.

12 Ibid.

13 Ibid.

14 Godin, Seth. 1999. *Permission Marketing: Turning Strangers into Friends and Friends Into Customers.* New York: Simon & Schuster.

15 White, Chad S. 2017. *Email Marketing Rules: Checklists, Frameworks, and 150 Best Practices for Business Success,* 3rd ed. Amazon Digital Services.

16 Ibid.

17 eMarketer 2019. "Behind the numbers" podcast: "The rise of D2C brands." Retrieved from https://soundcloud.com/behind-the-numbers.

18 *The Branding Journal.* "What is branding?" Retrieved from https://www.thebrandingjournal.com/2015/10/what-is-branding-definition.

19 Falls, Jason. 2018. "Understanding the direct vs. brand marketing conflict." Retrieved from https://socialmediaexplorer.com/content-sections/tools-and-tips/direct-vs-brand-marketing.

20 Ibid.

21 Ibid.

22 eMarketer. 2018. "Behind the numbers" podcast: "How retailers are using Pinterest." Retrieved from https://soundcloud.com/behind-the-numbers/how-retailers-are-using-pinterest-an-interview-with-amy-vener-retail-vertical-strategy-lead.

23 Criteo. 2018. The original Criteo webpage from which these figures were taken no longer exists, but for relevant information see "Strategies to re-engage lapsed shoppers" at https://www2.criteo.com/re-engage-lapsed-shoppers.

24 *Ad Age.* 2019. *Marketing Fact Pack.*

25 Duggan, Bill.2018. "Marketers continue to bring media chores in-house." Retrieved from https://www.mediavillage.com/article/marketers-continue-to-bring-media-chores-in-house.

26 Digiday. "Platform disintermediation of media agencies gains speed." 2018. https://digiday.com/marketing/platform-disintermediation-media-agencies-gains-speed/

27 Ibid.

28 Corbett, Michael. 2002. *The 33 Ruthless Rules of Local Advertising.* Hanover, MA: Pinnacle Books.

29 Heath, Chip and Heath, Dan. 2007. *Made to Stick: Why Some Stories Survive and Others Die.* New York: Random House.

30 Kotler, Philip and Keller, Keith. 2015. *A Framework for Marketing Management,* 6th ed. New York: Pearson.

31 "The Top10 Most Popular Websites of 2019." 2019. Retrieved from https://www.lifewire.com/most-popular-sites-3483140.

32 Kotler, Philip and Keller, Keith. 2015. *A Framework for Marketing Management,* 6th ed. New York: Pearson.

33 Corbett, Michael. 2002. *The 33 Ruthless Rules of Local Advertising.* Hanover, MA: Pinnacle Books.

34 Kotler, Philip and Keller, Keith. 2015. *A Framework for Marketing Management,* 6th ed. New York: Pearson.

35 Ibid.

36 Ibid.

37 Ibid.

17

Programmatic Marketing and Advertising

William A. Lederer

Media and marketing executives and their organizations are contending with profound changes in customer attitudes, media consumption, purchase behavior, the speed of technological innovation, and extreme media and marketing product and service vendor proliferation and consolidation.

Industry analysts predict that by 2023 US media firms, marketers, and those that enable them will invest $150 billion annually in media and marketing automation to produce more and higher-margin revenue and subsequent insights while seeking to reduce operating costs and headcount. Globally the programmatic market is roughly equal in size to annual US programmatic ad investment, but has a bit faster overall growth rate due to the early start that US has had.

In effect, both the supply-side and demand-side of the programmatic industry and those that enable them are engaged in a very expensive arms race in automating programmatic buying and selling of ad inventory. For those readers who sell or want to sell digital advertising, becoming more knowledgeable about programmatic advertising and marketing is a necessity.

What is Programmatic?

Programmatic advertising describes the automated serving of digital ads in real time based on individual ad impression opportunities. Programmatic marketing is a fully

Media Selling: Digital, Television, Audio, Print and Cross-Platform, Fifth Edition.
Charles Warner, William A. Lederer, and Brian Moroz.
© 2020 John Wiley & Sons, Inc. Published 2020 by John Wiley & Sons, Inc.

formed idea that programmatic media buying best practices and technology, originally developed for computerized buying of online display advertising, can be applied beyond display advertising or even beyond paid media to embrace all digital marketing activities. Programmatic marketing is about data and algorithmically driven targeting and campaign management being applied in an integrated fashion across all paid, earned, and owned digital and screen-based media.

Programmatic media is fully automated buying and selling of digital media using disparate data and typically algorithmically driven trading systems with direct access to publisher ad servers, ad exchanges, supply-side platforms, demand-side platforms, trading desks, and other auction-based electronic marketplaces, sellers, and buyers. Programmatic trading can be real-time or forward sold.

For our purposes, a programmatic algorithm embodies a systematic trading strategy that can be expressed by a set of rules or a computation procedure to derive results from data. A campaign is a specific marketing initiative run by an advertiser and identified by a time period and a specific objective or message.

Why Programmatic?

"I know I am wasting half of my advertising budget. I just don't know which half."

John Wanamaker

Well over 100 years ago, Philadelphia dry goods merchant John Wanamaker was one of the largest print advertisers of his day, and he famously shared his seemingly insurmountable challenge around wasteful media spending. His problem was the same as one faced by all advertisers who cannot measure the effectiveness of their advertising, improve the targeting and frequency of exposure to the audience receiving the message, or control the specific amount spent on the media opportunity.

In World War II, the United States spent 25–35 percent of its industrial output, used 2.4 million personnel, and built tens of thousands of bombers to destroy German cities and factories. British and Americans bombers dropped over 2.7 million tons of bombs on Germany in an effort to destroy the industrial capability of every major city in the country.[1] There was enormous waste in this process. Most of the bombs missed their targets by miles, requiring thousands of bombs to be dropped to hit one building, and a hit would happen if conditions were perfect, the weather was good, and enough bombers actually reached the target. To make matters worse, it was difficult to determine after the fact how much damage was done, or even if the target was hit at all. Think about that: it required one quarter to one third of the entire industrial output of the United States to hit industrial targets in Germany in World War II.

In the twenty-first century, the United States Air Force does not indiscriminately bomb cities and factories with fleets of thousands of bombers carrying tens of thousands of tons of dumb explosives. Instead, precision-guided munitions target the exact location at a specific moment in time with a defined impact at an exact cost. These weapons use targeting and feedback systems that are both accurate and precise.

The benefit of these precision-targeted missiles is more cost effective, there is less collateral damage, we can see what happened and estimate the impact of the attack, and there is greater accountability associated with the activity. Using precision-targeted missiles is more efficient, it is more effective, there is more transparency and greater control, and it benefits from the process of continuous improvement.

In the past, dumb bombs were delivered by airplanes in the general direction of the target in the hopes that something could be hit if enough munitions were dropped. In modern times, the expectation is that a bomb should be able to be delivered to within feet or even inches of its target while causing little to no damage to the surrounding area, and to understand the exact ramifications of that bomb. The problem faced by the Air Force is like the problem that is faced by advertisers because they both have a need for systematic process reengineering from end to end. This process encompasses targeting, measurement, and the high cost associated with the end-to-end process of creating an ad from planning, strategy, tracking, execution, optimization, billing, reconciliation, and, finally, reporting and analytics.

In modern media advertising and marketing, programmatic has been the biggest development since the advent of television and, interestingly, it owes its origins to the Arpanet, which was developed by the US military to improve and accelerate innovation more cost effectively.

Two other major contributors to programmatic advertising are financial and commodity electric trading and the enterprise-resource-planning industry. In the financial industry, activities moved from being labor intensive to electronic auction-based real-time marketplaces largely driven by algorithms instead of human-to-human contact. In the case of enterprise resource planning there is an entire ecosystem of technology and service providers supporting integrated automation systems intended to support greater control and efficiency in enterprises.

In both cases, the level of professionalism, training, and compensation increased dramatically for the underlying industries, though the total employment in those industries shrank over time. The labor saving became the dividend earned from the data and technology investments. Decision-making by industry participants was greatly improved by data and technology.

The Problem

Before the advent of computing and the Internet, advertisers had to carpet bomb their consumers with countless ads in print form, on the radio and television, and in other media such as billboards. This type of exposure was necessary because there was no way to precisely target a specific audience.

If an advertiser wanted to reach its target audience, it bought as many ads in the appropriate media as it could afford in the blind hope that some of those ads would reach the desired consumers. The analogy of bombers in World War II that had to drop thousands of bombs to hit one building dramatically and precisely illustrates the problem pre-programmatic advertisers had.

Carpet bombing with ads was the conventional wisdom for a hundred years until the advent of digital media, beginning with Internet advertising that started in the late 1990s, including display advertising and directory and search engine advertising on Yahoo and Google. Historically, the type of content was a proxy for an audience. For example, if there was programming on ESPN, there was an assumption that the audience was mostly male. If an advertiser bought ads on ESPN, a certain percentage of those ads might be on target, but it was highly likely that an advertiser would be paying for impressions that yielded no benefit. In other words, an advertiser was wasting money. Generating an impression is the main way in which the success of an ad is measured. This success is determined by the size, type, placement, and context of an ad that is actually served to an end user. However, creating a message that is not appropriate, that has an offer that is not impactful, that is delivered at the wrong time and place at too high a price to an audience that is irrelevant for the market, is a recipe for disaster.

The Stakeholders

The challenges that brought about the demand for programmatic approaches to buying and selling are different for each of the key stakeholders, such as audiences, advertising agencies, advertisers, publishers, and enablers.

Audiences and Agencies

Audiences include consumers, businesses, organizations, or whatever entities an advertiser is trying to reach.

A *media agency* is a company or entity that applies its expertise and technology to help marketers buy advertising from media sellers and marketplaces such as publishers, ad exchanges, ad networks, sales house, and so forth.

These stakeholders have a number of challenges and problems that programmatic buying and selling helps to address:

- The labor intensity of deploying impression-based digital and multichannel campaigns, particularly those that are smaller or are made of many different audience segments (a group composed of members of a target audience identified based on the webpages they visit, the actions they take such as making a purchase or completing a sign-up form, or data such as gender or geographical region), geographies, and offers.
- The stakeholders were facing pricing pressures and declining margins.
- The stakeholders were facing the mounting expense of data and technologies for servicing the digital media market.

Advertisers

Advertisers, whether B2C or B2B, with high-, mid-, or low-funnel marketing objectives faced the following problems:

- They increasingly want to know who the underlying target audience is.
- They have very little control and there is very little transparency associated with a media buy because neither the publisher nor the agency is forthcoming about the process.
- They are not sure what price to pay for the advertising. Comparative price information is minimal.
- The inability and unwillingness of the industry to make things easier for trading and measurement purposes and to increase accountability between the parties.

Publishers

Publishers are organizations that deliver content or a service to users. In many cases publishers depend on selling advertising mixed in with their content in order to fund the development, creation, and delivery of that content. In some other cases, advertising is a source of additional revenue. Publishers have traditionally sold on a direct basis to advertisers or agencies their best quality inventory. Less desirable inventory that cannot be sold directly is often sold through third-party resellers such as ad networks. More recently this less desirable inventory, sometimes referred to as *remnant inventory*, has been sold through supply-side platforms (SSPs) that place a publisher's inventory on electronic marketplaces, known as *exchanges*. As marketers move more and more toward automated or programmatic media buying, publishers are also moving to automated selling as they are adapting and learning how to effectively list their ad inventory in programmatic channels such as open exchanges and private exchanges.

Publishers need to address the following issues:

Publishers have a lot of unsold ad inventory. Inventory is the amount of ad impressions available on a digital property for a given ad size during a given time frame. With more targeting parameters, the amount of available inventory will change.

Publishers have difficulties managing their perishable remnant inventory. They get a lower price for an asset that is declining in price to zero as it gets closer to expiration. Like the value of an airplane seats or a hotel room is zero if it goes unoccupied on its expiration date.

The high cost of doing business in person. In-person selling, servicing, and administering business is expensive when these functions are not automated.

Publishers also need to understand how to sell to small advertising agencies or to a small advertiser that has a narrow need. These advertisers are not in a position to commit to a long-term or large commitment, but they often have limited advertising objectives against a narrow niche and may be willing to pay a relatively high price to reach a narrow target.

Publishers also need to deal with the following issues:

1 *Audience development.* When referring to audience development, we mean the application of a data-driven, cost-effective approach to creating more and better site traffic for the explicit purpose of greater publisher monetization. Audience development programs can leverage publisher data, analytics, media planning,

buying, and optimization capabilities across display, video, and other media channels.

2   *Monetization*. This is the process of converting existing traffic being sent to a particular website into revenue. Some ways of monetizing a website are by implementing pay-per-click (PPC) and cost-per-thousand (CPM) impressions advertising, or by driving conversions.

3   *Audience extension*. This is an application of behavioral targeting. Audience extension advertising allows advertisers to target a premium site audience, which is often sold out, across other sites that belong to the same ad network. The ad buy is then made at a lower CPM than running ads on the premium site alone. Audience extension is used for premium site audiences, which are especially sought after. Principles of audience extension are sometimes used by publishers to synthetically mimic the same or like audiences beyond owned-and-operated websites. That valuable audience is then partially recovered on other, sometimes less sought-after, channels on the same or other publishers' websites. Audience extension requires cookies or other audience identifiers as triggers for behavioral targeting techniques. An identifier is a value assigned to a particular user or device and is used to assist in ad-serving functionality. The identifier contains no personally identifiable information (PII), can be reset by the user at any time, and respects user options to limit or opt out of ad tracking. Identifiers are used for audience list targeting, frequency capping, and sequential creative rotation. Examples of identifiers are cookies, which are used on the web and the mobile web, mobile advertising IDs, which are used within mobile apps, and publisher provided identifiers (PPID), used for cross-screen serving.

Enablers

Enablers include:

*   Data and analytics vendors, data management platforms (DMPs), third-party data providers, attribution-models vendors, viewability vendors, and brand-safety vendors
*   Technology companies, supply-side platforms (SSPs), demand-side platforms (DSPs), and ad-serving platforms.
*   Ad networks, which are intermediaries in the process of digital media trading that sell publisher inventory to advertisers on a pre-sale basis. On behalf of multiple independent websites, an ad network relies on third-party data to package digital inventory based on certain characteristics, such as men, women, or teenagers. The packaged inventory, which is typically remnant rather than premium, is then sold to advertisers at a price determined by the network and/or negotiated between the buyer and seller.

Data providers source various types of data including market intelligence, audience intention, and publisher performance data. This data is then collated and packaged to sell to companies such as demand-side platforms (DSPs) and trading desks. Brought together in a DMP, the third-party data compliments the first-party data, which is owned and generated by the marketer, agency, or trading desk. This process allows for smarter bidding in ad auctions and for improved digital targeting of audience for smarter and less wasteful audience composition.

The History of Programmatic

Setting the Stage: Pre-1994

Before the current programmatic era, there were several media and marketing problems to be resolved. Effective solutions were not forthcoming, however, until technology solutions were widely available.

Before 1994, questions such as those listed below could not easily be answered except by directly surveying audience members or by making educated guesses. Some of the questions could not be answered at all due to insufficient time and a lack of appropriate technology.

These questions include:

- Is any anyone viewing an ad?
- To what effect?
- Is the ad pricing correct, too high or too low?
- What is the real cost to buy or sell ad inventory?
- What is the cost of servicing what is sold?
- What happens to remnant inventory?
- What is a fair value for the different types of inventory?
- What is the return on investment (ROI) on advertising?

Unless a publisher and those supporting the sale of advertising aggressively merchandise it, make a client aware of what is available, and stimulate the purchase, it is unlikely a buyer will systematically search out ad inventory to purchase. Furthermore, underlying the potential market demand for ad inventory is the tradeoff that exists between advertising effectiveness and advertising efficiency. Marketers are continually seeking to get as optimum a return on media investment as possible. However, it has only been in recent years that the technology existed to be able to measure the combination of stimuli and impact that make up a media and marketing campaign.

For years there was an inefficient market for advertising inventory. It was not entirely clear to publishers what to charge for different inventory because they did not know what it was worth to whom. A publisher was either selling at too high a price or too low a price, and there was no way of determining after fact which was the case.

Because of the weak linkage between exposure and consumer action in traditional advertising, benefits from upper-funnel metrics like awareness, exposure, consideration, and intent to buy were virtually impossible to measure. The closer that an advertiser is seeking to link media exposure to actual consumer behavior, measurement becomes more difficult and the available tools become slower and more expensive to pursue. The birth of the Internet would change the dynamics of ad measurement and ad effectiveness.

The emergence of digital: 1994–2000

With the advent of the first digital display ad banner and ad server in 1994, technological improvements reached the point where it became possible to match consumers to their actual buying behavior. The opportunity became how to better link ad messages to individual needs, interests, and desires, and to improve measurable impact and outcomes. In short, marketers could now use in-market and post-campaign data to advertise more effectively and at a lower cost. In effect, an advertiser could now link media exposure to an intended outcome. For their part, publishers could now match both specific content consumed by specific, identifiable audiences and relate this to behavior-based engagement and even to lower-funnel outcomes such as purchase and repurchase.

During this time tools were implemented that allowed speedier answers to be developed that could go beyond just attitudinal information like that which can be derived from survey results. These new tools collected actual behaviors, such as:

- Where on a screen did consumers click?
- Where did they go after they clicked?
- What did they do?
- Did they make a purchase?

These lower-funnel metrics were valuable and decidedly behavioral. The data could be collected in ways that were timelier and less expensive than previous methods. Before the Internet, very small samples sizes were used to estimate total audiences to radio and television programming. The Internet provided more precise measuring tools and statistics that resulted in larger sets of data that could be examined and analyzed.

In 1994 and onward, the Internet, as well as services such as CompuServe and AOL, became popular. Advertisers took advantage of these new digital advertising platforms by displaying ads that consisted of text links and, later, graphic banner ads. At the same time, paid subscription growth to newspapers and magazines was flattening due to the proliferation of free content on the Internet.

Ads in the form of a graphic image were called banners, which typically ran across a webpage or are positioned in a margin or other space reserved for ads. In addition to adhering to a standard size such 300 x 250 or 728 x 90 pixels, many websites limited the size of a file to a certain number of bytes so that the file would load and display quickly.

The main problem faced by advertisers in this period was the slow speed of transmission over dial-up modems, sometimes as slow as 300, 1200 or 9600 baud, or 960 characters per second. By contrast, a 1-mbps line, common in the twenty-first century, supports 125,000 characters per second. As technology advanced, the speed and quality of surfing the web improved, allowing for larger pages and more complex graphics to be displayed. To take advantage of the new, large audiences on the Internet, PPC ads appeared.

Advertisers bought these text or graphics banners from companies such as GOTO.COM based on keywords chosen as representative of their products or services.

Email became popular in this era, and the first commercial email address was created. Soon businesses realized the importance of email and began using email messaging systems for communication. Email software was unsophisticated, but that changed over time as new, more advanced email software platforms were developed.

Also, at this time, businesses began to allow consumers to use credit cards for online purchases. Credit card numbers were manually entered into plain text forms without any form of encryption, and verification was time-consuming and prone to error. Verification is the act of reviewing, inspecting, or testing, in order to establish and document that a product, service or system meets regulatory or technical standards. Despite the lack of any real security, theft and hacking were limited because hackers did not have the sophisticated set of tools that are available today.

In 1996, pure digital publishers began to flourish, and ad networks started to aggregate long-tail publishers' inventory. Long-tail publishers were small publishers and blogs that were ad supported and depended on ad networks and ad exchanges to monetize their sites.

An ad network is an intermediary that sells publisher inventory to advertisers on a pre-sale basis. On behalf of multiple independent websites, an ad network relies on third-party data to package a website's inventory based on certain characteristics. The packaged inventory, which is typically remnant rather than premium, is then sold to advertisers at a price determined by the network and/or negotiated between a buyer and seller.

Technology improved and made it possible for all parties to effectively use remnant ad inventory, which is also known as *backfill*. Remnant inventory is inventory that a publisher has failed to sell using its direct sales force and which, as mentioned earlier, is then redirected to third parties to sell on their behalf. In many cases a publisher requires that its identity not be disclosed so advertisers have to buy the ad inventory blind, or without knowing who the publisher is. This restriction is imposed by publishers to avoid adversely impacting the price of ad inventory that is sold directly by its sales force. However, some publishers experimented with direct selling remnant ad inventory themselves through their own branded private exchanges, which were often invitation-only exchanges for their most desirable customers. In a private ad exchange a publisher has more control over what ad inventory gets sold, to whom it is sold, and which bids to accept. In addition, publishers were finding that private ad exchanges were valuable sources of market intelligence that allowed them to track and evaluate media buyers' bidding behavior and ad inventory needs.

The first ad servers appeared in this era to service the ever-increasing number of ads that were being bought. An ad server is the technology and service that places ads on websites. Ad-serving technology companies provide software to websites and advertisers to serve ads, count them, choose the ads that will get the website or advertiser the highest price, and monitor the progress of different advertising campaigns.

Internet site directories such as DMOZ became popular because they helped organize the vast amount of information that was becoming available on the Internet. These directories were manually maintained lists of web resources separated by category. Volunteers devoted their time to maintain these lists of topics, subtopics, and associated websites, and to prevent spam entries from polluting them. For these lists, spam was defined as websites that were not relevant to the topic, were overly commercial, or existed only to serve ads, and had limited or irrelevant content.

Investors took notice of the burgeoning use of the Internet, and companies such as Amazon, eBay, and Zappos were founded to directly serve customers from their homes and businesses. These companies invented ecommerce, web analytics, and digital performance marketing.

Performance marketing refers to marketing techniques and campaigns by which the advertiser pays only for results. Performance marketing is an important part of digital marketing due to the tracking capabilities of the Internet. Purchase behavior can be measured by cost per action (CPA); cost per sale (CPS), which is a flat fee or sales commission; cost per lead, such as a filled-in web form; and cost per click (CPC).

These advances in technology allowed marketers to persuade mathematicians, physicists, and engineers, who were often called data scientists, to join them in their measurement efforts, resulting in ever-faster implementation and adoption of data analytics, which, in turn, resulted in more accurate recommendations and predictions of buying patterns.

Because of these advances and the greater adoption by the general public, directories such as Yahoo and Overture, and search engines like Altavista, and later Google, began to introduce dynamic bidding based on supply and demand and began to develop automated interfaces and analytics. These companies also began selling ad inventory globally.

It was not until the advent of search engines that dynamic bidding and pricing for ad inventory was introduced. Dynamic bidding means that a buyer and a seller could let the marketplace decide the price of the ad inventory impression by impression. Lead generation and direct response marketing were no longer fixed; rather prices were set dynamically in real time by marketplace participants. Also, advertising markets became globalized, as advances in global standardization and infrastructure help speed up the pace of real-time bidding (RTB) development and market access. Furthermore, as data connections became faster and more stable with the proliferation of broadband, DSL, and similar technologies, communication on how to optimize an individual ad impression could be sent around the world in a matter of milliseconds.

During this time, ad personalization became possible and important, because log-ins and permissions enabled dialogs with consumers to be conducted across multiple devices. Publishers and marketers discovered that delivering more relevant messages and experience clearly resulted in longer viewing times and better economic results. The entire market was, and still is, focused on searching for economic models that are viable and sustainable. By the year 2000, the technology was becoming more advanced, but the marketplace was changing rapidly, introducing new opportunities while at the same time creating many challenges to be overcome.

Setting the stage for programmatic: 2000–2007

Starting in the early 2000s, increased bandwidth and storage, combined with the availability of cheap and open software, distributed computing, and cloud computing reduced the cost of computation while the power of computing increased at an amazing rate.

Moore's Law, stated in 1965 by Gordon Moore, who was the co-founder founder of Fairchild Semiconductor and Intel, predicted that the number of transistors in a dense integrated circuit would double every two years. In the period between 2000 and 2007, an extremely rapid advance in technology combined with an equivalent lowering of costs, opened up the possibilities of innovative ways of solving problems and created new opportunities for publishers, marketers, agencies, and those that enable them.

However, the cost of figuring out the multiple possibilities was expensive, and there was not enough talent in the advertising industry to accelerate the process of innovation. In order to solve the various problems in some kind of cohesive fashion, dramatic investment was needed in the technology that drove digital media and marketing. This investment was not forthcoming from the incumbent leaders in broadcasting or print, in traditional advertising, or among the major advertisers. The capital came and continues to come from the venture capital community and wealthy individuals seeking outsized investment returns. Their motivation for profit is one of the key drivers for the current golden age that the advertising world has been in for the last decade.

Some advertising agencies figured out early on they could make more money in programmatic than they could using conventional media buying practices. Many of these opportunistic ad agencies gathered for themselves much of the profit from ad inventory that became available for purchase from publishers at prices far below what the advertisers had been paying previously for the same or similar inventory.

From a media publishers' perspective, programmatic has always represented an opportunity for a buyer to potentially know more about who their audience is and to place that audience in a specific context. Therefore, advertisers and agencies in the programmatic era have often preferred targeting ads based on *who* was reached more than *where* they were reached or *what* the context was. The exception is that today there is a greater awareness of factors related to brand safety and viewability. In the digital advertising industry, a viewable impression is a metric applied to ads which were actually viewable by a human when served. The measurement can be in part or entirely based on conditional parameters and is typically verified by a third-party vendor. There may or may not be a delivery guarantee between ad inventory buyers and sellers tied to a minimum threshold based on the viewability measurement. For example, a publisher might guarantee to an advertiser that 70 percent of all its ads will be viewable.

In this era, Google rolled out its new AdWords and AdSense programs, making it easier for businesses to monetize their web presence, and ad networks packaged premium inventory at scale. Google AdSense was a program in which enterprises can display Google advertisements on websites and earn revenue from hits that generate traffic for the Google search engines. Google AdWords was Google's paid search marketing program, the largest such program in the world and in most individual countries with notable exceptions such as China, which has Baidu, and Russia, which has Yandex.

Behavioral ad targeting and contextual ad targeting enabled advertisers to focus more precisely on their target audience. Behavioral targeting puts ads in front of people who should be more receptive to a particular message based on past Internet behavior, including online searches, clicks, purchases, and websites visited. Often, the use of cookies or mobile device IDs enables behavioral targeting. Contextual advertising is a form of targeted advertising for ads on websites or other media, such as content displayed in mobile browsers. The ads themselves are selected and served by algorithms based on the content displayed to a user.

After 2003, YouTube and other video sites launched user-generated videos and video ads, and agency trading desks formed. Digital agencies expanded globally, and social media emerged. Ad marketplaces and ad exchanges such as Right Media were further developed. These changes set the stage for the modern programmatic era.

Programmatic 1.0: 2008–2010

As a necessary condition for the programmatic era to really take hold in the early part of twenty-first century, there had to be a move to commodify and commoditize ad inventory and the processes of buying and selling that go with it.

Commodification is the standardization of an asset such that is can be compared to another like-kind asset in using specific and consistent dimensions and standards. Commoditization is making an asset widely available and interchangeable between multiple parties at scale.

Some of the drivers of change include the availability of immense computing power, which allows complex data to be computed in milliseconds, thus allowing for real-time marketing decisions. The vast volume of information needed requires inexpensive data storage to store billions of anonymized stored data points that can be used to forecast campaign-specific values for each individual ad space.

In this Programmatic 1.0 era, advertising technology continued to mature. Social media ads began to appear on Internet- or cellular-phone-based applications, and tools to share information among people increased exponentially. Social media includes popular networking websites such as Facebook and Twitter as well as bookmarking sites like Digg and Reddit. Social media includes blogging, forums, and any aspect of an interactive presence which allows individuals the ability to engage in conversations with one another, often as a discussion over a particular blog post, news article, or event.

Ad verification went from nice-to-have to need-to-have for advertisers and publishers in this era. Ad verification businesses are services that offer to validate that an advertiser's ad was delivered to the agreed-upon specification in an advertising insertion order (IO). There can be additional criteria such as above-the-fold placement, geographic targeting, and so on.

In-text ads became targeted and useful, and the newer, faster technologies enabled real-time bidding. Real-time bidding is a technology that uses highly specific data, algorithms, and automation to enable marketers to bid on ad inventory in microsecond auctions. During the time in which a user's webpage loads, which might be anywhere between 100 and 160 milliseconds, an advertiser or an agency places a bid for a specific ad impression, which is then served to the user once the page is loaded. Using data related to the user's cookie, in addition to other sources, an advertiser or agency is able to track users and match them with available ad impressions. This system allows for the delivery of an advertiser's message directly to a consumer in real time. See Exhibit 17.1 for an explanation of how the process of serving a programmatic ad works,

Exhibit 17.1   The life of a programmatic RTB ad impression

200 Milliseconds

Milliseconds	What occurs
0	Jane Doe clicks on a URL and the publisher's content begins to load in her browser.
10	Publisher may find information it has stored on Jane Doe, possibly in its data management platform.
30	Publisher sends available information to its ad server asking the ad server whether an ad campaign that an advertiser has placed with the publisher is available that would target Jane Doe. If there is a campaign matching Jane Doe's profile, an ad is served.
40	If no campaign targets Jane Doe, the server seeks to match the impression programmatically by requesting a response from selected traders, ad networks, and supply-side platforms.
65	If the impression is not cleared, the server may seek to clear the impression in a programmatic direct way via private exchanges. If the impression is not cleared, the request is sent to an open ad exchange in hopes of achieving liquidity, or selling the impression.
75	An open ad exchange sends a bid request containing information on Jane Doe's browser, website URL, and ad type to multiple bidders, including traders, ad networks, and demand-side platforms.
100	Each bidder processes the request, overlays it with additional user data and the marketer's targeting and budget rules. Each bidder's algorithm evaluates the request, selects the creative, and sends it along with an optimal bid price to the ad exchange.
125	The ad exchange selects the winning bid from bidder responses through a first-price auction.
150	The ad exchange sends the winning ad URL and price for the winning bid to the publisher's ad server, which tells Jane Doe's browser which ad to display.
175	Jane Doe's browser pulls the ad from the winning bidder's ad server and sends a matching ad to Jane Doe's browser. The browser displays the called-for web page and the matching ad.
200	The winning bidder's ad server receives ad tag data on Jane Doe's initial interaction experience. Did she interact with the ad in some way or not?

Source: Adapted from "The life of a programmatic RTB ad impression." https://www.mediacrossing.com/resources/infographics.

Programmatic is auction based because electronic auctions are the most effective and efficient way to achieve optimal price discovery by both buyers and sellers. These auctions use exchanges, which are real-time electronic exchanges in which ad inventory, typically at the individual impression level, is offered for sale and bid on in a sealed-bid auction in which bidders submit bids on "dark inventory" without knowing the bids of others participating in the auction.

There are several types of auctions. First-bid auctions need only one bid to win the auction. In this case, the exchanges and buyers come out ahead, but sellers lose. For second-bid, often called second-price, auctions, the second bid wins at a price of the first bid plus $.01 a CPC or CPM basis. For this type of second-price auction, exchanges win less often, buyers win, and sellers win. Finally, in futures auctions, buyers bid now, buy later, and deliver later. This future auction offers a hedge for both the buyer and seller, but requires market liquidity. Advertising assets are liquid when they can be bought and sold easily.

A DSP enables a marketer to utilize a single interface to perform programmatic and real-time bidding media buying. A DSP allows a marketer to manage bidding on and buying ad inventory and data across multiple ad exchanges, ad marketplaces, and data provider accounts.

Using data related to a user's cookie in addition to other sources, a marketer is able to track users and match them with available ad impressions. This process allows for the delivery of a marketer's message directly to a consumer in a live setting and in real time.

Programmatic media auctions are good news for both buyers and sellers because they provide a multitude of options for both.

Programmatic 2.0: 2010–present

From 2010 on, advertising has been undergoing tremendous change due to the rapid advance of technology. The marketplace is moving to take advantage of the new opportunities provided by fast and reliable communications, the Internet of Things, artificial intelligence, advanced modern browsers, the cloud, software as a service (SaaS), and other advances.

Because of the ubiquitous nature of Internet connections, smartphones, tablets, and other technologies, massive amounts of information is collected and stored constantly, which has led to the rise of Big Data, which refers to extremely large data sets and the technology that supports them and which is required to enable these technologies to be successful. Other technologies such as cloud computing and distributed computing are changing everything. In general, a computing cloud is a networked group of servers accessible through remote means. In ad tech, the cloud usually refers to cloud computing infrastructure on which an ad platform of some kind runs. Data or processes existing within such a network are usually said to be "in the cloud."

Microsoft and Yahoo recognized the value of exchanges and entered the market by building and buying exchanges, but then proceeded to stifle their innovation and growth. The executives at these companies then took their profits and moved on to create the next generation of programmatic, seeking to improve the state of the art for Programmatic 2.0.

Exchanges such as GoogleAdX, Xandr, OpenX, and Index next came to market. These services are used to manage display advertising sources. Advertisers and ad networks are buyers, while publishers and publisher networks are sellers on these exchanges.

Marketers and agencies needed to get a better understanding of their market, which led to the development of data-management platforms. These services provide a marketer, agency, or trading desk with a single integrated view of all campaign and audience data, helping with overall management and analysis of data. These functions enable a marketer or agency to target their advertising effectively in order to hit the right people at the right time with the right message. Examples of DMPs that entered the market at this time include Salesforce DMP, Oracle BlueKai, and Adobe Audience Manager.

To help manage the buying and selling process, which because of the proliferation of new services and technologies had become very complex, DSPs were created. These platforms enable a marketer to utilize a single interface to perform programmatic and real-time bidding. A DSP allows a marketer to manage bidding on and buying ad inventory and data across multiple ad exchanges, ad market-places, and data provider accounts. DSPs such as MediaMath, DBM, and Dataxu became dominant.

On the revenue side, supply-side platforms were rolled out to provide publishers with a technology platform that enabled them to better manage their ad impression inventory and to maximize revenue. Companies such as Rubicon, PubMatic, and Telaria serviced these technologies.

Rich media, mobile, social platforms, and video are growing in use, and are now a huge part of programmatic advertising. The Internet of Things has also grown and enabled still more advertising opportunities.

To give advertisers more options, geo-targeting was developed and implemented. This practice targets users based on their geographic location. This technology can also be used to target those near a competitor and can be served to desktop or mobile devices. Geo-targeting is becoming more granular, more real-time, and more precise every month. See Exhibit 17.2 to get a sense of how all the elements of a digital ad campaign are integrated to produce results for advertisers.

Exhibit 17.2   Typical digital ad campaign process

---

1   *Plan and budget* for a digital ad campaign and develop a media and measurement plan, including a testing calendar, and negotiate media, if necessary.

2   *Develop* an advertising plan to reach target audience segments with performance projections based on advertiser's benchmarks.

3   *Integrate* advertiser's target profile, CRM platform, campaign, and website first-party data with technographic, behavioral, contextual, ad demographic third-party data in a DMP and with cookie and cookieless synch/matching if desired.

4   *Assemble and store* audience segments in a DMP based on business needs. Create modeled and look-alike segments based on visitor and customer data files.

5   *Create* ads for multiple media ad formats such as display, video, social, and mobile, using best practices and past performance criteria. Tag relevant and destination URLs.

6   *Execute* utilizing a managed DSP to buy guaranteed ad RTB programmatic media.

7   *Analyze and report* activity, spending, ad campaign results against key performance indicators and adjust plans and budget in real time.

8   *Optimize* campaign performance, test additional audience segments, shift budgets, revise benchmarks.

9   *Advise* about future plan by consolidating campaign data back into DMP to generate new models.

Source: Adapted from iSocrates. Used with permission.

Agency trading desks

Agency trading desks developed as centralized or quasi-centralized centers of programmatic trading excellence. Trading desks such as Varick, Xaxis, Vivaki, Amnet, Affiperf, Goodway Group, and HX, were established by agency holding companies such as WPP and Omnicon in this 2010–present period. Independent trading desks also sprung up and began buying and selling media for themselves and for large- and medium-sized clients. Some of these independents include iSocrates, Programmatic Mechanics, and the Yellowhammer Group. See Figure 17.1 to see the core functions of a trading desk.

Private exchanges

In order to increase profits and give advertisers even more options, private exchanges were implemented. A private ad exchange is an exchange through which a publisher can directly auction and sell its ad inventory and, thus retain more control over bid selection, set dynamic reserves, and limit potential buyers through the use of invitation-only auctions. A private ad exchange is an auction marketplace in which a publisher can exclusively sell some or its entire ad inventory combined with its own proprietary data sets to obtain better bids. Higher bids improve revenues and yield, or the percentage of clicks vs. impres-

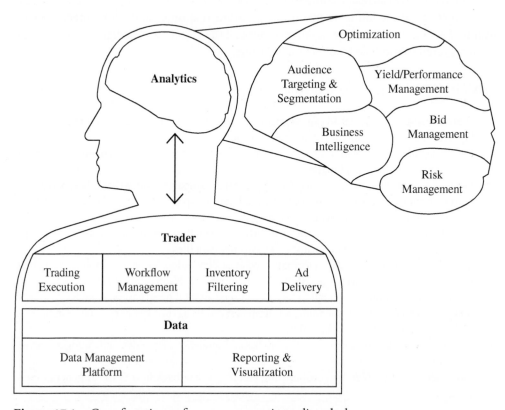

Figure 17.1   Core functions of a programmatic trading desk

sions on an ad within a specific page. A private ad exchange is the technology used by publishers to ensure maximum revenue generation from those who use programmatic media channels. An invitation-only auction sells a type of inventory that is unreserved, has auction-based pricing, and incorporates a one-seller-to-a-few-buyers type of participation. Other terms used in the market to describe invitation-only auctions of digital media inventory are *private marketplace*, *private auction*, *closed auction*, and *private access*.

A private marketplace functions similarly to an open auction in pricing and is determined in real-time based on what advertisers are willing to pay. The difference is that private-marketplace deals are more exclusive, because only a select group of invited buyers are permitted to bid in the auction, and negotiated fixed-rate prices are set in advance for each buyer through in-person negotiation.

Ad fraud and ad blocking

As always, there are side effects to new technologies. Criminals and greedy people have become clever, and because of that, ad fraud is becoming more common. Ad fraud is defined as the deliberate practice of attempting to serve ads that have no potential to be viewed by a human user. There are numerous types and sources of ad fraud, and ad fraud detection has become a critical tool for the buy side of the market.

In order to reduce exposure to advertising, consumer ad blocking is becoming more effective and ubiquitous. An ad blocker is a software product that prevents ads from appearing with the content the user is intentionally viewing. People block ads for a variety of reasons. For example, many of them find interrupt marketing ads annoying and even stressful. Interrupt marketing is intrusive by design, like an interstitial ad that comes between users and the content they are attempting to view or an autoplay or rollover ad that starts up without any intentional act on the part of the user.

Hackers and criminals have found vulnerabilities throughout the Internet infrastructure and have successfully been able to inject malicious code into many ads. These ads are known as *malvertisements*, and result in the spread of viruses on consumer machines of all types. This kind of attack demonstrates why security is of utmost importance and must be kept in mind as ad-servicing systems are built and rolled out.

Header bidding

Header bidding, also known as *advance bidding* or *pre-bidding*, is an advanced programmatic technique in which publishers offer inventory to multiple buyers including retargeters, market makers, and ad exchanges simultaneously (as opposed to sequentially as in waterfall mediation), before making calls to their ad servers. The transparency of the entire header-bidding process has always been a concern. When the marketplace is transparent, advertisers understand the biases and can work around them as needed. When the process is not transparent, questions such as "what steps are taken to prevent ad fraud," "how do they measure success?", and "what is the price for each part of the process?" cannot be easily answered.

Google, Facebook, and Amazon dominate the programmatic market, creating, in effect, a *walled garden*, which is a closed ecosystem in which all the operations are controlled by the ecosystem operator. In digital marketing, these three companies have reached the level of walled gardens, meaning they can force their clients to use their own marketing services.[2] These services include DMPs, DSPs, and dynamic creative optimization platforms.

Many advertisers wish to show different ads to different customers; for example, an advertiser might wish to show rain gear to people who live in rainy climates and sunblock to those who live in sunny climates. *Dynamic creatives* refers to having a few different creatives and choosing the most appropriate one for the user through some automated means such as audience segmentation or based on frequency and recency. Many platforms have rules about how much creatives can vary within the same placement. For example, there may be limitations placed on major advertisers on rotating brands on an unlimited basis.

One of the technologies showing great promise is Programmatic TV, which lets advertisers use the power of data-driven audience targeting and process automation to run incredibly effective campaigns on one of the world's most powerful mass ad media, television.

Advertisers need access to their information, and this is done by using a customer data platform, which is a marketer- or publisher-managed system that creates a persistent, unified customer database that is accessible to other systems. This structured data is then made available to other marketing systems.

Available types of programmatic and media channels

There are many options available for buying media, including IOs, automated IOs, DSPs, agency trading desks and marketers' in-house trading desks. Exhibit 17.3 outlines these different buying options and the different types of programmatic platforms.

Exhibit 17.3   Available media channels and types of programmatic platforms

Many media buying options	Types of programmatic platforms	Media channels
Insertion orders (IOs)	Direct	Television
Automated IOs	Programmatic direct	Video on demand
DSPs	Automated plus	Over the top
Agency trading desks	Guaranteed direct	Audio
Marketer in-house trading desk	Programmatic guaranteed	Desktop display
	Private marketplace	Mobile display
	Open exchange	Desktop video
	Non-O&O audience extension	Mobile video
	Non-O&O audience development	Social
		Native
		Search

Source: iSocrates presentation. Used with permission.

Several of the common programmatic methods for purchasing ads, as outlined in Exhibit 17.3 are described in more detail below.

- *Direct* is a traditional insertion order-based ad campaign delivered programmatically, but bought and sold between humans with very specific advertiser goals, such as a product purchase, level of brand awareness, store foot traffic, or the creation of a new customer account.
- *Programmatic direct* is a way to automate direct ad buys for set campaigns. Programmatic direct is the transactional methodology of automated direct sale of guaranteed advertising between advertiser and publisher.
- *Automated plus* is a type of inventory that is reserved, has fixed pricing, and incorporates a one-seller-to-one-buyer type of participation.
- *Guaranteed direct* is also known as automated guaranteed, premium or reserved. A buyer knows the desired audience and content, and buyers and sellers directly negotiate deals.
- *Programmatic guaranteed* is a one-to-one sale with fixed pricing and reserved inventory that is processed automatically. An automated transaction that takes place in the context of Open RTB. Publishers that make guaranteed deals and sell utilizing programmatic auction technology such as deal IDs are, in effect, selling through programmatic guaranteed. When this occurs, publishers and buyers negotiate a fixed price for reserved inventory, with the publisher linking the deal to the inventory in the RTB platform. To complete such a sale, the publisher needs a holistic view of both direct commitments and programmatic sales. Therefore, this type of transaction is limited to platforms like Smart RTB+.
- *Private marketplace* is an RTB auction by invitation only. One or more publishers invite buyers to bid on inventory, and the sites where the ads will run is known to the buyers.
- *Open exchange* is also called an *open auction*. In an open exchange many buyers can bid on the inventory of many different publishers in an auction format.
- *Non-O&O (owned & operated) audience extension*. Audience extension is an application of behavioral targeting. Audience extension allows advertisers to target a premium site audience, which is often sold out, across other owners' sites such as those not owned and operated by the original publisher.
- *Non-O&O audience development*. The term audience development describes activity which is undertaken specifically to meet the needs of existing and potential audiences. It can include aspects of marketing, commissioning, programming, education, customer care, and distribution. Most often, the term refers to using paid and earned media to drive site traffic to a publisher's digital property from non-endemic, or other publishers', properties.

Ads may be bought for several channels, including those listed in Exhibit 17.3. New technologies are being released on a regular basis, resulting in ever-more ad media channels to consider.

Programmatic media auctions

Programmatic is action-based because electronic auctions seem to be the most effective, efficient way to achieve optimal price discovery by both buyers and sellers. Programmatic auctioning makes use of a media exchange, which is a real-time electronic exchange in which ad inventory, typically at the individual impression level, is offered for sale and bid on in a sealed-bid auction whereby bidders submit bids on what is called *dark inventory* without knowing the bids of others participating in the auction.

There are three types of auctions:

1   First-price auction
    a   Need only one bid to win
    b   Exchanges win, buyers win, sellers lose in this type of auction because bids tend to be low.
2   Second-price auction
    a   Second bid wins at first bid + $.01 CPM
    b   Exchanges win less often, buyers win, sellers win
3   Futures
    a   Bid now, buy now, deliver later
    b   Offers a hedge for buyer and seller, but requires market liquidity

Typical tag-based approach to bidding

In tag-based integrations at publishers, the system is designed in such a way that every impression gets the highest competition possible, which requires the demand partner to pay the maximum CPM for an impression.

Every bid taking part in an auction through the publisher ecosystem will compete against these five layers of demand set-up:

1   Publisher-direct demand partners
2   Publisher waterfall partners
3   Google Ad Manager demand
4   Publisher indirect demand
5   Publisher SSP chooses the winning bidder after comparing the CPM prices offered in the waterfall, Google Ad Manager, and indirect demand. The final CPM will be sent to the publisher ad server for comparison with the best prices offered by the publisher direct demand.

Typical header-bidding approach

Header bidding is designed so that header-bidding demand partners face competition from the tag-based demand partners as well. This type of bidding adds real value for publishers. Header bidding (or advance bidding or pre-bidding), as mentioned in the

"Header Bidding" section of this chapter, is an advanced programmatic technique wherein publishers offer inventory to multiple buyers including retargeters, market makers, and ad exchanges simultaneously (as opposed to sequentially as in waterfall, or sequential, mediation) before making calls to their ad servers.

In header bidding a publisher selects a final bid from these three layers of completion:

1　Publisher SSP indirect demand
2　Publisher SSP header bidding partner
3　Tag-based demand partners via Google Ad Manager.

The biggest advantage of this approach to header bidding is that all header-bidding demand partners must beat bidding from AdX which increases competition and results in higher CPMs with improved fill rates. Latency in header-bidding demand partners is controlled programmatically.

Publishers minimize impression loss by adding fewer demand partners through the internal channel and maximize the yield by adding more demand in header bidding along with 100 percent fill partners in Google Ad Manager.

Finally, publisher inventory scanning tools such The Media Trust and Forensiq scan an impression to ensure clean delivery before impressions are actually served on a page.

Test Yourself

1. What is programmatic?
2. Who was John Wanamaker and what did he say about his advertising?
3. What were some of the problems advertisers had before the advent of programmatic?
4. What are some of the benefits of programmatic?
5. Who are the stakeholders in programmatic advertising marketing?
6. Why do we call 2007 to the present period The Golden Age of Programmatic?
7. What is real-time bidding?
8. How long is a typical programmatic bidding and delivery cycle?
9. What are some of the types of programmatic?
10. What are some of the media channels that are available to be planned and bought programmatically?
11. What is trade desk?
12. What are private exchanges?
13. What is a first-bid auction?
14. Explain header bidding.

Project

Go to an ecommerce website or app such as Amazon and search for a product that you might be interested in buying such as a watch, but make sure it is a relatively expensive watch, say, over $350. Then, over the next few weeks count the number of ads you receive for watches as you surf the web, especially to content sites such as the HuffPost, BuzzFeed, or *The New York Times*. Keep track of the number of times you see an ad for one brand of watch, indicating that you are being remarketed to, or retargeted. When you stop seeing ads for that particular brand of watch, count the number of times you saw the same ad. Do you think the advertiser had a frequency cap on the number of times the ad was served to you?

Resources

Adobe programmatic (www.adobe.com/experience-cloud/use-cases/programmatic-advertising. html)
Google programmatic information (www.thinkwithgoogle.com/marketing-resources/ programmatic)
iSocrates (www.isocrates.com/academy)
Oracle Blue Kai (www.oracle.com/marketingcloud/products/data-management-platform)
Xandr (www.xandr.com)

References

Busch, Oliver (Ed.). 2016. *Programmatic Advertising: The Successful Transformation to Automated, Data-Driven Marketing in Real Time*. Cham: Springer.

Dempster, Craig and Lee, John. 2015. *The Rise of the Platform Marketer: Performance Marketing with Google, Facebook, Twitter, Plus the Latest High-Growth Digital Advertising Platforms*. Hoboken, NJ: Wiley.

Smith, Mike. 2015. *Targeted: How Technology is Revolutionizing Advertising and The Way Companies Reach Consumers*. New York: AMACOM.

Wang, Jun, Zhang, Weinan and Yuan, Shuai. 2017. *Display Advertising With Real Time Bidding (RTB) and Behavioral Targeting (Foundations and Trends in Information Retrieval*. 2017. Boston, MA: Now Publishers.

Notes

1 Retrieved from https://en.wikipedia. org/wiki/Strategic_bombing_during_ World_War_II.

2 Poulpiquet, Pierre de. 2017. "What is a walled garden? And why it is the strategy of Google, Facebook, and Amazon ads platform." Retrieved from https:// medium.com/mediarithmics-what-is/ what-is-a-walled-garden-and-why-it-is- the-strategy-of-google-facebook-and- amazon-ads-platform-296ddeb784b1.

18

Measuring Advertising

William A. Lederer

Introduction
Charles Warner

The fourth edition of *Media Selling* contained a chapter titled Media Research, which contained information on the general principles of media research, including sampling, response bias, and media research concepts specific to the major media such as television, radio, newspapers, and magazines.

Since the fourth edition was published in 2009, digital advertising has overtaken television as the number one advertising medium, and measuring television has changed dramatically. The majority of magazines have digital versions, and printed newspapers are slowly being transitioned to digital-only distribution as owners abandon money-losing print editions. Furthermore, over 80 percent of digital advertising is bought and sold programmatically, and programmatic buying allows advertisers to target and buy specific, individual consumer impressions instead of broad audiences; therefore, the need for measuring mass audiences has diminished, and mass media such as television and radio are finding new methods for targeting life style, psychographic, and purchase-likely audience segments and new methods for estimating the size of their audiences.

Therefore, this chapter, in the sections that follow, written by industry programmatic expert, Bill Lederer, will discuss how advertising, especially digital advertising, is measured, because those selling advertising must understand how that advertising is measured and evaluated so they can help their customers get the results they need to survive and to succeed.

Media Selling: Digital, Television, Audio, Print and Cross-Platform, Fifth Edition.
Charles Warner, William A. Lederer, and Brian Moroz.
© 2020 John Wiley & Sons, Inc. Published 2020 by John Wiley & Sons, Inc.

The Job of Media Salespeople

Your objective as a salesperson for digital advertising is to get results for your customers, and in order to achieve that objective you need to understand how digital advertising is measured.

Media Research

General terminology

Target audience   The first step that an advertiser or an agency takes when planning a media investment is to define a target audience. A target audience is the most important marketing decision an advertiser will make because it drives all subsequent decisions and many of the decisions you make as a media salesperson about how to help a customer get results.

This core marketing decision is not always obvious; therefore, an advertiser may need your help. For example, everyone with a house needs carpets, but the carpet store's target audience is usually the person who makes the purchase decision. Customer research you have access to may reveal that women are the first to notice that the old carpet needs replacing, but it is a joint decision between two people in a household about which store to go to and which carpet to buy. The same research may find that the majority of carpet buyers are between the ages of 35 and 54. So the primary target audience for a carpet advertiser might be adults between the ages of 35 and 54, expressed in media shorthand as A35–54.

Target audience universe   Broadcast media coverage areas are defined in terms of counties. This Universe Estimate (UE) is the denominator that will be used to calculate ratings. Knowing that 75,000 people watch the early news on a television station is interesting, but to be meaningful for comparison purposes, it must be expressed as a percent of the people living in the area. Rating services such as Nielsen report this UE for every age/sex demographic.

Geography   When we think about where people live, it is usually in political or even postal terms: states, cities, counties, and perhaps Zip Codes. For media sales, what matters is the geographic area where the advertising can be seen or heard, although for research purposes, that area must be adjusted to reflect the counties reported in the US Census. For national television on the broadcast networks, cable, or syndication, the coverage area is the entire country. For local radio it is the counties that are covered by a station's signal, generally the Standard Metropolitan Statistical Area (SMSA). For local television, it is the counties in the Designated Market Area (DMA), which Nielsen defines as all the counties where the stations of a given city get the plurality of viewing. More about DMAs later in this chapter.

For digital content, the coverage can be geographically as precise or broad as desired through the use of geo-targeting, which is practice of targeting users (or eliminating exposure to them from campaigns) based on their geographic location. The global positioning system (GPS) is a satellite-based navigation system owned by the US Government. It is a global navigation satellite system that provides geo-location and time information to a GPS receiver, such as a cell phone, anywhere on the earth where there is an unobstructed line of sight to four or more GPS satellites.

Advertising impressions   An advertising impression is a single exposure of a message to one person in a target audience. This sounds simple, but the exact meaning of exposure is different for each medium and is governed by the way the medium is measured by the research companies.

For digital content, an impression refers to the display of an ad such as a banner, text, or video on a viewer's browser or mobile device. Even though an impression is recorded, it is not known if users actually paid attention to an ad unless they clicked through.

For television, an impression can mean the people who push a button on Nielsen's People Meter to indicate they are watching television. But, are they paying attention to the television set? Do they watch every minute of a commercial? Do they remember to punch out of the meter when they go to the bathroom or put the kids to bed? Do they continue watching during commercials? These are the kind of questions that are discussed at industry conferences, but the only thing that matters to you as a salesperson is the number reported by Nielsen.

Gross impressions   Just as cooks never talk about one bean or one pea in a recipe, advertisers never talk about one impression. The concept of gross impressions begins with the total number of people viewing a banner, text or video ad, watching a television program, or listening to a radio station at a given moment.

But the concept of gross impressions is more than that. It is the simple addition of the impressions every time an ad is displayed.

In a recent Super Bowl, a Bud Light commercial ran six times. Each time it was watched by about 20 million M25–54. By the end of the evening, Bud Light had accumulated about 120 million gross impressions (6 X 20 = 120,000,000). Note that the gross impressions number does not account for duplication. Surely some of the viewers saw the commercial several times, but gross impressions reflect the total media weight for the commercials that appeared in the game. The same concept applies over any period of time and any number of programs.

Rating   Talking about hundreds of millions of impressions is mind-boggling. It is much more meaningful to think of the impressions as the percent of the target audience universe. This percentage is called a *rating*.

The highest-rated television program is the Super Bowl, which might have an average rating of 40, which means that 40 percent of the television homes in America watched at least five minutes of the game. The rating of most prime-time network television programs is less than 5.0, and prime-time cable ratings are generally less than 1.0.

The same concept works in a local television market; although, because of the way a diary is formatted, ratings are expressed as an average-quarter-hour (AQH) audience instead of the average minute.

Gross rating points For planning purposes, advertisers add the ratings of all the programs where advertising appears to get gross rating points (GRPs). This is the same concept as gross impressions, only expressed as the sum of the rating points.

Gross rating points are typically used to describe the message weight per week or per month, although it can be used for any period of time. Following is an example of a schedule that will deliver 120 gross rating points a week:

Three commercials, each with a 15 rating	= 45 GRPs
Five commercials, each with a 10 rating	= 50 GRPs
Five commercials, each with a 5 rating	= <u>25 GRPs</u>
Total weekly GRPs	120 GRPs

Because GRPs are the simple addition of the ratings, there is no limit to the number of points that can be scheduled. Quick-serve restaurants, movies, and other heavy promotional advertisers typically run at least 250 GRPs in a week on television. Occasionally a television advertiser will run four or five hundred GRPs a week, giving viewers the feeling that they see the commercial every time they turn on a television set.

The GRP concept can be extended to other media such as radio, magazines, and newspapers; although translating the broadcast rating concept to other media is often messy, it can be done for rough estimating purposes. In magazines, for example, gross rating points equals the average issue audience multiplied by the number of ad insertions.

Reach and frequency It should be obvious that gross rating points do not account for duplication. The definition of *reach* is the percent of a target audience that is exposed to an ad at least once. The definition of *frequency* is the average number of times that a person who was reached sees an ad. These three concepts are bound together with the equation:

$$\text{Gross Rating Points} = \text{Reach} \times \text{Frequency}.$$

For example, a television schedule of 200 W25–54 GRPs in prime-time is a collection of spots whose W25–54 ratings add up to 200. Computer models based on Nielsen data tell us this schedule will be seen by (will reach) 61 percent of these women an average of about 3.3 times (61 x 3.3 = 198). Some will see the commercial only once, others will see it many times, but the average woman who was reached will see it 3.3 times. Conversely, 39 percent will never see the commercial.

Other terms that are sometimes used to describe reach are *cumulative audience* (referred to as *cume*), *net unduplicated audience*, or *net reach*. Each is correct, but in popular usage television media buyers are more likely to say, "The reach of these four programs is 60 percent."

The ad unit   Everything that is sold comes in some kind of unit. In the US, meat is sold in pounds, gasoline in gallons, fabric in yards, and so forth. For digital advertising the most common unit is a banner ad; in television and radio the unit of sale is typically a 15- or 30-second commercial; in magazines, the page; and in newspapers, the column inch.

Ad unit efficiency   The type of ad unit is merely descriptive, but the type of unit does not give any information about the efficiency of the unit based on how many people will see it. Advertisers and their agencies generally use cost-per-thousand (CPM) impressions as the measure of media efficiency. It is calculated by simply dividing the cost of the ad by thousands of impressions. For example, a 30-second commercial on "The Big Bang Theory" costs \$285,000; the average minute A18+ impressions = 18,630,000; therefore, the CPM for W25–54 = \$285,000 / 18,630 = \$15.30.

Cost-per-rating-point (CPP)   CPM is useful for comparing the efficiency of different programs, schedules, or media, but for planning purposes the cost-per-rating-point (CPP) metric is more practical. CPP is used when planning spot television or spot radio (see Chapter 22: Television for a definition of spot, or market-to-market, television). So if the "The Big Bang Theory" got a 5.0 rating and a 30-second commercial cost \$285,000, the CPP would be \$285,000 / 5 = \$57,000. Local television market CPP information can be obtained by paying for a subscription to SQUAD at www.sqad.com.

Digital

When they buy digital advertising, advertisers buy a certain number of ad impressions that are served to a user's computer browser on a smartphone, laptop, tablet, or other device. For example, one element of an online campaign may be 500,000 impressions served to visitors to one of ESPN's several websites or apps. These impressions might be purchased at a CPM of \$10.00 per thousand either direct from a salesperson or programmatically through a private exchange. A total ad buy is often tens of millions of impressions scattered over dozens of websites or apps. Delivering those impressions is the job of companies that are referred to as third-party ad servers, such as Google Ad Manager (formerly DoubleClick), that keep track of which sites should get how many impressions. The ad-serving companies deliver ads as they are requested by users' browsers, and then bill an advertiser when the required number of impressions has been reached.

Each occurrence of an ad being displayed is an impression. Engagement with an ad impression is the main way the success of an ad is measured, which, in turn, is determined by the size, type, placement, and context of the ad that is actually served to an end user.

However, a count of impressions does not say anything about the demographics of a website's or an app's visitors. Demographics are data about the size and characteristics of an audience.

Digital advertising depends on data, which are values of qualitative or quantitative variables, belonging to a set of items. In the past, the majority of people accessed the Internet used personal computers and desktop systems. However, mobile has become the way the vast majority of consumers access the Internet.

A mobile device ID is a unique identifier for a mobile device. The device ID cannot be linked to personally identifiable information (PII). Different operating systems use different identifiers: IDFA (iOS), AAID (Android), and Windows Advertising ID (Windows).

Digital ad effectiveness terminology

Marketers want to know how well their advertising is doing, so they have to measure ad effectiveness. Marketers use many different metrics to measure their advertising effectiveness, and the effectiveness of an advertising campaign usually increases over time with many different messages or exposures. But certain advertising objectives can be realized almost immediately using measuring techniques such as clicks, conversions, or registrations. Following are some of the terms advertisers and agencies use when evaluating how ads perform.

Unique visitor   Internet users may visit the same page or site many times, so it is important to be able to consolidate those visits into one statistic. This statistic is known as a *unique visitor*, often referred to as *uniques*, which is someone with a unique address who is viewing web content for the first time. Thus, a visitor who returns within the same day is not counted twice. The concept of unique visitors on the Internet is the same as the concept of cume, or cumulative audience, in broadcasting. Both count how many different people see or hear media content. A unique visitor count tells how many different people there are in an audience during a specified time period, usually a month, but not how many times they visited the site during that period of time.

Uniques are identified by unique user ID, which is sometimes called a UUID. A unique, anonymous user ID for a given user profile may be stored in a user's browser cookie and/or in a server-side cookie store. Ad traffickers are not permitted to associate these IDs in any way with personally identifiable information (PII), and user IDs do not necessarily equate to a unique individual. An individual may also be associated with multiple user IDs due to deleting cookies on their device or using multiple browsers and multiple devices. Additionally, for mobile devices, a unique user ID may be associated with multiple device IDs such as an Apple IDFA or an Open UDID.

Heat map   This is visual representation of user activity such as clicks and eye focus on a website. Heat maps are used to determine which pages and ads are being viewed and which are not.

Shopper ID   This, on the other hand, is information provided by a customer at the time of checkout, such as a telephone number, name and address, email address, loyalty card, or credit card.

Click   According to ad industry recommended guidelines, a click is when a visitor interacts with an ad. This does not apparently mean simply interacting with a rich media ad, but actually clicking on it so that the visitor is headed toward an advertiser's destination. It also does not mean that the visitor actually waits to fully arrive at the destination, but just that the visitor started going there. The click-through rate (CTR) measures the number of click-throughs received by an ad divided by the number of ad impressions. This is a key performance indicator for the effectiveness of digital ads. As you have read, one way to purchase ads is by cost-per click (CPC), in which the advertiser pays according to the number of clicks attributed to a campaign.

Pageview A pageview is an Internet or mobile user visiting a webpage on a given digital property. Pageviews are an important measurement of which pages are being visited on a website.

Conversion When a customer actually purchases a product or service, that is known as a conversion. This is an event showing a user has become a customer of the advertiser. The conversion event can be defined by various of actions, such as a successful page landing, a registration on the advertiser's website, an email subscription, making a deposit, or purchasing a product, for example. One way to measure conversion is through the use of a conversion pixel, which is a 1×1 image or a pixel placed on a webpage, such as a thank-you page, which is triggered whenever a conversion occurs.

In some cases, an advertiser pays according to consumers taking an action such as actually purchasing a product or service, registering for a download, or a completed a lead form. This type of payment is referred to as a cost-per-acquisition (CPA) model.

Attribution models These are composed of rules, or sets of rules, that determine how credit for sales and conversions is assigned to touchpoints in the conversion path. For example, the Last Interaction Model assigns 100 percent credit to the final touchpoints that immediately precede sales or conversions. Below are several other attribution models.

Probabilistic models use data points to guess who the consumer is on the other side of the screen. Knowing where a person is, what time it is, and the device in use help, but not with nearly 100 percent confidence. This type of data is considered less accurate than deterministic models.

Deterministic models consist of data that can accurately identify a consumer for targeting ads, such as a visitor's login information for a website. Other deterministic data points are credit cards, phone numbers, and email addresses.

First touch is an attribution model in which gives credit for the first impression a user saw. This may be used as an alternative to the last view/last click model, which gives credit for the last viewed or clicked ad.

Last click is an attribution model that pays out on the last impression that was clicked on by the user. This may be used as an alternative to the first-touch model, which gives credit for the first impression a user saw.

Last view is a type of attribution model that pays out on the last impression that was viewed by a user. This may be used as an alternative to the first-touch model, which gives credit for the first impression a user saw.

Screenshots   Once an ad campaign is complete, an advertiser is given screenshots of webpages or apps showing specific ads, for the purpose of proving to the advertiser that their ads ran in the way the advertiser wanted.

Yield   It is important that advertisers understand the yield of an ad, which is the percentage of clicks versus impressions on an ad within a specific page.

How advertisers get digital campaign information

Advertisers run campaigns, which are specific marketing initiatives, identified by a time period and a specific objective or message. In order to get a sense of how a campaign is performing, advertisers and their agencies can use a *dashboard*, which contains charts and graphs that provide a snapshot of campaign performance at a given point in time so evaluators can spot problems, or identify marketplace opportunities, and shift gears, if a better course of action is required.

Look-alike targeting   Defining a specific audience is important. *Look-alike targeting* is one method of determining an audience. Look-alike targeting is when a target audience is built using the attributes of a specific customer profile in order to find other users with the same interests.

The decision advertisers make about where, how, and whether to run a campaign is usually based on return on investment (ROI). This is a performance measure used to evaluate the efficiency of an investment or to compare the efficiency of a number of different investments. To calculate ROI, typically sales, is divided by the cost of an ad or campaign. Return on investment is a very popular metric because of its versatility and simplicity. That is, if an investment does not have a positive ROI, or if there are other opportunities with a higher ROI, then the investment should be not be undertaken.

Campaign optimization   Campaign optimization saves time and money while helping marketers achieve and improve upon business objectives, efficiently collect the necessary data to analyze marketing campaigns, and make informed data-driven business decisions. Campaign analysis not only helps marketers to reduce waste by making short term fixes to marketing campaign mix but can also provide the marketer with insight into maximizing the lifetime value of a customer over time.

Lift   In the context of yield management or product sales, lift is the percentage by which an ad was optimized. It is calculated by finding the percentage difference between the optimized group of ads and a control group of ads.

Activation   The execution of the marketing mix as part of the marketing process is called *activation*. The activation phase typically comes after the planning phase during which managers plan their marketing activities and is followed by a feedback phase in which results are evaluated with marketing analytics.

Using specific media, frequency determines how many times, on average, the individuals in your target audience should be exposed to your advertising message. It takes an average of three or many more exposures to an advertising message before consumers take action.

Acquisition   Users use the web regularly for shopping and other things. When they sign up, make a purchase, or perform some other desired action in response to an ad displayed on the Internet it is call an *acquisition*, and is also known as a *conversion* or *action*.

When an open slot of ad space is available on the Internet, a user's browser sends requests to ad exchanges or ad servers to send an ad. This request is known as an *ad call*. Ad calls include information from browser cookies and ad tag information such as publisher ID, size, location, referring URL, and other specifications and data needed for the ad to serve.

Frequency capping   This is a way to limit the showing of an ad over time. For example, an advertiser might want to avoid showing an ad to a specific user ID more than once per hour.

Tracking Ads

A substantial amount of information about end users is captured automatically as they surf the web. As ads and other elements are serviced, information is gathered about users. The various pieces of gathered information are called *attributes*, which are known information about a user that can be used to match them to ad content they would be interested in based on their demographics, segmentation, and retargeting information.

Identity graph   An identity graph is a database that houses all the known identifiers that correlate with individual customers. These are used to understand which ads to target to individual users.

Privacy is a big concern among consumers, and the use of personally identifiable information is declining. This is data that allows a user to be identified by their true identity, which includes their name, birth date, gender, and social security number, for example. Sites collect this via the registration process.

The following are some terms about tracking:

Bounce rate is the percentage of people who visit a website but leave without visiting any other page. Engagement is a measure of how consumers interact with ads about their involvement.

Clickstream is a recorded path of the pages a user requested in going through one or more websites. Clickstream information can help website owners understand how visitors are using their site and which pages are getting the most use. It can help advertisers understand how users get to the client's pages, what pages they look at, and how they go about ordering a product.

Cookies are small text files on the user's PC that identifies the user's browser so that they are recognized when they revisit a site. *Cookie syncing* is the process of matching the user IDs from one system to another. This allows supply-side platforms and demand-side platforms to identify the same browser for the purpose of retargeting browsers through the ad exchanges.

Analytics, also known as *web metrics*, collect the data about a website and its visitors. Analytics programs typically give performance data on clicks, time spent, pages viewed, website paths, and a variety of other information that can be found on Google Analytics. The proper use of web analytics allows website owners to improve their visitor experience, which often leads to higher ROI for profit-based sites.

Pixels are a method used track user data, and the information is used as a basis for analytics about the user and their actions as they surf the web. Originally, all pixels were literally snippets of code that called for a 1 X 1 transparent pixel to be delivered to a webpage by a third-party server. Nowadays, pixels may either be literal pixels or be Javascript based. When the pixel loads, the third-party server can record information such as the IP address of the user's computer, URL of the page, and time the page was viewed. (See also conversion pixel under "Conversion" above.) When more information is needed or must be reported to an additional party, a *piggyback* may be used. This term usually refers specifically to a piggybacked pixel. When pixel A has pixel B piggybacked on to it, then the firing of pixel A causes the firing of pixel B. This second firing can either be via a redirect or a server-side firing. Piggyback pixels may be used for tracking conversions in secondary systems.

Over time, people get tired of viewing advertisements due to saturation,or personal preferences, or for other reasons. This leads to *banner blindness*, which is the tendency of web visitors to ignore display ads when consuming content online, leading to low click rates, low visibility for advertisers, and low revenue for publishers.

A recent trend is for people to install software that removes ads from webpages. These are called *ad blockers*, and they are software products that prevents ads from appearing with the content the user is intentionally viewing. As discussed in Chapter 17, people block ads for a variety of reasons. For example, many of them find interrupt marketing ads annoying and even stressful. Interrupt marketing is intrusive by design, like an interstitial ad that comes between users and the content they are attempting to view or an autoplay or rollover ad that starts up without any intentional act on the part of the user.

Malicious individuals have come up with a number of ways to attempt to game the system. One of the most common is *click fraud*, which are clicks that are generated falsely, either by humans or artificially with the intent to creating a click on a search engine listing or text ad, forcing the advertiser to pay even though the click is not real. Search engines have measures to try and prevent this. Indicators of click fraud are a spike in clicks and can be monitored by collecting log file and visitor data.

Digital Measurement Services

Two research companies provide measurement of Internet traffic: Nielsen NetRatings, a division of Nielsen Online, and comScore. Both use a panel of respondents who agree to allow the research companies to put tracking software on their computer or smartphone. When respondents open their smartphones or logs into a computer, every keystroke is recorded and included in the tabulations.

A visitor to a website can go in and out many times, even in the same session. Each time will be recorded as an impression to the site, yielding a very large but inherently useless number. Web publishers such as the Huff Post use NetRatings or comScore to show the number of unique visitors over a 30-day period, counting each visitor only once.

Unlike other media where the base is essentially the total population in the geographic area served by a broadcast or print medium, an Internet rating can be calculated from three different bases, or universes:

1 *Total US population*. This base should be used when comparing an Internet rating to other media.
2 *Internet universe*. Persons age 2+ who had access to an Internet-accessible computer or device, whether or not they actually went online in the last month – roughly 85 percent of US population.
3 *Active universe*. Persons age 2+ who have used an Internet-accessible computer or device in the last 30 days – roughly 65–70 percent of the US population.

Typically, web publishers will report their audience in terms of the active universe in order to show the largest percentage.

For example, a comScore report may show the many ways of evaluating the visitors to a website. These evaluations might include the number of page views seen by each unique visitor, the number of sessions over the month, the time spent with the site per person, and other metrics. A report can be broken down by home and work samples. *Active reach* is computed against the active universe. *Universe reach* is computed against the Internet universe. The research firm comScore does not calculate reach against the total U.S. population.

Reports from comScore and Nielsen give a buyer a complete picture of the size and demographics of a website's visitors, but there is a big difference between this information and a television rating. When a commercial appears on a television program with five million viewers, we know that when it is finished, five million people will have seen it, or at least will have had the commercial displayed on their television set.

The Internet is different. For example, a comScore or Nielsen report on ESPN.com might show that over the course of a month, 600,000 uniques will have visited ESPN.com at least once. But that number is meaningless to the Internet advertiser who decides to buy only one million impressions. And, unlike television that delivers the impressions all at once, it takes time for the impressions to be delivered on the Internet. As each browser requests a page of content from ESPN.com, the third-party ad server sends it an ad. But the server handles many advertisers, so those one million impressions do not all go to the first million browsers. It takes time, days or even weeks for less-popular sites, before there will be enough requests for pages that the server can deliver the one-million impressions an advertiser wants. In short, television exposures are immediate, Internet exposures are delivered over a period of time, possibly several weeks.

The proper evaluative metric of a website for an advertiser is determined by the number of impressions that are bought, not by the total number of visitors. Media buyers use the comScore's PlanMetrix Reach/Frequency system or Nielsen NetRating's

WebRF program to show the net reach of an Internet campaign across many websites.

For example, an advertiser might buy 50 million page views (impressions) against a target of M18–34, focusing on sports websites. A comScore or Nielsen report defines the unique and total audience reach indicated by the number of impressions for each site. It may also reflect combined campaign or total site statistics in terms of gross rating points (reach x frequency), average frequency (OTS = opportunities to see), and total rating points (gross rating points for a defined audience target) for the base of the active audience universe.

The Top Five Questions Measurement Cannot Answer

Up to now we have discussed the general concepts and methodologies of measuring advertising. However, in the course of a salesperson's work, other questions come up for which there is no simple answer. These are the most important questions in media because they involve subtle judgments about what is best for a particular customer or a particular campaign.

The following frequently asked questions cannot be definitively answered because they depend on what is happening in the mind of each consumer. They are presented here to characterize them as "impossible" questions, to sensitize salespeople to the inevitable day when one of them comes up in the course of their work, and to provide something to say and ways to think about helping an advertiser make a reasonable judgment.

1 How much is enough?

This is the most common question, and it takes many forms. What is the least I can invest and still have an effective campaign? If I invest in X number of impressions against my primary target audience, am I delivering enough weight against the secondary target? My last campaign was wildly successful. I ran XX number of impressions and actually had to turn away customers. Next time, how much weight can I cut back and still be successful?

There are several approaches to answering this question that will put an advertiser in an effective ROI ballpark. If an advertiser has competitive sales and spending information, it is common to match the share of voice to the share of market. An advertiser with a 10 percent share of a market should be spending at least 10 percent of the media dollars spent in that industry. Certainly, an advertiser should look back at the experience with comparable products. For example, some industries have an historic advertising to sales ratio. Go to http://mediaselling.us/downloads/ to see the ad-to-sales ratios for 200 industries.

A widely accepted heuristic, or rule of thumb, is that an ad must be seen three or more times for it to be effective. While this sounds like a reasonable prescription, it finesses the question, "How many people can I afford to reach 3+ times?" In the end, and unfortunately, many advertising budgets are simply what remains after all other costs have been accounted for.

2 Which medium is most effective?

Effective at doing what? Different media have different strengths. Effectiveness is heavily dependent on the creative quality. Many people think television is the most effective medium, but other alternatives must be considered when television is not appropriate or affordable. There are virtually no independent, public domain studies of cross-media effectiveness. Advertisers who do conduct these studies treat the results as highly confidential. What publicly available research does exist comes from industry associations whose studies are designed to promote the value of their medium. As they say, "Don't ask your barber if you need a haircut." The best advice is to ensure the advertiser has matched the strength of the media to the marketing objectives.

3 What medium provides the best environment?

This question assumes there is a rub-off effect between the medium and the advertising message; however, as noted earlier, numerous studies have failed to quantify that effect, or even to confirm that it exists. We know that high-rated television programs attract more light viewers, but there is a heavy cost premium for these iconic programs. The first position in a commercial break has a larger audience than mid-break positions, but pod position is usually beyond a buyer's control or beyond their budget if pod position is charged for.

In magazines, an ad on the back cover is more likely to be read than one inside, but advertisers pay a premium for that position. Some advertisers believe a magazine ad near the front of the book is preferable, but since most insertion orders request "Far forward, right hand page" these (assumed to be) desirable positions are more likely to be given to advertisers running a heavy schedule. At the least, salespeople should ensure that advertisers running multiple insertions are given a fair rotation.

4 Which is better, flighting or continuity?

This age-old question concerns how a limited advertising budget should be scheduled over the year: In short bursts of heavy media weight followed by hiatus weeks of no activity (i.e., flighting) or continuous advertising at low weight? If the budget allows the advertiser to buy 1,600 GRPs a year, should they be scheduled in four four-week flights (total 16 weeks on-air) of 100 GRPs/week? Or would it be more effective to run for 40 weeks at 40 GRPs/week?

For products that are sold more or less evenly throughout the year, advertisers are guided by the "recency theory of advertising" that was proposed by media guru Erwin

Ephron. In contrast to the theory that three exposures are needed, the recency theory is based on research that shows a single exposure close to purchase is most effective. Since there is a steady demand for non-seasonal products, the advertiser should maintain a continuous presence on-air. The goal should be to maximize the total weekly reach points (the annual sum of each week's reach points). This is achieved by continuity scheduling.

However, continuity scheduling ignores the effect of competitors' advertising that may be flighted. Also, there is a need for synergy between the advertising and seasonal consumer or trade promotions. Finally, there is a reluctance to go below a perceived minimal level of about 50 GRPs per week. Most advertisers appreciate the importance of continuity, but given this minimum, they find continuity scheduling to be an ideal that is beyond their brand's budget.

5 When is my commercial worn out?

It is hard enough to know how impactful a commercial is when it is fresh. Commercial wearout is really a variation of the "How much is enough?" question. An industry rule-of-thumb is that a commercial is worn out when the heaviest viewers are exposed 26 times – somewhere around 1,000–1,500 GRPs. This has become a benchmark against which to judge a given campaign, but many questions remain. Does that rule apply to a single execution or to an entire campaign of similar but different creative executions? Over what period of time? What is the effect of hiatus periods? Is that target rating points or household rating points, which are usually larger?

One researcher sees an agenda behind the question. The agency wants to make a new commercial and the advertiser does not or vice versa. People who are closely involved with the lengthy creative process may be so close to the commercial that they will think it is worn out when in fact it has not even been aired.

It should be clear by now that there is no simple answer to these "How much is enough" questions of effective frequency, flighting versus continuity, minimum GRP levels, maximum hiatus weeks, media effectiveness, and wearout. Research can provide guidance, but in the end, it requires buyer and salesperson judgment to apply these general findings from the past to specific plans for the future in order to get the best results for customers

Test Yourself

1. What is the most important marketing decision an advertiser makes?
2. What is a DMA?
3. What is a rating?
4. How are gross impressions and GRPs calculated?
5. What is a cume?
6. What is PII?

7. What is "a unique"?
8. What are five attribution models?
9. What is lift?
10. Describe click fraud.
11. What are the five questions that measurement cannot answer?

Project

Listen to an eMarketer Weekly Review podcast and then go eMarketer.com and look for the report that shows the data reported in the podcast. Look at the sources for that data and then go the websites of the data providers to see if you can verify that eMarketer has reported the data accurately.

Resources

Ad Age (www.adage.com)
Adweek (www.adweek.com)
BPA Worldwide verified audience and research information (www.bpaww.com)
eMarketer strategic analysis of Internet trends (www.emarketer.com)
eMarketer's "Behind the Numbers" podcast (www.soundcloud.com/behind-the-numbers)
MediaPost (www.mediapost.com)
MRI Simmons (www.mrisimmons.com)
Nielsen Media Research (www.nielsenmedia.com)
SQAD subscription site for local and national CPP data (www.sqad.com)

References

Katz, Helen. 2019. *The Media Handbook, 7th Edition: A Complete Guide to Advertising, Media Selection, Planning, Research, and Buying.* New York: Routledge.

Martin, Dennis. 2014. *Media Flight Plan*, 7th ed. Saint George, UT: Deer Creek Publishing.

Sissors, Jack Z. and Baron, Roger B. 2010. *Advertising Media Planning*, 7th ed. New York: McGraw-Hill.

19

Selling Digital and Cross-Platform Advertising

Charles Warner

If you sell advertising in the media today, the odds are about nine out of ten that you are selling digital advertising in some form because in 2018 ad revenue in digital advertising surpassed ad revenue in all traditional media combined.[1] Also, virtually every traditional medium in today's media ecosystem – television, radio, newspapers, magazines, and out-of-home (OOH) – has a digital content or digital insertion component. For example, broadcast and cable television networks all have apps that allow consumers to stream content, including ads, to their smartphones or tablets. Virtually all local television and radio stations have websites and apps that carry advertising, as do practically all local newspapers and magazines. Figure 19.1 shows digital contribution to local media revenue in 2018.

Salespeople who sell for traditional media that have websites will often sell the online and offline media either separately or in some sort of bundled packages. Selling both online and offline channels is referred to as cross-platform selling. You will learn about the methods of selling television advertising in Chapter 22, of selling newspapers, or magazines, or OOH advertising in Chapter 23, and selling radio and podcasts in Chapter 24.

In this chapter you will learn about selling digital advertising only or as the digital component on a cross-platform basis.

The Landscape of Digital Advertising

As you learned in Chapter 16, in 2018 advertisers invested $10 billion more in digital advertising ($78.28 billion) than they invested in the number two medium, television

Media Selling: Digital, Television, Audio, Print and Cross-Platform, Fifth Edition.
Charles Warner, William A. Lederer, and Brian Moroz.
© 2020 John Wiley & Sons, Inc. Published 2020 by John Wiley & Sons, Inc.

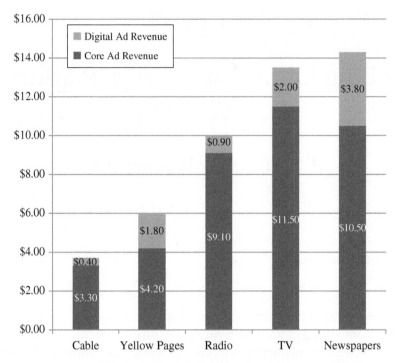

Figure 19.1   Digital's contribution to traditional local media in $billions
Source: *Radio Ink*. 2019. "Are you getting your fair share of digital revenue?" https://
radioink.com/2019/04/04/are-you-getting-your-fair-share-of-digital-revenue.

($68.21 billion), which included broadcast television, cable television, and syndicated television.[i] Advertisers invested $17.57 billion annually in 2018 in the number three medium, radio, which is about one-quarter of what advertisers invest in digital advertising.

Of the ad dollars invested in digital in 2018, about 60 percent was in mobile advertising, and the Google–Facebook duopoly gobbled up almost 58 percent (Google = 37.14 percent and Facebook = 20.57 percent) of all digital advertising investments.[2] The powerful duopoly also accumulated about 90 percent of the increase in digital investments in 2018 over 2017. In 2018, Amazon was third in digital ad revenue with 4.5 percent of the total, edging out Microsoft and Oath

---

[i] Broadcast syndication is the licensing of programs to multiple local stations without going through a network distribution system. In television there are two types of syndicated programs: first-run and off-network. "Jeopardy" and "Wheel of Fortune" are examples of first-run syndicated programs, and "Seinfeld" and "Everyone Loves Raymond" are examples of off-network syndicated programs. Advertisers and agencies can buy commercials on local television stations in syndicated programs on a market-by-market (spot TV) basis, and typically stations pay for a syndicated program in part by giving the syndicator two of the commercial positions in each showing of the program, which the syndication companies sell to national advertisers and their agencies.

(a now-defunct combination of AOL and Yahoo, owned by Verizon) which both had just over 3 percent of all digital ad revenue for the year.[3] In 2019, Amazon made a major advertising push that began with an announcement of the introduction of a new API for self-serve ads (see the Appendix for a glossary of digital advertising terms, including API).[4] The research firm eMarketer estimates that Amazon's share of online ad dollars will increase from 6.8 percent in 2018 to 7.6 percent in 2019 and to 8.6 percent in 2020.[5] Another reason for Amazon's growth is that many marketers are looking favorably at advertising on Amazon because they see the Amazon platform as having a more brand-safe environment than many of the sites that their ads appear on when they buy programmatically.[6]

The digital Goliaths

Google, Facebook, and Amazon dominate the digital advertising space for several reasons: (1) no ad-tech tax, (2) best return on investment ROI, (3) effective targeting, (4) ad-blocking software does not work on Amazon or apps, and (5) free support for large advertisers.

No ad-tech tax   Over 80 percent of all digital display ads are bought and sold programmatically. Buying ads programmatically has several advantages, among them being that programmatic buying allows advertisers to target individuals on a wide variety of dimensions: by age, by income, by gender, by lifestyle, by interests, by attitudes, by geography, by health, by purchase history, by browsing history, by occupation, by life stage, by purchase intentions, by content-type consumption, by credit history, and by residence type and tenure. Another advantage of programmatic is that it is often less expensive than buying from a salesperson.

On the other hand, there are some disadvantages of buying programmatically. One of those disadvantages is that there are costs involved in programmatic buying that do not go to the publisher of the content in which an ad is inserted. A programmatic buyer has to pay for automated demand-side platform (DSP) software to negotiate and place a buy, pay for an exchange on which available digital inventory is listed, pay for data from second- and third-party data providers for each dimension an advertiser wants to target, and pay for other services such as verification that a digital ad ran. All of these interactions with middleman companies have costs attached to them and, therefore, more than 50 percent of what an advertiser pays for a programmatic buy typically goes to a middleman company and not to the content publisher that runs the ad, as you learned in Chapter 17. These added costs are referred to as an *ad-tech tax*. Google, Facebook, and Amazon have their own first-party data that is included in the cost of their ads, so virtually 100 percent of what an advertiser pays for an ad goes to Google, Facebook, or Amazon and not to a middleman company. The net effect is that an advertiser gets more advertising bang for their buck on these three Goliaths than they get with most other programmatic buys. Also, buying ads on both Google and Facebook is very complex because they offer so many targeting, size, and placement options. Therefore, many advertisers use digital advertising agencies or marketing partners to execute digital ad buys on the two platforms. However, typically such agencies or marketing partners charge anywhere between 10 and 20 percent of the digital media budget to place advertising, but the 10–20 percent charge is still much less than a 50 percent or more ad-tech tax advertisers pay to buy programmatically on content, platforms, or networks other than Facebook or Google.

Best ROI   A February, 2018, article titled "Digital ad buyers say Google Search, Facebook deliver best ROI" reports on the results of a survey of digital ad buyers. Forty-eight percent of the responding buyers said Google search had the highest ROI, 30 percent said Facebook had the best ROI, only 8 percent cited ad exchanges and ad networks, only 4 percent said Instagram (owned by Facebook), and only 2 percent cited Twitter has having the best ROI.[7] Without imposing a tech tax, Google, Facebook, and Amazon have a built-in advantage, which goes a long way to explaining their Goliath status.

Effective targeting   Because Google, Facebook and Amazon use their own first-party data for targeting (and they have massive amounts of first-party data), their targeting dimensions and data tend to be more accurate than many second- and third-party data aggregators and data management platforms whose data are often outdated, messy, and inaccurate.

Ad-blocking software does not work on Amazon or apps   Google and Facebook also diligently try to impede ad-blocking software, which an estimated 21.5 percent of Americans Internet users have installed.[8] And a large majority of those who use ad-blocking software are millennials and Generation Zs, who are the most sought-after consumers.[9] It is also logical to assume that many people disable ad-blocking software when they are searching on Google because they want the search results and the ads associated with those results. Also, the vast majority of traffic to Facebook, Instagram, and Twitter comes from apps, and a user cannot block ads on an app. Ad-blocking software only works on a browser such as Chrome, Safari, or Firefox.

Free support for large advertisers   Google and Facebook manage large accounts free of charge. Neither company will reveal what the minimum yearly investment is in order for them to manage an account, but knowledgeable people in the industry estimate that for either of them to manage an account the investment must be about $1 million a year, with the potential for an even higher investment in subsequent years. Having a partner such as Google or Facebook do all the work involved in online auction bidding, scheduling, and optimization brings to mind the quip that "it's hard to compete against free."

David versus Goliath

David versus Goliath is a metaphor for an underdog being successful in the face of enormous odds. So, how does a digital David who does not sell for Google, Facebook, or Amazon be successful in the presence of these online Goliaths? There are three strategies that can be employed: (1) expertise, (2) inclusivity, and (3) focus on new opportunities.

Expertise   If we go back to the AESKOPP approach to selling introduced in Chapter 2 and discussed in detail in Chapter 4, the K in AESKOPP is for *knowledge*. In Chapter 4 knowledge was defined: "Knowledge means knowing the product you are selling in depth – knowing more about it than customers do so you can educate them. For sales-people, it means having information not only about their product and its underlying technology, but also about measurement and data analysis, about marketing, about advertising, about a customer's business, and about competitive media."

You learned about measurement in Chapter 18, you learned about advertising in Chapter 16, about marketing in Chapter 15, and about researching for customer insights and solutions in Chapter 10. In this chapter you are learning about selling digital media channels.

If you are currently selling digital advertising by itself or on a cross-platform basis, you may already be knowledgeable about the underlying technology. Or, if you are member of Generation Z and were born after 1996, you are probably familiar with much of the functionality of the Internet and have an intuitive understanding of how the Internet works and the many benefits it brings to people around the world. Being knowledgeable about how the Internet works and having an intuitive understanding does not make you an expert, which is important for you to be if you are going to reach the peak of your potential selling digital or cross-platform advertising.

In a *Harvard Business Review* article titled "Do you really know who your best sales-people are?" the authors of the article report on their research on the effectiveness of 800 salespeople.[10] The authors Ryals and Davies evaluated B2B salespeople on seven selling skills: (1) meeting preparation, (2) customer interaction, (3) company representation, (4) presentation rapport, (5) the sales pitch, (6) storytelling, and (7) rising to the challenge. Ryals and Davies discovered eight sales types in their observation of how the salespeople they studied performed in meetings with customers. Exhibit 19.1 shows the eight types of salespeople ranked in order of their effectiveness, the percentage of those observed in each type, and a description of each type.

Exhibit 19.1   Sales types

The Best

1   **Experts:** 9%
    Experts make selling seem effortless, keep customers, and consistently outperform their peers.

2   **Closers:** 13%
    Closers close some really big deals (typically in product sales rather than in service sales) and can effectively counter customer objections. But their smooth-talking style puts off some customers. They need mentoring in developing a lighter touch in order to improve the selling of services.

3   **Consultants:** 15%
    Consultants listen well and are good problem-solvers; they develop solutions that meet their customers' needs. But they tend to be one-dimensional and to forgo using valuable case studies that could boost sales. They too often leave money on the table, but they have the potential to become experts.

Exhibit 19.1   Sales types (cont'd)

The Rest

4   **Storytellers:** 7%

Storytellers are customer focused and love to provide case studies, but the often "talk through the sale" and waste too much time in long meetings that do not yield results. They do not read closing signals well.

5   **Focusers:** 19%

Focusers know their products well and believe deeply in their products, but they lack confidence. They often insist on detailing every product feature and, thus, may not be good listeners, so they do not hear their customers' needs.

6   **Narrators:** 15%

Narrators know their offerings and the market but are overly dependent on scripts. They cling desperately to marketing materials and fail to respond adequately to challenging questions and do not focus enough on customers.

7   **Aggressors:** 7%

Aggressors approach sales meetings purely as price negotiators. They can at times score big deals, and they rarely concede too much; however, too many customers dislike their combative approach. They need to be more self-aware and know the market better.

8   **Socializers:** 15%

Socializers may initially impress customers with their friendly chat about such things as children and cars, but they too often do not get past this chit-chat and, therefore, close few deals.

Adapted from Ryals, Lynette and Davies, Iain. 2010. "Do you really know who your best salespeople are?" *Harvard Business Review,* December.

If you strive to be an expert in selling digital or cross-platform advertising, you must understand the underlying functionality and technology of that advertising, which is much easier if you are a member of the Internet generation, or Generation Z. If so, you probably have an intuitive understanding of digital advertising, social media, and how the Internet works, but it is still a good idea to read and absorb the Glossary of Digital Advertising terms in the Appendix of this book. Study the Glossary carefully and make sure you are familiar with the terminology of digital advertising. Also, you should know the types of digital ads that are being served, the most prevalent of which are shown in Exhibit 19.2. Exhibit 19.2 also has some of the important terminology for video ads.

You should also go to the IAB New Ad Portfolio website https://www.iab.com/newadportfolio and click on the Ad Portfolio Guidelines and the FAQ links on the lower left part of the screen. Study the IAB New Standard Ad Unit Portfolio and the FAQs carefully so you understand the standard digital unit ad sizes and their aspect ratios and can explain them clearly to prospects and customers. These standard ad unit sizes for desktop and mobile do not apply to Google search results ads, to Google AdSense ads, or to Facebook ads, which have their own formats.

I also strongly recommend that you consider getting a Digital Media Certification from the IAB. Go to https://www.iab.com/certification-programs/iab-digital-media-sales-certification for the certification program. In the program you will learn: (1) How the digital advertising ecosystem works, (2) programmatic fundamentals, (3) digital ad formats, creative, and platforms, (4) ad serving terms and technology, (5) tools used for

Exhibit 19.2 Types of digital ads

Display is any ad other than a Google search ad, a classified ad, or video ad. Display ads can be a variety of sizes and often contain color, graphics, and pictures. They are created by an advertiser or an agency and ad-served to online content by means of ad tags inserted into the HTML code of a page.

Rollover ads (sometimes called *mouse-over ads*) are online ads that appear to be a static image until the cursor touches the image and activates it. Movement of the cursor over the image is known as a *rollover*. In the case of a rollover ad, activation usually causes an expansion of the ad.

Pop-up ads are an abused type of digital ads. Pop-ups open new windows on a device screen that partially or wholly cover a web browser window. Some search engines ban ads that create a certain number (or even any) pop-up ads.

Pop-under ads are ads that open in a new web browser window once you visit a particular page or take some other action. Pop-under ads are considered less annoying than pop-up ads because the new window appears behind the existing one.

Pre-roll ads are promotional video messages that play before the content a user has selected. Video ads are often repurposed television ads, sometimes shortened to 10 or 15 seconds because the 30-second standard for ads on television is not suitable for online videos, which are themselves frequently only a few minutes long.

An interstitial is a page that is inserted in the normal flow of editorial content structure on a website for the purpose of advertising or promotion. An interstitial ad can be more or less intrusive, and the reaction of viewers usually depends on how welcome or entertaining the message is.

Leaderboard is a standard display ad that is 728 pixels wide by 90 pixels high.

Medium Rectangle is a standard display ad that is 300 pixels wide by 250 pixels high.

Skyscraper is a standard display ad that is 160 pixels wide by 600 pixels high.

Rich media is advertising that contains perceptual or interactive elements more elaborate than the usual banner ad. Some studies have shown that rich media ads tend to be more effective than ordinary animated banner ads.

House ads are display ads promoting a product or service sold or provided by a publisher of a website on which it appears.

Video ads

Autoplay Video is audiovisual content, usually containing advertisements or promoted content, that starts automatically when a user goes to the host webpage. The purpose of autoplay is to get the user's attention, which it is bound to do so long as the user has sound turned on.

Video ad serving template (VAST) is an XML-based video ad serving protocol. It was created to provide a uniform way for video content to be transferred from ad servers to video players on web pages. For more details, see the Interactive Advertising Bureau (IAB) VAST documentation at https://www.iab.com/guidelines/digital-video-ad-serving-template-vast/.

Video player ad-serving interface definition (VPAID) VAST supports relatively simple in-stream video ad formats that are not executable. VPAID was created to support more interactive rich media video formats. For more information, see the Interactive Advertising Bureau (IAB) VPAID documentation at https://www.iab.com/guidelines/digital-video-player-ad-interface-definition-vpaid-2-0/.

In-banner video is a type of creative played in a standard banner rather than in a video player. Any banner placement may accommodate an in-banner video creative, if allowed by a publisher.

In-stream video is a video ad played before, during, or after the video content a publisher is delivering to a consumer.

booking, trafficking, and implementing campaigns, and (6) digital media standards, regulation, and compliance. Becoming certified by the IAB in digital media sales is an excellent first step in getting a job in selling digital media for several reasons, one of which is that even though you are reading this book and understand what is in it, have answered all the Test Yourself questions, and completed the Projects at the end of each chapter, it is possible that a hiring company has neither heard of nor read this book, but they have certainly heard of and value an IAB Digital Media certification.

Inclusiveness   In the 1970s, 1980s, and early 1990s, newspapers were the number one medium in total advertising revenue, about 12 percent of which was national advertising and 88 percent of which was local advertising.[11] There are several reasons that newspapers' total revenue ranked as number one, most notably because in many cities newspapers had a monopoly and could charge high rates as a result. Another reason is that before the invention of the smartphone, consumers not only read newspapers to keep up with the news, but also to look for deals, mostly from local retailers such as department stores and automotive dealers.

In those earlier decades, local television station salespeople sold hard against newspapers in order to get advertisers to switch. It was a negative sell: "Don't buy dull black-and-white, static newspaper ads. Buy television with sight, color, sound, and emotion." Television salespeople were successful, partly because of the drip-drip over the years of negatively selling against newspapers, but also because national advertisers, and especially their agencies, preferred television because of its huge reach. In the mid-1990s television became the number one medium in total advertising revenue.

Also, during those earlier decades magazine salespeople sold negatively against, newspapers, television, and other magazines. A typical magazine sales pitch might start something like this: "Don't buy *Ladies Home Journal* because its editor is going to be fired soon. Buy *Good Housekeeping*."[ii]

Thus, both local television and national magazine salespeople viewed selling advertising as a zero-sum game in which there could be only one winner and one loser. However, negative, zero-sum selling does not work today for the many reasons, which are detailed in Exhibit 19.3. This is the same as Exhibit 7.6, but is included in this chapter to emphasize the importance of *not* resorting to negative selling.

Another reason that negative selling is not viable is because of the fragmentation of the media that has accelerated in the digital era. In this era, advertising in one medium alone, not even in the Super Bowl, can reach enough people with enough frequency to make sufficient impact for a brand to be successful. In fact, Figure 19.2 shows how adding media platforms to an advertising campaign delivers increasingly higher ROIs with each media platform added.

You can see in Figure 19.2 that the first platform added to a campaign increased the ROI by 19 percent and that each addition platform added four percentage points to the campaign's ROI regardless of the percentage of the total campaign budget that went to each additional platform.

[ii] *Ladies Home Journal* and *Good Housekeeping* were two of the magazines that were referred to as the Seven Sisters. The other five were: *Better Homes and Garden, Family Circle, McCall's, Redbook,* and *Women's Day*.

Exhibit 19.3   Reasons for not knocking (or even mentioning) the competition

Reason	*Description*
Buyers hate it.	How would you like it if every conversation you had during a business day were negative, nasty, and mean spirited? You would probably become depressed. Buyers feel the same way.
You tear down the image of your medium.	After buyers hear how bad several competitors are, they begin to have a negative impression of the whole medium. Knocking the competition is destructive to your medium.
You waste time.	Customers' and buyers' time is limited; you usually have just few minutes to get their attention and make a presentation. If you spend time knocking the competition, you waste valuable time. Remember the old adage, "You can't sell what your competitors don't have." You can only sell the benefits of what you have to offer, so get on with it.
You lose credibility.	When you knock the competition, you are perceived as not being objective. Buyers say to themselves, "Of course you're badmouthing the competition; you're trying to sell me something. Why should I believe you?" Therefore, when you knock competitors, you lose credibility.
You lower your image.	Selling negatively puts your down in the gutter with other negatively selling salespeople. Stay above it; refuse to throw dirt. Buyers will appreciate your positive approach and like you better for it. If your competition goes low, you go high.
You can touch hidden sore spots.	You may not know if a customer or buyer has invested in advertising with a competitor (in your medium or another medium), so if you knock a competitor a buyer has invested in, you are insulting the buyer's judgment. When this happens, buyers become defensive and entrenched, and they vigorously defend their past decisions. Also, a buyer may like a salesperson (may even be dating the salesperson) and when you knock that salesperson's medium, you are knocking the salesperson and the buyer will become very defensive and defend their friend's product (and dislike yours). Remember, the media are an intangible product and, thus, salespeople become the surrogate for their products – they are the products in the minds of buyers.
You build competitors'importance andimage.	Did you ever see an ad in a magazine for Rolex that had a headline "We're better than a Timex?" Never mention the competition below you in rank position; all you do is elevate them to your level. If you mention competitors below you in rank position, buyers' reactions are "Why is this salesperson talking about that competitor? What is the salesperson afraid of?"

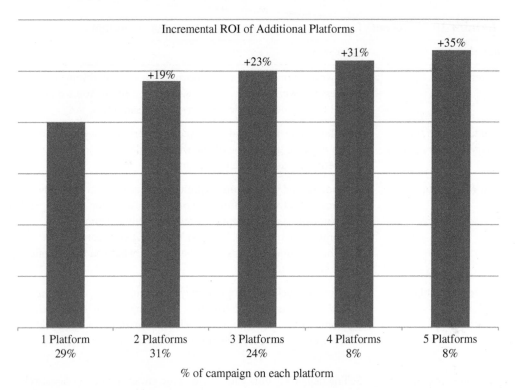

Figure 19.2   Advertising across platforms delivers higher ROI
Source: Analytic Partners, 2016. Analysis based on over 3,000 campaigns from 2010–2015.
https://www.linkedin.com/pulse/mega-post-30-most-important-takeaways-from-three-best-shane-o-leary.

Figure 19.3 demonstrates the economic principle of diminishing marginal returns. In other words, Figure 19.3 shows that adding five percentage points (from 30 to 35 percent) of reach to a prime-time television network schedule more than doubles the cost of Reach CPM. And going from 35 to 40 percent reach for the schedule costs 36 percent more for only 14 percent more reach.[iii]

Essentially, Figure 19.3 shows that increasing the reach of a prime-time television network schedule by five percentage points by adding more commercials to a campaign increases the Reach CPM and is, thus, inefficient. Figures 19.2 and 19.3 are like two sides of a coin that represents ad campaign efficiency. One side of the coin is Figure 19.2, which shows that adding media channels gives a campaign increasing marginal returns in ROI and, thus, adding platforms increases efficiency. Figure 19.3 is the other side of the coin that shows that adding reach to the same channel or platform, in this case network television, increases inefficiency.

[iii] Reach CPM means the cost-per-thousand of reaching unduplicated, different people. A CPM impressions number includes impressions that were seen or heard by some people two, three, four, five, or more times. A Reach CPM refers to the reach of new, unduplicated people. See also Chapter 18.

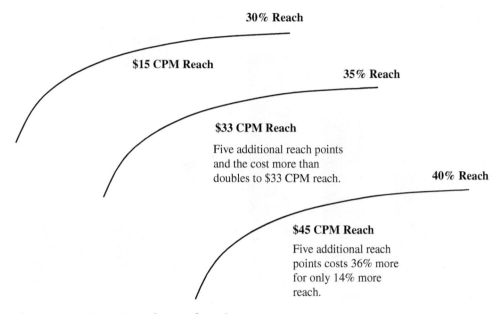

Figure 19.3 Incremental cost of reach
Source: Media Mix presentation at http://www/mediaselling.us/downloads.html.

Putting theory into practice

So, let's assume you are selling for an online newspaper in a top-25 market and are calling on Hess Jewelry. The jewelry store appeals to middle-income consumers and does not sell high-end, expensive jewelry or watches. The first thing you would do is conduct some research on the jewelry business, as you learned in Chapter 10. The second thing you would do is complete an Advertising Planner as described in Chapter 16 and seen in Exhibit 16.8. The third thing you would do is make some decisions about what media channels to recommend to Hess Jewelry, which you are familiar with if you completed the projects at the end of Chapters 3, 6, 7, and 13.

For the purposes of this chapter, we will assume the manager of Hess Jewelry is not Sy Abell, the manager described in the "Sales Dilemma," "Janet Creates Value," and "Janet Negotiates" cases that were referred to in the projects at the end of Chapters 3, 6, 7, and 13 but is a manager who has shared with you Hess's yearly sales figures and is more than willing to learn about what you are recommending. We will also assume that you know enough about the jewelry business to make some recommendations, which will be inclusive and include several media channels.

In order to estimate how to allocate Hess's advertising budget, you should first look at how people spend their time with the various media. See Figure 19.4 for time spent in the media and the total B2C ad revenue going to each medium. Keep in mind that the share of B2C ad revenue is weighted in favor large national advertisers such as GEICO, ATT, Samsung, and General Motors and that broadcast (television and radio) have a lower percentage of ad revenue than time spent more than likely because they lack precise, relevant measurement and, thus, accountability. Personalized, individually

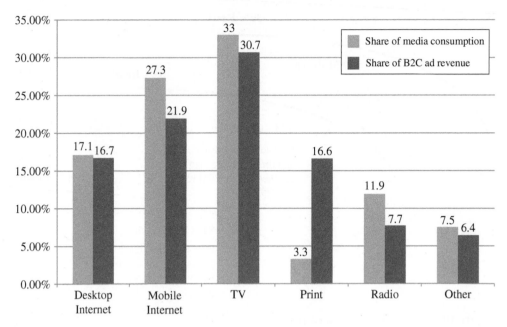

Figure 19.4 How ad spending aligns with media consumption, 2017
Source: IAB, PwC, eMarketer, Business Insider.

targeted, and, thus, accountable digital advertising has precise and relevant measurement that makes it much easier for advertisers to calculate ROI.

As you can see in Figure 19.4, if you combine desktop Internet and mobile Internet, the total Internet share of B2C ad spend is 16.7 + 21.9 = 38.6 percent, which tops television's 30.7 percent. Percent of ad spend (or investment, as you know I prefer) in desktop Internet is about the same as the percentage of time spent, whereas mobile Internet ad investment is 5.4 percentage points less than time spent, meaning that advertisers are investing less in mobile than they could be expected to. Keep in mind that these are 2017 figures and that mobile is the fastest growing of the advertising platforms, so by the end of 2020 many experts are predicting mobile ad investments will overtake total television ad investments.

Also, note in Figure 19.4 that the ad investment in the print versions of newspapers is totally out of whack with the small amount of time the average consumer spends reading a newspaper, which makes print newspapers a vulnerable target.

One way to get a prospect or client involved in thinking about how people spend their time with various media is to ask them how much time they spend watching a screen, and then ask if they spend more time on their television screen or on their smartphone screen. Then, ask how much time they spend reading the print version of their local newspaper. They will more than likely get the point without your saying anything negative about newspapers. On the other hand, they might be avid readers of a printed local newspaper and say, "I and all my friends read the newspaper every morning. Everybody reads the newspaper." If a client makes a statement similar to this, you might tell them the polo assumption story in Exhibit 19.4.

Exhibit 19.4   The polo assumption

In late 1960, the legendary salesperson for the CBS Television network, Frank Hussey, flew to Akron, OH to see the CEO of Firestone Tire and Rubber Company, Harvey Firestone, Jr. who was the patrician son of the founder of Firestone Tires, Harvey Firestone, Sr. Frank Hussey was an experienced salesperson who had visited many expensively decorated offices, but he was unexpectedly impressed with the opulent, walnut-paneled walls in Firestone's office. As Hussey approached the tire titan's desk, Firestone rose up, came from around his enormous desk, and asked in a friendly but somewhat condescending tone, "It's a pleasure to meet you. What may I do for you?"

"Mr. Firestone," Hussy said, "your prestigious name is on virtually every tire that is on the vast majority of cars that come out of Detroit. Your brand stands for the highest quality tire than can be manufactured. I have two cars, and I feel safe every time I or my wife drives one of our cars because the tires have your name on them."

"Yes, we are very proud of our tires," Firestone replied.

"CBS feels that our highest quality program, "Face the Nation," would be an ideal program for Firestone Tire and Rubber Company to sponsor. It would be two great companies partnering to bring a quality product to viewers who associate quality with both CBS and Firestone tires."

Seeming somewhat flattered and intrigued, Firestone replied, "Ummm … remind me. When is 'Face the Nation' on the air,'" Firestone asked.

Sensing interest, Hussey leaned in, "It's on Sunday afternoon at 2:30 p.m."

Firestone squinted, brought his fist up to his mouth contemplatively, and replied slowly, "Mmmm, 2:30 Sunday afternoon … no, I'm afraid that wouldn't work because *everybody* is playing polo on Sunday afternoon."

Exhibit 19.5 shows a budget that you as the salesperson created for Hess Jewelry based on information you received. That information follows.

The Hess Jewelry manager has indicated that his store's total yearly sales are $5 million. You looked at the Ad-Sales ratios for retail jewelry stores (see Ad-Sales Ratios in Exhibit 16.7 and in the Downloads section of *Media Selling's* website), which was 7.2 percent, so 7.2 percent of $5 million is an annual ad budget of $360,000.

Because of the excellent ROI of digital advertising, you are going to recommend that Hess invest 70 percent of its annual budget in digital advertising because of its ability to precisely target Hess's customers and potential customers. You are also going to recommend that Hess have a Facebook page, and then twice a year, four weeks before Christmas and four weeks before June (graduations and weddings) that Hess invest in highly geo-targeted and demo-targeted ads on Facebook to drive Facebook users to the Hess Jewelry Facebook page that will have special offers. Also, you recommend investing in Google search terms such as "jewelry stores," or "class rings." You might suggest that Google and Facebook be allocated 40 percent of Hess's digital ad budget. Also recommend that Hess go on Instagram frequently to promote special offers to fashion-oriented young people, and to go on Twitter to announce special sales of diamond rings and gold chains. Twitter and Instagram posts are free, so they do not require an advertising budget allocation.

You are also going to recommend that two percent of Hess's local digital ad budget be used for remarketing to people who visit Hess's website. You learned about remarketing,

Exhibit 19.5   Hess Jewelry ad budget

	Sales	Ad-Sales Ratio	Media Percent	Advertising Budget
Hess Jewelry	$5,000,000.00	7.20%		$360,000.00
Digital			70.00%	$252,000.00
Google+Facebook % of digital			40.00%	$100,800.00
Local digital % of digital budget			58.00%	$146,160.00
Remarketing % of local digital			2.00%	$2,923.20
Radio* – 52 weeks			20.00%	$72,000.00
Email			10.00%	$36,000.00
DailyNews % of local digital			98.00%	$143,236.80
DailyNews agency fee subtracted from local digital				$25,000.00
Remaining local digital to DailyNews			32.84%	$118,236.80
Total media budget			100.00%	$360,000.00

* Radio creative = live reads or host reads.

or retargeting, in Chapter 17, but the reason you recommend such a low percentage of the digital ad budget going to remarketing is because when you did your research for insights and solutions you learned from an eMarketer article titled "Fear of onerous return policies curb online purchases of clothing, jewelry" that it is highly likely that consumers are buying very little from the Hess website, even though the store has one, so remarketing efforts are probably not going to have a high payoff for Hess.[12]

You are going to recommend that Hess not invest in local television even though people spent 33 percent of their time watching television in 2017. Even though television viewing is going down at the rate of two–four percent per year, with sight, color, sound, and motion and its vast reach, television is still an excellent medium for branding for large, national advertisers that can invest enough in the medium to build a reasonable amount of frequency so as to make its television investments effective. However, a local retailer with one location, as in Hess's case, cannot invest enough in local television to build enough frequency to make a sufficient impact on sales. As Michael Corbett advises in *The 33 Rules of Local Advertising,* Rule #26 is "Use a proven scheduling formula."[13] As an element in a proven scheduling formula, Corbett includes, "Choose a medium you can dominate."[14] Hess cannot invest enough to dominate a television station or even a particular television time period. On the other hand if Hess had, say, four stores in the market each doing $5 million in sales and, therefore, an ad budget of $1,440,000 a year, then an investment in local television advertising might be an effective branding effort.

You are going to recommend that 20 percent of the budget go to radio in four-to-six-week flights in seasons of peak sales such as Christmas, Valentine's Day, graduation and June weddings on at least two stations that have audiences that fit Hess's target customers' profile. Hess can build relationships with local radio stations and do contests and remotes from the store in peak seasons, and the radio commercials should be live reads by popular radio personalities that are well connected to the community. A radio budget of $72,000 is enough to be able to dominate several time periods in peak seasons and, thus, build foot traffic for the store.

You are going to recommend that 10 percent of the ad budget be invested in email marketing campaigns. Four or five times a year a two-email campaign to Hess customers and prospects can be quite effective for a local retailer in promoting seasonal sales items.

Finally, you are going to recommend that Hess invest in TheDailyNews.com.

Take note of the order of your ad investment recommendations: Google, Facebook, digital remarketing, radio, email, and, finally, TheDailyNews.com. By ordering your recommendations the same way a two-sided argument is ordered (putting the other side first), you gain the Hess manager's trust and enhance your credibility. You demonstrate that you understand the jewelry business, Hess's business, and the strengths of multiple marketing channels, and that you are not greedy and are not putting your interests first.

Also, note that TheDailyNews.com is going to serve as Hess's advertising agency and is going to create Hess's Facebook page, place Facebook and Google ads, post Hess deals on Instagram and Twitter, which helps Hess achieve a presence in earned media, and manage and place the digital remarketing and email campaigns. TheDailyNews.com is going to charge a flat fee of $25,000 for doing the work of serving as Hess's agency, which will include updating and managing Hess's website. And $25,000 is a reasonable fee because it is only about seven percent of Hess's total annual ad budget and is less than the typical 10–15 percent fee most advertising agencies, digital agencies, or Google or Facebook marketing partners charge.

Investing in TheDailyNews.com and not the print version is efficient and effective because ads will be placed programmatically via a private exchange and targeted based on TheDailyNews.com's and Hess's first-party data. Hess's schedule on TheDailyNews.com will reach high-value customers because ads on TheDailyNews.com can be placed programmatically and augmented by TheDailyNews.com's early adoption of several artificial intelligence (AI) enhancements, which means they can be highly targeted and personalized locally to the demos, lifestyle, personality, browsing behavior, motivations, and even sentiment and mood of Hess's best potential customers, especially to those who are planning a wedding or a graduation.

Focus on new opportunities　　The third strategy that can be employed if you are selling digital or cross-platform content in order to fight against the digital Goliaths is to focus on new opportunities that have sprung up at both the local and national level. Three trends sales management and salespeople should track are: (1) retail-dominated digital ad investments will increase,[15] (2) more conventional brand marketers will embrace direct-to-consumer (DTC) marketing,[16] and (3) the exploding use of AI and augmented reality.[17]

Retail-dominated digital ad investments will increase. A report from eMarketer titled "Retail dominates digital ad spending in the US" estimates that retailers will invest $28.33 billion in digital ads in 2019, an increase of 18.7 percent over 2017, a figure that represents nearly 22 percent of all US digital ad spending."[18] The report also estimates a 21.9 percent increase for retail in 2019 and 2020.[19] The eMarketer report also estimates that the retail industry's investment in mobile ads in 2019 would total $19.41 billion, accounting for nearly 70 percent of retailers' digital ad spending. According to eMarketer, "that gives the retail industry a nearly 22 percent share of US mobile ad spending."[20]

The report estimates that in 2018 the automotive category was number two in digital ad investments, with $15.65 billion, and financial services was the number three category with $15.25 billion. These top-three categories (retail, automotive, and financial services) of digital ad spend represent an effective way to rank prospecting priorities, especially in selling local digital or cross-platform media.

Because retail is the number one category for investment in digital advertising, it is worth taking a closer look at retail and where the potential growth in retail is. "Growth" is not the first concept that comes to mind when thinking about the retail business. The explosive growth of Amazon, in addition to the effect that WalMart has had on the retail business, has changed the ecosystem of retail, especially on Main Street, or the downtown area of small and mid-sized cities and towns.

An Axios AM Deep Dive report in January 2019, looked at the retail business and its potential for growth. The report indicated that "If Main Street is going to be saved, enduring American vanity will be among the primary reasons."[21] For example, nail and waxing salons, "in addition to pet grooming shops, cosmetics stores, tattoo parlors, and gyms" all stand out as "improbable avatars of the future of retail, surviving and thriving amid the decades-long annihilation of mom-and-pop apparel, book, and hardware stores."[22] "A common theme among the victors: The offerings can't be easily replicated online."[23] The Axios report specified that the big picture for retail was that "the mainstays of retail – the mall and Main Street – have been picked apart by WalMart, discount chains like Dollar General and, of course, Amazon. Now, brick and mortar stores are stabilizing, and the industry is climbing out of the rubble to survey what has worked."[24] The Axios Report included data from the Bureau of Labor Statistics that showed the change in storefront per capita from 1990 to 2017. See Exhibit 19.6 for details.

Salespeople selling digital or cross-platform advertising should keep the list in Exhibit 19.5 in mind when they are prospecting for new business.

Exhibit 19.6   Changes in storefront per-capita, 1990–2017

1	Nail salons: + 247%	7	Sporting goods: –17%
2	Pet care: +162%	8	Furniture: –33%
3	Cosmetics: +95%	9	Shoes: –35%
4	Restaurants: +54%	10	Hardware: –44%
5	Gyms: +46%	11	Books: –46%
6	Supermarkets: –6%	12	Newsstands: –61%

Source: Allen, Mike. 2019. Axios Deep Dive. HYPERLINK https://www.axios.com/tag/deep-dive-future-of-retail.

More conventional brand marketers will embrace direct-to-consumer (DTC) marketing. Direct-to-consumer marketing brands "are digitally native brands that sell directly to consumers rather than through other retailers or middlemen."[25] The DTC brands are "solely responsible for sourcing, producing, marketing, and selling their products to shoppers."[26] Those shoppers are primarily millennial consumers, who are a "natural fit given the demographic's comfort with technology and willingness to try to new brands."[27] Such DTC brands as Allbirds, Everlane, Harry's, Hubble, Warby Parker, Away, Casper, and Blue Apron have eaten into the market share and profits of traditional brands.

In an eMarketer "Behind the Numbers" podcast, a discussion among eMarketer's category experts agreed that the DTC brand successes began with the Dollar Shave Club when a 2012 YouTube video featuring the Dollar Shave Club's founder went viral. The founder said that if viewers were paying $20 for a razor blade, $19 was going to Roger Federer.[28] The video emphasized that P&G's Gillette was funneling so much of the cost of their razor blades into marketing and that a consumer could buy blades just as good for a lot less money. The Dollar Shave Club had found a way to undercut the market leader by going direct to consumers.

DTC brands such as Warby Parker and Casper took the pain (and very high marginal profits) out of shopping for glasses and mattresses, and were very successful because these DTC brands were able to do an excellent job of explaining what they were and what their offers were. DTC brands were successful in part because of their close relationships with their customers. The brands got immediate feedback from customers and were able to customize and personalize their offers, which created great customer loyalty and advocacy.

Conventional media-based brands of such companies as P&G and Unilever saw their market shares decline, and so, rather than fight the DTC brands, in 2018 many traditional brands decided to "throw in the towel altogether and begin leveraging digital media to become direct sellers themselves."[29] One of the reasons big brands are shifting to a DTC model is because they realize that the only way to have a relationship with and understand their consumers is to cut out the middlemen and have a relationship with them directly.[30]

In 2018 the IAB published a report titled "Direct Brands to Watch" and listed 250 DTC brands. The list can be found at https://www.iab.com/iab250-2018/ and provides an excellent prospecting list for those selling digital media, especially those selling national digital media. Local digital salespeople should keep their antennae tuned to local retailers that might profit from moving to a DTC model and also look for local DTC businesses.

Exploding use of AI and augmented reality. In a CBS "60 Minutes" interview, one of the world's foremost experts, Kai-Fu Lee, told reporter Scott Pelle that he believed that AI "is going to change the world more than anything in the history of mankind. More than electricity."[31]

AI is certainly going to change marketing because, as Dan Rosenberg wrote in a *Harvard Business Review* article, it holds "great promise for making marketing more intelligent, efficient, consumer-friendly, and, ultimately, more effective."[32] As an example, the author wrote that AI-powered chatbots "use all the customer data at their disposal to answer questions and give advice to customers considering making a purchase," such as Sephora's Kik bot, which quizzes customers about their makeup preferences and then follows up with specific product information.[33] Another example is Under Armour's leveraging of IBM Watson's AI to create a personal health consultant that provides users with timely, evidence-based coaching around sleep, fitness, activity, and nutrition.[34]

Orchid Richardson in an article in IAB's AdExchanger writes that at least 80 percent of the digital market will be using AI in advertising in 2019.[35] Marketers have terabytes and petabytes of behavioral data, including personal data, location information, and individuals' interests that they can use to target prospects, and AI is a way to tame that data and take their marketing to the next level.[36] Richardson writes that soon "we'll start seeing unique web pages that are built on the fly just for us – a custom shopping catalog for one, compliments of AI."[37]

Furthermore, some marketers are now using digital marketing to test key messaging before making their television buys.[38] This testing provides another opportunity for digital media salespeople to explore.

In another technological advancement Apple plans to offer new iPhone and iPad models in 2020 that feature 3-D cameras that "steps up Apple's push into augmented reality."[39] Concerning the new iPhones and iPads, Bloomberg News reported that: "The rear-facing, longer-range 3-D camera is designed to scan the environment to create three-dimensional reconstructions of the real world. It will work up to about 15 feet from the device, the people said. That's in contrast with the current iPhone 3-D camera system, which points toward users and operates at distances of 25 to 50 centimeters to power Apple's Face ID facial-recognition feature."[40]

Augmented reality is predicted to give retail stores a big lift, especially with millennial and Generation Z shoppers. And with their high volume of foot traffic, supermarkets are ideal labs to test some of these bold new technologies, especially augmented reality.

Sales management and salespeople should keep a close eye on retailers, including grocery stores and supermarkets that might adopt augmented reality to enhance shoppers' experiences and develop relationships, in order to help these early-adopter retailers market and advertise their new technology.

Digital Marketing Agencies

The examples of selling local digital or cross-platform advertising in this book have involved selling for legacy media such as radio and television stations and a digital newspaper. However, beginning in 2004, another type of digital sales organization sprang up – local digital marketing agencies and solutions providers. The first, and still the largest, of these local digital marketing organizations is ReachLocal, founded by Zorik Gordon and five other entrepreneurs in 2004 with the objective of competing with the yellow pages.

In their peak revenue years, yellow pages had an estimated total revenue of $16 billion.[41] Yellow pages are telephone directories of businesses, organized by category rather than alphabetically by business name, and in which advertising is sold. The directories were originally printed on yellow paper, as opposed to white pages for non-commercial listings, and were started in the late 1880s by AT&T, and printed yellow pages books were distributed free to all residences and businesses within a given coverage area. The traditional term "yellow pages" is now also applied to online directories of businesses, which are usually updated annually. The yellow pages publishers generate profit by selling advertising space or listings under each category of business, and the advertising is sold by a direct sales force or by an approved certified marketing representative (CMR).

However, by 2004, Google had been in business for six years, and local businesses were starting to take notice of the effectiveness of search advertising. Also, several online companies, such as AOL's Digital Cities, were beginning to put business directories similar to yellow pages online. Gordon and his partners at ReachLocal recognized that small local businesses such as plumbers and locksmiths who advertised in the yellow pages were usually not technically sophisticated enough to navigate successfully the complex, but robust, Google Ad Words or other online business directory systems, so they founded ReachLocal to help local businesses get results from digital advertising. The founders of ReachLocal realized that all small business wanted was to "write a check and get calls" and not bother with the details of buying digital advertising.[42]

When Gannett, owner of *USA Today* and the largest number of newspapers in the US, bought ReachLocal in 2016 for an estimated $156 million, ReachLocal had over 1,300 employees in 68 offices in the United States, Australia, Brazil, Canada, Mexico, Germany, the Netherlands, New Zealand, Singapore, Austria, India, Belgium, and Japan, and served over 17,000 active clients.[43] A typical ReachLocal office in the United States consists of 10–15 salespeople who sell digital marketing solutions to small, medium-sized, and large business in markets that generally have a population of one million or more.

In early 2019, ReachLocal was still the largest local digital marketing solutions provider and was a certified Premiere Google Partner and Facebook Marketing Partner, but the competition for local digital business had increased substantially since it was founded. Today there are hundreds of digital marketing agencies that help businesses buy digital advertising and provide tech solutions, onboarding, and digital marketing solutions. A young person who has just graduated from college and hopes to have a career in digital marketing or selling digital advertising should consider applying to ReachLocal or one of the many other local digital marketing agencies that are certified Google Premiere Partners or certified Facebook Marketing Partners.

These local digital marketing agencies typically have excellent training programs that teach their salespeople many of the technical intricacies of selling and evangelizing digital marketing and advertising. In addition to learning about the digital plumbing, the ad delivery process, and ad-size specs, salespeople can begin establishing relationships with local businesses. And even though technical knowledge is important, digital marketing and advertising is "all about relationships," according to Zorik Gordon.[44] Once a salesperson has built strong relationships and accumulated a reasonably robust Rolodex of clients and contacts with local advertisers, moving to lucrative sales jobs at radio or television stations becomes a good option, or even opening their own digital agency is a possibility.

Hone your negotiating skills

Even though in the future more and more digital ad buying will be done programmatically, this does not necessarily mean that salespeople will be completely disintermediated.
In a MediaPost article titled "Dear humans: 82.5% of digital display ad buys are now done
programmatically," Joe Mandese writes that "the programmatic marketplace has exploded
as automatic technology replaces human haggling in processing display advertising inventory."[45] However, "supply-and-demand sides of the business are largely negotiating the
parameters of their programmatic deal-making before it hits the machines, either via
'programmatic direct' –the lion's share of all programmatic trading – or via 'private' markets that enable media traders and advertisers to leverage programmatic technology to
structure real-time buys based on their pre-negotiated terms and criteria."[46]

Thus, even though 82.5 percent of digital display inventory and a large part of video
ads are placed by programmatic automation, the "lion's share" of pricing is negotiated
in advance between human sellers and human buyers. Therefore, it behooves digital
media salespeople to cultivate relationships and brush up on the negotiating skills they
learned in Chapter 13.

Test Yourself

1. What is the number one advertising medium?
2. What is the digital duopoly?
3. What percentage of digital advertising does the duopoly have?
4. What are the five reasons the digital Goliaths dominate the digital advertising space?
5. What are three strategies for an underdog to be successful against the digital Goliaths?
6. What two media added together have the largest share of time spent with media?
7. What is the polo assumption?
8. Does the CPM Reach of adding additional reach to a campaign increase or decrease
   as you add commercials to a campaign?
9. What is one criterion for deciding what percentage of total sales an advertising
   budget should be?
10. If you were a salesperson for TheDailyNews.com, in what order would you place
    your recommended media investments?
11. In terms of changes in storefronts per capita 1990–2017, what are the three types of
    retailers that have the largest growth?
12. Why should a salesperson who sells digital or cross-platform advertising hone their
    negotiating skills?

Project

Assume you are selling digital advertising for a local television station in a market ranked
between 50 and 60. Digital ads are placed on the station's news website and app and in
its weather app, which is known to be fairly popular in the market. Assume you are

calling on a sports and athletic equipment retailer that has total yearly sales of $1 million, is not digitally sophisticated, and is putting 90 percent of its yearly budget on a local sports radio station. Create a spreadsheet that contains a recommended annual advertising budget for the sports and athletic equipment retailer using Exhibit 19.5 as a guide. Assume that your recommendations and proposal will include your television station acting as the customer's advertising agency. Make sure you give some thought to how you are going to rank order your recommendations.

References

Corbett, Michael with Stili, Dave. 2002. *The 33 Ruthless Rules of Local Advertising.* Hanover, MA: Pinnacle Books.

Resources

Facebook Marketing Partners (www.facebook.com/business/partner-directory)
IAB New Ad Portfolio (www.iab.com/newadportfolio)
IAB Digital Media Certification (www.iab.com/certification-programs/iab-digital-media-sales-certification)
IAB 250 Brands Worth Watching (www.iab.com/iab250-2018)
List of Facebook Marketing Partners and Agencies (www.advertisemint.com/a-complete-list-of-facebook-marketing-partners-and-advertising-agencies)

Notes

1   eMarketer. 2019. "The weekly listen: social misinformation, Pinterest IPO and ad-free Facebook." Retrieved from https://soundcloud.com/behind-the-numbers.

2   Fischer, Sara. 2019. Retrieved from https://www.axios.com/newsletters/axios-media-trends-1dfd7510-8393-4c57-946d-9e659cc7a4e4.html.

3   Ibid.

4   Pathak, Shareen. 2017. "Amazon's ad business will get another boost with the rollout of a new API for self-serve ads." Retrieved from https://digiday.com/marketing/amazons-ad-business-gets-another-boost-rollout--new-api-self-serve-ads.

5   eMarketer. 2018. "Amazon advertising 2018." Retrieved from https://www.emarketer.com/content/amazon-advertising-2019.

6   Sullivan, Laurie. 2017. "Brands turning to Amazon, Looking for safer display ad platforms." Retrieved from https://www.mediapost.com/publications/article/310859/brands-turing-to-amazon-looking-for-safer-display.html.

7   eMarketer. 2018. "Digital ad buyers say Google Search, Facebook deliver best ROI." Retrieved from https://www.emarketer.com/content/digital-ad-buyers-say-google-facebook-deliver-best-roi/

8   eMarketer. 2018. "Behind the Numbers" podcast: "The ad blocking elephant in the room." Retrieved from https://soundcloud.com/behind-the-numbers/.

9   Ibid.

10 Ryals, Lynette and Davies, Iain. 2011. "Do you really know who your best salespeople are?" *Harvard Business Review*, December.

11 "U.S. advertising volume (Coen/McCann-Erikson)." Retrieved from https://adage.com/datacenter/dataopup.php.

12 eMarketer. 2018. "Fear of onerous return policies curb online purchases of clothing, jewelry." Retrieved from https://retail.emarketer.com/article/fear-of-onerous-return-policies-curb-online-purchases-of-clothing-jewelry/5c4f79a5b979f10a1cc56a6c.

13 Corbett, Michael with Stili, Dave. 2002. *The 33 Ruthless Rules of Local Advertising*. Hanover, MA: Pinnacle Books.

14 Ibid.

15 eMarketer. 2018. "Retail dominates digital ad spend in U.S." Retrieved from https://retail.emarketer.com/retail-dominates-ad-spending-us/5b35210ebd40003b84918a2a.

16 Mandese, Joe. 2018. "Excuse me for being direct, but so will you." Retrieved from https://www.mediapost.com/publications/article/314419/excuse-me-for-being-direct-but-so-will-you.html.

17 Richardson, Orchid. 2018. "AI is eating advertising – And 2019 will be critical for getting it right." Retrieved from https://adexchanger.com/data-driven-thinking/ai-is-eating-advertising-and-2019-will-be-critical-for-getting-it-right.

18 eMarketer. 2018. "US retail digital ad spending 2019: Mobile and search continue to power a dominant vertical." Retrieved from https://www.emarketer.com/content/us-retail-digital-ad-spending-2019.

19 Ibid.

20 Ibid.

21 Allen, Mike. 2018. Retrieved from https://www.axios.com/newsletters/axios-deep-dives-4466a0da-aa4c-409a-863e-b8d8625e6411.html.

22 Ibid.

23 Ibid.

24 Ibid.

25 Pasquarelli, Adrianne. 2019. "Learn the ABCs of D-To-C." *Ad Age*, January 7.

26 Ibid.

27 Ibid.

28 eMarketer. 2019. "Behind the Numbers" podcast: "The rise of D2C brands." Retrieved from https://soundcloud.com/behind-the-numbers.

29 Mandese, Joe. 2018. "Excuse me for being direct, but so will you." Retrieved from http://www.mediapost.com/publications/article/314419/excuse-me-for-being-direct-but-so-will-you.html.

30 Ibid.

31 Axios. 2018. "'60 Minutes' warning: AI could take 40% of jobs." Retrieved from https://www.axios.com/artificial-intelligence-automation-jobs-robots-fbca4208-ffea-43c4-9bd3-8102b63caedb.html.

32 Rosenberg, Dan. 2018. "How marketers can start integrating AI in their work." *Harvard Business Review*. Retrieved from https://hbr.org/2018/05/how-marketers-can-start-integrating-ai-in-their-work.

33 Ibid.

34 Ibid.

35 Richardson, Orchid. 2019. "AI is eating advertising – And 2019 will be critical for getting it right." Retrieved from https://adexchangerawards.com/data-driven-thinking/ai-is-eating-advertising-and-2019-wii-be-citical-for-getting-it-right.

36 Ibid.

37 Ibid.

38 *Harvard Business Review*. 2018. "How leading marketers get ahead in today's data-driven world." Retrieved from https://hbr.org/sponsored/2018/05/how-leading-marketers-get-ahead-in-todays-data-driven-world.

39 Gurman, Mark and Wu, Debby. 2019. "Apple is planning 3-D cameras for new iPhones in AR push." Retrieved from https://www.bloomberg.com/news/articles/2019-01-30/apple-is-said-to-prep-new-3-d-camera-for-2020-iphones-in-ar-push.

40 Ibid.

41 LaMonica, Paul. "Let your fingers do the walking." Retrieved from https://money.cnn.com/2005/12/13/news/fortune500/yellow.

42 Personal interview with Zorik Gordon, February 18, 2019.

43 ReachLocal. Retrieved from https://en.wikipedia.org/wiki/ReachLocal.

44 Ibid.

45 Mandese, Joe. 2018. "Dear humans: 82.5% of display ad buys are done by machines." Retrieved from https://www.mediapost.com/publications/article/317296/dear-huan-825-of-display-ad-buys-are-ow-done.html.

46 Ibid.

20

Google and Search

Brian Moroz

Google began as a search engine company with a mandate. This was: "Organize the world's information and make it universally accessible and useful."

In the years since the founding of the company, it has grown to include products like Google Maps, YouTube, G Suite, Gmail, and many other products and services. Currently, Google is part of the parent company Alphabet, which includes companies invested in areas much further afield than Google originally planned for, including Life Sciences, Nest, and Sidewalk Labs.

Larry Page, Alphabet CEO, wrote the following to explain why Alphabet was founded:

> We've long believed that over time companies tend to get comfortable doing the same thing, just making incremental changes. But in the technology industry, where revolutionary ideas drive the next big growth areas, you need to be a bit uncomfortable to stay relevant.
>
> Our company is operating well today, but we think we can make it cleaner and more accountable. So we are creating a new company, called Alphabet. I am really excited to be running Alphabet as CEO with help from my capable partner, Sergey, as President.
>
> What is Alphabet? Alphabet is mostly a collection of companies. The largest of which, of course, is Google. This newer Google is a bit slimmed down, with the companies that are pretty far afield of our main Internet products contained in Alphabet instead. What do we mean by far afield? Good examples are our health efforts: Life Sciences (that works on

Media Selling: Digital, Television, Audio, Print and Cross-Platform, Fifth Edition.
Charles Warner, William A. Lederer, and Brian Moroz.
© 2020 John Wiley & Sons, Inc. Published 2020 by John Wiley & Sons, Inc.

the glucose-sensing contact lens), and Calico (focused on longevity). Fundamentally, we believe this allows us more management scale, as we can run things independently that aren't very related.

As of this writing, Alphabet is one of the top-five most valuable companies in the world. This is quite an accomplishment for a company that is only approaching 20 years old. Looking at companies by advertising revenue, Alphabet is the largest in the world, highly driven by Google.

To give a sense of how popular Google's products are, here are a few statistics:

- *Annual searches*: At least two trillion, though Google does not give out specific numbers
- *Estimated searched per minute*: 3.8 million, taken from third-party estimates
- *Estimated Gmail users*: Over one billion

Search ads remain a core of Google, and thus Alphabet's, business. In this chapter we will explore the search auction, keywords, bidding, quality score and ad rank, and touch on search as a direct response as well as a brand play.

A Brief History of the Google Ad Auction

As you read in Chapter 2, Google entered the online advertising market with a very different model than most of the previous media organizations or early search engines had attempted. Rather than a simple cost-per-thousand (CPM) model or a homepage take-over model, Google offered advertisers something different – an auction model. This model has been refined over time given the experience and feedback of many, many advertisers, from individuals selling homemade products to the world's largest corporations.

The search advertising auction model remains a cornerstone of the Google advertising suite, and understanding how it works is key to successful media selling even if you never personally consult with your clients on Google or search as a medium. A major percentage of Google's revenue continues to come from search advertising as marketers understand how effective such ads are for direct conversions and how they can be used for branding as well. While video ads and other more recent formats have come a long way, search is still a powerful place to be. The advertiser in search knows users are raising their hand at the specific moment of interest in a product, service, or category and know they can be there with a solution.

The knowledge in this chapter will assist you with your media selling career regardless of whether or not you ever actively sell search advertising. In the current market, savvy advertisers are planning their media buying and creative assets holistically, and want partners that understand how search blends with display, video, out of home, television, and so on. Few major advertisers look at any of their marketing in silos and your knowledge of the basics of the search ads marketplace will put you ahead of many of your competitors.

The Search Auction

Every time you go to Google, you type in a query. Often that query delivers search results accompanied by a few ads on the results page. How does this process take place? What are the inputs and levers that deliver search ads?

When a user searches for a keyword, any advertiser may enter the auction for that keyword to show their ad with the search results. Advertisers select keywords to bid on, attach ad text (and in some cases like shopping ads, images), and choose how much they are willing to pay per ad click.

When a search with that keyword is performed by a user on Google, the auction runs in fractions of a second to determine which ads will show on the search results page. The formula that Google uses to determine which ads show and in which order is not fully transparent but there are some specific guidelines for any advertiser which we will explore below.

Quoting from Google, the auction works in the following manner:

This is the process that happens with each Google search to decide which ads will appear for that specific search and in which order those ads will show on the page (or whether or not any ads will show at all): Each time a Google Ads ad is eligible to appear for a search, it goes through the ad auction. The auction determines whether or not the ad actually shows and in which ad position it will show on the page.

Here is how the auction works:

1   When someone searches, the Google Ads system finds all ads whose keywords match that search.
2   From those ads, the system ignores any that aren't eligible, like ads that target a different country or are disapproved based on a policy violation.
3   Of the remaining ads, only those with a sufficiently high Ad Rank may show. Ad Rank is a combination of your bid, ad quality, the Ad rank thresholds, the context of the person's search, and the expected impact of extensions and other ad formats.
    •   The most important thing to remember is that even if your competition bids higher than you, you can still win a higher position – at a lower price – with highly relevant keywords and ads.
    •   Since the auction process is repeated for every search on Google, each auction can have potentially different results depending on the competition at that moment. Therefore it's normal for you to see some fluctuation in your ad's position on the page and in whether or not your ad shows at all.[1]

Keywords

Keywords are the basis of your search campaign. They are the terms that you want your ad to appear on when someone searches for them. If you are selling bicycles, you may want to bid on keywords like "bicycles," "bikes," "road bike," "mountain bike," "kids bicycle" and so on. You would then match ad text and possibly images to each of the keywords to fill out what would appear when people searched for your keyword. If you win the auction for that specific search, your ad will appear. Your ad may appear alone but most often it will be part of several ads that run against that search. Major retailers such as Walmart or Macys may have literally hundreds of thousands of keywords that they bid on so that they can be there for almost any retail search, while niche brands may bid on only a few dozen keywords to make sure they only show when people are looking for their specific products. The majority of your media clients will likely fall somewhere in between. Keywords are refined by what are called *match types*. There are four categories of keyword match types.

Keyword match types

Broad match. With broad match, your ad may show if a search query contains your keyword terms in any order, with singular or plural forms, synonyms, stemmings (such as floor and flooring), related searches, and other relevant variations. This match type gives you the widest reach, but with the caveat that some users may not be searching for what you specifically are offering.

Here is an example of where your ad may show if you select broad match for the keyword "low-carb diet plan" (note that no capital letters are shown because the vast majority of searches are in lower case, plus algorithms don't distinguish between upper and lower cases):

- carb-free foods
- low-carb diets
- low caloric recipes
- mediterranean diet plans
- low-carbohydrate dietary plan

Phrase match. With phrase match, an ad may show only when someone searches on your exact phrase, or with additional words before or after, which narrows potential traffic compared to broad match, but provides increased relevancy.

Here is an example of where your ad may show if you select phrase match for the keyword "tennis shoes." What will not display an ad is if the user searches for "shoes for tennis," as this is not the exact phrase. Note that while misspellings are included, words out of order are not.

- tennis shoes
- red leather tennis shoes
- buy tennis shoes on sale
- red tenis shoes

Exact match. Exact match keywords will show ads on what are called *same-meaning* queries. This includes singular or plural forms, misspellings, word reordering and function word addition or removal. This category does provide fewer impressions and clicks than broad match, but is the most appropriate approach for tight control of when your ads are surfaced.

The following is an example of where your ad may show if you select exact match for the keyword "shoes for men." In this case, a search for "red shoes for men" would not place this ad in the auction.

- shoes men
- men shoes
- men shoe
- shoes for a man

Negative match. Negative match keywords exclude and filter out searches that are not useful for an advertiser. They prevent unwanted clicks. An example might be an advertiser selling dress shoes who adds the negative match word "running" to avoid people looking for running shoes. This is particularly helpful if your account has many broad match keywords and you want to avoid clicks that would not be useful to your brand or to the user searching.

Bids

Of course advertisers must pay for the ads they run on Google Search, but it is a very different model than is standard for traditional and most digital media. For search, Google uses a cost-per-click (CPC) model. Your search ad can show many times but you will not be charged unless a user clicks on your ad. You choose how much it is worth to you for that click, but Google will give you guidance on the general range that usually ensures your ad will show.

Some unusual keywords may have a very low minimum bid, and some may be very high indeed. Most keywords have an estimated average cost of around $1–2 per click, but some particularly valuable keywords can average $50 or more for each click. This doesn't mean a conversion, it merely means a user clicking on your ad to see what you offer, so clearly advertisers willing to spend at that level consider this lead generation quite valuable.

Quality Score

Possibly the most important factor in the auction is the Quality Score, which informs Ad Rank. Google's founders realized before launching the business that search engine users routinely ignored ads that had nothing to do with what they were searching for. The model in the early stages of search advertising followed the path that network television had laid out – sell advertising space at a set price in high traffic areas. Just as you may not own a car but be exposed to car insurance ads when watching television, early search engines would sell advertising inventory to whomever wanted the placement regardless of its usefulness to the searcher.

Google realized that if you want engagement, you should show ads relevant to the specific search being performed. Someone searching for bicycles is probably not, at that moment, interested in buying a refrigerator. Much better to show such a user advertisements for bicycle shops nearby, online bike stores and so on. This is the concept behind Quality Score – the more directly your ad connects to the keywords you are bidding on, and the better the user experience after clicking the ad, the more likely you are to show and have a preferred placement in the auction.

In short, Quality Score is a measurement of how useful and relevant the ad will be to the user. It is a dynamic score assigned to every keyword every time the auction is run and ads are shown which influences ranking on Search and Display ads.

The specifics of the Quality Score and Ad Rank are not completely defined by Google, as doing so would make gaming the system easy and common. However, Google does give some guidelines about what makes for a strong ad quality leading to a strong rank:

- Relevance to the search
- Expected click-through rate
- Landing page

Relevance to the search is how closely your ad aligns to the search itself. If someone is searching for "bicycle tires," an ad specific to bike tires may likely have a higher Quality Score and thus Ad Rank than an ad for bicycles in general, for instance. And either of those ads will have a better Quality Score and Ad Rank than an ad for shoes that is trying to bid on the keyword "bicycle tires."

Expected click-through rate is defined by Google as:

A keyword status that measures how likely it is that your ads will get clicked when shown for that keyword, irrespective of your ad's position, extensions, and other ad formats that may affect the prominence and visibility of your ads.

This status predicts whether your keyword is likely to lead to a click on your ads. Google Ads takes into account how well your keyword has performed in the past, based on your ad's position. The expected clickthrough rate (CTR) that Google Ads provides for a keyword in your account is an estimate based on the assumption that the search term will match that keyword exactly. At auction time (when someone's search terms triggers one of your ads), Google Ads calculates a more accurate expected CTR based on the search terms, type of device, and other auction-time factors.[2]

In practice, this means that over time your ads will have more predictable click-through rates, which may improve your Ad Rank score. It is helpful to learn from your campaigns, continue with keyword-ad matches that do well, and cull those that do not.

A *landing page* is the specific page you send users to after they click on your search ad. The landing page experience directly impacts your Quality Score and by extension your Ad Rank. A simple example of the landing page is a user who searches on Google for "Red Beach Cruiser Bicycle."

Our first advertiser is a big-box store and bids on those keywords. The landing page, i.e. the page you are sent to upon clicking the ad, is the homepage for the big-box store with every category of merchandise from clothing to gardening to appliances. This is a bad landing page experience, as you will have to click through many layers to get to the bicycle you specifically searched for and that the ad promised you.

Our second advertiser is another big-box store, but when you click on their ad it brings you right to the bicycle section of the website. This is a much better experience, and will improve the Quality Score and likely Ad Rank for this advertiser.

Our final advertiser is yet another big-box store, but one that understands search advertising very well. When you click on their ad, it brings you to a page of the available beach cruiser bicycles. This is the best landing page experience and will positively impact the Quality Score and likely the corresponding Ad Rank for the advertiser.

Ideally the advertiser would send the user to only red beach cruiser bikes, but sometimes website architecture make that impossible. The key is to link to a page as close to the exact ad you run as possible.

Ad rank

Ad Rank combines many factors to determine your ad position, if indeed your ad will show at that specific auction when an individual user types in the keywords that you have bid on. As mentioned, it is calculated by looking at the bid amount, your auction-time ad quality, the context of the person's search such as location, time of day, and many other factors. All of these factors mean that a bid alone does not determine your ad placement; this is not an auction where the highest bid wins the best spot. You may bid less than a competitor but rank higher in the actual ad placement because the quality of your ad is higher.

Here is an example of three advertisers:

CPC Bid	X	Quality Score	=	Ad Rank
$2		10		20
$4		4		16
$6		2		12

In this example, the lowest bidder had the highest Quality Score and, thus, is the first ad on the results page. This position underscores how much an ad relies on addressing a user's need to reach a solid placement in the results.

Search Advertising

Search for direct response

Search for direct response is the most traditional kind of search advertising. This kind of advertising is reacting to users who by searching for something, be it a product, a need, a question or a complaint, are showing that they are looking for a solution. Advertisers that have a solution want to be there when these users are most interested in something their product solves.

Examples of direct response search campaigns might be our bicycle seller bidding on keywords like "bike" or "buying a bicycle" and running an ad that sounds compelling to these shoppers. A fitness coach or a gym might run ads against keywords like "weight loss" or "exercise programs" or "how to do a pull up." A bank may run ads against keywords like "new checking account," "saving for retirement," and "home loan."

In all of the above cases, the advertiser is looking for people who are ready to buy a product of some sort, from a bike to a bank account. The expectation of the marketer is that clicks on these ads will result in sign ups, purchases, test drives, and so on. They are looking for specific, measurable and direct-to-the-bottom-line actions from potential customers who have shown interest in their product area.

Search for branding

Search is often seen as focused on direct response, a way to generate instant purchases or leads. It can, however, also be used for branding. This is possible by running ads alongside content that matches your brand. Websites can choose to run AdSense ads, which are Google Search or Display ads, on their site, and advertisers can select which websites best represent their brand message. If you are a publisher or individual with a site that focuses on mountain biking, you can opt into AdSense and determine how much space you would like to allow for ads. Google will match appropriate search and display advertisers for mountain biking content, and you will share in the ad revenue when anything is clicked.

In this way you can connect your search and display ads to content that connects with your brand message, and also reach users on sites that they enjoy and trust. This is an easy way to build in branding when running a search marketing campaign with essentially no operational overhead.

Technologies

AdSense

Google also has a product for online publishers called AdSense. If you or your company has a blog, a website, or publishes content online, you can monetize it by using AdSense. On the AdSense website Google indicates that:

> You just need three things to sign up for AdSense. … A Google account; Content created from scratch, [which] can include your website, blog, or other original content that complies with our program policies. This is where ads will be displayed so we want to make sure it's a nice place for everyone; The phone number and postal address associated with your bank account "so you can get paid. It's a must. ZIP Code and all.[3]

When you have an account set up as described above, you can select the ad size and the font color and size. Then Google's algorithms will check out your site to see if it meets their content standards (program policies) and to discover what the nature and focus of the content is so that it can place advertising on your site that is relevant to the content.

In about two days you will get a message that your site has been accepted (or rejected). If accepted, you will get in the acceptance email message several lines of code, called an *ad tag*, to insert on your site where you want it to appear. Within minutes of being updated and going live with the new Google ad tag, an ad for an advertiser relevant to your site will appear. If enough people click on the ads served on your site, you will get a check deposited in your bank account that represents 68 percent of the revenue generated by clicks on the ad. The threshold for payment for AdSense advertising is $100. If your website made $90 in January, you would not get a payment in February, but if you then made $10 in February, in March you would get your $100 payment.

It is difficult to make a lot of money with AdSense. A look at the math will tell you why. Let's say you have 100,000 page views in a month and the average click-through on the ads on your site is two percent, which is 2,000 click-throughs. If the average click-through rate for ads on your site is $0.25, then the total revenue would be $500, and 68 percent of $500 is $340.

YouTube

Google also owns YouTube, and YouTube channels can also be monetized in a similar manner to AdSense. If you have a YouTube channel, click on the Video Manager link and then click on the $ sign next to the video or channel you want to monetize by agreeing to let YouTube run ads on your content.

You'll need an AdSense account and at least 4,000 hours of watch time and a minimum of 1,000 subscribers to start earning money. YouTube takes 45 percent of the ad revenue and gives you 55 percent.

Google Help

There are millions of Google Ads, Ad Sense, and YouTube accounts, all of which have dashboards showing the owners all the important and necessary statistics for their individual campaigns and traffic. The Google Ads Help Center (https://support.google.com/adwords) can answer almost any question you have, as will the AdSense and YouTube Help Centers, and of course at higher levels of investment you will have a Google account team who is there to solve any issues that may arise.

Other Google products

Some of the other products Google provides free to anyone include:

- Gmail
- G Suite

- Drive – Documents, Sheets, Slides, and Photos
- Maps
- Hangouts
- Translate
- Play
- Calendar
- Assistant
- Chrome
- YouTube
- Google Local Services

Test Yourself

1. What is Google's mission?
2. Can advertisers win a bid on a search term if their bid is lower than a competitor's?
3. What is the difference between a *broad match* and a *phrase match*?
4. What is the definition of a Quality Score?
5. How is Ad Rank calculated?
6. Can search advertising be used for both direct response and branding?
7. What percentage of ad revenue does AdSense pay?

Project

Visit a local retail business – a locally owned clothing store or car dealership – and ask if they use Google Ads. If so, interview the person who handles buying Google Ads keywords and ask how it is working, and then ask to see their Google Analytics dashboard.

Notes

1 Retrieved from https://support.google. com/adwords/answer/142918?hl=en.

2 Retrieved from https://support.google. com/adwords/answer/1659696?hl=en.

3 Retrieved from https://www.google.com/ adsense/start/get-started.

21

Facebook and Social Media

Charles Warner

Facebook

On February 4, 2004, when Harvard sophomore, Mark Zuckerberg, in his Kirkland House third-floor dorm room "clicked a link on his account on Manage.com and Thefacebook.com went live," it was not the first online social media website.[1] In November 2001 a doctoral student in computer science at Stanford named Orkut Buyukkokten created Club Nexus that allowed people with a Stanford.edu address to create a profile using their real names and then list their campus "buddies."[2] Club Nexus had too many features and was difficult to use, so it fell out of favor.

The year before Zuckerberg created Thefacebook, Friendster had taken Harvard and many other college campuses by storm and had accumulated well over a million users nationwide. However, by February of 2004, Friendster had fallen into disfavor due to technical problems brought on by its rapid growth. Friendster's pages were painfully slow to load and the service was difficult to navigate and to use.[3]

The semester before, in September 2003, Zuckerberg, who had been writing computer code since he was 13, wrote a program called Course Match that allowed Harvard

Media Selling: Digital, Television, Audio, Print and Cross-Platform, Fifth Edition.
Charles Warner, William A. Lederer, and Brian Moroz.

students to pick classes based on who else was taking them, and it became fairly popular. His next project, which Zuckerberg completed in October of 2003, he called Facemash, "which gave the Harvard community its first look at his rebellious, irreverent side," and its purpose was to figure out who was the hottest person on campus.[4] Zuckerberg got into trouble with the Harvard authorities because he had surreptitiously found a way to get pictures of students from different houses at Harvard and posted those pictures without students' permission. For this infraction of Harvard rules, he was put on probation. Nevertheless, "the episode was a clear sign: Zuckerberg had a knack for making software people couldn't stop using."[5]

When the new semester rolled around in 2004, Zuckerberg had another project he was eagerly working on. On January 11, he went online and paid Register.com $35 to register the URL Thefacebook.com for one year.[6] For this new site, he borrowed ideas from his Course Mash and Facemash programs and from Friendster, which he was a member of. On Friendster, members were invited to create a profile of themselves, complete with information about themselves, their tastes in music, and other information. People on Friendster linked their profiles to the profiles of friends. The key insight Zuckerberg had was that people created their own profiles, posted a picture of themselves, *and* they had to use their real names. In 2003, in addition to Friendster, both LinkedIn and MySpace had also launched. LinkedIn was business oriented and, thus, was not popular with undergraduates at Harvard or other colleges, but MySpace was more popular because users could "create any identity they liked."[7]

When Chris DeWolfe and Tom Anderson launched MySpace, they put few restrictions on how you could use it. "If something had proven popular on the web, the commercially-minded pair wanted it in MySpace...it included games, a horoscope, and blogging along with a Friendster-like profile page for members."[8] The MySpace founders took a generally casual approach to just about everything, which suited its young members just fine. People could use HTML code to jazz up their profiles, which they did in many and often bizarre ways, which contributed to its "distinctive Times Square look – all flashing graphics and ribald images."[9]

But something else was happening that made the growth of social networking sites such as Friendster, MySpace, and Thefacebook possible – broadband Internet access rose from 15 percent to 25 percent during 2003, and broadband access meant faster uploading of images, and pages that loaded much quicker.[10] Lots of families with teenage girls got a broadband connection, and MySpace, with its sense of hipness, its ease in finding out about bands, and its often sexual postings, was like honey is to a bear to teenagers, especially to teenage girls. By the time Thefacebook launched in February 2004, the glitzy MySpace had more than one million users and was the country's dominant social network.

See Figure 21.1 for a timeline indicating when social media sites were launched.

Thefacebook's clean, uncluttered pages, its ease of use, its insistence on users giving their real identities, its simplicity – the "only thing you could do immediately was invite more friends" – and its limited distribution to only elite university students proved to be a winning combination.[11] During the spring semester of 2004, Zuckerberg and his roommate Dustin Moskovitz rolled out Thefacebook to Columbia on February 25, to Stanford on February 26, to Yale on February 29, to Dartmouth on March 7, and to other Ivy League schools where it became an essential social tool.[12] Thefacebook was growing at about 10,000 users a month because university students clamored for the social media tool

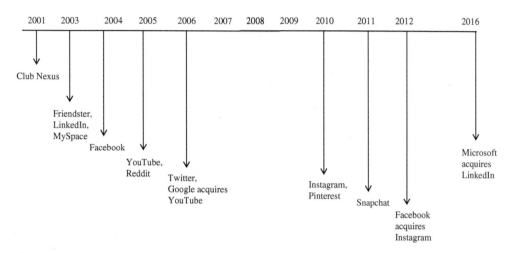

Figure 21.1 Social media timeline
Source: Kirkpatrick, David. 2010. *The Facebook Effect: The Inside Story of the Company That Is Connecting the World*. New York: Simon & Schuster.

to come to their campus. That summer Zuckerberg and Moskovitz moved to Palo Alto in Silicon Valley to raise the money they needed to keep up with the huge demand their social network was generating as "many students began to abandon their address books because they could use Thefacebook to contact anyone by simply entering their name."[13]

In November 2004, Thefacebook retained Y2M, an advertising representative company that specialized in selling ads in college newspapers, and Y2M sold its first ad deal to Paramount Pictures to promote "The Sponge-Bob SquarePants Movie" for $15,000 for 5 million impressions ($3 CPM).[14] Zuckerberg, like Larry Page and Sergey Brin at Google, was not fond of advertising. These founders were not focused on maximizing revenue, but on maximizing the user experience. However, Zuckerberg understood he had to put up with ads to fuel Thefacebook's incredible growth. Nevertheless, Zuckerberg put a caption on some ads that read: "We don't like these either, but they pay the bills," a caption that advertisers could not see because they could not log into Thefacebook because the service required a .edu email address from a limited number of colleges.[15]

In Palo Alto in the summer of 2004 Zuckerberg also found the investment money he needed with the help of Sean Parker, who introduced Thefacebook.com founder to LinkedIn founder Reid Hoffman, who, in turn, introduced him to Peter Thiel, an investor and co-founder of PayPal. Thiel loaned Thefacebook $500,000, which was eventually converted to a 10.2 percent share in the company and which at the time of the loan gave Thefacebook a valuation of $4.9 billion.[16]

A year later, in the summer of 2005, with Sean Parker now president and Zuckerberg CEO, the fledgling company paid another company, AboutFace, $200,000 to acquire the rights to the domain name Facebook.com, and on September 20, 2005, it officially changed its name.[17] In the fall of that year 85 percent of American college students were users of Facebook, and 60 percent of them returned to the site on a daily basis. Users were viewing 230 million pages daily, which translated into $1 million a month in ad revenue, which came mostly from ad networks placing low-priced display ads on the burgeoning social network.

In August 2006, Facebook made a transformational deal with Microsoft to have its ad network sell Facebook banner ads at a guaranteed CPM, but "Mark was adamant about preserving the user experience and the layout," which drove the Microsoft ad people crazy because it made it very hard to deliver standard Internet ad units.[18] Nevertheless, Microsoft's salespeople were successful, and Facebook ended 2006 with $44 million in ad revenue, twice what it had forecast before the Microsoft ad deal.[19] And in September 2006, Facebook opened to everyone at least 13 years old with a valid email address, which accelerated its explosive growth.

By the fall of 2007, half of Facebook's 50 million users were outside the US and advertising dollars were rolling in, but Zuckerberg did not want Facebook to be like network television, which he thought routinely interrupted viewers with irrelevant and inane advertising. Also, in 2007, Yahoo, Viacom's MTV, and Microsoft all wanted to buy Facebook because they saw the massive growth of young consumers who were avid Facebook fans. In October, Microsoft made a $240 million investment in Facebook for 1.6 percent ownership, which valued Facebook at $15 billion dollars. Microsoft made the deal in large part to renew its ad-selling contract with Facebook, but in the long and tense negotiations to seal the deal, Microsoft gave Facebook the right to sell 15 percent of its ad inventory on its own. Facebook lost no time in launching its new Facebook Ads self-service ad system, which hastened the transformation of digital advertising from mass media advertising carpet-bombing by large advertisers to precise, individual targeting available on a self-serve basis to all advertisers large and small.

In March 2008, Mark Zuckerberg hired Sheryl Sandberg to be chief operating officer (COO) of Facebook. Sandberg had been at Google since 2001 and "had built the search company's self-service ad business into one of the economic powerhouses of the web."[20] As Facebook's top advertising champion, Sandberg had deep experience with advertisers from her time at Google and a deep appreciation of digital advertising. She also knew that there was a deep corporate ambivalence toward advertising within Facebook, an attitude she had to work hard to overcome. Therefore, she began a series of meetings with top Facebook executives asking the question, "What business are we in?" Sandberg got Facebook's top managers involved because she knew that she needed alignment on the company's mission among all of Facebook's leadership team.[21]

These meetings on monetization of Facebook's huge user base came up with the concept that 70 percent of Facebook's revenue should come from advertising and that, whereas Google advertising helped people find the things they had already decided to buy, Facebook would help them decide what they wanted.[22] Google's search advertising fulfilled demand, but Facebook's advertising would generate demand, similar to the type of branding advertising that appeared on television.

A year after the Sandberg-led meetings on advertising, in May 2009, comScore Media Metrics reported that Facebook overtook MySpace as the number one social network website with 70.28 million US unique visitors versus MySpace's 70.26 million US unique visitors.[23] And at the end of 2009 Facebook announced that it had turned a profit for the first time in its history.

In April of 2012 Facebook made its first major acquisition by purchasing the 13-person startup, Instagram, from Kevin Systrom and Mike Keiger for $1 billion, $300 in cash and $700 million in Facebook stock. At the time of the Instagram purchase, a month before Facebook's initial public offering (IPO), its share price was $33 on the private marketplace.

In May of 2012, a month after its purchase of Instagram, Facebook had the biggest tech company IPO in history when it sold 421 million shares, or a little over 20 percent of its outstanding shares, for $38 a share, which valued Facebook at an astonishing $104 billion.[24]

In February 2014, 10 years after its launch in a Harvard dorm room, Facebook purchased the messaging app WhatsApp for $16 billion, $4 billion in cash and $12 billion in Facebook stock, which at the time was selling for $67.50 a share.

Since 2014, Facebook has continued to grow at an incredible pace, and at the beginning of 2019, the social media juggernaut had over 2.3 billion users worldwide, 1.5 billion people who use Facebook every day, and over seven million advertisers.[25] Of those 2.3 billion users, only 9.8 percent were in the United States.[26] In 2018, 80 percent of Facebook's traffic came from mobile devices, and in 2018 Facebook gobbled up about 22 percent of all US digital advertising, versus Google's 37 percent.[27] In March of 2019, Facebook stock was selling for $164.34 a share, which valued the company at $469 billion, making it the sixth most valuable company in the world.[28] The primary reason for Facebook's amazing success is because it is "the most targetable medium in history."[29]

The most targetable medium in history

Facebook can target advertising so effectively because: (1) Users give Facebook scads of information about themselves in their profiles – favorite movies, favorite music, favorite books, relationship status, hobbies, and interests – valuable information for an advertiser. (2) Users give Facebook massive amounts of information about themselves when they like a post, like their friends, like photos, and like brand and causes pages. By examining "likes," Facebook's algorithms can identify what people like, what they hate, and what their personalities are. For example, in 2016 researchers identified personality traits of American voters such as "a neurotic introvert, a religious extrovert, a fair-minded liberal, or a fan of the occult."[30] (3) Users give Facebook valuable information when they interact with ads or brand pages. Facebook's algorithms track which ads their users interact with, how long they spend on an ad or on a video, and whether they converted or not. (4) When advertisers use Facebook Pixel, a line of code advertisers put on their websites, an advertiser can track Facebook users' behavior when they come from Facebook to a website. Facebook SDK does the same kind of tracking for mobile app ads and interactions.

By collecting such vast quantities of data about its users, Facebook allows advertisers to target people with great precision, which is a "business mode that earns Facebook more ad revenue in a year than all American newspapers combined."[31]

Advertisers can buy ads on Facebook in three ways: (1) Buy self-serve ads on the Facebook Business/Ads platform.[32] (2) Buy ads on Facebook through a certified Facebook Marketing Partner. (3) Facebook, like Google, will manage accounts for large advertisers (close to a $1-million yearly investment or more). In some cases for very large advertisers, Facebook will embed one or more people in a company to strategize, manage, and optimize its Facebook advertising.

Buying Facebook ads

Whether you use Facebook's self-serve model and buy and manage your campaign your-self (by far the hardest way to buy Facebook advertising), or use a Marketing Partner, or have Facebook manage your large investment (by far the easiest way to buy Facebook), there are several steps all of these buying methods have to go through. These steps have been carefully thought through by Facebook and are an object lesson in how to plan and buy advertising. See Exhibit 21.1 for Facebook Ad's list of options.

All ads on Facebook, whether bought on a self-serve basis, through a Marketing Partner, or by Facebook managing a large account, are bought in an online automated, first-price, or first-bid, auction. Facebook allows ad buyers to employ several bidding strategies, as outlined in Exhibit 21.2. These bidding strategies are designed to give buy-ers options that fit with their advertising objectives and with their pocketbook. Also, bid strategies are cost control tools. They help control the cost when an ad is shown in the same way budgets help control overall ad investments. A bid strategy choice tells Facebook's bidding algorithms how to bid in ad auctions.

A bid is based on how much an advertiser values a served ad to someone in a target audience. Facebook sets a bid in alignment with a selected bid strategy. The strategy may include raising or lowering a bid on an auction-by-auction basis, which is called *pacing* a bid. The only time Facebook does not pace a bid is if the ads are not performing well. If an advertiser cares more about getting the most value from a budget, Facebook recom-mends the lowest-cost bid strategy. If an advertiser cares more about having a stable aver-age cost per optimization event, Facebook recommends the target cost bid strategy.

Once a bid is won, ads begin to be delivered. Facebook's delivery system determines to whom the ads are shown, when they are shown, and where they are shown, either on Facebook, on Instagram, or on an Audience Network, for example. Following are the steps that lead up to an ad being delivered:

1   During ad set creation an advertiser choses a target audience, such as people in France interested in cooking, and an optimization event, such as an app install.[i]

Exhibit 21.1   Facebook Ads options

Advertising objectives	Audiences	Ad formats	Placements
Brand awareness	Targeting specifically	Images	Facebook
Reach	Targeting broadly	Carousel	Messenger
Lead generation		Collections	Instagram
Increase brand		Video and slideshows	Audience network
consideration		Catalogs	Marketplace
Get product		stories	Placement optimization
conversions			
Messages			
dynamic ads			

Source: Facebook. https://www.facebook.com/business/help.

---

[i] An ad set is a group of ads. Facebook advertisers should have several different versions of an ad in a set. For example, ads with different background colors, different offers, or different headlines.

Exhibit 21.2   Bidding strategies

- **Highest value:** Facebook tries to maximize the amount of value generated by someone who clicked on an ad and then made a purchase within 1 or 7 days.
- **Minimum ROAS:** The ROAS (return on ad spend) for an ad set can be calculated by dividing the amount of money spent by purchasers within a conversion window (also known as conversion value) by the amount invested on the ad set. Setting a minimum ROAS is a constraint on Facebook's delivery system. This means it could lead to less delivery if a minimum is too high. However, if an advertiser has a specific goal for how much return it wants to get from ads, setting a minimum ROAS can help achieve it. If an advertiser is trying to attract new customers and can accept losing a little money in the short term because, the advertiser can make it up from new customers over time, and therefore, could set a minimum ROAS of 0.75, for example. A 0.75 ROAS is the equivalent of getting a 75% return on ad spend, which means if an advertiser invests $100 on an ad set, it would want to get at least $75 of value from purchases that happen within the conversion window.
- **Target cost:** The target-cost bid strategy used to be known as manual bidding, and it was set as an average. Facebook has made some improvements to the system so that this bidding strategy maintains more stable costs per result near the target that is set. Facebook now describes it as target cost to more accurately reflect how the strategy works, and its benefits and tradeoffs. Using this option tells Facebook to aim for the average cost to be within a 10% range of the amount that is entered. This option is best for staying at a specific cost per optimization event. Facebook may not be able to get an exact desired cost on average over the lifetime of a campaign, but Facebook will get as close to it as possible after the campaign has exited the learning stage. Also, not all optimization goals are available for target cost. Target cost is available for app install, conversion, lead generation, and product catalog sales campaigns. If an advertiser is not using one of those campaign types, this bid strategy is not available. If a target cost is $10 and the current average cost is $8, Facebook will seek out results that will get closer to $10. If maximizing the efficiency of a campaign budget is more important than maintaining a target cost, advertisers should use the lowest-cost bid strategy instead.
- **Lowest cost:** The lowest-cost bid strategy tells Facebook to bid with the goal of getting the lowest possible cost per optimization event while also spending the entire budget by the end of the day or by the ad set's (or campaign's) schedule. If an advertiser cares more about getting the most value from a budget, Facebook recommends the lowest-cost bid strategy. This bid strategy is best for spending a budget as efficiently as possible. For example, the lowest-cost bid strategy may produce costs that fluctuate more, but Facebook will always get the lowest-cost results available, and make the most efficient use of a budget.
- **Bid cap:** A bid cap tells Facebook the maximum it can spend in an auction. Bid caps are less flexible, which means they are more likely to constrain delivery than cost caps. This constraint occurs because bid caps limit what can be bid in every auction. If a bid cap is set, an advertiser has more control over a cost per optimization event, but if a cap set too low, there may be less delivery. For example, if a cap is set at $5 and 100 optimization events become available for $5.01 bids, Facebook will not bid on them. Facebook recommends a bid cap over a cost cap only if there is a need to tightly control the cost of every single optimization event.

Source: Facebook. https://www.facebook.com/business/help/245880322600819.

Facebook shows the ad to people in that target audience who are likely to get the desired optimization event, such as people in France interested in cooking who are likely to install the app being advertised.

2 Facebook shows people an ad from an ad set. If the ad set has multiple ads, Facebook shows each one equally at the beginning of a campaign. As the algorithms see how each ad performs, the highest-performing ad begins showing more than the others.

3 For every opportunity to show someone an ad, Facebook's algorithms hold an auction to determine which ad gets shown. The winner of the auction is not the highest bidder but the ad that creates the most value for people and for advertisers. Facebook recommends allowing the algorithms to show ads across all placements (Facebook, Instagram, Audience Networks, for example) for best results. This placement system is called *automatic placement*.

4 The longer Facebook shows an ad, the better sense it gets of when might be a good time to show it. For example, if an ad is getting better results in the morning, Facebook will start trying to show it more often in the morning.

From the above information, you can see how incredibly robust and complicated buying advertising on Facebook is. Nevertheless, over seven million advertisers, both big and small, have used Facebook to their advantage. In fact, small advertisers have been the biggest engine of growth, and many businesses, such as Hubble contact lenses, started from scratch and grew to being a large and profitable businesses using Facebook almost exclusively.[33] When Facebook had an outage for 12 hours in March 2019, several advertisers were hurt substantially. As reported in *Ad Age,* one direct-response advertiser that invests $19,000 a day, on the day of the outage generated only $2,000 in sales, when on a normal day it generates between $40,000 and $60,000.[34]

Facebook's troubles and future

On November 10, 2016, two days after Donald Trump's election as president of the United States, Mark Zuckerberg, in response to questions about Russian interference in the election, said that it was a "pretty crazy idea" that fake news on Facebook influenced the outcome of the election.[35] In March 2017, reports surfaced that Cambridge Analytica, a British consulting firm that ran Trump's digital ad campaign, had harvested data from well over 30 million Facebook users against Facebook's privacy policies and used the data to target Trump's Facebook campaign ads. In September 2017, Facebook revealed that as many as 150 million people may have seen posts by the Kremlin-linked Internet Research Agency, and in April 2018, Mark Zuckerberg testified before Congress and admitted his comment about Russian interference in the election and perhaps influencing its outcome as being "pretty crazy," were inappropriate.[36] Later in 2018, news accounts surfaced about how Facebook's COO, Sheryl Sandberg, hired a conservative opposition research firm to go after Facebook critic, George Soros, also a target of anti-Semitic extremists.[37]

However, in spite of all of Facebook's, Zuckerberg's, and Sandberg's bad press, Facebook's advertising business did not suffer. In a November 19, 2018 article in *Ad Age* titled "Facebook fumbles, advertisers shrug," Garret Sloane wrote: "Facebook advertisers are once again turning a blind eye to the issues plaguing the social media giant after a *New York Times* report detailed a pattern of willful stonewalling, delaying, and obfuscating around a series of urgent problems."[38] Also, research firm eMarketer in a March 1, 2019, report titled "Will Facebook scandal affect ad business?" projected that for the full year of 2019 Facebook's share of US digital ad dollars would increase from 21.8 percent in 2018 to 22.1 percent in 2019, while Google's share of US digital ad dollars would decline from 38.2 percent in 2018 to 37.2 percent in 2019.[39] Another eMarketer report in 2018 indicated that 86.3 percent of US marketers used Facebook.[40] Therefore, there is lots of evidence that in spite of Facebook's public relations problems, marketers worldwide still find enticing its ability to target consumers at an efficient return on investment.

Deep Throat's famous advice to Woodward and Bernstein to "follow the money" when the *Washington Post* reporters were investigating the Watergate break-in, has been repeated often as applying not only to criminal investigations but also to investing in the stock market and investing in advertising. If you follow advertising money, it is clear it is going toward Google and Facebook and away from newspapers, magazines, and television as the money follows eyeballs, especially young eyeballs, as they get more of their news from Facebook and social media, connect with friends and family on Facebook and social media, and buy goods and services on Facebook, Instagram, and social media.

See Exhibit 21.3 to see what percentage of B2C and B2B marketers used Facebook and other social media sites in 2018.

Furthermore, Facebook is addressing many of its problems by becoming more transparent and giving advertisers fewer targeting choices to avoid unlawful discrimination. See Exhibit 21.4 for a look at the changes Facebook made in 2018 and up to April 2019.

Exhibit 21.3   Leading social media used by B2C and B2B marketers as of January 2019

Facebook B2C	97%
Facebook B2B	91%
LinkedIn B2C	46%
Linked In B2B	80%
Twitter B2C	57%
Twitter B2B	67%
Instagram B2C	78%
Instagram B2B	66%
You Tube B2C	54%
You Tube B2B	54%
Pinterest B2C	30%
Pinterest B2B	25%
Snapchat B2C	7%
Snapchat B2B	4%

Source: Statista. https://www.statista.com/statistics/259382/social-media-platforms-used-by-b2b-and-b2c-marketers-worldwide.

Exhibit 21.4   Facebook changes

March, 2019*	Mark Zuckerberg announced in a blog post titled "A privacy-focused vision for social media" that Facebook in the future would build more privacy into all four of its products (Facebook, Instagram, Messenger, and WhatsApp), including encryption and ephemerality (Snapchat-like impermanence).
March, 2019**	Restricted demographic and location data to use for employment and credit ads.
March, 2019**	Banned anti-vaccination ads that promote misinformation about vaccines.
March, 2019***	Introduced an Ad Library functionality that allowed users to search for how much advertisers, including political issue advertisers, spent on ads, which Pages ads reference a topic such as immigration, what a Page's previous names were, what location a Page is managed from, and the option to report an ad policy violation.
February, 2019**	Removed Nazi terms that could be targeted such as Joseph Goebbles and neo-Nazi band Skrewdriver.
February, 2019**	Began showing users which companies used their information to target ads at them using Facebook's Custom Audiences product.
August, 2018**	Removed 5,000 targeting options after US Department of Housing and Urban Development (HUD) indicated that Facebook had violated the Fair Housing Act by allowing ads that discriminated against ethnic and religious groups.
April, 2018**	Updated Custom Audience rules so that advertisers must warrant that they have obtained the necessary rights and permissions to use data they upload to Facebook to create Custom Audiences for ad targeting. Users who have opted out must be removed from Custom Audiences.
April, 2018**	Required that advertisers verify their identity and location before they are able to place political and issue ads.
March, 2018**	Shut down its Partner Categories product, which enabled third-party data providers to offer their targeting services and data on Facebook.

Sources:

*Feldman, Brian. 2019. "Mark Zuckerberg's private Facebook is a supplement, not a replacement." http://nymag.com/intelligencer/2019/03/mark-zuckerberg-announces-new-privacy-features-on-facebook.html.

**eMarketer. 2019. "Here's how Facebook has restricted ad targeting." https://www.emarketer.com/content/here-s-how-facebook-has-restricted-ad-targeting.

***Constine, Josh. 2019. "Facebook launches searchable transparency library of all active ads." https://techcrunch.com/2019/03/28/facebook-ads-library.

Twitter

Twitter is a US-based online news and social networking service on which users post and interact with messages known as tweets. It was launched in July 2006, after being created by Jack Dorsey, Noah Glass, Biz Stone, and Evan Williams. The service rapidly gained worldwide popularity, and at the end of 2018, eMarketer estimated Twitter had 321 million average monthly users worldwide that generated $2.62 billion, 51.5 percent ($1.35 billion) of which was US ad revenue.[41] Tweets were originally restricted to 140 characters, but on November 7, 2017, this limit was doubled for all languages except Chinese, Japanese, and Korean. Registered users can post, like, and retweet tweets, but unregistered users can only read them.

In 2019, Twitter was one of the 10 most-visited websites, and has been described as "the SMS of the Internet."[42] Since 2015, Twitter has been a hotbed of debates and news covering politics of the United States, and during the 2016 US presidential election, Donald Trump communicated directly with the public through Twitter. By 2019, Trump had accumulated 59.3 million followers, and in terms of monthly interactions, Axios Media Trends newsletter reported that Donald Trump's Twitter account ranked number one in monthly interactions with 103.9 million. Ariana Grande was number two with 101.8 million Twitter interactions.[43] See Exhibit 21.5 for the top 20 Twitter accounts with the most followers.

In Exhibit 21.5 you can see that the people who have the most followers on Twitter are mostly celebrities, and the majority of those celebrities are pop singers. Only one of the top 20 (Ronaldo) is an athlete. However, looking at the number of followers is not the best way to evaluate the current popularity of or the interest in a celebrity, politician, or athlete. In order to evaluate which celebrities, politicians, athletes, or issues are currently most popular, or on the top of people's minds, you need to look at the number of *interactions* users have on social media platforms because just looking at followers can give you a distorted view of current popularity. For example, in Exhibit 21.5 Barack Obama is number two in total Twitter followers with 105,300,000, but that number was built up starting in, probably, 2007 and 2008 when he was first running for president and grew during his presidency from 2009 to 2016.

If you look at Exhibit 21.6, Obama does not appear in the top 10 in interactions on Twitter, Facebook, or Instagram. Likewise, Britney Spears and Justin Timberlake built up massive Twitter followers about the same time Obama did, but like the former president, have not kept up in the number of interactions on social media.

On the other hand, Donald Trump is number 13 in Twitter followers, but is number one in interactions on Twitter, which means that people on Twitter look at Trump's tweets, comment on them, or share them more than they do so with anyone else.

Looking at Exhibit 21.6, you can see that despite having less than half of Facebook's monthly active users (MAUs), Instagram's top 10 accounts generate five times more interactions than Facebook's most-engaged accounts. These numbers show the very high level of interactions users have on Instagram. Therefore, when evaluating the impact of celebrities, politicians, and issues it is important to look at the number of interactions, not at the number of followers or friends.

Also, the top accounts on each of the social media platforms reflect the type of people and issues the users of that platform interact with. For example, on Twitter, users interact with ideas, combative right- and left-wing ideologues, and conflict as entertainment; on Facebook people interact with faceless news, entertainment, and sports media brands; and on Instagram users interact with celebrities, personalities, lifestyles, aspirations, and influencers.[44]

Exhibit 21.5   Top 20 Twitter accounts with the most followers March 2019

Name	Followers (millions)
1 Katy Perry	107
2 Barack Obama	105.3
3 Justin Bieber	105.2
4 Rihanna	90.2
5 Taylor Swift	83.2
6 Lady Gaga	78.4
7 Ellen De Generes	77.3
8 Cristiano Ronaldo	77.2
9 YouTube	71.4
10 Justin Timberlake	64.8
11 Ariana Grande	61.6
12 Kim Kardashian	60.2
13 Donald Trump	59.3
14 Selena Gomez	57.3
15 Britney Spears	56.5
16 Twitter	56
17 CNN Breaking News	54.9
18 Shakira	51.1
19 Jimmy Fallon	50.9
20 Bill Gates	46.9

Source: Brand Watch. http://www.brandwatch.com/blog/most-twitter-followers.

Twitter facts[45]

- Number of tweets sent each day: 500 million
- Twitter only became profitable in 2017
- Number of people who on Twitter each month: 326,000[ii]
- Percent of Twitter's users who are not American: 80
- Percent of Twitter users who are reading news: 24
- Twitter is the numberone platform for government leaders worldwide
- Percent of Twitter ads that are more effective than television ads during live events: 11
- The best time to tweet is 3:00 p.m. weekdays
- Tweets with video attract 10 times more engagement than ads without video

---

[ii] In the third quarter of 2018 the number of monthly active users (MAUs) decreased from 326,000 to 321,000. Twitter attributed the losses to its ongoing effort of removing questionable accounts, and otherwise trying to improve the health of the service according to an eMarketer report titled "Four takeaways from Twitter's Q4 earnings: what advertisers need to know," which is available at https://www.emarketer.com/content/four-takeaways-from-twitter-s-q4-earnings-what-advertisers-need-to-know

Exhibit 21.6   Top 10 accounts by number of social media interactions in February 2019

		Interactions in millions			Interactions in millions	
Twitter						
1	Donald Trump	103.9	6	Brian Krasserstein[ii]	20.5
2	Ariana Grande	101.8	7	ESPN Sports Center	17.9
3	Bleacher Report	49.7	8	ye (Kanye West)	15.8
4	Alexandria Ocasio-Cortez	36.9	9	Ed Kasserstein[ii]	14.1
5	Charlie Kirk[i]	24.4	10	Kamala Harris	12.6
Facebook						
1	LADbible[iii]	121.3	6	Fox News	82.3
2	Cifras[iv]	115.3	7	Memes[vi]	81.7
3	UNILAD[v]	114.2	8	9GAG	81.0
4	Womenworking.com	92.8	9	Khaosod[vii]	73.3
5	Todo Imagenes	86.6	10	Power of Positivity	73.2
Instagram						
1	9GAG: Go Fun the World	812.8	6	Cristiano Ronaldo	477.4
2	Kylie[ix]	662.3	7	NFL	313.8
3	433[x]	568.3	8	therock[xi]	307.5
4	Ariana Grande	557.9	9	Kim Kardashian West	302.9
5	NBA	494.6	10	National Geographic	294.0

[i] Charlie Kirk is a left-wing ideologue.

[ii] The Kasserstein twin brothers are left-wing ideologues.

[iii] LADbible is the home of entertainment, viral video, trending content and the latest news.

[iv] Cifras is about Spanish music and musicians.

[v] UNILAD is a British Internet media company and website owned by LADbible Group. The company provides social news and entertainment with a social-first approach to their 60 million followers.

[vi] Memes is the home on Facebook of entertainment news.

[vii] Khaosod is a Facebook news site based in Bangkok, Thailand.

[viii] 9GAG: Go Fun the World is the home of funny pics, gifs, videos, gaming, anime, manga, movie, tv, cosplay, sport, food, memes, cute, fail, wtf photos.

[ix] Kylie is the celebrity Kylie Jenner. And owner of Kylie cosmetics.

[x] 433 is the world-wide Instagram home of football (soccer) fans and stars.

[xi] therock is celebrity and movie star Dwayne Johnson.

Source: CrowdTangle. Axios Media Trends. https://www.axios.com/newsletters/axios-media-trends-72b26dbd-6844-463d-851d-e89fbc291c59.html.

Buying Twitter ads

Twitter is similar to Facebook in that it uses a self-serve, first-price online auction model for buying ads and, like Facebook, asks advertisers to choose among several options for campaign objectives. Also, Twitter has two different advertising models: (1) Twitter Ads and (2) Twitter Promote Mode. See Exhibit 21.7 for guidelines for the two advertising models.

Exhibit 21.7   Twitter advertising guidelines

Twitter Ads*

- **Objective** Decide what you want your campaign to achieve: raise awareness of a specific Tweet, attract new followers, send traffic to your website, or increase engagement.
- **Audience** Use targeting features to choose the audience you want to reach. Select geographic areas, the followers of a notable account, or target people's interests.
- **Bidding** Twitter Ads run in an auction. Decide how much you will pay for each interaction, such as a new follower or a click to your website. Or use automatic bidding, which determines the best bid cost based on your budget and goals.
- **Budget** There's no minimum campaign spend. Choose a daily budget for your ads. Consider starting with at least $30 per day to consistently reach audiences throughout the day.
- **Creative** Select the Tweets you want to focus on in your campaign. Choosing four to five is a good start. Include strong call-to-actions, like "sign up" or "start today." Avoid #hashtags or @mentions in your copy so that your audience does not click away from your ad.

Twitter Promote Mode

- **Twitter Promote Mode** automates your brand marketing efforts for less than the price of a cup of coffee per day, enabling you to focus on creating your best Tweets. It is an affordable, always-on promotion engine, so whether you're building your personal brand or a business, Twitter Promote Mode grows your influence by automatically amplifying your message to a larger interested audience. For a set monthly fee, your Tweets and account will automatically be promoted. Reach up to 30,000 additional people and add an average of 30 new followers each month.
- **Promote Mode** works best for people who Tweet about their brand or product and want an automated, always-on advertising solution. Each day, your first 10 Tweets (that pass our quality filter) will be added to a Promoted Tweets campaign that targets your selected audience. Tweets that are promoted become Twitter Ads and appear with a small "Promoted" badge. Your Retweets, Quote Tweets, or replies will not be promoted. Typically, your first few Tweets of the day will receive the most promotion. Simply promote your brand as you normally do – Tweeting updates, links, and media that you want your target audience to see. Promote Mode does the rest.
- **Promoted Account** Promote Mode will also run a Promoted Account campaign which will increase your reach, attract visitors to your profile, and add followers interested in your brand. On average, accounts will reach 30,000 additional people and add 30 followers each month. Your performance may vary based on factors such as your account type, your targeting selection, and the type and frequency of your Tweets. In the future, higher priced tiers will be available for larger accounts that want to focus on reaching even more people.

---

* Twitter ads are called cards. The ads are not called banners because cards are small and come in the shape of a Tweet.

Source: "Choose your objective." https://business.twitter.com/en/solutions/twitter-ads.html;"Twitter Promote Mode help." https://business.twitter.com/en/help/twitter-promote-mode-help.html.

Twitter's troubles and future

Twitter has been criticized by many for allowing too much hate speech and too many conspiracy theorists to appear on its platform. Advertisers want a brand-safe environment, and many feel that Twitter does not always provide such an environment. Furthermore, the vast majority of Twitter's audience is on mobile phones, and, thus, ads on Twitter, which are small, often do not stand out. Although Twitter has huge reach, especially among government leaders worldwide, the social media platform has shown little or no growth in users, primarily because Twitter has purged many duplicate, bot-initiated, or controversial accounts. This lack of growth has hindered Twitter's ability to show the kind of significant revenue growth that other social platforms have experienced.

YouTube

YouTube was founded in 2005, and purchased by Google in 2006. Three former PayPal employees, Steve Chen, Chad Hurley, and Jawed Karim, created YouTube in February 2005, and Google purchased it in November 2006, for $1.65 billion. YouTube still operates as a Google subsidiary.

YouTube allows users to upload, view, rate, share, and comment on videos. It offers a wide variety of user-generated and corporate videos. Available content includes videos produced by individuals, clips from television programs, music videos, documentary films, audio recordings, movie teasers, occasional live streams, and other content such as video blogging, short original videos, and educational videos such as the Kahn Academy. Most of the videos on YouTube are uploaded by individuals, but media corporations including CBS, the BBC, and Hulu offer some of their content on YouTube as part of a YouTube partnership program.[46]

Unregistered users can only watch videos on the site, while registered users are permitted to upload an unlimited number of videos and add comments to videos. Videos deemed inappropriate are available only to registered users affirming themselves to be at least 18 years old. The vast majority of its videos are free to view, but there are exceptions, including subscription-based premium channels, film rentals, as well as YouTube Premium, a subscription service offering ad-free access to the website and access to exclusive content made in partnership with existing users.[47]

YouTube facts[48]

- Rank as most visited website in the world: #2
- Percent of all mobile Internet traffic: 37
- Number of people worldwide who use YouTube: 1.3 billion
- Number of people in the US who use YouTube: 260 million

- Hours of video uploaded to YouTube every minute: 300
- Number of videos watched on YouTube every day: 5 billion
- Number of YouTube visitors per day: 30 million
- Percent of 18–49-year-olds who watch YouTube in an average month: 80
- Percent of people who prefer online video platforms to live TV: 60
- Hours of video watched on YouTube each month: 3.25 billion
- Percent of YouTube's views from outside of the US: 80
- Percent of average mobile viewing that is up over previous year: 50
- Percent of YouTube's audience that is women: 38
- Percent of YouTube's audience that is men: 62
- Percent of users that are18–24: 11
- Percent of users that are 25–34: 23
- Percent of user that are 35–44: 26
- Percent of users that are 45–54: 16
- Percent of users that are 55+: 11
- YouTube overall and even YouTube on mobile alone reaches more 18–34 and 18–49-year-olds than any single cable network in the US
- Percent increase year-to-year (2109) in number of hours people spend watching videos on YouTube: 60
- Number of different languages people can navigate on YouTube: 76
- Percent of the Internet population reached by YouTube: 95
- Number of countries YouTube has launched a local version of: 88
- Percent increase in the number of advertisers running video ads on YouTube over previous year: 40

Buying YouTube ads

Advertisers can purchase video ads on YouTube by using the Google Ads self-serve platform, and they can target ads according to location, audience, interests, and budget.[49]

YouTube's troubles and future

Several major advertisers pulled their video advertising from YouTube in 2017 and 2018 because of videos that promoted terrorism, promoted fake news, provided a forum for abusive trolls, or even might have influenced the 2016 US presidential election. These actions by advertisers have put social media platforms on the defensive and most platforms, especially YouTube and Facebook, have responded by beefing up their efforts to police their content. This response involves a great deal of human intervention, and YouTube and Facebook have hired thousands of new staffers to monitor content. Algorithms have been developed to attempt to monitor offensive, especially hate-filled, content. However, even sophisticated algorithms often ban content that is not necessarily objectionable. Creators of content and advertising that algorithms turn down can appeal an algorithm's ruling to human monitors who can then make a judgment of content's or an ad's appropriateness.[50]

These attempts by YouTube have signaled to advertisers that YouTube's content is monitored more carefully than ever before, and is thus more brand safe, which has encouraged many advertisers to return to YouTube. The popular video-serving and video-sharing site is consistently the second most trafficked site (second to Google.com). And in 2019, the average time spent by adults per day with mobile devices (223 minutes, or three hours and 43 minutes) will surpass the average time spent by adults with television (222 minutes, or three hours and 42 minutes) which means that more time will be spent watching videos on YouTube.[51] So, as the eyeballs move to YouTube, so will the money. Therefore, the percentage of B2C and B2B businesses (as seen in Exhibit 21.3) that used YouTube in 2018 increased in 2019 and 2020.

Reddit

Reddit was founded by University of Virginia roommates Steve Huffman and Alexis Ohanian in 2005. Condé Nast Publications acquired the site in October 2006. In 2011, Reddit became an independent subsidiary of Condé Nast's parent company, Advance Publications. In October, 2014, Reddit raised $50 million in a funding round that included investors Marc Andreessen and Peter Thiel, and several other celebrities. Their investment valued the company at $500 million at that time. In July 2017, Reddit raised $200 million for a $1.8 billion valuation, with Advance Publications remaining the majority stakeholder.

Reddit is a social news aggregation, web content rating, and discussion website. Registered members submit content to the site such as links, text posts, and images, which are then voted up or down by other members. Posts are organized by subject into user-created areas called boards, which are known as *subreddits* that cover a variety of topics including news, science, movies, video games, music, books, fitness, food, and image-sharing. Submissions with more up-votes appear toward the top of their subreddit and, if they receive enough votes, ultimately appear on Reddit's front page. Despite strict rules prohibiting harassment, Reddit's administrators spend considerable resources on moderating the site, which often has objectionable material from hate groups and other extremists.

Reddit facts[52]

- Number of Reddit users: 330 million users
- Number of subreddits on Reddit: 853,824
- Number of Reddit communities: 50,000
- Number of countries with Reddit users: 217
- Number of monthly Reddit pageviews: 18 billion
- Number of daily votes on Reddit: 58 million

Exhibit 21.8   Reddit campaign objectives and bid options

Objective	Bid option
Brand awareness and reach	CPM (cost per thousand)
Traffic	CPC (cost per click)
Conversions	CPC
App installs	CPC
Video views	CPV (cost per view)

- The average visit length on Reddit: 16 minutes.
- Number of comments left on Reddit daily: 2.8 million
- Percent of Reddit content that is in English: 80
- Average daily time spent per visitor in the Reddit: 36 minutes.[53]
- Percent of Reddit's audience that is18–34: 25
- Percent of Reddit's audience that is 35–49: 23
- Percent of Reddit's audience that is over 45: 27[54]
- Percent of Reddit's audience that is women: 40
- Percent of Reddit's audience that is men: 60[55]

Buying Reddit ads

Reddit uses a self-serve, second-price auction model for buying ads, and advertisers can bid on a cost-per-thousand (CPM), cost-per-click (CPC), or cost-per-view (CPV) basis based on their campaign objectives. See Exhibit 21.8 for campaign objectives on Reddit and the bid options associated with each objective.

There are a number of targeting options on Reddit: by location (country, state, city, or ZIP code), by interests (news, entertainment, sports, gaming, style and fashion, healthy living, for example), by community (subreddit), by device, or by day and time of day. Also, advertisers can use the self-serve system or Reddit's Managed Sales Team will manage campaigns of large advertisers who invest $50,000 or more in any quarter.

Reddit's troubles and future

In 2018, Reddit completed a major cleanup of its platform because of brand-safety concerns by advertisers. Reddit revamped its ad model, and eMarketer estimated that it was on a path to more than triple its 2018 ad revenues by 2021, which means moving from $76.9 million in 2018 to $119 million in 2019 to $181.3 million in 2020 to $261.7 in 2021.[56]

Reddit positions itself as a "place where people can be their true selves" and as a "home for conversation." Reddit is also a good place to reach young men under 34, especially gamers; however, it still has brand-safety concerns for advertisers, which Reddit maintains that its "Anti-Evil Team" human moderators address on a daily basis. But, despite this emphasis on moderation and control, some major agencies and clients continue to shy away from Reddit because of brand-safety issues.

Snapchat and TikTok

Snapchat is another successful Internet company to be founded by men who went to Stanford University. It is a global image and video messaging app created by Evan Spiegel, Bobby Murphy, and Reggie Brown in 2011. A principal feature of Snapchat is that images and messages are ephemeral and are typically only available for a short period of time, usually two-to-ten seconds (the amount of time can be controlled by a user), before they become inaccessible to their recipients.[57] The app has evolved from originally just focusing on person-to-person photo sharing to currently featuring user-produced segments called *Stories*. Snapchat also has a Discover feature, which allows brands to show brief ad-supported content.

Stories allow users to post a series of video snaps that remain visible for 24 hours. Instagram replicated Stories successfully in 2016, and it has become a popular feature on that social media platform. Furthermore, Snapchatters have the option to save specific Snaps in a private storage area with the Memories feature. Snapchat also features longer videos called Originals, which consist of original video series, such as "Dead Girls Detective Agency," produced by a Snapchat–NBCUniversal joint venture. Major content creators such CBS, ESPN, Viacom, Discovery, the NBA, and the NFL have created content for Snapchat Originals.[58]

Snapchat facts[59]

- Daily active users: 186 million
- Total active users: 301 million
- US daily active users (DAUs): 79 million
- Average number of snaps daily: 3 billion
- Percent US penetration among 12–17-year-olds: 92
- Percent US penetration among 18–24 year olds: 94
- Percent of US adults who use Snapchat: 27
- Percent of US users who are under 34 years old: 53
- Percent of US users who are 18–24 years old: 28
- Percent of users globally who are female: 59
- Percent of college students who use Snapchat: 77
- Average number of snaps users send per day: 34
- Percent of daily active users who post a Story every day: 25
- Daily video views: 10 billion

- Percent of Snapchatters who use it because content disappears: 35
- Percent of Snapchatters who use it because their parents do not: 30
- Average number of minutes of in-app time spent daily per user: 30
- Average number of times per day daily users visit the app: 20
- Percent of US teens who use Snapchat: 79

Buying Snapchat Ads

Snapchat uses an online, automated, self-serve, first-price auction model to sell its ads, much like Facebook, Instagram, YouTube, and Twitter do; however, Snapchat ads last 10 seconds or less. To purchase ads on Snapchat, (1) create a Snapchat account, (2) set up a Business account, (3) create an Ad Account, (4) go to Ad Manager to create ads, create audiences, and create and launch campaigns. It has similar campaign objectives and targeting options as other social media platforms do, as can be seen in Exhibit 21.9.

Snapchat also offers several different bidding options, which are outlined in Exhibit 21.10.

Exhibit 21.9   Snapchat ad campaign objectives

Awareness Increase awareness of a brand or product across Snapchat. Available ad types: Filters, Story Ad, Snap Ad with Long Form Video, Website, AR Lens, or Top Snap Only. Available optimization goals: Shares, Story Opens, or Impressions

Consideration (1) App Installs: Send Snapchatters to the App Store to download an app. Available ad types: Snap Ad with App Install, or Story Ad. Available optimization goals: Impressions, Swipe Ups, or App Installs. (2) Drive Traffic To Website: Send Snapchatters directly to a website. Available ad types: Snap Ad with Website or Collection Ad. Available optimization goals: Swipe Ups. (3) Drive Traffic To App: Send Snapchatters to an advertiser's app or to a third-party app. Available ad types: Snap Ad with Deep Link or Collection Ad. Available optimization goals: Swipe Ups. (4) Engagement: Get more Snapchatters to share a Filter, or open a Story Ad. Available ad types: Filters, Story Ad, or Snap Ad with augmented reality (AR) Lens. Available optimization goals: Shares or Story Ad Opens. (5) Video Views: Promote a brand or product to Snapchatters through video. Available ad types: Snap Ad with Long Form Video or Top Snap Only. Available optimization goals: Video Views. (6) Lead Gen: Generate leads for a business. Available ad types: Story Ad, Snap Ad with Website, or Collection Ad. Available optimization goals: Story Opens, Swipe Ups, or Pixel Sign Ups.

Conversions (1) Web Conversion: Drive specific actions on a website. Available ad types: Snap Ad with Website. Available optimization goals: Pixel Purchases, Pixel Sign Ups. (2) Catalog Sales: Drive online product sales. Available ad types: Story Ad, Snap Ad with Deep Link or Web View, or Collection Ad. Available optimization goals: Swipe Ups, Pixel Purchases, App Purchases, or Story Opens.

Source: Based on "Campaign objectives." https://businesshelp.snapchat.com/en-US/article/campaign-objectives.

Exhibit 21.10   Snapchat bidding strategies

Auto-Bidding This bidding strategy allows Snapchat to set the bid on an advertiser's behalf to get the most ad objective actions given the budget and target audience. When auto-bidding is enabled, Snapchat will try to optimize for the most efficient cost per objective such that it is consistent with ads targeted to similar audiences on the platform. However, Snapchat cannot guarantee that a campaign will deliver in full due to variables such as the creative interaction rate, current auction dynamics, target audience size, and so forth.

Additionally, when creating a campaign, an advertiser can use the auto-bid feature, which will automatically set bids that are optimized for campaign objectives while staying within a budget. Auto-bidding does not increase the bid price incrementally to ensure a campaign will deliver in full. Rather, when auto-bidding is enabled Snapchat will try to optimize ad set performance so that it is consistent with similar ads targeted to the same audience on the platform. Auto-bid is the default selection.

Max bid This bidding strategy tells Snapchat the maximum amount Snapchat can bid for an advertiser while Snapchat tries to achieve the most efficient cost-per-acquisition (CPA) possible. A suggested bid range will appear below a bid amount, if available. This suggested range is based on many factors, including current auction dynamics and targeted audience. This range is intended to give a reference point when setting a max bid. Estimates are optimization objective specific and should help deliver against a specified daily budget. While bidding within the suggested range simplifies setup, other variables may lead to a campaign not delivering in full. To give an ad set a better chance to spend through its daily budget, Snapchat encourages bidding on the higher end of the suggested range. Max bidding tells Snapchat not to bid above a max bid amount. If the max bid amount is too low, an advertiser may not be able to spend its budget in full. This bidding strategy is only available for Swipes, App Install events, Long Form Video Views, Shares, Pixel events, and Story Opens ad objectives.

Target cost This bidding strategy tells Snapchat to make its best effort to keep an advertiser's average CPA at or below the amount set by the ad set end date. This bidding strategy is only available for Swipes, App Install events, Long Form Video Views, Shares, Pixel events, and Story Opens ad objectives. If the target cost is too low, advertisers may be unable to spend their entire budget. Changing the target cost may also result in a campaign CPA that is higher than the current desired one.

Suggested bids When an advertiser creates a campaign, a suggested bid will appear under the Bid & Goal field. A suggested bid is a recommended range based on average platform performance intended to give a reference point when setting a bid. These estimates are optimization objective specific and should help deliver against a specified daily budget. While they will help an advertiser bid more effectively, there is no guarantee that a campaign will deliver in full. In order to give an ad set a better chance to spend through its daily budget, Snapchat encourages bidding on the higher end of the suggested range. While Snapchat's bid suggestions are currently based on average platform performance, Snapchat may use a different methodology in the future.

Source: Based on "Bidding strategies." https://businesshelp.snapchat.com/en-US/article/bidding-strategies.

Snapchat's troubles and future

A redesign of Snapchat in 2018 was publicly criticized by celebrity Kylie Jenner on Twitter. Because Jenner has a huge number of teen followers, the tweet not only hurt Snapchat's image among teens but also hurt its stock price – the market value of the company dropped almost $1 billion soon after Jenner's tweet. Later in 2018 Snapchat experienced the first drop in user numbers since its launch, which many analysts blamed on a redesign of the app. CEO Evan Spiegel received a petition signed by 1.2 million users calling for the redesign to be reversed. Snapchat soon changed the design and users began returning. In spite of the redesign and users returning, as of April 2019, the social media app has lost over 50 percent of its $33 billion market valuation since its much-anticipated IPO on March 2, 2017.

However, because teenagers grew up with smartphones, they are mobile natives and know nothing else. About 95 percent of US teens have a smartphone, and 45 percent of US teens stay online "almost constantly."[60] And even though Snapchat usage among teens (69 percent) is third behind YouTube (85 percent) and Instagram (72 percent), the percent of teens that use Snapchat "most often" is number one with 35 percent, ahead of YouTube with 32 percent and Instagram in third place.[61] Snapchat is designed for quick updates, and due to the ephemerality of snaps, it is built for constant updating because of teens' fear of missing out (FOMO).

Because of Snapchat's immense popularity and usage by teenagers, it is an effective advertising vehicle for reaching them with targeted advertising. Also, some recent moves such as paying influencers who create popular content, launching a gaming platform, a "new round of original shows," and "actively courting UK advertisers" all bode well for Snapchat's future.[62] In 2019, eMarketer estimated that Snapchat's revenue would increase 24.3 percent in 2019 and another 21.5 percent in 2020 to reach $1.01billion.[63]

TikTok

At the end of 2018, TikTok was the number one most downloaded app on both iPhones and Android phones worldwide.[64] There are some estimates that indicate that in the summer of 2019, TikTok may have about one billion monthly users, making it the third most popular social media app in the world behind Facebook and YouTube.

The TikTok mobile app allows users to create a short video of themselves which often features music in the background, and can be sped up, slowed down, or edited. To create a music video, users can choose background music from a wide variety of music genres, edit it with a filter, and record a 6–15-second video with speed adjustments before uploading it.[65]

TikTok has very heavy use by teenagers in the US and 21–25-year-olds in South Asia, where it is the number one app in terms of downloads. The average user of TikTok views the app 52 minutes a day and checks in 43 times a day. According to some studies, just over 40 percent of users open the app 21–50 times per day, with close to 30 percent more opening it 51 times or more.[66]

TikTok sells several different types of ads, based on the country the advertiser lives in and offers fairly granular targeting, but the guidelines for bidding for ads and the type of ads offered are not clear from the TikTok advertising website.[67] Even though ads on TikTok may reach a sizeable audience, the biggest question for advertisers is asking if TikTok provides a brand-safe environment.

According to Tik Tok's service agreement, the app is not for users under 16 years old and TikTok claims it will terminate accounts where necessary. However, investigations by several newspapers and online newsletters revealed that the personal information of hundreds of child users was being exposed publicly on TikTok. Disturbing selfie videos with sexually suggestive themes or actions implying self-harm were discovered on the app, along with suspicious adults using the platform to stalk and court teenage girls.[68]

Whether or not TikTok is just another teenage fad or has long-term staying power is a question about which it is too early to make a reasonable prediction. What is not in doubt is that TikTok in the summer of 2019 had a huge global audience of young people.

Pinterest

Pinterest is a free website on which users can register and then upload, save, sort, and manage images – known as *pins* – and other media content such as videos in another format known as *boards* or *pinboards*. The images on pinboards range from art supplies to apparel to recipes to hairstyles to travel locations, and users can follow other users' pinboards if they have similar tastes and interests. Pinterest was founded by Ben Silbermann, Paul Sciarra, and Evan Sharp in 2011, as a "catalog of ideas," and soon after it went live, co-founder and current CEO, Ben Silbermann, personally wrote to the site's first 5,000 users offering his personal phone number and even meeting with some of its users.[69]

Pinterest does not view itself as social media, but instead describes itself as a "visual discovery engine."[70] It helps people find the things they love, whether they are planning a wedding, putting up pictures of a wedding they loved, remodeling, gardening, or doing an arts and craft project.

Content can also be found outside Pinterest and uploaded to a pinboard by means of a Pin It button, which can be downloaded to a bookmark bar on a web browser. Some websites and apps include red-and-white Pin It buttons on items, which allows Pinterest users to pin the items from other websites directly to Pinterest.[71]

In one case study of a fashion website, users visiting from Pinterest spent $180 compared to $85 spent from users coming from Facebook. These users spent less time on the company's website, choosing instead to browse from the company's pinboard. Further brand studies have continued to show Pinterest is more effective at driving sales than other forms of social media. A study carried out by Wolfgang Digital found that site traffic originating from Pinterest Business pages was more engaged and spent up to five times longer on site.[72]

Pinterest provides partners and advertisers with a dashboard, called Pinterest Analytics, similar to Google Analytics, that shows data on pins, pinners, repins, and repinners. Pinterest Analytics also collects data that depicts the percentage of change within a specific time to determine if a product is more popular on a specific day during the week or slowly becoming unpopular. This information helps marketers and their agencies alter their strategies and change content in order to optimize its appeal. The Most Clicked tab in Pinterest Analytics demonstrates products that are more likely to sell.

Retailers such The Gap, Chobani, Nordstrom, and West Elm use Pinterest to gather online referrals that link users with similar interests to each other and to a retailer.[73]

Pinterest facts[74]

- Total number of people using Pinterest every month: 250 million
- People in the US using Pinterest every month: 77.4 million (31 percent of total)
- Percent of US women aged 25–54 Pinterest reaches monthly: 83
- Percent of new sign-ups in 2018 that were men: 50
- Percent of new sign-ups that were outside the US: 80
- Top five countries for Pinterest users: America, Brazil, India, Turkey, Russia
- Percent of Americans 18–49 who use Pinterest: 34
- High-income and educated US households are twice as likely to use Pinterest as low-income and less-educated US households
- Percent increase in pins in under two years: 75
- Number of images pinned in 2018: 175 billion
- Percent of Pinterest users on mobile: 80
- Percent of users who try the ideas they find on Pinterest: 98
- Percent of millennials who have discovered products on Pinterest: 59 (Facebook = 78 percent, Instagram and Pinterest = 59 percent, Twitter = 34 percent, and Snapchat = 22 percent)
- Percent of weekly users who use Pinterest to make purchase decisions: 90
- Percent more traffic Pinterest delivers to shopping sites than Facebook: 33

Buying Pinterest ads

Pinterest has an easy-to-use ad-buying system that explains how to buy ads and promote pins. Buying ads on Pinterest is not as complicated as doing so on Facebook, primarily because it does not have as many targeting opportunities. On Pinterest there are only three basic targeting strategies: (1) interest targeting, (2) keyword targeting, and (3) audience targeting. Under the audience targeting option, the types of audiences that you can target are: (1) a list of your customers that you upload to Pinterest, (2) your website visitors for which you must install appropriate tags, (3) engagement, and (4) actalikes, or targeting people whose online behavior mirrors the behavior of known customers.[75]

In terms of interest targeting, Exhibit 21.11 shows the top 10 interest areas on Pinterest.

Exhibit 21.11   Pinterest interest categories

Interest Category	Percent of US users who like category
Art, art supplies and hobbies	48
Flowers, food, drinks, and gifts	47
Home, garden, and pool/spa	45
Health and beauty	45
Clothes and apparel	37
Entertainment (books, music, etc.)	34
Jewelry, handbags, and accessories	23
Sporting goods	16
Footwear	13
Baby gear	7

Source: "Most popular Pinterest categories in the United States as of February 2017."
https://www.statista.com/statistics/251048/most-popular-categories-browsed-on-pinterest.

Bidding strategies on Pinterest are also pretty straightforward. "Every campaign has a different bid floor. Within each campaign type, different countries have different floors. The minimum bid will depend on which countries you select your campaign to target. The bid floor for each country is then converted to the US dollar (USD) equivalent based on the current exchange rate. The minimum bid will be the highest of the different floors for the different countries.

"For example, if you have a CPC campaign targeting US, UK, Canada, the bid floors are $0.10, £0.07, and $0.10 respectively. We convert these bid floors to USD then set the minimum as the highest price, which would be $0.10."[76]

Pinterest's troubles and future

Since Pinterest launched in 2011, the company has made every effort to make it "positive and respectful" and free of controversial or hate-filled pins.[77] Therefore, Pinterest has been able to avoid much of the controversy over privacy and objectionable content that has plagued many other popular social media apps.

Pinterest is also one of the fastest growing websites in terms of revenue, primarily because all sizes and types of retailers use Pinterest extensively and successfully. In October 2018, eMarketer forecast that in 2018 Pinterest revenue would grow 43.8 percent to $553,300, would grow 39.4 percent in 2019 to $771,4000, and would grow almost 30 percent in 2020 to slightly over $1 billion.[iii]

[iii] The October 2018 eMarketer report is no longer available online because in 2019 eMarketer changed the pricing model of some of its reports, which are available only on its paid service, eMarketer Plus.

Because of Pinterest's relatively brand-safe environment and "incredibly strong connection with consumers," its future is less fraught with many of the negatives other social media sites face, and its prospects for steady growth, if not spectacular, are solid.[78]

Pinterest's IPO in April 2019 saw its stock price rise from an initial offer of $15–$17 per share to $19 by the end of the first trading day, which valued the company at $10 billion.

LinkedIn

LinkedIn was founded in December, 2002, and was launched in May, 2003, by Stanford graduate Reid Hoffman and several colleagues from PayPal, where he worked at the time, and from Socialnet.com, which he had also founded.

LinkedIn is used primarily for professional networking, including employers posting available jobs and job seekers posting their resumes, experience, and likeness in a profile. LinkedIn members not only create profiles, but also make connections to LinkedIn members and non-members. The website and app have become the largest business and professionally oriented social media site in the world; even many high-schoolers have LinkedIn profiles that they hope will aid them in getting jobs. And recruiting companies such as ZipRecruiter.com scrape LinkedIn data extensively to find job candidates with relevant skills and experience for employers seeking to hire people.

In June, 2016 Microsoft acquired LinkedIn for $26.3 billion, which was the company's largest ever acquisition because Microsoft apparently saw the opportunity to integrate LinkedIn with its Office product suite to better integrate the professional social network's vast connections and data with Microsoft's Office and other offerings.[79]

LinkedIn facts[80]

- Total number of people using LinkedIn: 610 million
- Total number of active monthly users: 260 million
- Total number of LinkedIn users in the US: 154 million
- Number of new LinkedIn members per second: 2
- Number of LinkedIn users who are senior-level influencers: 61 million
- Number of LinkedIn users who are senior-level decision-makers: 40 million
- Percent of LinkedIn users who are male: 56
- Percent of millennials who use LinkedIn: 13
- Percent of all Internet male users on LinkedIn: 28
- Percent of LinkedIn users who earn more than $75,000 a year: 44
- LinkedIn is the number one channel B2B marketers use to distribute content
- Percent of B2B marketers that use LinkedIn to distribute content: 94
- Percent of B2B marketers that use LinkedIn in their marketing mix: 92
- Percent of LinkedIn article readers who are in upper-level management positions: 45

- Percent of business leads that come from LinkedIn versus 13 percent on Twitter and 7 percent on Facebook: 80
- LinkedIn has over 26 million companies and 15 million job listings
- More than 90 percent of recruiters use LinkedIn regularly

Buying LinkedIn ads

LinkedIn features three types of ads: sponsored content, sponsored InMail, and text ads. *Sponsored content* is native advertising in LinkedIn's News Feed. *InMail* reaches a target audience in the LinkedIn inbox with personalized messages that tend to drive more conversions than regular email.

LinkedIn also offers several precision targeting opportunities. Marketers can target LinkedIn members who visited their website and can reach decision-makers at their specific target accounts. An individual or a company can give LinkedIn access to its contacts and ads can be targeted just to those contacts. With LinkedIn, advertisers target a quality audience in a professional context: "Market to influencers, decision-makers, and executives who act on new opportunities, and combine targeting criteria to build the ideal persona: IT decision makers, C-level executives, prospective students, small business owners, and more."[81]

Ads can be purchased on LinkedIn by means of its online auction model, and bids can be either cost-per-click (CPC), cost-per-thousand (CPM), or cost-per-send (CPS). In a CPS model, advertisers only pay when sponsored InMail messages are successfully delivered. B2B advertisers use CPS to drive highly qualified leads or event registrations.

There are three ways for advertisers to control their advertising investment on LinkedIn:

1   *Total budget.* If advertisers want their campaigns to deliver as fast as possible for a specific budget, then they should set a total budget limit on their campaign.
2   *Daily budget.* If advertisers want to set up a campaign that is always on, then they should set a daily budget.
3   *Setting bids.* Advertisers should set the maximum amount they are willing to pay for clicks, impressions, or delivered InMails. Advertisers will never pay more than the price they bid.

LinkedIn's future

LinkedIn provides B2B advertisers with a brand-safe, interactive environment, especially for marketers with limited budgets. LinkedIn should be the primary digital advertising choice for B2B advertisers, because no site or app reaches more decision-makers or high-level executives than LinkedIn. In the 2018 fiscal year, LinkedIn revenue was $5.3 billion compared to $2.3 billion in 2017, a whopping 130 percent increase, and in the first quarter of 2019 Microsoft-owned LinkedIn showed a 33 percent revenue increase over the first quarter in 2018.[82] This revenue is chiefly driven by Talent Solutions – the LinkedIn tool that helps employers find talent – and because of the low unemployment rate in the US and, thus, the general difficulty in finding good talent, LinkedIn's future is quite rosy.

The Future of Sales Jobs in Social Media

Even though advertisers can buy all of the social media platforms covered above on a self-serve basis, these companies need salespeople to evangelize their platforms and educate advertisers and buyers how to buy their particular platform, because each social media platform has different buying interfaces, different types of ads, different pricing options, and different campaign goals and objectives.

Also, Google, YouTube, Facebook, Twitter, and several other social media companies have sales or business development staffs that partner with major accounts and manage those accounts. These sales teams do the bidding for inventory, optimize campaigns, and create ads for the accounts they manage. Some of the most desirable sales jobs in the media are at Google, YouTube, and Facebook. The majority of these jobs are in New York.

An excellent way to get a sales job for these major social media companies is to start in a sales support job and then work your way up to selling. Also, sales support, or as you learned in Chapter 14, customer success, jobs are, in reality, sales positions. Remember that the mission of sales is to get customers and to keep them, and keeping them is more profitable than developing new business. Therefore, customer success jobs focus on getting results for customers and also getting renewals at increased investment levels. Getting results for customers and getting renewals can be very satisfying, more satisfying to many people than developing new business – it is service selling rather than missionary selling.

Go to Google, Facebook, or other social media websites, then go to their Careers section, look for open jobs in sales or sales support, and apply online. I have suggested to many of my graduate students to follow the above advice, and it is has been successful for several of them.

Test Yourself

1. Who founded Thefacebook.com and where was it started?
2. Was Facebook the first social media website?
3. Originally, Facebook was only in a limited number of colleges. What league were most of those colleges in?
4. Who did Mark Zuckerberg hire in 2008 as Facebook's COO?
5. Why has Facebook been called "the most targeted medium in history?"
6. What are the three ways to buy Facebook ads?
7. How many characters are now allowed in a Twitter tweet?
8. What celebrity is number one in monthly interactions on Twitter with 103.9 million?

9. Are the majority of Twitter users American?
10. What company owns YouTube?
11. How many total users worldwide use YouTube?
12. What company owns Reddit?
13. Is Reddit's audience primarily men or women?
14. What is the defining differentiation feature of Snapchat?
15. What percent of US teens use Snapchat?
16. What social media site is known as "a visual discovery engine?"
17. What is LinkedIn's defining differentiation feature?

Projects

1   In the market in which you live, choose a local B2C retailer and create a social media advertising campaign using the sites covered in this chapter. Match the demographics and interests of the retailer's target audience with the sites you select to advertise in and decide what the best way to buy these sites is (self-serve or through a marketing partner).
2   Do the same exercise in #1 for a B2B marketer.

References

Kirkpatrick, David. 2010. *The Facebook Effect: The Inside Story of the Company that is* Connecting the World. New York: Simon & Schuster.

Notes

1   Kirkpatrick, David. 2010. *The Facebook Effect: The Inside Story of the Company that is Connecting the World*. New York: Simon & Schuster.
2   Ibid.
3   Ibid.
4   Ibid.
5   Ibid.
6   Ibid.
7   Ibid.
8   Ibid.
9   Ibid.
10   Ibid.
11   Ibid.
12   Ibid.
13   Ibid.
14   Ibid.
15   Ibid.
16   Ibid.
17   Ibid.
18   Ibid.
19   Ibid.
20   Ibid.
21   Ibid.
22   Ibid.
23   "comScore: 2019. "Facebook Passed MySpace in the US for the First Time." Retrieved from https://www.adweek.com/digital/comscore-facebook-passed-myspace-in-the-us-for-the-first-time-in-may.

24 Wikipedia. Retrieved from https://en.wikipedia.org/wiki/Initial_public_offering_of_Facebook#Valuation

25 Facebook. https://www.facebook.com/business/marketing/facebook.

26 eMarketer. 2019. "US social trends for 2019." Retrieved from https://www.emarketer.com/content/us-social-trends-for-2019.

27 Retrieved from https://zephoria.com/top-15-valuable-facebook-statistics and from https://www.emarketer.com/content/will-facebook-s-latest-scandal-affect-its-ad-business.

28 Wikipedia. Retrieved from http://en.wikipedia.org/wiki/facebook.

29 Kirkpatrick, David. 2010. *The Facebook Effect: The Inside Story of the Company That Is Connecting the World*. New York: Simon & Schuster.

30 Rosenberg, Matthew, Confessore, Nicholas, and Cadwalladr, Carole. "How Trump consultants exploited the Facebook data of millions." Retrived from https://www.nytimes.com/2018/03/17/us/politics/cambridge-analytica-trump-campaign.html.

31 Osnos, Evan. 2018. "Can Mark Zuckerberg fix Facebook before it breaks democracy?" Retrieved from https://www.newyorker.com/magazine/2018/09/17/can-mark-zuckerberg-fix-facebook-before-it-breaks-democracy.

32 Facebook. https://www.facebook.com/business/help.

33 Helm, Burt. 2017. "How Facebook's oracular algorithm determines the fates of start-ups." Retrieved from https://www.nytimes.com/2017/11/02/magazine/how-facebooks-oracular-algorithm-determines-the-fates-of-start-ups.html.

34 Sloane, Garett. 2019. "Advertisers grapple with Facebook's outage." *Ad Age*, March 18.

35 Jeffrey, Clara and Bauerlein, Monika. 2019. "With friends like these…". *Mother Jones*, March–April.

36 Ibid.

37 Ibid.

38 Sloane, Garett. November 19, 2018. "Facebook fumbles, advertisers shrug." *Advertising Age*.

39 eMarketer. 2019. "Will latest Facebook scandal affect ad business?" Retrieved from https://www.emarketer.com/content/will-facebook-s-latest-scandal-affect-its-ad-business.

40 eMarketer. 2018. "How many marketers are using Facebook." Retrieved from https://www.emarketer.com/content/will-facebook-s-latest-scandal-affect-its-ad-business.

41 eMarketer. 2018. "Four takeaways from Twitter's Q4 earnings: What advertisers need to know." Retrieved from https://www.emarketer.com/content/four-takeaways-from-twitter-s-q4-earnings-what-advertisers-need-to-know.

42 Twitter. Retrieved from https://en.wikipedia.org/wiki/Twitter.

43 Fischer, Sara. 2019. Retrieved from https://www.axios.com/newsletters/axios-media-trends-72b26dbd-6844-463d-851d-e89fbc291c59.html.

44 Ibid.

45 "General Twitter stats." Retrieved from https://blog.hootsuite.com/twitter-statistics.

46 YouTube. https://en.wikipedia.org/wiki/YouTube.

47 Ibid.

48 "37 Mind blowing facts, figures and statistics from YouTube 2019." Retrieved from https://merchdope.com/youtube-stats.

49 YouTube. https://www.youtube.com/yt/advertise/signup.

50 eMarketer. https://www.emarketer.com/content/policing-video-content-on-youtube-facebook-and-twitter

51 eMarketer. 2019. "Mobile soon to pass TV in time spent." Retrieved from https://www.emarketer.com/content/mobile-soon-to-pass-tv-in-time-spent.

52 "80 Amazing Reddit statistics and facts." Retrieved from https://expandedramblings.com/index.php/reddit-stats.

53   See https://www.redditinc.com/advertising.

54   Ibid.

55   Ibid.

56   eMarketer. 2019. "Reddit to cross $100 in ad revenue in 2019." Retrieved from https://www.emarketer.com/newsroom/index.php/reddit-to-cross-100-million-in-ad-revenues-in-2019.

57   Snapchat. Retrieved from https://en.wikipedia.org/wiki/Snapchat.

58   Spangler, Todd. 2018. "Snapchat sets slate of new scripted originals and documentaries, doubling down on mobile TV." Retrieved from https://variety.com/2018/digital/news/snap-snapchat-originals-scripted-shows-1202973565.

59   "Snapchat statistics and revenue." 2018." Retrieved from http://www.businessofapps.com/data/snapchat-statistics/#2.

60   eMarketer. 2018. "Constantly on: Teens and social media." Retrieved from https://soundcloud.com/behind-the-numbers/constantly-on-teens-and-social-media.

61   Ibid.

62   eMarketer. 2019. "Snapchat's US ad business will soldier on, growing 24.3% this year." Retrieved from https://www.emarketer.com/content/snapchat-s-us-ad-business-will-soldier-on-growing-24-3-this-year.

63   Ibid.

64   https://en.wikipedia.org/wiki/TikTok.

65   Ibid.

66   Iqbal, Monsoor. 2019. "TikTok revenue and usage statistics (2019)." Retrieved from https://www.businessofapps.com/data/tik-tok-statistics/#2.

67   https://ads.tiktok.com/i18n.

68   Zhang, Karen. 2018. "TikTok, currently the world's most popular iPhone app, under fire over lack of privacy settings." Retrieved from https://www.thestar.com.my/tech/tech-news/2018/05/28/tiktok-currently-the-worlds-most-popular-iphone-app-under-fire-over-lack-of-privacy-settings.

69   Wikipedia. Retrieved from https://en.wikipedia.org/wiki/Pinterest.

70   eMarketer. 2019. "The weekly listen: Social misinformation, Pinterest's IPO, and ad-free Facebook." Retrieved from https://soundcloud.com/behind-the-numbers/the-weekly-listen-social-misinformation-pinterest-ipo-and-ad-free-facebook-feb-22-2019.

71   Ibid.

72   Ibid.

73   Ibid.

74   "23 Pinterest statistics that matter to marketers in 2019." Retrieved from https://blog.hootsuite.com/pinterest-statistics-for-business.

75   "Audiences." Retrieved from https://ads.pinterest.com/audiences.

76   "Understanding bids." Retrieved from https://help.pinterest.com/en/business/article/set-your-bid.

77   https://en.wikipdipedia.org/wiki/Pinterest.

78   Minsky, Jeff. 2019. "Something You May Find Pinteresting." Retrieved from https://www.mediavillage.com/article/something-you-may-find-pinteresting.

79   https://en.wikipedia.org/wiki/LinkedIn.

80   Aslam, Salman. 2019. "LinkedIn by the numbers: Stats, demographics & fun facts." Retrieved from https://www.omnicoreagency.com/linkedin-statistics.

81   Retrieved from https://business.linkedin.com/marketing-solutions/ad-targeting.

82   Iqbal, Monsoor. 2019. "LinkedIn revenue and usage statistics (2019)." Retrieved from http://www.businessofapps.com/data/linkedin-statistics.

22

Television

Charles Warner

What Is Television?

Close your eyes and say the word "television" out loud.

What image came into you head? Was it your favorite television program, such as "Game of Thrones" or "Survivor" or "Sunday Night Football?" If you do this exercise with a group of, say, 10 people, how many different answers do you think you might get? Some answers might involve broadcast television network programming, such as "NFL Sunday Night Football" that is free and is supported by advertising. Some answers might involve cable television network programming, such as "Game of Thrones," that is on HBO and for which subscribers pay a fee each month to be able to watch. Some answers might involve a favorite local television station news program, such as "Eyewitness News at 6:00 p.m.," which is supported by national and local advertisers and political ads at election time. Some answers might involve programming, such as provided by Netflix, that is delivered to television sets via the Internet and that is accessed on a smart TV or by using a ROKU, Google Chromecast, or Apple TV device.

In other words, "television" is not a single visual entity, it is a video experience that is delivered in several different ways – over-the-air broadcast, cable, satellite, IPTV

Media Selling: Digital, Television, Audio, Print and Cross-Platform, Fifth Edition.
Charles Warner, William A. Lederer, and Brian Moroz.

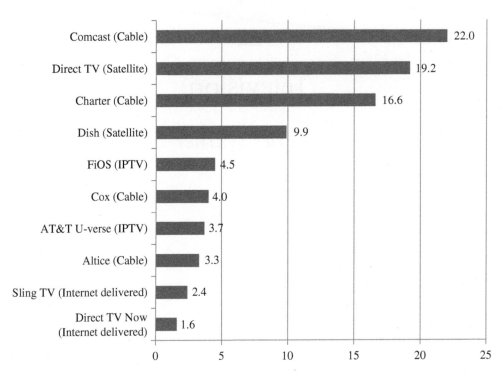

Figure 22.1   Pay TV subscribers in the US (in millions)
Source: Adapted from Statista. https://www.statista.com/chart/6994/pay-tv-providers-in-the-us.

(Internet Protocol Television), and OTT (over-the-top, or streaming) – and is funded in two different ways – advertising or subscription, and sometimes both.[i]

There are 120,000,000 homes in America with at least one television set. Approximately 58 percent of those homes have a digital video recorder, just over 54 percent of those homes have OTT, and 73 percent of those homes have some form of Pay TV, which is simply television that is delivered via cable, satellite, IPTV, or OTT. Figure 22.1 shows the various Pay TV providers that cumulatively reach 87.2 million homes.

In the following sections, we will describe the various types of television and provide some insights into how advertising is sold in ad-supported television.

Broadcast Television Networks

When network television first began in 1947 (NBC and DuMont) and 1948 (CBS), telephone lines connected local television stations that had signed an affiliation contract with a network. In return for carrying network programs on the same day and same time as other stations, a network would pay stations a negotiated fee based on the potential

---

[i] See the Glossary in the Appendix for definitions of Satellite TV, IPTV, and OTT.

size of an audience a station could reach. Thus, stations in New York, Los Angeles, and Chicago were paid higher affiliation fees than stations in Pittsburgh, Phoenix, or Peoria.

In the 1950s and early 1960s, when television was relatively novel and there were only three networks (ABC, CBS, and NBC), top-rated prime-time (8:00–11:00 p.m. EST) programs such as "I Love Lucy" and "Gunsmoke" would often have a 20 rating, meaning that 20 percent of all the households in America were estimated to watch that particular program. This massive reach into consumers' households gave advertisers an unprecedented opportunity to reach people with highly effective advertising that employed sight, sound, motion, and emotion in order to persuade consumers to buy products and services.

In the decades before the Internet, because of the enormous reach of network television and the effectiveness of television commercials, prime-time network programs were in high demand, and advertisers would wait in line to sponsor top-rated programs, which garnered higher and higher prices each year. In the 1950s and in the 1960s, due to the strong demand and the relative scarcity of highly rated prime-time commercial inventory, the two top-rated television networks, CBS and NBC, sucked up the vast majority of television advertising dollars. To counter this dominance, in 1962, Oliver Treyz, the president of the low-rated ABC Television Network, decided to premiere all of ABC's programs in the week after Labor Day to appeal to the Big Three Detroit auto manufacturers that made huge investments in television network advertising and that debuted their new car models the week after Labor Day every year.[1] ABC's programming debut strategy was so successful that CBS and NBC soon followed ABC's lead.[2]

But the fall debut of ABC's new programming was not Treyz's only innovation. In 1962 ABC had to overcome relatively low ratings as compared to CBS and NBC; therefore, Treyz asked the television rating company, Nielsen, to break down its household ratings into demographic segments that included an 18-49 segment that encompassed younger people that advertisers craved and a demographic that ABC's youth-oriented programming appealed to.[3] Treyz also realized that advertisers were more willing to place bets in the spring on a new program in the coming fall if they had a guarantee of a certain level of viewership for that program. ABC's new pricing structure was based on how much an advertiser would pay to reach a thousand viewers, and thus the cost-per-thousand (CPM) pricing model was established.[4]

The clustering of television networks' premiere programs in the early fall and the high demand for the commercial inventory in those programs led the three networks to require that advertisers commit the majority of their fall prime-time television ad budgets the previous spring. In return for these early commitments, the networks would guarantee audience rating levels and CPMs and give advertisers a 15 to 40 percent discount off the prices they would have to pay if they purchased the same advertising during the same quarter that the advertising was to run. This quarterly ad purchasing process is known as the *scatter market*. The process of placing prime-time ad buys in the spring for fall programming is called the *upfront market*, or *upfront*, and persists to the present time.

The upfronts typically occur in the second and third weeks in May each year when all seven broadcast television networks (ABC, CBS, Fox, NBC, the CW, Univision, and Telemundo) and the major cable television networks trot out their biggest stars and hype their fall programming lineups. Typically, the broadcast networks sell up to 80 percent of their fall prime-time commercial inventory in the upfront, and the cable networks sell up to 50 percent of their prime-time inventory. In the past several years the broadcast networks have received rate increases of 5 to 10 percent over previous years, even in the face of steadily declining ratings, and especially among the advertiser-coveted 18–49 demographic, which declined 38 percent in the five years from 2014 to 2018 inclusive.[5]

Why do advertisers continue to pay more for steadily diminishing audiences? There are several reasons, three of which were reported in a 2019 Jack Myers Report: (1) advertisers believe they get relevant audience reach, (2) they buy from trusted media partners, and (3) they buy in a brand-safe environment.[6] Another reason for the continued success of the upfronts is live sports programming.

About 58 percent of American homes use a DVR to record television programs so they can be watched later, and the vast majority of DVR users fast forward through commercials.[7] However, research has shown that viewers rarely record live sports programming because they want to see the action and know what the score is in real time, and, therefore will not record sports programming and, thus, will watch in-game commercials. Not only do viewers tend to watch commercials in live sports programming, but also eight of the top-ten rated broadcast network programs in 2018 were NFL games, and the top-rated cable television network program is ESPN's "Monday Night Football." Therefore, live sports in general and NFL football in particular are the most sought-after programming by advertisers in the upfront market, and the networks would have a hard time surviving without NFL programming.[8]

Another reason major advertisers continue to pay a little more for television ads that reach fewer people each year is because audiences are more fragmented than ever before and there are fewer and fewer media vehicles that can reach huge audiences simultaneously. According to Edmund Lee of *The New York Times,* "In the current cultural climate, programs that millions prefer to watch in real time, in campfire moments of togetherness, have become rare and especially valuable. A viral YouTube video may generate billions of views, but they don't occur at the same time."[9]

Also, advertisers like the impact of 30-second commercials on network television – commercials that are created to appeal to the broadest swath of consumers as possible. Such mass-appeal commercials are less effective on the Internet where video ads are much shorter. However, even though ads on the Internet allow advertisers to target consumers whose purchases are tracked purchase by purchase, many major advertisers that buy digital advertising programmatically are wary of the Internet's unregulated content, which can place an ad next to hate speech or other inappropriate content.

Broadcast network television provides advertisers with a guaranteed, regulated, brand-safe environment and continues to be attractive to major advertisers who want to reach a mass audience with 30-second commercials.

How broadcast network television ads are sold

Fewer than 50 high-ranking, experienced broadcast television network sales executives and high-ranking advertising agency holding company media executives negotiate about $9 billion worth of advertising in the broadcast network upfront each year. This relatively small, exclusive group of negotiators, primarily women, have developed a close, trusting personal

Exhibit 22.1   "Young Sheldon" CPMs

Average total viewers = 11,138,000
Percent Adults 18–49 in US. = 42.3%
11,138,000 X 0.423 = Adults 18–49 viewing "Young Sheldon" = 4,822,754
4,822,754 ÷1000 = 4,823
Cost of 30-second commercial = $213,536
$213,536 ÷4,823 = $44.27 CPM Adults 18–49
Average viewers = 11,138,000
11,138,000 ÷1000 = 11,138
30-second commercial cost = $213,536
$213,536 ÷ 11,138 = $19.17 CPM Viewers

Source: Viewer information: "TV Series Finale." 2018. https://tvseriesfinale.com/tv-show/young-sheldon-season-two-ratings; Population information: "So how many millennials are there in the USanyway? (Updated). 2018. https://www.marketingcharts.com/featured-30401; Cost information: Poggi, Jeannie. 2018. "Here's how much it costs to advertise in TV's biggest shows." https://adage.com/article/media/tv-pricing-chart/315120.

relationship over the years of dealing with each other. Broadcast network salespeople are the royalty of media selling, and they are the quintessential example of service selling

Upfront deals typically involve a guaranteed CPM based on the audience delivery of a program. For example, a 30-second commercial in CBS's program "Young Sheldon" would be priced at $213,536.[10] If an advertiser were guaranteed a CPM of $20 for total viewers, that would mean that if the average audience for "Young Sheldon" for 16 episodes were 11,138,000, the CPM guarantee would be met. See Exhibit 22.1, which shows the CPM calculations.

Normally, upfront CPM or rating guarantees are considered fulfilled if the actual CPM or rating is within 10 percent of the guarantee. Thus, in the example in Exhibit 22.1, if the guarantee was a $20.00 CPM total viewers and the actual CPM was between $18.00 and $22.00, the CPMs would be within the parameters of the guarantee. If, however, the average viewers of "Young Sheldon" for the 16 programs purchased in an upfront deal were only 9,000,000, then the CPM would be $23.73, and CBS would owe the advertiser makegoods, or enough free ads to make up for the audience shortfall.

Because of the practice of guarantees in the upfront market, the networks typically guarantee audience levels that are slightly higher than they expect because they would rather underperform and give advertisers makegoods than overperform their audience estimates, which meant they did not charge enough. Also, typically the networks allow agencies to cancel, often referred to as *recapture*, up to half of a schedule committed for in the upfront market.

Fighting the digital duopoly

In 2017, in order to try to quell the switching of television dollars to the two digital advertising Goliaths, Google and Facebook, at least two networks – cable network A&E and broadcast network NBCU – offered a limited number of advertisers guaranteed deals based on business outcomes.[11] In A&E's case, the initial business outcomes guarantees focused on the number of website visits or in-store foot traffic to an advertiser's business.[12] A&E worked with Data Plus Math, a television attribution company that attributes business outcomes to commercials, and also estimates cross-screen exposure of those commercials.[13] NBCU made a deal with STX films to guarantee ticket sales for the movie *The Upside*, starring Bryan Cranston and Kevin Hart. And in 2018 AMC, Discovery, and the Turner cable networks joined the group of networks offering business-outcomes guarantees to a small number of advertisers.[14]

This switch in pricing strategy from guaranteed CPMs and ratings to guaranteed business outcomes is in response to the dominance of Google and Facebook in the advertising ecosystem. As digital advertising revenue overtook television advertising revenue and as marketers began shifting budgets from television to digital because they could attribute returns on investment (ROIs) and business outcomes to digital advertising, television networks had to adapt. One of the ways media companies tried to adapt, in addition to guaranteeing business outcomes, was to restructure their sales organizations in order to aggregate their advertising inventory into one sales organization. For example, NBCU used to have separate television and digital sales staffs, but in 2018 it combined them into one sales organization. That same year the Walt Disney Company, that owns ABC, ESPN, and the Disney cable networks, finalized combining all of the separate sales staffs of those organizations into one sales organization, named Disney Advertising Sales, and put it under the leadership of Rita Ferro, formerly head of ABC Television sales.

Another way that the television networks are adapting is to embrace addressable advertising. In 2018, a consortium of NBCU, CBS, Disney Media Networks, Discovery, AMC Networks, Turner, AT&T's Xander, Hearst TV, and Comcast's FreeWheel automated planning, buying, and selling platform, cooperated in an attempt to establish the standards for addressable television advertising.[15]

"Addressable advertising has long been ballyhooed as the holy grail of television advertising," according to a 2019 *Ad Age* article.[16] However, after a decade of talking about the benefits of being able to target individuals the way digital advertising does, the problems of delivering digital-type individual targeting has been elusive, cumbersome, and controversial. Addressable advertising is delivered to smart television sets that are connected to the Internet and through a set-top box provided by a cable system operator such as Comcast, Spectrum (owned by Charter), or Cox Cable.

However, of the 120 million television homes in the US, only approximately 44 percent of them can be served addressable advertising through a cable set-top box. And of those 120 million homes, only about 60 percent are connected to the Internet via a broadband Internet service provided by a cable system operator. Those connected television homes can be served ads on other devices such as smartphones while they are watching television. In other words, in a household with a smart, Internet-connected television set, if a person watching an NFL game is also browsing the Internet on their smartphone (76 percent of people check their email while watching TV[17]), that person can be served a relevant ad on their smartphone – perhaps a BMW ad just after they watched a Mercedes ad in the NFL game. Because both the smart television and the smartphone are connected to the Internet via a WiFi network, a smart chip in the television set can track all devises on that home's WiFi network.

This tracking ability scares some people who like their privacy, but advertisers love it because it allows them to serve relevant, targeted advertising and, thus, try to compete with the type of accountability for advertising that Google and Facebook provide.

Nevertheless, some of the networks hesitate to embrace addressable advertising because they would be selling off slices of their total audience to advertisers that only want to reach specific segments of that audience, and that slicing involves a great deal of math and technology. Reluctant networks are afraid that they might not be able to sell enough audience slices to make a profit.[18]

Cable Television Networks

The first cable television network was HBO, which debuted in 1972 and was distributed by microwave relays to local cable systems. In 1975, HBO became the first satellite distributed cable network. HBO was, and still is, a premium channel, which means that it carries no advertising, and subscribers to local cable systems must pay a premium monthly fee over and above the monthly fee they pay for basic cable service, which in 1975 consisted primarily of channels dedicated to local television stations that were affiliated with the three television networks. In 1976, Ted Turner distributed his local Atlanta independent UHF television station, WTCG, via satellite to local cable systems. Turner subsequently changed the WTCG call sign to WTBS (Turner Broadcasting System), and local cable systems that were typically restricted technologically to 20 channels in the 1970s put WTBS on a basic tier that carried advertising-supported programming. In 1977, Pat Robertson's Christian Broadcasting Network (CBN) became the second ad-supported cable network, followed in 1979 by Nickelodeon, C-Span, and ESPN. Ted Turner's all-news channel, CNN debuted in 1980 as did BET and the USA network, and in 1981 MTV debuted on August 1.

The business model of these early ad-supported cable television networks was to pay a yearly fee to cable systems to carry them based on the number of subscribers a cable system had, and then the cable networks hoped that they sold enough advertising to cover the fees paid to local systems and give them a profit. However, in January 1983, ESPN President and CEO, Bill Grimes, decided that ESPN, which would lose $41 million in 1982, could no longer afford to pay cable systems $0.10 a year per subscriber and would instead ask cable systems to pay ESPN $0.10 per month per subscriber.[19]

Because of ESPN's immense popularity among sports fans, local cable systems who were originally reluctant to pay ESPN's fees eventually did so not only because of ESPN's popularity but also because ESPN accounted for a majority of local cable systems' ad revenue that was generated by the systems' ad sales staffs to local advertisers. Soon MTV, CNN, and other cable networks followed Grimes's and ESPN's lead and began charging local cable systems for carriage. This new business model gave cable networks two income streams: per-subscriber carriage fees from local cable systems and advertising revenue.[20]

Furthermore, as the technology of cable's coaxial cables improved and the capacity to carry more signals increased, so did the number of cable networks. Not only did basic ad-supported networks such as Lifetime, Oxygen, and A&E increase in number, but also premium networks such as the Discovery networks, Disney, and the History Channel increased.

With the proliferation of cable networks and cable television's penetration into a majority of US homes, in the 1990s viewing to cable television overtook viewing to broadcast television. However, because there are over 100 cable networks and only five English-speaking broadcast networks, even though total viewing to cable television is larger than viewing to broadcast television, viewing to the average broadcast television network program is much larger than to the average cable television network program.

Therefore, in the upfront, the broadcast networks dominate the calendar because of the greater reach of their programming, especially sports programming, and only the highest-rated cable networks, such as A&E networks and the Viacom networks (Country Music Television, or CMT, Logo, MTV, MTV2, Comedy Central, Nickelodeon, Nick at Nite, VH1, and BET) make upfront presentations.

Some cable networks are included in the upfront pitches of their parent companies. For example, MSNBC is included in NBCU's upfront presentation, ESPN is included in Disney's upfront presentation, and CNN, TBS, and TNT, acquired by AT&T early in 2019, are included in Xander's (AT&T's media division) upfront presentation.

How cable network television ads are sold

What is evident in the 2019 upfront calendar of presentations is how the media is consolidating.[21] For example, ESPN, before 2018, even though it was 80 percent owned by the Walt Disney Company, operated separately, had its own sales force, and made a big splash with its upfront presentations. However, in 2019, ESPN was included in the Disney upfront presentation, and its sales force had been integrated into a Disney Advertising Sales division that included ESPN, ABC Television, FX, the Disney Channel, Disney Junior, the National Geographic Network, and the Freeform network (teenage appeal). Another example of consolidation is Xander Media, AT&T's media unit that was created when AT&T bought Time Warner, which includes the CNN, TBS, and TNT cable networks.

The same small group of experienced executives and agency negotiators that complete broadcast television upfront deals worth about $9 billion wrapped up about $11 billion for the cable networks in the upfront in 2019 for a total television upfront of about $20 billion, or 29 percent of an estimated $70 billion total television advertising marketplace in 2019.

Syndicated Television

Syndicated television consists of two types of programs, first-run and off-network, that are sold to individual local television stations to air exclusively in their markets. Examples of first-run syndicated programs are the game shows "Jeopardy" and "Wheel of Fortune." These first-run programs are produced specifically to sell directly to local stations and not to a national network. Examples of off-network syndicated programs are the sitcoms "Seinfeld" and "Everybody Loves Raymond."

The most successful syndicated television program of all time was "The Oprah Winfrey Show," often referred to simply as "Oprah," that aired nationally for 25 seasons

Exhibit 22.2 Television daypart definitions	
Daypart Name	*Daypart Definition*
Early Morning	5:00 – 9:00 a.m.
Morning Daytime	9:00 a.m. – 12:00 p.m.
Afternoon Daytime (Eastern Time, Pacific Time)	12:00 – 4:00 p.m.
Afternoon Daytime (Central Time, Mountain Time)	12:00 – 3:00 p.m.
Early Fringe (Eastern Time, Pacific Time)	4:00 – 6:00 p.m.
Early Fringe (Central Time, Mountain Time)	3:00 – 5:00 p.m.
Early News (Eastern Time, Pacific Time)	6:00 – 7:00 p.m.
Early News (Central Time, Mountain Time)	5:00 – 6:00 p.m.
Prime Access (Eastern Time, Pacific Time)	7:00 – 8:00 p.m.
Prime Access (Central Time, Mountain Time)	6:00 – 7:00 p.m.
Prime Time (Eastern Time, Pacific Time)	8:00 – 11:00 p.m.
Prime Time (Central Time, Mountain Time)	7:00 – 10:00 p.m.
Late News (Eastern Time, Pacific Time)	11:00 – 11:30 p.m.
Late News (Central Time, Mountain Time)	10:00 – 10:30 p.m.
Late Fringe (Eastern Time, Pacific Time)	11:30 p.m. – 1:00 a.m.
Late Fringe (Central Time, Mountain Time)	10:30 p.m. – 12:00 a.m.
Overnight (Eastern Time, Pacific Time)	1:00 – 5:00 a.m.
Overnight (Central Time, Mountain Time)	12:00 – 5:00 a.m.

from September 8, 1986, to May 25, 2011. It remains the highest-rated daytime talk show in American television history.[22]

The syndicated first-run game shows "Jeopardy" and "Wheel of Fortune" typically run on network-affiliated local television stations in the Prime Access time period of 7:00–7:30 p.m. (See Exhibit 22.2 for television daypart definitions.) Off-network syndicated programs such as "Seinfeld" typically run on independent, non-network-affiliated television stations, in prime time or on Fox- or CW-affiliated stations because those networks provide less prime-time programming than ABC, CBS, or NBC does.

How syndicated program ads are sold

Commercial time on syndicated programming typically has eight minutes per half hour, and in some cases 10 minutes per half hour. Of those eight or 10 minutes of commercial time, six or eight of those minutes are sold by a local television station's local or national sales organization and two minutes are typically sold by the syndicator. A television station might give back to a syndicator the two minutes of commercial time, and, in return, a syndicator will reduce the cost of licensing a syndicated program to that station.

Broadcast National Spot Television

When television is bought on a market-by-market basis, not on a network basis, this buying strategy is referred to as *spot television*. When network television is purchased, the same number of commercials generally run on all television stations affiliated with the network on which the commercials appear. However, a national brand such as MacDonald's does not have equal sales levels in all of the markets in which commercials on a network appear; therefore, MacDonald's might want to put more commercial weight in markets where sales are lagging. In such a situation, MacDonald's would instruct its media agency to buy spot television in those markets where it needs the extra advertising weight.

Spot television buys are placed by agencies by contacting representative companies, called *reps*. National reps are sales organizations that represent local television stations outside of their local markets. All of the major television networks own stations, called O&Os (owned and operated), in the country's largest markets, and these O&Os have their own rep organizations, often referred to as CBS TV spot sales or ABC TV spot sales, for example. ABC owns eight television stations, CBS owns 28 television stations, Fox owns 17 stations, NBCU and Telemundo own 40 stations in 28 markets, and Univision owns 27 stations, and all of these televisions station groups have their own national rep organizations.

Non-owned-and-operated stations retain one of two national rep firms: the Katz Television Group and Cox Reps. The Katz Television Group, the largest television rep company, represents 800 local television stations and has offices in 15 US cities. These two national rep firms sell the vast majority of national spot television in the US, and that national spot revenue represents anywhere from 30 to 50 percent of a local television station's revenue, depending on the size of a station's market. A station in a large market such as San Francisco would have close to 50 percent or more of its total revenue come from national spot, while a station in a smaller market such as Columbia, MO, would have 30 percent or less of its total revenue come from national spot.

How broadcast national spot television ads are sold

The broadcast national spot television buying and selling process begins when a media agency buyer calls, emails, or uses an automated online platform to send a request for proposal (RFP) to a national rep salesperson. Selling spot television for a rep company is strictly a reactive process. Reps do very little prospecting because rep selling is another example of service selling.

Using the example of a client such as McDonalds, here's how a spot television buy would happen:

1 A television buyer at OMP, McDonald's media agency, would call her television rep salesperson at Katz Television and give that salesperson the details of an upcoming spot television campaign and the due date for the rep to submit avails (short for availabilities, or available commercial inventory) in, say, 25 markets. The buyer might indicate that McDonald's primary target audience is Adults 18–34, and secondary target audience is Men 25–54. The buyer wants Early Morning, Prime Access, and Late Fringe avails, she wants to buy 300 ratings points a week, and proposals are due in one week.
2 The rep salesperson knows the buyer, has a relationship with her because of handling several previous McDonald's spot buys, and repeats all of the information that he's been given to confirm that he understands the parameters of the buy, and then he

makes an appointment to see the buyer. The rep salesperson tells the buyer that he represents strong stations in all of the 25 markets she's buying and that he'd like to have the buyer's first available appointment. It is this initial request by the rep that emphasizes the importance of having a relationship with the buyer. If the rep salesperson has a good, trusting relationship with the buyer, the rep can probably get the buyer's first available appointment, which is important because the rep knows that the first call will more than likely be the most memorable (remember the concepts of primacy and recency) and it also gives the rep the opportunity to advocate for also being able to come back after other reps have presented in order to adjust the offering to make the buy even better for the buyer.

3   The rep salesperson then submits all the information into automated software programs that are connected to the inventory-control and yield-management software platforms at all of the Katz-represented television stations. These software platforms are essentially SSPs (supply-side platforms) that automatically show what inventory is available, what the ratings are for each avail, and what the suggested price ranges are. The rating information is typically based on Nielsen, although more and more stations are now subscribing to comScore ratings.

4   After the software automatically generates avails and pricing, the rep salesperson typically calls a local television station's National Sales Manager (NSM), whose job is to interact with a station's national rep firm and strategize on how to best secure national spot business.

5   The NSM will typically update the rep salesperson on current programming, upcoming special events, and added-value opportunities such as sponsorships or promotions that are available. The NSM is aware of a station's current daypart sell-out levels, current demand for each daypart based on outstanding avail requests and proposals, and what pricing levels have the best possibility for clearance. The SSP software reports that the NSM looks at keeps track of every local and national proposal that is pending, thus giving the NSM a good barometer on demand on the station's inventory. The software also analyzes historic demand patterns as well, and, thus, can recommend pricing levels based on past and current demand and current ratings for each avail.

6   Once the rep salesperson has discussed pricing strategy and programming or added-value opportunities with each station's NSM, if time permits such discussions, the salesperson will input the information into another software platform that generates a specific proposal for the McDonald's spot buy.

7   Next, the salesperson or a salesperson's coordinator creates a presentation that includes the proposal and its benefits and advantages to present to the buyer.

8   In the typical 10-minute meeting with the buyer, the rep salesperson uses the presentation as an opening for the negotiating that inevitably follows in subsequent calls.[23]

Because there is fixed supply of desirable television station commercial inventory, the price of that inventory fluctuates according to demand. Therefore, television rates are highest when demand is highest in the fourth quarter (October, November, and December) and second quarter (April, May, and June) of the year. When demand determines the price of a scarce resource, prices will always be negotiable. In digital advertising, negotiating is typically handled programmatically via real-time bidding (RTB) in which algorithms bid on individual impressions for a specific consumer who is defined by multiple data points. But in spot television, the buyer is not buying impression by impression, but is buying exposure opportunities to a broad demographic, such as Adults 18–34.

Let's assume the buyer has a budget for 300 rating points per week per market in 25 markets for a four-week flight. Let's assume that the cost-per-rating-point (CPP) in one of the Katz Television markets the buyer is buying is $300, which would mean that the buyer's budget in that market would be $90,000 per week, or a total of $360,000 for four weeks. Let's also assume that the four weeks are in the high-demand month of June. The rep salesperson's job is to try to get as high percentage of that $360,000 budget as realistically possible. Therefore, the rep salesperson would price the three proposals offered (remember Chapter 12: Proposing) in such a way as to give to give the buyer a better price for getting a higher share of the budget.

"Realistically" is the key word in the sentence in the above paragraph, "The rep sales-person's job is to try to get as high percentage of that $360,000 budget as realistically possible." What is realistic from the buyer's perspective is different from what is consid-ered realistic from the represented station's perspective, which is different from the rep salesperson's perspective of what is realistic.

These dilemmas make rep selling particularly challenging. A rep's customers are the stations they represent, because the stations give rep companies a commission on all business it sells. A rep's consumers are the agencies they sell to. A station's ideal outcome would be to get 100 percent of every national spot television buy at the highest possible rates. An agency buyer's ideal outcome would be to give a station a share of budget in line with a station's share of audience in the demo requested and at the lowest possible rates. A rep salesperson's job is make both the customer (a station) and the consumer (an agency) feel like they got a good deal.

Therefore, a rep salesperson's challenge is to lower the expectations of both the sta-tion's NSM for getting a 100 percent share of budget and high rates, and of the buyer of getting low rates. Trust is the key to success. A station's NSM must trust the salesperson to get the best deal possible for the station and a buyer must trust the salesperson to get the best rates possible in light of demand in the market.

When negotiating, a rep salesperson must keep in mind the agency buyer's goals of: (1) getting low rates, (2) getting the favorable first position in a commercial pod, (3) getting added value such as bonus (free) spots or opening or closing billboards for a program or event sponsorship, (4) social media support, (5) station contact with or entertainment of local clients (in the case of a MacDonald's spot buy, entertaining the owner of one or several local MacDonald's franchises), and, probably most important, (6) 100 percent posting.[ii] The rep salesperson must also balance the buyer's goals with

---

[ii] The term posting refers to a post-buy affidavit that an agency receives from a station that shows the exact dates and times that each commercial in a campaign ran. For example, if the buyer for the MacDonald's campaign bought 20 spots a week on a station equally distributed in the Early Morning, Early News, Prime Access, and Late News time periods and the affidavit showed that all 20 spots ran equally distributed in all four time periods, the buyer would be pleased because she "posted 100 percent." Sending the affidavits and checking them against what was purchased are all done electronically.

the represented station's goals: (1) getting a high share of the budget, (2) getting high rates, (3) having maximum flexibility to move and preempt spots, and (4) giving no added value such a bonus spots, sponsorships, or local client entertainment.[iii]

Because the experience levels of agency media buyers vary dramatically from highly experienced, tough negotiators to young, relatively inexperienced, underpaid, and over-worked, an effective national rep salesperson must be flexible enough to be a tough, effective negotiator as well as a nurturing educator, depending on the situation and how experienced a media buyer is.

Cable National Spot Television

The process for selling cable national spot television is essentially the same as selling broadcast national spot television with one major exception: there is essentially only one cable national spot rep firm – NCC Media. NCC Media was founded as National Cable Communications in 1981 to represent local cable systems, cable interconnects, and satel-lite and telco (FiOS and AT&TU-verse, for example) service on a national level.

The process of buying cable national spot is essentially the same as the process of buying broadcast national spot with the exception that buying spot cable is somewhat more complicated because there are opportunities to buy more targeted ads because most cable and satellite (multichannel video program distributors (MVPDs) offer set-top-box addressable advertising which can target ads to homes such as to new car buying intenders or to homes in upscale ZIP codes.

Broadcast Local Television

There are 1,374 commercial television stations in the US – 1,004 UHF stations and 370 VHF stations.[24] UHF stands for *ultra high frequency* and includes channels 14–69 on the electromagnetic spectrum. VHF stands for *very high frequency* and includes channels 2–13 on the electromagnetic spectrum. These commercial television stations are located in 210 designated market areas (DMAs) as defined by Nielsen, which essentially include the population and homes within, roughly, a 75-mile radius of television station transmit-ters. Nielsen has meters installed in 56 of those 210 DMAs in a sample of homes. These meters collect data on who in the home is watching television on what set, on what

---

[iii] Flexibility to move spots anywhere in a pod of commercials, to move spots within program-ming or in a time period, and to preempt spots is important to television station sales manage-ment in order to maximize revenue. Preempting spots means moving them from the program or time period initially purchased to another time period to make way for a spot that has been pur-chased at a higher rate. For example, a spot purchased in Early News with a 3.0 rating might be preempted for a higher-priced spot and the advertiser given three makegood spots in Early Morning with a 1.0 rating.

channel, and for how long they watch. This data is electronically transferred every night to a Nielsen data center in Florida. Nielsen algorithms aggregate the data and next day produce overnight quarter-hour ratings for each station in metered markets.[25]

To learn more about how the Nielsen ratings work, go to the Nielsen Ratings Academy online at http://ratingsacademy.nielsen.com/television-101.

Markets are typically identified by the largest city, which is usually located in the center of the market region. However, geography and the fact that some metropolitan areas have large cities separated by some distance can make markets have unusual shapes and result in two, three, or more names being used to identify a single region (such as Wichita-Hutchinson, Kansas; Chico-Redding, California; Albany-Schenectady-Troy, New York; and Harrisburg-Lebanon-Lancaster-York, Pennsylvania.[26]

How broadcast local television ads are sold

Broadcast and cable networks, syndicated television, and national spot television are not the only media that are fighting the digital duopoly. Local television stations are also experiencing revenue declines because more and more local advertisers are switching their advertising budgets to Google and Facebook.

A headline in the April 3, 2019, *TV News Check* (TVN) read "Facebook, Google Dominate Local Ad Market." The *TVN* article further stated:

> Broadcasters wondering where local advertising dollars are going need only to click on Facebook. Since 2012, when the social media giant began offering simple do-it-yourself ad buying, it has "blossomed into the most popular form of local marketing" with 24 consecutive quarters of 30% growth or more, according to a new report from Borrell Associates, *2019 Benchmarking Local Media's Digital Revenues.*
>
> "Those expecting the social media juggernaut to collapse due to data breaches, fake news and reports of click fraud may have more hope than reality in their expectations," the report says.[27]

The article also reports than 74 percent of local ad buyers surveyed said that they felt Facebook was moderately to extremely effective, and that local ad agencies felt even stronger as 85 percent rated Facebook as moderately to extremely effective. The article also reports that digital-only media surged to nearly $60 billion in local revenue in 2018 and that Google and Facebook accounted for more than 70 percent of that total.

What strategies can local television station sales management employ to counteract both steadily declining ad revenue that goes to the duopoly? This is a question I asked Tim Warner (no relation), Director of Sales of WTHR-TV in Indianapolis. The reason I talked to Tim is because when I interviewed Leo MacCourtney, President of the Katz Television Group, I asked MacCourtney which of the 800+ television stations that Katz represented had the best sales management. "WTHR-TV in Indianapolis," was his immediate answer.

WTHR-TV on channel 13 is the NBC-affiliated station in the country's number 28 DMA, which has approximately one million television homes.[28] Reporting to Tim Warner are a Research Director, a Local Sales Manager, a National Sales Manager, and a Digital Sales Manager. WTHR-TV has 11 salespeople (six females and five males) and one digital salesperson (the Digital Sales Manager), all of whom account for 55 percent of the station's revenue (national spot accounts for 45 percent). Seven of the 11 salespeople call on local advertising agencies and four salespeople focus on calling direct on clients.

The WTHR-TV salespeople are paid a relatively low base salary plus a percent commission on everything they sell. They get three times the base commission percentage for selling new business and three times the base commission percentage for selling digital inventory on the station's website, on its diginets, and in its weather and its traffic apps.[iv] The salespeople also receive quarterly and yearly bonuses based on hitting their digital, diginets such as MeTV, new business, and overall station budgets, or revenue goals. I mention how the WTHR-TV salespeople are compensated because it is an example of the principle that sales compensation should reflect the overall sales strategy of an organization, and as the sales strategy changes, such as emphasizing the sale of digital inventory, compensation should be adjusted.

The salespeople use the Matrix CRM software system to manage their interactions and communications with their accounts and the WideOrbit software system that empowers television sales teams to build proposals with a full suite of tools leveraging real-time account information, inventory availability, as well as audience research and delivery of both linear and digital inventory.[29]

Sales management assigns accounts according to relationships. The WTHR-TV salespeople have developed strong relationships over the years with local advertisers, and Tim Warner believes that those relationships are the best weapons the station has in fighting the competition from Google and Facebook. The WTHR-TV Account Executives are marketing experts trusted by their accounts to get results for them with television and digital ads. Furthermore, the salespeople are also experts in selling special events such as the Olympics on NBC and locally produced events such as Prince Harry and Meghan Markle's Royal wedding.[v]

In my interview with Director of Sales Tim Warner, he gave me his view of the advantages of being a local television salesperson: (1) they do very well financially (low-to-mid six-figures), (2) they learn to sell digital as well television ads, because, eventually, virtually all advertising will be digital, (3) they are not tied to a desk all day, (4) they call on a wide variety of accounts and people, thus learning how to deal with and empathize with a diverse range of personalities, (5) they can be quite creative in ways to get results for clients, and (6) they learn about a wide variety of businesses. This list of advantages is as good a reminder as I know of as to the advantages of being a media salesperson.

[iv] See the Glossary in the Appendix for a description of a diginet.

[v] WTHR-TV sent a crew to London to cover the Royal Wedding in May, 2018. It is unusual for a local television station in the middle of the United States to send a production crew so far away to cover any event, but WTHR-TV has a tradition of covering such special events and selling coverage to local advertisers. Tim Warner indicated that, even though the coverage was expensive, the station made a profit, which is a tribute to the local sales staff.

Cable Local Television

Multiple systems operators (MSOs), typically referred to as MVPDs (multichannel video programming distributor), also have sales staffs calling on local advertisers. The sales process and the software used for selling cable local television is largely the same as selling broadcast local television.

The cable networks typically give local systems one two-minute break, or pod, per hour to sell locally. Therefore, local cable salespeople are selling ads in Fox News, ESPN, and CNN programming. But because there are up to 500 channels or more on most cable systems, the local cable audience is fragmented and the ratings of all but the most poplar cable networks such as Fox News, MSNBC, HGTV, TNT, USA, ESPN, CNN, Discovery, and Hallmark are so low that there is not much demand for ads in them. Therefore, with the scarcity principle not applicable, prices for local cable are much lower than those for local broadcast stations. Low ad rates mean less revenue and, thus, lower commissions for salespeople.

The future of sales jobs in television

Even though broadcast and cable television audiences are slowly diminishing as viewers cut the cable chord and move to subscription services such as Netflix, Hulu, HBO Go, and Amazon Prime Video, television as we know it today will not disappear entirely, and there will be an ongoing need for salespeople who understand how to help customers navigate through the complex details of buying addressable Advanced TV inventory, which will require a knowledge of both television and programmatic.

If you are trying to break into television sales outside of top-tier markets, then selling for a small- or medium-sized market television station or local cable system is a good place to start, learn the business, and begin to build relationships with local advertisers and agencies.

If you are trying to break into television sales in New York, Los Angeles, or Chicago, a good place to start is as an assistant buyer or a buyer at a media agency so you can learn the lexicon of the business, learn the intricacies of buying programmatically, and get to meet sales managers from major media companies.

Sales jobs for local television stations and local cable systems are often posted on job sites such as Indeed, Glassdoor, CareerBuilder, LinkedIn, or Zip Recruiter (see links in Resources section below).

Test Yourself

1. How may television homes were there in the US in 2019?
2. What is the upfront?
3. What are three reasons why advertisers pay more for declining ratings on broadcast network television?
4. What percent of US television homes have DVRs?
5. Why is NFL football so important to television networks?

6. What are makegoods?
7. What were the first two networks to guarantee business outcomes to advertisers?
8. What was the first cable television network?
9. What are the two types of syndicated television programs?
10. What is spot television?
11. How many DMAs are there in the US.?
12. What is a diginet?
13. Give four examples of diginet programming.

Project

First, go to the Research section on the TvB ("Local Media Marketing Solutions") web-site (https://www.tvb.org/Public/Research.aspx) and on the drop-down menu click on the following selections: Purchase Funnel 2019, Media Comparison Study, Seasonal Retail Reports, Competitive Media, and Measurement. Next, from the information in those sections create a PowerPoint presentation to sell a Back-To-School promotion to a department store for a local television station WAAA-TV (fictitious station). Your presentation should be at least 10 slides and not more than 20 slides.

Resources

Ad Age (www.adage.com)
CareerBuilder job searches (www.careerbuilder.com)
GlassDoor job searches (www.glassdoor.com)
LinkedIn job searches (wwwlinkedin.com/jobs)
Indeed job searches (www.indeed.com)
Nielsen Ratings Academy (http://ratingsacademy.nielsen.com/television-101)
Nielsen DMAs (https://mediatracks.com/resources/nielsen-dma-rankings-2019)
Television Bureau of Advertising (TvB) (https://www.tvb.org/Public/Research.aspx)
Video Bureau of Advertising (VAB – formerly Cable Television Bureau of Advertising) (thevab.com)
ZipRecruiter job searches (www.ziprecruiter.com)

Notes

1 MediaVillage. 2019. "History's moment in media: How 'Upfront' became a noun over decades of ad sales innovation." Retrieved from https://www.mediavillage.com/article/historys-moment-in-media-how-upfront-became-a-noun-over-decades-of-ad-sales-innovation.

2 Ibid.

3 Ibid.

4 Ibid.

5 Lee, Edmund. 2019. "As TV industry's $20 billion week starts, signs that streaming isn't king yet." Retrieved from https://www.nytimes.com/2019/05/12/business/media/network-upfronts-television-streaming-advertising.html.

6 Myers, Jack. 2019. "Upfront 2019: Look for this canary in the coal mine." Retrieved from https://www.mediavillage.com/article/upfront-2019-look-for-this-canary-in-the-coal-mine/

7 eMarketer. 2019. "The shelf life of TV ads, and now DVRs might be wasting money." Retrieved from https://soundcloud.com/behind-the-numbers/the-shelf-life-of-tv-ads-and-how-dvrs-might-be-wasting-money-may-13-2019.

8 Crupi, Anthony. 2019. "Network TV can't survive without the NFL." Retrieved from https://adage.com/article/media/top-50-u-s-broadcasts-2018/316102

9 Lee, Edmund. 2019. "As TB industry's $20 billion week starts, signs that streaming isn't king yet." Retrieved from https://www.nytimes.com/2019/05/12/business/media/network-upfronts-television-streaming-advertising.html.

10 "So here's how much it costs to advertise in TV's biggest shows." 2018. Retrieved from https://adage.com/article/media/tv-pricing-chart/315120.

11 Friedman, Wayne. 2018. "A&E offers limited guarantee deals based on business outcomes." Retrieved from https://www.mediapost.com/publications/article/318976/ae-offers-limited-guarantee-deals-based-on-busine.html.

12 Ibid.

13 Ibid.

14 Poggi, Jeanine. 2018. "How to navigate TV attribution." Retrieved from https://adage.com/article/media/navigate-tv-attribution/317005.

15 Poggi, Jeanine. 2019. "TV net tackle addressable advertising." Retrieved from https://adage.com/article/media/tv-networks-partner-standardize-addressable-advertising/316937

16 Ibid.

17 "Most popular smartphone activities of second screen users in the United States while watching TV as of January 2019." Retrieved from https://www.statista.com/statistics/455377/smartphone-usage-while-watching-tv.

18 Wolk, Alan. 2018. "The Upfronts: Where do we go from here?" Retrieved from https://www.firbes.com/sites/alanwolk/2018/05/14/the-upfronts-where-do-we-go-from-here/#6a48391f5665.

19 Parsons, Patrick. 2008. *Blue Skies: A History of Cable Television*. Philadelphia, PA: Temple University Press.

20 Ibid.

21 "TV Upfront 2019 calendar: The latest updates." 2019. Retrieved from https://adage.com/article/special-report-tv-upfront/tv-upfront-digital-newfront-2019-calendar/316640.

22 https://en.wikipedia.org/wiki/The_Oprah_Winfrey_Show.

23 Personal conversation with Leo MacCourtney, President, Katz Television Group, April, 2019.

24 FCC. "Broadcast Station Totals as of December 31, 2019." Retrieved from https://www.fcc.gov/document/broadcast-station-totals-december-31-2019.

25 http://en-us.nielsen.com/sitelets/cls/documents/nielsen/Local-Measurement-Methodology-Ex.pdf.

26 https://en.wikipedia.org/wiki/Media_market.

27 TVN. 2018. "Facebook, Google dominant in local ad market." Retrieved from https://tvnewscheck.com/article/233267/facebook-google-dominate-in-local-ad-market.

28 MediaTracks Communications. 2019. "Nielsen DMA rankings 2019." Retrieved from https://mediatracks.com/resources/nielsen-dma-rankings-2019.

29 https://www.wideorbit.com/products.

23

Print and Out of Home

Charles Warner

Newspapers

In April, 2019, legendary investor Warren Buffett told an interviewer with Yahoo Finance that "newspapers are toast."[1]

Buffett, through BH Media, a division of his Berkshire-Hathaway holding company, bought his home-town newspaper, the *Omaha World Herald* in 2011, and in 2012, expanded his newspaper holdings when BH Media bought Media General and its 63 newspapers.[2] At that time Buffet thought newspapers were a good investment. However, by 2019, he had obviously come to a much different conclusion.

What happened to make one of America's most successful investors – he is the world's third richest person – finally conclude that newspapers were "toast?"[3] Here are some of the reasons:

The Internet   The Internet completely disrupted the advertising and media ecosystem, and few media responded more slowly to this disruption than the newspaper industry did. As early as 1994 when The Monster Board was established online and provided free job listings that began to eat into lucrative Help Wanted newspaper classified advertising, the newspaper industry did not fully understand The Monster Board's threat.[4] In 1996, the Monster Board became just Monster (www.monster.com). Then, when Craig Newmark established Craig's List (www.craigslist.com) online in 1995, that allowed people to list items for sale free of charge, the newspaper industry could have pivoted to a new business model, but it did not fully understand the Craig's List threat either.[5] The

Media Selling: Digital, Television, Audio, Print and Cross-Platform, Fifth Edition.
Charles Warner, William A. Lederer, and Brian Moroz.

main reason that the small one- or two-line all-text Help Wanted and classified ads were so profitable was because of the way that newspapers sold advertising, which was on a per-line basis so that the cost of classified ads was much higher on a per-line basis than the bulk rates many larger advertisers paid. For clarification of per-line rates and bulk discounts, see the "How newspapers are sold" section below.

The Internet was also disruptive because it allowed production and distribution costs of digital content to virtually disappear, or to be so low as to make them virtually free, and as a result anyone with a computer could become a publisher. Thousands of free blogs and newsletters sprouted, and as dandelions do on a lawn, this new, free content tended to take nutrients away from healthy plants, in other words, take away readers from newspapers.

In his 2009 book titled *Free: The Future of a Radical Price,* author Chris Anderson makes that point that it is extremely difficult to compete against free, and in his opinion the only way for an established company to compete successfully was to offer a free or free-mium product. A freemium product is a simple, bare-bones product that is made available free, with the expectation that when consumers try the product, they will like it and then will be willing to pay for a premium model with lots more features. *The New York Times* took a similar approach in 1996 when, on January 22, the paper of record put a free version of the newspaper on its website (www.nytimes.com).[6] The *Times* was confident that readers would: (1) find the content so intriguing and valuable that they would pay more for it and would subscribe in order to get more in-depth articles, and (2) generate sufficient traffic so that enough digital advertising could be sold to make up for the steady losses in print advertising revenue.

However, over the next 15 years, the *Times* and other newspapers realized that taking Anderson's advice had been the wrong long-term strategy, as clearly laid out in a 2011 *Harvard Business Review* article. The authors of the article conducted research on companies that had offered their products free, and their conclusion was:

> We have found no examples of companies in the non-digital realm that have prevailed against rivals with free offerings. In fact, in two-thirds of the battles that have progressed far enough to be judged, incumbents (both digital and physical) made the wrong choice. In a handful of instances, companies that should not have taken action did so immediately by introducing their own free offering – hurting their revenues and profitability. They should have either waited and allowed the attacker to self-destruct or recognized that the two could peacefully coexist.[7]

In 2016, *The New York Times* changed its policy and set up a paywall that charged people for reading the paper. The *Wall Street Journal (WSJ)* was the first major newspaper to establish a paywall in 1997, and the Murdoch-owned *WSJ* has continually experimented using sophisticated artificial intelligence (AI) and algorithms to find ways to entice readers of a few free articles to become subscribers.[8] However, the vast majority of newspapers do not have the resources to use expensive AI software to experiment on effective ways to entice people to subscribe, and so more and more newspapers are switching to digital editions as the *Pittsburgh Post-Gazette* did in July 2019, when it announced the phasing out its printed newspaper and its intention to become digital-only.[9]

Internet shopping   When the Internet had become a viable advertising vehicle by 1996, primarily on AOL and Yahoo, newspapers were the number one medium in advertising revenue, just slightly higher than total television (cable, broadcast, and spot).[10] At that time department stores were the largest advertisers in newspapers, but the Internet, led by the AOL Shopping Channel, brought with it a new functionality that allowed people to become aware of a product, then if it appealed to them, to ask for more information about the product, and then act to buy the product. Consumers were able to do their shopping on a computer and never have to leave their home.

As consumers began to shop more and more online, led by the growth of Amazon and other ecommerce sites, major advertisers such as department stores began switching part or most of their budgets out of newspapers and putting them online where they got a much better return on investment (ROI), especially with Google's and other sites' cost-per-click (CPC) pricing model.

Programmatic   When programmatic buying and selling of online ads was introduced in 2007, with the facility to target advertising more precisely, and when the Great Recession hit the US economy in 2008, these two occurrences accelerated both the growth of digital advertising and the decline of newspaper advertising.

Prior to the massive Internet disruption, many newspaper owners, particularly those who privately owned their papers, often thought of newspapers as being a public trust that were necessary to keep voters informed and to keep our democracy free. However, as public conglomerates began buying newspapers, too often their primary mission changed from being a public trust to making a profit. Also, even private owners realized that without profits, a company cannot sustain itself. Therefore, newspapers began transforming into digital businesses "hoping that strategy would save them from the accelerating decline of print."[11]

In the last decade and a half there has been a "parade of newspaper closures and large-scale layoffs."[12] Almost 1,800 newspapers closed between 2004 and 2018, leaving 200 counties in the US with no newspaper.[13] At the same time, about 400 online-only local news websites sprang up to fill the void, but these sites are mostly in large cities and affluent areas.[14] "It's hard to see a future where newspapers persist," according to Nicco Mele, Director of the Shorenstein Center for Media, Politics, and Public Policy at Harvard. Mele predicts that half of the surviving newspapers will be gone by 2021.[15]

Newspaper industry attempted solutions

As advertising revenue continues its precipitous decline, newspapers that survive are trying to develop new revenue streams because digital ad dollars do not come close to replacing print ad dollars, which traditionally have had high CPMs. Large, nationally distributed newspapers with both print and paywalled digital editions are surviving, but while Google and Facebook have siphoned ad dollars away from all newspapers, local publishers have been hit the hardest, with 77 percent of local ad dollars going to the two digital Goliaths, which take only 58 percent of national ad dollars.[16]

New revenue streams   The most common way newspapers are trying to develop new revenue streams is to convert print subscriptions to digital subscriptions. Only a few nationally distributed, well-edited, and well-written papers, such as The *Wall Street Journal,* the *Washington Post*, and the *Boston Globe* have been successful in converting readers to digital subscriptions.[17]

In addition to converting print subscribers to digital subscribers, many newspapers have developed other revenue streams: video ads; branded or sponsored content; events; memberships; ecommerce; related businesses such as education, trips, crosswords, recipes, jobs, and children's editions; donations; and micropayments.[18]

Consolidation   Another way that the newspaper industry is attempting to solve declining revenues is to merge or consolidate in hopes of saving money on back-office support jobs such as accounting and human resources (HR) functions. The biggest of such consolidations was publicized in the summer of 2019, when GateHouse, one of the two largest newspaper groups, announced it was purchasing Gannett, the largest newspaper group in the country to create a "megachain like the US has never seen."[19] One out of every six daily newspapers in the country will be owned by the new megachain, and the hope of the new company will be to "buy two or three more years to figure out how to make money in digital."[20]

Newspaper revenue

Circulation revenue   Print versions of daily newspapers are sold to consumers either by subscription or on a single-issue basis. Subscribers receive their papers via home delivery, either through "little merchant" walking carriers or adult motor route carriers. Single issues are purchased out of vending machines or over the counter at various news outlets including, but not limited to, newsstands, vending machines, street hawkers, grocery stores, and so forth. A number of newspapers are also available to businesses, hotels and motels, and travelers on a bulk-purchase basis. Regardless of how consumers receive a newspaper, an individual newspaper's circulation is the combined total of paid subscriptions, single-copy sales, and bulk sales. In the past, circulation revenue traditionally amounted to 20–25 percent of print newspapers' total revenue. For comparison purposes and to show how much more important total subscription revenue currently is, *The New York Times* had print circulation, or subscribers, at the end of 2018, of one million and digital subscribers of 3.3 million. Total subscription revenue of both print and digital accounted for 60 percent of the *Times*'s revenue in 2018.[21]

Advertising revenue   Unlike other media that base audience projections on sampling techniques, such as Nielsen ratings in television and radio, print editions of newspapers base their advertising rates on average weekly circulation and the size and placement of an ad.

Newspapers rely on outside circulation auditing firms to provide independent verification of their circulation numbers. Most large daily newspapers are audited by the

Alliance for Audited Media (AAM), which was established in 1914 as the Audit Bureau of Circulation, but changed its name to the Alliance for Audited Media in 2012.[22] The AAM has rules and requirements that all of its members must follow in order to obtain an acceptable audit. The standardization of the auditing process gives advertisers a high level of confidence in a newspaper's circulation claims. In addition, the audits provide advertisers with a consistent format that merges with their own customer databases for more convenient market analysis. The purpose of the auditing process of print newspapers is to give advertisers a high degree of comfort with the numbers presented to them by newspaper salespeople.

Audits not only provide average paid circulation figures but also record how many of the papers were purchased through discount programs and at regular price. Circulation data available for newspapers include the number of copies delivered by various methods – newspaper carriers, dealers or agents, street vendors, over-the-counter, and vending machine sales, and by the US Postal Service – for the newspaper's city zone, retail trading zone (RTZ), and areas outside the RTZ. Audit reports typically report circulation by community and by ZIP code. An audit report will also provide advertisers with an estimate of occupied households within each of the newspaper's circulation measurement areas to enable advertisers to easily calculate the newspaper's household penetration in the communities or ZIP codes most important to an advertiser.

Newspaper salespeople need to know and understand their newspaper's circulation patterns in order to advise advertisers on how best to utilize their newspaper. Salespeople should also know their competition's coverage in key ZIP codes and be able to talk about duplication of reach and readership.

Newspaper salespeople also need to understand how to help advertisers navigate a newspaper's Byzantine and highly complicated rate structure. Go to *The New York Times*'s online Media Kit at https://nytmediakit.com/index.php to see an example of how complex a newspaper's rate structure can be.

How newspapers are sold

Newspapers have historically separated the editorial and business functions. The editor makes decisions about editorial content and the publisher makes decisions about business and advertising. However, the wall separating "church and state" has been, if not broken, at least lowered considerably as digital editions have become more prominent. The mounds of data about readers of digital newspapers and what kind of articles they read, the number of articles they read, and for how long they read them provided by analytic platforms such as Chart Beat give both the editorial and marketing departments invaluable information for making decisions to keep readers engaged. These decisions about improving engagement with and the popularity of content as well as the decisions about promoting that content often lie jointly with both the editorial department and the marketing department as they cooperate to grow engagement, readership, and advertising.

Generally, newspapers that have both print and digital editions have two sales staffs: a print staff and a digital staff. You learned how to sell digital advertising in Chapter 17:

Programmatic Marketing and Advertising, Chapter 18: Measuring Advertising, and Chapter 19: Selling Digital and Cross-Platform Advertising, so the remainder of this newspaper section will deal with selling just newspaper print advertising and is based largely on content in the fourth edition of *Media Selling*, which was published in 2009, when newspapers were struggling, but were not yet "toast."

Newspaper advertising comes in all shapes and sizes. An effective newspaper ad might consist of only three lines of carefully worded copy and placed in the Merchandise for Sale category in the classified section, or it could be a multipage section behind the main news section. Newspapers are organized to accommodate all types of advertising from both big and small advertisers. Advertising in newspapers is typically divided into four categories: classified, classified display, display, and pre-printed inserts.

Classified advertising   Even though classified advertising in newspapers has been hurt significantly by free Internet services such as Craig's List, Monster.com, Amazon, and eBay, classifieds is still an important source of ad revenue for newspapers. Classified ads, also called *want ads*, appear in small, type under indexed headings, which identify the type of product or service advertised. Many newspapers also offer bold headlines, color type, and logos in the classified section in order to help improve the readership of individual ads. These small ads, often numbering more than one million per year for large metropolitan newspapers, provide strong newspaper readership and interactivity with readers. Classified ads are usually sold on a per-line basis and appear in the classified sections of the newspaper. Generally, these sections have 10 columns per page. Some papers have six, eight, or nine columns. These small ads inform readers where yard sales are being held, what used cars are for sale, who is trying to sell their exercise equipment, and so on. A number of service businesses also use these classified ads because they can afford to advertise every day. This increased frequency enables consumers to know where to look for contact information when they are in need of someone to trim their trees, mow their lawns, or clean their gutters.

Classified display ads   Classified display advertising differs from regular classified in several ways. The copy usually occupies more space. It is surrounded by a bold border and often features product illustrations, bold type and headlines, and / or company logos. The most common users of classified display advertising are automobile dealers, realtors, and employers or recruiters. By placing these similar advertisements in one section of the paper, newspapers make it easy for readers to comparison shop for services such as these. At the same time, the shopping environment works for advertisers because consumers know where to look for the ads of interest to them when they are in the market for a new or used car or truck, a new home, or a new job.

Display ads   Display advertising (often called ROP – run of paper, or run of press) is the term used to describe the bold advertisements found in sections of the newspaper other than the classified section. These display ads usually occupy fairly large spaces, but can vary in size from one column inch (one and 7 / 8s inches wide by one inch deep) to a

126 column-inch-page, six columns or 12 inches wide by 21.5 inches deep. Display ads are surrounded by bold or graphic borders and are not placed under specific headers, as happens with classified display ads. These display ads may be promotional, offering price and merchandise information, brand or image building, or a combination of these styles and formats. Advertisers like display ads because they can squeeze a lot of product and price information into each ad. This gives consumers more product options to consider. And, it increases the likelihood that one or more of their advertised items will appeal to potential customers.

Display advertising is often divided into two major categories: local, also referred to as *retail*, and national, often referred to as *general*. Newspapers rely heavily on local retail advertising, which is usually sold in bulk annual contracts at the paper's most attractive rates. Local display advertising is sold by the newspaper's salespeople through direct sales calls on local store owners or managers or at regional and national chain store offices. In most cases, an advertiser is treated as a local account if it operates a retail or service outlet within the newspaper's market area. National display advertising has been a declining segment for newspapers. Much of the traditional national display advertising, which consisted of manufacturers' product coupons, has shifted away from display ads to coupon ads in the Sunday coupon supplements, to pre-printed inserts, and, even more so, to digital advertising.

Pre-printed inserts   Pre-printed inserts are distributed primarily through Sunday newspapers across the country. Newspaper pre-prints, or inserts, are advertising circulars that are not printed as part of the daily or Sunday newspaper but are distributed through the newspaper. Many advertisers, particularly national chain stores, use inserts because they can gain economies of scale by printing millions of copies at a time and shipping them in bulk to the newspapers they select to distribute their advertising messages. Pre-prints also provide advertisers with more options for running full-color advertisements and for choosing higher grades of paper. Pre-print advertisers can usually print and distribute more pages of advertising through this method. In addition, pre-print advertising enables advertisers to zone their distribution to targeted areas, usually ZIP codes, around each of their stores or service areas. By maximizing the space available for product display and targeting the distribution, advertisers feel they can make their advertising investment more effective and more efficient. Pre-printed inserts are produced by national firms such as Valassis and News America.

The future of newspaper jobs

With the exception of a handful of big city, nationally distributed newspapers, if a large majority of newspapers are "toast," what is the future of newspaper jobs in general, and sales jobs in particular? Editorial jobs will continue to decline as newspapers cut staff to reduce costs, switch to digital editions, or go out of business, and sales jobs will switch from selling print editions to selling digital editions. Also, as more and more new digital news sites appear in markets not served or underserved by a local newspaper, the job of editor and publisher will merge. The editor will write or supervise writing the content and then will sell that content to advertisers. This new business model of merging church and state will create opportunities and jobs for enterprising people who can do both – write intriguing content and sell digital advertising.

Magazines

Magazines are one of the oldest media in the world, and have played a vital role in the history of advertising. Since they first appeared in the early 1800s, magazines have been documenting the cultures, events, and opinions of the world.

In the late 1800s, magazines were read by only a small percentage of the population, primarily upper-class people. Magazines at that time were small, soft-cover books that carried stories of limited appeal, tended to take a European, aristocratic approach, and were expensive to produce and distribute. Therefore, only relatively wealthy and well-educated people could afford them.[23]

In the late1800s, a large percentage of the country's populations were reading news-papers and weekly tabloids. The magazine production process was expensive in the 1800s and technologically limited; printing 100,000 copies took a very long time, for example. And, until the United States Congress created second-class mail in 1879, the Post Office would only carry magazines a short distance, and doing so was quite expensive.[24]

In 1883, a Scotsman named S.S. McClure dropped the price of his magazine, *McClure's,* a general interest magazine, to only 15 cents. It became very successful and widely read. Not long after, a rival publisher lowered the price of its magazine to 10 cents, from 25 cents. This price-cutting set off a new age mass distribution, as publishers realized that dropping cover prices could lead to increased circulation.[25]

However, magazines still looked like and read like books. There were no headlines or continued stories, and pictures were confined to small sizes, but the design and produc-tion of magazines would soon change. In the 1890s, sketch artists were employed by magazines and assigned to cover events and stories. The artists sent back to their maga-zines dramatic and romantic interpretations of the world.[26]

By the 1930s, magazines were bringing in more and more advertising, and this surg-ing revenue made it possible to sell magazines to readers at below production costs. Thus, publishers could lower cover prices and increase circulation. Magazines no longer counted on the single revenue stream of circulation dollars, and they began to attract increasing numbers of readers, which they then sold to advertisers.[27]

National advertisers continued to increase their investment in magazine ads in the 1940s and 1950s, led mostly by fashion and beauty magazines. Since the 1970s, there have been continual changes in magazine design and technology, and the medium has grown because of its innovative approach to finding more and more areas of interest so that people continue to justify paying more for magazines than ever before, and paying for more magazines.

The current state of magazines

Innovations in production and distribution have allowed advertisers to insert two or three different versions of an ad in selected editions, such as regional editions, of a magazine. New editorial segments continue to be developed, and readers are still intrigued by attractive, up-to-the-minute design. Publishers and editors are being continually challenged in their approach by other media, and are looking for ways to stay original, unique, and relevant, including moving their magazine's content to the web. Today circulation figures typically contain both print and digital readership under the label of "Magazines 360°."[28]

Magazines have increased total readership of print plus digital editions fairly consistently, according to the Association of Magazine Media, an organization formerly known as the Magazine Publishers Association, which is still referred to and labels itself as the MPA. Figure 23.1 shows five years of percentage of growth of Magazines 360°. By including digital readership of magazines and expressing growth in percentage terms, the MPA can tell an effective story of growth.

Exhibit 23.1 shows the total audience (print and digital) of the top 10 magazines for 2018 in thousands. Total audience is estimated by aggregating subscribers and pass-along readers, such as readers in doctors' offices, and visits to the digital and mobile editions, plus views of magazine videos online.

No example of the current state of the magazine industry is as typical as the status of the magazine with the largest total brand audience for the full year of 2018 – *ESPN: The Magazine*. Note in Exhibit 23.1 that *ESPN: The Magazine* was ranked number eight in Print + Digital Audience, but ranked number one in Unique Visitors on the Web, Mobile Web, Video, and Total Brand Audience. Also note that *ESPN: The Magazine* had by far the biggest lead over the number two magazine in the Video category, which is not surprising considering that ESPN's magazine's web editions had access to ESPN's cable television's video highlights.

Magazine 360°
Percent Growth in Total Magazine Media 360° Since Launch

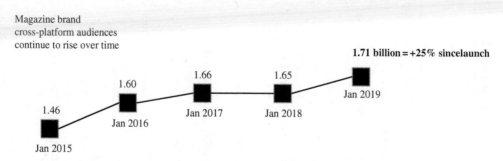

Magazine brand
cross-platform audiences
continue to rise over time

1.71 billion = +25% sincelaunch

1.66

1.65

1.60

Jan 2019

1.46

Jan 2017   Jan 2018

Jan 2016

Jan 2015

Percent Growth in Total Magazine Media Audience Vs. Same Month a Year Ago

Figure 23.1   Magazine growth
Source: Print + Digital : GfK MRI and Ipsos Online. comScore. Used with permission of the MPA.

Exhibit 23.1 Top 10 magazine brands

Magazine Media 360°
Top 10 Magazine Brands
Average Audience (000) – Full Year 2018

Print + Digital		Web-desktop/laptop		Mobile web		Video		Total brand audience	
Brand	Audience	Brand	Unique visitors	Brand	Unique visitors	Brand	Unique viewers	Brand	Total
1 AARP	38,755	ESPN The Magazine	19,958	ESPN The Magazine	44,994	ESPN The Magazine	23,525	ESPN The Magazine	105,530
2 People	37,447	WebMD Magazine	12,396	People	37,971	Vanity Fair	9,410	People	87,552
3 Better Homes & Gardens	34,059	Allrecipes	9,141	WebMD Magazine	33,984	Vogue	7,390	WebMD Magazine	56,923
4 National Geographic	31,730	People	6,608	Allrecipes	32,395	Wired	7,292	Allrecipes	51,637
5 Good Housekeeping	18,878	New York Magazine	6,509	New York Magazine	22,984	GQ	6,840	AARP	48,257
6 Reader's Digest	18,166	The Atlantic	5,592	Cosmopolitan	16,588	Bon Appétit	5,775	Better Homes & Gardens	42,900
7 Sports Illustrated	17,204	Taste of Home	3,931	US Weekly	15,223	People	5,525	National Geographic	38,841
8 ESPN The Magazine	17,053	Wired	3,331	Good Housekeeping	13,503	Glamour	4,409	Cosmopolitan	36,930
9 Southern Living	15,722	Sports Illustrated	3,189	The Atlantic	13,095	The New Yorker	3,607	Good Housekeeping	36,904
10 Women's Day	15,137	The New Yorker	3,177	Entertainment Weekly	12,564	Allure	3,175	Sports Illustrated	33,234

Sources: Print+Digital Editions – GfK MRI Survey of the American Consumer®, GfK MRI Accessed Prototype, OR Ipsos Affluent Survey USA. Web (Desktop/Laptop) – comScore Media Metrix®. Mobile Web – comScore Mobile Metrix. Video – comScore Video Metrix. Used with permission.

Since *ESPN: The Magazine* launched in 1998 as a biweekly (26 issues a year) broadsheet (larger than standard magazine size), it has cut the number of print editions it published from 26 to 20 to 16 to 12, and on April 30, 2019, it announced it was ceasing its print edition and would be an online-only magazine.[29] In the mid-2000s, *ESPN: The Magazine* had $150 million in ad revenue and profits of $30 to $40 million.[30] However, steadily increasing production and distribution costs for the large print magazine on high-quality paper stock and the inclusion of many high-definition color photographs ate into those profits, and by 2017 it was losing money.[31] Therefore, the inevitable happened for *ESPN: The Magazine*, ESPN killed its print edition, and it will be inevitable that eventually the vast majority of magazines will switch to digital-only publication for the same reasons *ESPN: The Magazine* did.

How magazines are sold

With the inevitability of most magazines becoming digital, the way magazines have been traditionally sold by offering full-page, half-page, front- and back-cover glossy ads will be "toast," as Warren Buffett would say. This inevitability means that those who are interested in selling magazine content, must know how to educate advertisers and buyers on: (1) the benefits and advantages of magazine media advertising in general, (2) the benefits and advantages of advertising in their specific magazine media or group of magazines, and (3) how to buy their magazine media or group of magazines programmatically, typically with larger publishers in a private marketplace (PMP). Examples of a group of magazines would be a Young Women's Group or a Fashion and Luxury Group. These magazine groups can be seen on Hearst's website (www.hearst.com/magazines/digital-media).

Following are a few examples of the benefits and advantages of magazine media advertising.

Americans of all ages read print and digital magazines   The MPA 2019 *Magazine Media Factbook* includes Fall 2018 research by MRI Simmons that shows that 91 percent of adults, 93 percent of people under 35, and 94 percent of those under 25 read magazine media in the last six months (print and digital editions).[32] These facts are important to use when selling against newspapers and television, especially television news, which tend to have a large proportion of their audience in the 55+ and 65+ age groups, which are generally not that desirable to many advertisers.

Magazine media provide valuable information   Another study that is referenced in the MPA *2019 Magazine Media Factbook* shows that the magazine media provide more valued information, conversation, and purchase inspiration than websites or ad-supported television networks. See Exhibit 23.2 for details.

Magazine media get strong support on social media   Remember from Chapter 15: Marketing in which the concept of Marketing 4.0 is described that "Recent research across industries shows that most customers believe more in the F-Factor (friends,

Exhibit 23.2   Magazine media provide valued information, conversation, and purchase inspiration

Index	Magazine Media	Websites	Ad-supported TV networks
A way to learn about new products	137	103	80
Gets me to try new things	131	100	81
Inspires me to buy things	125	107	79
I like to kick back and wind down with this	125	83	115
Gives me something to talk about	118	95	100
Get valuable information from this	115	104	83
Provides info that helps me make decisions	114	108	81
I bring up things from this medium in conversation	112	90	100

Note: Data for each medium based on levels of agreement with the above statements for users of a set of vehicles in each medium.

Index: An index is a percentage of adults who used a set of vehicles in each medium vs. percentage of adults who used these vehicles in any medium.

Source: MRI-Simmons Engagement Study, Spring, 2018. Used with permission from the MPA.

families, Facebook fans and Twitter followers) than in marketing communications." Therefore, in the era of Marketing 4.0 earned media is vitally important, not only because it is credible, but also because it is free. Earned media is the last step in a customer's five-step shopping journey of Aware, Appeal, Ask, Act, and Advocate. Magazine media do especially well acquiring friends and likes on earned media platforms such as Facebook, Twitter, and Instagram, as seen in Exhibit 23.3. Note at the top of Exhibit 23.3 that devoted magazine readers have a higher index on the number of friends they have on social media than devoted Internet users, devoted television viewers, and devoted radio listeners do (definitions of devoted users, viewers, and listeners are in the exhibit's Note.)

The reason accumulating friends, likes, and thumbs-up and having a positive self-image on social media are important is because people with lots of friends and a positive self-image are typically strong, credible influencers. Exhibit 23.4 reinforces the notion that devoted magazine media readers on social media tend to have high engagement and influence.

Magazine media provide excellent ROI   Also from the MPA 2019 *Magazine Media Factbook,* a series of 2,200 studies conducted by Nielsen Catalina Solution for Meredith magazine brands from 2004- 2017, showed the Meredith magazine brands had higher ROI than television, radio, and digital video. See Figure 23.2 for details.

The Meredith magazine brand study is not necessarily definitive research that can be applied to all magazine media; that is not necessarily the MPA's intent in making it available. The value of the Meredith magazine brand study is for salespeople to be able to use the information to anchor in advertisers' and buyers' minds the concept that magazine media generally have an excellent ROI compared to other media. The Meredith magazine media slide is available on the MPA's website (www.magazine.org) in the Research & Resources section.

Exhibit 23.3   Magazine readers have *real* friends

Devoted magazine readers have the most friends[+] and spread their ideas over the widest social circle.

Number of friends among devoted media users (index)

	Magazines	Internet[++]	TV	Radio
20 or more	177	88	11	144
15 or more	168	88	103	155
10 or more	158	84	101	134
8 or more	149	88	105	134

Self-perception (index)

	Magazines	Internet	TV	Radio
Have a wide social circle and enjoy it	131	93	85	125
My friendship group is a really important part of my life[+++]	128	95	93	101
Get energy by being in a group of people	122	98	103	110
Enjoy entertaining people at home[+++]	116	93	93	105

[+]Real people – not social media.

[++]Includes Internet magazine activity

[+++]Definitely agree

Note: Devoted magazine readers are defined as those who read printed magazines at least several times per week or digital magazines more than once a day. Devoted Internet users are those who use it at least 31 hours per week. Devoted radio listeners are those who listen to FM Radio at least two hours a day or AM radio at least one hour a day. Devoted TV viewers are defined as those who watch live or "catch up" TV at least 31 hours per week. Each group represents approximately the same proportion of US adults 18+. Source: YouGov Profiles, December 2018. Used with permission of the MPA

The MPA, like other associations that promote media industries, such as the Internet (IAB), television (TvB), cable television (VAB), radio (RAB), out-of-home (OAAA), and newspapers (NMA), provide research information and sales material for association members to use to sell their medium; therefore, all associations' sales material is biased in favor of the media these organizations represent. Advertisers and buyers understand that these biases exist, but, nevertheless, they usually find media industry association information useful in weighing the strengths and weaknesses of the media they consider for a buy.

The future of magazine media jobs

The number of consumer print magazines has remained fairly constant over the years, even though the more popular consumer magazines are moving to web-only editions.[33] Because magazine entrepreneurs continually find niches of interest such as online gaming and AI as new industries are created and as people have more free time because of automation and AI, the magazine media are more than likely viable in the long term. In other words, they are not "toast."

Exhibit 23.4 Magazine brands are the original (and still the most powerful) influencers.*

Magazine media	Facebook	Twitter	Instagram
Total Likes/Followers	525,234,324	267,450,519	320,452,938
Total Engagement Actions	166,284,083	44,837,458	908,855,360
Total Publisher Posts	248,612	305,338	32,499
Engagement Factor+ (median)	**220**	27	4,500
Non-magazine media			
Total Likes/Followers	754,976,749	421,967,421	239,095,183
Total Engagement Actions	656,612,721	164,877,748	1,153,956,328
Total Publisher Posts	453,966	633,642	59,369
Engagement Factor+ (median)	214	29	2,604

$$^{*}\text{Social media engagement factor} = \frac{\text{Social media actions}}{\text{Publisher posts}}$$

Source: Automatic collection through the social networks' APIs (Application Program Interface) collected by CrowdTangle. Used with permission from the MPA.

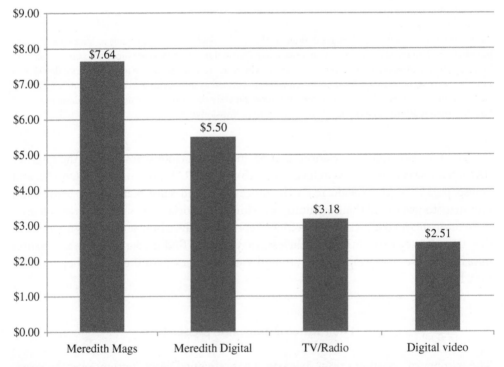

Figure 23.2 Meredith magazine brands' comparative ROIs Note: ROI = incremental sales generated per media dollar spent, no margin applied, Across over 2,200 studies. Source: Nielsen Catalina Solutions. Multi-Media Studies Effect Studies from 2004–2017. Used with permission of the MPA.

Also, trade magazines, mostly digital editions, continue to flourish as new industries blossom, and these trade magazine media, as well as consumer magazine media, will need salespeople or, as mentioned above, editors/salespeople to educate advertisers about the benefits and advantages of their content.

Out of Home (OHH)

Out of home (OHH) is the oldest advertising medium; some say as old as prehistoric people writing on cave walls. Although OOH was formerly referred to as *outdoor* advertising or *billboard* advertising, as advertising displays began appearing inside airport terminals, malls, and supermarkets, the industry had to change its name to include of all types of out-of-home advertising.

OOH advertising has had slow but reasonably steady growth ever since the 1930s when small signs, such as, during the early years of highway travel, Burma-Shave posted a series of six small signs, each one of which showed part of a commercial message that typically ended with a humorous quip.[34] Since that time, as people travel more in cars, sit in bus-stop shelters, walk through airports, and use subways in major cities, they are exposed to high-definition, dynamic, digital displays that grab their attention and remind them to buy tickets to movies, watch "Game of Thrones," buy coffee, stop at McDonalds, or drink Coca-Cola. OOH advertising has the great advantage of recency, or being the last advertising consumers see or are aware of before they enter a store to make a purchase.

The current state of OOH

Since the explosion of smartphone usage, beginning with the iPhone introduction in 2007, OOH advertising has also exploded, growing faster than any other medium except for digital and mobile advertising. According to an online article in Recode, "Digital technology is also driving growth in outdoor ads. Our mobile phones and digital footprints create a much more precise picture of where we are and what we're spending. In, turn, ad buyers can better understand the impact of outdoor advertising."[35]

Technology, location, and creativity are defining OOH today, according to a MediaVillage article.[36] For example, technology enables advertisers to use mobile phone location data provided by such companies as Place IQ to understand audience composition and location with such precision that an ad for a discount on a latte can be delivered to a person with a mobile phone who is walking past the location of a coffee shop with a personalized, creative message, such as "Hey, there is a 20% discount on your favorite pumpkin-spiced latte right now!"

Location data melded with database technology and can also be utilized to change OOH displays to reach targeted groups of traveling consumers with dynamic creative tied to the news of the day, to an event, or to a special offer nearby, as more and more OOH companies such as Clear Channel, Lamar, and Outfront Media (formerly CBS Outdoor) in the US and JCDecaux worldwide adopt self-service programmatic buying.

The leading programmatic company in the OOH space is Adomni, which incorporates audience data into the OOH search, buying, and reporting processes. For no extra cost to advertisers, billboard, and display owners or to affiliate partners, such as Lamar, Adomni provides audience data and insights.[37] Using the Adomni OOH search engine, advertisers can discover and then instantly purchase the best OOH ad inventory that fits their budget with locations that have the highest composition of their intended audience.[38]

Currently, OOH advertising has an energetic, graphically enticing quality that appeals to most younger consumers, and, in contrast to other media, cannot be overlooked by skipping, fast-forwarding, or paying more to avoid ads: "Out-of-home media is a full-funnel solution, providing mass awareness with comparably low CPMs, while also providing a last-touch opportunity before consumers reach their destination."[39]

The future of jobs in OOH

Because OOH is the third-fastest growing advertising medium behind digital and mobile advertising, job prospects are quite positive, especially if you are technically proficient. Selling OOH advertising may not be as glamorous to many as selling television, selling for Google or Facebook, selling magazines, or selling radio; however, for that reason the demand for OOH sales jobs is not as great as for the more top-of-the-mind, glitzier media. Therefore, selling OOH advertising might well provide an excellent opportunity for those starting out in media sales.

Test Yourself

1. What are three reasons why Warren Buffett said that newspapers are "toast?"
2. What are two solutions to declining circulation and advertising revenue that the newspaper industry is attempting?
3. What are the four types of newspaper advertising?
4. What did S.S. McClure do?
5. What was the effect that advertising revenue had on magazine cover prices and subscription rates?
6. What does the term "Magazines 360°" mean?
7. What happened to *ESPN: The Magazine*?
8. What are four benefits of magazine media advertising?
9. What caused the recent explosion of OOH advertising?
10. Can advertising on digital OOH displays be purchased programmatically?

Project

First, go to the MPA Factbook area in the Research and Resources section of the MPA website (https://www.magazine.org/Magazine/Research_and_Resources/

MPA_Factbook/Magazine/Research_and_Resources_Pages/MPA_Factbook.aspx) and download the MPA Factbook PPT file. Next, using the slides from the Factbook, create a presentation for a Fashion and Luxury magazine group to the cosmetics advertiser L'Oreal that educates the advertiser on the benefits and advantages of advertising in your Fashion and Luxury group. The presentation should consist of at least 25 slides and not more than 50 slides.

References

Anderson, Chris. 2009. *Free: The Future of a Radical Price*. New York: Hyperion Press.

Bryce, David, Dyer, Jeffrey H., and Hatch, Nile W. 2011. *"Competing against free."* *Harvard Business Review*, June.

MPA. 2019. *Magazine Media Factbook*. Available at https://www.magazine.org/Magazine/Research_and_Resources/MPA_Factbook/Magazine/Research_and_Resources_Pages/MPA_Factbook.aspx.

Resources

Adomni OOH programmatic (www.adomni.com)

Association of Magazine Media (MPA) (www.magazine.org)

Conde Nast magazines (www.condenast.com/advertising)

Hearst magazines (www.hearst.com/magazines/digital-media)

Meredith magazines (www.meredith.com/marketing-capabilities/digital)

National Newspaper Association audits for smaller markets (www.nnaweb.org)

News Media Alliance audits for large markets (www.newsmediaalliance.org)

Outdoor Advertising Association of America (www.oaaa.org)

Pew Research Center: State of the News Media 2019 (www.pewresearch.org/topics/state-of-the-news-media)

Notes

1 Chiglinsky, Katherine and Smith, Gary. 2019. "Warren Buffett sees most newspapers as 'toast' after ad decline." Retrieved from https://www.bloomberg.com/news/articles/2019-04-23/warren-buffett-sees-most-newspapers-as-toast-after-ad-decline.

2 Smith, Aaron. 2012. "Warren Buffett buys into 'declining' newspapers. Retrieved from https://money.cnn.com/2012/05/17/news/companies/buffett-newspapers/index.htm.

3 Forbes. 2019. "Billionaires: the richest people in the world." Retrieved from https://www.forbes.com/billionaires/#4dcb9640251c.

4 https://en.wikipedia.org/wiki/Monster.com.

5 https://simple.wikipedia.org/wiki/Craigslist.

6 Lewis, Peter. 1996. "The New York Times introduces a web site." Retrieved from https://www.nytimes.

com/1996/01/22/business/the-new-york-times-introduces-a-web-site.html.

7　　Bryce, David, Dyer, Jeffrey H., and Hatch, Nile W. 2011. "Competing against free." *Harvard Business Review*, June.

8　　Sangal, Aditi. 2019. "Inside the Wall Street Journal's subscription strategy." Retrieved from:https://digiday.com/podcast/inside-wall-street-journals-subscription-strategy.

9　　Deitch, Charlie. 2019. "Updated: Pittsburgh Post-Gazette to 'phase out' all print operations and become fully digital." Retrieved from https://www.pittsburghcurrent.com/pittsburgh-post-gazette-to-phase-out-all-print-operations-to-become-fully-digital.

10　Lightcap, Bradford Colton and Peek, William Anthony. 2012. "The effects of digital media on advertising markets." Retrieved from https://sites.duke.edu/djepapers/files/2016/10/lightcap-peek-dje.pdf.

11　Hagey, Keach, Alpert, Lucas, and Serkez, Yaryna. 2019. "In news industry, a stark divide between haves and have-nots." Retrieved from https://www.wsj.com/graphics/local-newspapers-stark-divide.

12　Ibid.

13　Ibid.

14　Ibid.

15　Ibid.

16　Ibid.

17　Ibid.

18　eMarketer. 2018. "The challenges publishers face in monitizing digital content." Retrieved from https://www.emarketer.com/content/the-challenges-publishers-face-in-monitizing-digital-content.

19　Doctor, Ken. 2019. "It's looking like Gannett will be acquired by GateHouse – Creating a newspaper megachain like the U.S. has never seen." Retrieved from https://www.niemanlab.org/2019/07/newsonomics-its-looking-like-gannett-will-be-acquired-by-gatehouse-creating-a-newspaper-megachain-like-the-u-s-has-never-seen.

20　Ibid.

21　Peiser, Jaclyn. 2019. "The New York Times Co. reports $709 million in digital revenue in 2018." Retrieved from https://www.nytimes.com/2019/02/06/business/media/new-york-times-earnings-digital-subscriptions.html.

22　https://en.wikipedia.org/wiki/Alliance_for_Audited_Media.

23　Kleiner, Art. 1979. "A history of magazines on a timeline." *Co-Evolution Quarterly*.

24　Ibid.

25　Ibid.

26　Ibid.

27　Ibid.

28　MPA. 2019. *Magazine Media Factbook*. Retrieved from https://www.magazine.org/Magazine/Research_and_Resources/MPA_Factbook/Magazine/Research_and_Resources_Pages/MPA_Factbook.aspx.

29　Tracy, Marc and Draper, Kevin. 2019. "End of the line (in print, anyway) for ESPN: The Magazine." Retrieved from https://www.nytimes.com/2019/04/30/sports/espn-magazine-print-closes.html.

30　Strauss, Ben. 2019. "ESPN The Magazine will cease print edition." Retrieved from https://www.washingtonpost.com/sports/2019/04/30/espn-magazine-is-closing-down/.

31　Ibid.

32　MPA. 2019. *Magazine Media Factbook*. Retrieved from https://www.magazine.org/Magazine/Research_and_Resources/MPA_Factbook/Magazine/Research_and_Resources_Pages/MPA_Factbook.aspx.

33　Statista. 2018. "U.S. Magazine Industry – Statistics & Facts." Retrieved from https://www.statista.com/topics/1265/magazines.

34　https://en.wikipedia.org/wiki/Burma-Shave.

35　Molla, Rani. 2018. "Outdoor advertising is bigger than ever." Retrieved from https://www.vox.com/2018/9/25/17897656/billboards-outdoor-advertising-ads.

36　Senese, Jodi. 2019. "How technology, location and creativity are defining OOH in 2019." Retrieved from https://www.mediavillage.com/article/how-technology-location-and-creativity-are-defining-ooh-in-2019.

37 Babb, Nicholas. 2019. "The science of OOH audience-based buying (Part 2 of 3)." Retrieved from https://www.mediavillage.com/article/the-science-of-ooh-audience-based-buying-part-2-of-3.

38 Ibid.

39 Winston, Nathan. 2019. "Antifragile: How Advertising's oldest medium became stronger than ever in the digital age." Retrieved from https://www.mediavillage.com/article/antifragile-how-advertisings-oldest-medium-became-stronger-than-ever-in-the-digital-age.

24

Audio

Charles Warner

Radio

The distinction of being America's first licensed commercial radio station is claimed by a number of broadcasters, but Pittsburgh's KDKA, which broadcast Federal election returns in November of 1920, is generally considered to be the first.[i]

When radio hit the airwaves in the early 1920s, radio programming was provided to the public primarily to give it a reason to buy radio receivers. The Westinghouse Electric and Manufacturing Company, the company that owned KDKA, was in the radio receiver manufacturing business. Westinghouse also was a partner with American Telephone & Telegraph Company (AT&T) and Radio Corporation of America (RCA) in owning several radio stations and creating the first radio network, NBC.

One of the stations that the Westinghouse–AT&T–RCA partnership owned was WEAF in New York.[ii] The station's primary business model was to charge people to talk on the air, which was sort of like making a phone call to lots of people. When the station got an inquiry from a real estate developer who wanted to talk about his new apartment

---

[i] The history of radio section of this chapter has been adapted from Chapter 21: Radio in *Media Selling, 4th Edition*. That chapter was written by Paul Talbot,

[ii] WEAF subsequently changed its call letters to WRCA, then to WNBC, and, finally, to WFAN, which was the first spots-talk radio station and was still on the air with that format in the summer of 2019.

complex in Queens, the station charged him $50 and allowed him to talk for 10 minutes. It turned out to be the first radio commercial. Here is how that first radio ad began:

> Let me enjoin upon you as you value your health and your hopes and your home happiness, to get away from the solid masses of brick, where the meager opening admitting a slant of sunlight is mockingly called a light shaft, and where children grow up starved for a run over a patch of grass and the sight of a tree. Friends, you owe it to yourself and your family to leave the congested city and enjoy what nature intended you to enjoy. Visit our new apartment homes in Hawthorne Court, Jackson Heights, where you may enjoy life in a friendly environment.

On the night its first ad was broadcast in 1922, radio was the domain of hobbyists and early adopters; however, in the explosion of interest in radio after restrictions of technology were lifted following the First World War, there was a flood of new radio adopters and broadcast bedlam blotted the airwaves because the new stations that sprang up did not have assigned frequencies.

Five years later the Federal Government made its first attempt to bring regulatory order to the radio dial with the establishment of the Federal Radio Commission (FRC) in 1927. The FRC assigned frequencies, established a broadcasting band between 500 and 1,500 kilocycles, and gave the best-funded stations with the most powerful transmitters the best dial positions, which allowed signals to travel farther at night and more clearly during the day. Out of radio's awkward birth, two men emerged who laid the foundational structure of the broadcasting business that largely remains intact today. One was a gruff Russian immigrant who looked like he slept in his clothing. He placed his bets on tubes, receivers, and transmitters. The other was a debonair American tobacco heir with hundreds of suits in his closet. This man placed his bets on crooners and comedians. Each built a radio network. Each was a visionary. Each was a fierce competitor. And each can take credit as being a founding father of today's media businesses that sell advertising.

The immigrant was David Sarnoff. Sarnoff's journey from a village in southern Russia to the executive suite of NBC lead through the tough New York City neighborhood of Hell's Kitchen where he delivered telegrams. He learned Morse code, made a name for himself reporting the details of the sinking of the "Titanic," and in 1916 he sent a memo to the president of the Marconi Company suggesting that radio could be used, as he put it, as a "music box." A few years later Sarnoff was the guiding force behind the establishment of the National Broadcasting Company (NBC), and the nation's first radio networks that appeared in the fall of 1926.

The tobacco heir was William S. Paley. After graduating from the Wharton School of Finance and Economics at the University of Pennsylvania in 1922, he went to work for his family's Philadelphia-based cigar business, the Congress Cigar Company. Every day the Paley factories manufactured a million and a half cigars, most notably the popular La Palina. In 1927, Paley was a Vice President of the Congress Cigar Company when United Independent Broadcasters (UIB), a ramshackle radio network which included Philadelphia's WCAU, approached his family for an investment. Paley's father was skeptical. But the family had seen the impact on sales attributable to the "La Palina Hour" broadcast on WCAU.

A deal was struck and in September, 1928, William Paley showed up for work at the UIB offices in New York's Paramount Building. The company had 16 employees. Within a year there was a new name, the Columbia Broadcasting System (CBS), and enough new affiliates – radio stations in different markets linked together into one network – for Paley to tell advertisers that his fledgling network was the nation's largest.

Paley and Sarnoff battled through the 1930s and 1940s to attract the mass audiences that would interest national advertisers. They raided each other's talent and courted each other's clients. Americans loved what these two men put on the air. The first radio show to attract a national audience to tune in at a specific time was "Amos 'n' Andy." It began a 19-year run on NBC-owned radio station WMAQ in 1928.[1] Radio programmers and advertising agency producers swept through the nation's vaudeville theaters searching for talent.[iii] They found people like Ed Wynn, Burns and Allen, and Jack Benny. In 1900 there were more than two thousand vaudeville theaters. By 1930, fewer than a hundred remained. The audiences had gone to radio.

Comedy was served up in the easily duplicated structure of the variety show, which featured an announcer, an orchestra, a straight man, sketches, stand-ups, puns, punchlines, and characters who captured the flavor of the audience's diverse ethnicity with exaggerated accents. Every show had a sponsor. Performers wove the name of the product into their scripts. Jack Benny launched every show with the invocation "Jell-O, again."

While radio's largest audiences were delivered by comedians, everything from opera to boxing filled the airwaves. Americans were enthralled. In a landmark 1937 study funded by the Rockefeller Fund, *The Psychology of Radio* found that for every telephone in the country there were two radios. Seventy-eight million Americans, which at the time were just over 60 percent of the US population, were regular listeners. Women liked music, men liked sports, the poor listened more than the well-to-do, and 95 percent of the people surveyed said that they would rather listen to a man's voice than a woman's.[2]

Radio geared itself up to deliver the news in the late 1930s. There was fierce opposition and intense political pressure from newspaper publishers not to broadcast news, but, nevertheless, as World War II unfolded, radio networks deployed journalists to report on the war. Edward R. Murrow's broadcasts from London, air-raid sirens blaring in the background, brought the war into America's living rooms. News became a staple of radio.

World War II was radio's last big story. In 1946 there were nine television stations in the United States. Eight years later there would be 354. By 1954 common wisdom suggested that radio was an unnecessary medium. The popular programs and their stars left radio for television. Radio networks were, for the most part, dismantled. Television captured the nation's fancy, created new stars, and crafted new definitions of leisure.

[iii] In the early days of radio, the two networks, NBC and CBS, sold blocks of airtime to advertisers, such as Sunday from 8:00 to 8:30 p.m., and to advertising agencies. The agencies produced radio programs for their advertisers, which means that the agencies not only wrote the commercials, but also wrote the scripts for the programs, hired the talent, and produced and directed the shows.

But radio stations did not go the way of vaudeville. The opposite took place. In 1948 there were 1,621 AM stations. By 1960 the number of AM stations more than doubled to 3,483 and there were 700 FM stations.[3] And beginning in 1960 the number of FM radio stations increased dramatically.

Inventor Edwin Armstrong developed FM radio in the 1930s, and in 1937 the Federal Communications Commission (FCC) granted the first FM broadcast license to W1XOJ in Paxton, Massachusetts. In 1940, Armstrong demonstrated FM broadcasting in a long-distance relay network that proved that FM was a viable medium. However, during World War II, the FCC froze the development of broadcast technologies, so it was not until after the war, in 1945, that Armstrong took up further development of FM. Armstrong's efforts were thwarted by RCA CEO David Sarnoff, who was afraid Armstrong's FM network would hamper the growth of NBC. Sarnoff lobbied for use of higher frequencies for FM than Armstrong's system used, and eventually Sarnoff's expensive lobbying won. In 1945, the FCC allocated 100 channels on the higher frequencies of 88–107 MHz.

Even though FM had much higher, static-free sound quality than AM, FM did not take off and become widely popular with listeners until the introduction of high-fidelity recording equipment and, especially, high-fidelity records, which were developed in the late 1950s.

Beginning in 1960, broadcasters began to increase their investments in FM programming, especially music programming, in order to expand their market reach. Because advertisers put their radio advertising budgets on AM stations, most FM stations in the1960s were commercial free or were limited to just a few commercials. Therefore, FM stations acquired the reputation of being commercial free or having "the most music," as many FM stations promoted themselves. Also, FM stations were helped by introduction in 1961 of FM stereo.

By 1970 the total number of radio stations had grown to 6,352, of which 2,083 were FM stations – a growth of almost 300 percent in the number of FM stations since 1960.

Radio, both AM and FM stations, still mattered after the introduction of television because the medium struck out on a different path from television. Television was a national, mass-appeal medium. Radio evolved into primarily a local medium with segmented audiences. Radio stations chose programming formats to deliver well-defined audience segments to listeners who liked news and talk, oldies music, heavy-metal, rock 'n' roll, country music, or classical music. Television owned the living room, but radio owned the kitchen, the bedroom, the car, the backyard, and eventually the beach. The dawn of the transistor in 1954 turned radio into a portable medium. Audiences grew. Revenues rose. And shifting social patterns dealt the medium strong cards as young people and African Americans turned to radio for entertainment and music they wanted but could not find on television.

Advertisers have bought radio advertising since 1922, when Hawthorne Court's owner first talked about his apartments, and ever since it has been a vital platform for marketers who wanted to reach the vast majority of the American population.

The current state of radio

As of March 31, 2019, there were 4,613 AM stations and 6,762 FM stations, for a total of 11,375 commercial radio stations in the United States.[4] Radio as a medium is thriving, or as Mark Twain quipped, "the report of my death has been grossly exaggerated."

When the FCC unfroze television station licenses in 1952 and the sale of television sets exploded to become the fastest growing appliance in history, many advertisers and agencies declared that radio was dead. But, as you can see from the above history of radio, the medium's death was exaggerated and it thrived by switching programming from comedy and drama shows to music and news-talk formats.

Furthermore, radio did not become "toast" because of the Internet disruption that devastated other media. Radio was not hurt as much as the print and television industries were. Radio maintained most of its listeners and held on to its impressive mass reach and total revenue by expanding its digital offerings and increasing the number of sponsored off-air events such as concerts and music festivals. Exhibit 24.1 shows total radio revenue for 2017 and 2018.

Note in Exhibit 24.1 that radio is not a high-growth industry, but its revenue manages to inch up little-by-little in spite of it operating under the radar of many advertisers and especially under the radar of most young media buyers who grew up in the Internet era. But even before digital advertising steamrolled over television and print, radio was a difficult sale to most national brand marketers because they were influenced by their agencies, and the majority of those agencies loved television and consciously overlooked radio. Agency creative directors got paid high salaries for making expensive television commercials and taking advertisers to exotic commercial-shoot locations; and when agencies pitched for new business, they showed prospective clients their successful television campaigns. Radio was seldom mentioned for several reasons: (1) radio was not a glamorous medium; (2) compared to the cost of creating and producing a television commercial, creating a radio commercial cost very little, and, therefore, agencies could not charge clients a lot for producing them; and (3) it took just a few highly skilled negotiators to execute a $10-million-dollar television network campaign, but it might take a media department of 25 people or more to execute a $10 million radio campaign. In other words, television was much more glamorous and profitable for agencies than radio.

Exhibit 24.1 Radio revenue in billions of dollars 2017 vs. 2018

	2017	*2018*	*YTY % change*
Local	$10.3	$10.4	+1%
Local %	58.5%	58.4%	
Digital	$1.2	$1.3	+1%
Digital %	6.8%	7.3%	
Off-Air	$2.4	$2.5	+1%
Off-Air %	13.6%	14.0%	
Network	$1.1	$1.1	–
Network %	6.3%	6.2%	
National Spot	$2.6	$2.5	–3.8%
National Spot %	14.8%	14.0%	
TOTAL	$17.6	$17.8	+1%

Source: InsideRadio. 2018. "Kagan: Radio revenues climb 1.1% to $17.8 billion in 2018."https://www.insideradio.com/kagan-radio-revenues-climb-to-billion-in/fa5faeee-7a94-11e8-b009-07a867dfdbc9.html.

Nevertheless, over the years since the introduction of the Internet, radio has, to a large degree, maintained its audience, and its revenue has steadily crept upwards. In 1996, the last year newspapers were the number one medium (television was second), radio was in third place, slightly ahead of magazines. In 2018, as you saw in Exhibit 16.3, radio was still in third place in revenue, behind the Internet and television. Why has radio, media's unglamorous stepchild, held on to its third-place position in total media revenue over the years? There are four reasons:

Reach As other media audiences fragmented because of the disruption of the Internet, radio maintained its audience, and in 2019 had the largest US reach of any medium.

Results As you can see in Exhibit 24.1, radio is primarily a local medium, and local advertisers continue to get good results and competitive returns on investment (ROIs) from radio advertising. Radio delivers for local services such as lawyers, accountants, financial services, and for retailers such as car dealers, restaurants, and jewelers.

New revenue streams Radio, led by Bob Pittman, CEO of iHeart Media, has digitized and streamed online most of its content and has developed off-air revenue such as concerts, live events,group travel, education, such as cooking classes, websites, podcasts, and advertising and marketing services.[iv]

Consolidation Like newspapers, magazines, and television, the radio industry has consolidated to cut back-office costs, to negotiate with suppliers such as Nielsen, and to negotiate with large national advertisers.[v] In 2018, iHeart Media ranked number one in number of stations owned (855) and revenue ($6.33 billion, or 36 percent of total 2018 radio revenue). In 2018, Entercom Communication was ranked number three in the number of stations owned (235) and ranked number two in radio revenue ($1.43 billion). In 2018, Cumulus Media ranked number two in number of stations (448) and ranked number three in revenue ($1.14 billion).

iHeart, Entercom, Cumulus, and other station group owners such as Beasley and Emmis own clusters of radio stations in large- and medium-sized markets. Congress passed the Telecommunications Act of 1996 that expanded the limit of the number of radio stations any one company could own in a market, depending on the size of

---

[iv] For a description of the type of marketing services many radio stations offer see references to the Zimmer Radio and Marketing Group in Chapter 2: Selling In the Digital Era.

[v] Remember in Chapter 15: Marketing the example of a marketing solution provided by iHeart Media to 21st Century Fox to promote the opening of the movie "Bohemian Rhapsody?" As part of a package to buy a schedule on many of iHeart's radio stations, iHeart arranged to play Queen's six-minute song "Bohemian Rhapsody" simultaneously at 9:00 a.m. on a Thursday morning on 650 iHeart radio stations. Such a massive, coordinated promotion would only be possible with a company that could guarantee clearance on a large number of stations and would only be attractive to a national advertiser if such a promotion could deliver nationwide coverage.

the market.[5] Ownership restrictions are based on a sliding scale that varies by the size of the market:

- In a radio market with 45 or more stations, an entity may own up to eight radio stations, no more than five of which may be in the same service (AM or FM).
- In a radio market with between 30 and 44 radio stations, an entity may own up to seven radio stations, no more than four of which may be in the same service.
- In a radio market hosting between 15 and 29 radio stations, an entity may own up to six radio stations, no more than four of which may be in the same service.
- In a radio market with 14 or fewer radio stations, an entity may own up to five radio stations, no more than three of which may be in the same service, as long as the entity does not own more than 50 percent of all radio stations in that market.[6]

Because of these ownership rules, in 1996 companies such as Clear Channel Communications (now iHeart Media), Cumulus Media, and Entercom went on a radio station buying spree to accumulate stations. As a result of this buying spree and the eventual consolidation that followed, independently owned stations declined in number as the large, consolidated radio companies dominated ownership of radio stations, especially in larger markets. Exhibit 24.2 shows an analysis of the ownership, station type (AM or FM), and formats of the 10 top radio stations in the top five radio markets, which iHeart, Cumulus, and Entercom, as you can see, dominate.

There are 269 radio markets measured by Nielsen Audio, from the number-one market, New York, to number 269, Las Cruces-Deming, NM. Therefore, an analysis of only the 10 top-rated stations in only the top five markets (50 stations out of over 11,000) is certainly not a random sample, so the Exhibit 24.2 analysis of these stations is not a statistically representative depiction of US radio. Instead, the analysis does give a snapshot

Exhibit 24.2 Analysis of ownership, station type (AM or FM), and format of the top 10 radio stations in the top five markets in June, 2019.

- iHeart owned 16 of the top 10 radio stations in the ratings in the top five radio markets (New York, Los Angeles, Chicago, San Francisco, and Dallas-Fort Worth).
- Entercom owned 13 of the top 10 radio stations in the ratings in the top five markets.
- Cumulus owned 7 of the top 10 radio stations in the ratings in the top five radio markets.
- FM stations dominate in the ratings.
- All of the top 10 rated stations in Los Angeles were FM stations.
- Only six of the top 10 radio stations in the top five markets (50 stations) were AM stations.
  - Of those six AM stations, four were all news or news-talk (WINS, WBBM, KCBS, and WBAP) and two were all sports (WSCR and KNBR). Also, all the stations but WINS were 50,000-watt, clear-channel stations, which means they had excellent signals, especially at night when most of these stations could be heard within a 1,000-mile radius.
- The highest rated AM station in the top five markets was Entercom's all-news KCBS-AM in San Francisco.
- The number one station in the ratings in San Francisco is NPR-affiliated KQED-FM, the only public, educational station to be in the top 10 in any of the top five markets.

Source: Radio Online. 2019. "Nielsen audio ratings." https://ratings.radio-online.com/content/arb001.

of the current state of radio and reflects some overall trends that in all probability will not be reversed in the near future. These trends are:

- FM stations dominate in the ratings.
- iHeart Media dominates radio in top markets. For example, five of the top 10 stations in New York are owned by iHeart.
- Unless they are 50,000-watt, clear-channel stations, the vast majority of AM stations are not competitive in the ratings.
- NPR-affiliated FM stations play an important role in the radio panoply.

How radio is sold

In 1964, in order to help radio salespeople fight against the onslaught of television that was slowing radio advertising revenue growth, the Radio Advertising Bureau (RAB) had radio personality and comedian, Stan Freberg, create a one-minute ad to promote the use of radio. See Exhibit 24.3 for a script of that spot. You get a sense of the ad's impact from the script, but it is a much better experience to listen to it. You can find it on YouTube (https://www.youtube.com/watch?v=qPbvFv6BJvU).

In the 1950s, 1960s, 1970s, and 1980s radio salespeople had to scrap for every dollar and sell against newspapers and television on a local level, and against television and magazines on a national level. They had to sell creatively and emphasize radio's effectiveness based on the medium's ability to stretch listeners' imaginations by using what is known as the *theater of the mind*. Salespeople also sold radio based on the power of the human voice to grab people emotionally and based on the unparalleled effectiveness of popular local personalities endorsing products by reading commercials live on the air.

In the 1990s, 2000s, and 2010s radio salespeople had to fight the further encroachment on their revenue streams of the Internet and Goliaths such as Google and Facebook. But radio not only survived, it prevailed. It prevailed through creative selling and by emphasizing radio's strengths, humanness, and strong emotional connection to listeners. It also prevailed by not selling radio as an alternative to television or digital advertising but as a strong combination with these two powerful media. Radio salespeople did not try to beat the competition; they joined them. In November, 2018, radio's sales efforts at selling radio in combination with other media was given a big boost when Nielsen announced that it had added radio to its widely used cross-media planning tool, Nielsen Media Impact. This tool allows users to determine cross-media reach, frequency, and duplication using advanced audience segments, and, thus, radio can be readily compared to other national media.[7]

See Exhibit 24.4 for a list of the advantages and benefits about their medium that help salespeople keep radio growing.

The future of radio jobs

The future prospects for radio sales jobs are excellent. There are 11,375 radio stations in America, and the vast majority of them exist on some sort of advertising revenue. There

Exhibit 24.3 RAB Stan Freberg spot

VOICE:	"Radio? Why should I advertise on the radio? There's nothing to look at. No pictures."
FREBERG:	"You can do things on radio you couldn't possibly do on TV."
VOICE: "	That'll be the day."
FREBERG:	"OK, watch this: OK, people, now when I gave you the cue, I want the 700-foot high mountain of whipped cream to roll into Lake Michigan, which has been drained and filled with hot chocolate, then the Royal Canadian Air Force will fly overhead towing a ten-ton maraschino cherry, which will be dropped into the whipped cream to the cheering of 25,000 extras.
	"All right, cue the mountain."

(SOUND OF LOGS ROLLING AND A BIG SPLASH)

"OK, cue the Air Force."

(SOUND OF AIRPLANES)

"OK, cue the cherry."

(SOUND OF CHERRY DROPPING INTO WHIPPED CREAM)

"OK, cue the 25,000 extras."

(SOUND OF CHEERING MULTITUDE)

"Now, do you want to try that on television?"

VOICE:	"Well…"
FREBERG:	"You see, radio is a very special medium because it stretches the imagination."
VOICE:	"Doesn't television stretch the imagination?"
FREBERG:	"Up to 27 inches."

Source: RAB. 1964. Stan Freberg spot. https://www.youtube.com/watch?v=qPbvFv6BJvU.

are opportunities in market number 269 and market number one. Selling local radio is not as numbers oriented as selling local television is, and in most small- and medium-sized markets salespeople not only sell radio advertising but also create commercials or write the copy for live reads. Radio salespeople also learn how to sell remote broadcasts, sponsorships of parades and live concerts, and other off-air revenue-producing promotions, trips, or educational opportunities. They also establish relationships with local advertisers, which can lead to jobs in television, ad agencies, or digital agencies such as ReachLocal.

Furthermore, as pointed out in by Tim Warner, Director of Sales of WTHR-TV (see in Chapter 22: Television), basically the same advantages of selling local television apply to selling local radio: (1) radio salespeople typically do well financially, (2) they learn to sell digital as well as audio ads, because, eventually, virtually all advertising will be digital, (3) they are not tied to a desk all day, (4) they call on a wide variety of accounts and people, thus they learn how to deal with and empathize with a diverse range of personalities, (5) they can be quite creative in ways to get results for clients, and (6) they learn about a wide variety of businesses. Furthermore, if you are passionate about a particular genre of music such as hip hop, or heavy metal, rock 'n' roll, jazz, oldies, or classical, radio has the advantage for salespeople of allowing them to be associated with and evangelize the music they love.

Exhibit 24.4   Benefits and advantages of radio

1   Nielsen Audio figures show radio is the number one reach medium. Radio reaches 92 percent of adult consumer weekly, 91 percent of millennials weekly, and 87 percent of teens weekly.

2   Radio reaches 53.6 million more adults each month than search sites and apps such as Google, Yahoo, and Bing.

3   Radio reaches 66.7 million more adults each month than social media sites or apps such as Facebook, Snapchat, Instagram, and Twitter.

4   Radio added to a television-only campaign and increased ROI by over 20 percent in one study.

5   Forty-four percent of Americans are light television viewers that account for only nine percent of total television viewing. Radio reaches 90 percent of those light television viewers.

6   The heaviest television viewing quintile (20%) view an average of 10.1 hours a day. The lightest television viewing quintile tune in an average of only 12 minutes per day.

7   Radio's heaviest listeners are considerably more upscale than television's and are 74 percent more likely to reside in a home with household income over $100,000, are 40 percent more likely to have graduated from college, and are 165 percent more likely to be employed full time than television's heaviest viewers.

8   Precise targeting is not a substitute for mass reach. Marketers' livelihoods depend on reaching a lot of people to try to persuade a few of them to include the marketer's brand in their consideration set and to purchase it.

9   Radio is an intimate medium in an increasingly impersonal world.

10   Music on radio acts as a time machine that transports people back to an exact place and time, often better than any picture or video.

11   Radio enables advertisers to deliver well-crafted and refined audio messages of various lengths by a trusted friend – a local personality who is popular and tied to the community.

12   Radio reaches consumers in places other media cannot, often while they are a mobile or a captive audience. Radio is one of the few media that people can enjoy while they are doing other things such as driving or walking.

13   Radio is the most trusted medium, 81 percent more trustworthy than cable television, 27 percent more trustworthy than network television, and two times more trustworthy than social media.

Source for items 1–8: McCurdy, Bob. 2019. "The uninformed are everywhere." https://radioink.com/2019/07/21/the-uninformed-are-everywhere. Source for item 13: Moss. E.B. 2019. "Radio scores as most trusted medium: iHeart Media shares survey results." https://www.mediavillage.com/article/radio-scores-as-most-trusted-medium-iheartmedia-shares-survey-results.

There are also opportunities in radio national representative companies such as Katz Radio and even in network radio.

Podcasts

Podcasts are Internet radio on demand, which means listeners do not have to tune in at a specific time but can listen whenever it is convenient for them; or as Rion Swartz, head of marketing for LegalZoom, said in an interview, compared to terrestrial radio, podcast advertisers are "not at the mercy of people changing stations."[8]

The invention of podcasting is attributed to MTV personality Adam Curry and software developer Dave Winer when they distributed their audio shows "Morning Coffee Notes" and "Daily Street Code "via a real simple syndication (RSS) feed in 2004.[9] That same year the term *podcast* was first mentioned by Ben Hammersley in a *Guardian* newspaper article in which he suggested possible names for the new audio medium, the "pod" of podcast is borrowed from Apple's "iPod" digital media player; and the "cast" of podcast is borrowed from radio's "broadcast."[10]

In 2005, Apple released iTunes version 4.9 for the iPod that contained support for podcasts, thus making discovery of podcasts relatively easy, and in 2006 Steve Jobs demonstrated how to make a podcast in his Macworld keynote address. That same year, host Ira Glass's "This American Life," a popular radio program on NPR stations, made its debut as a free podcast and went on to not only become the nation's most popular podcast, but it also spawned NPR's "Planet Money," "Serial," and "S-Town."

In 2009, abrasive comedian Marc Maron began his "WTF" podcast after his show was cancelled by liberal talk radio network Air America. "WTF" gained a large following and is one of several popular podcasts that extended the reach and awareness of podcasts as a medium. By 2012, Edison Research stated that 29 percent of Americans had listened to podcasts, and the audiences to podcast has grown dramatically since then to become an important advertising vehicle, especially for direct-to-consumer (DTC) marketers.[11]

In 2014, "Serial," a podcast spinoff from "This American Life," became a sensation. The 12 episodes of season one have been downloaded 175 million times since its debut, making it the most downloaded podcast of all time. "Serial's" unparalleled success put podcasts on the media map and intrigued not only a huge audience but also radio group operators such as iHeart, Entercom, Cumulus, Emmis, and Beasley – all companies added podcasting to their repertoire of content offerings.

The current state of podcasting

As of March, 2019, there were 660,000 podcasts on virtually every topic imaginable.[12] Research firm eMarketer estimated that the number of listeners to podcasts in 2019 would climb to 76.4 million, and by 2020 would move up to 78.9 million.[13] In terms of advertising revenue, eMarketer estimated that in 2019 podcast dollars would total $678.7 million and by 2021 they would hit $1.045 billion.[14]

As of June, 2019, the 10 most popular podcasts, according to PodTrac were: (1) "The Daily" (The NY Times), (2) "Stuff You Should Know" (iHeart Media), (3) "This American Life" (NPR), (4) "Up First" (NPR), (5) "The Ben Shapiro Show" (The Daily Wire), (6) "RadioLab" (NPR), (7) "Pardon My Take" (Barstool Sports), (8) "Planet Money" (NPR), (9) "TED Radio Hour" (NPR), and (10) "Wait, Wait…Don't Tell Me" (NPR).[15]

How podcasts are sold

In spite of podcasts' relatively small audiences, especially when compared to the massive reach of radio, advertisers, especially direct marketers, find podcasts' audiences highly desirable and their commercials very effective, especially when read by a podcast's host.

In this section, you will learn how podcasts' audiences are *measured*, how the ads in podcasts are *structured*, how podcasts are *priced* and those prices are negotiated, about the *IAB Podcast Upfront*, and about *podcast networks*.

Podcast measurement   Until the end of 2018, the only way to measure the audience of a podcast was to count how many times it had been downloaded. Metrics advertisers and agencies prefer, such as the number of unique visitors, how long visitors were engaged, number of clicks on an ad, or ad listener demographics were, for the most part, not available for podcasts. Tracking and measuring podcast performance is challenging, because once a podcast file is downloaded onto a device, it is difficult to know how much of a podcast has actually been listened to or whether it was listened to it at all. Because podcasts are downloaded for future listening, it requires a highly technical solution to measure how the ads they contain are consumed.

Nevertheless, podcast advertisers have found methods other than counting downloads to evaluate their investments in podcasts:

1   *Unique downloads.* The number of times a podcast has been downloaded is not an accurate method of estimating a podcast's audience. The Interactive Advertising Bureau (IAB) recommends using unique downloads to measure the size of a podcast's listening audience. A unique download is a statistic in which multiple individual download requests are attributed to the same overall download request. Therefore, rather than tallying up the raw requests online from a user, those requests are shown as one unique download.[16]

2   *Subscribers.* The best way to understand the size of a podcast's subscriber base is to look at the degree of consistency in download totals between each episode. The larger the number of consistent downloads, the larger the subscriber base probably is. Look at the first 48 to 72 hours after a podcast is published because it is that time frame that is typically dominated by subscribers.[17]

3   *Context.* How niche is a podcast? If a podcast is about politics in a town of 100,000 people and has 5,000 consistent unique downloads (5 percent of the population), an audience of 5,000 would be significant and, thus, attractive to local advertisers. However, if a podcast is about news or politics in the entire US and, therefore, had a potential audience in the hundreds of million people, an audience of 5,000 would be

way too small for advertisers to consider. For example, the number one podcast, "The Daily," in June, 2019, had an estimated audience of eight million monthly unique listeners.[18]

4   *Lead generation.* Advertisers that put a podcast link on their website can track conversions. For example, when an advertiser such as ZipRecruiter has a commercial in "The Ezra Klein Show" and host Ezra Klein reads the ZipRecruiter commercial, he will urge listeners to go to "ZipRecruiter.com slash E.Z.R.A. to get a free trial." By closely tracking visitors to their website link, advertisers can determine the number of conversions a podcast generated.

5   *Reviews and likes.* Podcast listener reviews on iTunes, Google Play, and other download platforms area also helpful to advertisers and podcast producers to get a sense of listener engagement and loyalty. Social media likes also help for the same reason and because people are advocating for a podcast.

By 2019, several organizations had developed systems that measured podcasts more precisely. Apple Podcast Analytics became one of the most widely used measurement tools, in December 2018 NPR announced a new podcast measurement tool called RAD, and in 2019 Nielsen announced a qualitative podcast measurement service it called Nielsen Podcast Listener Buying Power that allowed advertisers to target audiences with specific interests and buying habits. Experts predict that by 2021 podcasts will be measured as precisely as other digital advertising is. This increased precision will be another boost to podcast advertising.

Podcast ad structure   Podcasts generally have one 15-second pre-roll position, one or two 60-second mid-roll positions, depending on the length of the podcast, and one 15-second post-roll position. For a typical 20- to 30-minute podcast, there is just one mid-roll commercial position and one sponsor. For longer podcasts there might be two sponsors. Pre-roll and post-roll positions are typically used to promote a publisher's other podcasts, or do like "The Daily" does and use these positions to promote subscriptions.

Podcast pricing   Because, as of 2019, the number of thousands of actual listeners to a podcast could generally not not be determined accurately, podcasts are sold on one of three pricing models: (1) On an estimated cost-per-thousand (CPM) basis according to the number of unique downloads. CPMs generally run anywhere from $18 to $40, or even higher for top-rated podcasts such as "The Daily" or "Stuff You Should Know."[19] (2) On a cost-per-acquisition (CPA) pricing model that is based on the number of customers that are sent to and who take action on a website. For example, a financial services company might pay $300 for each customer that opens an account as a result of hearing a podcast ad and going to the /(podcast link) and opening an account. (3) On a flat-rate sponsorship basis. This sponsorship model works well for podcasts that are just starting up and do not have a track record of downloads or listener information.

Because the vast majority of podcast advertising is not yet bought and sold programmatically, each podcast buy typically is negotiated separately. Most pre- and post-roll positions are used by publishers for promotion; however, depending on the size of an ad buy, many podcast publishers, if asked in a negotiation, will give pre-roll or post-roll positions to a sponsor that makes a reasonably large multi-episode commitment.

IAB Podcast Upfront   In 2017 the IAB held the first Podcast Upfront market, and at the 2018 IAB Podcast Upfront many major media organizations such as iHeart, NPR, Turner Broadcasting, Univision, and Cumulus's radio network Westwood One show-cased new podcasts to the interest of major advertisers and agencies.[20] In the future the Podcast Upfront will be a major marketplace for major podcast publishers and large national advertisers, just as the television network upfront is.

Podcast networks   Podcast networks such as Midroll (owned by podcast platform Stitcher), AdvertiseCast, PodGrid, Archer Avenue, Authentic Shows, PodcastOne, Earwolf Podcast Network, and Megaphone (owned by Panoply Media) represent and sell ads in a large number of podcasts. A podcast network is similar to a national televi-sion or radio rep firm. Some podcast networks concentrate on selling podcasts with similar content, such as content that appeals to women of all ages, but most networks sell the aggregated mass audience of all the podcasts they represent. One of the largest podcast networks, Midroll, claims on its website that, "Podcast advertising is a digital audio platform reaching 90 million educated, affluent and mobile listeners every month, who are open to hearing your brand's message. Midroll connects you to 300+ shows, downloaded more than 150 million times a month. Because we specialize in host-read ads, listeners pay attention and remember what they hear."

The future of podcasting

The future of podcasting is excellent because it is one of the few high-growth media left. As podcasting growth accelerates and becomes a viable mass medium for both direct and brand marketers, the following trends will define podcasting:

Consolidation   As has happened in the Internet, television, newspaper, magazine, and radio industries, podcasters will consolidate, and in the future there will be fewer and fewer small players and just a handful of large players that remain in business. Major podcast companies such as NPR, iHeart, and Entercom will continue to grow and become even more dominant. Consolidation not only allows podcast publishers to cut back-office costs but also to aggregate podcast audiences to sell to advertisers and to use their platforms to promote podcasts they produce. Consolidation also makes it possible to take a longer-term view and not only invest in new genres of podcasts but also to offer them to a global audience as iHeart did when it announced in August, 2019, that it was going to make available in early 2020 the megahit podcast "Stuff You Should Know" and five other iHeart podcasts in Spanish, Hindi, Portuguese, French, and German.

Subscriptions   More and more publishers of podcasts will adopt a subscription model and charge for podcasts. In 2019, online subscription music service Spotify bought Gimlet Media (a major podcast publishing company), Anchor (a podcast production firm), and Parcast (a producer of crime and mystery shows), so it could offer a variety of podcasts to its subscribers. When Spotify bought Gimlet and Anchor, CEO Daniel Ek admitted that he did not originally realize that "audio – not just music – would be the future of Spotify" when he founded Spotify in 2006.[21]

Also in 2019, the subscription podcast service Luminary announced its lineup of sub-scription-based, commercial-free podcasts. The Luminary podcasts include shows by Malcolm Gladwell, Lena Dunham, Conan O'Brien, Trevor Noah, Guy Raz, known for "How I Built This," and Adam Davidson, known for being a creator of the award-winning podcast "Planet Money."[22] When interviewed by *The New York Times* when he announced Luminary's all-star lineup, co-founder and CEO, Matt Sacks, said, "We want to become synonymous with podcasting in the same way Netflix has become synony-mous with streaming." Luminary charges subscribers $7.99 a month, and in addition to its ad-free, star-studded podcasts it also offers a free area, where listeners can play any of the estimated over 600,000 ad-supported and non-exclusive podcasts in the market. Luminary is offering ad-supported podcasts in order to compete with other podcast plat-forms such as Stitcher, Pocket Casts, Overcast, and Castbox.

The future of sales jobs in podcasting

Because podcasting is the fastest growing medium, the prospects for sales jobs are excel-lent. However, because of consolidation, the future of sales jobs is not in selling indi-vidual or a small network of podcasts, but in selling for large companies such as iHeart, Entercom, or NPR, or for podcast networks such as Midroll or AdvertiseCast.

Test Yourself

1. What commercial US radio station was the first to be licensed?
2. What were the names of two visionaries who built the radio industry and estab-lished the basic business model for modern media?
3. Who developed FM radio?
4. How many commercial radio stations were there in the US in 2019?
5. What rank position does radio hold in terms of media revenue?
6. What two media rank above radio in revenue?
7. What are four reasons radio has held on to its third-place revenue rank?
8. Explain the concept of the *theater of the mind* and why it is important for radio.
9. What is the "pod" part of podcasting named after?
10. What was the most popular podcast of all time?
11. What are two trends that will define podcasting's future?

Project

Assume you are educating a direct-to-consumer (DTC) advertiser about Vox Media's podcast, "Today Explained." Create a PowerPoint presentation on the benefits of adver-tising in "Today Explained." Do not mention audience size, number of downloads, or price (investment).

Resources

BIA Advisory Services media insights (www.biakelsey.com)
Borrell Associates local advertising insights (www.borrellassociates.com)
Hot Pod News podcasting news (www.hotpodnews.com)
Math and Magic with Bob Pittman podcast (www.iheart.com/podcast/1119-math-magic-31150153)
MediaPost media news (www.mediapost.com)
MediaVillage media and advertising analysis (www.mediavillage.com)
Podcast Business Journal (www.podcastbusinessjournal.com)
PodTrac podcast measurement (analytics.podtrac.com)
Radio Advertising Bureau (RAB) (www.rab.com)
Radio Ink radio news (www.radioink.com)
Radio Ink sales advice (www.radioink.com/author/bmccurdy>)
YouTube Stan Freberg spot (www.youtube.com/watch?v=qPbvFv6BJvU)

Notes

1 Encyclopedia Britannica. "Amos 'n' Andy Show." Retrieved from https://www.britannica.com/topic/Amos-n-Andy-American-radio-program.

2 Douglas, Susan J. 1999. *Listening In*. Times Books.

3 FCC. 1960. "Annual Report to Congress." Retrieved from https://www.fcc.gov/reports-research/reports/annual-reports-congress/26th-annual-report-congress-1960.

4 FCC. 2019."Broadcast Station total as of March 31, 2019." Retrieved from https://www.fcc.gov/document/broadcast-station-totals-march-31-2019.

5 Retrieved from https://en.wikipedia.org/wiki/Federal_Communications_Commission#Telecommunications_Act_of_1996

6 FCC. 2019. Retrieved from https://www.fcc.gov/consumers/guides/fccs-review-broadcast-ownership-rules

7 Friedman, Wayne. 2018. "Nielsen cross-media planning tool adds radio." Retrieved from https://mediapost.com/publications/article/328103/nielsen-cross-media-planning-tool-adds-radtio.html.

8 eMarketer. 2019. "What LegalZoom learned over 7 years of podcast advertising." Retrieved from https://www.emarketer.com/content/legalzoom-talks-best-practices-for-podcast-advertisers.

9 Sternberg, Adam. 2019. "The Great Podrush has only begun." *New York,* March 18–31.

10 Retrieved from https://internationalpodcastday.com/what-is-podcast.

11 International Podcast Day. "Podcast Historical Timeline and Milestones." Retrieved from https://www.internationalpodcastday.com/podcasting-history.

12 Sternberg, Adam. 2019. "The Great Podrush Has Only Begun." New York. March 18–31.

13 eMarketer. 2019. "Podcasts: A small but significant audience." Retrieved from https://www.emarketer.com/content/podcasts-a-small-but-significant-audience.

14 eMarketer. 2019. "Podcast advertising revenues will surpass $1 billion by 2021." Retrieved from https://www.emarketer.com/content/podcast-advertising-revenue-will-surpass-1-billion-by-2021.

15 Ibid.

16 Booth, Katherine. 2018. "Podcast metrics: How to measure your performance (with such little data). Retrieved from https://impactbnd.com/blog/how-to-measure-podcast-metrics-performance.

17 Ibid.

18 BusinessInsider. 2019. "The New York Times is extending its podcast 'The Daily' to a newsletter as it tries to turn listeners into paying subscribers." Retrieved from https://www.businessinsider.com/the-new-york-times-is-launching-a-newsletter-for-the-daily-podcast-2019-2?r=US&IR=T.

19 Dumas, John Lee. 2019. "Podcast sponsorships: The ultimate guide." Retrieved from https://www.eofire.com/podcast-sponsorships.

20 Moss, E.B. 2018. "Top takeaways from the IAB Podcast Upfront – Part 1." Retrieved from https://www.mediavillage.com/article/takeaways-from-the-iab-podcast-upfront-part-1.

21 Russell, Jon. 2019. "Spotify says it paid $340m For Gimlet and Anchor." https://techcrunch.com/2019/02/14/spotify-gimlet-anchor-340-million/

22 Barnes, Brooks. 2019. "With big stars and paid subscription, Luminary aims to be the Netflix of podcasts." Retrieved from https://www.nytimes.com/2019/03/03/business/media/luminary-media-podcast-app.html.

25

Time Management

Charles Warner

In the years that I have been involved in the media as a salesperson, a sales manager, a sales consultant, and a teacher of media sales, the two questions I have been asked the most are: (1) from sales managers, "Where do I find good salespeople?" and (2) from salespeople and students, "How do I find the time to get everything done?"

I would hope that at least one answer to the first question is, "To find good salespeople, look for a person who has read *Media Selling, 5th Edition.*"

Some answers to the second question follow.

Characteristics of Time

Time is a finite, non-renewable resource, which means that there is a fixed amount – 24 hours in a day – and, thus, everyone on earth has exactly the same amount of time. No one has any more than 24 hours, and no one has any less. Because time ticks by relentlessly one second at a time, once a second is gone, it cannot be recovered. Time is not like money because it cannot be stored, saved, replaced, made up, or overspent. Time passes inexorably forward one tick at a time; therefore, there are only two things that you can do with time: use it or waste it. A concept such as, "I can *save* ten minutes by driving this alternate route," is logically flawed because time cannot be saved in a bank and used later. The 24 hours of time that you have must be managed, because

Media Selling: Digital, Television, Audio, Print and Cross-Platform, Fifth Edition.
Charles Warner, William A. Lederer, and Brian Moroz.
© 2020 John Wiley & Sons, Inc. Published 2020 by John Wiley & Sons, Inc.

there is exactly the same amount of time for everyone, both you and your competitors. Therefore, one of the best ways to win over your competition is to manage your time better than they do.

In order to manage how you use your time, you have to take the following four steps in time management: planning, organizing, controlling, and evaluating. What these four steps do is allow you to work smarter, not work harder.

Planning

Planning begins with setting goals on a yearly basis and setting objectives on a monthly, weekly, and daily basis. In this book, I define the difference between a goal and an objective as being that goals are long-term (a year or more) and objectives are shorter term (less than a year).

Yearly

Planning begins anew each year with a written list of goals, or what you want to accomplish in the coming year – your map. You must write down your goals because you not only must keep track of them as the year progresses but also because when you write your goals down, you increase your commitment to them. Here are the three elements of a goal that you want to write down:

Overall goals   What outcomes do you want? For example, if you are a salesperson whose compensation is based to a large degree on commissions or on receiving a bonus based on hitting a budget or quota, then you might set a goal of increasing your income by 15 percent. A goal must be measureable. For example, a goal of "increasing my income" is not useful because it is too indefinite, not measureable. Also, when you set your yearly goals, do not have more than five because if you have more than five, you tend to lose the ability to focus.

Task goals   What are the tasks, or activities, that you must undertake in order to achieve each of your goals? If you do not have tasks assigned that are necessary for you to achieve a goal, then that goal becomes a vague intention, not a concrete, measureable goal. Tasks are the path to a final destination. For example, if your goal is to increase your income by 15 percent, the tasks, or activities, that you must complete might be: (1) make 20 more prospecting calls every week, (2) make 10 more client presentations every week, and (3) make twice as many contacts weekly with current clients than you did the previous year. These goals are all measureable.

Improvement goals   Set four or six improvement goals in a year so that you can focus on one improvement goal for either three or two months. For example, six improvement goals might be: (1) improve listening skills, (2) improve Excel skills, (3) improve

PowerPoint skills, (4) improve question-asking skills, (5) improve understanding of artificial intelligence (AI), and (6) lose 10 pounds. Note that all the improvement areas do not have to be business related; some can be personal. Your improvement goals require that you become an *ultralearner*.[1]

In his 2019 book, *Ultralearning: Master Hard Skills, Outsmart the Competition, and Accelerate Your Career,* author Scott Young synthesizes research on learning and writes that being an ultralearner requires intense focus, concentration, and drill, or deliberate practice, as you learned in Chapter 8: The New Buying and Selling Process. Young describes ultralearning as, "A strategy for acquiring skills and knowledge that is both self-directed and intense."[2] Young proposes nine principles of ultralearning, the majority of them based on focus, practice, feedback, and experimenting. He emphasizes that, because of computerization, automation, and outsourcing, in today's business world there is "skills polarization" – top performers do a lot better than everyone else.[3] Young quotes the economist Tyler Cowen, who believes that, "Average is over."[4]

Yearly planning is more general in nature and not bogged down with specific details. In other words, you do not have a yearly To-Do list, instead you draw a map of where you want to go and the route to get you there. Later in this section you will learn how to organize monthly, weekly, and daily To-Do lists to set reminders to complete the activities and tasks that will help you achieve: (1) your three type of goals, (2) your team's goals, (3) your supervisor's goals, and (4) your organization's goals.

Organizing

Once you have your yearly plan, the next step is to organize the tasks that will help you achieve your overall goals and your improvement goals, which you do on a monthly, weekly, and daily basis. You also need to organize your desk, your computer, and your written communication to be as efficient as possible in order to help you achieve your monthly, weekly, and daily objectives.

Monthly

Every month, review your progress toward achieving your yearly overall goals, task goals, and improvement goals, and make adjustments if necessary. Remember from Chapter 4: The AESKOPP Approach, Attitude, and Goal Setting that goals must be moderately difficult and challenging, but not so difficult as to make them unachievable.

At the beginning of each month you need to synthesize the two most important time management tools: (1) your To-Do list, and (2) your calendar.

To-Do lists These are a tool that everybody uses in some form, but few use them as well as they could. Most To-Do lists are too long. The longer they are, the worse they are. Similarly, long To-Do lists are depressing; and the longer they are, the more depressing they are. Long To-Do lists cause us to play unconscious tricks on ourselves. We tend to do lots of little things first in order to give ourselves achievement feedback. We desperately want to be successful, to win, so we unconsciously choose the easiest and most fun things to do first so we will feel successful. Another unconscious thing that happens is a matter of perception. Have you ever been near to an airport and watched planes coming in for a landing? Have you noticed that a huge airplane such as a 727 jet looks as though it is approaching very slowly, particularly in comparison to a small air-plane such as a Cessna two-seated propeller airplane, which looks as though it is coming in fairly fast. In reality the jet is going faster than the Cessna, but because of its size we perceive that the jet is going slowly, and we perceive that the much smaller Cessna is going faster. Our perception is warped by size.

The same warped perception occurs with time. The things we like to do go fast, and the things we do not like to do go very slowly – they seem to take forever. In order to manage our time well, we have to be aware of this perceptual bias and cor-rect for it.

Therefore, in order to solve the overly long To-Do list problem, do the following:

1   Label each item with a priority number of 1, 2, or 3.
2   Scrub your To-Do list at the beginning of every month to eliminate anything on it that is not a 1, 2, or 3 priority.
3   Check with your boss or your team leader on your priorities. This is an absolutely necessary step. Over the years I have learned that one of the biggest reasons people get fired is because they have different priorities than their boss or team leader does. If everyone on team has the same priorities, then they all agree on the best route to reach their common destination, to accomplish their mutual goals and objectives.
4   Put a deadline on each item so you will know by what date an item has to be completed.
5   Look at your calendar for the upcoming month and enter previously scheduled appointments, then fit in tasks according to agreed-upon priorities.

Calendars   Calendars are the second most important arrow in your task-management quiver. It is vital that you have only one calendar that synchs with your computer, tablet, and mobile phone. Do not have a calendar on your mobile phone and another calendar on your desk or in an appointment book. Most sales organizations have shared calendars so everyone on a team can see what everyone else is doing.

Weekly

At the beginning of each week, look at last week's calendar for appointments, tasks, and meetings for items that need to be carried over to the coming week. Scrub your To-Do list again, reset the priorities if necessary, and include the deadline date for each item. Next, synthesize the To-Do list with your calendar.

Daily

Daily To-Do lists are the most useful To-Do lists if you have sovereignty, or control, over your time. If you have a job that contains a set routine of tasks that need to be accomplished virtually the same way in the same order every day, you do not need a daily To-Do list because every day is essentially the same. However, if you have control over your time, a daily To-Do list is a vital tool. Following are practices that will make your daily To-Do list more effective:

1   Set a time in your daily routine to create you daily To-Do list. First thing in the morning is usually the best time.

2   Look at your email. *Delete* unnecessary ones, *refer,* or forward, emails that are appropriate for someone else to take action on, or *act* on an email if it will take two minutes of less. Do not reply to emails unless it is vitally important that you do so, and, most important, *never* "Reply All" to emails unless it is absolutely necessary that everyone on the email list read your reply. Remember how many times that you have received a reply to a group email with just an inane, "OK" or "I'm in." You didn't need to know that, so the reply was irrelevant and time wasting. Always think twice or three times before you "Reply All."

3   Unsubscribe to emails that you do not need. Everyone is inundated with unnecessary, time-wasting emails, so get rid of them.

4   Be tough on yourself. Do the hardest, least fun, and most difficult tasks first. Correct for the perception that fun things get done quickly.

5   Save the easiest, most fun tasks for last in your day because by doing so you have something to look forward to, which, in turn, will make you much happier when you go home after work.

6   Set a time limit on each appointment and meeting. If you have set a 45-minute time limit for a call on an agency buyer and the buyer keep you waiting for 40 minutes, tell the receptionist that you are leaving and will reschedule the appointment. Do not let other people control your time agenda.

7   If you add one item to your To-Do list during the day, drop another item. If your boss asks you to do something, or in other words, adds an item to your To-Do list, ask the boss which other item to drop. For example, if the boss asks you to create a presentation, say something like, "Sure, I can add that to my To-Do list. Here's my list; which item would you like me drop?" If you allow others to control your To-Do list, it is no longer your list, it is their list.

8   Break big tasks into smaller chunks and work interrupted on those chunks (some time-management consultants refer to this practice as *chunking*). Then work on that project chunk until it is finished. Close your email program and email notifications, close your browser, and use a mobile phone answering and scam-filtering app such as YouMail so you do not have to answer your phone unless it is an important call, such as a customer calling.

9   Do not put too many items on your daily To-Do list. You want to make yourself feel like a winner, not like a loser. If you have 12 items on you daily To-Do list and you only get 10 completed by the end of the day, you feel awful. You'll say to

yourself, "I didn't get enough done. I didn't have enough time." On the other hand, if you had nine items on your daily To-Do list and you get 10 completed, you feel great at the end of the day. You'll say to yourself, "Wow, did I get a lot done today! I feel great!"

10   The final organizational tip, and the most common time-management advice that is given in every book I have read about time management and every time-management seminar I have given is: Do just one task until it is finished. If you get interrupted, go back to the task. Do not look at anything else online. Do not make a phone call. *Do just one task until it is finished.*

There are literally hundreds of time-management and task-management software programs and apps. Most sales organizations or a company you work for most likely have time – and task-management functionality as part of a system such as Matrix or Efficio or HubSpot. But if you if have to get a To-Do program or app for yourself, see the Resources section at the end of this chapter for some suggestions.

Organize your desk and your computer   Your desktop should be as uncluttered as possible and have on it the minimum number of things, such as a notebook and pens. If your job, such as a sales job, requires that you be on the phone a lot, use an untethered headset, ear buds, or Air Pods so you can be hands-free and can take notes.

It is vital that you take notes on all of your business calls. I recommend using the Rocketbook system for taking notes. With a special Rocketbook notebook you can order online, you take notes with a Pilot Frixion pen. When you are finished taking notes in your Rocketbook, you scan your note pages with your smartphone and they are distributed up to seven different destinations, such as to your email, to your Google Drive, to your boss's email, to a shared drive, or to a Slack account if that is appropriate. With the Rocketbook system, you have digital copies of all of your notes, your notes can be distributed to multiple destinations, and you can erase your notes using a wet cloth to wipe off the plastic notebook page.

Do not use PostIt notes because you tend to get in the habit of taking notes on things to do, or addresses, or phone numbers and paste them all over your computer screen, desk top, and even old coffee mugs. Once you have more than three PostIt notes posted in your desk area, none of them stands out and they become wallpaper—something you never notice. Instead of using PostIt notes, write every reminder on a To-Do list that you scrub weekly and daily.

Organize your written communications   Analyze all the emails, proposals, presentations, customer success communications, and, in fact, all correspondence you send out and look for wording, phrases, paragraphs, and entire documents that are repeated often, and then create templates. Properly label the templates and store them on a shared drive so everyone on your team or organization can use them and not have to retype things over and over again.

Organize everyone's time   Consider creating a policy for your team or your organization (after getting everyone's buy-in) of *no-interrupt hours*. Some organizations call them *quiet hours,* but they are essentially the same concept. For example, when I was VP and general manager of WNBC-AM in New York (now WFAN-AM), I established 9:00–10:00 a.m. as a no-interrupt hour every workday. No one could call anyone internally at the station, drop by their desk, or start up a casual conversation between 9:00 and 10:00 a.m. unless, of course, there was an emergency. People loved the no-interrupt hour. They opened their mail, made calls, and worked on chunks of tasks, and then at 10:00 a.m. there was a beehive of activity and conversations around the coffee machine.

Controlling

Rule #1: *Learn to say "no."* But say "no" in a polite way. For example, if you are concentrating on a chunking task and a colleague interrupts you to chat, say something like, "I'd love to chat with you, but I've got to finish this task. May I get back to you in an hour?" It is difficult to say "no" to conversations and distractions in an open office environment, so rather than continually saying "no" to colleagues, many companies, such as Google, that have open office configurations provide small, single-desk offices where employees can work alone, be free of interruptions, and concentrate. But, whatever the office configuration is or your company culture is, it is vital that you are able to have uninterrupted time so you can focus on what you are doing.

Rule #2: *Eliminate distractions.* Many experts who study how we use our time believe that we tend to interrupt ourselves, that we are the initiating cause of most of our distractions. We go to Facebook, we text or respond to texts, we check Instagram, or we peek at what is happening on Twitter. Cal Newport, who writes extensively about work habits, believes that for most people, especially young people, Facebook, Instagram, and Twitter are addictive distractions and recommends we simply say "no" to these time wasters. In Newport's book *Digital Minimalism,* the author quotes Bill Maher, who said on his HBO show "Real Time," "The tycoons of social media have to stop pretending that they're friendly nerd gods building a better world and admit they're just tobacco farmers in T-shirts selling an addictive product to children. Because, let's face it, checking your 'likes' is the new smoking."[5] You might be sensible enough not to smoke because you know smoking is bad for your health, but use Instagram intensely without realizing that it is bad for your mental health.

Rule #3: *Set a specific time for callbacks.* It is usually best to schedule callbacks early in the morning before 9:00 a.m. or after 5:00 p.m. because you are most apt to find people free at those times.

Rule #4: *Allow time in your daily schedule for interruptions.* If you are not a manager, allow about an eighth of your time, or an hour a day, for interruptions. If you are a manager allow about a quarter of your time, or two hours a day, for interruptions. Remember, if you are a manager, a critical part of your job is to be interrupted, to be available to your team for answers, support, and facilitation.

Evaluating

The evaluating step in time management involves keeping a time log every six months to track everything you do in a typical day and then objectively evaluating how you spent your time. Pick a workday that you think is pretty typical, begin the log when you get up in the morning, and write down every activity. Your log might look something like the log in Exhibit 25.1.

Exhibit 25.1   Time log

Activity	Time
Get up, get dressed and put on makeup	7:00–7:30
Breakfast at Starbucks	7:30–8:15
Commute to work	8:15–8:45
Planning my day, email	8:45–9:30
Sales meeting	9:30–10:30
Chat with colleagues	10:30–10:45
Prospecting calls	10:45–11:30
Coffee break, gossip	11:30–12:00
Commute to lunch with client	12:00–12:30
Lunch with client	12:30–1:30
Commute back to office	1:30–2:00
Report to sales manager on lunch	2:00–2:10
Return client and agency calls	2:10–2:40
Work on client presentations	2:40–3:30
Coffee break, gossip	3:30–3:45
Work on client presentations	3:45–4:15
Discuss RFP response with sales manager	4:15–4:40
Set up appointments for coming week	4:40–5:30
Work on RFP response	5:30–6:00
Beers with colleagues at Hooters	6:00–700
Commute home	7:00–7:30
Cook and eat dinner with partner	7:30–8:30
Watch Netflix	8:30–10:30
Facebook, Twitter, and Instagram	10:30–12:00
Watch TV	12:00–12:30
Go to bed	12:30

Look at Exhibit 25.1 and evaluate it based on what your see. Is there is anything you might eliminate, or combine, or do at a different time? For example at 2:00 you talked to your sales manager about your lunch meeting with a client, and you also met with your sales manager at 4:15 to discuss an RFP response. You could have put a note in a manila folder titled "Sales Manager" on your desk or in a folder on your mobile phone (you want your "Sales Manager" folder to be portable) so you can put items in it to talk to your sales manager about, and then have one meeting at the end of the day to discuss several items instead of interrupting the manager several times with a single item.

Also, you wasted an hour and a half from 10:30 to 12:00 in the evening on Facebook, Twitter, and Instagram when you could have been exercising to lose 10 pounds (one of your yearly improvement goals) or practicing creating Excel spreadsheets (another improvement goal).

You might say, "But I need some down time." Well, you had two hours of relaxing down time for two hours from 8:30 to 10:30, which probably is enough time to relax, so invest two hours from 10:30 to 12:30 in improving your knowledge or skills instead of wasting it on social media and watching television. Furthermore, to make certain that you are being as productive as possible, you should take into consideration your metabolism and natural rhythm cycles. Are you a lark, or an early morning person, or an owl, a late night person? Larks and owls are defined by Daniel Pink in his book *When: The Scientific Secrets of Perfect Timing*. Pink believes that we should schedule our most important work when we are most alert. Therefore, if you are an owl and working on a major project, work on the project at night when you do your best thinking. On the other hand, if you are a lark, you should probably schedule your most important projects early it the morning, in the above example, say from 5:00 to 7:00 in the morning, and you would probably schedule your bedtime at 10:00 p.m.

Summary

Time management consists of planning, organizing, controlling, and evaluating how you invest your time. Do yearly planning to set a road map of where you want to go, then organize your To-Do list on a monthly, weekly, and daily basis. Do not be fooled by misperceptions of time, schedule harder tasks first, divide big tasks into smaller chunks of time, and work on just one thing until it is finished.

Managing time is more about managing distractions than managing time hour by hour. Intense, distraction-free focus is critical to success. Get off of social media and schedule your most important tasks based on whether you are a lark or an owl.

Test Yourself

1. Can time be saved in a bank like money?
2. What potentially is your biggest edge over your competition?
3. What are the four elements of time management?
4. What are three types of goals you should have when you do you yearly planning?
5. What are five ways to solve To-Do list problems?
6. What are the four rules for controlling your time?

Project

Pick a fairly typical workday and keep a time log of everything you do that day, and then evaluate your time log. Can you eliminate some time wasters? Can you combine two tasks or meetings? How many times were you interrupted, and who did the interrupting (including yourself)? How much time did you waste on social media? How much time did you invest in achieving improvement goals?

References

Newport, Cal. 2016. *Deep Work: Rules for Focused Success in a Digital World.* Grand Central Publishing.

Newport, Cal. 2019. *Digital Minimalism: Choosing a Focused Life in a Noisy World.* Portfolio.

Pink, Daniel. 2019. *When: The Scientific Secrets of Perfect Timing.* New York: Riverhead Books.

Young, Scott. 2019. *Ultralearning: Master Hard Skills, Outsmart the Competition, and Accelerate Your Career.* New York: Harper Business.

Zahariades, Damon. 2017. *Fast Focus: A Quick-Start Guide to Mastering Your Attention, Ignoring Distractions, and Getting More Done in Less Time.* Amazon Digital Services.

Resources

Google Keep To-Do list extension (keep.google.com) Monday task-management platform (monday.com) Rocketbook not-taking platform (getrocketbook.com) Wrike task-management platform (wrike.com)

Notes

1 Young, Scott. 2019. *Ultralearning: Master Hard Skills, Outsmart the Competition, and Accelerate Your Career.* New York: Harper Business.

2 Ibid.

3 Ibid.

4 Ibid.

5 Newport, Cal. 2019. *Digital Minimalism: Choosing a Focused Life in a Noisy World.* New York: Portfolio.

Appendix: Digital Advertising Glossary*

Ad Blockers   Ad blocking software filters content and blocks ads on a webpage that loads on a browser. The software targets ads like pop-ups, banner ads, sticky ads, interstitial ads, or auto-playing videos to allow users to surf the web without distractions or interruptions in their browsing experience.

Ad Completion   An ad completion occurs when a video ad plays through to the end.

Ad Exchange   An ad exchange is a technology platform that facilitates the programmatic buying and selling of media advertising inventory from multiple sources. Prices for the inventory are determined through real-time bidding (RTB).

Ad Fraud   Ad fraud is when a company knowingly serves ads that no one will actually see in order to drive views and revenue. For example, a website can use bots to automatically refresh its pages in order to register a high number of page views and appear more attractive as a source for inventory on programmatic exchanges.

Ad Tags   Ad tags are lines of code in an ad space on a website that specify the location of a file, image, or video so that that content can be found and served in the ad space.

AI   Artificial intelligence (AI) is an area of computer science that emphasizes the creation of intelligent machines that work and react like humans. Some of the activities computers with artificial intelligence are designed for include speech recognition, learning, planning, writing articles, and problem-solving,

Algorithm   An algorithm is a step-by-step method of solving a problem and is commonly used for data processing, calculations, and other related computer and mathematical operations. An algorithm is also used to manipulate data in various ways, such as inserting a new data item, searching for a particular item or sorting an item.

Ad Network   An ad network is a company that connects websites with advertising to sell, then aggregates that ad inventory for advertisers to buy, usually on programmatic exchanges. Ad networks are often organized by demographics (e.g., women 18–49) or interest (e.g., sports).

AMP   Accelerated mobile page is a project initiated by Google in an attempt to standardize the technology that will allow pages, apps, and ads to load faster on smartphones.

AOR   Agency of record is the advertising agency authorized to purchase advertising on behalf of a company with which they have an agency contract. There could be an AOR for planning media or an AOR for buying media.

API   An application programming interface is a set of routines, protocols, and tools for building software applications. An API expresses a software component in terms of its operations, inputs, outputs, and underlying types.

Ad Server   An ad server is a company whose software technology distributes ads to websites and then reports on how the ad performed.

Ad Tech   Ad tech, short for advertising technology, refers to all technologies, software, and services used for delivering, controlling, evaluating, and targeting digital ads.

Auction   This refers to buying ads on Google, Facebook, or programmatically based on a real-time bid-and-ask process. There are two prevalent types of auctions: Google features a second-price auction in which the winner of an online auction pays the price the second-place bidder bid plus one cent, and a first-price auction, such as in header bidding, in which the winner pays the price that was bid.

Audience Extension   Audience extension is a process used in advertising technology that attempts to expand a target audience's size while ensuring relevancy and maximizing engagement. The extension process takes a known audience segment and catalogs various shared characteristics that can be used to target people who bear similarities and are therefore likely to become customers.

Augmented Reality   This is an enhanced version of reality created by the use of technology to overlay digital information on an image of something being viewed through a device (such as a smartphone camera or screen).

Behavioral Targeting   Behavioral targeting is a technique used by advertisers and publishers to utilize a user's previous web browsing behavior to customize the types of ads that are served.

Bid Shaving   In March, 2019, Google announced it was switching from a second-price auction model on its exchange and ad server to a first-price auction model. It had switched its bid models by the end of 2019 in all areas where it did not control the end-to-end buying experience. In a first-price auction, buyers can use bid-shaving algorithms to ensure that they do not overpay.

Blockchain   A blockchain is a distributed database consisting of a ledger of transactions that is shared across a network of computers. The records that networks accept are added to a unique block of data assigned a person, company, or organization. Each block contains a unique code called a hash.

Bot A bot is a software application that runs automated tasks that are usually both simple and structurally repetitive at a substantially higher frequency than would be possible for a human or group of humans. In 2018, approximately 52 percent of Internet traffic came from bots.[1]

Bounce Rate A bounce rate is the percentage of visitors to a website who leave the site without visiting a second page.

Brand Lift This is the increase in effectiveness measurements (for example, message recall) between respondents who did not view the ad and those who did.

Bumper Ad Six-second video ads are sometimes referred to as bumper ads.

Byte A group of binary digits or bits, typically eight, that operate as a single unit, is called a byte. A byte is the smallest unit of a computer memory. A *kilobyte* is 1,024 bytes. A *megabyte* is one thousand kilobytes, or a million bytes. A *gigabyte* is 1,024 megabytes, or a billion bytes. A *terabyte* is 1,024 gigabytes, or a million million bytes. A *petabyte* is 1,024 terabytes. An *exabyte* is 1,024 petabytes or a billion billion bytes. A *zettabyte* is 1,024 exabytes, or mathematically 10^{21}. A *yottabyte* is 1,024 exabytes, or mathematically 10^{24}.

Chatbot A chatbot is a particular type of bot that is used most often by marketers to communicate with and respond to questions from customers, typically in an online or mobile environment.

Click Fraud Click fraud refers to clicks on an ad that are generated falsely, either by humans or artificially by a bot with the intention of creating a click on an ad that causes an advertiser to pay even though the click is not real. Indicators of click fraud are an unusual and sudden spike in clicks from the same IP address.

Connected TV Connected TV refers to any television set that is connected to the Internet and can access content beyond what is available via the normal offering from a cable provider.

Contextual Targeting A form of targeted advertising that appears on websites, mobile browsers, or other ad-supported devices. Ads are selected and served by automated systems according the demographic, behavioral, and life-style profile of an online user and based on the content displayed.

Cookie A cookie is message given to a web browser by a web server. The browser stores the information in a small text file on the browser. The information is then sent back to the server each time the browser requests a page from the server.

CPA Cost per acquisition is the price paid by an advertiser to a publisher when a user takes an action as a result of seeing an ad, such as opening an account or purchasing a relatively expensive product or service.

---

[1] Fisher, Sarah. "Most Internet traffic comes from bots." https://www.axios.com/most-internet-traffic-comes-from-bots-fake-news-31f25b93-eedf-4abb-b7cf-7656d9263272.html.

CPC   Cost per click is the price paid by an advertiser to a publisher or platform for a single click on an ad. The vast majority of Google search ads are CPC.

CPCV   Cost per completed view, or the price paid by an advertiser to the publisher once a video has been viewed through completion.

CPE   Cost per engagement. With the CPE bidding strategy impressions are free and advertisers only pay when users actively engage with ads (for example, when they click, watch, roll-over, or take another similar action).

CPI   Cost per install is a pricing method that only charges when an app is downloaded.

CPM   Cost per mille (thousand), or cost-per-thousand impressions. With a CPM pricing method an advertiser pays a set price for every thousand impressions served regardless of any action taken by users. Digital video ads, television, cable, and radio are typically purchased on a CPM basis.

CPP   Cost per (rating) point. Spot and network television are often purchased on a cost-per-point basis, with one rating point equal to one percent of a target population. For example, the CPP of a one rating of women 18–49.

CPV   Cost per view is a pricing method in which advertisers pay for each time their video is played.

CTR   Click-through rate is the number of clicks an ad receives divided by the number of impressions an ad has. A CTR of greater than two percent is considered very good.

Data Aggregator   A company, similar to a DMP, that aggregates second- and third-party data from various sources and then sells it to marketers typically as a data resource for a programmatic buy.

DMP   A data management platform is a data warehouse in which first-party, second-party, and third-party data are often combined with data such as cookies (browsing data), IDs, demographic, life-style, and other data. These melded data sets are stored and then used to generate audience segments, which in turn, are used to target specific users with digital ads.

Daypart   Traditionally used for television and radio buying. Dayparts are blocks of time that divide the day into segments (for example, Prime Time, or 8:00–11:00 p.m. EST and PST, 7:00–10:00 p.m. CST and MST).

Deal ID   A unique piece of code assigned to an automated ad buy, used to match buyers and sellers and based on a variety of criteria negotiated beforehand.

Diginet   Diginets got their start due to the availability of extra channels when high-definition television came online, and they have grown due to the unexpected rise of so-called cable television cord-cutters and cord-nevers. Instead of subscribing to expensive cable packages, people who abandon their cable subscription pair inexpensive over-the-air antennae with over-the-top streaming subscriptions and get programs from MeTv, This TV, Cozi TV, Bounce, Escape, Grit, and Laff.[2]

---

[2] Albiniak, Page. 2018. TV Technology. https://www.tvtechnology.com/news/diginets-come-of-age.

DTC More and more consumer package goods (CPG) companies are using DTC (direct-to-consumer) marketing to sell directly to consumers. Dollar Shave Club and Warby Parker are examples of DTC companies. Also referred to as B2C-D, or business-to-consumer direct marketing.

Display Advertising A form of non-video online advertising where an advertiser's message is shown on a webpage, generally set off in a box at the top or bottom or to one side of content of a page

DMA Designated market areas are defined by Nielsen. DMAs divide the country into different regional markets by population centers that are within approximately a 75-mile radius from television station antennae. For example, the San Francisco Bay Area DMA, which includes towns such as Oakland and San Jose.

DOOH Digital out-of-home advertising is out-of-home advertising on displays (screens) that reach consumers when they are on the go, such as on the streets, on in commercial locations, or in waiting areas.

DSP Demand-side platforms consist of automation software that allows advertisers to buy ads across a range of publisher sites through online programmatic exchanges. DSPs facilitate advertisers being able to target and optimize trillions of impressions without having to negotiate in person with hundreds or thousands of media salespeople.

DVR A digital video recorder is attached to a cable box and records selected programs for later viewing.

DAI Dynamic ad insertion expands advertising opportunities by allowing advertisers to serve ads that can be swapped in and out of video-on-demand content depending on the profile of a user.

eCPM Effective cost per mille (thousand) is calculated by dividing the revenue generated by an ad campaign by the number of ad impressions of that campaign expressed in thousands.

Fill Rate The ratio of ad requests that are successfully filled on a website or in an app in relation to the total number of ad requests made, expressed as a percentage.

First-party data This is data directly collected by a marketer, typically through e-commerce sites, in retail stores, and on company websites, about the actions users take while on that site.

First-Price Auction When buying programmatically or on an online auction, an advertiser with the highest bid for an impression wins the bid and pays the price it bid.

Flooring Strategies Publishers often use a flooring strategy to make sure they price the inventory they put up for sale programmatically on an exchange such that it has a minimum price they will accept. Publishers set a floor price on their SSPs (supply-side platforms.)

Freemium A freemium product is a simple, bare-bones product that is made available free. The hope is that when consumers try the product, they will like it, and will be willing to pay for a premium model with lots more features.

Frequency   Frequency is the average number of times an ad is delivered to an average user in a specified time period. For example, weekly frequency or monthly frequency.

Geo-targeting   This refers to showing ads to people based on their mobile device's location, ZIP code information they submit when registering on a site, or GPS coordinates collected by a website.

GRP   Gross rating point is the standard currency that broadcast television has used to plan, purchase, and measure advertising campaigns since the 1950s. GRPs are calculated by adding up the target demographic rating points of each commercial in a TV schedule.

GUI   A graphical user interface is a form of user interface that allows users to interact with electronic devices through graphical icons and visual indicators such as secondary notation, instead of text-based user interfaces, typed command labels, or text navigation.

Hashing   Hashing is an encryption process to secure untampered message transmission on data transactions such as on a blockchain. A math formula on the sender's side generates a unique hash number based on the message, then the hash is encrypted and transmitted along with the message itself. After the data package is received, the receiver generates another hash number and if this matches the encrypted hash, there is a high probability that the original message has been transmitted intact.

Hashtag   A hashtag is a name or phrase on Twitter preceded by a #. People can follow hashtags and get all the Tweets posted on that hashtag, such as #MeToo.

Header Bidding   Header bidding is a method of buying inventory programmatically by means of an auction conducted by publishers outside of their primary ad server, which allows advertisers to cherry-pick high priority, or premium, impressions. Advertisers will only win impressions in the header auction if their bids are high enough.

Index   An index of users of a product is a percentage that shows how much more or less of a product a group of users use than the average user (100 percent) does. Thus, an index of 137 means that the identified group of users use 37 percent more of the product than the average group of users does. An index of 80 means that the identified group of users use 20 percent less of the product than the average group of users does.

In-Stream   This is an ad that appears within a piece of content. For example, a pre-roll ad attached to a YouTube video or a Promoted Tweet in a Twitter feed.

Insertion   An insertion is the actual placement of an advertisement, digital or otherwise, as recorded by an ad server.

Insertion Order (IO)   An insertion order is a purchase order, or contract, between a seller of advertising and a buyer, typically sent via email.

Interactive In-App Pre-Roll   This refers to video ads containing rich media or interactive functionality running in-app on smartphones or tablets.

Interactive Pre-Roll   This refers to in-stream video ads that play before video content and feature interactive and rich media elements, such as overlays, video galleries, microsites and/or zip code locators.

Interconnect   An interconnect is a sales organization that is created by two or more cable MSOs and MVPDs in a DMA – a market area designated by Nielsen – that aggregates local cable commercial inventory from cooperating video distributors to make it easier to purchase a large swath of the local cable households within a DMA. For example, the San Francisco interconnect includes Direct TV, AT&T U-verse Dish, Comcast, and Altice.

Interstitial Ad   An interstitial is an ad that covers the interface of its host app and is typically displayed at natural transition points in the flow of an app, such as between activities or during the pause between levels in a game.

IPTV   Internet protocol television is television delivered over the Internet via a privately managed network such a FiOS or AT&T U-verse. IPTV is generally of higher quality than Internet-based streaming services such as Netflix, which are delivered directly to a TV set and during which, at times, viewers see the spinning circle indicating buffering.

KPI   A key performance indicator is a measure of how effectively a company is achieving important, predetermined business objectives.

Last Look   A last-look strategy gave preferred buyers and Google itself the privilege that after an online auction was completed, Google itself or one of its preferred advertisers could pay a penny more than an ostensibly winning bid to buy an impression. This practice stopped when Google went to a first-bid auction model on its non-controlled inventory.

Leaderboard   A standard IAB-defined 728 × 90 ad unit that stretches across the top of a screen.

Linear TV   This is live television that is watched as scheduled; it stands in contrast to pre-recorded or video on demand (VOD) television.

LUMAscape   LUMAscape refers to graphic representations of the crowded, complex ecosystems of the ad tech, display, video, and mobile advertising, which can be found at https://lumapartners.com/content/lumascapes/display-ad-tech-lumascape.

Machine Learning   Machine learning is a method of data analysis that automates analytical model building. It is a branch of artificial intelligence based on the idea that systems can learn from data, identify patterns, and make decisions with minimal human intervention.

Makegoods   Makegoods are additional ad impressions which are negotiated in order to make up for a shortfall of impressions delivered versus the commitments agreed upon in an IO.

Medium Rectangle   A standard IAB-defined 300 x 250 ad unit that typically appears at the top right area of a screen.

Message Recall   This is a measurement used to evaluate an ad's effectiveness in driving a viewer's ability to remember a brand or the message it intended to communicate. It is typically measured using a survey methodology.

Mid-Roll   Mid-roll is a form of online video ad placement where the ad is played during a break in the middle of the content video.

Mobile Pre-Roll   This refers to video ads running on smartphones or tablet devices where the ad is played before video content begins. It can be in-stream or in-app.

MRC   The Media Rating Council is a body whose mission is to insure that audience measurements by companies such as Nielsen and comScore are valid, reliable, and effective.

MVPD   Multichannel video programming distribution is a service that provides multiple television channels such as a cable or satellite television service like Comcast, DirecTV, DISH, Spectrum, or Cox, which were often formerly known as cable operators or multisystem operators.

Open Exchange   A digital programmatic advertising marketplace for aggregated inventory from multiple partners where buyers can bid programmatically to purchase impressions and that is open to all buyers.

Opt In   Opt in refers to a consumer giving a company permission to send marketing emails or to use data collected from or about the consumer in order to market the company's products and services.

Optimization   Algorithms automatically analyze the performance of different versions of an ad and then only serve the best-performing versions. For example, if one version of an ad has a blue background and another has a yellow background, and more people click on the ad with the blue background, the algorithm will henceforth serve only the blue-background ad.

OTT   Over the top refers to content accessed via the Internet without the involvement of a television service provider. OTT includes subscription video on demand (SVOD) services such as Netflix and Hulu.

Page Request   A page request is the opportunity for an HTML document to appear in a browser window as a direct result of a user's interaction with a website.

PII   Personally identifiable information is digital information that can be used, on its own or together with other information, to attribute online activity to a specific individual.

Pixel   A pixel is the smallest unit of a digital image or graphic that can be displayed and represented on a digital display device such as on a smartphone screen. Pixels are combined to form a complete image, video, text, or anything visible on a screen. A pixel is also known as a picture element.

PMP   A private marketplace is where publishers invite selected buyers to bid on their inventory which gives advertisers more knowledge of and control over the environment in which their ads appear even though it is more expensive than inventory bought in an open exchange.

Pod A pod is a series of commercials, sometimes as many as eight or nine, grouped together back-to-back on broadcast and cable television. The first position in the pod is considered to be the most valuable, and many advertisers are willing to pay a premium to get this desired placement.

Post-Roll Ad This is a video ad that appears after video content plays.

Pre-Roll Ad This is a video ad that appears directly preceding any video content that subsequently plays.

Programmatic Ad Buying This refers to the use of automation software to purchase digital advertising on a digital platform that enables an advertiser to reach the right person, at the right time, in the right place, and at the right price in a real-time auction environment. Programmatic buying allows advertisers to create complex media plans easily by means of automation and to implement, manage, and optimize ad campaigns seamlessly.

Programmatic Direct This is a programmatic ad buy done directly between a publisher and advertiser, not through an open ad exchange, and on an invitation-only basis and which gives advertisers access to premium inventory.

Programmatic Guaranteed This is a programmatic deal negotiated in advance between a publisher and a buyer with a fixed budget amount, guaranteed impressions delivery, and guaranteed CPM pricing.

PTV Programmatic TV is a technology that enables brands and agencies to buy TV ads programmatically. Television sets must be attached to a cable box and the ads inserted by local systems in local ad breaks.

RTB Real-time bidding is programmatically buying and selling of digital ad impressions through real-time auctions that happen within milliseconds.

Remarketing Remarketed ads are a form of digital targeted ads that are served to people who have already visited a website, looked at a product, or bought a product.

Reward Video This refers to video ads that give people who view an entire video ad some kind of reward such as coins or an extra life in a game. Completion and engagement rates on reward videos are extremely high.

Retargeting This is the same as remarketing.

RON Run of network is the scheduling of digital advertising by an ad network that positions ads across the sites it represents at its own discretion.

ROS Run of site is the scheduling of digital advertising by a website for ads that places the ads at its discretion, often at a lower cost to an advertiser than purchasing of specific site positions.

Satellite TV This is the name for television from providers such DirecTV that sends encrypted signals by a satellite via radio waves to a set-top box.

Scatter Market   This is term for buying network television advertising in the same quarter that the advertising will run.

Second-Party Data   This is when a marketer makes its first-party data available to another company which then uses it to target its advertising. For example, a retailer such as CVS makes its data available to P&G so the P&G can target its add more effectively based on purchase behavior.

Second-Price Auction   This is Google's bid model for all its products where it controls the end-to-end buying experience, such as on YouTube, Google Search, AdSense for Search and other Google properties. In a second-price auction if an advertiser wins an online bid for an impression with a bid of $10 and the second place bid was $3.00, the advertiser does not pay $7, but pays what the second-place bidder bid plus a penny, or $3.01.

Sell-Through Rate   This the percentage of a publisher's ad inventory that is sold.

Set-Top Box   A set-top box is an electronic device that connects to a television set that provides connectivity to the Internet, game consoles, or cable systems.

Skippable Pre-Roll   This refers to in-stream video ads that allow viewers to skip ahead to non-advertisement video content after playing for a few seconds, especially on YouTube.

Skyscraper   A skyscraper is a tall, thin online standard IAB-defined160 x 600 ad unit on the right side of a screen.

SOV   Share of voice is a single brand's percentage of the total advertising spend in a category over a specified time period. For example, Chevrolet might have a 20 percent SOV of all automotive advertising in the first six months of a year.

SPO   Supply path optimization is a strategy used by programmatic buyers and that helps them grapple with resellers and duplicate auctions. SPO helps programmatic buyers find the best route to getting a fair price for online inventory.

Spot Television (or Radio)   Spot television or radio means buying on a market-by-market basis. For example, a spot television campaign might include the top 25 markets, or a select group of northern US markets in two winter months to advertise snow chains for tires.

SSP   A supply-side platform is software used by publishers to sell advertising programmatically. SSPs also assist publishers evaluate, price, and manage their ad inventory in order to maximize revenue.

Standard Pre-Roll   This refers to in-stream video ads that play before video content plays.

Target Audience   A target audience is the intended audience for an ad, usually defined in terms of specific demographics (age and gender) and psychographics (interests, lifestyles), and online behaviors.

Tech Tax   Tech tax refers to the additional costs marketers pay to middlemen such as trading desks, DSPs, DMPs, ad exchanges, and second- and third-party data for buying ads programmatically. Some estimates indicate that of $100 spent on a programmatic buy only $50 or less winds up with an online publisher; the other $50 is the tech tax, or the cost of executing the buy and purchasing data for targeting the ads.

Third-Party Ad Server These are independent companies that utilize software platforms that serve digital ads and manage, store, track, and analyze the data for online advertising campaigns.

Third-Party Data This is information that an established data company collects indirectly or aggregates from others and then sells to ad buyers.

Trading Desk A trading desk is a dedicated team of people within an agency or client organization that executes programmatic media buying.

UDID UDID is a line of code that is a unique user or device identifier; it is assigned to that device or user and lasts until the device is reset or the account is deleted.

Upfront Market Buying television advertising in May in programs that will run the following fall. In return for making commitments five months before programming airs, advertisers receive discounts from what they would pay in the Scatter Market and guaranteed ratings and CPMs.

VAST A video ad-serving template is a universally used XML code tag for serving ads to digital video players.

vCPM A viewable CPM is cost-per-thousand for viewable ads served. The calculation for vCPM is CPM divided by a viewability rate.

Viewability Viewability is a metric that addresses an ad's opportunity to be seen by a viewer.

Viewable Completion This is when a video is viewable at the end of ad play.

Viewable Impression As defined by the Media Ratings Council, a viewable video impression is one where 50 percent of a video player's pixels are in view in an active browser tab for any two consecutive seconds.

Virtual Reality This refers to a computer-generated simulation of a three-dimensional image or environment that can be interacted with in a seemingly real or physical way by a person using special electronic equipment, such as a helmet with a screen inside or gloves fitted with sensors.

Voice Assistant A voice assistant is an AI-driven system consisting of software that recognize voice commands and responds. Amazon's Alexa and Apple's Siri are examples of voice assistants.

VTR View-through rate is a measurement of how many people saw an ad and eventually visited the website advertised in the ad.

Widget A widget is an element of a graphical user interface (GUI) that displays information or provides a specific way for a user to interact with the operating system or an application. Widgets include icons, pull-down menus, buttons, selection boxes, progress indicators, on-off checkmarks, scroll bars, windows, window edges (that let you resize the window), toggle buttons, form, and many other devices for displaying information and for inviting, accepting, and responding to user actions.

Yield Yield is the percentage of clicks versus impressions on an ad within a specific page. It is also called referred to as ad click rate.

Yield Management Yield management is AI-type software, often included in a publisher's SSP, that helps a publisher identify, manage, package, and price ad inventory in order to maximize revenue based on current demand for that inventory.

Zapping Zapping is the practice of changing television channels by means of a remote control device to avoid commercial interruptions.

Zipping Zipping is fast-forwarding through commercials during the playback of programs on a DVR device.

Notes

* This glossary has been expanded on and adapted from Tube Mogul's "Ad Glossary." https:// www.tubemogul.com/glossary.
1 Fisher, Sarah. "Most Internet traffic comes from bots." https://www.axios.com/most-internet-traffic-comesfrom-bots-fake-news-31f25b93-eedf-4abb-b7cf-7656d9263272.html.
2 Albiniak, Page. 2018. TV Technology. https://www.tvtechnology.com/news/diginets-come-of-age.

Index

Media Selling: Digital, Television, Audio, Print and Cross-Platform, Fifth Edition.
Charles Warner, William A. Lederer, and Brian Moroz.
© 2020 John Wiley & Sons, Inc. Published 2020 by John Wiley & Sons, Inc.